To Our Students

ABOUT THE AUTHORS

Charles E. Faupel is Professor of Sociology and Director of Graduate Studies at Auburn University in Auburn, Alabama. He received his Ph.D. from the University of Delaware in 1981. He researches primarily in the areas of criminology, with a special emphasis on drug use, and in the sociology of the environment. He is author/editor of five other books, including Shooting Dope: Career Patterns of Hard-Core Heroin Users, published by the University of Florida Press. Dr. Faupel has also published in numerous sociology journals, including Social Problems, Social Forces, Sociological Spectrum, Qualitative Sociology and Urban Life (now Journal of Contemporary Ethnography). He is also currently editor of Sociological Inquiry, the official journal of Alpha Kappa Delta, the international sociological honorary society. Avocationally, he has recently become involved in research on country music careers.

Alan M. Horowitz is an associate professor of sociology with the University of Delaware's Parallel Program, a position he has held for more than twenty years. His graduate work in sociology was completed at the University of Delaware. This is his first book-length publication. He has published previously in the journals Social Forces, Sociological Quarterly, Sociological Inquiry, the International Journal of Contemporary Sociology, and others. He has been nominated for the University of Delaware's "Excellence in Teaching" and "Excellence in Undergraduate Advisement" awards and has twice won an award for "Teaching Adult Students" from the Division of Continuing Education. His areas of teaching and research interest are the sociology of deviance, the sociology of drug use, and the sociology of law.

Greg S. Weaver is an associate professor of criminology at Auburn University, a position held since 1997. Greg completed his PhD in Sociology in 1997 from the University of Nebraska. He is a former probation officer with the Florida Department of Corrections. His primary research interests focus on lethal violence and substance use. Major publications include articles in *Deviant Behavior,* The Journal of Criminal Law and Criminology (forthcoming), The Journal of Social Psychology, and Sociological Inquiry (forthcoming).

BRIEF CONTENTS

CONTENTS

C h a p t e r   3

Classifying Psychoactive Drugs   65

Chapter   **8**

Health Correlates of Drug Use   *239*

Chapter   **9**

Drugs and the Economy   *273*

C h a p t e r   14
Drug Policy for the Twenty-First Century   *439*

PREFACE

Sociology of American Drug Use is written with a very targeted readership in mind, namely sociology undergraduates, or undergraduates in criminology and criminal justice programs with a strong sociological focus. All three authors are sociologically trained criminologists, and all have taught courses in the sociology of drug use. This text is borne out of the frustration that the authors have had in finding a text that is appropriate for the courses that we teach.

Like many of you, we have taught a number of criminology courses, most of which are organized around predictable themes—measurement of crime, problems with such measurement, theoretical perspectives on crime, social correlates of crime, and societal reaction to crime. These same themes, which will be familiar to criminologically oriented faculty, function as the foundation for this text.

ORGANIZATION

The first section, "A Sociological Approach to Drug Use," provides an overview of some of the basic concepts and issues involved in the study of drug use from a sociological perspective. Chapter 1, "The Sociological Study of Drug Use," lays out the foundation for a sociology of drug use by identifying and defining some of the basic concepts that any student of the sociology of drug use must know. This chapter focuses especially on the *social construction* of drug use as a social problem. Chapter 2, "A Brief History of Drugs in America" provides a valuable historical context for understanding drug use in this country, from prior to our founding as a nation to the present day. Chapter 3, "Classifying Psychoactive Drugs," presents a pharmacological typology of drugs. While the emphasis of this book is the social context of drug use and drug experience, drugs do differ in the ways that they affect the central nervous system. This typology, which is commonly used in the field today, provides students with an important grounding in the pharmacology of drugs and drug use. Because of their importance in recent years, we have added a sixth category to this typology entitled "CNS Stabilizers," which comprises those drugs designed to *moderate* extremes of moods. Two specific types of drugs are included in this category: those drugs which seek to moderate the extremes associated with attention deficit hyperactive disorder (e.g., ritalin), and the various families of antidepressants. Chapter 4, "Theoretical Explanations for Drug Use" summarizes the theories that have been used to explain initiation into drug use and/or addiction. This chapter focuses heavily on *sociological* theories, though it also summarizes other important theories from the fields of philosophy, biology and psychology as well. Chapter 5, "Subcultures of Drug Use," is a logical extension of Chapter 4. This chapter underscores the importance of social and cultural context in understanding drug use. Here we also examine four specific drug subcultures: Rastifarianism, the Native American Church, the Rave subculture, and the street heroin subculture. The chapter concludes with a discussion of the "career" dynamics of drug use. Chapter 6, "Official and Unofficial Data Sources," provides students with an extensive discussion of the major sources of information that researchers utilize in coming to an *empirical* understanding of drug use. This chapter underscores the importance of empirical observation as a basis for theorizing as well as policy making.

The second section, "Social Correlates of Drug Use," focuses on some of the predominant social features that tend to be associated with drug use in America. Much of the material contained in these chapters is not addressed in many texts on drug use, an omission due in part to the fact that there are very few comprehensive textbooks in this area that are written from a strongly sociological perspective. Chapter 7 highlights some of the demographic and occupational correlates of substance use and misuse. Specifically, gender, race and age are examined as demographic correlates. This chapter also examines medicine, the military, sports, and law enforcement as occupational contexts for drug use. Chapter 8 presents some of the major health correlates associated with the use of psychoactive substances. This chapter focuses not only on the negative consequences of drug use, but also on some of the ways in which drugs can positively impact our health. Three specific issues are addressed in this regard, namely medical marijuana, unrestricted use of narcotics in terminally-ill patients, and the use of alcohol in moderation. Chapter 9 discusses the economic dimension of drug use. This chapter takes both a "macroeconomic" look at the drug industry, highlighting the impact of the drug trade on the larger economy both in the United States and other countries; and a "microeconomic" examination of the underground economy of drug use. The chapter also examines the problems of drugs in the workplace and the response of business and industry to this use. Chapter 10 addresses the relationship between drug use and crime. This relationship is examined both theoretically and empirically. The common sense notion that drug use causes crime through either direct pharmacological action or through economic compulsion is critically analyzed, and alternative ways of understanding the drugs-crime nexus are also explored.

The final section of the text, "Societal Reaction to Drug Use," explores important areas of drug policy. The material in this section represents, possibly, the most important contribution that the discipline of sociology can make to our understanding of drug use. Drug use occurs within the context of social policies which profoundly shape the experiences and the consequences of use. The nexus between social policy and the consequences of that policy on the behavior which it is intended to affect is not always clear, and there is perhaps no policy issue in which this is more the case than drug policy. This is an area that begs for clear, non-partisan empirical knowledge that comes from social science disciplines such as sociology. Chapter 11, examines the broad policy options of prohibition, legalization and decriminalization. This chapter examines the benefits and the limitations of each of these options. A fourth broad policy option, *harm-reduction,* is introduced as an alternative to minimize the negative impacts of drug use in American society. Chapter 12, entitled "Therapeutic Responses to Drug Use," focuses on drug treatment. There are a variety of philosophies governing the treatment of substance abuse which are addressed in this chapter. The chapter further examines the effectiveness of the various types, or "modalities" of drug treatment. Chapter 13 focuses on "Preventive Responses to Drug Use." This chapter examines two broad preventive initiatives, namely drug education and drug testing. The final chapter of the text, "Drug Policy for the Twenty-First Century," is, admittedly, somewhat speculative as we attempt to offer creative suggestions for a workable drug policy for the century ahead. Our suggestions are based upon a commitment to harm-reduction. While there are certainly differences of opinion regarding what harm-reduction means and how it should be implemented, this is a philosophical ideal to which we are committed. While the details of what such a policy might look like are beyond the scope of this chapter and this text, we do try to provide some specific ideas as to some of the elements that might comprise such a policy.

PEDAGOGICAL AIDS

Working together, the authors and the editors have created a number of learning tools to help students master the material presented in the text:

- Chapter-opening overviews and outlines function together to provide a valuable guide to the chapter's coverage.
- Unique "Drugs and Everyday Life" boxes in every chapter contain information that is part of the "everyday life" of drug users,

researchers, policy makers, or practitioners. Some examples of "Drugs and Everyday Life" boxes:

- the subculture of alcohol use among police officers
- the vernacular of the heroin subculture
- the history of Project DARE and the great gap between its popularity and promotion as an effective approach to drug education and what we know empirically about its effectiveness

- End-of-chapter review materials—a summary, list of key terms, and review questions—provide students with ample resources when studying for exams.
- Unique "Critical Inquiry Questions" at the end of each chapter require the student go beyond merely repeating information found in the text and can be used as a basis for lively class discussion, as material for more structured debates, or as a stimulus for paper topics.
- Finally, a comprehensive glossary at the end of the book functions as an important reference as students proceed through the text.

INSTRUCTOR SUPPLEMENT

As a full service publisher of quality educational products, McGraw-Hill does much more than just sell textbooks. We also create and publish supplements for use with those textbooks. Accompanying this text is a comprehensive **Instructor's Manual/Testbank** featuring lecture notes, student activities, classroom discussion questions, a complete testbank, and more. The **Instructor's Manual/Testbank** is provided free of charge to instructors. Orders of new (versus used) textbooks help McGraw-Hill defray the substantial cost of developing supplements like this.

ACKNOWLEDGMENTS

Any major writing project that is successful is a team effort. As authors, we are keenly aware of the importance of teamwork in the division of labor on this book. We recognize, moreover, that there were several other team members who contributed in important ways to this text. We want to recognize, first, Lindsey Topping and Dara Ranson for the many hours of library research that they contributed. Lindsey and Dara are graduates of the criminology program at Auburn and were two of the very best students that we had, hence our decision to invite them to participate in this project.

We are also keenly appreciative of the contributions made by the substantive reviewers of this manuscript:

Don Barrett—California State University, San Marcos

Willie Edwards—Texas A&M University

Gil McCann—University of Vermont

Sylvia Mignon—University of Massachusetts, Boston

Leah Moore—University of Central Florida

James Orcutt—Florida State University

The critiques and suggestions of these individuals were invaluable and have contributed, in our view to a significantly improved text.

We also want to recognize our colleagues at Auburn University both faculty and staff. While these individuals did not directly contribute to the content of the book, their words of encouragement, their assistance in getting versions of manuscripts ready for mailing, and their willingness to act as sounding boards is deeply appreciated. We are also very appreciative of the sabbatical provided to Alan Horowitz which allowed him precious needed time for work on this text. Finally, we want to acknowledge the editorial staff at McGraw-Hill who so patiently worked with us as first time text book authors. We know that we must have created at least a few headaches for you and we so appreciate your gentle forebearance.

A SOCIOLOGICAL APPROACH TO DRUG USE

THE SOCIOLOGICAL STUDY OF DRUG USE

Five suburban Philadelphia high school girls, four of them honor students, die in an accident after their car leaves the road and hits a tree; all five had been "huffing" the fumes of a well-known cleaning product shortly before their death. An elderly woman in rural West Virginia takes OxyContin, a potent synthetic narcotic for pain caused by bone cancer; she sells some of her prescription to a young addict for $40 per pill, a stash which he promptly pulverizes and inhales. Two members of the Native American Church of North America ingest peyote, a naturally occurring hallucinogenic drug, in a church-sponsored religious ritual in Oregon; because they violated state law in doing so, they are fired from their jobs as drug abuse counselors. A son of one of this country's best known politicians dies in a hotel room from the effects of mixing heroin and cocaine in a concoction known as a "speedball"; his brother is later arrested aboard an airplane for behaving erratically and for heroin possession. An Olympic track and field star is disqualified from competition for using anabolic steroids, which are on the banned substances list; his wife, a multiple gold medal winner, is tainted by the scandal. These scenarios all happened to real people and are descriptive of the range of drug-related issues this textbook investigates.

Ours is a country of drug users. This statement is not a pejorative one; we are not saying that being a drug user is a bad thing; nor, certainly, are we saying that it is a good thing. Rather, we are simply stating a social fact. The overwhelming majority of Americans, adolescents and older, use substances that have a *psychoactive* effect and can, from a biochemical perspective, be considered "drugs." **Psychoactive drugs** affect the functioning of the mind in some way, and hence influence our thought processes, our emotional responses, how we perceive the world around us, the mood we are in, and more. We, the authors, are not claiming that most of us are drug *abusers,* or that most of us are taking great risks, or even that most of us are using *illegal* drugs or legal drugs in an illegal way. But we do routinely use substances that are legal and may even be widely promoted—substances such as caffeine, nicotine, alcohol, and some prescription drugs—in our daily lives. Consider the number of college students who start their days with a cigarette and a strong cup of coffee, who don't feel "right" until they've done so. Of course, a sizeable minority of the American people also use drugs that are currently illegal, many of whose psychoactive effects are harmful to the user and possibly to others. This is also a social fact, albeit one with profound consequences to American society. It is estimated that Americans, who make up only about 5 percent of the world's population, consume perhaps 50 percent of the world's supply of cocaine. The American hunger for illegal drugs will be given the greatest scrutiny in this textbook, though our patterns of alcohol and tobacco use and abuse also are of considerable interest to us. It is safe to say that all facets of American life are touched by psychoactive drug use or abuse.

This introductory chapter introduces you to the basics of a *sociological* perspective on drugs and drug use. We begin this chapter by comparing the sociological perspective with the perspectives provided by other scientific disciplines. This discussion is followed by an explanation of some of the basic terminology that is essential to understanding the nature of drug use in society. We examine terms such as *drug effects, dependence, addiction, drug use,* and *drug abuse,* and yes, even the term *drug,* all through the lens of the sociological framework. We also introduce briefly the importance of classifying drugs, a topic that will be taken up in greater detail in Chapter 3. Finally, we conclude the chapter with a sociological examination of the "drug problem."

A Sociological Approach to Studying Drug Use

This textbook is a *sociological* investigation of drug use in America. It is likely that many, if not most of the students reading *The Sociology of American Drug Use* have had previous courses in sociology and have a working knowledge of the sociological perspective and of sociological concepts such as *culture, social structure,* and *society.* Regardless, a brief explanation of a sociological approach to the phenomenon of drug use is in order. To the sociologist, drugs are more than just chemical substances, the effects of which can be studied in laboratory experiments. They are also social and cultural phenomena. How we define what is and is not a drug, the meanings we attach to drugs and their use, the sorts of drugs we use and the manner in which we use them, and the overall societal impact of drug use are all influenced by social and cultural factors.

Drugs may be researched and theorized about from any number of academic perspectives; each has specific theoretical questions they are interested in and specific methods of conducting research. One of the tenets of scientific inquiry is that the answers you seek are predicated on the questions you ask. Different research questions will yield different answers. Clinical **pharmacology** is the study of how the biochemical substances we know as "drugs" affect the structure and function of the human body. Pharmacologists are interested in how drugs work as pharmacological entities, testable by experiments; they pay relatively less attention to the role of social or environmental influences on drug effects. Pharmacologists interested in the absorption and distribution patterns of cocaine by the human body, for example, have an important research agenda. They might ask: "What are the factors that promote or block absorption of cocaine into the bloodstream?" Courses in pharmacology, or more specifically psychopharmacology, which focus on the action of psychoactive drugs, would be of great benefit to nursing students in college, to premedical or medical students, to those studying for a career in clinical pharmacology, or perhaps those wishing to be drug and alcohol counselors. They might be of somewhat less importance to the college student who is looking to be a police officer or who is seeking other employment within the criminal justice system. The student who is interested in the social science dimensions of deviant or disapproved of behavior wouldn't find her answers there. Drug and alcohol counselors would certainly need additional grounding in research on drug abuse that looks at extra-pharmacological factors. And the individuals who want to understand the consequences of the drug abuse of a family member or friend might also wish to look elsewhere. Social scientific perspectives on drugs would be of great value to them.

Drugs are much more than just chemical substances to sociologists and other social scientists. "In addition to their inherent pharmacological properties, drugs are also taken *in certain ways, by certain people, for certain reasons;* moreover, they are also social, cultural, political, and symbolic phenomena . . ." (Goode, 1999:27, emphasis in the original). Pharmacologists simply aren't interested, professionally, in studying these dimensions of drugs. Nor should they be.

In their exhibit on "Cocaine-Use Research and the Social Sciences," Inciardi and Rothman (1990:12–13) acknowledge that cocaine use is sufficiently widespread to stimulate considerable research from the perspectives of each of the social sciences. *Anthropologists,* whose focus is often on traditional, nonindustrial societies, have examined the practice of coca-leaf chewing by the indigenous peoples of the Andes mountains of South America where coca has been grown and chewed for centuries. (Cocaine is derived from the coca plant.) In studying the coca rituals and beliefs of these people, they may note that coca-chewing is a mildly stimulating pastime considered comparable to our well-established practice of taking a coffee break. Coca leaves contain relatively small amounts of active stimulant, and chewing them releases the substance into their system quite slowly. The role of coca use as an aspect of peasant folk medicine, in brewed coca tea for example, might also considered; as could be the religious properties of coca, which was associated with the divine by the Incan people (see Weil, 1972 on natural drug use; Goode, 1999:275).

Political scientists, with their emphasis on political and governmental processes, and the means by which power is acquired and used, might be concerned with issues like the destabilizing or corrupting effects of cocaine trafficking on a government's functioning, such as in Colombia since the 1980s, or on the relationships between the governments of multiple countries (consider recent tensions between Peru and the United States over coca eradication policies). The considerable amount of money and influence wielded by drug-trafficking cartels, who have a vested interest in reducing governmental control of their operations, may be profoundly corrupting of democratic process. Other interests of political scientists might concern the political debates at the origin of many of our drug laws and of drug legislation in general (a topic we look at in Chapter 2). A number of scholars (among them Brecher, et. al. 1972; Musto, 1987; Grinspoon and Bakalar, 1976) have argued that the anticocaine legislation of the early 1900s was racist in its implementation and enforcement, being based on mythologies that black Americans would be especially likely to use cocaine and especially violent if they used the drug. The use of political power to control an "undesirable" segment of society for its alleged drug abuse is of interest to sociologists as well, whose scope of study overlaps with the political scientist.

The economics of the "crack" cocaine trade, the effect of windfall drug-dealing profits on a country's economy, or the impact of drug abuse on economic productivity might be of interest to *economists*. Colombia, home of the famous Medellin and Cali cocaine cartels, was affected throughout the 1980s by the billions of dollars a year that cocaine brought to the country's economy. (Inciardi, 1992:203–231) Flooded with money, specifically U.S. dollars, the Colombian currency was devalued and hyperinflation ensued. A black market in American dollars thrived; American automobiles sold for several times their asking price in the United States. Conversely, Americans were estimated to be spending upwards of 100 billion dollars a year on illegal drugs in the 1980s (estimates for today are far lower as drug prices have dropped and so have consumption rates when compared with 20 years ago). This is money that largely was unavailable to aid the bottom line of legitimate industries (Mills, 1987, Nadelmann, 1989).

Historians, who study drug use throughout American history, help to remind us that forms of drug use which concern us today, often were practiced, albeit in somewhat different forms many years ago. The recreational use of psychoactive drugs was not invented yesterday or by the "hippies" of the 1960s, despite what the popular belief might be. David F. Musto (2001), a professor of child psychiatry and the history of medicine at Yale University, and a recognized expert on drug use in the United States in the nineteenth and early twentieth century, writes that the recreational use of inhalants dates back to the early nineteenth century. At his own Ivy League university in the 1820s, students staged "ether frolics" and used nitrous oxide (known then and now as "laughing gas") at parties. So, college students and others today who do "whipits" are continuing a centuries-old practice. Inhalation-based drug experiences are more covert today, because while nitrous oxide is legally available, using it for intoxication is currently illegal. We know a great deal more about the damage done by inhalant abuse today than we did many years ago. Just because a substance that alters one's consciousness (but has other, more common uses) can be purchased legally should never lead one to conclude that it is therefore safe to use. As historians remind us, the legal status of chemical substances changes not just when harm is recognized, but for many other social and political reasons as well (Goode, 1975).

Each of the social sciences mentioned so far differs from sociology in that they are disciplines focused on a relatively narrow slice of human behavior (political behavior, economic behavior, etc.). *Psychologists* engaged in drug studies differ from sociologists, not in the scope of the discipline as both study the full range of human behavior but in its focus on the individual as the unit of analysis, whereas sociologists study human behavior within social groups ranging from the very small to the quite large. Psychologists might be interested in studying what personality characteristics are found in those who are more likely to use drugs such as cocaine. They are also interested in the effects of cocaine use on one's personality, on thinking, on emotions, on motivation. Psychic dependence on the drug's mood elevation or induced feelings of well-being, which fosters compulsive cocaine use known as "binging" may be studied by psychologists who wish to understand the brain-behavior link. And psychologists would be interested in the link between drug abuse and psychosis: Does abusing drugs lead to psychotic episodes? Or are those with serious underlying mental illnesses more likely to abuse drugs? Or are both possible?

Rothman and Inciardi (1990, p. 13) claim that *sociologists* have been especially concerned with studying patterns of cocaine use and abuse (as well as that of other drugs) in the United States. Sociologists collect and analyze data on the *incidence* and *prevalence* of cocaine use in the U.S. That is, they are concerned with how frequently someone takes a dose of a given drug (incidence) and what segment of the population has used a given drug, or drugs in general, in a specified period of time (prevalence), ranging from their lifetime ("Have they ever used, even once?") to daily ("Have they used in the last 24 hours?"). Unlike psychologists, who attempt to predict an individual's behavior, including drug-using behavior, by researching factors *endogenous* to an individual, sociologists look at the linkage between the behavioral patterns of subgroups in the society and the *exogenous* factors to which they are exposed.

What combination of theoretical points of view and approaches to conducting research is characteristic of sociological approaches to the study of drug use in America? Note that we say *approaches*, not approach. We do so because while there are common elements composing their discipline about which all sociologists agree, there are many research and theory-based issues about which sociologists might legitimately differ, such as what methods to use when conducting social research or what general theories of society inform their professional work. *Sociology is a general behavioral science*, which studies all forms of human behavior, including those studied by more narrowly focused disciplines like political science (there are political sociologists, for example). You would have a difficult time coming up with a type of social behavior that has not been studied by sociologists. The *focus of sociologists is on social groups and their structure, organization, and cultural elements*. When studying social behavior—including drug use and abuse, drug trafficking, and drug control—the sociologist is ever mindful of the social forces which shape that behavior and the group response to that behavior. To that end, sociology reminds us that human behavior exists within a social and cultural context which cannot be ignored. Ignoring the social dimensions of drug-oriented behavior leads to incomplete or distorted research and theory according to sociologists.

There are four important ways that a sociological view of the world affects the academic understanding of drugs in American society. Most of what is written in this textbook directly or indirectly touches on one or more of these dimensions.

- To define what a drug is, or is not, we must look beyond the biochemical substances studied by pharmacologists and include the social contexts within which social definitions take place. What the concept "drug" means is affected by a variety of social influences.
- To understand psychoactive drug effects, we must have an awareness of social factors that influence the way that drugs affect those who take them and how those users experience their drug taking independent of any pharmacological processes that are occurring.
- Drug use, drug abuse, and drug addiction and/or dependence are all social constructions. That is, the meaning attached to each of these ideas is a matter of social negotiation. We will be defining these concepts for you, but we ask you to recognize that other professionals in this field, with other interests, may disagree with our interpretation.
- To comprehend our society's concern over the social problem of drug abuse, we must investigate not only the objective harm done by and to drug abusers but also the subjective dimensions of concern. Social problems are both conditions that cause observable harm and subjectively constructed campaigns led by those who claim that something is harmful.

The impact of drug abuse in this society profoundly affects our social institutions and our social relationships. Drug abuse affects all aspects of social life: family dynamics are strained, economic productivity decreases, the health care system has increased demands placed on it, and the landscape of crime and justice shifts. In short, drug abuse raises the costs of running a society, it is associated with a host of social pathologies, and it is destructive of interpersonal trust.

THE SOCIOLOGICAL DEFINITION OF *DRUG*

This may seem like an unnecessary section of this book. After all, we all know what a drug is, don't we? You might find, were you to do a survey of people in your community that there is agreement among them as to whether substance A or B should count as a drug. But what would be the basis for that decision? Would your respondents be considering the *psychopharmacological* actions of the substance in question? That is, would they be thinking of drugs as chemical substances that alter the way we feel or think or the ways in which our bodies function? Without question, drugs are such chemical entities. It is likely, however, that those examples considered drugs by the subjects of your survey weren't selected on this basis alone. An additional dimension would be whether your survey respondents would classify Drug A or Drug B as "good drugs" or "bad drugs." This distinction is particularly influenced by extrapharmacological factors of a social, cultural, or political nature. Many Americans consider marijuana to be a drug but do not consider alcohol to be a drug, yet both are substances which have a *psychoactive effect* on those who use a sufficient dose of them. Psychoactive drugs—which exert an influence on our *central nervous system* and have the capacity to alter our moods or emotion, our sensation or perception, or our cognition (thinking)— are the central subject of this textbook. Psychoactivity alone, though, doesn't explain why marijuana is more frequently thought of as a drug than is alcohol, a substance that in many ways is more powerful and has a wider range of psychoactive effects and societal consequences than does marijuana. Alcohol's effect on motor skills performance, such as driving a car, is more profound. Alcohol abuse precipitates violent behavior, from getting in fights to rape to homicide, in ways marijuana does not (Parker, 1995). Where there is interpersonal violence in America, alcohol is likely to be a contributing factor. It isn't the level of actual social harm done by abusing a particular substance that leads to its being considered a drug, or a dangerous drug, or a bad drug. Purported social harm is used to indict certain practices that are deemed unacceptable, however. What leads the public—at a given point in time, since public attitudes change—to label a substance as a drug is a complex process of **social construction.**

Sociologists are particularly interested in understanding the social and cultural factors that influence common perceptions of what drugs are and are not. For sociologists, the political climate matters, the prevailing culture matters, a society's awareness of a threat in its midst matters. Drugs are multidimensional phenomena. They are pharmacological substances that affect human anatomy and physiology, the structure and functioning of the human body, to be sure. But they are also political and economic phenomena, they are grounded in our history and our folklore and in our popular culture, they are an integral part of our national psyche. We must take these varied contexts into consideration when naming, classifying, evaluating, and judging drugs. Consider the following from sociologist Erich Goode (1999, p. 58): ". . . any accurate and valid definition of drugs must include the social, cultural, and contextual dimension. The concept drug is in part a cultural artifact, a social fabrication, applied to certain types of substances in specific contexts or settings. *A drug is something that has been defined by certain segments of the society as a drug.*" [emphasis in the original]

According to this perspective, what is most important is how social elements get defined by a society, at a specific point in time. It recognizes the variability of social concern and societal responses about things we might call "drugs." Currently, marijuana is viewed as a "drug," its recreational use is illegal in all states (though not necessarily a *criminal offense*, as it has been decriminalized in eleven states). With the exception of some "dry" counties or municipalities, and, of course, for those who are under the age of 21, alcohol is legal, available, and widely promoted. It wasn't always so. Seventy-five years ago, during Prohibition, alcohol consumption was illegal by federal law as a result of the Eighteenth Amendment to the Constitution of the United States. Marijuana use, in contrast, was a legal, though somewhat disreputable, pursuit in every state. Sociologists stress that one's status as a criminal or as a societal outsider (Becker, 1963:1–18) is always the result of being associated with behaviors whose prevailing social definitions deem them unacceptable. In the public mind, being a user of drugs (meaning: "bad" drugs) conveys such disrepute based on images of drug use as dirty, destructive, dangerous or the like.

The point being made by sociologists is that while the chemical properties of a substance certainly matter, what gets defined as a drug, and hence which practices get defined as drug use or abuse, hinges on the social and political perspectives that prevail. The "reality" of drug use is a social and political phenomenon (Goode, 1975). It shifts with the times and with changes in the groups who wield political power and moral influence (see Gusfield, 1963, on shifting perceptions of drinkers of alcohol). A commonly used phrase in sociology is that "reality is socially constructed." This may be applied to the definition and assessment of drugs in America. We are somewhat relativistic when we define something as a "drug." We distinguish "drugs" from "drink," though both act pharmacologically on our bodies. We distinguish "drugs" from "medicine," because they are purported to be used for different purposes. Yet sometimes a substance shifts in the collective wisdom from medicine to drug, as was the case with OxyContin in the years 2000–2002. Throughout this book, but particularly in Chapter 2, we will see that the drugs with which we are most concerned, the "most dangerous drugs," go through cycles of public recognition.

PSYCHOACTIVE DRUG EFFECTS

One of the most commonly asked questions by students in a course on the Sociology of Drug Use, or by the population in general, is: "What effect does taking a drug have on the user?" As we shall soon see, this is an imprecise question, because the questioner may have several different goals in mind. She might be asking, "If I take this drug, how will it make me feel?" Alternatively, the intention might be to discover whether any deleterious effects of using this substance might be likely, as in: "If I take this drug, might it lead me to go crazy?" (As in the popular myth that anyone who "trips" on LSD seven times—or is it 11?—is legally insane.) Or perhaps the intention is to ferret out long-term consequences of using a particular drug on one's health and well-being. We really are talking about several different kinds of effects associated with psychoactive drug use—*objective drug effects, subjective drug effects, and chronic drug effects.* Each will be discussed now.

Objective drug effects are those which are the result of being under the influence of a substance and which can be measured reliably. While they are less likely to be the reasons motivating drug use in the first place, they are quite valuable to researchers and scientists. For example, users of marijuana frequently experience a *tachycardial effect.* That is, smoking marijuana produces a measurable increase in one's heart rate. This effect doesn't generally motivate people to use the drug; in fact, the elevated heart rate may be experienced by the user as an uncomfortable anxious

DRUGS AND EVERYDAY LIFE

The Social Construction of "Hillbilly Heroin"

The public perception of a psychoactive drug can shift radically, often in a very short period of time. A recent such case is that of OxyContin, a powerful brand-name pharmaceutical narcotic manufactured by Purdue Pharma, which was the subject of increasing public and media attention, particularly in the spring and summer of 2001. OxyContin, a pill of varying strengths of timed-release oxycodone—a painkiller found in much smaller amounts in Percocet and Percodan—is intended to be used once every 12 hours by patients with chronic pain like that found in many cancer sufferers (Waldman, 2001, p. E3). Fueled by concern about the abuse of the drug by addicts who were circumventing the time-release mechanism of the drug by crushing the pills and either snorting or injecting it, OxyContin quickly was elevated to "most dangerous drug" status by society's opinion makers. It was given the catchy nickname of "hillbilly heroin" because it penetrated rural areas, for example West Virginia and Kentucky, where illegal drugs like heroin aren't as widely available (Tough, 2001, p. 33; McGraw, 2001, p. 108). Consider the following lead-in from an article in a youth-oriented magazine, one not ordinarily known for antidrug hysteria: "OxyContin was supposed to be a miracle— the strongest, safest painkiller ever. But when some junkies found out that its rush could rival pure heroin's, an epidemic was born. Talk to the addicts, hear the tales of teenage drugstore cowboys and old ladies getting jacked for their stash, and the `miracle drug' sounds anything but wonderful. Here's what went wrong." (McGraw, 2001, p. 107) Note the emotionally laden language, the invoking of the bogeyman of "pure heroin" and the warning of an incipient epidemic. When a media campaign is under-way to discredit a substance or its use, such rhetorical devices are common (Goode, 1990;

Reinarman, 2000). Heroin, fairly or not, has had a decades long reputation as a scourge, a demon drug. Although it is a highly effective pain reliever, and is an analog of morphine (heroin breaks down into morphine in the bloodstream; the heroin user tests morphine positive), heroin has no recognized medical utility and hence is a Schedule I drug (discussed in Chapter 2), because of its demonization. Comparing OxyContin in any way to heroin— as in its alliterative nickname "hillbilly heroin"—contributes to its demonization as well. Likewise, the use of "epidemic" to describe OxyContin abuse may be overheated. While it had been associated with perhaps a hundred or more deaths by mid-2002, this should be put in the context of true epidemics—about 17,000 deaths from using illegal drugs per year (Office of National Drug Control Policy, 2002), upwards of 150,000 deaths per year directly or indirectly associated with alcohol abuse (National Center for Health Statistics, 2001) or the approximately 430,000 premature deaths a year from smoking-related causes reported by the Centers for Disease Control and Prevention (Goode, 1999, p. 197). OxyContin abuse statistics also need to be compared with the more than 1,000,000 patients who used the drug in 2000 and the 6.5 million prescriptions written that same year (Tough, 2001, p. 37).

As an opioid drug, OxyContin is an addictive substance. That is, it has the potential to render users physically dependent, even in those who use the medicine in prescribed ways. Yet for someone who suffers from severe and intractable pain, being addicted to something that reliably brings relief may be a minor consequence. The term "addiction" may be misused in ideological campaigns, as those with vested interests use OxyContin as a springboard for their own agendas. Letters to the editor of the *New York Times* and *New York Times*

continued

continued from previous page

Magazine, in response to stories about OxyContin during the Summer of 2001, represented many such interests. The General Counsel for Purdue Pharma, the manufacturer, reminded us of all of the people being helped by the drug, and castigated the newspaper for using misleading statistics and fostering an atmosphere of fear. The president of Odyssey House, a New York area system of drug rehabilitation centers, touted his company's record in treating all kinds of addiction, and argued OxyContin addiction can be combated successfully. A recovering substance abuser said "throwing money at the problem" by paying for

rehab was not the answer, and touted 12-step programs which are free and address the reasons for addiction. And the president and CEO of The Partnership for a Drug-Free America, the "this is your brain on drugs" people, saw this as a platform to oppose the legalization of currently illegal drugs. With such diverse positions being presented, one can see that "the social construction of reality" for OxyContin and, by extension, other drugs as well, is a complex ideological process in which empirical evidence of the consequences of a drug's abuse or its potential for abuse gets buried by the actions of claims-makers ∎

---

feeling. Yet this knowledge is valuable, since it would seem to indicate that individuals with underlying heart conditions should be especially cautious about smoking marijuana, because for them the risks of doing so might be greater than for other individuals. Drugs affect different users in different ways; the health history of the user, among many other factors, is relevant to the consequences he or she might experience from using drugs. Remember, risk associated with drug use is not an either-or proposition; degree of risk varies along a continuum from slight to quite serious.

Another objective drug effect, one with far greater consequences, can be seen in the discoordinating effects of alcohol intoxication. Nearly every reader of this text is aware of the effect of alcohol in sufficient doses on speech and motor coordination. One's performance in driving a car, a measurable skill, is adversely affected by alcohol consumption, and the degree of diminished performance, correlated with blood-alcohol concentration, is reliably shown in study after study. Researchers can then pinpoint how much alcohol one would need to consume, on average, to yield a particular level of increased risk. And public policy makers could employ such data in setting laws, as in the recent movement to have states lower the threshold for DUI offenses from the once standard .10 percent BAC to the more restrictive .08 percent, an increasingly common change in state laws.

To sum up, objective drug effects are measurable effects resulting from the direct ingestion of a drug or drugs by a user. They are observable, independent of whatever the user believes that he or she is experiencing. Marijuana intoxication is associated with decreased driving performance, though not as clearly so as is alcohol intoxication. Yet a significant number of marijuana smokers believe themselves to be better drivers when "high," mistakenly so. They confuse the subjective experience of their greater awareness of the need to be careful when driving stoned with their objective driving performance while affected by marijuana. Objective drug effects matter to the study of drug use in America, and are of some interest to sociologists, yet in many ways subjective effects are the more valuable to look at. And they are certainly more controversial.

Subjective drug effects are those which cannot be measured on a consistent scale, and are grounded in the experiential reality of the user. Note that just because an outside observer may not be able to measure such effects doesn't make them any less real. Perhaps an example of subjective reality in an allied field will be helpful here. As of early 2001, hospitals are required to ask their patients about the level of pain they are experiencing and to make pain management a higher therapeutic priority. Patients are asked to rate their current pain on a scale of 1–10, something which they are generally able to do. We are aware that one person's pain experience may differ from another's, based on factors such as tolerance for pain, and that the reporting of pain may be mediated through factors such as gender ("tough men don't show they are hurting"). So two patients undergoing similar treatment may report subjectively experienced levels of pain that are quite different.

So it is with subjective drug effects—the use of a particular drug may yield different experiences for different users. These differences may be heightened further because of the difficulty one has in precisely articulating subjective effects. We know about subjective effects primarily through user-reported experiences, as opposed to first-hand observation, and such reportage is often imprecise because drug experiences may be so personal and profound that an agreed upon vocabulary of effects is not possible. Obviously, this makes them somewhat tougher to study by sociologists and other drug researchers. They are also more controversial, since it is easier to make claims about subjective drug effects that are wildly divergent and that support different (pro-drug or antidrug, let's say) agendas. There is great difficulty evaluating the "rightness" of perspectives based on subjective experience, just as there is with many other social issues today, such as abortion or capital punishment.

What is the experience of being "high" like? Is being high on marijuana like being drunk on alcohol? How are the similarities and differences articulated? Here you see how hard it is to explain to others, to sociologists who are studying drug use, or to those who might wish to experiment with a drug themselves, about the subjective nature of drug experience. These experiences may or may not be related to objective, observable changes in the user's vital signs, blood chemistry, or appearance. In other words, subjective drug effects may be more than the user's psychic experience of changes in objective conditions. They may be wholly unique phenomena *sui generis*—in and of themselves.

LSD (lysergic acid diethylamide-25), commonly known as "acid," is a potent drug which provides a wide range of profound subjective experiences for its users, experiences that they may have difficulty articulating to others who might wish to know what their drug "trip" was like. Imagine an experience where one's senses cross heretofore unheard of boundaries—attributing colors to different musical sounds, for example, or reporting that one could "taste" musical notes. Or consider the "eureka experience"

(Goode, 1999:247) where one makes connections between things that now appear to the user to represent some important truth (but will seem silly or incomprehensible if explained to an observer). A female college student told one of the authors of the following experience: "I had come to the great 'aha.' And that was that Herman Munster (of the TV show *The Munsters*) and Prince (the musical artist) were one and the same person, because you never saw them in the same place and the shoes they wore were identical." Needless to say, she had great difficulty persuading others at the time that the green and physically imposing Munster was one and the same with the diminutive Prince. Given that LSD renders its users extremely emotionally labile, she was distraught when no one else could see her point of view, since conveying this important truth to others had become a mission for her. Days later, sober, she could understand why her fellows had not bought into the Munster-Prince unified theory of pop culture.

For the most part, subjective effects are the ones that users seek, that motivate them to use psychoactive drugs initially, regularly, or even habitually. Experiencing a "high," "tripping," having a sense of drug-induced well-being, are all subjective effects. It must be noted that while pleasurable subjective drug experience may be sought by users, that not all such effects are pleasurable and may, in fact, result in profoundly uncomfortable sensations or experiences. Powerful drugs may yield powerfully negative subjective experiences, such as sensations of paranoia, or of being suffocated, or of experiencing nightmares from which one may not easily awaken. Traumatic drug experiences, while relatively rare occurrences, can indelibly implant themselves on unfortunate users.

Subjective drug effects are influenced by many factors that are of particular interest to sociologists and other behavioral scientists. One's expectations prior to a drug using experience, or one's emotional state or mood, known as the user's **set,** can influence whether one gets intoxicated and whether that intoxication is defined as pleasurable or not. It can also influence the behavior one considered appropriate while intoxicated. Experimental psychologist Kim Fromme and her associates have done research on "alcohol outcome expectancies," using "of age" student subjects in a simulated tavern. Some of her research subjects would be served mixed drinks containing a measured amount of alcohol, while others would drink nonalcoholic counterparts of similar appearance, and some subjects would be given some of each. Subjects often would report feeling intoxicated and they "acted drunk," even when no or little alcohol had been consumed, because they were around others who had imbibed alcohol and their behavioral expectations were adjusted accordingly. Behaviors that might seem purely alcohol-induced, Fromme argues, including risk-taking sexual behaviors, may be products more of one's expectations of the alcohol experience than of pharmacological disinhibition, including the expectation held by many college men that the consequences of coercing sex are reduced when alcohol is a factor (Fromme and Wendel, 1995). This is important, because it leads us away from the simplistic assessment that the pharmacological action of drugs alone *causes* a host of unwanted and risky behaviors, and leads us toward looking at psychological and sociocultural influences on our comportment "under the influence."

These emotional states and expectations, the drug user's **set,** is a concept frequently paired with the **setting** within which drug use is to take place. Setting, the environment in which drug use takes place, has a number of dimensions: physical surroundings, the presence or absence of others and one's relationship to those present, and the legal and political climate that prevails. All of these affect the comfort level of the user, and being comfortable or uncomfortable in a drug-using episode can alter the nature of the experience. This isn't difficult to see. If one wishes to use a substance—say marijuana—in an environment where there are well-known social or legal consequences for doing so, the behavior will be more surreptitious due to fear of being discovered, and this can result in feeling suspicious or paranoid of others. It is not the pharmacological action of the marijuana that is causing such feelings (though the tachycardial effect mentioned previously might play a modest role), it is the "unsafe" environment. The experience of drugs like marijuana, and especially hallucinogenics like LSD, whose impact on cognition and mood are pronounced, may be altered profoundly by how one perceives the immediate and social environments. Set and setting are important, nonpharmacological influences on the nature of subjective drug experience.

There are also pharmacological influences on objective and subjective drug effects which are worthy of mention. **Route of administration,** the method by which drugs are introduced into one's physiological system can greatly alter the effects of using the drug. There are many such routes of administration: "mainlining," intravenous injection directly into the bloodstream; "skin-popping," or subcutaneous injection; "snorting" or intranasal administration; smoking or inhaling vapors; oral ingestion where one swallows a solid or liquid containing the active ingredient; and transdermal absorption through the skin, as with a nicotine or fentanyl patch, are some of them. They vary in the speed and efficiency of the onset of effects. Intravenous injection and smoking are extremely rapid, effects being felt within a matter of seconds (there is some disagreement in the drug research literature about which of these is faster, though the effects of IV injection are more profound). Drugs that are swallowed take effect or "kick in" much more slowly, taking perhaps 30–60 minutes in many cases. That time-lag may make it harder for the user to connect the effects experienced with the substance ingested, especially in *polydrug use* situations, those where an individual is using multiple substances in the same time period. Coca products, for example, may be injected in solution form, smoked in rock ("crack") form, snorted in powdered form, or even orally ingested, as with chewing coca leaves or drinking brewed coca tea (or in Coca-Cola in its earliest formulations a century ago). The intensity and duration of the drug-using episode will vary with different routes of administration. The route of administration one chooses to employ may be affected by drug-using peers or by financial considerations, so we can see that social processes remain important factors on drug effects and experiences.

Other pharmacological factors influencing psychoactive drug effects are *dose, potency, purity, tolerance,* and *drug interaction.* Most drugs have effects that are dose-related, with known **effective doses** and **lethal doses.** Pharmaceuticals have recommended **therapeutic doses.** What is the dose that is most often appropriate for the effect one wishes to achieve? Anabolic steroids have a therapeutically recommended dose, appropriate for tissue repair. Yet someone who is interested in increasing muscle and strength rapidly will seek a much higher effective dose, many times the therapeutic dose, which yields the desired benefits but does so with greatly enhanced risks. Or consider drinkers of alcohol, who might seek the gentle relaxation which one mixed drink and a slightly elevated blood alcohol level provides, or may desire as binge-drinking college students do, a greater level of intoxication in which one would feel "drunk." The latter effect might be found at a blood alcohol level of 0.15 percent (though many drink beyond that point), not all that far from the median *lethal* dose for alcohol which is right around 0.40 percent. The ratio between effective and lethal dose for alcohol, being relatively narrow, makes lethal levels of alcohol intoxication a possibility, particularly for the naive drinker who might be talked into drinking games. In contrast, marijuana, a less toxic drug, has a lethal dose that is virtually unreachable.

Potency and **purity** are allied terms. Potency refers to the strength of the drug in question, and refers to how much of that drug is necessary for an effective dose. The more potent the drug, the smaller is the effective dose. LSD is an extremely potent drug, with an effective dose of perhaps 100 micrograms; about one ten-thousandth of a gram. An aspirin-sized tablet (325 mg.) of pure LSD would yield around 3,250 doses! Drugs like marijuana or psilocybin mushrooms, grown naturally, have a variable potency, though they are far less potent than LSD. Marijuana cultivators can breed strains of the cannabis plant with higher levels of THC (delta-9-tetrahydrocannabinol), its active ingredient, that would be more in demand and fetch a higher price because of the increased potency. In contrast, purity refers to the percentage of the drug sample that is actually the drug itself. Marijuana, whatever its potency, is generally 100% pure (though it may be occasionally mixed with other drugs). Powdered street drugs, like heroin and cocaine, may vary widely in purity; some samples containing little drug and much inactive ingredient or adulterant, with other samples having higher rates of purity. In recent years, the purity of street drug samples has been increasing, due to a glut of drugs on the market. A user not used to higher levels of purity might be at greater risk of overdose, perhaps fatally so. Recent emergency room data show an increase in overdose cases for both heroin and cocaine (Office of National Drug Control Policy, 2002:110–111).

Tolerance is a pharmacological phenomenon which develops in some users of some drugs. Tolerance is a cumulative resistance to the pharmacological effects of drugs. In drugs where tolerance may develop in users—among them LSD, alcohol, and the narcotics—regular, chronic, or habitual use may raise the effective dose for such users. Consider the case of the individual who can "drink others under the table"; he or she may have developed a tolerance to alcohol, which may serve as a warning sign that alcohol dependence or alcoholism has begun to set in. Drug tolerance and **drug dependence** are believed to be related phenomena. At the very least, behaviorally and pharmacologically, experienced drinkers have subjective drug effects different from the inexperienced drinker. Interestingly, though the effective dose of such drinkers is higher, moving closer to the known lethal dose, by virtue of their drinking experience, such users are less likely to die of acute alcohol intoxication. The chronic or cumulative effects of alcohol abuse are another story, as we shall see shortly.

Finally, we must consider **drug interaction** effects. These are vitally important for two reasons: polydrug use, the mixing of substances, is an extremely common practice; and when drugs are mixed together, their cumulative effect may be synergistic, antagonistic, or idiosyncratic, and hence dangerous. This is true for both recreational drug use and the use of pharmaceutical drugs for medical purposes. For this reason, physicians ask their patients for lists of all current medications (especially elderly patients who take pills for more ailments and whose livers metabolize drugs more slowly) and pharmacies have computerized records which "flag" potentially dangerous combinations.[1] One form of danger is known as *synergy* or **synergistic effects.** Synergy is the condition where two or more drugs taken in combination have an effect that is greater than a simple additive effect. Many drugs, particularly central nervous *depressants* like quaaludes or tranquilizers or narcotic pain relievers, when combined with alcohol (itself a CNS depressant), exhibit synergy, often dangerously so. Some drugs are **antagonistic** to one another, and cancel out each other's effects. Some drugs in combination have **idiosyncratic effects,** where the effect of one of the drugs is greatly heightened by the presence of the other drug, whose effect is muted. Or the effects of both drugs are heightened, as with the injectable heroin-cocaine mix known as a "speedball." An awareness of the ways in which drugs—legal and illegal, recreational and therapeutic—interact, is critical for users and health practitioners alike. **Chronic effects** are those that accumulate over time as one continues to use or abuse a particular substance. They are, for the most part, objective health-related consequences of a history of drug abuse. Perhaps this is most easily understood by looking at tobacco smoking. Tobacco does little harm to the vast majority of users in any given episode of use. While we have been warned by the Surgeon General about the deleterious effects of smoking since the 1960s, such warnings are not of the "one puff could lead to insanity or to lung cancer" variety. Rather, we are confronted with powerful evidence that many years of smoking tobacco products, most notably cigarettes, is associated with some of America's leading causes of death, among them chronic lung disorders such as lung cancer and emphysema, and heart disease. Recent estimates of smoking related deaths range from 400,000–450,000 people a year. Clearly, the chronic effects of tobacco consumption contribute mightily to mortality (death) and morbidity (sickness) statistics.

Another chronic effect of drug abuse is addiction, a concept we deal with elsewhere in this chapter. Despite alarmist claims to the contrary, no drug is "instantly addictive," regardless of its potential for producing dependency in its user. Addiction results from regular and repeated instances of the use of a drug by an individual. It must be noted that while there is no magic timetable for when addiction occurs, as drugs vary in their addictive potential from low to quite high, and users vary somewhat in terms of their susceptibility to addiction, the biochemical alterations occurring within the addict are the result of an accumulative process and hence must be considered chronic effects.

DRUG USE, DRUG ABUSE, AND DRUG ADDICTION

So far in this chapter, the concepts of "drug use" and "drug abuse" have appeared repeatedly. They are often conflated by casual observers of the drug scene, by the mass media, and by those who may have an ideological axe to grind. It is time for us to differentiate these terms, because they are not interchangeable and should not be used interchangeably by anyone who takes the study of psychoactive drugs in America seriously. **Drug use** is an extremely broad concept, for it refers to the consumption of any chemical substance that acts like a drug or that is believed to act like a drug. This includes a wide range of both legal and illegal substances. It includes every level of involvement with psychoactive substances, from the most occasional user to the frequent social user to the person who uses habitually, perhaps due to drug dependence. When we wrote earlier that ours is a nation of psychoactive drug users, and that this is a social fact and not a pejorative viewpoint on the American people, we were acknowledging the universality of drug using in this country. And the majority of this drug use is socially acceptable and even promoted. We joke about needing our caffeine "fix" in the mornings, but rarely does going into a coffee shop require surreptitiousness. The majority of American adults drink alcoholic beverages in any given month; lifetime prevalence approaches six out of every seven of us (SAMHSA, 2000). After work or college classes, drinking establishments attract the thirsty, the overworked, and the stressed-out with "happy hours" or "attitude adjustment sessions;" societal protest is minimal. The point is, the *use* of substances that alter emotion and mood is ingrained in American society. That is why we can say that drug use is an American way of life. The broadness and ubiquity of psychoactive drug use makes "drug use" a less useful concept than "drug abuse."

There are those who argue—usually on religious, moral or ethical grounds—that using anything psychoactive constitutes **drug abuse.** While it is not a mainstream cultural position, it should be acknowledged. Students at Brigham Young University, which is run according to Latter

Day Saints' principles (the Mormon Church), sign a pledge that they will abstain from all drugs, even soft drinks containing caffeine. Violation of this pledge is considered drug abuse in the eyes of school administrators. Other colleges and universities, other religious organizations, have similar bans. As mentioned previously, this is not a widely held position. Much more widely believed by the public at large, and some drug abuse professionals, is that the recreational use of any *illegal* drug constitutes drug abuse. After all, the word "abuse" connotes a negative evaluation of a practice; the "abuser" is a wrongdoer, a violator of acceptable standards of behavior. And it is also wrong to do things that are against the law. So why not combine the two, allowing the criminal law to be the arbiter of whether a practice qualifies as drug abuse or not?

We believe that the "any use of an illegal drug constitutes drug abuse" argument is overly simplistic and falls short in two important areas. First, it fails in any way to distinguish the degree of involvement one has with drugs; the one-time-only user of an illegal drug and the habitual user are lumped together and are tarred with the same damning brush. Drug abuse should not be considered an all-or-nothing phenomenon, where smoking marijuana once, or a few times, is equated with hard core, intractable, consequential behavior. The second shortcoming, and the more critical, is that it legalistically assumes that the law assesses with impartiality and scientific precision, those drugs whose use represents a threat and hence should be designated as abusive.

Drug legislation is not created in a social and political vacuum, by legislators who rely on the best drug research available. Drugs are not politically neutral entities, either, about which we can be dispassionate. Legislation is a process that is always swayed by the prevailing political winds; drug legislation is especially political. The distinction between "legal drugs" and "illegal drugs" is a political one, not a scientific one. This doesn't mean that it is worthless or unimportant. It matters vitally which substances can lead to legal consequences for those who use them. But it is a great mistake to assume that drugs which are illegal are inevitably harmful and that the use of their legal counterparts is essentially a risk-free endeavor. Yet we make this mistake all of the time, dichotomizing "good" drugs from "bad" on the basis of legal status alone, and in doing so attribute far greater wisdom to the legislative process than it deserves.

As sociologists, we believe that it makes much more sense to assess whether drug involvement should be considered drug abuse by looking at the individual, interpersonal, and social consequences of drug-involved behavior. This restores the concept of *social harm*, allows us to ground our understanding of drug abuse in measurable adversity, and permits us to see abuse on a sliding scale from slight to great, since the consequences of actions are not of uniform severity. Let us therefore define **drug abuse** as *"the use of a substance or substances in such a way that it leads to measurable personal, interpersonal, or social consequences."* (Adapted from Fuqua, 1978:8–9) Many of these consequences will come from over involvement with a substance, some will come from misusing a substance, and still others will be the result of bad luck. We mention the last of these because while most episodes of drug use result in no harm whatsoever, one should never assume that using a drug, even a relatively benign one, is entirely without risk. And while we can calculate the probability of risk to some extent, by attending to the many factors that affect the pharmacological action of a drug, there are no guarantees of safety.

What are some of the consequences that might stem from drug involvement? Impaired physical and mental functioning is one. Every human physiological system is potentially affected: the cardiovascular system by drugs that accelerate the development of heart disease or by stimulant drugs such as cocaine which may overstimulate the heart; the respiratory system, by drugs that are smoked or inhaled, contributing to chronic obstructive lung diseases or lung cancer; the central nervous system, which may experience irreversible damage to brain functioning. The damage may be done by legal drugs like tobacco products and alcohol as well as illegal drugs such as heroin, cocaine, and marijuana. That is why judging abuse by legal status alone is an inappropriate strategy.

Or consider the following interpersonal and social consequences of the overuse or misuse of drugs, which potentially affect every social role that we might be called on to play, within every social institution.

- Fathers and mothers who abdicate parenting roles, because they are debilitated by a drug's effects, or because they are wrapped up in the pursuit of the drugs or the money with which to purchase drugs.
- Significant others who withdraw from intimacy and commitment because of drug involvement. When drug abuse enters a relationship, it becomes an unhealthy love triangle which tends to squeeze out the nonabusing partner.
- Religious or spiritual individuals whose relationship with God withers as drug abusing becomes more central to their lives. In very real ways, drug abusers pursue false gods, seeking comfort and meaning in chemicals.
- Committed students whose love of learning and outstanding academic records get thrust aside by over involvement with drugs. A history of drug abusing can often be intuited by looking at student transcripts that follow all too predictable patterns.
- Once productive employees whose absences become more frequent, whose postlunch break performance declines, whose interaction with co-workers suffers are often abusing drugs. Lost potential productivity due to drug abuse was estimated to be more than $110 billion in 2000 (Office of National Drug Control Policy, 2002, p. 70).
- Law-abiding people who find that their moral objections to committing crimes dissolve when drug hunger requires money that they cannot earn legitimately. The sharp increase in prison populations in the last generation is primarily fueled by increased penalties for drug-related crimes.

Perhaps this paints an overly pessimistic view of drug abuse; however, it is important for students to recognize that drug abuse has the potential to utterly destroy lives, and not just the lives of the abusers themselves but often those who are tied to them in a variety of social relationships. Remember that drug use is not the same as drug abuse; it is rhetorical over-reach, a convenient myth that those who wage war on drugs would like us to believe. Any drug may be used safely by some, even the drugs about which we are most frequently warned. Not all drug abusers are irreparably harmed. Drug abuse, while it has serious consequences, and is one of our nation's social problems, may not be the scourge that some have painted it to be. But it is surely a fact of life in American society that has consequences, now and in the future.

No concept in the study of drugs has been as variably used and as misused as **drug addiction.** Addiction is a disease where a misconfigured brain chemistry produces drug cravings. No it's not. It is a product of moral breakdown or moral inferiority that comes from associating oneself with undesirable drugs. Really? Drugs have negative associations in our society, therefore addiction must be pejorative as well. The concept of addiction has been broadened beyond the realm of chemical abuse. Public discourse—talk shows, self-help advocates—now refers to gambling as an addiction, to sex and love addiction, to refined sugar and simple carbohydrate addiction, to Internet addiction, and more. In science, and sociology adheres to principles of scientific inquiry and method, concepts need precise definition, as precise as language allows for. In the realm of drug studies, we have been extremely imprecise when we talk about "drug abuse," "the dangerous drug problem," and especially about "drug addiction." We need to clear up this conceptual confusion.

Addiction originally was used to connote an "enslavement" of a person to a substance, which became the master (see Brecher, 1972). When drugs began to be studied scientifically in the 1800s, what became known as a "classical" model of addiction emerged, one which focused on physical addiction, on craving and on drug withdrawal, as in the following definition from a recent drugs text: "Addiction is a drug craving accompanied by physical dependence, which motivates continued usage, resulting in a tolerance to a drug's effects and a syndrome of identifiable symptoms when the drug is abruptly withdrawn." (Inciardi and McElrath, 1998, p. xiii)

To become addicted in the classical sense, one must use a potentially addictive drug, in adequate doses and for a sufficiently long time, that one undergoes biochemical alterations that produce such a physical dependence. All narcotic drugs are physically addicting, as are most other central nervous system depressants, including alcohol. Nicotine, a stimulant, is also an addicting drug. Not all drugs, however, regardless of how frequently they are used, produce such a physical dependence in their users. Cannabis products like marijuana and hashish do not. Hallucinogenic drugs like LSD, peyote, and ecstasy do not. Most stimulants, including cocaine and the amphetamines, are not physically addicting. This may sound like semantic hair-splitting, but a drug may not be physically addicting yet be powerfully habit-forming. Cocaine clearly is such a drug, as it is used habitually and harmfully by many. In other words, physical addiction is just one type of **drug dependence.** Dependence can also exist at the psychological level and at the behavioral level as well.

Why don't we simply speak of drug dependency then, rather than of both drug addiction and nonaddictive drug dependency? What is the value of maintaining separate researching and theorizing on drug addiction? We will understand physical withdrawal symptoms better—some are dangerous, even life-threatening while others are merely uncomfortable—which allows us to make *detoxification* a safer process. Drug treatment programs will have higher success rates as the phenomenon of addiction is understood more fully. Alfred Lindesmith (1938), a giant in the field of understanding drug addiction, constructed a sociological theory of addiction which focused on how the pain associated with opiate withdrawal made it more difficult to perform a variety of social roles, and often led the addict to continue using to keep those painful symptoms at bay. An awareness of this might reduce relapse, which at one time was seen as an inevitable part of the addiction process. Alan Leshner, the former Director of the National Institute on Drug Abuse, claims that drug addiction treatment is as successful as treatment for other chronic diseases as diabetes, high blood pressure, and asthma (Leshner, 1999, p. 1321). The profound changes in brain functioning wrought by addiction make addiction a brain disease according to Leshner, but one that is eminently treatable.

Increasingly, researchers have focused their attention on the role of *psychological* (or *psychic*) *dependence,* both with drugs that have a potential to be physically addicting and those which do not. The reason for the increasing attention being paid to the concept of psychological dependence starting in the 1970s—a period of rising rates of drug usage—seemed clear. Users of drugs that were not physically addicting, particularly cocaine, were exhibiting patterns of drug dependence very similar to physically addicting substances. If the dependence was not physical, which meant that there weren't physical cravings or withdrawal symptoms when the drug was removed, then what could explain continued abuse of these drugs, even in the face of accumulating negative consequences? Lindesmith (1938) emphasized avoidance of withdrawal symptoms as the primary motivator for continued opiate use by the addict, downplaying the role of the pursuit of euphoria, which he felt wasn't experienced once true addiction set in. He argued that his theory of addiction was truly sociological, because one could only interpret the distress of drug withdrawal within a cultural pattern of knowledge and beliefs about drugs. More modern drug theorists take issue with Lindesmith's contention that pursuing euphoria does not drive addicts to continue using. Addicts who have undergone detoxification and remained "clean" for periods of time relapse back into opiate use. And as mentioned before, nonaddicting drugs were being abused in patterns similar to the opiates. Why? McAuliffe and Gordon (1974) challenged Lindesmith and theorized that pursuit of euphoria, of feeling good through using chemicals, might be the answer. Psychologists argue that substance use (among a wide range of pleasurable practices), can be highly *reinforcing,* and such reinforcement might be at the core of psychological dependence. We've all heard of the laboratory rats who will push a lever many hundreds of times if there is a possibility of receiving a small dose of cocaine. Positive pharmacological reinforcement would seem to explain this. Could such findings be transferred to human subjects as well? Could this be the key to compulsive drug abuse, even among drugs that are physically addicting? Are drugs so pleasurable for some abusers that they will risk serious consequences of continued use to their health and to their social relationships?

The answer seems to be yes, though the existence of psychological dependence is somewhat harder to establish than is the existence of physical addiction. Drug users may be physically addicted, psychologically dependent, or both. Physically addicting drugs, heroin for example, may also produce profound psychological dependence. Psychological dependence would seem to be especially useful in explaining patterns of cocaine dependence, since cocaine seems to be the most reinforcing of all drugs. Research subjects who are given cocaine, but are unaware that is what they have taken, report higher levels of pleasure than with any other drug (Grinspoon and Bakalar, 1976). With an estimated 2.7 million hardcore cocaine users, in this country those who use the drug more frequently than ten times in a week (ONDCP, 2002, p. 68), we must be interested in explaining compulsive drug abuse. While psychological dependence is still a concept in formation, it seems to be a useful tool for understanding and possibly controlling, compulsive and consequential drug abusing behavior.

SOCIOLOGY AND THE CLASSIFICATION OF DRUGS

Chapter 3 of this book presents a *taxonomy of drugs,* a classification schema by which we can understand similarities and differences between substances we consider to be drugs. It is worth mentioning here, albeit briefly, the role that sociology plays in understanding drug classification, when it asks the question, "How do social and political influences affect the way our society classifies drugs?" Some drug classifications are made on the basis of pharmacological or biochemical factors, largely outside the scope of sociology. Whether a drug is deemed psychoactive or not is based on whether the chemical substance acts on the central nervous system (CNS). The *type* of influence on the CNS is likewise largely pharmacological; a CNS stimulant like cocaine and a CNS depressant like heroin have widely divergent effects. A user who desires to use one when she is actually using the other will experience unwanted drug effects, regardless of how powerful her expectations, as was vividly demonstrated when the Uma Thurman character in the film *Pulp Fiction* had a seizure after snorting high-grade heroin she mistook for cocaine.

A number of drug classification dimensions are very much influenced by social and political forces, including: whether drugs are considered medically useful or not; whether drugs should be legalized or not; and whether a drug is seen as having a high potential for addiction or abuse or not. As we will see in Chapter 2, these factors are at the root of how the federal government classifies psychoactive drugs. Consider the current debate over whether marijuana has legitimate medicinal properties that might benefit those with glaucoma or AIDS or certain forms of cancer. Is marijuana "medicine" or is it merely a "drug." Physicians find themselves at odds with most politicians who are upset with promarijuana activists. The debate has pitted different levels of government against one another (State of California: pro, Federal Government: con). This clearly indicates that something other than scientific reliance on empirical evidence is going on here. Political ideologies, vested social interests, images of morality, and public opinion affect how marijuana will be classified. The sociological perspective recognizes and assesses the roles these factors play in the debate.

Definitions of drugs and drug use are widely variable. Earlier in the 20th century, marijuana was known as "the devil's weed," Causing sexual agression and crazed bahavior. Today, marijuana is believed to cause apathy and disinterest among users, a phenomenon called "the amotivational syndrome."

UNDERSTANDING SOCIAL CONCERN ABOUT THE "DRUG PROBLEM"

We have discussed how, from a sociological point of view, the concepts of "drug," "drug abuse," "drug addiction," and "drug classification" are all socially constructed concepts, acquiring diverse meanings in different social contexts. To these social constructions we wish to add one other: "the drug problem." How the American drug problem, or more accurately drug problems, are understood as a product of our time and place, and the social and political forces that predominate. This does not mean that drug problems are social fabrications, woven out of thin air. We are arguing that the presence of objectively harmful conditions is relevant but not sufficient for us to understand why some forms of drug use are labeled as problematic and others are not. In other words, the way our society considers drugs to be a threat, which we certainly do, is not a purely scientific decision. Many interests—moral, political, economic—weigh in on what our "drug problem" is and what we ought to be doing about it. This is an important point: that the drug policies that emerge in any era are based on the way we construct, and hence come to understand, the "drug problem."

Our collective governments—federal, state, and local—control the use or distribution of a great many psychoactive substances. They also permit, but regulate, many drugs, including prescribed pharmaceuticals, tobacco products, and alcohol. Still others are essentially unregulated, like over-the-counter medications and caffeine. How substances are classified are based as much on perceived threat as anything else. How harmful/dangerous/threatening is substance _____ perceived to be? And by whom? Obviously, some people or groups in our society have more power to influence our perceptions than others. There is political advantage to be gained from declaring certain drugs to be harmful and conducting campaigns against them. Drug controls in this society are influenced by political lobbyists representing interests supporting or fighting the criminalization of the use of a particular drug. The history of drug controls in America, which we will cover in Chapter 2, makes this clear.

Sociologist Howard Becker (1963) calls individuals or groups who argue that they are the ones who should define "the reality" of drugs and their users, **moral entrepreneurs** (sometimes this concept appears as "politico-moral entrepreneurs"). Moral entrepreneurs take it upon themselves to tell us what we should be threatened by and what we should, as a society, do about that threat. Accordingly, defining "the drug problem" and implementing drug controls is a moral and political enterprise. Think of the range of societal actors who might benefit professionally from placing drugs in a negative light and having us be "at war" with drugs: politicians who are trying to build political capital by declaring themselves tough on drugs (in today's climate, few politicians get reelected by pushing for drug legalization or for fewer restrictions); religious leaders who preach that drug use is a sign of moral breakdown or turning away from God; and law enforcement personnel who argue that drug users commit more crimes and make their jobs much harder. To the extent that these groups have power or access to the powerful (and access to the media to get their message out), they shape the perception that drugs are a serious problem in America and something must be done now. Critics, such as Troy Duster (1970), say that this leads to the dangerous practice of "legislating morality," using the law to uphold the primacy of one among several competing moral ideologies.

Moral entrepreneurs, at their most successful, generate a subjective concern over drugs that is out of proportion with the objective threat. Such a situation is called a "moral panic" (Goode, 1990), a "drug scare" (Reinarman, 2000), or a "drug panic" (Jenkins, 2001). Sociologist Craig Reinarman writes: "Drug 'wars,' anti-drug crusades, and other periods of marked public concern about drugs are never merely reactions to the various troubles people can have with drugs. These drug scares are recurring cultural and political phenomena *in their own right* and must, therefore, be understood sociologically on their own terms . . . especially so for U.S. society, which has had *recurring* anti-drug crusades and a *history* of repressive anti-drug laws." (2000, p. 147; emphases in the original). There have been many such drug scares scattered over the last hundred years, ranging from concern over "demon alcohol" by temperance movement leaders in the early 1900s, which led to the Volstead Act of 1919 and Prohibition (Gusfield, 1963), to the "reefer madness" scare of the 1930s, fostered by the then head of the Federal Bureau of Narcotics (today it is the Drug Enforcement Administration), Harry Anslinger, which led to the Marihuana Tax Act of 1937, to the overheated rhetoric and exploding social concern of the crack cocaine scare of the late 1980s. Drug scares create a "crisis mentality" in the minds of Americans, who believe that the drug scourge threatens to overwhelm our society. This may be seen most astonishingly in a September 1989 *New York Times*/CBS News poll which found that 64 percent of the respondents, five out of every eight people, answered that drugs were the most important concern of our country (Goode, 1999:71)! As we have stated before, drug abuse produces consequences about which we should be justly concerned. But they are not now, nor have they ever been, the greatest threat to American society, least not in objective terms.

Reinarman (2000, p. 151–153) and Goode (1999, p. 73–75) discuss the ingredients, the objective and especially the subjective factors, which can serve as a "recipe" for drug hysteria and the repressive drug laws that often follow them. Drug scares are built upon kernels of truth; people do abuse drugs, and drug scares often follow an increase in drug abuse or deaths from drug abuse. This would be an objective factor. The mass media magnify the problem by engaging in what Reinarman calls "the routinization of caricature," arguing that worst-case scenarios are more typical than they are, in order to sell the news. Moral entrepreneurs and prominent spokespersons make claims about the social evil of drugs and create and enforce rules prohibiting them, often furthering their own vested interests. Professional interest groups—churches, law enforcement agencies, the drug treatment industry, and others—compete for definitional "ownership" of the problem by claiming that their special knowledge makes them the legitimate authority. Clearly, the media, moral entrepreneurs, and interest groups "pop" the kernel of truth, making it both larger and somehow less substantial than it was. This inflation of the problem occurs against a historical context of conflict between groups in the society, which creates a "level of cultural anxiety that provides fertile ideological soil" (Reinarman, 2000, p. 152) for drug prohibition. Drug scares have often included a conception of a "dangerous class" of folk-devil drug abusers about whom we should be wary. The combination of a disreputable and immoral group (often based on thinly veiled racist or ethnic assumptions) and a substance which is said to increase the threat to we who are "innocent," is a powerful ideological weapon. Finally, "(d)rugs are richly functional scapegoats. They provide elites with fig leaves to place over unsightly social ills that are endemic to the social system over which they preside. And they provide the public with a restricted aperture of attribution in which only a chemical bogeyman or the lone deviants who ingest it are seen as the cause of a cornucopia of complex problems (Reinarman, 2000, p. 153)." This is part of the American tendency to embrace simplistic and individualistic explanations for problems that really demand nuanced and complex social investigation. Sociologists must reject such simplicity in their research projects and in their theorizing.

SUMMARY: SOCIOLOGISTS ON AMERICAN DRUG USE

While there are many intellectual approaches to studying and understanding drug use, we will be focusing our attention on only one of them, the sociological approach. Sociology, because it is a social science, looks at empirical evidence about drugs. It also points out when others are being patently unscientific. Much of what we "know" about drugs is untrue, or partially true, because our society permits the debate over drugs to be distorted by ideology, morality, and partisan politics. Sociologists stress that the social context of drug use is vital to understanding its meaning. Whether a psychoactive substance is considered a drug or not involves contextual interpretation. So does the divide between "good" drugs and "bad," between safe and unsafe, between medically useful and not. Harmfulness gets determined not by objective standards but by political persuasiveness. The "drug problem" and solutions to said problem are grounded in prevailing cultural beliefs, however unscientifically generated they may be. With great zeal, drugs are presented to us as being "dangerous" or "highly addicting" or "an epidemic" or "a plague" or "a crisis" (see Jenkins, 2001) to whip up subjective concern. Sociologists help us make sense of the divide between such concern and the empirical reality or actual social harm done by drugs.

As you read this textbook, we ask you to examine critically your own beliefs, favorable or unfavorable, about drugs. Are you willing to set aside some of what you know, if you can be shown that it is built on faulty assumptions? We hope so. Sociology is about learning "truths" and coming up with more valid beliefs about social phenomena, including drugs. As we are instructed by the eminent sociologist Peter Berger, "there is a debunking motif inherent in sociological consciousness. . . . The sociological frame of reference . . . carries with it a logical imperative to unmask the pretensions and the propaganda by which men cloak their actions with each other (Berger, 1963, p. 38)." Drugs are complex social phenomena, and we hope that students reading this book are willing to understand the difference between facts and value judgments, and between science and ideology.

KEY TERMS

antagonistic effect
chronic effect
dose
drug
drug abuse
drug addiction
drug dependence
drug interaction
drug use

effective dose
idiosyncratic effect
lethal dose
moral entrepreneur
objective drug effect
pharmacology
potency
psychoactive drug
purity

route of administration
set
setting
social construction
subjective drug effect
synergistic effect
therapeutic dose
tolerance

REVIEW QUESTIONS

1. What is the *sociological approach* to studying drug use, and how is it similar to and different from the approach used by other behavioral sciences?

2. What are the four important ways in which a sociological view affects the academic understanding of drugs in American society? Do you understand why each of them is sociological?

3. Explain the sociological argument that the concept of "drug" is a "cultural artifact, a social fabrication." What might make accepting this social constructionist argument difficult for some?

4. Why is it useful in studying drugs to divide drug *effects* into three types: objective, subjective, and chronic?

5. What are the pharmacological and nonpharmacological factors which influence both objective and subjective drug effects?

6. The text defines *drug abuse* as drug involvement that "leads to measurable personal, interpersonal, or social consequences." What are some of the most significant consequences of drug abuse?

7. Compare and contrast the concepts of *drug addiction* and *psychological dependence* on drugs. Why is it useful to distinguish between the two?

8. Historically, to what extent has the shaping of the American "drug problem" been a *political and moral enterprise*, rather than a scientific one?

CRITICAL INQUIRY QUESTIONS

1. Studying sociology can be uncomfortable for some students because the discipline challenges many of the beliefs they hold dear. How does the sociological perspective, as laid out in this chapter, challenge beliefs that you hold regarding drugs and drug users in American society?

2. Do you support the notion that the sociological perspective on drugs and drug use manages to achieve a balance between cultural and social structural factors on the one hand and biochemical or pharmacological features of drugs on the other? Or would you contend that sociology underweights the pharmacological dimensions of drugs and drug use? Explain your decision.

NOTES

1. The concern here is over "drug misuse," where prescription medications or over-the-counter drugs are used in inappropriate ways. The more our population ages, the greater the likelihood that drug misuse and its consequences will rise.

A Brief History of Drug Use and Drug Controls in America

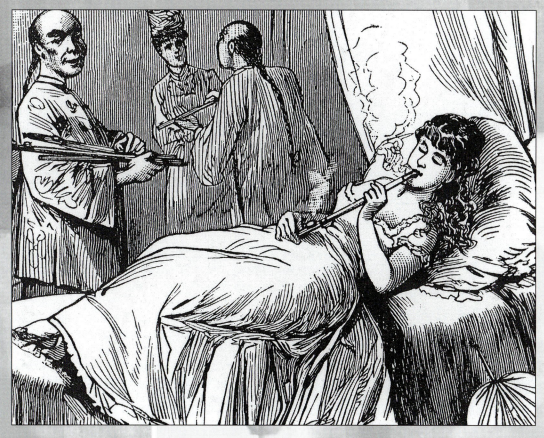

We established in the last chapter that drug use and abuse are *socially constructed* problems. By that we mean that whether drug use is seen as a problem is defined by the social context of which that behavior is a part. It is difficult, however, to understand that the problem of drug abuse is socially constructed when we observe people dying from drug overdoses, becoming addicted to the point of neglecting their families and other social roles, and suffering from physical ailments such as hepatitis B, AIDS, and cardiac disease—to name just a few— that result from drug abuse. Are these not direct, objective consequences of the use of the drug? History helps us understand how such problems, which seem to be so intrinsic to the drugs themselves, are often the result of much larger social and political processes. That is why sociologist Peter Berger (1963) describes the sociologist and the historian as fellow travelers with a close intellectual bond. History is also important because it provides valuable lessons for future public policy and practice. Failure to consider the lessons of history when it comes to drug use and drug policy stifles our ability to move beyond emotionally laden rhetoric and to avoid knee-jerk reactions to this rhetoric. As philosopher George Santayana (1905, p. 284) wrote, "those who cannot remember the past are condemned to repeat it." Indeed, we shall see how relevant Santayana's observation is to the study of drugs in American history, since we have often repeated our mistakes. Before examining the American experience with drug use and drug policy, however, we begin by looking back further into global history as a context for the American drug experience. We will then focus our attention on drug use in nineteenth and twentieth-century America.

DRUGS THROUGH THE AGES

Drug use and abuse are not unique to American society, nor to contemporary global experience. Drug-taking has been found in most societies that have existed over the last 10 thousand years or so, prompting sociologist Erich Goode to describe drug practices as coming "very close to being a cultural universal (1999:56)."

Perhaps the oldest known mind-altering substance consumed by humans was *mead,* an alcoholic drink made from honey, which was first produced about 8000 B.C. Other forms of fermented alcohol such as beer and berry wines appeared by about 6000 B.C. Because yeast is neutralized by alcohol, the highest level of alcoholic content that can be produced through natural fermentation is about 15 percent. Higher-concentration beverages can only be produced through an elaborate process of distillation, which has a much more recent history, probably around A.D. 800. Today, distilled liquors are usually measured in *proof*—the highest concentration possible being 200 proof—or pure, 100 percent alcohol.[1]

Opium and its derivatives also have a long history of use and abuse. The earliest known reference to opium is about 4000 B.C. when mention is made of a "joy plant" on a Sumerian tablet (Ray, 1978). Recent evidence also suggests a very early use of opium in Switzerland, by the Neolithic period in the fourth millennium B.C. (Booth, 1998; Merlin, 1984). Ancient Greek culture was particularly fond of the poppy plant, and its legends contain several references to opium, which is derived from the poppy. Here, opium was used medicinally, recreationally, and ritualistically. Hippocrates was also fond of opium as a medicine, and believed that the white poppy juice, mixed with nettle seeds would cure a host of ailments (Booth, 1998).

The use of opium as a ritualistic and pleasure drug in Greek culture is also apparent. Its presence is evident in Greek literature, including Homer's *Odyssey*. Homer makes reference to "nepenthe," the "drug of forgetfulness:"

> Helen, daughter of Zeus, poured a drug, nepenthe, into the wine they were drinking which made them forget all evil. Those who drank of the mixture did not shed a tear all day long, even if their mother or father had died, even if a brother or beloved son was killed before their own eyes by the weapons of the enemy (Booth, 1998, p. 18).

Opium was also used as a poison in these early cultures. We are told that Agrippa, the second wife of Emperor Claudius slipped it into the wine of Britannicus, rightful heir to the Roman throne, so that her own son Nero would take on the royalty. The drug was even used as a more palatable form of suicide, an alternative to some of the more hideous methods available, such as falling on one's own sword (Scott, 1969).

Other drugs have been targeted at various points in history as both "problems" and "cures." One such drug is caffeine, usually consumed in the form of coffee. Legend has it that coffee was first discovered when an ancient Arabian goat herdsman named Kaldi could not understand why his goats were bouncing about so energetically all over the hillside. When he investigated, he discovered wild red berries that the goats were eating. He tried them himself and, as the story goes, he experienced the first coffee high! As we have seen with so many drugs, as caffeine became more widely known, it was believed to have special curative powers. An Arabian medical text from around A.D. 900 suggested that coffee was a panacea for everything from curing measles to lust (Ray, 1978).

Coffee, and caffeine generally, is arguably the most widely used drug today, though we do not usually think of it as a drug. It is indeed a drug, however, and it was not always so widely tolerated as it is today. A certain group of women in England published a pamphlet in 1674 entitled *The Women's Petition Against Coffee*. It read, in part:

> Our countrymen's palates are become as fanatical as their Brains; how else is't possible they should *Apostatize* from the good old primitive way of ale-drinking, to run a *Whoreing* after such variety of destructive Foreign Liquors, to trifle away their time, scald their *Chops,* and spend their *Money,* all for a little *base, black, thick, nasty bitter stinking, nauseous* Puddle water . . . (Meyer, 1954; cited in Ray, 1978, p. 187).

Concern with caffeine consumption was expressed in the United States as well. One medical professional categorized coffee addiction with addictions to narcotics and alcohol when he claimed that it induced delusional states. He went on to note:

> a prominent general in a noted battle in the Civil War; after drinking several cups of coffee he appeared on the front of the line, exposing himself with great recklessness, shouting and waving his hat as if in a delirium, giving orders and swearing in the most extraordinary manner. He was supposed to be intoxicated. Afterward it was found that he had used nothing but coffee (Crothers, 1902, pp. 303–304; cited in Brecher, 1972; p. 197).

Dr. Crothers went on to claim that coffee drinkers will often become less than satisfied with coffee, and go on to more destructive drugs such as narcotics. This is a very familiar claim, and one that we often hear regarding marijuana today. Coffee was then, as marijuana is today, considered a "gateway drug." (See Chapter 4 for further discussion of this argument.)

Tobacco has also had an uneven social history, with periods of tolerance followed by periods of intolerance. During one such period in the early seventeenth century in England, King James I was especially anxious to rid his country of tobacco. His strategy was to identify tobacco with evil foreigners who represented a threat to a civilized way of life—a strategy not unlike what would be used centuries later in this country with early drug laws having racist origins. Yet while it has been villified, tobacco has also enjoyed strong support from the medical community throughout much of its pharmacological history, having been touted as a cure for headaches, abscesses, and even the common cold. Not until the 1890s was tobacco removed from *The United States Pharmacopeia,* a document analogous to today's *Physician's Desk Reference,* which contains information on drugs used for treating various maladies. To be part of a society's pharmacopeia is to have a recognized medical utility, an important part of the way psychoactive drugs get classified. Such was our 400-year dance with the medical marvel tobacco.

The *recreational* use of tobacco did not, of course, end in the 1890s, nor did it begin there. Almost certainly before they even arrived home from their explorations, Columbus and his crew were enjoying the pleasures of this drug. These sailors discovered early that "drinking" (inhaling) the smoke of tobacco provides energy when that is needed, but also eases tensions during times of anxiety. From the late 1700s to roughly 1900, however, tobacco *smoking* gave way to other forms of tobacco use, primarily chewing and snuff dipping. During this time ordinances were passed which actually forbade the use of smoking tobacco in some cities. It would not be until about 1920 that the use of smoking tobacco would once again surpass other forms of tobacco use.

Marijuana has a long history dating to at least 2737 B.C. when is found the earliest known reference to cannabis in a pharmacy book written by the Chinese emperor Shen Nung. Here it is referred to as "Liberator of Sin" suggesting doubt and uncertainty about the euphoric effects of the drug.

The emperor did, however, recognize certain medicinal benefits to marijuana, though we would not recognize them today. Marijuana did not make its way into the New World until about 1545, when the Spaniards introduced it into Chile. It was also introduced into North America in Jamestown in 1611, where it was cultivated for its fiber. It came to be a fairly important part of the agricultural economy in the colonies. One writer has pointed out that "Virginia awarded bounties for hemp culture and manufacture, and imposed penalties upon those who did not produce it" (Boyce, 1900, p. 35; cited in Brecher, 1972, p. 403). Even George Washington grew hemp on his Mount Vernon estate, and while he was no doubt growing it for its fibrous content, evidence from his diary suggests that he was also interested in its pharmacological properties:

May 12–13, 1765:   Sowed Hemp at Muddy hole by Swamp
August 7, 1765:   —began to separate the Male from the Female
                      Hemp . . . rather too late (Andrews and Vinkenoog, 1967,
                      p. 34; cited in Brecher, 1972, p. 403).

The assertion that Washington was concerned about the pharmacology of the hemp rests on the recognition even at that time, that the potency of the marijuana resin was enhanced if the male and female plants were separated before they had the opportunity to pollinate.

Marijuana had clearly found a place early on in American life. By the mid-nineteenth century, it was being touted as a remedy for a variety of ills, and later in the century, extracts of marijuana were marketed by major pharmaceutical firms of that day. Its use as a recreational drug was also discovered by this time, and particularly during prohibition, when alcohol was illegal, marijuana became a drug of choice among tens, even hundreds of thousands of Americans.

We highlight this early history here, not to provide an exhaustive account of drug use throughout history, but to simply document the fact that drugs have been part of recorded human history virtually from the beginning. Moreover, societal reaction to drug use can also be observed throughout history, though the drugs being praised or villified have varied greatly. We shall discover in the sections that follow that the American drug experience is also varied as is American reaction to drug use.

NINETEENTH-CENTURY AMERICA: A "DOPE-FIEND'S PARADISE"

Nineteenth-century America can be characterized as among other things, a century of widespread medicinal and recreational drug use. Edward Brecher (1972) has noted that the use of drugs, particularly narcotics, was so prevalent in the 1800s that this century could appropriately be described as a "dope fiend's paradise."

NARCOTICS USE IN THE NINETEENTH CENTURY

Opium and its derivatives were readily available through prescriptions given to patients for a variety of complaints. They were available in over-the-counter preparations under a variety of brand name **patent medicines** that were popularized early in the nineteenth century. Young (1961) has noted that, whereas in 1771 there were no American brands of patent medicines marketed commercially, by 1804 some 80–90 brands were being advertised in a New York catalog of medicines. Some of the brands appearing in the nineteenth century included *Dr. James' Cordial, McMunn's Elixir of Opium*, and *Mrs. Winslow's Soothing Syrup* (a mixture especially marketed as a teething syrup for infants, containing morphine sulfate). Other preparations contained cannabis indica, chloral hydrate, and cocaine. A popular method of marketing these medicines, especially during the last two decades of the nineteenth century, was the medicine show. These were rather elaborate performances, complete with magic or other forms of entertainment, culminating in a "pitch man" who, when the crowd was sufficiently worked up, convinced them of the need for the tonics available for sale (Young, 1961). There essentially was no regulation of these products, and prior to the Pure Food and Drug Act of 1906, patent medicines and soothing syrups were not even required to have their ingredients listed on the bottle.

Nineteenth-century physicians became so enamored of morphine's pharmacology that it was commonly referred to in this profession as G.O.M.—*God's Own Medicine*, a reference introduced by the eminent Canadian physician Sir William Osler who was an expert in treating addiction and himself a narcotics addict (Booth, 1998). Most of the consumers of these drugs were middle-class women, many of whom became addicted as a result of using narcotics to treat physical symptoms. Brecher (1972) notes that one textbook in the late nineteenth century listed 54 symptoms that are treatable by morphine. These symptoms included angina, diabetes, insanity, menstrual cramps, and even nymphomania! Morphine is a pain reliever with wonderful therapeutic properties, but as was often the case in the nineteenth century for a variety of substances, advocates overstated the benefits. Morphine use became especially prevalent during the Civil War to treat wounded soldiers. So widespread was morphine abuse during the war that dependence on it would eventually come to be called "soldier's disease." This drug was so widely received that many confederate states grew the poppy plant for its morphine production during the war, and the federal government did not make its cultivation illegal until 1942.

Morphine also came to be viewed as an alternative to recreational drinking and as a form of treatment for opium addiction. Dr. J. R. Black, in a scientific paper read to colleagues, noted that morphine ". . . is less inimical to healthy life than alcohol . . . [It] calms in place of exciting the baser passions, and hence is less productive of acts of violence and crime; in short . . . the use of morphine in place of alcohol is but a choice of evils, and by far the lesser" (Black, 1889; quoted from Brecher, 1972, p. 8). Many physicians attempted to convert alcoholics to morphine, a practice that continued into the 1930s and even early

DRUGS AND EVERYDAY LIFE

WHEN RUM SHALL CEASE TO REIGN

Written to the tune of "When Johnny Comes Marching Home"

Get ready for the jubilee,
    Hurrah! Hurrah!
When this our country shall be free,
    Hurrah! Hurrah!
The girls will sing, the boys will shout,
    When alcohol is driven out:
And we'll all feel gay when whiskey is no more.
And we'll all feel gay when whiskey is no more.

We're only children now, you know,
    Hurrah! Hurrah!
But temp'rance children always grow,
    Hurrah! Hurrah!
The girls will all be women then,
    The boys, of course, will all be men,
And we'll all fight rum 'till rum shall be no more.
And we'll all fight rum 'till rum shall be no more.

From Maine to California,
    Hurrah! Hurrah!
From Delaware to Canada,
    Hurrah! Hurrah!
The struggle now is going on,
    And when the mighty victory's won,
We'll all feel gay that whiskey reigns no more.
We'll all feel gay that whiskey reigns no more.

It will not do to simply say,
    Hurrah! Hurrah!
But do your duty, then you may
    Hurrah! Hurrah!
Assist the weak, yourself deny,
    Stand by the right, and bye and bye,
We'll all feel gay that whiskey reigns no more.
We'll all feel gay that whiskey reigns no more ■

—*Edward Carswell*

Source: Reprinted in Elton Shaw (ed.), *The Curse of Drink* (1909)

1940s by many older doctors (Brecher, 1972). The use of morphine was further spread when, by the late nineteenth century, the medical profession was recognizing the addictive potential of opium and came to believe that the use of morphine in place of opium might be a cure for opium addiction. More particularly, with the invention of the hypodermic syringe in 1853, many in the field believed that *injection* of morphine was less addictive than the orally ingested opium. We now know that this is not the case, and, indeed, mainline injection is a particularly addictive method of administration.

The waning years of the nineteenth century witnessed the introduction of a new, semi-synthetic narcotic which would later become the scourge of the twentieth century. This new "wonder drug" was *heroin*, so named because of the "heroic" powers it was alleged to possess (derived from the German *heroisch*, which means heroic or powerful). Heroin was developed in 1874 but not marketed commercially until 1898, by the German pharmaceutical company Bayerische AG, more commonly known as Bayer Laboratories, makers of Bayer aspirin. It was initially marketed as a powerful analgesic and a cough suppressant but soon became touted as an effective cure for morphine and opium addiction, continuing the fruitless pursuit of finding a nonaddictive narcotic. The nation's honeymoon with heroin was short-lived, however, and by 1910, Bayer had removed heroin from its pharmacopeia. Heroin was discovered to be powerfully addicting and would be the object of intensive law enforcement for the remainder of the twentieth century.

The historical circumstances that gave rise to America's concern with opiates in the late nineteenth century are important to note. Throughout the latter half of the nineteenth century, tens of thousands of Chinese men and boys immigrated into the United States, working on the railroads during the great Western expansion. They brought with them their opium-smoking habits along with other customs. In time, these Chinese immigrants moved into cities that were mushrooming in the West, working for low-wages and incurring the hostility of residents of these cities. Suddenly, opium was defined as a major problem. Many women—the principal users of narcotics besides the Chinese—were frequenting opium dens, incurring the wrath and fear of their husbands and the city fathers. All of this culminated in the first antinarcotics law in the country, an ordinance enacted in San Francisco in 1875, ". . . forbidding the practice under penalty of a heavy fine or imprisonment or both" (Terry and Pellens, 1928, p. 73). Opium smoking had been practiced by San Franciscans for years, but only when the use of this drug came to be identified with the Chinese, a despised and feared minority group, was this practice denounced. This is a pattern that we will observe with other drugs as well—*a tendency to villify minorities and minority drug use when that minority is perceived as a threat to the dominant community.*

ALCOHOL USE IN THE NINETEENTH CENTURY

Alcohol had been widely tolerated in America prior to the nineteenth century, though drunkenness was not generally accepted. Most of the early colonists drank beer and hard cider, though by the 1700s distilled liquors were becoming increasingly available. They drank quite a bit by contemporary standards, seemingly at odds with the Puritan reputation of the colonists. There were voices of concern over the overuse of alcohol during this time, most notably by Philadelphia psychiatrist Benjamin Rush, one of the signers of the Declaration of Independence. He went so far as to label it a destructive disease (Lender and Martin, 1987). These voices were not given a great deal of credence, however, and the practice and the legal status of drinking remained relatively unchanged. In short, it was not perceived to be a social problem.

Social drinking continued to be commonplace throughout much of the nineteenth century, and in amounts greater than the previous century. As the western frontier expanded, many of the original settlers and explorers were single men, isolated from their families and other human contact. Drinking was often quite unrestrained, and frequently coincided with gambling, fighting and womanizing. It was during this time that Native American tribes were also introduced to alcohol by western frontiersmen. The belief was, generally, that as long as one's drinking was not harmful to others, it was not a social concern (Lender and Martin, 1987).

The mid-nineteenth century witnessed a massive immigration of Europeans, initially from Ireland, who brought robust drinking habits with them. Americans had little love for the Irish. Most were very poor, and no doubt willing to work for wages much lower than domestic labor. They were also overwhelmingly Roman Catholic with a strong allegiance to the Church and to the hierarchical order which it represented. The Irish were indeed an alien culture in American society, one that was both feared and despised. Irish drinking habits became a symbol of moral inferiority, and America's tolerance of alcohol diminished substantially (Lender and Martin, 1987).

Organized opposition to alcohol also began to emerge in the nineteenth century. The first evidence of any real organized effort to oppose alcohol came in 1811 at the General Assembly of the Presbyterian Church held that year in Philadelphia. Benjamin Rush, by now up in years, implored those in attendance to deliver strong temperance messages from their pulpits, which they did. The Presbyterian effort was mirrored by other denominations including the Methodists, Baptists, and others. These efforts eventually resulted in the formation of the American Society for the Promotion of Temperance (later shortened to the American Temperance Society) in 1826. The goals of this organization were truly **temperance**—moderation, not abstinence—except for distilled liquors which were seen to be intrinsically evil. There were, to be sure, numerous voices for **prohibition** (abstinence), but it would be until the late nineteenth century that prohibition would emerge as a strong political force in America—the culmination of which would not be seen until the early twentieth century (Lender and Martin, 1987). The strong prohibition sentiment can be seen in collections of stories that tell of the horrible evils of alcohol and the consequences that it wreaks on families. One such collection edited by Elton R. Shaw (1909) is entitled *The Curse of Drink; or Stories of Hell's Commerce*. Stories such as "A Bottle of Tears," "Married to a Drunkard," and "The Saloon Keeper's Daughter," all ostensibly true, describe the horrors of alcohol on individual and family life. Some have direct reference to the Irish as in "Timmy Flannigan and His Promotion" and "Tom M'Hardy's Battlements." Songs and poems were also written, often to popular tunes of the time, to galvanize prohibitionist support as Prohibitionist sentiment was being mobilized with greater fervor by the waning years of the nineteenth century.

COCAINE USE IN THE NINETEENTH CENTURY

The chewing of coca leaves has been practiced for centuries by Native American tribes, particularly the Incas. The earliest record that we have of such activity is found in a grave in Peru which is dated to about A.D. 500. By A.D. 1000 the coca leaf was used as part of religious ritual in the Inca civilization, and was even used as a form of monetary exchange.

The coca leaf was introduced into the European world when the Spanish *conquistadors* invaded Peru and established a European presence there. The coca leaf was not immediately popular in Europe, and when it did finally catch the imagination of the European people it was used in prepared drinks

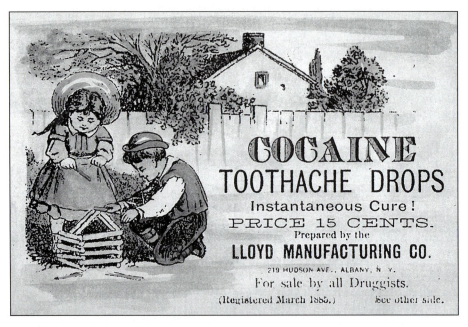

Remedies containing narcotics, cocaine and alcohol were widely available and highly marketed during the nineteenth century. Some were targated for use by children.

rather than chewed as it had been in the New World. A particularly popular drink in Europe was *Mariani's Wine,* which was a red wine containing coca, and named after its manufacturer Signor Angelo Mariani.

Cocaine, the alkaloid base and active ingredient in the coca leaf, was not isolated until 1844. The drug enjoyed about a half-century honeymoon period, being touted as a cure for both depression and morphine addiction (Brecher, 1972; Ray, 1978). Perhaps the most notable cocaine user was Sigmund Freud, the father of psychoanalysis. Freud found that the drug was almost instantaneously helpful in overcoming his own depression. He almost immediately recommended it to his fiancée, Martha Bernays, and his close friend Ernst von Fleischl, who was suffering from morphine addiction. Freud was so elated with the drug that he referred to it as "the magical drug" and promptly wrote a medical treatise, *The Cocaine Papers,* on its benefits that was published within two months of his own initial experimentation in 1884. We get a glimpse into Freud's early high regard for the drug in a letter to Martha Bernays:

> If it goes well, I will write an essay on it and I expect it will win its place in therapeutics, by the side of morphium and superior to it. I have other hopes and intentions about it. I take very small doses of it regularly against depression and against indigestion, and with the most brilliant success. I hope it will be able to abolish the most intractable vomiting, even when this is due to severe pain; in short it is only now that I feel I am a doctor, since I have helped one patient and hope to help more (Jones, 1953, p. 81).

His enthusiasm was short-lived however, when a year later his friend von Fleischl developed a full-fledged cocaine psychosis, complete with hallucinations of snakes crawling over his skin (Brecher, 1972). Freud would later denounce the use of cocaine and by 1890 the dependency potential of cocaine was fully appreciated by medical practitioners.

Cocaine, like opium and its derivatives, was also an ingredient in many of the popular patent medicines of the time which were marketed under various names such as *Coca Cordial.* Pharmaceutical companies, such as Parke-Davis, openly advertised cocaine in their products, which included coca-leaf cigarettes, tablets, hypodermic injections, sprays and ointments (Musto, 1973). In addition to patent medicines, the beverage industry discovered cocaine. About the time that Freud was experimenting with cocaine, an Atlanta druggist, Dr. John Stythe Pemberton was developing a beverage that included extracts from the coca plant. Initially, he combined it with alcohol, naming it *French Wine Coca—Ideal Nerve and Tonic Stimulant,* which he marketed in 1885. The following year he developed yet another product which replaced the alcohol with an extract of the kola nut, which contains about 2 percent caffeine. This product was named *Coca Cola,* a beverage that in modified form (minus the coca extract) is the biggest-selling soft drink today (Brecher, 1972).

By the end of the nineteenth century, cocaine was generally regarded as a public menace. Musto (1973) points out that it was widely believed that cocaine spurred violence against whites by African Americans in the South. Stories also abounded of black men on cocaine with superhuman strength and that cocaine use by blacks improved their pistol marksmanship. One of the more incredible myths was that cocaine rendered black users impenetrable by .32 caliber bullets which supposedly resulted in many southern police departments issuing .38 caliber handguns to their officers. There beliefs almost certainly contributed to the eventual vilification of cocaine. There is, of course, no evidence that cocaine had this effect on African Americans of that day (or any other day), but the troublesome aspect of this belief is the reaction that it spurred. This fear coincided with a peak period in the lynching of blacks in the South. Once again, we see the consequences of racist thought and action, and of how a drug scare can be fomented based on little or no evidence.

MARIJUANA USE IN THE NINETEENTH CENTURY

As we have seen, marijuana has been part of the American experience practically since the founding of the colonies in New England. Its use in medical practice spanned the nineteenth and part of the twentieth century. The drug was accepted into the *United States Pharmacopeia* in 1850 and remained there until 1942. It was recommended for a variety of ailments, including neuralgia, gout, rheumatism, hysteria, insanity, uterine hemorrhage tetanus, and many other maladies. It was also believed to act as an aphrodisiac and an appetite accelerant, a generally recognized effect today (Brecher, 1972). Pharmaceutical companies, such as Parke-Davis, Squibb and Lilly, marketed fluid extracts of the drug to meet growing medical demands and one company, Grimault and Sons, marketed marijuana cigarettes for use by asthma patients. By the early twentieth century, as other drugs became more available, medical dependency on marijuana declined, though the medical community continued to accept the medical legitimacy of marijuana until the passing of the Marihuana Tax Act of 1937 (Brecher, 1972).

Marijuana was also widely used *recreationally* in the nineteenth century. Several accounts have been written of the experiences of marijuana users, some of these in highly regarded magazines of the time, including *Putnams* and *Harper's New Monthly Magazine*. Recreational use at this time was typically referred to as "hashish eating," suggesting that the hashish resin was used, often baked into other foods but also taken directly in liquid form. (Brecher, 1972).

Recreational use of marijuana did not become widely popular until the early twentieth century, however. The efforts of the Women's Christian Temperance Union, and other groups seeking to outlaw alcohol were rewarded when the Eighteenth Amendment, ratified in 1919 and implemented one year later, and the subsequent Volstead Act made the manufacture and sale of alcohol illegal on a national basis. The impact of this legislation on marijuana consumption was almost immediate. Marijuana use and possession was not illegal at this time, and "tea pads"—marijuana smoking establishments—were established throughout the major cities of the United States. It is estimated that by 1930 there were 500 such establishments in New York City alone (Brecher, 1972). Brecher further reports that it was smoked in exclusive gentlemen's clubs. Cultivation of the cannabis plant became commonplace throughout the United States; it can be grown pretty much anywhere.

There was, to be sure, heightened concern over the use of this drug during the 1920s because of its easy availability. Of particular concern was access to marijuana by children. The concern over marijuana was fueled by reports in the Southwest that Mexican immigrants were bringing the drug into the country. Fears were heightened as a series of articles linking marijuana use and crime were published in a New Orleans newspaper about the same time (Ray, 1978). Once again, public reaction intensified as drugs become identified with ethnic minorities. This concern would ultimately result in the passage of the Marihuana Tax Act in 1937 which had the effect of outlawing marijuana distribution at the federal level.

THE TWENTIETH CENTURY: AGE OF LEGAL REPRESSION AND EXPERIMENTATION

The nation's fascination with drug use in the early 1900s gave way to a sober awareness of the abuse potential of these substances by the end of the century. Moreover, we have seen that these drugs lost their innocence as their use became associated with ethnic minorities who were perceived as a threat by those in dominant racial groups who held political power. As a consequence, the twentieth century witnessed a rather strong social and legal reaction against the use of drugs, particularly the four categories of drugs that we have discussed above. The mood of the nation was both reflected in and, to some extent at least, shaped by men such as Richmond Pearson Hobson, a celebrated Navy Captain. After unsuccessfully attempting to mobilize public opinion against a growing "yellow peril" (the Japanese), he turned his attention to alcohol as the "great destroyer." Hobson eloquently portrayed the battle against alcohol as the battle between good and evil, positing that "95 percent of all acts and crimes of violence are committed by drunkards" (Epstein, 1977, p. 24). He theorized that alcohol attacked "the top of the brain . . . since the upper brain is the physical basis of thought, feeling, judgment, self-control, and it is the physical organ of the will, of the consciousness of God, of the sense of right and wrong, of ideas of justice, duty, love, mercy, self-sacrifice and all that makes character" (Epstein, 1977, p. 24). Furthermore, he maintained that the effect of alcohol on "negroes" was a degeneration "to the level of the cannibal." Similarly, alcohol caused "peacable redmen" to become "savages" when drinking alcohol (Epstein, 1977, p. 25).

Ironically, Hobson's very success as a *moral entrepreneur* (see Chapter 1) left him once again in search of a cause. The Prohibition movement succeeded in making alcohol illegal across the country, but unfortunately for Hobson's theorizing, the crime rate did not go down significantly as a result. In the meantime, the Harrison Narcotics Act of 1914 was drawing the nation's attention to the evils associated with cocaine, opium, morphine, and heroin. Hobson saw another opportunity for a moral crusade. In 1928, he claimed over national radio, "Most of the daylight robberies, daring holdups, cruel murders, and similar crimes of violence are now known to be committed chiefly by drug addicts who constitute the primary cause of our alarming crime wave . . ." (Epstein, 1977, p. 28). Hobson's explanation for how these drugs caused crime was remarkably similar to what he said a decade earlier about alcohol:

> The entire brain is immediately affected when narcotics are taken into the system. The upper cerebral regions, whose more delicate tissues, apparently the most recently developed and containing the shrine of the spirit, all those attributes of the man which raise him above the level of the beast, are at first tremendously stimulated and then—quite soon—destroyed. . . . At the same time the tissues of the lower brain, where reside all the selfish instincts and impulses, receive the same powerful stimulation. With the restraining forces of the higher nature gone, the addict feels no compunction whatever in committing any act that will contribute to a perverted supposition of his own comfort or welfare (Epstein, 1977, p. 27).

Already by 1875, as we have seen, city governments were enacting ordinances against opiate use. This wave of lawmaking was followed by national legislation beginning very early in the twentieth century. In this section, we examine the following pieces of national antidrug legislation: the *Pure Food and Drug Act* of 1906; the *Harrison Narcotics Act* of 1914; the *Eighteenth Amendment* and the *Volstead Act* of 1919–1920; the *Marihuana Tax*

Act of 1937; the *Controlled Substances Act* of 1970; and the *Anti-Drug Abuse Act* of 1988. In addition, we will briefly examine antismoking efforts in the latter part of the century, commonly known as the Great American Smokeout, and the recent litigation against tobacco companies.

PURE FOOD AND DRUG ACT OF 1906

The **Pure Food and Drug Act** was a sweeping policy change that had as its goal making food and drugs safer for American consumers. The drugs primarily targeted by this Act were the unregulated patent medicines, concoctions which contained narcotics, cocaine, cannabis extracts and other psychoactive drugs. The Pure Food and Drug Act was the culmination of more than a quarter-century of advocacy that was met with strong opposition from the business sector, which was making a good profit from patent medicines affected by this legislation. A series of events took place which resulted in the successful passage of the Pure Food and Drug Act of 1906. The American Medical Association (AMA) began to take a more active interest in regulating the patent medicine industry, as did the American Pharmaceutical Association (APhA). There were also exposés written on the patent medicine industry and published in widely circulated magazines. Samuel Hopkins Adams wrote an impassioned series in *Colliers* under the series title *The Great American Fraud*, in which he severely attacked the patent medicine industry (Brecher, 1972). Perhaps the triggering event for the Pure Food and Drug Act, however, was Upton Sinclair's disturbing exposé of the meat packing industry in Chicago, a thinly veiled novel titled *The Jungle*, published in 1906. Sinclair's portrayal was so disturbing that President Theodore Roosevelt sent investigators to Chicago to verify Sinclair's charges. Their report confirmed Sinclair's claims and identified further problems as well (Ihde, 1982). Later that year the Pure Food and Drug Act was enacted into law.

The Pure Food and Drug Act required, among other things, that manufacturers of patent medicines indicate on their labeling whether certain specified drugs, including alcohol and narcotics, were contained therein. Later amendments to the Act would also require a listing of quantities and concentrations of these drugs. The Act was, essentially, a truth-in-advertising act that had the effect of protecting both addicts and innocent consumers from undue concentrations that could result in health problems (Brecher, 1972; Young, 1961). Whatever safeguarding effect that this Act would have on the lives of addicts, however, was short-lived. Merely eight years later, in 1914, Congress would pass the **Harrison Narcotics Act**, which, in effect, made distribution of narcotics a federal offense, and would shift the federal focus from health concerns to socio-legal ones.

THE HARRISON NARCOTICS ACT OF 1914

The origins of the Harrison Narcotics Act can be traced back to the midnineteenth century's concern over Chinese opium use and the early antiopium ordinances passed, first in San Francisco and then in other Western cities. America's concern and sensitivity over narcotics rose considerably throughout the last 30 years of the nineteenth century.

Following the Spanish-American War in 1898, the United States gained control over a number of Spanish colonies, including Puerto Rico, Guam, and the Philippines. American occupation of the Philippines revealed that the Spanish had operated an opium distribution monopoly. Episcopal Bishop Charles Henry Brent, perhaps the first American missionary to the Philippines, quickly learned of the opium monopoly and determined to address the opium problem there. Bishop Brent was assigned to head a commission, known as the Brent Commission, to study alternatives to dealing with the narcotics distribution problem in the Philippines. The Brent Commission urged international intervention and control of narcotics, realizing that this was, indeed, an international, not merely a national problem. This resonated well with the State Department. Two opium wars had already been fought in 1839 and 1858 over the British bringing "cut rate" opium from India into China, undercutting trade for Chinese opium. Moreover, American businessmen in China had been complaining that much of the Chinese trade was being diverted for British opium, making American trade more difficult. American missionaries to China were also raising concerns about what high levels of opium consumption were doing to the Chinese people (Brecher, 1972; Musto, 1973).

An international group representing 13 nations, known as the Shanghai Opium Commission, chaired by Bishop Brent, met in Shanghai in 1909 to discuss and make recommendations for international narcotics control. Several recommendations came out of this conference; however, failing to get the representative nations to agree to a second meeting, the United States began an active effort to organize an effort at international narcotics control. Two years following the meeting of the Shanghai Commission, representatives from twelve nations met at The Hague in the Netherlands to further discuss international control of narcotics. In this conference, participating representatives hammered out the first international narcotics agreement, in what was known as The Hague Convention of 1912. The Convention was not immediately enforced, however, because only 12 of the 46 powers of the world were at the table. Moreover, Germany—not one of the original 12 nations at the table—questioned the resolve of the United States to enact their own legislation to implement the provisions of the Convention. If the United States was to avoid international embarrassment, it would be necessary to enact comprehensive federal legislation (Musto, 1973).

The United States thus began to consider domestic legislation, which eventually became known as the Harrison Act in 1914, named after Representative Francis Burton Harrison who promoted the bill in the House of Representatives. Very little was mentioned about the evils of narcotics throughout the congressional debates, which lasted several days. Rather, the issue was debated on the basis of international obligation that the United States had incurred at The Hague (Brecher, 1972). Neither the morality of narcotics use or addiction, nor crime and other antisocial behavior that we now associate with narcotics use, were part of the debates. Indeed, crime and antisocial behavior were not major problems stemming from narcotics use until after the criminalization of these drugs.

Because the federal government has only very limited powers to criminalize behavior, the Harrison Narcotics Act of 1914 was written in language that ostensibly imposed a tax on importers and distributors of narcotics. Indeed, the official title of the Harrison Act was *An Act to provide for the registration of, with collectors of internal revenue, and to impose a special tax upon all persons who produce, import, manufacture, compound, deal in, dispense, sell, distribute, or give away opium or coca leaves, their salts, derivatives, or preparations, and for other purposes* (United States Congress, 1914—cited in Brecher, 1972).

The Harrison Act was, *prima facie,* a revenue measure. It required that medical practitioners—doctors and pharmacists—as well as manufacturers and importers of narcotics (which in the language of this Act also included cocaine, a non-narcotic stimulant) register with the U.S. government, obtain a license, pay a modest fee for this privilege and a small excise tax (one cent per ounce), and maintain paperwork on all drug transactions (Brecher, 1972; Lindesmith, 1965). Patent medicines, incidentally, were exempt from the licensing, taxation and reporting provisions provided that they maintained specified minimum concentrations of narcotics in their remedies. The Pure Food and Drug Act had earlier required labeling of these concentrations and made provision for testing of them.

The Harrison Act, while on the face of it merely a revenue act, made it unlawful to sell, barter, or give away narcotics except in pursuance of a written order of the person to whom the drug is to be sold, an order that must be on a special form issued by the Internal Revenue Service (Terry and Pellens, 1928). The exception to this provision was the

> distribution . . . to a patient by a physician, dentist, or veterinary surgeon registered under this Act in the course of his professional practice only . . ."
> (Terry and Pellens, 1928, p. 985).

The last phrase—*in the course of his professional practice only*—was something of a hook. This phrase would later be interpreted by law enforcement agencies and by the courts to mean that prescribing narcotics to addicts for maintenance purposes was *not* within the course of professional practice. Law enforcement agencies reasoned that addiction was not a disease, and hence opiates prescribed to addicts were not administered in the course of professional practice. The *effect* of the Harrison Act, therefore, even though ostensibly a revenue measure, was to criminalize narcotics for all but narrowly circumscribed medical purposes. Indeed, many physicians were arrested, convicted and imprisoned for distributing drugs to addicts following the Harrison Act.

That physicians would interpret prescribing heroin and morphine to addicts for maintenance purposes as being an acceptable professional practice is not difficult to understand. Narcotics addiction is tenacious, and efforts to cure addicts had not often been successful. Hence, physicians, having taken the Hippocratic Oath, felt bound to alleviate the suffering of their patients. The Oath reads, in part, "I will follow that method of treatment which according to my ability and judgment, I consider for the benefit of my patient . . . (modern version)." Relief of withdrawal symptoms was clearly in keeping with the spirit of this tradition.

The Supreme Court generally sided with the interpretation of the Harrison Act held by law enforcement, however. Five cases were particularly significant. The first, *U.S. v. Jin Fuey Moy* (United States Supreme Court, 1916), concluded that the possession of drugs by addicts was illegal under the provisions of the Harrison Act. The defense for this case argued that the section of the Act which stated that unregistered persons possessing narcotics were presumed guilty of violation applied only to *those who were required to register*—namely doctors and pharmacists. The Court ruled otherwise, which essentially made criminals of all addicts who were in possession of narcotics that were not prescribed by a registered physician (Lindesmith, 1965).

A second case, *Webb et al. v. U.S.* (1919) directly addressed the legality of physicians prescribing maintenance dosages to addicts. In this case, Dr. Webb, a practicing physician in Memphis, Tennessee, had been prescribing narcotics to addict-patients. Dr. Webb was indicted under provisions of the Harrison Act. The Supreme Court issued a very short opinion in which they concluded that ". . . to call such an order for the use of morphine a physician's prescription would be so plain a perversion of meaning that no discussion of the subject is required. (United States Supreme Court, 1919). The Webb case was upheld one year later in *Jin Fuey Moy v. U.S.* (1920). A closely related case in 1922 upheld the findings of the latter *Jin Fuey Moy* decision in that the physician in question (Dr. Behrman) was prescribing such large doses of narcotics and cocaine that the court maintained that no reasonable interpretation could conclude that they were being prescribed for medical purposes (United States Supreme Court, 1922). With the Behrman case, the criminal status of the addict seemed sealed.

One final case, *Lindner v. U.S.* (1925), softened the impact of these prior cases, however. In this case, Dr. Charles Lindner, a Seattle physician, prescribed only four tablets to a patient who later reported him to authorities. Lindner was convicted on the basis of the prior interpretations of the Harrison Act; however, his conviction was reversed by the high court which argued that the small amount of drug prescribed must be considered when considering the legality of prescribing narcotics, even to addicts. With this decision, the court modified its previous stance and left open the door to prescription for maintenance purposes, at least in smaller dosages. Addiction was not a crime, in and of itself, nor was the addict to be considered a criminal. Rather, *Lindner* held that those addicted to narcotics are "diseased and proper subjects for medical treatment." This position was bolstered further in the 1962 case of *Robinson v. California,* which struck down a California statute that made it a misdemeanor to "be addicted to the use of narcotics." The *status* of being an addict could not be construed as a criminal status, as it would violate the Eighth and Fourteenth Amendments ban on cruel and unusual punishment. An individual cannot be criminalized, therefore, for looking sickly or for having needle marks on the arm. *Being an addict is an illness and is hence different from using an addictive drug, which may be declared illegal,* though the two may obviously be related (United States Supreme Court, 1962). The Supreme Court seemed to be arguing for a public health response to the problem of addiction, rather than a criminal justice response. Our century-long policy of criminalization speaks otherwise.

Consequences of the Harrison Act   The Harrison Act and the subsequent Supreme Court decisions that interpreted this Act, have been the cornerstone of American drug policy throughout most of the twentieth century. Two decades later, another influential act, the Marihuana Tax Act, would use the basic architecture of the Harrison Act to criminalize marijuana. More importantly, the Harrison Act established a prohibitionist policy and a repressive mind set toward recreational drug use that has characterized twentieth-century America. Indeed, it was the *defining* drug legislation until 1970, when Congress passed the Controlled Substances Act.

One result of the Harrison Act as well as earlier narcotics legislation was a substitution of these drugs with other legal **functional alternatives.** An early alternative to narcotics that was especially popular among women (who, along with the Chinese, were the primary users of narcotics) was barbiturates. The barbiturates enjoyed widespread popularity during the early part of the twentieth century, even though potential problems were recognized as early as 1905 when the first barbiturate intoxication and withdrawal symptoms were noted. They continued to be used, however, and it was not until 1942 that concern among the medical community was heightened by an article appearing in *Hygiea* (since renamed *Today's Health*), warning of the potential dangers of nonmedical use of barbiturates. Other articles would soon follow, including an article with the provocative title "Thrill Pills Can Kill You" in the popular and prestigious *Collier's* in 1949 (Brecher, 1972). This was followed by a 1950s study demonstrating the addictive potential and withdrawal hazards of barbiturates. As a result of these and other reports, doctors became more hesitant to prescribe barbiturates, though they continued to be quite widely prescribed well into the 1970s.

When the addictive potential of barbiturates came to be realized, alternatives were sought, resulting in the development of sedatives and minor tranquilizers as whole new classes of drugs. Among the sedatives, methaqualone was most popular. It was synthesized in the 1950s in India, and was initially believed to be an effective antimalarial agent (Inciardi, 1992). When its sedative qualities were discovered, it was introduced as a safer alternative to barbiturates. Known on the street as "ludes," "Vitamin Q," and a variety of other names, this drug became very popular among the 60s generation. Unfortunately, a darker side of the drug soon emerged, as violence and other antisocial behaviors became linked with it. Nausea, dizziness and even overdose became increasingly common. The result of this was a reclassification of the drug from a Schedule II to a Schedule I, which denotes that the drug has no medical utility, and carries with it stronger law enforcement response (see Table 2.1 later in this chapter).

Side effects from the sedatives set the pharmaceutical companies in search of still another alternative, the *minor tranquilizers*. The most popular, and most widely prescribed of the minor tranquilizers was the wonder drug Valium. At the peak of its popularity in 1975, there were 61.3 million prescriptions (including refills) for Valium. Millions of Americans, especially women who were the primary consumers of Valium, became addicted. This tendency, to replace one form of addiction with another did not go unnoticed. Muriel Nellis, in her widely read critique of the prescription drug industry entitled *The Female Fix* observes:

> just as heroin was perceived as a treatment for morphine addiction, now methadone is the addictive substitute for heroin. . . . In the same continuum of reduced risk, barbiturates and other heavy sedatives were replaced by the so-called minor tranquilizers. But this breakthrough foisted more of these drugs on larger populations—for a wider variety of milder nondisease conditions. (Nellis, 1980, pp. 8–9).

Prescriptions for Valium declined after 1975 because of the concern over addiction and other adverse effects. There would never again be such a surge of popularity for Valium. This does not mean, however, that minor tranquilizers have been removed from the mood-disorder pharmacopeia. Just as the patent for Valium was approaching expiration, a new drug, Xanax, was introduced in 1981. Halcion, another benzodiazepine, followed shortly.

Doctors have learned to be cautious in prescribing Valium, and now Xanax and Halcion. The popularity of these drugs, however, have created a huge underground market, which has gained the title "gray market" for these prescription drugs. Unlike heroin, cocaine, and methamphetamines, which are illegally manufactured, illegal Valium and other prescription tranquilizers are usually diverted from pharmacies, hospitals, and doctor's offices. Sometimes, patients will "physician hop"—visit several doctors complaining of the same symptoms and get several prescriptions filled at different drug stores. Another way in which prescription drugs are diverted to the streets is by burglarizing pharmacies and doctor's offices. In some cases, clever criminals surreptitiously obtain "script pads" from doctor's offices and forge their own prescriptions. However obtained, these drugs are then resold through illegitimate channels for prices much higher than the prescription cost.

In addition to the search for functional alternatives, the Harrison Narcotics Act encouraged the development of a drug using-criminal subculture. This topic is explored more thoroughly in Chapters 5 and 10, but we would point out here that when drugs are made illegal, those who continue to use these drugs are faced with a number of problems—including locating dependable supplies of the drug, raising the funds to purchase illegal drugs, which are always more expensive than legal substances, and avoiding detection by the police, among others—for which they inevitably turn to each other for assistance and mutual support. Because illegal users must typically rely on criminal means of income, they cultivate relationships with other criminals as mentors, business associates, and friends. The criminalization of narcotics thus provided a legal milieu which encouraged the emergence of an underground subculture centered around the acquisition and use of illegal substances.

The Eighteenth Amendment and the Volstead Act

Prior to the late nineteenth century, opposition to alcohol was framed primarily in terms of *temperance* rather than prohibition, reflected in the name of the leading alcohol opposition group of the time, the *American Temperance Society*. Among other things, this call for temperance resulted in the establishment of many breweries throughout the United States, which would replace the distilleries and encourage the consumption of beer rather than the more potent distilled spirits. Many of these breweries were owned by Germans, a factor that would later play into the movement to constitutionally prohibit alcohol. The breweries were very effective in marketing the beers that they produced, alcohol consumption (albeit of beer) rose, and the temperance voices soon took on more strident prohibitionist tones (Ray, 1978).

The movement to prohibit alcohol began in the mid-nineteenth century when several states, led by Maine in 1851, enacted statewide prohibition statutes. Until the twentieth century, however, the movement to prohibit alcohol was characterized by a series of starts and stops: states would enact prohibition legislation only to repeal those statutes a few years later. A political party, the National Prohibition Party, was organized in 1874 specifically for purposes of promoting a prohibition agenda. More significant, however, was the establishment of the Anti-Saloon League in 1895. This was a nonpartisan organization which lobbied with all political parties, promising to bring votes to whoever would support national prohibition. The Anti-Saloon League also worked with ministers and church groups to gain political support by preaching a prohibitionist message in the pulpits of America. By 1903, more than one-third of the nation lived in states which had enacted prohibition legislation, a figure that would increase to about 50 percent of the population by 1913. This year (1913) also saw the passage of the Webb-Kenyon Act, which banned shipment of intoxicating liquors from wet to dry states (Lender and Martin, 1987).

The momentum for national prohibition was clearly gaining. The elections of 1916 placed into office so many "dry" candidates that congressional action authorizing a national vote on a constitutional amendment would almost be certain. Such a resolution was authored by Andrew Volstead, Representative from Minnesota, and passed both houses of Congress by December of 1917. Within a month, Mississippi became the first state to ratify a constitutional amendment. The thirty-sixth state to ratify (the minimum needed for the three-fourths of states required) was Nebraska, on January 16, 1919. (All but two states—Connecticut and Rhode Island—eventually ratified.). Later that year, Congress passed the **National Prohibition**

Act (also known as the Volstead Act), a piece of enabling legislation which cleared the way for the practical implementation of Prohibition. As stipulated by the constitution, one year following Nebraska's ratification, on January 16, 1920, the Eighteenth Amendment went into effect (Lender and Martin, 1987; Ray, 1978). The Amendment was short, consisting of three small sections:

> *Section 1.* After one year from the ratification of this article the manufacture, sale, or transportation of intoxicating liquors within, the importation thereof into, or the exportation thereof from the United States and all territories subject to the jurisdiction thereof for beverage purposes is hereby prohibited.
>
> *Section 2.* The Congress and the several States shall have concurrent power to enforce this article by appropriate legislation.
>
> *Section 3.* This article shall be inoperative unless it shall have been ratified as an amendment to the Constitution by the legislatures of the several States, as provided in the Constitution, within seven years from the date of the submission hereof to the States by the Congress.

The Eighteenth Amendment remained in effect for 13 years, from 1920 to 1933. But the political landscape had shifted, and those supporting the reintroduction of legal alcohol had the numbers in their favor. On February 20, 1933, Congress passed legislation proposing a repeal of Prohibition, and sent it to the states for ratification. By December of that year, the thirty-sixth state ratified the Twenty-First Amendment repealing prohibition. This Amendment, too, was direct and to the point:

> *Section 1.* The eighteenth article of amendment to the Constitution of the United States is hereby repealed.
>
> *Section 2.* The transportation or importation into any State, Territory, or possession of the United States for delivery or use therein of intoxicating liquors, in violation of the laws thereof, is hereby prohibited.
>
> *Section 3.* This article shall be inoperative unless it shall have been ratified as an amendment to the Constitution by conventions in the several States, as provided in the Constitution, within seven years from the date of the submission hereof to the States by the Congress.

Individual states also began repealing statewide legislation during this time. Predictably, Mississippi, which had been the first state to ratify the Eighteenth Amendment, was the last state to lift statewide prohibition, in 1966 (Brecher, 1972; Ray, 1978).

It is somewhat difficult to assess the impact of alcohol prohibition on American society. Early assessments of prohibition dismissed it as a total failure, insisting that the country, and especially women, were drinking more than ever. Clarence Darrow and co-author Victor Yarros promoted such a popular view in *Prohibition Mania* (1927). More careful analysis, however, has failed to confirm this popular view. Numerous studies have suggested that the overall amount of alcohol consumption did indeed decline during Prohibition. Moreover, indicators of alcoholism and other alcohol problems, such as hospital admissions, arrests for drunkenness and drinking-related diseases suggest an overall decline in alcohol consumption during these years (Lender and Martin, 1987). Other research presents a more complex picture, however. Economist Mark Thornton (1991) suggests that while there was initially a sharp decline in drinking levels after the Eighteenth Amendment went into effect, there was a gradual increase thereafter, reaching pre-Prohibition levels by the end of the 1920s. Furthermore, economist Clark Warburton (1932) presents data suggesting that distilled liquor consumption comprised a much larger percentage of the overall alcohol consumption in the United States during the years of Prohibition. Moreover, the *illegal* alcohol most available during this period was distilled in nature—moonshine—and often very toxic. Hence, the risks for toxic reactions and other health problems associated with Prohibition-era alcohol use increased dramatically (Lender and Martin, 1987). Such observations lend support to "The Iron Law of Prohibition," which states that the more repressive the law enforcement efforts, the more potent a prohibited substance becomes (Cowan, 1986). While Cowan was referring to narcotics in this case, the same general principle can probably be applied to alcohol and other substances as well.

There are, of course, other costs that have been borne in American society because of Prohibition. Perhaps most significantly, it was during this era that organized crime first gained a substantial foothold in American economic life (Lender and Martin, 1987). These costs must also be considered when considering the success or failure of Prohibition. Most historians and social scientists agree that Prohibition was, on balance, a failed experiment.

THE MARIHUANA TAX ACT OF 1937

Cannabis products were quite widely used as recreational drugs in the early twentieth century, and particularly in the 1920s when alcohol was prohibited. Both narcotics and alcohol were illegal during this time and even if one were willing to break the law, the price of alcohol became prohibitively expensive. Consequently, many people began smoking marijuana as a functional alternative to alcohol and opium.

America's courtship with recreational marijuana in the 1920s was an uneasy one, however. The 1920s was a period of considerable Mexican immigration to Southern states from Louisiana to California, and extending up to Colorado and Utah (Musto, 1973). Mexicans coming into America, some legally and others illegally, brought marijuana with them, much as the Chinese brought opium with them a half-century earlier. While cheap Mexican labor was welcomed by farmers, these neighbors from south of the border were also feared and were believed to be responsible for crimes and other forms of deviant behavior. Because marijuana smoking was part of their cultural experience, we find once again a pattern of vilification of both Mexicans as an ethnic minority and marijuana as their drug of choice. Marijuana quickly came to be seen as a cause of violence and crime among Mexican immigrants. It should not be surprising that many of the border states and surrounding states were early advocates of criminalization and became the first to pass statewide laws prohibiting marijuana.

Despite these concerns, only 16 states had passed marijuana legislation by 1930. That year, the Federal Bureau of Narcotics was formed in the Treasury Department with Harry J. Anslinger as its Commissioner. Initially, the Bureau was not especially concerned with marijuana use, as is evidenced in the following 1932 report:

> A great deal of public interest has been aroused by newspaper articles appearing from time to time on the evils of the abuse of marihuana. . . . This publicity tends to magnify the extent of the evil and lends color to an inference that there is an alarming spread of the improper use of the drug, whereas the actual increase in such use may not have been inordinately large (Bureau of Narcotics, 1932, p. 51; cited in Becker, 1963, p. 138).

Commissioner Anslinger, however, became personally interested in combating marijuana use. He began a three-fold strategy of moral entrepreneurship for doing so. First, he began *lobbying in state legislatures* for adoption of antimarijuana laws. In his report for 1935, Anslinger stressed the importance of state legislation:

> In the absence of Federal legislation on the subject, the States and cities should rightfully assume the responsibility for providing vigorous measures for the extinction of this lethal weed . . . (Bureau of Narcotics, 1936, p. 30; cited in Brecher, 1972, p. 413).

Largely as a result of Anslinger's sustained lobbying effort at the state level, 46 of the then 48 states adopted antimarijuana laws by 1937. This, despite the fact that marijuana was almost certainly declining in use anyway because of the lifting of prohibition on alcohol.

Anslinger's second strategy was to *launch a massive public opinion campaign*. The Bureau did this by feeding information from its files to newspapers, magazines, and tabloids. These accounts were often filled with half-truths, and had the effect of mobilizing public support for national prohibition as well as complying with state laws prohibiting marijuana use. One such story, printed in *American Magazine* captures the tenor of information being conveyed to the public:

> An entire family was murdered by a youthful addict in Florida. When officers arrived at the home they found the youth staggering about in a human slaughterhouse. With an ax he had killed his father, mother, two brothers, and a sister. He seemed to be in a daze. . . . He had no recollection of having committed the multiple crime. The officers knew him ordinarily as a sane, rather quiet young man; now he was pitifully crazed. They sought the reason. They boy said he had been in the habit of smoking something which youthful friends called "muggles," a childish name for marihuana (Anslinger and Cooper, 1937, pp. 19, 50).

The final strategy employed by the Bureau of Narcotics was to *seek federal legislation* that would prohibit the distribution of marijuana. Again,

Commissioner Anslinger was adamant regarding the need for federal legislation. In his 1936 report, Anslinger states:

> In the absence of additional Federal legislation, the Bureau of Narcotics can therefore carry on no war of its own against this traffic . . . the drug has come into wide and increasing abuse in many states, and the Bureau of Narcotics has therefore been endeavoring to impress upon the various States the urgent need for vigorous enforcement of local cannabis laws (Bureau of Narcotics, 1937, p. 59; cited in Becker, 1963, p. 140).

As with the Harrison Narcotic Act, the **Marihuana Tax Act** was framed as a revenue measure to avoid constitutional problems. Marijuana was used for certain medical purposes at that time. Hence, as with the Harrison Act some 20 years earlier, physicians, dentists, veterinarians, and other established medical professionals were required to register with the federal government and pay a nominal tax. The language of this act also stipulated that these medical professionals must administer marijuana "in the course of their professional practice." Hence, individuals possessing or distributing marijuana without registering and obtaining a tax stamp, or administering the drug in a manner not in keeping with the course of their professional practice, would be subject to sanction.

The public's concern over marijuana, which had been agitated by Anslinger's entrepreneurial campaign, faded once the Tax Act had been passed. The 1940s and 1950s were periods of minimal marijuana concern and marijuana usage. Yet the legacy of the Marihuana Tax Act, as with the Harrison Act, was enormous: it would be the defining legislation for marijuana control until the introduction of the *Controlled Substances Act of 1970* which superceded it. We turn to a discussion of that legislation now.

RENEWED DRUG EXPERIMENTATION AND THE CONTROLLED SUBSTANCES ACT OF 1970

Following the heightened level of concern over marijuana in the 1930s were a couple of decades of relative calm as our national attention was focused on World War II, returning GI's, establishing families, building the economy and so forth. While it would be inaccurate to say that there was *no* governmental or public concern about drug use during the 1940s, 1950s and early 1960s, it was at a low ebb. There were some initiatives, to be sure, such as the Boggs Act in 1951. This Act placed mandatory minimum sentences for drug law violators, and in the process made penalties much higher. Perhaps more significantly, marijuana and narcotics were lumped together for the first time at the federal level as the Act provided for uniform penalties for violations of either the Narcotics Drug Import and Export Act *or* the Marihuana Tax Act (Bonnie and Whitebread, 1970). As significant as this legislation was, it would be the 1960s until the nation's attention would become fixated once again on recreational drugs.

The first "scare" that would herald a new age of drug experimentation was almost accidental. The drug was *toluene,* an organic solvent found in model airplane glue. The first recorded event of glue-sniffing seems to have occurred in 1959, though children were certainly breathing the fumes from tubes of cement much earlier than that. On August 2, 1959, *Empire,* the Sunday supplement to the *Denver Post* featured an article with the headline, "Some Glues are Dangerous: Heavy Inhalation Can Cause Anemia or Brain Damage." The article went on to report how young children were getting high from toluene, and even provided quite explicit information about their techniques for sniffing. This and other stories only increased the fascination with the drug, and experts were soon warning that the drug could be fatal. Many juvenile arrests were made, even though this drug was not yet prohibited by law. Laws were soon passed in several states that would make glue sniffing illegal. It was not long before the media across the country were filled with reports of deaths caused by glue sniffing. When these claims were carefully investigated, it turns out that there a total of nine alleged deaths, each one reported several times as reporters would use secondary sources, which have a tendency to multiply a single case many times over. When these nine deaths were carefully investigated, six of them were found to be due to asphyxiation resulting from the victim's head being covered by an air-tight plastic bag—not due to glue fumes at all! It was suspected that the seventh death was an asphyxiation case as well. An eighth case involved a juvenile who had been ill, and had sniffed gasoline fumes, but was not known to have sniffed glue. The final case was also questioned, as the victim had not been seen sniffing glue before his death, and moreover, there was no evidence of toluene in his body during autopsy (Brecher, 1972).

The glue-sniffing scare is instructive. As is so frequently the case when it comes to juvenile drug use, the publicity surrounding drugs—even when it is negative—only serves to pique the fascination of young people. It is interesting to note that at the beginning of the 1960s, the most popular form of inhalant among young people was gasoline fumes. By the end of that decade, the incidence of gasoline-fume inhalation was about the same as it was in the beginning of the decade. Glue-sniffing, however, had skyrocketed (Brecher, 1972). It seems that sometimes the best-intentioned publicity campaigns can have the most adverse effects. We will address some of these issues in Chapter 13.

The 1960s also witnessed a renewed interest in marijuana among America's youth who used it in part as a symbol of protest against establishment morality. It was at this time that a widespread subculture of marijuana use among middle class youth developed. The drug became variously known as *pot, herb, weed,* and *reefer* among this generation of users. Studies revealed that by 1979 more than 50 percent of teenagers were at least experimenting with marijuana over the 12 months prior to their being questioned.

As the decade of the 1960s progressed, establishment norms were increasingly being challenged by the nation's youth—and especially the middle class youth. Variously called the "Woodstock Generation," the "Hippie Generation," and the "Boomer Generation," this was the large adolescent and college-aged cohort who was challenging many accepted cultural mores and the established hierarchy. Consider these last two verses from the seminal 1964 rallying cry, "The Times They Are A-Changin'" by poet-folk singer Bob Dylan:

> Come mothers and fathers/Throughout the land
> And don't criticize/What you can't understand
> Your sons and your daughters/Are beyond your command
> Your old road is rapidly agin'. . . .
> The line it is drawn/The curse it is cast
> The slow one now/Will later be fast
> As the present now/Will later be past
> The order is rapidly fadin.
> And the first one now/Will later be last
> For the times they are a changin'

Establishment norms were also challenged by the use of hallucinogenic drugs, or, as they were known by the users of that day, *psychedelics*. By far the most notorious of these was *d-lysergic acid diethylamide* (LSD). This semi-synthetic hallucinogenic was discovered almost accidentally by a Swiss chemist by the name of Albert Hoffman. Hoffman first synthesized the drug in the laboratories of Sandoz Pharmaceutical Company and promptly set it on the shelf where it would sit for five years. Then, in the afternoon of April 16, 1943, Hoffman would make a "mind bending" discovery: he accidentally took the world's first LSD "trip." Hoffman would recount his experience a short time later:

> Last Friday, the 16th of April, I was forced to interrupt my work in the laboratory in the middle of the afternoon, and go home to seek care, since I was overcome by a remarkable uneasiness combined with a slight dizziness. At home I lay down and fell into a not unpleasant, intoxicated-like state which was characterized by an extremely exciting fantasy. In a twilight condition with closed eyes (I found the daylight to be annoyingly bright), there crowded before me without interruption, fantastic pictures of extraordinary plasticity, with an intensive, kaleidoscopic play of colors. After about two hours this condition disappeared (Stoll, 1947, p. 60; cited in Liska, 1990, p. 284).

The recreational use of LSD was promoted by a young Harvard University professor, Timothy Leary. Leary was a highly respected clinical psychology professor at Harvard who had taught classes, collaborated on several text-books, and until his encounter with LSD, was a most uncontroversial fig-ure. While in Mexico, he experimented with psilocybin, and would later experiment with LSD. He began holding sessions with students off cam-pus, touting the marvels of these drugs, and in many cases introducing his students to them. Leary was sincere in his belief that LSD was truly a mind-expanding (psychedelic rather than hallucinogenic) drug that could change the human nervous system in positive ways. Because these young, edu-cated, affluent drug users were not so easily dismissed as criminal or otherwise disposable, there was a felt need for legislation that would dis-courage such rampant drug use among the cream of our nation's youth, while at the same time not impose sanctions that would destroy their fu-tures. One such piece of legislation was that Narcotic Addict Rehabilitation

Act (NARA) in 1966 which authorized the courts to order civil commitment for purposes of drug treatment as an alternative to prison sentences (a policy that is being received favorably today in states like California). It was, not coincidentally, about this time when methadone maintenance became widely available as a treatment option for heroin addiction.

The most significant legislation, however, was passed by Congress in 1970. This was the *Comprehensive Drug Abuse Prevention and Control Act*. Title II of that Act, known as the **Controlled Substances Act** (CSA), essentially incorporates all changes in drug laws that have occurred since the passage of the Harrison Act in 1914 (Shulgin, 1992; Winger, Hoffman, and Woods, 1992; McDowell and Spitz, 1999). Hence, the CSA supersedes prior legislation and remains the defining legislation for current drug law policy. Furthermore, this legislation contains provisions that place strict requirements on record-keeping, inventory control, and security (Drug Enforcement Administration, 1999). Finally, and most importantly for purposes of this discussion, the Controlled Substances Act classifies or "schedules" drugs for purposes of legal sanction (refer to Table 2.1). The CSA does not itself much focus on specific substances, but rather establishes a set of common standards that are associated with the dangerousness of a drug (Bureau of Justice Statistics, 1992). The primary criteria that are ostensibly used in scheduling a drug are (1) identifying the medical uses of a drug; (2) determining the abuse potential of particular substances; and (3) assessing threats to human safety (Shulgin, 1992; Drug Enforcement Administration, 1996). These criteria are used to determine both whether a drug should be controlled and if so, to place the substance in the appropriate schedule (McDowell and Spitz, 1999). The Controlled Substances Act contains five different **drug schedules**—Schedule I through Schedule V. A lower schedule number indicates a higher potential for abuse. The determination of where on the schedule a specific drug should be placed lies with the Administrator of the DEA, and is a highly political process. Examples of drugs in each of the schedules, as well as definitions of abuse potential, medical utility, and legal availability of these drugs are provided in Table 2.1.

The Process of Scheduling   The process through which a drug is added to one of the five schedules is understandably complex and sometimes controversial. The Drug Enforcement Administration plays an important role in this process. Newly developed drugs automatically undergo a medical and scientific evaluation by the Department of Health and Human Services in order to identify if scheduling in accordance with the Controlled Substances Act is warranted. This evaluation, which includes a partially binding recommendation, is forwarded to the Drug Enforcement Administration for review (Bureau of Justice Statistics, 1992). As noted by Shulgin (1992) the scheduling or enforcement status of a drug may change if a previously unidentified health hazard or abuse potential becomes apparent.

Proceedings to schedule a drug per the Controlled Substances Act may be initiated by the Administrator of the Drug Enforcement Administration, the Department of Health and Human Services, or by petition of any interested party (Drug Enforcement Administration, 1996). At this time, the

TABLE 2.1	A Summary of Drug Scheduling of the Controlled Substances Act of 1970			
Schedule	Examples	Abuse Potential	Medical Use	Available by Prescription
I	Heroin, LSD, MDMA, quaaludes, marijuana	High	None	No
II	Morphine, Cocaine, amphetamines	High	Limited	Yes (No refills)
III	Barbiturates, non-narcotic analgesics, anabolic steroids	Moderate	Yes	Yes (5x in 6 months)
IV	Valium, Librium, Equanil, Miltown	Low	Yes	Yes
V	Over the counter cough medications with codeine; antidiarrheals	Low	Yes	Not required, but available only by licensed pharmacist to persons 18 and older; sale must be recorded

Source: Goode, Erich, *Drugs in American Society* (4th ed.), 1993; and Leavitt, Fred, *Drugs and Behavior* 93rd ed.), 1995.

Administrator of the DEA requests that a scientific and medical evaluation of the drug by the Department of Health and Human Services be conducted to explore the previously mentioned criteria of medical use, abuse potential, and associated safety concerns (Drug Enforcement Administration, 1999). This evaluation also includes a partially binding recommendation on whether the drug should be placed into a particular schedule (Bureau of Justice Statistics, 1992). However, the Administrator of the DEA has the ultimate authority in this regard (Shulgin, 1992; Drug Enforcement Administration, 1999).

Concerns in Drug Scheduling   There is some concern that the DEA, particularly the Administrator, has excessive influence over the scheduling process, and may be unduly influenced by political rather than by scientific considerations (Shulgin, 1992; Kleber, 1994). Not only does the Administrator of the DEA often initiate scheduling proceedings, but also plays a significant role in scheduling itself. For example, any evaluation conducted on a drug by the Department of Health and Human Services for scheduling purposes is binding only when the recommendation is to *not* schedule a substance (Drug Enforcement Administration, 1999). Placement into a specific schedule is determined ultimately by the Administrator of the DEA.

A second issue of importance concerns how scheduling decisions impact the availability and use of drugs for medical purposes. McDowell and

Spitz (1999) specifically note the controversy that surrounds the medical use of marijuana, a Schedule I drug. Recall that Schedule I substances are considered to have no accepted medical use and therefore cannot be obtained by prescription. Cocaine, in contrast, is located in Schedule II because it does have limited medical uses—even though it is generally considered to be the more dangerous of the two. Kleber (1994), on the other hand, suggests that a measure of the support for medical use of marijuana is political because the negative consequences of use outweigh benefits that have yet to be proven. As a result, he contends that the Department of Health and Human Services, not the DEA, should define medical use for the Controlled Substances Act so that decisions are based upon scientific grounds.

The Controlled Substances Act established a new threshold in drug policy. Politically, the issue of drug control was muted in the 1970s as the nation addressed other pressing problems, such as a dignified retreat from the Vietnam War and a searing energy crisis. The drug issue would once again emerge, however, under the presidency of Ronald Reagan in the 1980s.

ANTI-DRUG ABUSE ACT OF 1988

Several events occurred in the 1980s which resulted in a renewed federal interest in drug control. A conservative president, Ronald Reagan, was elected. Reagan made federal drug control, particularly "supply side" (law enforcement) initiatives a high priority. First Lady Nancy Reagan complemented her husband's drug priorities by making drugs her focus with her "Just Say No" campaign against drug use. Additionally, two high profile athletes— Len Bias, a basketball player at the University of Maryland, and Don Rogers, a defensive back for the Cleveland Browns—died within a month of each other in 1987 due to alleged cocaine overdose. The 1980s also witnessed the introduction and widespread popularity of crack cocaine, a cheaper, ready to use, but highly dependence-producing form of cocaine. This was also the decade that a new fatal disease was introduced, Acquired Immuno-Deficiency Syndrome (AIDS). The connection between AIDS and IV drug use was quickly recognized. As a result of all of these events, the nation was again, by the end of the decade, focused on drug use.

A series of laws were enacted in the 1980s that represented a return to more repressive drug policies. In 1984, Congress passed the Sentencing Reform Act which once again placed mandatory minimum sentences for those convicted of drug offenses. This was a return to a policy instituted in 1951 by the Boggs Act, but which had been lifted by the Controlled Substances Act in 1970. Two years later, Congress passed the Anti-Drug Abuse Act of 1986 which, among other things, placed differential mandatory minimum sentences on powder and crack cocaine. Essentially, the penalty for selling 5 grams of crack cocaine (5 years) was equivalent to the penalty for possession of *500 grams* of powder cocaine (Musto, 1999). This was, needless to say, a controversial piece of legislation, with many suggesting that the new law was blatantly classist and racist. (Crack is a drug used primarily by lower class and minority individuals.) It is not surprising, therefore, that drugs and drug policy was a major issue in the 1988 presidential campaign which placed the first George Bush in the White House.

This was the social and political context for the **Anti-Drug Abuse Act of 1988.** This act was multifaceted and addressed a broad range of concerns. First, it addressed alcohol and especially the problem of drunk driving in the United States, by requiring warning labels on all beverage alcohol and by providing federal dollars to states that vigorously addressed the problem of drunk driving. This act also reinstituted the federal death penalty for major drug traffickers. Also included in the act were provisions to combat money laundering and asset forfeiture of those arrested for drug violations (Musto, 1999). This latter provision has also proved to be quite controversial because assets could be seized even prior to an individual being found guilty in a court of law. Finally, the 1988 legislation addressed the fears of drugs in schools and in the workplace by establishing the Drug Free Workplace (see Chapters 9 and 13), and enacting the Drug-Free Schools and Communities Act Amendments of 1989. These amendments required schools to establish a system for maintaining drug-free environments, to inform students and teachers of the penalties for drug use and sale, and to provide information on available treatment (Musto, 1999). These provisions established the basis for drug testing in the workplace and in the schools discussed in Chapter 13.

The Drug Abuse Act of 1988, along with the 1984 and 1986 legislation, profoundly affected our criminal justice system, though not always in a positive way. These laws have largely been responsible for serious jail and prison overcrowding. Between 1985 and 1996, the number of prisoners in federal, state and county facilities rose by about 100 percent. Those sentenced for drug offenses accounted for about half of this increase (Musto, 1999). Perhaps the positive side of this is that as we have incarcerated more and more of our drug offenders, both crime rates and overall drug use have been declining or at least staying level since the late 1980s (with blips upward for specific drugs in the early 1990s). It is not clear, of course, how much of this is due to our nation's tough drug laws and how much is due to a graying of the population or other demographic or cultural factors.

THE GREAT AMERICAN SMOKEOUT AND THE ONSET OF TOBACCO LITIGATION

The 1960s witnessed a renewed concern over the health hazards associated with smoking. Low tar and nicotine cigarettes were introduced for the first time, and in 1964 the Surgeon General of the United States issued the famous report on smoking and health, which ultimately resulted in cigarette manufacturers being required to put a warning label that "cigarette smoking may be hazardous to your health" on every package of cigarettes (Surgeon General, 1964). The 1970s witnessed the enactment of several state laws which would restrict smoking; by 1978, 33 states and Washington D.C. had passed restrictive measures as to where one could and could not smoke in public places.

The American Cancer Society has also been quite successful in its campaigns to get people to quit smoking, organizing its first *Great American Smokeout* in 1977 (American Cancer Society, n.d.). The event has been held annually for about a quarter of a century, and more people quit smoking on that day than any other day of the year, including New Year's. Unfortunately, more than 90 percent of those who try to quit without seeking treatment fail, most within a week (National Institute on Drug Abuse, 1998).

Other groups have also participated in promoting a smoke-free environment. Groups such as ASH (Action on Smoking and Health) and GASP (Group Against Smokers' Pollution) have been striving to designate public areas as smoke-free out of their concern for "passive" or "secondary" smoke. These and other groups which make up what has come to be called the "non-smokers liberation movement" (Matchan, 1977) have successfully banned smoking from many public areas such as schools, hospitals, certain lobby areas, and other public places. More recently, two small-town lawyers from Mississippi brought suit against the tobacco companies in 1997. Tobacco industries had been sued before, but these suits were almost always unsuccessful because the tobacco companies managed to convince juries with the argument that victims themselves brought on their own demise by voluntarily smoking in the face of evidence of tobacco's ill health effects. However, in 1997 the Attorney General of Mississippi, Mike Moore, with his law school classmate Dick Scruggs, took on the companies on behalf of state taxpayers to recoup money spent on health care. They were able to show that the tobacco companies themselves knew about the potential dangers of smoking and suppressed that information. Their efforts were eventually joined by some 40 other states in the lawsuit that some would say has finally brought the tobacco industry to its knees. The industry agreed to pay some $368 billion in health-related damages; to discontinue billboard advertising; and to withdraw ads using the "smooth character" Joe Camel because of their appeal to children (Frontline, 1998). In 2000, a jury in Florida found tobacco producers and distributors liable for lying about the dangers of nicotine and for suppressing evidence that they had conspired to boost amounts of nicotine to hasten addiction. This decision, in essence, declared cigarettes to be nicotine-delivery devices.

There is some evidence that the efforts of antismoking groups have been effective. According to the Economic Research Service of the Department of Agriculture (cited in Goode, 1993, p. 258), per capita consumption of cigarettes in the United States declined from an all time high of 4,345 (cigarettes per year) in 1963, to 2,926 in 1990—representing a steady decline since 1963 and lower than any time since the early 1940s. This decline has continued throughout the 1990s, though at a slower rate. It is estimated that overall cigarette consumption has declined by about 2 percent annually throughout the 90s, and per capita consumption was estimated to be at 2,399 in 1997 (Capehart, 1998).

SUMMARY

We have examined all too briefly the history of drug use in America. Most of this history has focused on the nineteenth and twentieth century. This is so for one primary reason: these consecutive centuries contrast sharply with regard to attitudes and societal responses to drug use. The nineteenth century had wide open availability of most types of drugs. Virtually no controls were placed on the manufacture, distribution, possession, or use of psychoactive drugs. The twentieth century represented a complete swing of the pendulum to a repressive control strategy on most forms of recreational drug use. There is perhaps no other area of public policy that has experienced such a sea-change.

What might we learn from this history? Hopefully, this question will be answered, in part at least, with discussions in the chapters to follow. There are, however, several points that we might want to consider at the present time before proceeding further:

- Characteristics of drugs, such as addictiveness, health consequences, and their criminogenic potential are clearly *not* merely a matter of pharmacology as many presume. These characteristics are *socially defined* as we have seen, by examining the shift in our understanding and policies toward drug use and addiction between the nineteenth and twentieth centuries.
- Drug policy is fickle, and subject to factors totally unrelated to the harmfulness (or lack thereof) of drugs; such factors include racial prejudice, economic interests and political entrepreneurship.
- We have seen in this contrast the extremes of drug policy—from one of laissez faire nonintervention to one of considerable repression; neither policy has seemed satisfactory. We must search out solutions that can realistically reduce the damage that drug use, and societal reaction to drug use, can cause.

As you explore the remaining chapters of this text, we urge you to keep these first two chapters in mind. They establish an important conceptual, theoretical, and historical context for interpreting contemporary issues and knowledge on the landscape today.

KEY TERMS

Anti-Drug Abuse Act of 1988
Controlled Substances Act
drug schedules
functional alternative
Harrison Narcotics Act
    of 1914

Marihuana Tax Act
    of 1937
National Prohibition
    (Volstead) Act
patent medicine
prohibition

Pure Food and Drug Act
    of 1906
temperence

REVIEW QUESTIONS

1. "The sociologist and the historian are fellow travelers with a close intellectual bond." How does understanding the history of American drug use and drug control help us understand contemporary drug issues?

2. Nineteenth-century America is described by one researcher as a "dope-fiend's paradise." What evidence is presented to support this contention? Do not try to validate the concept of "dope-fiend," one with which the authors are uncomfortable. Rather, assess the evidence that drugs, particularly narcotics, were widely available and used.

3. Related to number 2, above, the demographic profile of narcotics users in the late 1800s was quite different from that of today. Who were the more frequent users then, and who are they now? Why did the characteristics of the typical user shift, and what are the implications of this?

4. Discuss the history of organized opposition to alcohol in America from Benjamin Rush through the temperance movements to national prohibition as the result of the Eighteenth Amendment. What were the reasons cited by alcohol's foes? Are they different from those who would seek to put limits on drinking today?

5. What are the social and political factors that led to the enacting of the Harrison Narcotics Act of 1914, America's first sweeping drug law? What were the provisions of the act? How did subsequent Supreme Court decisions limit and alter the Harrison Act's provisions?

6. Throughout the twentieth century, how did politico-moral entrepreneurs whip up public concern, hence public support, for drug control campaigns? What does this say about the "rationality" of the law, a principle endorsed by many Americans?

7. The Controlled Substances Act, which "scheduled" drugs for purposes of legal sanction, assessed the medical utility and potential for abuse or threat to human safety for drugs. Schedule I substances—including marijuana and heroin—have *no recognized* medical benefit, a contention that some scientists and physicians challenge. Discuss the process of scheduling drugs and the concerns over that process.

CRITICAL INQUIRY QUESTIONS

1. A survey of drugs through human history reveals that chemical substances which were once touted as "miraculous" later are condemned as a "scourge." [Occasionally, the process goes in the other direction.] This is true of heroin, cocaine, and many other drugs. From what you have read in the first two chapters, is this due to advancement in scientific knowledge, to change in the prevailing social and political climate, or possibly to something else?

2. Many antidrug laws originated to control groups of purported users who were from some "undesirable" ethnic or racial minority group. Is this particular to drug legislation, or is it consistent with using the law in a broader context of social control of minorities?

NOTE

1. The term "proof" came from early colonial days when alcohol was used to ignite gunpowder. Gunpowder would ignite at about a 50 percent concentration of alcohol, which was then considered "100 proof." This was, essentially, full proof that the alcohol was strong enough to ignite the gunpowder. Pure alcohol is therefore 200 proof.

CLASSIFYING PSYCHOACTIVE DRUGS

You may ask, "Why classify drugs? What purpose does it serve?" Scientists classify information for much the same reason that everybody else does. Confronted with a multitude of "data," this information must be placed into categories for it to be meaningful. Hence, plants and animals are classified first into a family, then a genus, then a species, etc. These categories are based on particular qualities that the scientists are looking for, and individual plants and animals which possess those qualities are placed into a particular category. Only by classifying the world in this way, can the scientist comprehend the

chapter OUTLINE

world in a meaningful way. Scientists call these classification schemes **taxonomies.**

The classification of psychoactive drugs serves the same sort of purpose that taxonomies do in science generally. In the first place, classification allows drug researchers and practitioners to make sense of the many substances that are collectively referred to as "drugs." But, while these substances share some things in common (e.g., they are all ingested into a living organism), there are also many ways in which they are different. These differences can then provide a basis for classification. One classification scheme was introduced in Chapter 2. This classification system, which is more commonly known as a "Schedule of Drugs" is essentially a *legal taxonomy.* While it purports to arrange drugs according to their addictive potential and medical utility, it is used primarily as a mechanism for determination of criminal sanctions.

Still another classification scheme, introduced by Erich Goode (1999) categorizes drugs on the basis of their *intended function.* Goode distinguishes between drugs which are recognized as drugs for their *medical utility, psychoactivity, illegality,* or *public definition* as a drug (p. 60). Among these broad functions, the one which we use to define "drug" for this text is psychoactivity. *That is, this text is concerned with those substances which in some way affect the operation of the central nervous system.* This narrows the range of substances substantially. We are not, for example, interested in penicillin or birth control pills in this text. But among psychoactive substances, there is still a broad range of drugs that, while sharing the characteristic of affecting the central nervous system in some fashion, nevertheless differ from each other in some important respects.

The remainder of this chapter identifies and discusses a classification scheme which focuses only on psychoactive drugs—a classification scheme which we call a *pharmacological taxonomy.* This taxonomy, which is commonly used among drug researchers and practitioners, classifies drugs on the basis of their psycho-pharmacological effect. Classifying psychoactive drugs according to their pharmacological effect requires consideration of the *way in which these drugs affect the central nervous system.* We now know that most drugs affect the central nervous system through one or more **neurotransmitters.** While many neurotransmitters have been discovered, those which are most closely connected with psychoactive drugs are *acetycholine, norepinephrine, dopamine, serotonin,* *gamma-aminobutyric acid (GABA), N-methyl-D-aspartate (NMDA), endorphins* and the *cannabinoids* (Moak and Anton, 1999). These neurotransmitters are chemicals released by neurons into a small space between two neurons called a **synapse.** These chemical neurotransmitters are specifically targeted to a single cell and are very specific in the message that they provide (Ray and Ksir, 1999). Most of the psychoactive drugs that we discuss in this text affect in some way one or more of the neurotransmitters discussed above. We could classify drugs according to the type of neurotransmitter activated. The problem with this is that some drugs involve more than one neurotransmitter. Furthermore, while such a taxonomy might be meaningful to pharmacologists, it is less useful to social scientists, counselors, policy makers and lay persons who are much more interested in the actual effect that drugs have on the central nervous system and, in turn, behavior and mood. The classification system in Table 3.1 is the one most widely used by researchers and practitioners in the field today. We are adding one category to this widely used taxonomy, which we are calling "CNS Stabilizers," referring to drugs that help to stabilize mood and behavior. This taxonomy is not exhaustive. Some drugs, such as the steroids, more directly affect hormonal production. We will not be discussing these drugs in this chapter as part of this taxonomy, but we will discuss them in some of the later chapters as they are relevant to certain occupational domains as well as posing certain health concerns.

TABLE 3.1	A Pharmacological Taxonomy of Psychoactive Drugs	
Type	**Effect on CNS**	**Examples**
Narcotics	Generally depressant; also analgesic and soporific effects	Drugs which derive from the poppy plant or are chemically very similar: Opium, morphine, codeine, heroin, methadone, dilaudid
Depressants	Slow down the activity of the central nervous system	alcohol, barbiturates, tranquilizers, sedatives, inhalants such as gasoline fumes and toluene in glue, ether
Stimulants	Speed up the activity of the central nervous system	cocaine, crack, amphetamines, caffeine, nicotine
Hallucinogens	Cause extreme sensory distortion, and cross-sensory stimulation	LSD, psilocybin, mescaline, PCP, nutmeg
CNS Stabilizers	Leveling of moods; reduce extremes of emotional/ behavioral states	antidepressants, lithium, ritalin
Marijuana	Slight depressant effect; mildly euphoric	marijuana, hashish

NARCOTICS

Our English word **narcotic** comes from the Greek word *narkotikos,* which means "to benumb." Indeed, as we shall see below, this is one of the principal effects that the narcotic drugs have. When we think of "drug abuse," an image that commonly comes to mind is the narcotics addict, emaciated, unkempt, and willing to do anything for his or her next "fix." This is, furthermore, an image that often drives public policy and plays on the fears of drugs by Americans. There are, however, many *misunderstandings* about narcotic drugs—misconceptions ranging all the way from just what qualifies as a narcotic, to the powers that narcotic drugs have over individuals. We begin this section by examining the various drugs make up this taxonomic category. This discussion will be followed by a brief discussion of the pharmacological effects that these drugs have on the human organism.

WHAT ARE THE NARCOTICS?

There is probably no category of drugs which have been more *misidentified* than the narcotics. Popular culture has identified everything from marijuana to cocaine to heroin as a narcotic at some time or another. Furthermore, the *legal culture* defines narcotics as those drugs which are

Many psychoactive drugs are derived from natural sources, such as the poppy plant or mushrooms. Other drugs are "synthetic," meaning that they are compounds that have been synthesized in a laboratory.

potentially dangerous and have high addictive potential. Our use of the term narcotic in this text, however, is driven by the *pharmacological* definition. At the risk of oversimplification, narcotic drugs are those that derive from *Papaver somniferum*—the opium poppy plant—or those drugs which have a chemical structure similar to those deriving from the poppy plant but which are synthetically produced in a laboratory. For this reason, the narcotics are also sometimes generally referred to as *opioids;* or, if derived from the opium alkaloid itself these "natural" or "semisynthetic" narcotics are referred to more specifically as *opiates* (Stine and Kosten, 1999). The poppy plant is grown in various parts of the world, but most successfully in areas of the middle and far east, known as the "golden crescent" and "golden triangle" respectively. We examine some of the more commonly used narcotics below.

THE NATURAL NARCOTICS

The natural narcotics are those drugs which derive directly from the poppy plant, and do not involve the use or mixture of any other chemical compounds. We will look at three of the most commonly used natural narcotics below: opium, morphine, and codeine.

Opium   Our word opium comes from the Greek word, *opion,* which means "poppy juice." That is exactly what opium is—the milky extract of the seeds of the poppy plant. Before they completely ripen, the poppy seeds are slit open to drain, which, when dried, forms a sticky brown substance called opium. Through the years, opium has been used both medically and recreationally (see Chapter 2). Recreationally, it is quite typically smoked in an opium pipe which entails filtering the vapor of the burning residual through water and inhaling deeply into the lungs.

Morphine   The discovery of morphine and codeine in the early nineteenth century represents a major threshold in the medical use of narcotics. Morphine was first isolated as the primary active ingredient in opium by a young, 20-year old German scientist by the name of Frederich Sertürner. Sertürner named his discovery *morphium* after Morpheus, the Greek god of dreams. Ironically, his wife would later die of an overdose of it (Lingeman, 1974). Morphine is a particularly strong narcotic, some 10 times stronger than opium. It was at one time quite widely used as a recreational drug, with names such as *M, morph, morpho, dreamer, monkey, stuff,* and *Miss Emma.* Heroin has largely displaced morphine as the drug of choice among recreational users.

Codeine   The discovery of morphine opened up the field of chemistry to pursue other derivatives, resulting in some 30 different alkaloids over the next few decades (Ray and Ksir, 1999). Perhaps the most important of these came in 1832 in the form of codeine, a narcotic used largely for its analgesic effect. Literally translated from the Greek, "poppy head," codeine quickly caught on as both an analgesic, and an antitussin—a cough suppressant. Many cough formulas using codeine as the active ingredient were patented and sold over the counter as late as 1970. Codeine was also commonly used recreationally in this form by youthful users, and known as *schoolboy* on the street. Codeine is not nearly as potent as morphine, and requires at least twelve times the dose to achieve the same analgesic effect as morphine (Liska, 2000). For this reason, it has been much more popular among physicians as an analgesic when the more powerful morphine is not required.

The Semisynthetic Narcotics

"Semisynthetics" are a classification of narcotics which are the product of a synthesis of naturally occurring narcotics with other chemical substances. The following discussion highlights three of the most commonly used semisynthetics: *heroin, dilaudid,* and *oxycodone.*

Heroin   The story of heroin begins in 1874. It was in that year that two acetyl groups—which essentially share the chemical properties of vinegar—were attached to morphine, to form *diacetylmorphine,* or more commonly, heroin. Named for its "heroic" powers, this new drug was substantially more powerful than morphine (Ray and Ksir, 1999). Moreover, it was initially believed and reported that heroin was not an addictive drug, and that it was effective in eliminating morphine withdrawal symptoms (Lipton and Maranda, 1983). Within about a decade the addictive potential of heroin would be clearly evident. Because of its phenomenally addictive power, there is no accepted medical use of heroin in the United States today, though in Britain and a handful of other countries the drug is used for certain medical purposes including the legal maintenance of narcotics addicts (Liska, 2000). Heroin is, however, a drug of choice among recreational narcotics users. Some of the more common street names for heroin are *smack, horse, H, shit,* and *dope* among many other "brand" names given by dealers of heroin to identify their supplies (Goldstein et al., 1984).

Dilaudid   Dilaudid (*dihydromorphone*) is a very powerful narcotic, from two to eight times the potency of morphine (Carroll, 1989). Dilaudid is a prescribed medication for the most extreme forms of pain, and in some cases, for cough suppression. Because of its potency, however, physicians do not readily prescribe it, though it is a drug of choice among addicted medical professionals (see Chapter 7). In addition, it seems to be the narcotic of choice among heroin addicts when supplies of heroin are temporarily low or cut off (Inciardi, 1992). The 1988 film *Drug Store Cowboy,* which is based on an unpublished novel by James Fogle, depicts the use of dilaudid by a veteran narcotics addict who describes dilaudid as ". . . the best pharmaceutical dope money can buy."

Oxycodone Oxycodone is synthesized from a minor constituent of opium known as thebaine. It is similar chemically to codeine, but more potent, and potentially more addictive. Medically, oxycodone is usually administered as *Percodan®*, which is a combination of oxycodone and aspirin; or *Percocet®*, an oxycodone and acetaminophen combination. Both of these combinations have made their way into the underground economy, and are either taken orally, or may be dissolved in water and mainlined. A new and stronger form of oxycodone was developed and patented in 1996 under the trade name *OxyContin®*. This new drug was originally produced in 10, 20, 40 and 80 milligram tablets and in July, 2000, a 160 milligram tablet was introduced. Percodan® and Percocet®, by contrast contain 5 and 2.25 milligrams of oxycodone respectively. OxyContin® is not only a more powerful form of oxycodone, but it is a controlled release drug which acts for up to 12 hours, making it especially effective as a pain treatment. OxyContin® has attracted attention as a popular recreational "club drug" recently on national media, which raises concerns about its strong abusive potential. Used recreationally, the drug has been chewed, crushed and snorted, and dissolved in water and injected. When used in these ways, the controlled release function is no longer effective, leading to rapid release and absorption of the drug (National Drug Intelligence Center, 2001).

THE SYNTHETIC NARCOTICS

The synthetic narcotics are those drugs which have no origin in the poppy plant—i.e., are manufactured from beginning to end in a laboratory—but which, nevertheless, have a chemical structure and pharmacological effect which mimics that of the natural narcotics. There are many synthetics available today. We briefly examine five of these that are commonly used: *methadone;* the synthetic analgesics, *Demerol*, *Darvon*, and *Talwin;* and *Fentanyl*.

Methadone Methadone was first synthesized by chemists in Germany in the 1940s, due to a shortage of morphine. It was not until the 1960s however, that this drug came to be used as a treatment for heroin addiction, which is its primary use today. Methadone is a drug that is usually taken orally in liquid form—most often mixed with orange juice or some other pleasant-tasting medium. Because it is usually swallowed, it takes much longer to take effect than heroin, which is usually mainlined. More importantly, it has an effective action of 24–36 hours, compared with heroin's 4–5 hour effect, therefore requiring only a single dosage daily. It is this quality which has made methadone a particularly appealing drug in some treatment circles. Because methadone is taken orally, not intravenously, it produces less in the way of deleterious health consequences and, it is believed, should be less addicting (Drug Enforcement Administration, 1997). Methadone maintenance as a treatment program is discussed more fully in

Chapter 12. Methadone is sometimes used as a drug of preference by recreational drug users who gain access to the drug by other users who have diverted it from methadone maintenance clinics (Inciardi, 1977b). Methadone is often referred to on the street as *Dollies* or *Dolls*.

The Synthetic Analgesics: Demerol, Darvon, and Talwin   Discovered in 1939, Demerol (*meperidine*) is primarily used as an analgesic. It is stronger than codeine, though only about 15 percent as potent as morphine (Liska, 2000). It is commonly used in childbirth to relieve labor and delivery pain. It is also commonly prescribed for postoperative discomfort (Drug Enforcement Administration, 1997). Demerol does produce euphoria, particularly when injected, and for that reason is a popular substitute for heroin by addicts who are temporarily cut off from their suppliers. Contrary to early belief, Demerol is an addictive drug, as many physicians discovered when they began to prescribe and use it for minor pain (Liska, 2000).

Darvon (*propoxyphene*) is almost always administered orally, and is the least potent of all the narcotics we have discussed, except perhaps for opium. It is usually taken as an analgesic for mild to moderate pain. Darvon is often manufactured in combination with other analgesics such as acetaminophen (where it is called *Darvocet-N*) and aspirin. Darvon is not a popular drug for recreational use because of potentially severe side effects, such as depression and psychosis. Physicians are strongly warned against prescribing this drug to suicidal or extremely depressed patients (Liska, 2000).

Another popular narcotic analgesic is Talwin (*pentazocine*). Talwin has greater analgesic effect than Darvon, and is used for moderate to severe pain. It is capable of producing physical dependence, though it is generally considered to have low abuse potential. While Talwin is considered a synthetic narcotic, it does have some *antagonistic* effect (Liska, 2000). As you shall see in Chapter 12, narcotics antagonists are drugs that block the effects of other narcotic drugs by keeping them from binding to the brain receptors that will in turn cause euphoria. Talwin seems to have a narcotic effect of its own, but its chemical structure also has features similar to the narcotic antagonists.

Fentanyl   Fentanyl was first synthesized in the late 1950s in Belgium and was medically introduced as an anaesthetic under the trade name of *Sublimaze*. It is used during and following surgery for pain relief. Analogues of the original drug were produced shortly thereafter, and by the mid-1970s, the drug was being used illicitly, first in medical circles and eventually in the street culture. Today, over a dozen analogues are manufactured in clandestine laboratories. Known by street users as *china white* or sometimes *P dope* (Stine and Kosten, 1999), this is an extremely potent narcotic, many times more potent than most heroin available on the street, and some 100 times more potent than morphine (Drug Enforcement Administration, 1997; Liska, 2000).

Pharmacological Features of Narcotics

The narcotics have several pharmacological features in common which, taken together, distinguish them from the other categories of drugs we discuss in this text. These features are: *addictive potential, analgesic effect,* and *euphoria.*

Addictive Potential   The narcotics are perhaps the most addictive of all drugs, at least from a strictly physiological point of view. Those addicted to heroin and other narcotics describe having a "monkey on their back," which drives them to go back again and again to score more drugs. Research by Inciardi (1979), for example, suggests a very rapid transition from experimental to addictive heroin use: among males, only about six months; among females, less than two months.[1] Clearly, with a few notable exceptions such as crack cocaine (see below) narcotics have a seduction almost unparalleled among recreational drugs.

Early efforts to explain this addiction relied on theories of weak moral character, or personality attributes that were prone to addiction, commonly known as the "addictive personality" (Chein et al., 1964; Platt, 1975). These early attempts at explaining the physiological basis for addiction notwithstanding, it would not be until the 1970s that medical science would approach an understanding of the complex chemical and physiological basis for this addiction. The key to understanding the physiological basis for addiction, it turns out, is in the chemistry of the brain itself. Scientists have discovered that the brain and the pituitary gland produce morphine-like chemical neurotransmitters, the first of which were named *enkephalins,* and later chemical discoveries which were named **endorphins** (a contraction of the words "endogenous morphine"). Addiction to the natural and synthetic opiates results when the brain and pituitary gland cease or diminish production of the body's own chemical narcotics because the heroin or other ingested narcotics attach to the receptor sites and fool the brain into thinking it does not need to produce enkephalins or endorphins. When an individual ceases taking narcotics for whatever reason, the organism experiences acute withdrawal because brain chemical production has been curtailed (Carroll, 1989; Liska, 2000; Stine and Kosten, 1999). Chapter 4 further explores the biochemical basis for narcotics addiction, as well as addiction to other types of drugs.

It is important to point out that there are also psychological and social factors in addiction to narcotics. The late Norman Zinberg (1984) brought to the attention of the scientific community that many individuals who use narcotics *never* become addicted. Zinberg emphasized the importance of drug *set* (the psychological predisposition of drug users) and *setting* (the social context of drug use) as important factors in drug addiction. These social dynamics contributing to drug addiction and the experience of drug use generally, are discussed more fully in Chapter 1.

Analgesic Effects   The blocking of pain is the most important of the intended effects of the narcotics. As we have pointed out earlier in this section, morphine, dilaudid, codeine, Darvon and Demerol are all prescribed primarily for their analgesic properties, and indeed, most if not all of the narcotics have been used for this purpose at one time or another. The narcotics are arguably the most effective analgesic available to modern medicine. The mechanism of analgesic action is also found in the endorphins and their receptors found throughout the human body. When the human organism experiences pain endorphins are sent to those receptors to alleviate the discomfort. Narcotics, having a similar molecular structure and with the ability to attach to the same receptors, accomplish the same result (Liska, 2000).

Euphoria   All the drugs that we are examining in this chapter are psychoactive, meaning that they affect the functioning of the central nervous system. The narcotics, however, have a rather unique euphoric effect. This effect has been variously described as a "warm feeling," "floating," and simply "at peace with the world." Lingeman (1974, p. 104), describes the euphoric effects of narcotics in a medical setting as ". . . a subjective state of well-being produced by the patient's dramatic release from pain and the anxieties and tensions accompanying it." The euphoria produced by narcotics is a strong motivator for continued use. While most experienced heroin addicts seldom experience the desired state of euphoria after they become fully addicted because of the large quantity of the drug it would take to achieve this state, addicts often report that they are "chasing that first high." While the euphoria is an important psychological motivation for continued use, most addicts are content to merely ease or forestall the *jones*—withdrawal symptoms resulting from a lack of the drug.

Other Effects   In addition to their addictive potential, analgesic effect and euphoria, the narcotics produce numerous other physiological reactions. One such effect is suppression of the cough reflex, or what is called an *antitussive* effect. The narcotic that has been used for this purpose historically is codeine, though other narcotics could accomplish this as well. The narcotics also produce an *antidiarrheal* effect. Indeed, long-term opiate users sometimes experience constipation because of this narcotic effect. Another symptom associated with opiate use is *constriction of the pupils* of the eye. A rather harmless effect, such constriction is often used as an indicator that an individual has been using opiates (Liska, 2000; Stine and Kosten, 1999).

A final physiological symptom associated with narcotics use which does have potential health ramifications is a decrease in central nervous system activity, especially the rate of respiration. This symptom is one shared with other depressants such as alcohol and barbiturates. This feature of narcotics is the basis for overdose, and death resulting from overdose. Theoretically, if one consumes a large enough amount of narcotics in high enough concentrations, the respiratory system can slow down to such an extent that the brain literally suffocates because of a lack of sufficient oxygen (Liska, 2000; Stine and Kosten, 1999). There is a great debate in the field about how dangerous heroin and other narcotics are in this regard. Clearly, other factors contribute to most so-called overdose deaths. We will discuss these health consequences of narcotics use in more detail in Chapter 8.

DEPRESSANTS

The **depressants** share one feature in common with the narcotics—they both act to slow down central nervous system processes. Depressants do not produce many of the other (analgesic, antitussive, etc.) effects of narcotics, however. Depressants fall into five broad categories: *alcohol, barbiturates, tranquilizers, sedatives,* and *inhalants.*

ALCOHOL

Alcohol[2] comes in three forms: *beer, wine,* and *distilled spirits. Beer,* which is normally the least concentrated of all forms of alcoholic beverages, is produced by the fermentation of grains, usually barley. Most commercial beers in the United States today contain only about 4 percent alcohol content. These are called *lager* beers. More concentrated are *malt liquors,* which contain 4 to 5 percent alcohol. Ales comprise the high end of the alcohol content, with 6 to 7 percent alcohol (Carroll, 1989). More recently, "ice beers" have been introduced. This process involves freezing the beer and removing some of the ice to produce a slightly higher concentration of alcohol. (Ray and Ksir, 1999).

Wine is also produced through fermentation. Wine can be produced from just about any fruit available. Most fruits include sugar which, when combined with yeast and water, will produce the necessary fermentation. Most wines contain a maximum of 15 percent alcoholic content, (normally 10 to 15 percent), or two to three times the concentration in commercially made beers (Carroll, 1989). Some wines are "fortified" with distilled spirits, and may contain as much as 20 percent alcohol (Ray and Ksir, 1999).

Distilled spirits are produced by heating fermented solution until the alcohol boils. This solution is usually a grain mash, but in the case of brandies and liqueurs, wine may also be distilled. The vapors are then captured and allowed to condense. Because alcohol has a lower boiling point than does water, it is possible to capture the more pure alcohol vapors before the water boils, and thus, when condensed a much more concentrated alcohol residue remains. Distilled beverages generally range in concentration from 80 to 100 proof—or 40 to 50 percent alcohol content (Carroll, 1989).

While beers, wines and distilled spirits contain varying concentrations of alcohol, the typical serving sizes contain approximately the same amount of ethyl content. This is referred to as the principle of "equivalent amounts." Three individuals—one drinking a 12 oz. can of beer, a second drinking a 4-ounce glass of wine, and a third consuming a 1.25 ounce shot of whiskey—are all consuming about the same amount of alcohol—approximately one-half ounce (Carroll, 1989).

Product	Gross Weight	Percent Alcohol	Net Alcohol Consumed
Beer	12 oz.	4%	$12 \times .04 = 0.48$ oz.
Wine	4 oz.	12%	$4 \times .12 = 0.48$ oz.
Distilled Spirits	1.25 oz.	40%	$1.25 \times .40 = 0.50$ oz.

Alcohol **intoxication** is usually measured in terms of **blood-alcohol content** (BAC). BAC refers to the proportion of the content of one's blood supply is made up of alcohol, measured in grams per 100 milliliters. A blood alcohol content of 0.10, for example (the legal threshold of intoxication in most states), means that alcohol comprises .10 gram per 100 milliliters of blood (otherwise stated as one tenth of one percent alcohol). Table 3.2 highlights the behavioral effects of varying levels of blood-alcohol content in the typical individual. It should be pointed out that there are at least two factors which seem to affect the relationship between BAC and behavioral performance—these are the *rate of increase* of BAC and the level of tolerance one has developed to alcohol. The faster rate of increase (resulting from hard and fast drinking), the greater the effect on motor performance; and the greater tolerance that one has developed to alcohol, the *lower* the impact on performance (Ray and Ksir, 1999).

BARBITURATES

Barbiturates is the term given to a family of central nervous system depressants that were developed and widely prescribed from the late nineteenth

TABLE 3.2	Performance Indicators at Select Alcohol Blood Alcohol Concentrations
Percent BAC	**Performance Indicators**
0.05	Lowered alertness; lowered inhibitions; impaired judgment
0.10	Increased reaction time; impaired motor function and coordination
0.15	Significant increases in reaction time
0.20	Lowered sensory awareness; substantial impairment of motor function
0.25	Staggering and other signs of seriously impaired motor function
0.30	Stuporous, but probably conscious; totally unaware of surroundings
0.35	Coma; minimal level causing death (LD1, meaning that about 1 percent of people with .35 concentration will die)
0.40	LD50—about half of people with BAC of .40 will die
0.80	LD100—virtually anyone at this level will die

Source: Adapted from Ray and Ksir, 1999, p. 222.

century until the 1950s, when doctors became more wary of addiction potential. More than 2,500 barbiturates have been synthesized, though only about 50 were ever marketed for human consumption. Today, only about 20 percent of all prescriptions for depressants are for barbiturates (Drug Enforcement Administration, 1997). The barbiturates are typically categorized into "short acting," "intermediate acting," and "long acting," referring to the amount of time it takes for the drug to take effect, and also the duration of the effective time. Short-acting barbiturates are generally used as anesthesia for short-term surgical procedures. They typically take effect within one minute when intravenously injected and have a duration of action of no more than three hours. Because of their extremely short duration, these barbiturates are not commonly used for recreational purposes. Intermediate-acting barbiturates generally take only about 15 to 45 minutes to take effect, and may work for up to six hours. They are most commonly used to induce sleep, and quickly replaced alcohol, chloral hydrate, bromides, and the opiates, which had been commonly used for this purpose. Commonly used intermediate acting barbiturates are Seconal, Amytal, Tuinal and Nembutal, which, along with others in this category, bear some resemblance to alcohol in their effects. They produce the euphoria and disinhibition characteristic of an alcohol high, and often a similar hangover effect as well. Long-acting barbiturates, such as Luminal, are used primarily for daytime sedation where a longer action period is required. It has also been demonstrated that these drugs increase aggressiveness (Cherek, Spiga, and Steinberg, 1989). These barbiturates take up to an hour to take effect, but their duration may be as long as 16 hours. The relatively slow onset of these barbiturates discourage their recreational use (Carroll, 1989).

The barbiturates were popular as recreational drugs, especially during the 1960s. According to Brecher (1972), much of this popularity can be attributed to the negative publicity that surrounded them in earlier years. They became a source of fascination for thrill seekers. The barbiturates were marketed on the streets under such names as *reds, blues, yellows, barbs, yellow jackets, goofballs, Christmas trees, red devils* and many others. Used nonmedically, barbiturates can have very serious consequences, including fatalities due to overdose and sudden withdrawal.

NON-BARBITURATE SEDATIVES

The oldest non-barbiturate sedative is *chloral hydrate*, first synthesized in 1862. It is still in use today, but has not been prescribed with any frequency since the introduction of barbiturates about the turn of the century. Chloral hydrate is perhaps best known today as "Mickey Finn" or "knock-out drops." When mixed with alcohol, chloral hydrate is especially potent and quick acting, and is used to intentionally cause deep sedation for purposes of robbery, kidnaping, or otherwise victimizing a subject. Because of the synergistic effect that chloral hydrate has when mixed with alcohol, the Mickey Finn is a potentially toxic and fatal concoction (Inciardi, 1977a).

What we more commonly know today as *sedatives* were developed in response to the concerns over the potentially addictive affects of the barbiturates. One of the early sedatives was *glutethimide,* synthesized in 1954, and marketed as Doriden and Dormtabs. Glutethemide was a treatment for insomnia, and was supposedly less toxic and addictive than the barbiturates. Unfortunately, it was found to be both addictive and more toxic than the barbiburates it was designed to replace. Glutethimide was succeeded in 1965 by yet another sedative, *methaqualone,* most commonly known by its trade name Quaalude in the United States. In England and Europe, it was more commonly marketed under the names Sopor or Mandrax. Street users generally refer to the drug simply as *ludes* or *sopers* (Lingeman, 1974; Ray and Ksir, 1999). This drug was considered to be much safer than the earlier glutethimide, but—in part because of its reputation for being safer— was much more widely abused. Ironically, when Controlled Substances Act rescheduling of many drugs occurred in 1991, *methaqualone* was transferred to Schedule I while *glutethimide,* was moved only to Schedule II (Drug Enforcement Administration, 1997).

TRANQUILIZERS

The tranquilizers are generally divided into two broad categories—*major tranquilizers* and *minor tranquilizers.*

Major Tranquilizers   The major tranquilizers are almost exclusively limited to medical contexts, and while they are occasionally used recreationally, there is not widespread use or abuse of these drugs. The major tranquilizers are grouped into four broad families: *phenothiazines, thioxanthines, butyrophenones,* and *Rauwolfia alkaloids.* The most commonly used are the *phenothiazines,* which are marketed under trade names such as Thorazine and Mellaril. Contrary to popular opinion, the term "major tranquilizer" does not refer to the extent of their use or abuse. Rather, it has to do with the nature of their impact on the human body and the types of symptoms which call for their use. The major tranquilizers, also called *antipsychotics* are used almost exclusively to treat the symptoms of schizophrenia and other psychotic states—if you will, "major" mental illnesses. They have been found to effectively reduce hallucinations and delusions, and the anxieties associated with them (Liska, 2000).

Minor Tranquilizers   The minor tranquilizers are used to treat a variety of disorders which generally fall under the category of *anxiety disorders,* or "minor" forms of mental illness. Because of this, some prefer the term *antianxiety agents* or *ataractics* when referring to these drugs. The two most commonly prescribed categories, or "families" of minor tranquilizers are *meprobamate* and the *benzodiazepines.* Meprobamate was the first of the minor tranquilizers to be synthesized under the trade name of Miltown, but when the addictive potential of Miltown became apparent, the benzodiazepines were introduced, initially as Librium followed by Valium. Valium quickly became the most widely prescribed drug in America. At the peak of its popularity, in 1975, there were 61.3 million prescriptions (including refills) for Valium (Goode, 1999). Millions of Americans, especially women, who were the primary consumers of Valium, became addicted. Valium use declined significantly by the early 1980s, partly because doctors became more hesitant to prescribe Valium, but perhaps mostly because the patent on Valium was running out, and the manufacturer, Hoffman-Laroche, ceased marketing the drug so heavily (Consumer Reports, 1993). This did not signal the end of minor tranquilizer use, however. New benzodiazepines, most notably Xanax and Halcion were introduced in the 1980s. It was believed that these drugs would not have the addictive potential of Valium because they are processed and eliminated from the body in less than half a day. These drugs are typically prescribed to be taken three times a day rather than the one-a-day dosage for Valium. Clinical studies soon found that these rapidly eliminating drugs have an even stronger rebound effect and addictive potential than does Valium. These findings were too late for many Americans who were already dependent on these drugs. By 1987, Xanax had become the fourth leading drug on the prescription drug list (Consumer Reports, 1993). On the street, the tranquilizers go by names such as *blues, heavenly blues, valley girl, vals, valums, tranqs,* and *valo* among other slang terms.

A very recent benzodiazepine with a very troublesome record is *flunitrazepam,* marketed under the trade name of *Rohypnol.* Better known as *roofies, rophies, roach, rope. Mexican Valium,* or simply the *date rape drug,* this drug has never been approved in the United States, although there are over 50 countries which have approved it for insomnia (see Drugs and Everyday Life). Rohypnol usually begins to take effect within 20 minutes and reaches peak effectiveness within a couple of hours. Rohypnol use in the United States has been especially popular among males to facilitate untoward and unwanted sexual advances. This drug is nearly ten times as strong as Valium, and not only sedates an individual, making her powerless to resist, but also causes temporary *anterograde* amnesia,[3] so that victims often do not recall any details of an assault or sexual misadventure. At a cost of only about $5 per tablet, many high school and college males find this to be a cheap form of sexual thrill. The federal government is responding more harshly to this "date rape drug." In 1983, it was categorized as a Schedule IV drug, but it was moved up to Schedule III in 1995, requiring much more careful record keeping and monitoring of distribution records. The DEA is currently considering moving it up to Schedule I because of the recent abuses that have been observed. While most well known as a date rape drug, Rolypnol is probably used more for other purposes. Commonly used at rave parties and other social occasions at which drugs are used, Rohypnol produces profound intoxication and is said to enhance the effect of heroin and to modulate the effects of cocaine (Drug Enforcement Administration, 1999).

DRUGS AND EVERYDAY LIFE

Date Rape and Roofies

Flunitrazepam, which is marketed under the brand name Rohypnol and is commonly known as roofies, belongs to the benzodiazepine class of drugs. Rohypnol has never been approved for medical use in the United States, therefore, doctors cannot prescribe it and pharmacists cannot sell it. However, it is legally prescribed in over 50 other countries and is widely available in Mexico, Colombia, and Europe, where it is used for the treatment of insomnia and as a pre-anesthetic. Therefore, it was placed into Schedule IV of the Controlled Substances Act in 1984 due to international treaty obligations and was moved to Schedule III in 1995. Like other benzodiazepines (such as Valium, Librium, Xanax, and Halcion), Rohypnol's pharmacological effects include sedation, muscle relaxation, reduction in anxiety, and prevention of convulsions. However, Rohypnol's sedative effects are approximately 7 to 10 times more potent than diazepam (Valium). The effects of Rohypnol appear approximately 15 to 20 minutes after administration and last approximately four to six hours. Some residual effects can be found 12 hours or more after administration.

Rohypnol causes partial amnesia; individuals are unable to remember certain events that they experienced while under the influence of the drug. This effect is particularly dangerous when Rohypnol is used to aid in the commission of sexual assault; victims may not be able to clearly recall the assault, the assailant, or the events surrounding the assault.

It is difficult to estimate just how many Rohypnol-facilitated rapes have occurred in the United States. Very often, biological samples are taken from the victim at a time when the effects of the drug have already passed and only residual amounts remain in the body fluids. These residual amounts are difficult, if not impossible, to detect using standard screening assays available in the United States. If Rohypnol exposure is to be detected at all, urine samples need to be collected within 72 hours and subjected to sensitive analytical tests. The problem is compounded by the onset of amnesia after ingestion of the drug, which causes the victim to be uncertain about the facts surrounding the rape. This uncertainty may lead to critical delays or even reluctance to report the rape and to provide appropriate biological samples for toxicology testing.

While Rohypnol has become widely known for its use as a date-rape drug, it is abused more frequently for other reasons. It is abused by high school students, college students, street gang members, rave party attendees, and heroin and cocaine abusers to produce profound intoxication, boost the high of heroin, and modulate the effects of cocaine. Rohypnol is usually consumed orally, is often combined with alcohol, and is abused by crushing tablets and snorting the powder.

Rohypnol abuse causes a number of adverse effects in the abuser, including drowsiness, dizziness, loss of motor control, lack of coordination, slurred speech, confusion, and gastrointestinal disturbances, lasting 12 or more hours. Higher doses produce respiratory depression. Chronic use of Rohypnol can result in physical dependence and the appearance of withdrawal syndrome when the drug is discontinued. Rohypnol impairs cognitive and psychomotor functions affecting reaction time and driving skill. The use of this drug in combination with alcohol is a particular concern as both substances potentiate each other's toxicity. ■

Source: DEA:
www.usdoj.gov/dea/concern/rohypnol.htm

INHALANTS

The inhalants are CNS depressants dispensed in vapor form which are breathed. They come in a variety of commercial products, most of which are not intended for medical use. These volatile substances can be found in more than 1,000 common household products, and because of their use in these commercial products, they are readily available to children. The mind-altering effect of these substances has a very long history, dating to ancient times. Preble and Laury (1967) note, for example, that in the ancient Greek, Judaic, Egyptian, and Babylonian worlds there is strong evidence that the aroma of burnt spices and other natural vapors were enjoyed and even used as part of worship rituals. These religious practices continue today in the Jewish Havdalah service, which represents the end of the Sabbath. As our knowledge of chemistry developed, many synthetic solvents were developed which produced even stronger psychoactive effects. We can categorize most inhalants as either *organic solvents* or *anaesthetics*.

Organic Solvents   Almost universally, organic solvents are commercial products which have been legally manufactured for uses other than human consumption. Most of the organic solvents are petroleum distillates, and include such products as gasoline, lighter fluids, paint thinners, varnishes and lacquers, dry cleaning products, and model glue (toluene) among others. All of these products, when inhaled intensely, are capable of producing extreme physiological reactions, sometimes resembling the hallucinogenic drugs, discussed below. These are all depressants in their pharmacological impact on the CNS, however, and in most cases their effects resemble extreme alcohol inebriation. The organic inhalants can be taken in several ways. They can be sniffed directly from the container they are in, squeezed into paper bags, as was toluene during the 1960s experimentation with that drug, or they may be "huffed" from a rag that is soaked with the substance, and often placed in a bag so that the vapors are not dispersed into the atmosphere. This practice seems to be most common among rural and suburban teens and pre-teens (Drug Enforcement Administration, 1999).

Anaesthetics   Many of the anaesthetic inhalants are used for medical purposes, but have been discovered by recreational drug users for the high that they can experience. Perhaps the oldest of the anaesthetics is *nitrous oxide* (N_2O), discovered in 1776 by Sir Joseph Priestly, and almost simultaneously by Sir Humphrey Davy. Davy discovered that when inhaled, the drug produced a rush of excitement and a compulsion to laugh loudly which resulted in it being referred to as "laughing gas." Medical uses for nitrous oxide were not discovered until later, when a dentist by the name of Horace Wells quite accidentally discovered its ability to stop pain. By the mid-1840s, this drug was recognized as a medical breakthrough (Brecher, 1972). Today the drug continues to be used recreationally, though not on a large scale. Its users, who suck the drug out of gas-filled balloons, call the practice "doing whippits." The high is extremely short-lived (Ray and Ksir, 1999).

Two other inhalants that have been used both medically and recreationally are *ether* and *chloroform*. Ether is produced when distilled alcohol was combined with sulfuric acid. The drug has been used in medicine as an anaesthetic since the early 1700s, but became a popular drug of choice during prohibition. *Chloroform* is a nineteenth-century discovery that was used both recreationally because of its intoxicating effect, and, by the mid-nineteenth century, was used medically as an analgesic during childbirth. Its medical use was discontinued as the potential for overdose was soon discovered, and for the same reason, it is no longer commonly used as a recreational drug (Brecher, 1972).

PHARMACOLOGICAL FEATURES OF THE DEPRESSANTS

The common pharmacological feature which unites all depressants is their tendency to depress the actions of the central nervous system, and to slow down physiological processes dependent on the CNS. The respiratory system slows down, the heart rate decreases, thought processes slow down, and reaction time increases. This feature of the depressants poses several health threats that are discussed more fully in Chapter 8.

Another effect shared by most of the depressants is that they interact with one another and with certain other drugs, particularly the narcotics, in a synergistic fashion, which can result in overdose-like symptoms (Brady, Myrick, and Malcolm, 1999). Finally, studies have demonstrated that most of the depressants produce both tolerance and dependence over time, which means that the user requires higher levels of the drug to achieve the same effect (tolerance) and withdrawal symptoms are experienced when use of the drug is discontinued, resulting in potentially dangerous withdrawal symptoms (Brady, Myrick, and Malcolm, 1999; Moak and Anton, 1999; Ray and Ksir, 1999).

Beyond the pharmacological effects of the depressants generally, alcohol affects the human organism in numerous and unique ways. Most of the CNS depressants act primarily through the *gamma-aminobutyric acid* (GABA) neurotransmitter system (Brady, Myrick, and Malcolm, 1999). Alcohol, however, affects multiple neurotransmitter systems, including serotonin, dopamine, endorphin, GABA and NMBA (Kranzler and Anton, 1994). Other properties of alcohol pose unique risks to the human organism which, along with other health correlates of the depressants, is discussed much more fully in Chapter 8.

STIMULANTS

The **stimulants** share one important pharmacological characteristic—they stimulate the central nervous system. This feature of the stimulants leads to some common physiological effects, which are discussed at the end of this section and in Chapter 8. Some of the stimulants, such as cocaine and its derivatives are well-known for their abuse potential. Others are not even considered drugs by many people. These "non-drug drugs" include nicotine and caffeine–drugs which are used by millions of Americans today.

COCAINE

Cocaine is derived from the leaves of the coca plant (scientifically known as *Erythroxylon coca*), which is grown primarily in the high-altitude regions of South America, principally in Colombia, Peru, Ecuador, and Bolivia. A coca paste is formed by pulverizing the coca leaf and soaking it in alcohol and benzol (a petroleum distillate), draining the solution and adding sulfuric acid. Cocaine crystals containing about a 90 percent cocaine concentration (compared with about a 1 percent concentration in the coca leaf) are left as a residue. These crystals are known as coca paste (Inciardi, 1992). The paste is then usually transformed into a powder form, *cocaine hydrochloride,* by diluting it with other substances such as milk sugar or lactose. Powdered cocaine is quite typically sniffed or "snorted" nasally, but it may also be smoked or injected directly into the bloodstream. The latter practice is often in combination with heroin use, and is called *speedballing.* When used recreationally, cocaine has been referred to variously as *coke, C, big C, lady snow, toot, blow,* and *girl,* among many others. The term "girl" is used to differentiate cocaine from heroin ("boy") when used in a speedball. Cocaine has always been attractive as a recreational drug and was particularly popular in the disco culture of the 1970s among upwardly mobile young people. Its use peaked during the 1980s, and has generally declined since (National Institute on Drug Abuse, n.d.a). The potentially dangerous consequences of cocaine, which were at one time denied by users and professionals alike, were highlighted by the closely timed deaths of University of Maryland basketball star Len Bias and Cleveland Browns defensive back Don Rogers.

Freebase   Freebase cocaine became popular during the 1970s. It is a form of cocaine that is smoked. Cocaine in powder form has a very high melting point and therefore is very difficult to ingest in this form. Freebase is formed by treating powder cocaine with a liquid base such as ammonia to remove the hydrochloric acid. The free standing cocaine base (hence, "freebase") is then dissolved, typically in ether, that forms crystals with much lower melting points. It is then melted in a glass pipe and the vapors inhaled. The more concentrated form of cocaine, combined with the form in which it is inhaled, makes freebasing a particularly quick and potent form of high. Because the solution that the freebase is combined with is usually ether or some other volatile substance, freebasing has proven to be a potentially dangerous pastime (Inciardi, 1992). One of the more well-known cases of injury caused by freebasing was the comedian Richard Pryor, who was severely burned while freebasing. Freebasing declined with the emergence of the more stable "crack" cocaine.

Crack   Crack cocaine first emerged in the mid-1980s and has been considered by many to be the scourge of the 1990s. Chitwood et al. (1996, p. 1) document that the first major media mention of crack was "(b)uried within the pages of the Monday edition of the prestigious *New York Times*." It was a most casual mention, and inappropriately confused crack with freebase. But it caught the attention of other media, and in less than a year there were over a thousand stories in major media outlets focusing on crack cocaine. By 1986, the DEA felt compelled to respond to the hysteria that was being generated by the media. In actuality, crack was, at this time, restricted to inner city neighborhoods in a small number of major cities. It was not the epidemic that the media were constructing (Inciardi, 1992).

Crack is manufactured by mixing the powdered cocaine hydrochloride with ammonia, or more typically with sodium bicarbonate (baking soda) and water and then heating to remove the hydrochloride. What remains is a cocaine-sodium or cocaine-ammonia mixture, which is typically about 30–40 percent pure. It is then heated, and the vapors inhaled. The name "crack" derives from the crackling sound that is made, caused by the baking soda heating (Inciardi, 1992). Because crack is so cheap—typically about $3 to $5 for a "rock"—it is highly attractive to young users who have very limited resources to purchase more expensive drugs. Crack is, as Reinarman and Levine (1997) point out, primarily a marketing innovation. It takes substances already available and repackages them in a new and less expensive form, allowing distributors to reach a new clientele—young, minority, inner city youth. It is seductive, however, in that the high from crack is very immediate (crossing the blood-brain barrier within about six seconds), intense and very short-lasting, leaving the user with a craving for more (Inciardi, 1992). Crack users quickly find themselves craving more of the drug than they can afford, and many spontaneous, poorly planned crimes which frequently turn violent are committed by crack users seeking fast money. During the late 1980s and early 1990s, we witnessed the emergence of a crack subculture, complete with argot, crack houses, crack dealers, and crack paraphernalia (see Chapter 5). Crack goes by many names in the subculture of crack use, some of which include *caps, caviar, cookies, hard rock, jelly beans, kryptonite, rooster,* and *white tornado* among others. Of great concern to public health officials is the spread of HIV among regular crack users, as many will readily prostitute themselves—often within the crack houses—for rocks of crack cocaine (Inciardi, 1993, 1996). We take up this issue in greater detail in Chapter 8. There is some evidence for a downturn in the use of crack during the 1990s (Office of National Drug Control Policy, 1998), though surveys of high school students suggest a level or perhaps even slight increase in crack use as measured in 30-day and annual prevalence (Johnston, O'Malley and Bachman, 2002).

PRESCRIPTION STIMULANTS

Normally referred to as amphetamines,[4] these powerful CNS stimulants have some similarities to cocaine, but are usually longer lasting and more pervasively impact the body. There are three broad families of amphetamines: *levoamphetamine* (Benzedrine), *dextroamphetamine* (Dexedrine), and *methamphetamine* (Methedrine). The amphetamines are rather recent additions to the medical and recreational pharmacopeia. Their discovery followed on the heels of discovering the chemical structure of epinephrine (adrenalin). Epinephrine is also found naturally in certain herbs, and had been used by the Chinese for some 5,000 years as well as in Russia and among the Native Americans and Spaniards in the southwestern United States (Grinspoon and Hedblom, 1975). Seeking to develop a drug that could, in effect, imitate the effect of adrenalin, chemists first isolated ephedrine, the active ingredient in epinephrine in 1887, though it would not be until 1932 that this drug would make its way into routine medical practice. The drug was marketed as Benzedrine, and it was used to clear bronchial passages by shrinking the enlarged nasal mucosa. Other discoveries soon followed. Only three years after it was first marketed, scientists learned that Benzedrine was very effective in treating narcolepsy, a disorder which causes victims to suddenly fall asleep for no apparent reason. The drug would later be used by truck drivers, students and others who needed to maintain alertness for long hours without sleep. Then in 1939, a discovery was made that would eventually place amphetamines in hundreds of thousands of American households. Studies of patients being treated for narcolepsy revealed that they had a significant reduction in appetite. Our cultural preoccupation with thinness created a demand for this new wonder drug, and by mid-century a generation of women had discovered the marvels of "black beauties" (biphetamines) (Liska, 2000). While there is some question as to how effective they are as *anorectics* (inducing weight loss) compared with maintaining careful diets, in the short run at least, patients are able to facilitate weight loss. The FDA no longer approves amphetamines for long-term weight control, but other amphetamine-like drugs have been developed for this purpose (Liska, 2000; Ray and Ksir, 1999).

The *methamphetamines* are the most recently developed of the amphetamines. This family of amphetamines is much more powerful than either Benzedrine or Dexadrine. Moreover, it has a more rapid onset than do the other amphetamines. Perhaps most significantly, however, methamphetamine is produced in powder form which makes it much more amenable to snorting, smoking, or mainline injection. Consequently, this drug has come into wide recreational use and abuse, under the street names of *meth, crank, speed, go, chalk, fire, glass, crystal, crystal meth,* and, *ice.* "Smoking" methamphetamines actually involves heating the substance in a container over a flame and inhaling the fumes through a straw or glass pipe. Intravenous use of the drug has been documented among U.S. servicemen since the 1950s (Brecher, 1972); however, this method of use did not spread among civilians until the 1960s. It was particularly popular among heroin addicts, who used the powder methampetamine in place of cocaine in the preparation of speedballs. (In fact, this is probably where it took on the nickname "speed.")

Figure 3.1 Clandestine laboratory seizures reported to DEA EPIC Calendar Year 1999.

Total clandestine lab seizures: 7,528. Over 97 percent of clan lab seizures were methamphetamine labs.

Source: DEA EPIC, September 2000.

The introduction of methamphetamine was also significant because this is a drug that can be manufactured quite easily in home kitchens or basement laboratories, often called "speed labs." Brecher (1972) notes that when the government began to tighten up legal distribution of methamphetamine, these homemade speed labs sprang up all across the United States, making it virtually impossible for the government to control its spread. In 1999, the Drug Enforcement Administration seized more than 7,500 clandestine labs, virtually all of which were methamphetamine labs (Drug Enforcement Administration, 1999). See Figure 3.1.

Speed was a particularly attractive drug because it provided a powerful "rush" which has been compared to an intense sexual orgasm. Unlike cocaine, however, the high that is afforded by speed lasts much longer and the user does not feel the need to re-inject nearly so often. The late 1990s has witnessed a dramatic increase in the abuse of methamphetamines (or "crank") among the young, particularly in the West, but also in the Southeast and Midwest (Albertson, Derlet and Van Hoozen, 1999).

NICOTINE

The only medium in which nicotine is conveyed is tobacco. So, our discussion of nicotine is really the story of tobacco. Today, there is no recognized medical use for tobacco, though this was not always the case as we have seen in Chapter 2. There are, today, an estimated 48 million adults in the United States who smoke cigarettes, in addition to millions of others who use other tobacco products. Nearly half of regular cigarette smokers will eventually die or experience one or more severe disabilities as a result of their smoking. More than 430,000 deaths each year (or 1 in 5) can be attributed to tobacco (Centers for Disease Control, 2000b). The physiological dangers associated with tobacco smoking are immense. Arguably, no other drug poses as many physiological risks to the human organism as does tobacco. Yet, this is a drug that has historically been treated rather lightly by policy makers, treatment specialists and educators.

The addictive potential of nicotine has been a source of controversy recently, with tobacco companies making strong denials of this claim. Clearly, there is evidence of withdrawal symptoms, including irritability, anxiety, headaches, drowsiness and gastrointestinal problems among heavy smokers. Moreover, if we measure addiction by compulsive reinforcement, there is perhaps no other drug that produces quite the dependence and need for reinforcement as tobacco. Studies conducted prior to the Great American Smokeout emphasis of the 1980s revealed that 85 percent of adolescents who smoked more than one cigarette went on to become regular users. Moreover, of those who went on to become regular users, some 85 percent continued regular smoking patterns at least until age 60. If these statistics are accurate, more than 70 percent of adolescents who smoked more than one cigarette (i.e., went beyond the experimental trying out of a cigarette) would go on to become regular smokers for the rest of their lives (Russell, 1971; cited in Brecher, 1972). Another study found that nearly 70 percent of American smokers smoke more than 15 cigarettes per day (National Clearinghouse for Smoking and Health, 1969; cited in Brecher, 1972). This is an average of one cigarette (read, one "hit") per hour. No other drug commands this level of reinforcement. If we use the frequency of reinforcement as a measure, tobacco is clearly the most addicting drug there is, a reality underscored by C. Everett Koop, Surgeon General during the Reagan administration. It is estimated that more than 80 percent of current adult smokers started smoking before the age of 18. (Centers for Disease Control, 1994). This is of particular concern today, as recent studies are reporting increasing rates of tobacco use among high school and even middle school students through the 1990s. A recent study by the Centers for Disease Control (2000a), revealed that 13 percent of middle school students and 35 percent of high school students use some form of tobacco product. These findings are confirmed with studies by University of Michigan researchers, which show an increase in cigarette use among high school seniors through 1997, when 36.5 percent of seniors reported using cigarettes within the last 30 days. This percentage has declined slightly since 1997 (Johnston, O'Malley and Bachman, 2002). Some of the increased attractiveness of tobacco to younger users has come in the form of "bidi" and "kretek," two forms of tobacco which are imported from India and Indonesia respectively, and are flavored with cloves, fruit, and other flavorings.

CAFFEINE

The story of *caffeine* as a psychoactive drug is, for the most part, the story of coffee. We would point out, however, that caffeine itself is part of a larger family of drugs known as the *xanthines*. The word "xanthine" is a Greek term meaning "yellow," which is the color of the residue of xanthines when heated with nitric acid until dry. In addition to caffeine, the xanthines also comprise *theophylline* and *theobromine*. The last two categories of xanthines are not commonly consumed for their psychoactive effect, though theobromine is a substantial ingredient in cocoa and chocolate, as well as in cola soft drinks. Caffeine is the primary psychoactive ingredient in coffee, as well as some teas and cola drinks (Ray, 1978).

Some of the psychoactive effects of caffeine consumption are positive and intended. Caffeine is included in many over-the-counter preparations such as Anacin, which are used primarily in the treatment of headaches. College students and truck drivers use this drug both in tablet and liquid (coffee) form to stay awake. While commonly used, and not even considered by most people to be a drug, the stimulant potential of caffeine is greatly underestimated by most users. Certainly, while caffeine overdoses are highly unlikely (it would take the equivalent of about 100 cups of coffee within a two or three hour period to die from an overdose), caffeine has produced some bizarre reactions. Sensory disturbances have been reported, such as seeing flashes of light. Like other stimulants, caffeine increases heart rate, blood pressure and metabolism rates, as well as gastrointestinal activity (Ray and Ksir, 1999). These and other physiological symptoms of the stimulants are discussed below.

PHARMACOLOGICAL FEATURES OF THE STIMULANTS

The stimulants affect primarily the dopamine and serotonin neurotransmitter systems as well as the hormonal norepinephrine system (Weaver and Schnoll, 1999). The stimulants accelerate CNS activity, which results in symptoms such as increases in heart rate, blood pressure, metabolism, and generally, an increase in the electrical activity of the cerebral cortex. In low to moderate dosages, these symptoms do not pose health risks for most people, though in higher dosages there is certainly the risk for cardiovascular problems. There is also evidence that the stimulants produce both tolerance and dependance. This is particularly true of cocaine as we discuss below, but all of the stimulants show these symptoms. Some classic withdrawal symptoms include depression, anxiety, problems with memory and suicide ideation (Weaver and Schnoll, 1999; Ray and Ksir, 1999). These drugs also produce some positive effects, including a reduction in appetite and inhibition of one's ability to sleep. When used in normal dosages, studies have found a heightened level of mental acuteness and motor coordination, along with increased levels of energy. Because these drugs are taken in different media, the stimulants also have their own unique effects on the human organism.

Methamphetamine poses potentially severe consequences for the regular and heavy user. Because it induces such a high level of energy over a long period of time, users experience sleeplessness, often for many days in a row. Prolonged heavy use of methamphetamine is also believed to induce psychotic-like episodes, involving hallucinations of insects crawling just under the skin—a phenomenon experts call *formication.* (Liska, 2000).

Cocaine is somewhat unique in how rapidly and intensely it produces euphoria, whether taken as powder or rock (crack). Crack is particularly intense, but compared with other stimulants, powder cocaine is very intense as well. Not surprisingly, there has been a great deal of debate over the years regarding the addictive quality of cocaine. It was long believed that dependence on cocaine was a purely psychological phenomenon, that the pleasurable experience of cocaine was highly reinforcing psychologically. Researchers have recently discovered regions deep within the brain that produce pleasurable feelings. One area that appears to be particularly responsive to cocaine is an area called the ventral tagmental area (VTA), which releases large amounts of *dopamine,* which are transmitted to the synapse between neurons and which bind to specialized proteins called *dopamine receptors.* Scientists have found that cocaine blocks the removal of dopamine from the synapse, resulting in the accumulation of dopamine, thereby resulting in more continuous stimulation of the receiving neurons and hence, the euphoria that users experience (National Institute on Drug Abuse, 1999). There is even some suggestion that a tolerance for cocaine may develop, requiring the user to use ever larger amounts of cocaine to achieve a similar effect. This would explain, for example, why lab rats and other animals will forego food for cocaine, or will push a lever thousands of times for a dose of cocaine. This continues to be debated as more research on the physiology of cocaine use is being conducted. Clearly, however, cocaine in all its forms is highly reinforcing, producing an intense desire for more of the drug. This seems to be a feature of other stimulants as well, but recent research on cocaine addiction has been especially enlightening in this area (National Institute on Drug Abuse, 1999; Weaver and Schnoll, 1999).

HALLUCINOGENS

When most people think about the **hallucinogens,** they think of LSD, a powerful hallucinogen that rose to prominence during the 1960s. The hallucinogens have a long history, however, which precedes LSD by centuries, even millennia. The remainder of this section will examine two broad categories of hallucinogens—the *natural hallucinogens* and *synthetic hallucinogens.*

THE NATURAL HALLUCINOGENS

Grinspoon and Bakalar (1979) suggest that of the approximately 5,000 known alkaloid plants that exist throughout the world, probably about one hundred or so would be considered hallucinogenic. The natural hallucinogens have been used for thousands of years as intoxicants, healing remedies, and as part of religious rites. Throughout most of this history, these drugs were not used recreationally, but under the watchful eye of medical or religious specialists (Grinspoon and Bakalar, 1979). It is impossible to examine all of the naturally occurring hallucinogens here, but we will be looking at some of the more common ones in use today.

Peyote and Mescaline   Peyote is interesting historically, as this is a drug that has been in continuous use as part of religious rituals from before written history to the present day. This drug, which is part of the cactus *Lophophora williamsii*, has been used by native peoples in America as a component in their religious rituals long before Europeans discovered this land. Spanish explorers who moved into Mexico discovered the use of this plant and noted that it had extreme effects on its users. Early missionaries into Mexico and the southwest United States attempted to stop its use, but this only forced it underground and led to the establishment of a peyote-based religion among Native American peoples. It was used largely underground in Native American religious practice until the establishment in 1918 of the Native American Church of the United States. Despite attempts to make the use of this drug illegal in religious practice, with the official establishment of the Native American church these attempts failed on grounds of interfering with free religious expression (Grinspoon and Bakalar, 1979).

The entire *Lophophora williamsii* cactus has hallucinogenic qualities, though only the portion above the ground can easily be consumed. The upper portion of the cactus, or crown, is typically sliced into "mescal buttons" and eaten. The primary active ingredient in the mescal buttons is *mescaline*, which is usually taken in a powder or capsule form. Mescaline became quite popular among recreational drug users in the 1960s along with LSD and other hallucinogenic drugs. It was preferred over LSD by many because it does not produce as intense an effect and often less nausea and other unwanted effects. The psychedelic effect of mescaline is primarily visual distortion, though it does also produce some **synesthesia.** (Drug Enforcement Administration, 1997; Ray and Ksir, 1999). Recreational users refer to mescaline as *Big Chief, Mescal, Mesc, Buttons,* and *Cactus.*

Psilocybin   A derivative of the *Psilocybe mexicana* mushroom, psilocybin has become a popular drug among recreational hallucinogenic drug users. This drug is also used by some Native Americans in religious rituals, and was used as early as 1000 B.C. in Guatemala among the Aztecs. Psilocybin was first isolated in the *Psilocybe mexicana* mushroom in 1958 by Albert Hoffman, who 20 years earlier had discovered LSD (Ray and Ksir, 1999). Psilocybin has many of the same effects as peyote and mescaline. Time and space perception are affected, and subjects are reported to be more suggestible and distracted. Emotions become more labile and extreme, swinging from extreme euphoria and hilarity to deep depression. The effect, however, is more mild than with either peyote or LSD (Grinspoon and Bakalar, 1979). Slang terms for psilocybin include *shrooms, magic mushrooms, sacred mushroom, caps, liberty caps,* and *purple passion.*

SYNTHETIC AND SEMISYNTHETIC HALLUCINOGENS

The synthetic and semisynthetic hallucinogens are those which are substantially synthesized in a laboratory setting. We look at some of the more commonly used synthetics here.

LSD   Laboratory-synthesized hallucinogens begin with the discovery of LSD[5] (*d-lysergic acid diethylamide*), known on the street as *microdot, blotter, acid, window panes, Bart Simpson, Bartman, blue heaven, tabs,* and most commonly, *acid.* LSD is arguably the most potent drug known to human kind. Normal doses are measured in *micro*grams—1/1000 of a milligram. The effective dose of 50 micrograms is but one-twentieth of a milligram. LSD is considered to be about 5,000 times more potent than mescaline and some 200 times more potent than psilocybin (Ray and Ksir, 1999). A single ounce of the drug would provide enough for about 300,000 doses! Because of its extreme potency, LSD is taken via another medium of transmission, such as in a small sugar cube or on blotter paper.

LSD is the combination of lysergic acid (not itself an hallucinogen)—which is found in *ergot,* a fungus that grows on various grains—with diethylamide, a synthetic compound. Hence, LSD is technically a *semisynthetic* hallucinogen. LSD produces all the effects of hallucinogens that we cited earlier. Because these experiences are often very intense, users may experience anxiety or panic (see Chapter 1 for a discussion of the importance of *set* and *setting* for how these drugs are experienced). The so-called "bad trip" results from these intense experiences where the user is at a loss to make sense of what is happening, and typically, other users are not around to help "normalize" or explain that these experiences are to be expected (Grinspoon and Bakalar, 1979).

Despite the potency of the drug and its potential for bizarre hallucinogenic reactions, LSD is almost surely not the evil menace that the hysteria purported it to be during the height of our concern in the decades of the 1960s and 1970s. Perhaps the most common allegation regarding LSD use is the occurrence of flashbacks, even years after discontinuing use. There seems to be no question about whether these occur. There is, however, some disagreement as to *why* they occur. Some see these flashbacks as a result of the pharmacological effect of LSD on the brain and nervous system. A more commonly accepted explanation, however, is that the human mind captures extreme experiences that are replayed at later times. War veterans frequently experience this phenomenon. A study by William McGlothlin and David Arnold (1971) revealed that among 247 LSD users, eight reported symptoms that might be serious enough to call a flashback.

A related concern regarding LSD use is the belief that it induces psychotic reactions—reactions that might result in great panic or even suicide. Again, severe reactions do occur. Sociologist Howard Becker (1967) has suggested, however, that the likelihood of such an experience is *socially* derived. In his research, Becker found that those users who were given LSD in clinical settings, where abnormal reactions were *expected*, generally experienced the severe symptoms. All their actions while under the influence of the drug were met with reactions of shock and horror. The situation was defined as one of abnormality. This was a far different response than those users who first used in the context of an experienced subculture of use, which defined these actions and subjective experiences as normal. Becker found far fewer incidents of so-called psychotic episodes in this context. Becker's findings only emphasize the importance that *setting* plays in the nature of one's experience using LSD. A related concern is the potential for LSD to induce suicide attempts. There have been a small number of suicide attempts among LSD users, but several qualifying factors must be noted. One of these is the *set*, or psychological disposition of the user while using the drug. Those users who are already highly depressed upon using LSD will very possibly be at higher risk for suicide given the tendency of LSD to make one more emotionally labile anyway. It must also be remembered that because LSD greatly affects spatial perception, many apparent attempted suicides may be nothing more than an inability to correctly perceive one's environment (which may account for people walking out of multistory windows, for example).

A major charge against LSD that sent shockwaves through communities was that it causes genetic (chromosomal) damage. The concern was first raised in a March 1967 article appearing in *Science,* a popular but highly respected journal (Cohen, Marinello, and Back, 1967). It was reported that subjects exposed to repeated dosages of LSD were many more times likely to have white blood cell chromosomal damage than were nonexposed subjects. News of this study spread quickly across the country, and soon the popular media was speculating about the risks of giving birth to deformed or retarded infants. Unfortunately, because the popular press is not constrained to the same level of scientific rigor that scientific reporting is, the fine details are often overlooked. The reports fail to mention that white blood cell damage bears no necessary relationship to germ cells, which are the cells involved in reproduction. The media further failed to report that white blood cell chromosomal damage can be caused in many ways—by x-rays, viral infections, and even heavy use of caffeine! (Brecher, 1972).

Ecstasy   A relatively recent addition to the pharmacopeia of drugs is the powerful drug *ecstasy*. Scientifically, this drug is referred to as MDMA (which stands for its chemical structure, *3–4 methylenedioxymethamphetamine*). It was first synthesized in 1912 by a German pharmaceutical company for possible use as an appetite suppressant. Ecstasy has both hallucinogenic mescaline and amphetamine-like qualities and today is used almost exclusively as a recreational drug (Drug Enforcement Administration, 1999). It is marketed on the street as *Ecstasy, XTC, Adam, Clarity, Lover's Speed,* or most commonly, simply *X.* Ecstasy is a particularly powerful stimulant, and has been linked to brain damage in the form of damaging the nerve endings that release serotonin. This is believed to result in memory loss among ecstasy users (Mathias, 1999). Warnings of harm notwithstanding, and in spite of its expensiveness ($25 a hit in 2000), it remains a very popular club drug. This is likely due to its association with "rave culture," or rave parties, which are often quite psychedelic themselves, complete with trance-like music and wild color schemes. Raves also generally last until after dawn, so the stimulant component of the drug is attractive as well.

PCP (Phencyclidine)   PCP was originally developed as an anaesthetic, and was tested for human use in the 1950s. It was discontinued, however, because of the side effects of confusion and delirium that it caused, though it was marketed and used as an animal anesthetic under the trade name Sernalyn (Ray and Ksir, 1999). The drug did, however, become popular among recreational drug users. It is commonly known on the street as *angel dust, rocket fuel, embalming fluid,* and *wack,* among other names. PCP, which comes in powder form, is often sprinkled on marijuana leaves to "spike" the smoke. When used in this form, it is often called *killer weed, killer joint,* or *crystal supergrass.* It is easily manufactured in makeshift labs and requires very little knowledge of chemistry.

Ketamine   Ketamine hydrochloride was also developed as a general anaesthetic for human and animal use. This drug produces effects very similar to PCP, though users claim that it is superior to PCP or LSD because its effects are more short-lived, typically about an hour, though some of its effects can last up to a day. Ketamine is a relatively recent drug to be used recreationally, and is known on the street as *k, ket, vitamin k, special k,* and *psychedelic heroin.* It is used by a relatively small number of primarily teenagers, though that number is increasing, as this is also a drug associated with rave culture (Drug Enforcement Administration, 1999; Stephens, 1999).

PHARMACOLOGICAL FEATURES OF THE HALLUCINOGENS

The hallucinogens are a category of drugs which have a very unique psychoactive effect on the user. There has been controversy over the years as to the exact nature of this effect. Those who see these drugs as dangerous tend to describe these effects as *hallucinogenic,* suggesting psychotic episodes, hallucinations, and the like. During the 1960s and 1970s, when LSD was more prominently defended, this image was contested.

Users defined their experience as *mind expanding,* rather than hallucinogenic, and preferred the term **psychedelic.** Both terms—*hallucinogenic* and *psychedelic*—are politically loaded terms. It is not surprising that today, in the midst of a strong antidrug culture, the term *hallucinogenic* is the preferred term. The truth of the matter is that both terms are less than adequate in describing what transpires when one uses these drugs. While there are some effects which are unique to each of the hallucinogens, they all share some characteristics in common. Goode (1999), building on the pioneering work of Harvard psychiatrist Lester Grinspoon and his colleague James Bakalar (1979), identifies nine subjective effects that the hallucinogens tend to share, most of which involve distortion of sensory perceptions:

- *Synesthesia*—Where the user tends to "smell" colors, or "see" sounds as bright colors. Indeed, the psychedelic motifs and lighting designs that can still be seen in many nightclubs derive directly from this experience.
- *Eidetic imagery*—Sometimes called "eyeball movies," where the user, with eyes closed, sees visual images as though watching a motion picture.
- *Multilevel reality*—An experience that involves seeing the same object or event from a variety of levels or perspectives.
- *Fluidity*—Objects are in continual flux, much like an amoeba.
- *Subjective exaggeration*—Involves either multiplying the number or size of objects or events. An LSD user described an incident to one of the authors of this text of being on LSD and having to go to the bathroom to urinate. He described how he felt like a giant 12 feet tall standing over a commode with an opening the size of the dime. He went on to describe how challenging it was to "hit the target" when he urinated. What he was experiencing was a substantial spatial distortion.
- *Emotional lability*—Great swings in mood and temperament.
- *Timelessness*—Time ceases to be relevant, even ceases to exist in the mind of the user.
- *Ambivalence*—The experience of both good and bad emotions during the same episode, perhaps during the same moment in time.
- *Sensory overload*—A sense of being bombarded with stimuli and not being able to process it adequately (Goode, 1999; pp. 245–248).

In addition to these subjective effects, Jacobs (1987) has identified certain "psychic" effects, which include sudden changes of affect, isolation, and other-worldly sensations. He also suggests a "somatic" effect, which might include nausea, tingling of skin, dizziness, tremors, and sudden reflexes. These experiences, which are certainly shaped by social and psychological factors, are also a function of the unique chemistry of the hallucinogens. While not all users of hallucinogens experience all these symptoms, these are experiences that have been reported by users of various drugs in this category.

PCP is somewhat unique among the hallucinogens in that it is primarily an anesthetic that shares some properties with other hallucinogenic drugs such as LSD (Goode, 1999). It can produce very strong and severe reactions in users. A moderate dose causes feelings of estrangement and detachment, numbness, slurred speech and loss of coordination. In large doses, the user also experiences auditory hallucinations and image distortion and in some cases amnesia. Very high dosages of PCP can cause seizures, comas, and even death, although most reported deaths occur from accidental injury during a trip (Drug Enforcement Administration, 1999).

The risk of overdosing on hallucinogenic drugs is extremely low. Most of the drugs in this category have a high effective dose/lethal dose ratio. The lethal dose for LSD is about 400 times what it takes for an effective dose, and not surprisingly, there has not been a single verified case of LSD overdose. Mescaline has a much lower ratio—the lethal dose being about 10 to 30 times the effective dose (Ray and Ksir, 1999).

Finally, the hallucinogens produce a high level of tolerance, and quite quickly. It is difficult to produce the desired effect after several days of use, a pattern characteristic of LSD, psilocybin, and mescaline. Moreover, there is a cross-tolerance between these drugs. Tolerance for these drugs abates rather rapidly, however, usually after only a few days. Because of this pattern of tolerance, users of hallucinogens typically "trip" on only a sporadic basis (Stephens, 1999). Dependence, characterized by withdrawal symptoms, is extremely rare among hallucinogenic users; indeed, these drugs have the *lowest* rate of dependency development (Gable, 1993, Stephens, 1999). The one exception to this is PCP which generates a moderate to high rate of dependency.

CNS STABILIZERS

CNS Stabilizers comprise a novel category of drugs that do not fit neatly into any of the other psychoactive categories, but which, nevertheless, share an important characteristic in common: they tend to stabilize moods and/or behaviors. These are not drugs, at least in the way that they are used, that depress the activity of the central nervous system; nor do they stimulate it. Rather, their function is to level or moderate extremes of psychological functioning. There are two major types of drugs included in this category. The first category includes drugs that serve to reduce the level of hyperactivity and distraction, a condition defined by the 4th edition of the *Diagnostic and Statistical Manual* of the American Psychiatric Association (DSM-IV) as Attention Deficit Hyperactive Disorder (ADHD). The second category consists of the *antidepressants*, which have become widely prescribed in recent years.

ADHD STABILIZERS

The year 1937 marked a most remarkable and paradoxical discovery in medical science: amphetamines, which are stimulants, were effective in controlling hyperactivity in children, a condition that would later be linked with attention deficit disorder (ADHD) (formally referred to as Minimal Brain Dysfunction), affecting an estimated 5 to 10 percent of the general population (Volkow et al., 1998). This is a paradox, because common sense would dictate that to treat such a condition with a stimulant would only increase the level of activity and/or distraction. The primary drug of choice which is used today to control hyperactivity is methylphenidate, commonly known as *Ritalin*. Less commonly, *Cylert* (pemoline), Dexedrine and other stimulants are also used. All of these drugs are CNS stimulants; however, among individuals with ADHD, they act upon the central nervous system in unique ways to *lower* the level of hyperactivity and attention deficit. The mechanism by which this takes place is believed to be in the ability of these drugs to block the dopamine transporters, thereby increasing the synaptic concentration of dopamine (Volkow et al., 1998). Moreover, recent research has found that the use of these drugs promotes self-esteem, cognition, social and family functioning, and greatly lowers the risk of substance abuse among those diagnosed with ADHD (Beiderman et al., 1999; Spencer et al., 1996).

The use of Ritalin has risen dramatically in the past ten years. It has been suggested that between 1990 and 1996, its use increased sixfold, and that approximately 6 percent of American boys are prescribed Ritalin for ADHD (Bromfield, 1996). Many medical experts believe that Ritalin is being greatly overprescribed, while others make the case that because of its effectiveness, it might actually underprescribed (Weiner, 1996). Also of concern, *Ritalin* has been used by persons for whom it has not been prescribed for a variety of reasons, including appetite suppression, staving off sleep, increased cognitive focus, and for euphoria. The Community Epidemiology Work Group (CEWG—see Chapter 6) has reported the misuse of Ritalin in numerous cities, especially among middle-class users. Those who misuse the drug for these purposes typically take them orally or intranasally, though some inject it intravenously, in some cases mixing it with heroin and/or cocaine in what is commonly known as a "speedball" (National Institute on Drug Abuse, n.d.b.). While Ritalin is not widely abused, the DEA has defined it as a Schedule II drug, indicating a high level of abuse potential (Drug Enforcement Administration, 1997).

ANTIDEPRESSANTS

Perhaps no area of psychoactive pharmacology has advanced more in recent years than the development and refinement of antidepressant medication. Within a few years of its discovery in 1937, the standard treatment for depression has been electric shock, or electroconvulsive therapy (ECT).

While it is still used today, the popularity of ECT has waned considerably since the 1970s. This treatment is regarded by many as primitive and inhumane, a reaction prompted in part by media depictions such as that found in the highly successful 1975 film *One Flew Over the Cuckoo's Nest* starring Jack Nicholson (Sabbatini, n.d.). While antianxiety medications of various sorts—tranquilizers and other depressants—had been available for years, these drugs were not effective for treating depression, or manic-depression (now called bipolar disorder) (Goode, 1999).

Drugs introduced specifically for the treatment of depression first appeared in 1955 in the form of *monoamine oxidase inhibitors* (MAO). These drugs, which were initially introduced for the treatment of tuberculosis, were found to have a substantial mood-elevating effect. Because of severe side effects when taken with certain foods, including severe headaches, heart palpitations, nausea and severe hypertension, these early antidepressants have been all but discontinued (Pletscher, 1991; Ray and Ksir, 1999).

A second "family" of antidepressants, known as the *tricyclics,* was developed in the late 1950s. These drugs were also discovered quite by accident in the process of searching for a more effective antihistamine. It was discovered that, while not effective for everyone, these drugs were quite effective in lessening the severity of depressive mood disorders (Ray and Ksir, 1999). Indeed, there is some evidence suggesting that for severe depression, the tricyclics may be more effective than the newer generation serotonin reuptake inhibitors, which are most widely prescribed for depression today (Boyce and Judd, 1999). While tricyclics are still in use today for treating depression, untoward side effects, including the possibility of lethal dosages, has resulted in physicians and psychiatrists preferring a newer, more stable family of antidepressants known as *selective serotonin reuptake inhibitors (SSRIs).*

The *SSRIs* work to increase the level of serotonin at the synapse between neurons. **Serotonin** is a neurotransmitter, which is the key to conducting electrical activity across the **synapse,** the microscopic space (only a few millionths of a millimeter) between neurons (Liska, 2000). Normally, serotonin released into the synapse that does not immediately bind with receptors will be eliminated (a process called *reuptake*), sometimes too quickly resulting in less than adequate transmission of neurological impulses. By inhibiting the reuptake process, more serotonin remains in the synapse for a longer period of time, thereby maximizing the neurotransmission process (Williams College Neuroscience, 1998).

There are a number of SSRIs that have been developed since *fluoxetine* (Prozac) was first introduced in 1987, though Prozac remains the most popular. Others include *sertraline* (Zoloft), *paroxetine* (Paxil), and *venlafaxine* (Effexor). All work on the same basic principle of inhibiting serotonin reuptake. The SSRIs do not have the serious side effects of the earlier tricyclics, but there are some, including nausea, vomiting, drowsiness, and tremors (Barbey and Roose, 1998). A widely circulated 1990 clinical study by Martin Teicher and his colleagues (1990), raised considerable fear among medical professionals regarding suicide ideation among patients using the drug to treat depression. This warning, which was based on six clinically depressed patients, was followed up by several other similar reports alleging the same thing, as well as other symptoms of *akathisia,* or heightened agitation, which could possibly lead to violent behavior (Healy, 2000). A controversy flared when David Healy, psychiatrist and eminent scholar at the University of Wales College of Medicine, had a job offer revoked from the Centre for Addiction and Mental Health at the University of Toronto because he claimed harmful effects of Prozac and other drugs that were manufactured by Eli Lilly Pharmaceuticals (Birmingham, 2001; Canadian Association of University Teachers, 2001). The company was a major financial supporter of the Centre. A media frenzy also ensued, as both print and electronic media, including the tabloids in both versions, ran feature stories on the Prozac scare (Hegarty, 1995). Law suits were also filed against Eli Lilly on behalf of patients who had injured themselves while on the drug as well as victims of Prozac patients, including the children of a man who killed himself and his wife while taking the drug (Bourguignon, n.d.; Zuckoff, 2000).

In point of fact, while clinical studies have demonstrated that there has been suicide ideation, and even instances of bizarre and violent behavior among Prozac patients, there is little evidence to support the inferences drawn from these studies, nor the allegations mounted in the media and the courtrooms. Research by Jick, Dean and Jick (1995), examining suicides among patients taking various antidepressants reveals that Prozac was less implicated in the suicides than the earlier tricyclics. A summary of studies, conducted by David Hegarty (1995), confirms the Jick et al. (1995) research that the risk for suicide ideation or aggression is no more, and probably considerably less than other antidepressants. Indeed, it has been suggested that any increase in suicide ideation may be the result of heightened expectations of such thoughts as a result of the media hype (Iosnnou, 1992).

A final drug that has been used to treat depression is *lithium.* Lithium was initially proposed in the 1940s as a salt substitute in heart patients until it was discovered that high levels of lithium could be toxic and even fatal. Research in the late 1940s in Australia revealed that lithium was quite effective in sedating manic patients, though it was not until 1970 that the FDA approved its use as a treatment for depression (Ray and Ksir, 1999). Lithium has been most effective in the treatment of bipolar disorder (manic-depression), with only modest effectiveness with unipolar, or simple, depression. The mechanism by which lithium controls mood extremes is still being researched, but one known effect of the drug is the increased synthesis of serotonin (Ray and Ksir, 1999).

There are some serious risks associated with the use of lithium. Excessive concentrations of the drug can lead to a state of confusion, loss of coordination, convulsions, and ultimately death. Fortunately, it is quite easy to monitor blood levels so that dosage adjustments can be made.

Clinical evidence continues to show that the benefits of lithium for bipolar patients are favorable enough to outweigh the risks. Research has suggested that is has been especially effective in the reduction of suicide among bipolar patients (Baldessarini, Tondo and Hennen, 1999; Tondo, Hennen and Baldessarini, 2001). While there has been a trend away from lithium as a treatment, some in the medical research community continue to urge its use (Baldessarini and Tondo, 2000, 2001; Baldessarini, Tondo, Hennen and Viguera, 2002).

MARIJUANA

Marijuana consists of the leaves and flowering tops of the *Cannabis* plant. There are actually three species of the cannbis plant, all of which can be used for recreational or medicinal use, though not all are as effective. The most widely used species in this country is *Cannabis sativa,* which originated in Asia, but is now grown worldwide and commonly in the United States and Canada. It is also *Cannabis sativa* that is used for hemp fiber in rope and other materials. *Cannabis indica* is a second species of the plant, which is substantially more potent than *Cannabis sativa,* but not as widely grown. Still a third species is *Cannabis ruderalis,* which is grown primarily in Russia, and has little psychoactive substance in it. There is also nonpsychoactive cannabis, hemp, used for its fiber for clothing and other purposes.

Marijuana is known on the street as *pot, grass, reefer, mary jane,* and *apupulco gold* among other names. Marijuana and marijuana products are consumed in many ways. Most commonly, it is smoked as a hand-rolled cigarette, commonly called a *joint.* Sometimes, however, it is smoked in a pipe (known as a bowl) or a *bong,* where the smoke is typically filtered through water before being taken into the lungs. Other methods of consumption are also used. Many users prefer the more potent resin from the flowering tops of the female marijuana plant, which is known as *hashish* or simply *hash.* Hashish can be smoked, but it is often eaten in cookies, brownies, and other baked goods. Hashish is more often found in Europe or Asia than in the United States. An even more concentrated form of marijuana is *hash oil* which is prepared by boiling the hash resin in a solvent and filtering out the remaining solids (Ray and Ksir, 1999).

The active ingredient in marijuana is *delta-9 tetrahydrocannabinol,* normally known simply as "THC." THC is but one of 61 cannabinoids—chemicals which are unique to the Cannabis plant—and more than 400 total chemicals found in the marijuana plant. The THC content of marijuana varies widely across the species and forms discussed above, and indeed, varies widely even with species. *Cannabis sativa,* for example, typically contains about 2 to 5 percent THC, though it can range from less than 1 percent to about 8 percent. *Cannabis indica,* which is not grown in North America at all, is more potent than *Cannabis sativa*. *Hashish* generally ranges between 2 and 8 percent, but can be as high as 14 percent, and hash oil may contain more than 50 percent THC content (Ray and Ksir, 1999).

SOME MISCONCEPTIONS ABOUT MARIJUANA USE

Because of its widespread popularity, and because of antimarijuana campaigns since the 1930s, marijuana has been an alleged culprit in many types of mental, behavioral, and physical disorders. We now know several of these allegations not to be true, and there are serious doubts about others. Any sociological assessment of such charges must account for social factors that may come into play in users' experiences of this, or any other drug. That is to say, we must be cognizant of the *setting* in which marijuana is used. Only by accounting for the impact of these contextual factors can we appropriately assess the impact of the drug itself; that is, its pharmacological effect.

One of the primary charges brought against marijuana in the 1970s and still widely believed today is that marijuana destroys ambition, induces laziness, and generally decreases the motivation of the user to engage in constructive activity. Psychologists have referred to this as the **amotivational syndrome.** This is an interesting charge, because it is almost diametrically opposed to an earlier charge launched by Harry Anslinger, first Director of the Bureau of Narcotics, that marijuana use incited violence, sexual aggression, and other aggressive forms of behavior (Anslinger and Tompkins, 1953). What has changed are the *social conditions* under which marijuana is used. Marijuana was largely confined to inner-city, lower class neighborhoods in the late 1930s and 1940s. Users were individuals who were largely segregated from middle class America, and they were greatly feared. It was easy to play on these fears, and the Bureau of Narcotics did precisely this in a number of ways. The 1960s and 1970s users were, by contrast, favored sons and daughters of professional middle class families. The earlier imagery was not credible. What was credible, however, was the allegation that these young people had lost their drive and ambition. Many were flunking out of college and opting for alternative lifestyles. We can hardly blame this on the marijuana, however! There is simply no convincing data that marijuana has a direct causal relationship on motivation (Joy, Watson and Benson, 1999). Many of these teens were (and are) predisposed to rejecting the values of hard work and getting ahead even before they ever start using marijuana. There have indeed been studies that have shown lower academic achievement on the part of chronic marijuana users. In most cases, however, this pattern was also observed *prior* to the onset of marijuana use (e.g., see Johnston, 1973). There is, furthermore, the fact that when an individual begins to use marijuana, he or she begins to associate with other users who do not reinforce the "Protestant ethic" of hard work and material success. There is a *normative* component to marijuana use which puts pressure on the user to conform to *subcultural* expectations. All these factors make a direct causal linkage between marijuana use and the amotivational syndrome extremely doubtful. Finally, there is the demographic reality that adolescence is a time of rebellion; a time of rejecting parental values for a season to explore the world for one's self. For many young people, this involves experimentation generally with alternative lifestyles, which may involve marijuana. Marijuana may, in fact, be a component of an amotivational syndrome that we observe among many young people in college. It is but one of *many* factors that converge during this time in life, however, and we must be careful not to single out this lone "cause." We must recognize that the amotivational syndrome is a *lifestyle* feature that is much broader than simply using marijuana.

Another characterization of marijuana that is promoted by our nation's drug enforcement officials is that this drug inevitably leads to the use of other, more serious, dangerous and expensive drugs. The current labeling of this allegation is that marijuana is a **gateway drug.** Past researchers and practitioners have also referred to it as the *stepping-stone hypothesis* and the *slippery-slope hypothesis.* All these terms refer to essentially the same thing—that once started down a path of drug use, beginning with marijuana, it is difficult to turn back, and users find it necessary to go on to more potent drugs to achieve a satisfactory "high." There is a measure of truth to this hypothesis. There is by now almost irrefutable evidence that marijuana users are more likely to use other drugs than those who do not use marijuana. And the evidence is strong that they used marijuana at an earlier age than they used the other drugs. Indeed, there are strong relationships between *all* forms of psychoactive drug use (including alcohol and tobacco) and the use of other more expensive psychoactive drugs. Once again, we must be careful in how we *interpret* these data. There are, specifically, two fallacies that we must be careful to avoid as we interpret such empirical evidence. One fallacy we would call the *inevitability fallacy.* This fallacy, which is very much a part of a common cultural understanding, is that those individuals who use marijuana, at least beyond a brief experimental level, will inevitably (or at least will be very likely to) go on to use other more potent drugs. The evidence simply does not support such a proposition. Examining the *Monitoring the Future* study, for example, we can observe that in 1997, 34.8 percent of 10th graders smoked marijuana within the past year; however, two years later (which we would assume to be a reasonable time span to be going on to other drugs), only 8.1 percent of the same cohort (now seniors) used LSD, 1.8 percent used PCP, 6.2 percent used cocaine, 2.7 percent used crack, and 1.1 percent used heroin (Johnston et al., 1999). Clearly, the *overwhelming majority* of individuals who smoke marijuana never go on to use more potent drugs. Part of the problem with the logic of the *inevitability fallacy* is that there is a tendency to examine the issue backwards. We tend to look at heroin addicts or crack addicts and find that most of them used marijuana before they went on to using other drugs. This is certainly true.

It is also true that most of them first used tobacco, alcohol, caffeine, and soda pop!

The second fallacy we call the *causal fallacy*. This fallacy states that *those marijuana users who do go on to use more potent drugs* are compelled to do so because of the intrinsic nature of the drug or drug experience. Generally, the argument goes, marijuana users are not satisfied with the high that marijuana can give and feel the need to go on and experiment with other drugs. Goode (1999) refers to this as the "intrinsic school," which uses the metaphor of the conveyor belt. Users get on the belt by using marijuana, and they are carried away down the path of increasingly dangerous drug use. Joy, Watson and Benson (1999) reserve the term *stepping stone hypothesis* to refer to this pharmacologically driven movement to other drugs. Social scientists who have studied this issue carefully have generally rejected such an explanation. Rather, they suggest that marijuana use is a *socially significant* step in the process of drug involvement. Indeed, research by Kandel and her associates suggests that the "real" gateway drugs are either alcohol or tobacco (Kandel, 1975; Kandel and Yamaguchi, 1993; Kandel, Yamaguchi, and Chen, 1992). Joy, Watson and Benson (1999) suggest that what is significant about marijuana in the progression to other types of drugs such as heroin and cocaine, is that marijuana is the first *illicit* drug used for most people. Marijuana is a threshold of sorts which represents a willingness to engage in behavior beyond what is generally accepted in society. Goode (1999) advances this idea further in what he calls the "socio-cultural" model. Those who use marijuana are more likely to get involved in peer groups that promote anticonventional activity. After initial contact with close friends who turn them on to marijuana, they are introduced to others in a subculture of drug use, who may also be using cocaine or other drugs, and perhaps even committing criminal acts. If the developing marijuana user continues this association, there is, of course, a greater likelihood that his or her behavior will increasingly reflect these subcultural values and ideals. This is a process of socialization that is no different from the socialization that takes place in the military, in churches, and indeed, in drug treatment programs! This understanding of the cause of progression, however, suggests a much different intervention strategy than does the "intrinsic school." We address the issues of intervention in Chapters 12–15, where we examine societal reaction to drug use.

PHARMACOLOGICAL FEATURES OF MARIJUANA USE

As reported by users, marijuana produces a sense of well-being and euphoria, a distorted sense of time, which is associated with short-term memory loss, and heightened physical and emotional sensitivity. Other effects include reduction in anxiety and alternating periods of talkativeness and laughter, followed by introspection and lethargy (Joy, Watson and Benson, 1999). As we have already pointed out, these experiences cannot be fully understood apart from an understanding of the *set* and especially the *setting* of the marijuana user. Scientists have, in recent years, identified neurochemical factors which seem to be related as well. About 1990, investigators discovered a specific neuro-receptor for cannabinoids in various regions of the brain. These areas of the brain correspond to long-established effects of marijuana use on fragmented thought patterns, short-term memory and motor coordination (Stephens, 1999).

There is very little evidence that marijuana produces tolerance, and to the extent that it does, the tolerance is very short-lived (Joy, Watson, and Benson, 1999). For years it was believed by many users that marijuana use results in a "reverse tolerance"—that the more one uses the drug the *less* one needs to achieve the desired effect. This phenomenon has never been produced under controlled experimental conditions, however, and it is believed that this effect may be due to the users' learning to inhale more deeply and efficiently (Stephens, 1999). Studies have, however, found evidence of withdrawal symptoms, especially among heavy users, and when withdrawal is sudden. Irritability, insomnia, sweating, restlessness, nausea, cramping, and loss of appetite are commonly reported (Joy, Watson, and Benson, 1999; Stephens, 1999). Most users, however, do not experience these symptoms, and when they do, they are mild at worst.

Summary

Classification is an intrinsic and essential part of science as well as social life in general. We classify people according to their sex, their weight and height, hair color, and even the region of the country they are from. We classify objects into animate and inanimate; the living world into plant and animal. Classification allows us to order the world around us. The term that scientists use for the classification schemes that they develop is *taxonomy*.

This is also why we classify drugs. While there are any number of dimensions which might be used as the basis for classifying drugs, the most common, and we believe most helpful, is *the impact of the drug on the central nervous system.* We have termed this classification system a *pharmacological taxonomy* because it classifies drugs based on their pharmacology, which is to say, how those drugs affect the central nervous system. The six broad categories included in this taxonomy are: *narcotics, other depressants, stimulants, hallucinogens, CNS stabilizers*, and *marijuana.* Each of these drugs affects the user in different ways. Moreover, it is important to remember that the effects that these drugs have on the user depend not only on the pharmacology of the drugs, but also on the *set* and *setting* of the use of these drugs. As we have seen in Chapter 1, the frame of mind of the user (set) and the external circumstances in which drugs are used (setting) also profoundly influence the effect that drugs have on individual subjective states and behavior. Mode of ingestion also affects how a drug acts upon the central nervous system. Pharmacology is, in short, but one component of a complex set of factors which, together, account for both subjective and behavioral responses to drug use. Pharmacology is an important component, however. Regardless of set or setting, stimulants are going to affect the user in a different way than are depressants. Moreover, when a user consumes more than a single drug, the pharmacology of those drugs will determine, to a large extent, whether the user *enhances* his or her experience or whether he or she suffers an overdose or other negative consequences. Pharmacology is thus an important piece of a larger puzzle that must be in place to fully understand the impact of drug use on human and social experience.

Key Terms

amotivational syndrome	gateway drug	psychedelic
blood-alcohol content (BAC)	hallucinogens	serotonin
CNS Stabilizers	intoxication	stimulant
depressants	marijuana	synapse
endorphin	narcotic	synesthesia
	neurotransmitter	taxonomy

REVIEW QUESTIONS

1. What are the pharmacological features and medical uses of the narcotics? Why has this category of drugs been mislabeled so often by politicians, the media, and society at large?

2. What are the pharmacological properties of alcohol? In what ways is alcohol's social and cultural stature at odds with its pharmacological dimensions?

3. What makes inhalants attractive for the relatively young, despite some pretty serious consequences of inhalant abuse?

4. Crack cocaine dominated concern over drug abuse in this country from the late 1980s through much of the 1990s. How does crack achieve such a powerful hold over many of its users? How did crack dependency transform communities where crack smoking was widespread?

5. Much of hallucinogenic drug use, both recreationally and ritually, occurs within subcultures (e.g., rave culture, Native American ceremonies) in American society. Are there pharmacological reasons why this might be so?

6. Psychotherapeutic drug use (e.g., the use of CNS stabilizers) has increased in recent years. Based on what you've read about their properties *and* your knowledge of contemporary America, why would you say this is so?

7. Marijuana is a drug which is misunderstood both by those who stress its harmfulness and by those who tout its benefits. What are some of the most prominent marijuana myths and fallacies?

CRITICAL INQUIRY QUESTIONS

1. Pharmaceutical depressants and stimulants, which are intended for medical purposes, were much more widely used to get high a generation ago than they are today. What are the social and legal reasons why this is so? If these pharmaceuticals have been replaced by street drugs today, what might be some of the personal and societal effects?

2. Ask your friends (family, dorm mates) to assess which drugs, from a list you will provide, are "most harmful." Attempt to construct a list of drugs ranked by their pharmacological harmfulness. How would you account for discrepancies between the two lists?

NOTES

1. Inciardi found that males, on average, first used heroin at 18.7 years of age; their "continued" use of heroin began, on average, at age 19.2. The average age for first heroin use among females was 18.2; first "continued" use was age 18.4.

2. More precisely, we are referring to *ethyl alcohol*. This is but one family of alcohol compounds, and the only one that is safe for human consumption. The other two types of alcohol are methyl and isopropyl. Neither of these can be metabolized by the body, and hence are toxic.

3. *Anterograde* amnesia is distinguished from *retrograde* amnesia in that individuals suffering from the former remember events from their past except for the period of their intoxication. Retrograde amnesia involves the losing of memory of all or significant portions of past events in one's life.

4. Not all the prescription stimulants are in the amphetamine family. Ritalin, for example, is not technically an amphetamine. Its structure and effect are very similar, however, and hence, we are considering it and other prescription stimulants in the same category for purposes of this discussion. We will also be examining Ritalin as a CNS stabilizer later in the chapter.

5. Sometimes the drug is referred to as "LSD-25." The "25" has reference to the fact that LSD was the 25th derivative of lysergic acid to be synthesized.

THEORETICAL EXPLANATIONS FOR DRUG USE AND ADDICTION

This chapter examines various scientific theories that have been offered for drug use and addiction. Simply stated, a *scientific theory* is an explanation for the relationship between two or more phenomena that can be verified or falsified with empirical evidence. Empirical evidence is that which is observed: either through one of the five natural senses—touch, smell, sight, hearing or tasting; or with the use of special instruments such as microscopes, telescopes, seismographs, or survey questionnaires. When sociologists and other thinkers work to explain drug use and addiction, they desire to construct theories that are scientific in nature.

Some theories prove to be better than others in that empirical testing tends to support the explanation contained in these theories. A theory that is not supported by the evidence is no less scientific because its hypotheses are not supported, however. Indeed, the very fact that such a theory *fails* to find support is evidence that it is scientific! Its failure to find support may be because it does not, in fact, explain the evidence; or it may be because of problems with the data or with the measurement of the data. None of these problems renders our theory in question unscientific. The theories that are discussed in this chapter ostensibly meet the test for being scientific in nature.

You may wonder why it is important to develop theories in the first place. The answer is quite simple, really—without theory, we would have nothing more than a series of descriptions of things observed. We would not know *why* these things exist as they do, because explaining *why* (or *how)* is the essence of theory. If we do not know why events occur as they do, we would not be able to predict their occurring in the future. Moreover, understanding why something occurs as it does provides a basis for taking preventive action. If we know why a group of people abuse drugs, we can gear social and governmental policy appropriately to reduce the occurrence of abuse.

We are not usually interested in developing theories merely for the sake of explaining, though fundamental explanation is the essential role of the basic sciences. Those of us who are basic scientists are pleased to let our work end there. We know, however, that there are greater rewards of good theory. When we theorize well, and when those theoretical explanations are supported repeatedly by empirical data, we offer a solid foundation for both prediction and intervention efforts. Without theory, such efforts would be random and would not be particularly effective.

Before talking about specific theories, we need to clarify what it is that we are theorizing *about*. The phenomena of drug use, abuse, and addiction are complex and involve different behaviors and dynamics as we have already discussed in Chapter 1. The reasons one first uses drugs, for example, are almost surely quite different from the reasons that one goes on to become addicted to these substances. Moreover, factors involved in initial experimentation with drugs are likely to be very different from those factors leading to relapse after a period of abstinence. There is an extensive literature on each of these aspects of drug use.

TABLE 4.1	A Taxonomy of Theories of Drug Use	
	Behavior to Be Explained	
Theoretical Level	**Onset of Use**	**Addiction**
Nature	Weil	
Biological		Neurochemical Explanations Biogenetic Explanations
Psychological	Psychoanalytic Theories Personality Theories	Psychoanalytic Theories Personality Theories Behavioral Theories
Sociological	Differential Association Theory Differential Reinforcement Theory Becker's Learning Theory Social Control Theory Strain Theory	Differential Reinforcement Theory Becker's Learning Theory Winick's Integrated Theory Strain Theory Cultural Deviance Theory Conflict Theory

Source: Adapted from Mary C. Ritz and Michael J. Kuhar, "Psychostimulant Drugs and a Dopamine Hypothesis Regarding Addiction: Update on Recent Research." In S. Wonnacott and G.G. Lunt (eds.), *Neurochemistry of Drug Dependence.* London: Portland Press, 1993, p. 52.

Table 4.1 presents a framework for organizing theories of drug use. You will also notice that there are various levels of explanation for drug use and addiction. These are *nature theories, biological theories, psychological theories,* and *sociological theories.* The discussion in this chapter is organized around this typology. Some of these approaches tend to be more focused on initiation into drug *use,* while other levels of explanation tend to focus on addiction. Some biological and sociological theories also tackle the question of why rates of drug use vary for different segments of the population or how drug use is distributed in our society, a pursuit known as *drug epidemiology,* which is discussed in Chapter 6. For these reasons, complete theoretical understanding of the phenomena of drug use and addiction requires an awareness of multiple types of theory.

NATURE THEORIES

Nature theories suggest that initial drug use and drug addiction result from an intrinsic character of human nature itself. Discussions grounded in human nature are often controversial and unpopular in academic circles. They are argued by many to be less scientific than biological, psychological, or sociological theories, because "human nature" is seen as slippery to conceptualize and hence difficult to put to empirical test. Nature theories are different from biological theories, which focus on how biological features of individuals who become addicted are different from individuals who do not become addicted. Nature theories, by contrast, proclaim that proneness to drug use and addiction is a human universal.

The earliest nature theories had strong moral overtones. The addict was seen as "weak-willed" and not able to control his or her impulses. There was a moral inferiority implied in this notion. These early ideas of drug addiction easily blended moral judgments of drugs, drug use and the drug user with biological and "disease" metaphors as they sought to paint a vivid picture of the perils of addiction. More recent nature theories do not impose a moral evaluation on drug use or human nature—or at least not a *negative* moral evaluation. Well-known alternative medicine guru Andrew Weil suggests that the desire to alter consciousness is universal. He states, "It is my belief that the desire to alter consciousness periodically is an innate, normal drive analogous to hunger or the sexual drive" (1986, p. 19). Chemical agents are, of course only one route to altered consciousness. Young children experience such a state when they spin themselves into dizziness. Altered states are also reported by athletes and daredevils as a motivation to engage in otherwise painful or risky behavior (e.g., seeking a "runner's high"). The use of chemical substances is, however, a very common and popular route to altered consciousness. Weil points out that in every known culture (with the exception of Eskimo culture) there are indigenously grown intoxicants and established rituals for using them.

As children grow older, they learn that they can experience a similar state of consciousness by "huffing" the fumes of the model airplane glue they are using or gasoline fumes at the filling station. The world of chemical agents is introduced in a variety of ways. Cultural taboos, of course, force much of this activity underground. Because of social disapproval, most people will not go on to use chemicals as adults, except for alcohol and caffeine, which are approved for use in our society and indeed in most societies. Some people go on to use other drugs, of course, and what distinguishes them from alcohol users, Weil argues, is merely the form of expression that their altered consciousness takes.

Drug use is, according to Weil, an expression of the universal drive to achieve altered states of consciousness. The "goodness" or "badness" of this drive might be questioned, but it is universal. The question that remains, however, is why this drive leads to different forms of consciousness-altering behavior—for some individuals it involves drugs; others are driven to sexual excess; still others to daring adventures involving high rates of speed or altitude. Weil's argument about altered states of consciousness cannot explain why this drive is expressed differently. Weil's theory is grounded in the idea that because the desire for an altered state of consciousness is universal, we must not presume that it is bad, though certain means to attain it involve excessive risk to the individual and to others, and therefore may be considered behaviorally undesirable. For Weil, "human nature" does not excuse the choosing of harmful or threatening variations of consciousness alteration.

BIOLOGICAL THEORIES

Biological theories are theories of addiction which suggest that people become addicted to chemical substances because of biological predispositions. Nineteenth-century theories of addiction used biological "disease" metaphors in their attempts to explain drug addiction. These theories were a product of their time. Darwinian theories of evolution were having a broad effect on scientific thought; addiction was seen as a disease which was "communicable" to unwary others. An underlying belief was that drugs were "toxins" that built up in the body and destroyed or damaged bodily organs, thereby resulting in addiction and a loss of behavioral control. "Detoxification" strategies emerged in response to this understanding, both for addiction to alcohol and other drugs. Early biological theorizing only vaguely defined the biological character of addiction, preferring the power of rhetoric to systematic observation.

Since then, medical researchers and others have attempted to refine our understanding of the biological basis of addiction. Contemporary explanations focusing on biological characteristics can be broadly classified as either chemical/pharmacological or genetic in nature.

NEUROCHEMICAL EXPLANATIONS

The specific nature of *neurochemical explanations* varies with the type of drug in question. All of them, however, identify the biological source of addiction in the *neurotransmission* mechanism of the human organism. Sunderwirth (1985, p. 12) defines neurotransmission as *"the mechanism by which signals or impulses are sent from one nerve cell (neuron) to the other."*

A major breakthrough in biological understanding of *opiate* addiction came with the work of Vincent Dole and Marie Nyswander. Dole and Nyswander began treating heroin addicts with methadone, a synthetic narcotic, in 1963 and within two years time noted a considerable drop in the level of criminality and heroin use of addicts in treatment. Their treatment was predicated on the observation that heroin addicts develop a *tolerance* for heroin, and that if given methadone, an oral medication which was much longer-lasting than heroin, the felt need for heroin would not be present (Dole, Nyswander, and Warner, 1968). In the decades since Dole and Nyswander's groundbreaking research on methadone, researchers have discovered the instrumental role that neurotransmitters play in addictions to various types of drugs. In the case of narcotics, protein peptides in the brain which serve as transmission agents for electrical messages regarding pain, stress, and mood, from one brain cell to another were discovered (Fishbein and Pease, 1990; Terenius, 1993). The remarkable discovery that provided clues as to the neurological basis of addiction is that these peptides are extremely similar in chemical structure to opiate drugs. Hence, when an individual consumes opiate drugs such as heroin, the receptor sites in the brain accept these opiates as though they were endogenous peptides. This is why, after a period of time, the narcotics addict merely feels "normal" after taking heroin unless they take an unusually large dose. It is also the reason that addicts experience physiological withdrawal symptoms. There is a period of time after the cessation of heroin use until the brain can produce endogenous peptides to send to receptor cells. The result is an experience of muscle cramps, diarrhea, profuse sweating, and other unpleasant symptoms during this interim period when there is a lack of either external or internal chemical neurotransmitters—which may last from several hours to two or three days depending on the level of tolerance that one has developed.

Neurochemical explanations for addictions to other drugs are similar, though the specific mechanisms vary. Stimulants, particularly cocaine and the amphetamines, are said to affect the neurotransmitter *dopamine* as well as *norepinephrine* and *serotonin*. These drugs do not imitate dopamine, as is the case with narcotics, but rather block the reabsorption of dopamine by the sender cell. Since dopamine triggers reward mechanisms in the brain, when it is blocked from reabsorption by cocaine, the user experiences an intense high. Researchers have also recently discovered that when a chronic cocaine user ceases using cocaine, withdrawal symptoms occur because the brain has been getting the message that there is too much dopamine resulting in less dopamine being fired in the first place. The result is depression and underarousal during periods of withdrawal. This is a phenomenon that has only recently been understood. Prior to the 1980s, it was believed that cocaine did not produce physical dependence, and that addiction to cocaine was purely psychological. The discovery of these mechanisms has added a new dimension to our understanding of cocaine addiction (Fishbein and Pease, 1990; Gawin, 1991). This research does not answer why some people are more prone to addiction than others, however. We begin our search for the answer to this question by looking at *biogenetic* explanations for addiction.

BIOGENETIC EXPLANATIONS

Most research focusing on genetic predisposition to drug abuse and addiction has focused quite specifically on alcohol, though there has been some research which shows a link between genetics and tobacco use (Collins, 1985). Unlike neurochemical theories which have isolated specific biological mechanisms which cause dependency symptoms, the genetic linkage is based largely on epidemiological studies. There are four broad types of epidemiological studies that assess the genetic linkage to alcoholism: studies of *animals, family patterns, twins,* and *adoptees.*

Animal Studies   Studies conducted on animals (mostly rats) have shown that it is possible to breed strains that have a decided preference for alcohol over water when given a choice. In most of these studies, rats are given free access to food, alcohol, and water. Typically, rats preferring alcohol over water are then bred together, as are rats preferring water over alcohol.

Results show that after several generations, the preference for alcohol is even greater in the alcohol-preference breed, and even lower in the water-preference breed. (Logue, 1986). Schuckit (1983) has further noted that some strains of rats consume as much as 80 percent of their fluid intake in the form of alcohol while other strains preferred water almost exclusively.

Family Pattern Studies   Marc Schuckit (1985) has noted that a familial linkage to alcoholism has been documented for more than a century. There appears to be a direct relationship between the risk for becoming alcoholic and the number of alcoholic family members as well as the genetic closeness of these family members. Cotton (1979) observed that direct offspring of alcoholics tend to be about three to five times more likely to become alcoholic than offspring of nonalcoholics. Schuckit's (1985) research suggests that individuals in families with a history of alcoholism tend to react less intensely to moderate doses of ethanol than do individuals in the lower-risk, nonalcoholic family group. Schuckit suggests that this may render individuals in high-risk families less capable of discerning appropriate boundaries to drinking behavior.

Twin Studies   Because of the difficulty in separating genetic influences from environmental influences in family studies, researchers have examined alcoholism patterns among twins, comparing monozygote (MZ) twins with dizygote (DZ) twins. MZ twins, more commonly known as identical twins, are those which share 100 percent of their genetic material, as they split after an egg has been fertilized. DZ twins, or fraternal twins, are the result of separate eggs, and hence are as different genetically as nontwin siblings. Theoretically, if there is a genetic basis for alcoholism, symptoms should be much more evident in MZ twins than in DZ twins. Studies of twins yield somewhat mixed results, but a genetic factor is suggested. Rates of alcoholism are much more similar among MZ twins than among DZ twins, a finding which is particularly consistent for men (Sher, 1991). Sher also reports that other selected aspects of alcohol behavior, such as willingness to drive drunk, general attitudes about alcohol, and binge drinking may also have a genetic link.

Adoption Studies   Perhaps the strongest evidence for a genetic link to alcoholism comes from research among adoptees which has been conducted most comprehensively in Scandinavia. These studies examine individuals with alcoholic biological parents who have been adopted by nonalcoholic parents at or near birth. Alcoholism rates for these individuals are compared with those adoptees who were born to nonalcoholic parents, who also live with nonalcoholic parents. The results are remarkably consistent, showing a much higher likelihood of alcoholism among those children born to alcoholic parents, even though they are raised by nonalcoholic parents. Again, the genetic influence seems to be more consistently present among males (Schuckit, 1983; Sher, 1991).

In Search of a Cause   The epidemiological studies provide evidence that is convincing, and cannot be ignored in the search for the etiology of alcoholism. There are, however, three questions that remain to be answered by these studies, as convincing as they are. *First,* can we generalize from these studies of alcoholics to other types of drug addicts? This remains an open question because there simply is not a sufficient body of research from which to draw any sound conclusions regarding genetic linkages to other types of substance abuse. *Second,* these studies do not explain *all* of the variation. Clearly, there are other factors that contribute to alcoholism. These *environmental* factors will be taken up in our discussion of psychological and sociological theories of addiction.

There is a *third* question that is not answered by these epidemiological studies, namely, *what is the bio-genetic mechanism that causes a predisposition toward alcoholism?* Schuckit (1983) suggests several possible mechanisms, though conclusive linkages have yet to be established. Some studies suggest that the rate of absorption and metabolism of ethanol (alcohol) may be under genetic control. One study by Vesell (1975), for example, suggested that the rate of metabolism for ethanol was more similar between MZ twins than between DZ twins. Other studies suggest that there may be a difference in central nervous system sensitivity to alcohol that is genetically related. If so, susceptibility to neurotransmitter factors discussed above may itself have a genetic basis. Still other research points to the possibility that there may be inherited vulnerability to *consequences* of chronic alcohol use, such as cirrhosis of the liver. Finally, it has been suggested that there may be a link between certain inherited personality traits and/or psychiatric disorders and the risk for alcoholism (Schuckit, 1983). These factors are generally identified and examined by psychologists.

PSYCHOLOGICAL THEORIES

Psychological theories of drug use and addiction, like biological theories, focus on the individual user, and characteristics of that individual which somehow differentiate him or her from nonusers. Unlike biological theories, however, which identify neurochemical and genetic features of drug addicts which predispose them to substance abuse, psychological theories look at the nature and quality of individual *experiences* which might make one susceptible to drug use, abuse, or addiction. There are four broad types of psychological explanations: *psychoanalytic explanations, personality theories, behavioral explanations,* and *social psychological ones.*

PSYCHOANALYTIC EXPLANATIONS
Psychoanalytic theories comprise a range of explanations which identify the cause of abuse and addiction to be abnormal personality development or

adjustment. Addiction is seen as a "sickness" or "pathology," the result of an unhealthy development process which is often traced to early childhood experiences. Many of these explanations draw upon Sigmund Freud's general theory of human development. Each stage of development poses its own challenges and needs to the developing child/adolescent, theorizes Freud. Failure to meet the challenges or the needs of the individual may result in an emotional "fixation" at that stage such that the individual does not adequately develop emotionally beyond that point. In the search for "compensatory gratification" to fill the emotional void left by unfilled needs and challenges, the individual may engage in certain forms of drug use or other deviant behavior. The "high" or relief sought with the help of the drug, is a surrogate ideal, a substitute value, a chemical mythology, which normally would be supplied by the internal sense of meaning, goal directedness, and value orientation (Wurmser, 1981; pp. 147–148). Raskin, Petty and Warren (1957) suggest that the user is one who is not able to make the necessary adjustments required in normal daily living. Drug abuse is a mechanism for alleviating the frustrations and stress resulting from the inability to adjust to these conflicting demands. Psychoanalytic explanations are not especially influential in contemporary theorizing about drugs.

PERSONALITY THEORIES

Some have suggested that those who use or abuse drugs have personalities that are somehow different from those of nonabusers. Jessor (1979, p. 343) defines personality as "that set of relatively enduring psychological attributes that characterize a person and constitute the dimensions of individual differences, including values, attitudes, needs, beliefs, expectations, moral orientations, and other such essentially sociocognitive variables." These personality traits are usually phrased in evaluative and negative terms. Some of the earliest studies suggested that addicts tended to have *psychopathic* or *sociopathic personalities*, (Kolb, 1925), now usually referred to as *antisocial personality disorders*. Other psychologists suggested that those who abused drugs or who became dependent on them suffered from an **addictive personality** or *addiction-prone personality*. This idea is rooted largely in a "disease model," which sees addiction as a pathology which is caused by some inadequacy in the individual. Isidor Chein and his colleagues (1964) identified the inadequate personality as a causative factor. They suggest that a lack of goals, interests, and emotional expression predisposes them to drug use and addiction. While the idea of an "addictive personality" remains popular among the general public and among some sectors of the treatment community (Nakken, 1988) most scholarship has rejected this concept. Part of the reason that it has fallen into disrepute as an explanation for addiction is that the early empirical research supporting this concept was quite seriously flawed (Gendreau and Gendreau, 1970; Platt and Labate, 1976). Moreover, it has become increasingly apparent that the search for a single personality type to explain addiction has not been productive. Psychologists have, rather, identified several personality characteristics that would appear to predispose an individual to addiction. These variables include low self-esteem, an inability to trust, and a higher-than-normal need for stimulation and sensation-seeking (Platt and Labate, 1976; Cox, 1985).

A review of the literature regarding personality characteristics of marijuana users led Jerome Jaffe (1979) to three generalizations which are consistent with a multicharacteristic understanding of personality variables. *First,* Jaffe suggests that marijuana users tend to score high on scales of nonconventionality. Factors related to nonconventionality include a sense of alienation, critical beliefs about the larger society, and lower rates of religiosity. *Second,* Jaffe concludes that marijuana users are open to new experiences. They are more spontaneous in nature and receptive to uncertainty and change. *Third,* marijuana users manifest lower rates of conventional achievement value and achievement satisfaction. Jaffe is careful to point out that these personality characteristics may be history or culture-bound.

While personality correlates continue to be examined as predisposing factors in substance abuse, it is often difficult to distinguish the personality attributes from the behaviors they are attempting to explain. To suggest that "sensation-seeking" individuals are more likely to abuse drugs, for example, seems hardly explanatory. Drug-using behavior *is* sensation-seeking! Similarly, the fact that marijuana users score higher on nonconventionality should hardly be surprising since the use of marijuana, though common, is itself an unconventional behavior. These explanations of addiction frequently identify causes attributed to personality features but which are perilously close to the very behavior that they are trying to explain. We call such explanations *tautologies,*[1] a methodological dilemma which sociologists work hard to avoid when theorizing.

BEHAVIORAL THEORIES

Unlike psychoanalytic theories, which focus on early, inner, unconscious drives and deeply rooted personality features, behavioral theory is focused on *behaviors* and the stimuli which elicit those behaviors. The foundation for behavioral theory was established with the work of a Russian physiologist by the name of Ivan Pavlov who discovered that dogs could be conditioned to salivate at the sound of a bell because of the association that they made between the bell and food when both were presented at the same time. Pavlov's ideas of "classical conditioning" were extended by the American behaviorist B.F. Skinner, who suggested that certain behavior is *reinforced* when it is rewarded consistently, an idea known as **operant conditioning.** Psychologist Albert Bandura (1969) extended the notion of operant conditioning even further by suggesting that individuals *model* their behavior after significant others, whose opinion and relationship they value.

Psychologists have applied principles of behavioral theory to the use of and addiction to drugs. McAuliffe (1975) identified three reinforcing effects of opiates which keep users coming back: *euphoria, cessation of withdrawal effects,* and *related analgesic effects.* Crowley (1981) distinguishes between *primary reinforcers* and *secondary reinforcers.* Primary reinforcers are those objects or situations which are directly pleasurable, such as food or sexual activity. Certain kinds of drug use, Crowley states, are primary reinforcers in that these drugs produce an intrinsically pleasurable experience. Secondary reinforcers, on the other hand, are those objects or situations which are pleasurable because of the associations that people make with them—a classical and/or operant conditioning response. Crowley describes how the smoking of dried banana peel became a fad in some circles for its presumed hallucinogenic effect. Banana peel has no such primary effect, but the association made between smoking the peel and the psychedelic music, peer group enjoyment, and other aspects of the "banana grass" subculture reinforced the behavior. Crowley also identifies the importance of "negative reinforcement," which is a reinforcing effect that results from the termination of a painful or punishing condition. Withdrawal from narcotics, for example, may be a painful experience, and continued use of these drugs serves to terminate the withdrawal symptoms. Narcotics are thus not only a primary *positive* reinforcer because of the euphoria produced, but a *negative* reinforcer for the relief of the pain that they also produce.

Cognitive behavioral theories also recognize the role of operant conditioning in producing a behavioral response when certain stimuli are present. These theories explicitly recognize, however, that response to stimuli is not automatic. Rather, when stimuli are presented, a cognitive, or thought process begins to unfold which, in turn, results in behavior. It is this cognitive component to response that distinguishes human response from animal response according to cognitive theorists. The classic cognitive theory of addiction was developed by sociologist Alfred Lindesmith (1938). Lindesmith titled the article in which he developed this theory "A Sociological Theory of Addiction," but in fact this was, and remains, perhaps the best articulation of a cognitive behavioral framework for understanding addiction. He suggested that addiction to narcotics cannot be accounted for by positive reinforcements of euphoria, for there are many individuals who have used narcotics and experienced the euphoric effects, but do not become addicted. Moreover, addiction cannot be accounted for merely by the absence of withdrawal distress that results from self-medication of narcotics during times of withdrawal. According to Lindesmith, only when there is a cognitive connection made between the use of narcotics and the alleviation of withdrawal symptoms does the felt need for the drug arise. That is, only when the would-be addict comes to *recognize* the effect of narcotics in producing withdrawal relief does that individual come to feel a need for the drug. This *cognitive recognition* is the necessary condition for addiction to develop, according to Lindesmith.

The behavioral theories are similar in many ways to some of the sociological theories that we will be discussing next. As we shall see, some of the sociological theories—particularly those commonly known as "social learning theories"—draw many of their ideas from the work of the behaviorists.

Sociological Theories

General sociological theories of drug use and abuse are most often derived from categories of theory originally created to explain crime and delinquency. These theories include: *social process theories, social structural theories, societal reaction theories,* and *conflict theories.* Each of these theoretical approaches attempts to answer different theoretical questions. However, all focus explicitly on the *social environment* of the user, the hallmark of sociological theory. Keep in mind our Chapter 1 discussion on how sociologists approach the study of drugs.

Social Process Theories

Social process theories tend to be social psychological or microsociological in nature. That is, these theories seek to explain the process by which social norms, expectations, values, and other social and cultural forces are translated into individual behavior. Social process theories are, essentially a link between psychological theories (particularly behavioral theories) which we have discussed above, and social structural theories which are addressed in the next section. We can distinguish between two types of social process theories: *social learning theories* and *social control theories,* both of which are relevant to the understanding of drug use and addiction.

Social Learning Theories

Social learning theories begin with the assumption that individuals are not "born" to be drug users, but acquire the penchants, values, and skills to do so through a process of socialization. The first major theoretical statement

Drug use, and the subsequent experience of getting high, are learned in the process of interaction with other users, according to social learning theorists

from a social learning perspective was Edwin Sutherland's *differential association* theory (1939). Sutherland's theory is quite simple. Essentially, it proposes that criminal behavior is learned in association with others who positively value such behavior. Adapted for the study of drug users, his argument is that individuals become involved in a drug culture by associating with others who characterize drug behavior in positive terms. Sutherland further recognizes that our relationships with people vary in *frequency* of interaction, *duration* of those interactions, the *priority* or importance of those relationships, and the *intensity* with which we interact. Hence, those people whom we highly admire and with whom we interact frequently, over a long period of time, and/or intensely will have a much greater impact on our proclivity to become drug involved than less significant relationships involving less frequent and intense involvement.

Sutherland's theory has been extended by the work of Ronald Akers (1969), who focuses on the process of **differential reinforcement.** This theory blends elements of differential association with behavioral theory in psychology. Akers suggests that behavior is reinforced through the rewards obtained in interaction with others. The individuals and groups with which we interact control the reinforcements that we receive. Hence, if we associate primarily with law-abiding or nondrug-using people, law-abiding behavior will be reinforced.

In his 1992 work on the sociology of drug use, Akers suggests that, initially, there is a *social reinforcement* for drug use by one's peers: "In the initiation of drug use, exposure to definitions favorable to drugs and differential association with other users who provide models and social reinforcement for use are critical" (p. 97). Akers goes on to say, "Many who are exposed to deviant subcultures define drugs in positive terms from the beginning or are exposed to drug-tolerant attitudes" (p. 99). Reinforcement comes not only from social peers, however. The drugs themselves often provide an intrinsic reinforcement to the users. Akers suggests that if the initial drug effects are pleasant, drug use is positively reinforced, and it is more likely that use will continue than if the results are unpleasant. Akers also recognizes that once one becomes addicted, particularly to opiates and other physiologically addicting substances, the motive for continued use may be a *negative reinforcement*—a way of avoiding the pain of not having the drug. While the inherent reinforcing effects of the drugs are recognized, Akers' general theory is profoundly *social* in nature. The key to understanding why some people begin and continue to use drugs lies in the nature of the reinforcements provided by one's social groups and significant others.

Another social learning explanation that has been developed especially for understanding drug-using behavior has been offered by Howard Becker (1963, 1967). Becker argues that the user who experiments with marijuana (1963) does not automatically experience the effects of the drug. Rather, the user of the drug must engage in a learning process in order to experience the positive effects of the drug. There are several components to this learning. First, the novice user must *learn the technique* of using the drug. The marijuana user must learn to inhale deeply, and to hold the marijuana in the lungs for a period of time. The correct technique for smoking is usually learned in the context of marijuana-smoking peers. A similar learning process is reported by narcotics users. They must learn how to "cook" (prepare) the heroin, to "tie up," (prepare their veins) and to insert the needle through the wall of the vein without going all the way through the other wall (Faupel, 1991). Failure to learn these techniques will require them to be dependent on another addict to "get them off."

It is not enough to learn the technique for smoking (or shooting) if one is going to have a "successful" drug experience. One must also learn to perceive the effects of these drugs. Drugs may produce certain physiological symptoms, but if these symptoms are not recognized as being caused by the drug, the user will not experience it as a high. That is, the subjective effects of the drugs may be perceived as sleepiness or dizziness or a host of other experiences, but not as a "high." One of the functions of the drug-using subculture is to "normalize" these experiences. The user is told that this is a normal experience and to be expected when using the particular drug in question. These associates thus serve to *define the experience* as a normal result of using the drug. Moreover, the drug subculture also serves to define these subjective states as *pleasurable.* Lacking such an interpretation, the novice user may well decide that this is not a pleasant experience, and will not care to repeat it. Truth be told, initial experiences with drugs ranging from alcohol and marijuana to heroin are often unpleasant and uncomfortable. Faupel (1991) reports that veteran heroin users, recalling their initiation into heroin use, would recall gut-wrenching nausea which would be met with smiles of understanding from their friends. Yet in the words of one female addict, "the more I puked, the higher I got." While intrinsically a *negative* experience by just about any standard, these experiences were redefined for the beginning user as something to be appreciated and enjoyed. Becker's learning theory, in sum, suggests that if one is to continue substance use of any type beyond an initial experimental use, the user must literally "learn" to get high. All of this learning takes place in a social context, typically among more experienced users, who are mentors of sorts in this educational process.

Social Control Theories

Social control theories begin with a fundamentally different premise than do learning theories. Human beings do not need to *learn* the motives and predispositions to engage in drug use and criminal behavior, as learning theorists contend. Such predispositions are built into the very fabric of human nature, in which we are naturally predisposed to maximize selfish wants and needs, and drug use may be a quick and easy way of achieving these ends. According to control theorists, what must be explained is *why most people do NOT engage in such hedonistic behaviors.*

The most concise statement representing control theory comes from Travis Hirschi (1969) who contends that selfish behavior is thwarted and

DRUGS AND EVERYDAY LIFE

Becoming a Heroin User

Charles Faupel, in his book *Shooting Dope*, identifies "drug availability" as a critical determinant of one's level of involvement as a heroin addict. The following excerpt from that book highlights the importance of learning how to self-inject as a factor in drug availability, and the process that this learning entails:

> There is one final avenue to increased availability that was essential to the transition to the stable-addict phase among the participants in this study, namely, learning the skills and techniques required for self-injection. Almost without exception participants reported dramatic increases in their heroin consumption once they had learned to "spike" themselves. As Gloria recalled, "It wasn't hard for me to learn to spike my own arm—so he (a friend) didn't have to do it anymore. I did it myself. . . . I went on and on, and it got to be so big that it got to the point I wasn't selling, I was just using."
>
> While Gloria mastered self-injection with relative ease, this was not the case for many of the respondents. Some of them had an aversion to needles that had to be overcome. Moreover, it was necessary to learn to "tie up"

to expose a vein. Many addicts initially found it difficult to control *rolling* (moving) veins; and having done that, to know at what depth to insert the syringe to avoid extending the needle through both walls of the vein. These addicts also had to learn what mixtures of water to add to the powdered heroin, how long to cook the heroin, and how to draw the mixture into the syringe, avoiding air bubbles and straining impurities. All of this is a complex process, and most users do not become adept at it without considerable practice.

Learning to self-inject is an important milestone in an addict's career because it signifies an independence from older, more experienced addicts and gives users increased stature and respect in the subculture. Little Italy summarized how this rite of passage affected his relationships: "They came back, fixed me up with a shot. I hit. I was hitting myself, man. And they were smiling, 'Oh Man, you know how to hit yourself too now, huh?' So I done graduated. I'm one of the big boys now" ■

Source: Charles E. Faupel, *Shooting Dope: Career Contingencies of Hard-Core Heroin Users*. Gainesville, FL: University of Florida Press, 1991, pp. 69–70.

conformity assured to the extent that young people are appropriately "bonded" to conventional society. Hirschi identifies four elements to this "social bond:" *attachment, commitment, involvement,* and *belief*. These elements and their explanations are presented in Table 4.2.

Hirschi suggests that these elements of the social bond provide certain stakes or interests in conformity. Nonconforming behavior jeopardizes the attachments that one has developed with caring adults; or the payoff for the investments involved in commitment. Similarly, behavior that violates one's belief in the integrity of the moral order produces dissonance. However, when one or more of these bonds are lacking or weak, the individual has less at stake and is therefore at higher risk for delinquency, drug use, or other forms of antisocial behavior.

TABLE 4.2	Hirschi's Social Bond Theory
Attachment	Emotional bonds developed with others who represent conventional values and authority
Commitment	Investment of time, effort and other resources into conventional lines of activity, the fruits of which could be jeopardized if one were to engage in activities such as drug use or delinquency
Involvement	Filling up one's time with conventional activities such as sports or other after-school activities, so that there is little time for illegal activities
Belief	Cognitive affirmation of conventional values and morality

Control theory has not been subjected to as much testing or elaboration, and what has been done has not provided much support for control theory. One study by Burkett and Warren (1987) found indirect support for the theory. Examining both religiosity (a measure of religious commitment) and peer associations together, Burkett and Warren found that religiosity did not have a direct impact on marijuana use, but it did have an impact on the types of peers with which one associated. Peer associations (a social learning variable) then had a direct impact on the level of marijuana use. Ironically, while control theory has found considerable support for other types of delinquent behavior (Hirschi, 1969; Van Voorhis et al., 1988; Agnew and Peterson, 1989; Junger-Tas, 1992), the theory is not particularly effective in explaining drug use.[2] When it is operative, it appears that social control variables have their greatest impact in the choice of friends with which one associates. This is, of course, an important contribution and should not be minimized for as these studies and others in the tradition of learning theory make convincingly clear, friendship patterns have a powerful effect on the likelihood of drug use. We address this process governing friendship patterns and recruitment into drug use in the following section.

Subcultural Recruitment and Socialization: An Integrated Perspective

Erich Goode (1970, 1999) and Bruce Johnson (1973) find that young people who smoke marijuana tend to share a number of characteristics in common. They tend to be less religious than nonsmokers, more sexually permissive, and more likely to hold left-wing political views. These common characteristics, according to Goode, provide a basis for interaction and mutual attraction. Among drug users there is, even before one begins using drugs, a selective recruitment process at work that draws these individuals together into a common network and subculture. Would-be marijuana users are not recruited randomly into this subculture, but are drawn to it because of the common world view and lifestyle characteristics of others in the network. Nonusers, by contrast, tend to become involved in friendship networks that are more compatible with conventional values.

Once recruited into such a drug-using peer network, socialization begins to unfold. While parents and schools as well as other conventional socialization agents such as religion exert influence in the life of an adolescent, peer groups are particularly powerful agents of socialization when it comes to making immediate lifestyle choices. Denise Kandel (1973), who has perhaps studied adolescent drug use patterns more than any other single scholar, suggests that while parents may exert preliminary influence by example in the use of alcohol, the use of drugs is primarily the result of socialization among peers. Later research by Kandel and Davies (1991) further revealed that drug users tended to have even greater intimacy with peers than did nonusers. And they found that the further along in the sequence of drug use one was, the greater the likelihood that one had a closest friend who used that drug. This most recent research suggests that while parental and general peer group influence may play a greater role in entry-level drug use such as alcohol, as the adolescent progresses to illegal drug use such as marijuana and especially other more expensive drugs, he or she will more deliberately seek out like-minded peers.

This body of research, which supports what Goode (1999) has called the "selective interaction/socialization" model, suggests that both social control and social learning processes are at work in the process of becoming a drug user. Social control factors are primarily at work in the selection of peer associations—people seek out friends who are most closely aligned with their lifestyle and world view. Once this peer-selection process has taken place, however, social learning principles become dominant in one's choices to initiate and continue involvement in drug using sequences.

SOCIAL STRUCTURAL THEORIES

When we talk about "social structural theories," we are referring to explanations that attempt to explain why certain *categories* of people tend to be more involved in drug use and/or crime than other categories. These epidemiological theories attempt to explain differential levels of *crime and drug use rates* among different segments of the population. This focus separates social structural theories from earlier theories which look for links between *individual* drug users and the social environment of which they are a part. Over the years, two distinct approaches to structural explanations have developed. These are known as *strain theories* and *cultural deviance* theories respectively.

Strain Theory

Strain theory is often called *anomie theory*. Sociologist Robert Merton provided the basis by which strain theory could be applied to drug use and other deviant behaviors. Merton's theory saw social structure in primarily economic or social class terms. In "Social Structure and Anomie" (1938), Merton states that there are two elements of society that interact to produce varying levels of strain. The first element is socially defined goals which are held out as desirable. In American society, these goals are typically material in nature;

we tend to define success in materialistic terms. The second element of his model is the socially approved of means for obtaining these goals. Young people go to college to get higher paying jobs, thus pursuing the socially defined goal of material success through a socially approved mean.

The problem is that the acceptance of socially defined goals of material success in a particular sector of society does not necessarily mean that socially approved means are acknowledged with the same level of commitment; or, that commitment to socially approved means is accompanied by a commitment to the goals. The disjuncture between socially approved goals and socially accepted means for obtaining those goals, produces strain which may result in deviance, such as drug use. In particular, Merton argued that the drug user was likely to be someone who rejected both socially defined goals and the accepted means by which to achieve them. He called such a person a **retreatist,** in effect a societal dropout who has retreated into his own isolated world. Heroin and alcohol were cited as especially prominent in the world of the retreatist because they provide an "escape" from the demanding realities of life.

Merton's ideas were later elaborated upon by Richard Cloward and Lloyd Ohlin (1960). Their *differential opportunity theory* posits that retreatism occurs only after attempts to achieve the American dream have proven unsuccessful. Cloward and Ohlin claim that most individuals first attempt to achieve the socially defined goals of material success through legitimate means. Failing that, attempts are made to attain these goals illegitimately through one or more types of criminal activities. Only when these attempts fail does one give up and drop out, turning to drugs as an escape. Cloward and Ohlin suggest that these retreatists are **double failures** who have failed to achieve the American dream of material success through either legitimate or illegitimate means. The only option is to retreat into a world of drug use and addiction (1960, pp. 179–183).

Strain theory has not stood up particularly well under empirical scrutiny as an explanation of drug abuse and addiction. Lindesmith and Gagnon (1964) challenged the efficacy of strain theory in explaining drug *addiction*. While it may explain initial experimentation with heroin for some individuals they argue, it falls short in explaining addiction. Indeed, the very lifestyle of the heroin addict precludes Cloward and Ohlin's scenario:

> If, as is commonly reported, the addict's habit costs him as much as from $10 to $50 a day (note: late 1960s) seven days a week, one may argue that it is no mean feat to raise these amounts. The user who supports himself by stealing finds that the value of stolen goods is heavily discounted by the fence, and if his habit costs him twenty-five dollars per day he may have to steal goods worth from $75 to $100 to meet his daily expenses. . . . From this, one might reasonably argue that addicts are quite successful criminals (Lindesmith and Gagnon, 1964, p. 176.)

This observation is directly addressed by an early ethnographic study of drug users in New York, which found little evidence to support the ideas in strain theory. Examining the economics of the heroin-using lifestyle, Preble and

Casey (1969) convincingly made the case that the heroin user is *anything but* a social dropout trying to escape an otherwise harsh existence. They write,

> Heroin use today by lower class, primarily minority group, persons does not provide for them a euphoric escape from the psychological and social problems which derive from ghetto life. On the contrary, it provides a motivation and rationale for the pursuit of a meaningful life, albeit a socially deviant one. The activities these individuals engage in and the relationships they have in the course of their quest for heroin are far more important than the minimal analgesic and euphoric effects of the small amount of heroin available to them. . . . the heroin user is, in a way, like the compulsively hard-working business executive whose ostensible goal is the acquisition of money, but whose real satisfaction is in meeting the inordinate challenge he creates for himself (p. 21).

Other ethnographic studies have also challenged the double failure characterization of drug addiction (e.g., see Agar, 1973, Biernacki, 1979; Faupel, 1991). The weight of evidence from post-1960s ethnographic studies strongly suggests a very active and even criminally successful lifestyle among heroin addicts and users of other expensive drugs.

The empirical evidence has quite clearly spoken: strain or anomie does not explain much in the way of drug abuse or drug addiction. It is a seductive theory which "makes sense" to those of us who are not part of the drug-using world. Why else would anyone use drugs or become addicted? Surely, they would prefer another lifestyle! Only in failing in that attempt would they withdraw into a world of drug use and addiction. The evidence suggests, however, that, indeed, many addicts *do* freely choose a drug-using lifestyle, indeed preferring it to nine-to-five routines.

Cultural Deviance Theories

Cultural deviance theories have their genesis with sociologists at the University of Chicago who were attempting to understand patterns of urban crime and delinquency in the 1920s and 1930s, and who essentially concluded that cultural traditions often promoted crime. An early explanation was developed by Clifford Shaw and Henry McKay (1972), who believed that drug use and other forms of delinquency were the result of "transitional neighborhoods" where there were high rates of residential turnover and lack of a strong community to encourage conventional values. Children growing up in these areas often lacked adequate supervision, and grew up under the influence of delinquent gangs which passed on delinquent values. "Delinquent gangs" morphed into "criminal or drug-using subcultures" in later formulations of cultural deviance theory.

The application of cultural deviance ideas specifically to subcultures of drug users received support from John O'Donnell (1967) in his research on addicts in the federal treatment facility in Lexington, Kentucky. Comparing drug addiction prior to 1914, when the Harrison Narcotics Act effectively criminalized the possession and distribution of drugs, with post-1914 periods, O'Donnell found evidence of the emergence of a drug subculture. O'Donnell suggested that with the criminalization of narcotics, continuing drug users experienced a common problem: how to maintain access to sources of drugs. This involved a host of other problems, such as the learning of criminal skills to support their habit, and learning to avoid detection and arrest. He writes:

> When drugs were in short supply, they could be obtained from others. Information could be traded on where and how drugs could be obtained. Skills, which before had been unnecessary were now needed, and could be transmitted from one addict to another. These included criminal skills: how to commit burglaries or forge prescriptions; how to administer narcotics by the intravenous route; how to process paregoric so the residue could be injected; and how to 'make' doctors. Addicts could support each other in the attitudes and values needed to maintain addiction in the face of mounting public disapproval" (O'Donnell, 1967, pp. 78–79).

The criminalization of drug use, according to O'Donnell, resulted in the emergence of a distinct *drug subculture* for the first time in American history.

Johnson (1973) also employs a subcultural perspective to explain marijuana use. He suggests that the overriding characteristic, called a "conduct norm," shared by subcultures of marijuana use is the mandate to smoke marijuana. Corresponding to this conduct norm are supporting values and belief systems which reinforce the importance of the norm. Johnson further explains that regardless of the diversity of the marijuana subculture in other ways, such as social class or lifestyle, marijuana users recognize each other by virtue of the fact that they smoke marijuana. Johnson (1980) later extended his theory to account for other drug-specific subcultures, arguing that special conduct norms can also be observed for the alcohol abuse subculture, heroin-injection subculture, and the multiple-drug-use subculture. Each has its own conduct norms, but also its own rituals, argot, and values that support the use of particular drugs.

It should be pointed out that cultural deviance theory, especially as formulated by Johnson, carries within it certain features of social learning theory, a process theory. Johnson understands, for example, that it is within the context of drug subcultures that individuals learn the conduct norms associated with using drugs. The *structural* features of cultural deviance theories, however, emphasize the importance of one's "social location" in relation to subcultures of crime and drug use as explanatory variables. The social learning process that takes place within these subcultures is more or less assumed.

An Integrated Structural Theory

Drug researcher and sociologist Charles Winick proposed a theory in 1974 which combined elements of both strain theory and cultural deviance theory. Winick contended that drug dependence is a function of three factors: (1) access to drugs; (2) disengagements from normative proscriptions against drug use; and (3) role strain and/or role deprivation. *Access* to drugs refers to the various means by which drugs become available to users. Drug users can enhance access in a variety of ways, including connecting with wholesale dealers; learning new and more lucrative criminal skills and learning how to inject one's self, rather than being dependent on others to help one "get off" (Faupel, 1991).[3] Greater access to drugs provides greater opportunities for getting high, which is posited as increasing the likelihood of abuse or dependence. Involvement in the drug subculture is a valuable asset in increasing availability to levels required for addiction to develop. *Disengagement from proscriptions* against drug use refers to the process by which young drug users counteract conventional morality which places heavy taboos on drug use, or at least on certain kinds of drug use. Sykes and Matza (1957) identified five "techniques of neutralization" that delinquents use to disengage from conventional norms. Similar techniques are used by drug abusers to provide a justification for behavior that had once represented a violation of their own ethical standards. These techniques of disengagement are typically learned as addicts become immersed in the subculture of drug use.

The third element of Winick's theory, and the one which he stresses most strongly, is *role strain* and *role deprivation.* Role strain, for Winick, involves perceived difficulty in meeting the obligations of a social position, while role deprivation refers to the termination of a significant and important position in the individual's life. Both increase an individual's vulnerability to drug abuse and addiction, particularly if the first two elements of his theory are present. Winick points out that physicians, for example, frequently experience role strain because of their busy schedules which, combined with easy access to drugs, makes them vulnerable to addiction. Physicians may also experience role deprivation in a number of ways, such as failing board exams or leaving the security of medical school to set up their own practice. Faupel (1991) also identified the importance of role strain/role deprivation in what he termed the "life structure" of users, which was a critical element in predicting level of drug use. Individuals who maintained a highly structured daily routine were much better able to manage their drug consumption than individuals who led more chaotic lifestyles. With disruptions to life structure caused by increased pressure from police, the loss of a job, the breaking up of a relationship, or a particularly lucrative criminal event the user is already well on his or her way to becoming, in Faupel's terms, a "free-wheeling addict," with little or no control over an escalating habit. Life structure features, including role strain and role deprivation, clearly play an important part in predisposing one toward drug addiction.

SOCIETAL REACTION THEORIES

Societal reaction theories represent a fundamental paradigm shift with regard to explaining drug use and deviant behavior generally. The very question that we are trying to answer shifts from "Why do individuals (or categories of individuals) engage in problematic drug-using behavior?" to "Why does *society* respond to this particular type of behavior in the way that it does?"

The societal reaction theory that is most relevant to the issue of drug use is *labeling theory*. Labeling theory has its intellectual roots in the *symbolic interactionist* tradition. Interactionists such as George Herbert Mead, Herbert Blumer and others suggested early on that social reality is a *constructed* phenomenon. That is, while there are concrete social phenomena that may be observed and measured objectively, the *meanings* we assign to those phenomena are mediated by our social and cultural experiences. An example will help illustrate this.

In recent years, concern over alcohol abuse in our society as a whole and on college campuses specifically, has led to a reduction in tolerance over drunkenness and the "Three Vs"—violence, vandalism, and vomiting—which are said to result from it. In an effort to put a name on the vilified phenomenon, moral entrepreneurs in government and private entities like the Robert Wood Johnson Foundation have crusaded against *binge drinking* by college students. A well-funded media campaign against binge drinking and *binge drinkers,* has focused on what is said to be the objective and unassailable harm of the practice. The authorized meaning imputed to binge drinking is that of a scourge, which all concerned parties must work toward reducing if not eliminating. It sounds pretty definitive—the practice is so objectively harmful that it shouldn't be debated or defended.

Before we declare the case closed, consider the definition of binge drinking that is being used—consumption of five or more alcoholic drinks (four for women) in one session of drinking, at least once in a two-week period. A session of drinking might refer to an evening, or the duration of a party, possibly four hours or more. Consuming four or five drinks in that time period might raise one's *blood alcohol concentration* (BAC) to the legal level of intoxication, but probably not much above it. So even an occasional drinker might fit the operative definition of *binge drinking*. No wonder college binge drinking rates are often 40 percent or higher. For most college students, this threshold for binge drinking is likely to be assigned a nonproblematic meaning, one quite at odds with the (perhaps well-intentioned) antidrinking crusaders. One group's serious public threat is another's cherished practice. We can say this without minimizing the fact that alcohol abuse is potentially damaging to one's health or academic performance. We are simply recognizing that "binge drinking" is a social construction, the reality of which is predicated by where one is positioned on this issue. The degree of harmfulness is in the eyes of the beholder.

We have also addressed the issue of social construction of the reality of drug use in Chapter 1. There we learned that some drugs are defined as acceptable in American society, even glamorous. Drinking champagne or gourmet coffee distinguish one as having an elegant palate. Smoking marijuana or dropping LSD may render one a social pariah in his or her community. Yet it is difficult to make the case that one drug is intrinsically more damaging than another. These judgments are also social constructions. The recognition of the social construction of reality is, in part, the legacy of symbolic interactionism.

There are three basic questions that labeling theory brings to the table in its attempt to understand drug use and addiction.

1. *Why are certain drug-using behaviors defined as deviant, and others not?*
2. *Why do certain individuals who engage in these drug-using behaviors acquire a deviant label, while others who engage in the same behavior are not so labeled?*
3. *What are the social and interpersonal consequences and implications of this labeling process?*

We address each of these questions in the paragraphs that follow.

The Defining of Deviant Behavior   As we have already seen in Chapter 1, the social construction of drug use as a deviant behavior is rarely a rational process, if by "rationality" we mean that there is an objective assessment of the pharmacological dangers inherent in using particular drugs. Rather, according to labeling theory the social construction is much more typically based on the vested interests and ideologies of those who have power and access to deviance-defining processes, such as legislative bodies or the mass media. This process of *moral entrepreneurship* was analyzed by Becker (1963) where he traced the initial criminalization of marijuana by the newly formed Federal Bureau of Narcotics (the precursor of the Drug Enforcement Administration, the DEA). The FBN, headed by Harry Anslinger, conducted a "reefer madness" campaign, which was particularly instrumental in the legislation process and in the shaping of public opinion. Not coincidentally, the success of this criminalization effort led to a big increase in the FBN budget.

The moral entrepreneurship process was also identified by Joseph Gusfield (1963) with regard to alcohol prohibition. Gusfield demonstrated that the prohibition movement, and the defining of alcohol consumption as a socially unacceptable behavior, was the end result of a political and public opinion battle between the more established and often-abstinent Protestant middle class and the more newly immigrated Catholic, typically ethnic minority blue collar populations for which drinking was an integrated part of social life. More recently, Ruth Peterson (1985) did a content-analysis of the Comprehensive Drug Abuse Prevention and Control Act of 1970. Her analysis revealed a *reduction* in penalties for possession of certain types of drugs, particularly marijuana. Penalties were substantially *increased*, however, for drug sales. Analysis of the documents revealed that the aim of the legislation was to send a clear message regarding society's disapproval of drug use, but to do it in such a way so as to protect the privileged position of the "cream of American youth" from the full weight of the existing law, while at the same time singling out drug dealers who were perceived to be of more marginal social status (Peterson, 1985, p. 264). Peterson's analysis of how the legislative process defines drug using and drug dealing behaviors differently also has implications for the second question addressed by labeling theory: "Why are some individuals singled out and labeled for certain behaviors while others who engage in the same behaviors are not?"

The Differential Labeling of Individuals   Labeling theory suggests that the primary factors in who is labeled a criminal, drug addict, or any other type of deviant, are *characteristics of the individual* rather than the characteristics of the acts in which they engage. Typically, those individuals most likely to be labeled and identified as "drug addicts" are those who are racial minorities, of lower socio-economic status, or who have been otherwise marginalized by society. Peterson's (1985) analysis, discussed in the preceding section, suggests that the writers of the Comprehensive Drug Abuse Prevention and Control Act of 1970 in a very concerted fashion (though perhaps not intentionally) singled out these marginalized segments of the population to bear the greatest impact of the law. We also see this differential labeling process take place when homeless alcoholics are occasionally "rounded up" and put into the paddy wagon and carried off to the "drunk tank," while their middle- and upper-class counterparts are protected by the privacy of their homes and the confidentiality of their psychiatrists. We have also observed a disparity over the past decade or so in the way crack versus cocaine users are treated by the criminal justice system. While these are not exactly the same drug because of the way that crack is manufactured and ingested, cocaine is the principle ingredient nevertheless, and the overall effect of both drugs is pharmacologically very similar. The primary difference between these two drugs is not their pharmacology, but rather their *demography*. Crack cocaine is a preferred drug among younger users and those with less means to purchase drugs. Powder cocaine, which is much more expensive on a "per hit" basis, is much more likely to be indulged in by older and more mainstream members of society.

The Impact of Labeling   Much of the focus of labeling theory has been upon the consequences of labeling for the individual labeled in some undesirable way. Once labeled, the theory goes, the individual takes on a new, devalued social identity. Goffman (1963) refers to this new deviant identity as a **stigma;** Becker (1963) denotes it as the *master status*. Regardless of nomenclature, the public designation as a "deviant"—pothead, junkie, crack whore, or drunk—powerfully changes one's public identity. Moreover, consistent with the perspective of symbolic interactionism, in which labeling theory is rooted, this public identity inevitably shapes one's self concept. Schur (1971) suggests that concurrent with public labeling is a process of "role engulfment" whereby more and more of an individual's self-concept is centered around the deviant identity. Not only is the individual defined by *others* as a deviant, but now defines *him- or herself* as a deviant as well.

Such self-definition has profound implications for subsequent behavior. According to labeling theory, individuals are likely to act in a way that is consistent with their self-concept. Edwin Lemert (1951) distinguishes between primary deviance and secondary deviance to capture this idea. **Primary deviance,** according to Lemert, consists of those rule violations that are often inadvertent, and which most everyone engages in from time to time. These are not the acts of a career deviant or of one who thinks of

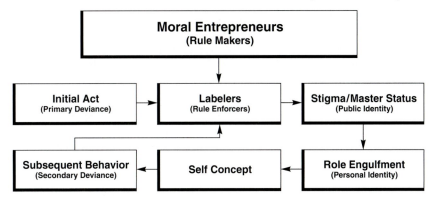

Figure 4.1 **The Dynamics of Labeling Theory**

him or herself as a deviant; they are the variety of indiscretions that, if detected and made public *could* be the basis for labeling and role engulfment. When such a labeling process takes place and one's self-concept takes on a deviant character such as a "pothead" or "dope fiend," subsequent behavior that conforms to the deviant self-identity is referred to by Lemert as **secondary deviance.** Unlike primary deviance, which is usually occasional and sporadic, secondary deviance is routine and systematic as it reflects the new identity that the publicly labeled drug user has internalized. Rather than occasionally experimenting with drugs, or using them socially from time to time, the labeled user now uses on a regular basis; drug-related activities and identities have now become a central focus.

Figure 4.1 depicts the sequence of events involved in the labeling process. The making of rules sets in motion a labeling process that typically begins following the commitment of an initial act of drug use (or other form of deviance).[4] Once labeled, a process of role engulfment takes place and the self concept begins a metamorphosis. According to labeling theory, the result is a much more systematic pattern of secondary deviant behavior. There are, moreover, labeling implications of secondary deviance itself. Such behavior serves to reinforce the perceptions of the labelers, whether these be teachers, police, or other community agents. The cycle of labeling then escalates, and the public identity of the drug user becomes even more firmly entrenched. Barring some form of external intervention, the dynamics of labeling theory suggest that drug-using and/or other deviant behavior patterns will eventually take the form of a full-blown drug-using "career" in which an individual organizes major portions of his or her life around drug use and the activities associated with that use. Labeling theory contains within it some profound policy implications which are discussed in Chapters 11 and 12.

CONFLICT THEORIES

The decade of the 1960s provided sociologists with ample evidence that assumptions some of them had been making regarding the harmonious and fundamental fairness of American society might need to be reworked. Our national complacency was shaken by racial protests and violence in urban areas from coast to coast. The Vietnam War was challenged by millions as imperialistic and unnecessary. And societal elites found that their wealth and power could make them objects of scorn to many. These societal divisions gave rise to new ways of thinking about larger issues—racism, poverty, abuses of political power, and deteriorating cities among them—facing America. A number of critical, macro-societal arguments emerged under the rubric of *conflict theory*. As critical arguments, they challenged the legitimacy of American social institutions and of entrenched structures of power. As "macro" approaches, they examined the larger structural forces that affected communities and American society as a whole. This made them different from other sociological theories of drug use we've covered which focused on how *individuals* are situated with American culture and social structures.

An example of a sociologist who writes about social problems, crime, and drug abuse from a conflict perspective is Elliott Currie (1985, 1993). Currie is primarily concerned with the abuse of crack cocaine and heroin in our inner cities and how utterly destructive of families and community it can be. In fact, conflict theory is most useful in explaining such drug abuse, rather than, say, patterns of drinking and pot-smoking by affluent suburban teens. He says that higher rates of crack and heroin dependency are found in these urban centers because meaningful economic opportunities are scarce and because perceived powerlessness and alienation is so crippling. Going further, he argues that the dearth of economic options and the marginalization of entire communities is systematic and intended politically. The "War on Drugs" conducted by government has done little to reduce these structural conditions, and hence has had little impact on the kinds of chronic drug dependency plaguing the cities (Currie, 1993). Support for this may be seen in government data sets which show that while occasional cocaine use was down sharply from 1988–2000, in the same period "hardcore" use was largely unchanged (ONDCP, 2001:142).

For conflict theorists, drug policy, to be meaningful, must attack the economic and political conditions which polarize us at a macro-societal level. It must be noted that social and political support for such a policy shift is not strong. Both major political parties, save for a relatively few legislators, would dismiss widespread economic restructuring as "extreme" or "radical." Conflict theorists would not be surprised by this, given that the greatest harmful consequences of drug abuse are being felt by those who are most dissimilar demographically from the politicians themselves. The scourge of drug abuse victimizes most those who have the least clout and autonomy in our society. And the devastation of drug dependency helps to silence their voices more completely. Conflict theorists are pessimistic that this degrading cycle will be broken any time soon.

SUMMARY

The theories that we have highlighted in this chapter are but some of the most widely recognized explanations for drug use and addiction. While recognizing various approaches to understanding drug use and addiction, we have emphasized sociological theories in this chapter. This has been intentional. Drug use, perhaps more than any form of deviant or criminal behavior, has suffered from a very narrow, individualistic casual understanding among policy makers, practitioners, and in the popular press. Our intent is not to deny the reality of biological and psychological factors, but rather to expand our understanding of the etiology of drug use to include *cultural* and *structural* factors which are at work predisposing certain categories of individuals toward the use of drugs—*or certain types of drugs*—while other categories of persons are not so vulnerable to the use these kinds of drugs. The sociological perspective, we believe, is at least as important as biological and psychological dimensions for sound drug-use policies for the twenty-first century.

KEY TERMS

addictive personality
differential reinforcement
double failure

operant conditioning
primary deviance
retreatist

secondary deviance
stigma

REVIEW QUESTIONS

1. What is meant by the term "scientific theory"? Why is it important that theories of drug use, abuse, or addiction be scientific theories?

2. Dr. Andrew Weil, an advocate for thinking about drug use in new ways, believes that "the desire to alter consciousness periodically is an innate, normal drive." What evidence does he provide to support this claim?

3. Why are neurochemical theories more successful at explaining drug addiction or dependency than initial drug involvement?

4. How useful is the concept of the addiction-prone personality? What are the arguments, pro and con, for its existence?

5. Behaviorist psychological theories focus on the *reinforcing effects* of drug use—primary and secondary reinforcement, positive and negative reinforcement. Show you understand the concept of reinforcement and can distinguish between the different types.

6. In what ways are social learning theories such as "differential association" and "differential reinforcement" similar to and different from behaviorist psychological theories?

7. Both social control theory and anomie theory are described as being largely

unsupported by drug research. Where do these approaches fall short in the eyes of their critics? How is Winick's "integrated structural" approach an improvement?

8. What are the basic tenets of labeling theory (aka social reaction theory)? How does labeling theory mesh with the idea of drug reality being socially constructed?

CRITICAL INQUIRY QUESTIONS

1. Most sociological theories of drug use were originally formulated to explain the broader concepts of criminal and deviant behavior. How successful are these theories at adapting to the explanation of drug use, abuse, and addiction?

2. Is it compelling to argue that much of nonabusive involvement with drugs stems from the personal or interpersonal or social rewards of drug use, and hence the user may be making rational behavioral choices? Why or why not?

NOTES

1. A "tautology" is an explanatory statement in which the explanatory variable (in this case personality attributes) is the same or a very similar measure as the variable to be explained (in this case drug-using behavior). Hence, when we suggest that marijuana use (a sensation-seeking behavior) is caused by a sensation-seeking personality feature, we have not explained much. It is, essentially, a circular reasoning.

2. At least one recent study by Durkin, Wolfe, and Clark (1999) does find support for control theory as a predictor of binge drinking among college students. This study seems to be an exception. It does suggest, however, that more research needs to be done testing the postulates of control theory among middle-class college students specifically with regard to excessive drinking behavior. There may be a different process at work here than that which takes place when

adolescents make the decision to use illegal drugs.

3. Learning how to inject one's self increases access in two ways. First, the individual does not have to wait for an experienced user to assist in the self-medication process and hence can use the drug whenever the felt need arises. Second, most experienced users demand drugs in exchange for their services in assisting newer users to inject. This results in less drugs for the one needing this service.

4. The labeling process need not necessarily begin with an act of primary deviance. In many cases, the rule enforcers wrongly assume that an individual has committed a deviant act and will publicly label them. The consequences are often the same—a public identity is established, thereby resulting in the formation of a deviant self concept and, in turn, secondary deviance.

SUBCULTURES OF DRUG USE

Whenever drugs are used, there is a social context for that use, regardless of the type of drug that is being consumed. Alcohol, for example, is often used to celebrate festive occasions, whether it be a wedding or getting off from work. Coffee is typically consumed at mealtimes or during scheduled coffee breaks. Marijuana is often smoked at rock concerts, or sitting around in a circle listening to rock music on a CD player. To suggest that there is always a social context for drug use certainly does not mean that drugs are always consumed in the physical presence of other people. Often they are deliberately used away from the presence of others, as witnessed by the lone alcoholic, the closet cocaine user, the independent Marlboro Man. Even in these instances, however, drug use has a social context. These drugs must be obtained from other people, whether on the street or in a grocery store. The use of these drugs contributes to the shaping of identities and reputations, and almost always affects the relationships that users have with others. All of these circumstances comprise the social context of drug use. Indeed, the understanding that drug use takes place in a social context is the very premise of the sociology of drug use and of this book.

The social setting in which *illicit* drugs are used is often quite different from that of legal drugs. It is not uncommon for illegal drug users to form **drug subcultures**—groups which are a part of the cultural mainstream and often share many of the values and goals of the cultural mainstream, but nevertheless maintain a distinctive lifestyle which is integrated around the use of illegal drugs. This chapter examines these unique social settings of drug use. The chapter is divided into three parts. The first part of the chapter describes the nature of drug using subcultures by (1) exploring how and why these subcultures form and the functions they fulfill for users of illicit drugs; and (2) discussing some of the essential features of drug subcultures. The second section focuses on four specific subcultures of drug use: the *Rave Ecstacy-Using Subculture*, the *Rastafarian Marijuana-Using Subculture*, the *Native American Church Peyote-Using Subculture* and the *Street-Heroin Subculture*. The final part of the chapter focuses on the careers of drug users, with a specific focus on heroin-using criminal careers, and how these careers are shaped by the subculture in which they develop.

WHAT ARE SUBCULTURES?

The subculture concept is widely used today and is found in nearly every introductory sociology text on the market. It is a concept of fairly recent origins, however, first introduced in the 1940s (Gordon, 1947). As the concept is used today, subculture usually connotes normative and ideological features of a segment of the population and frequent interaction among these individuals, which provide a basis for common identity. Commenting specifically on subcultures of drug use,

O'Donnell (1967:75) has stated, "whatever else a subculture is, it implies contact between its members, learning from each other and recognition of oneself as a member of the group."

Deviant subcultures are those which are organized around behavior patterns which are to some degree in conflict with dominant cultural norms and values. Numerous deviant subcultures have been identified in the literature, including subcultures of prostitutes (Bryan, 1966), gamblers (Hayano, 1982), homosexuals (Harris, 1973) and nudists (Weinberg, 1966) among others. Drug-using subcultures are also deviant in nature, and are organized around the use of one or more (usually illegal) drugs. Johnson (1973, p. 9) defines drug subcultures as ". . . those conduct norms, social situations, role definitions and performances, and values that govern the use of illegal drugs and the intentional nonmedical use of prescription drugs."

THE FORMATION OF DRUG-USING SUBCULTURES

Drug subcultures are generally found where drugs are illegal or at least strongly disapproved. It has been observed, for example, that heroin and cocaine using subcultures began to appear following the Harrison Act in 1914 (Lindesmith, 1965; O'Donnell, 1967). Similarly the subculture of marijuana use became evident following the Marihuana Tax Act in 1937 (Becker, 1963, Brecher, 1972), and the psychedelic subculture of the 1960s was at least in part a response to strong public disapproval (Brecher, 1972; Grinspoon and Bakalar, 1979). Cross-cultural researchers have identified an analogous watershed in Jamaican history when, one morning in April 1963, all Rastafari in the country were made subject to arrest. Troops were even given authority to shoot anyone who resisted arrest. Marijuana, or *ganja*, was not only part of the Rastafari religion, but part of Jamaican culture for many years. However, this shift in public policy led to a widespread media campaign that portrayed ganja users as potentially violent, thereby legitimating the arrest of thousands of Jamaicans. All of this only reinforced a core subculture of ganja users, many of whom were closely connected with Rastafarianism (Campbell, 1980).

It is not a coincidence that drug subcultures tend to form under conditions where the use of these drugs are strongly disapproved. In what is now considered to be the classic explanation for the formation of deviant subcultures, Albert Cohen (1955) states that:

> The crucial condition for the emergence of new cultural forms is the existence, *in effective interaction with one another, of a number of actors with similar problems of adjustment* (p. 59; emphasis in original).

Cohen maintains that all human behavior is essentially "problem solving" in nature, and when a number of individuals experience the same or similar problems, it is natural that they come together to find group solutions to their common problems.

Where drugs are made illegal or are socially disapproved, there are a number of problems encountered by users: how to obtain drugs; how to obtain the money to purchase drugs which are almost surely more costly than they would be if they were obtained legally; how to manage spoiled identities; how to avoid potential health risks; and how to avoid detection and arrest. Furthermore, users must maintain values and ideologies which are consistent with their behavior. These supports are not generally available when drug use and other behaviors associated with this use are socially disapproved, and can be found only among others who share this lifestyle. In this way, the prohibition of drugs has itself contributed to the emergence and maintenance of drug subcultures as Lindesmith (1965) and others have noted.

Recent research by Golub and Johnson (1999, 2001) suggests that this may be going on currently, at least in New York City, with the emergence of a "blunts" subculture among youth. Blunts are quite literally marijuana *cigars*, formed by removing the tobacco contents from a cigar and replacing it with marijuana. It is preferred to marijuana cigarettes because it burns more slowly. Golub and Johnson (1999) trace the emergence of the "blunts generation" to youth born in the 1970s who had witnessed the dangers of cocaine, crack, and heroin use. These drugs pose both observable health risks and social costs of apprehension and incarceration. According to Golub and Johnson, the new "blunts generation" is a direct response to these external forces. Moreover, the values and ideology of this new generation of drug user is maintained in their music, particularly "hip-hop" music, on T-shirts and through other media (Golub and Johnson, 2001).

CHARACTERISTICS OF DRUG SUBCULTURES

Drug researchers have identified several characteristics of drug-using subcultures. Goode (1970, pp. 21–22), for example, suggests that the following features tend to characterize drug subcultures:

- Drug use is usually done in a group setting.
- Others with whom one uses drugs are usually intimates, intimates of intimates, or potential intimates, rather than strangers.
- One generally has long-standing and continuing social relations with others in the subculture.
- There is a certain degree of value-consensus within the subculture.
- A value-convergence will occur as a result of progressive group involvement.
- Drug-using activity maintains the group's cohesion and reaffirms its social bond by acting it out.
- Participants in the subculture view the activity as a legitimate basis for identity, defining themselves and others on the basis of whether they have participated in the activity.

Goode's summary underscores the social and cultural basis for understanding drug-using behavior. Similarly, Fiddle (1963) identifies the following features of addict subcultures: (1) an ideology which justifies their behavior; (2) an expectation that new members will perpetrate the system; (3) specialized argot and cryptic means of communication; (4) an elaborate informational system; (5) rituals; and (6) strong personal relationships between addicts and a high degree of group identification. More recently, Smeja and Rojek (1986) suggest that there are at least three principal components to a drug subculture, namely a drug-oriented value system, distinctive conduct norms, and special subcultural roles which define the rights and duties of each member and position in the subculture. Castro (2001), suggests that drug subcultures are comprised of unique language, symbols, meaning-systems, beliefs, and practices. These and other attempts at definition help to focus on the social and cultural features of the world of drug use.

In the section that follows, we examine four drug subcultures which feature characteristics highlighted above. Each of these subcultures is unique with regard to the type of drug that is primarily used in the subculture. The rave subculture which has recently emerged among high school and college students is primarily focused on the use of ecstacy, though there are other drugs used in rave settings as well. Rastifarians are primarily marijuana users, and participants in the Native American Church use peyote. Participants in the street addict subculture use a variety of drugs including cocaine, crack, and heroin among others. These subcultures also are comprised of different kinds of people demographically. Rave participants are usually young and quite typically middle class, whereas street addicts are more likely to be lower class and often minority youth and young adults. Rastifarians and Native American Church members are also ethnically distinctive. All these groups, however, share features which set them apart from the larger culture and bond them to one another ideologically, symbolically, and normatively.

FOUR SUBCULTURES OF DRUG USE

RASTAFARIANISM

Rasta . . . A term that evokes a number of images: The rhythmic beat and liberation message of reggae music (Spencer, 1998); dreadlocks, the matted, shoulder-length hair that for some symbolizes African heritage and for others is believed to be an antenna of sorts for receiving divine messages (Johnson-Hill, 1995); or the sacramental use of *ganja* (Marijuana) as a part of worship (Campbell, 1980; Johnson-Hill, 1995). Particularly in relation to the use of ganja, Rastafarianism—as a culture and a religious belief system—offers unique opportunities to examine the importance of behavior, identity, and the corresponding reactions to them.

At least in a symbolic sense, the origin of Rastafarianism can be traced to the countries of Ethiopia and Israel. The birth of the religion is generally linked with the coronation of Ras Tafari, a black nationalist leader, as emperor of Ethiopia in 1930. Its development and early popularity occurred in Jamaica, however, promoted by Marcus Garvey, a Jamaican apologist for African culture whose views were widely read (Lewis, 1998). During the decade of the 1930s, the economic and social conditions experienced there have given rise to an intriguing yet controversial set of beliefs, primarily as a response to poverty and limited economic opportunity (Savishinsky, 1998). Rastafarianism as a religion is closely intertwined and an integral part of the culture itself. Although originating in Jamaica, Rastafarianism, or Rasta, has spread abroad. In the United States, Rasta began to receive increased attention during the 1970s, due in part to immigration of a large number of Jamaicans to the United States as well as to the diffusion of the music genre. It was during this period that reggae, most notably the music of Bob Marley, increased in popularity (Taylor, 1984). Largely through reggae music, tenets of the Rastafarian culture and religion (particularly promarijuana themes) attracted the attention of many, including the criminal justice system. The use of ganja by followers of Rastafari during worship reflects both symbolic and manifest responses to domination by those in power (Johnson-Hill, 1995).

According to Rastafarianism, ganja is a sacramental herb, not a drug. Substance abuse (including alcohol) is discouraged. Ganja use is considered appropriate based on the principle of *ital livity*. This notion emphasizes a sense of naturalness in various aspects of life such as a vegetarian diet and the use of herbs for healing purposes (Hepner, 1998).[1] The use of ganja is justified in part upon a reference to herbs in the Old Testament book of Genesis (Kitzinger, 1969). According to belief, its use is sacramental in nature, being no different than the use of incense during a Roman Catholic mass (Kitzinger, 1969; Lewis, 1993). Used during individual meditation and group meetings, ganja is an integral element of worship (Johnson-Hill, 1995). Ganja—whether eaten, brewed into a tea, or smoked—is believed to be a mechanism through which one can gain a greater understanding of God. Furthermore, ganja is believed to allow one to see through the distorted perceptions of God that have been corrupted by others (Breiner, 1985/1986).

In some ways, the aforementioned negative backlash was inevitable. Clearly, fundamental elements of Rastafarianism reflect the clash with the white, middle-class, capitalist establishment frequently referred to metaphorically by believers as "Babylon" (Johnson-Hill, 1995). Breiner (1985/1986) notes that Babylon also refers to the location named Jamaica by Europeans, for the Rastafarian a place of captivity dominated by the West. In relation to the use of ganja, not only is its use offensive to the establishment but, according to followers, it assists the Rastafarian in realizing the many truths that are being withheld by Babylon (Kitzinger, 1969; Johnson-Hill, 1995). According to some, it is the mockery of capitalism and authority that has resulted in Rasta culture being defined as deviant and followers becoming targets. Nonetheless, the use of ganja appears to be influential in this manner.

It is no surprise, then, that ganja use is a source of controversy. For example, a 1963 Jamaican press campaign implied that users of ganja were prone to violence (Campbell, 1980). Hepner (1998) suggests that law enforcement and media portrayals perpetuate notions that violence and drug trafficking are key elements of Rastafarianism, both of which are strenuously disputed by followers. Such characterizations are remarkably similar to the "Reefer Madness" hysteria that led to the passage of the Marihuana Tax Act of 1937. Several observers, however, assert that a number of nonfollowers have adopted Rasta dress and mannerisms in order to "cloak" their violent and criminal activity within the context of a religion (Campbell, 1980; Lewis, 1989; Murrell 1998).

The extent to which Rastafarianism is a unified belief system is quite debatable, and even though "official" documents exist, doctrines are not formalized (Murrell and Taylor, 1998). The following, adapted from Taylor (1984), identifies several basic elements that are generally agreed upon by most followers.

- Most central to the Rastafarian belief system is the acknowledgment of *Haile Selassie as the living God.* Haile Selassie, emperor of Ethiopia from 1930–1935, is generally regarded as a "Messiah" to most followers of Rastafarianism. During the 1930s, a number of impoverished Jamaicans turned to their African roots and looked toward Selassie for deliverance from the Great Depression and oppression at the hands of Babylon (Lewis, 1993). For some believers, the ascension of Selassie was viewed as fulfillment of the Old Testament prophecies of the coming of the Messiah, while others view him as the incarnation of Jesus (Murrell and Taylor, 1998).
- *The black person is the reincarnation of the ancient Israelite.* Followers of Rastafarianism view their situation of poverty and oppression as being similar to the ancient Israelites, who frequently experienced hardships at the hands of others. Particular emphasis is placed on the enslavement of the Israelite and their exile into "Babylon." In fact, some contend that Haile Selassie is a descendent of King Solomon (Murrell (1998). The religious nature of Rastafarianism is enhanced because followers often consider themselves to be Israelites as well.
- Believers await the *exodus to Heaven (Ethiopia)* and the beginning of an age in which the *black man (superior to whites) will eventually rule the world* (Taylor, 1984).

In light of these principles, Lewis (1989) correctly suggests it is rather ironic that in the United States, reggae music is popular among the white middle class.

The controversial practice of ritual ganja use raises a particularly complex question: *Does the guarantee of freedom of religion in the U.S. Constitution extend to situations in which drugs are used during worship?* Legally speaking, the answer to this question is "sometimes." The line between religious expression and exploitation is a fine one, and it is extremely difficult to distinguish between legitimate versus frivolous claims. A good example of the latter occurred in the 1960s when the Neo-American Boohoo Church, whose theme song was "Row, Row, Row Your Boat," was prohibited from the sacramental use of LSD (Liska, 2000). Likewise, the sacramental use of marijuana by Rastafarians or others is not permitted, in part because it is classified as a Schedule I substance of the Controlled Substances Act of 1970. Lawrence (1990) notes that the Ethiopian

Zion Coptic Church, a Miami group whose beliefs are remarkably similar to Rastafarianism, failed in its attempt to obtain the right to use marijuana during worship (*Olsen* v. *DEA*, 878 F.2d 1458). This case is cited frequently as justification for the prohibition of ritual ganja use by Rastafarians.

On the other hand, there are noteworthy examples of the United States government allowing the use of controlled substances during worship. For example, in the Prohibition era between 1920 and 1933, the Roman Catholic Church was permitted to serve wine during communion. Perhaps the most interesting example of drug use during worship can be found in the Native American Church. In 1993, this practice was legally protected when President Clinton signed into law the Religious Freedom Restoration Act. This act in effect served to overturn a 1990 Supreme Court decision which stated that ritual peyote use was not protected under the first amendment (Peregoy, Echo-Hawk, and Botsford, 1995). The following section discusses the use of peyote among followers of the Native American Church.

THE NATIVE AMERICAN CHURCH

For thousands of years, Indian tribes in Mexico have utilized the peyote cactus during religious rituals (Institute for Substance Abuse Research, 1990). While the Native American Church was first incorporated in 1918 in Oklahoma, use of peyote in North America is believed to have begun in the early seventeenth century (Peregoy et al., 1995). Following the Civil War, Native American religion experienced particularly acute oppression. Native American beliefs did not accommodate well to European cultural traditions. Because traditional Native American religion contained a plethora of spirits, calling on these various spirits and seeing visions provided hope for these oppressed peoples, and gave the shamans who received these visions extraordinary power at the same time. Visions were often induced by self-torture and other machinations. As the quest for visions became more important to Native Americans, they began to seek alternative ways of inducing them, including chemically through tobacco, the jimson weed, and the mescal bean, as well as through peyote which had by now proliferated throughout many Native American reservations. Peyote offered a more peaceful response to Native American oppression than earlier visionary movements which promised the decimation of the white race, among other doomsday scenarios. As one anthropologist, Vittorio Lanternari, put it, "Peyotism, too, like the Ghost Dance, contained a messianic message; but whereas the Ghost Dance promised restoration of the past, Peyotism announced a new dispensation, and a renewal of Indian culture" (Lanternari, 1965, p. 81; cited in Anderson, 1996, p. 40). Current membership is estimated to be between 250,000 and 400,000 persons worldwide (Ray and Ksir, 1999; *The Economist*, 1999). Similar to Rastafarianism, the extent to which elements of Christianity are present differs by congregation. Generally speaking, church doctrine consists of a combination of Christianity and native beliefs. The sacramental use of peyote however, is commonplace.

Peyote is harvested by removing and then drying the crown of the cactus. The crowns, whether left whole or cut into pieces, are frequently referred to as "buttons." The buttons from the peyote cactus contain the psychoactive substance *mescaline* which, when eaten, smoked, or brewed into a tea can cause the user to experience hallucinations and kaleidoscope-like sensations. A typical dose of 4–12 buttons may last up to 10 hours. Usually, the substance is consumed during dusk-to-dawn rituals that include prayer, singing, and dancing. It is during these ceremonies that users experience God through the intermediary of nature, where he resides (Kiyanni and Csordas, 1997; Liska, 2000). In a symbolic sense, the use of the substance allows the believer to travel on what is frequently referred to as the "Peyote Road," which emphasizes respect for oneself, nature, and others (Kiyaani and Csordas, 1997).

As mentioned previously, the Religious Freedom Restoration Act of 1993 effectively overturned a 1990 U.S. Supreme Court decision (*Employment Division of Oregon* v. *Smith*, 494 U.S. 872) declaring that ritual use of peyote was not protected under the First Amendment. In *Smith*, followers of the Native American Church lost their jobs as a result of peyote use. Essentially, the Act precludes the federal and state governments from prohibiting the use, possession, or transportation of peyote for legitimate religious purposes (Peregoy et al., 1995). Exclusive of the provisions pertaining to the Native American Church, peyote is a Schedule I substance under the Controlled Substances Act of 1970 and possession of it is a crime. Interestingly, these exclusions granted to the Native American Church are based on political, not religious grounds. The protection to use peyote during worship is based on the justification that because Indian tribes lived in this country prior to passage of the U.S. Constitution, an element of sovereignty is recognized for a practice that has existed for centuries (Lawrence, 1990).

In the United States production and distribution of peyote for use during religious rituals is strictly monitored and controlled (Peregoy et al., 1995)[2] and use and/or abuse by nonmembers is extremely rare (Julien, 2001). The peyote cactus grows naturally in Mexico and in limited areas of Texas. Traveling to Mexico or Texas to obtain peyote is part of a lengthy and elaborate ritual (Ray and Ksir, 1999). Regulations include restrictions on both the user and the producer. As mentioned previously, ritual use of peyote is limited to members of the Native American Church only, and membership in the church is restricted to persons of at least one-quarter Indian ancestry. Presently, legitimate outlets for peyote are located in only four Texas counties, and seven individuals are licensed distributors, or *Peyoteros*. Individuals who harvest and distribute peyote to members of the Native American Church are required to follow a myriad of both federal and state regulations, including annual registration (Lawrence, 1990; *The Economist*, 1999).

THE RAVE SUBCULTURE

Based on the criteria outlined previously in this chapter, inclusion of the rave "scene" as a drug subculture is somewhat debatable. But to the extent that raves are a source of identity to participants, and because drug use occurs frequently at these parties, its inclusion is warranted. In essence, raves have evolved from an event into a party culture. A rave is defined as a dance party distinguishable in terms of music, clothing, paraphernalia, and in many instances drug use (National Drug Intelligence Center, 2001). While not all persons who attend rave parties use drugs, these substances are widely available. Use of these "club drugs," either singly or in various combinations, enhances the effect of the distinctive music played at raves. The music is usually electronically produced and is characterized as having a fast, repetitive beat and is often accompanied by psychedelic lights, smoke, fog, and water sprayed to assist in cooling participants (Weir, 2000; Keefe, 2001). Participants frequently dress in layered, loose-fitting, androgynous clothing that can be easily removed as they become overheated from dancing. Accessories and paraphernalia are usually brightly colored, and many "ravers" utilize lollipops or baby pacifiers as a remedy for the involuntary teeth grinding that often accompanies the use of club drugs (Weir, 2001; National Drug Intelligence Center, 2001).

Rave parties originated in Europe during the 1980s and have become popular in the United States as well (Marshall, 2001). Most parties are advertised as "alcohol free," so there are usually no age restrictions for admission (provided the cover charge, often in excess of $50 can be afforded), and parents are less hesitant to allow teenagers to attend. During the latter part of the 1990s, a number of popular media accounts highlighted the increasing popularity of raves, and rave parties were openly advertised using highly symbolic representations to stimulate interest in these events. Media reporting on these events often provided detailed accounts from party-goers of how drug use enhanced the experience. Information on the negative effects of these substances was minimal, and it was believed that if used "responsibly," club drugs posed little danger (National Drug Intelligence Center, 2001).

Drugs associated with parties are used to accentuate the rave experience by enhancing perceptions and visual stimulation. Substances commonly

used tend to have stimulant and/or hallucinogenic properties, including MDMA (Ecstacy), Ketamine, GHB, Rohypnol, and LSD (Drug Enforcement Administration, 2000). Club drugs possessing stimulant and/or hallucinogenic qualities are popular because they allow one to dance for hours without experiencing fatigue, and the visual and auditory sensations are dramatically enhanced (National Drug Intelligence Center, 2001).

In recent years, raves have come under increasing scrutiny because of concerns associated with drug use (Weir, 2000). A number of studies suggest that use of club drugs may result in a number of negative physical consequences, such as physical impairment, memory loss, and irreversible brain damage. Furthermore, death can result when club drugs are used in combination with other substances such as alcohol, cocaine, or heroin (National Institute on Drug Abuse, 1999).

THE STREET-HEROIN SUBCULTURE

The street-heroin subculture is comprised largely (though not exclusively) of inner-city youth and adults who are also quite heavily involved in criminal activity to sustain their drug-using lifestyles. Contrary to popular belief, however, street heroin addicts are not indiscriminate in their criminal activities, nor can they be dismissed as "moral degenerates" who willingly abandon all ethical constraint in their pursuit of heroin. The lifestyle and behavior of heroin-addicted criminals can only be understood in the subcultural context in which they live their lives. Our discussion of the heroin subculture is organized around four broadly defined components which are consistent with the characteristics of drug subcultures made by those observers of the drug scene that were discussed in the previous section. These four components are: (1) boundary-maintenance mechanisms; (2) distinctive norms, values, and ideologies; (3) specialized knowledge and skills; and (4) a distinctive social organization which provides a basis for a social identity within the subculture.

Boundary-Maintenance Mechanisms   Wherever there are identifiable social groups there are ways to distinguish between members of those groups and all others who are not members. We refer to these mechanisms for distinguishing between "in-groups" and "out-groups" as **boundary-maintenance mechanisms.** In a socially deviant world such as that inhabited by the street heroin user, these boundary-maintenance mechanisms become mandatory. Illicit drug users are often pariahs in their communities, despised by the respectable establishment, and subject to frequent surveillance and harassment by law enforcement agencies. Consequently, these individuals must be able to determine who can be trusted as a fellow member of the subculture. Two boundary-maintenance mechanisms which have evolved among heroin users and are quite effective are the use of specialized **argot,** and the assignment of **monikers,** otherwise known as *nicknames* or *street names*.

A specialized *argot* refers to the use of language in a way which is not shared by members of the larger culture. Such vernacular allows addicts to communicate with one another so that those who are not familiar with these specialized meanings—i.e., those who are not in the subculture—are effectively excluded from meaningful interaction. The description of vernacular among black heroin users by Iglehart (Drugs and Everyday Life insert) vividly demonstrates how the specialized use of language can serve to exclude outsiders from effective participation in the heroin subculture.

Iglehart (1985) suggests that while the pressures of stigmatization and threats by law enforcement necessitate the creation and use of such argot, to be overheard using such argot by the unitiated carries its own risk. Iglehart observes, in fact, that addicts often shift into standard English when interacting with outsiders.

Even more important than excluding outsiders, being able to converse in the subcultural vernacular provides a basis for cohesiveness among participants in the subculture. Street argot is often a metaphorical description of common experiences and problems faced by heroin users, and a shorthand means of communicating important information between them. In this way, the lexicon of the heroin subculture provides a basis for a common identity among street users.

Finally, it should be pointed out that just as there is regional variation in dialect and connotation in language in the straight world, such regional differences can also be observed in the drug-using world (Agar, 1973). While there are certainly commonalities of vernacular among drug users regardless of where they live and work, there are also many subtle differences. Agar (1973, p. 43) notes, for example, that the term "junkie" is commonly used throughout the United States to refer to a heroin addict (although even here, some restrict the use of "junkie" to refer to an addict that is especially "strung out.") The term "jones" on the other hand, is sometimes used to refer to a heroin habit, while in other places, refers to heroin itself. The glossary provided in the Drugs and Everyday Life closeup was derived from research among East Coast, Wilmington, Delaware area heroin addicts. Those readers who are more familiar with drug subcultures might find it interesting to compare the definitions provided in this glossary with their understanding of these terms which derive from different geographical regions, or from nonheroin drug subcultures.

Participants in drug-using subcultures often take a different name than that given to them at birth. These *monikers,* or *street names* are not taken or assigned arbitrarily. They are typically applied to symbolize some aspect of a participant's personality, biography, physique, or some other identifiable characteristic feature. Examples of such names include "Taxi-cab Mike," "Bent Over Bennie," "Put Your Lights Out Bernie," "Hanky-Panky Marie," and "Stone-Face Eddie."[3]

These appellations are not unique to drug-using subcultures. A similar process occurs among professional criminals (Inciardi, 1975), religious cults (Zellner, 2001), and in prisons and other total institutions (Irwin, 1980). Indeed, most young boys and many young girls have had the experience of being given a nickname. These experiences are not unlike those of participants in drug subcultures who are given street names. Importantly, these

DRUGS AND EVERYDAY LIFE

The Language of the Heroin Subculture

Vernacular in the Black Inner City Heroin Lifestyle

We laid around, shot the beast . . . up and down in the street, bullshit in the street, messin' around . . . I seen a guy I know coming from work and borrowed a pound off him. So that there was cop street. We got the half, and then we had problems who's gonna oil it . . . none of our cribs was cool . . . galleries ain't where it's at . . . two dollars a person to get in. They works, the shit all dirty . . . most of the guys like old houses— I case them out if I can. (Mr. Ben, age 27, Philadelphia)

Those outside the Black heroin lifestyle may be totally confused by the above statement. Yet, within the Black heroin subculture, it is easily understood. Mr. Ben was socializing and talking. He borrowed five dollars, which meant he now had enough money, approximately $20, to buy a half a quarter-teaspoon of heroin. Where to inject it then became a problem. He and the other heroin users couldn't use their living quarters for activities unacceptable to outsiders. The shooting galleries, which, for a fee, supply shelter and paraphernalia for injection, weren't desirable, perhaps because the paraphernalia is often unsanitary. Most people Mr. Ben knows prefer abandoned houses; he tries to investigate them in advance to make sure each is a relatively safe place in which to inject heroin.

Commonly Used Argot in the Heroin Subculture

bag—The most basic unit in which heroin is bought and sold on the street, typically about 90 milligrams.

big sting—A particularly lucrative score from a criminal hustle.

boost—To shoplift.

boy—Heroin. This is a term often used when *speedballing.* Heroin is referred to as the *boy* and cocaine as the *girl.*

bundle—The bulk equivalent of about 25 bags available from wholesale dealers.

chasing the bag—All the activities involved in securing heroin for consumption, including *hustling,* locating *connections, copping,* etc.

cook—To prepare heroin for use; done by mixing heroin with water and heating it with a match or cigarette lighter until it dissolves.

cop—To purchase heroin.

crib—One's home.

cut—To dilute heroin; or the dilutant in heroin.

fix—A shot of heroin.

hustle—Criminal or quasi-criminal means of obtaining money for drugs.

jones—Withdrawal symptoms experienced when withdrawing from heroin.

juggling—Small time dealing.

main hustle—One's primary *hustle.*

mainline—To inject heroin directly into the vein.

panic—A shortage of heroin in an area, often intentionally created by wholesale dealers.

re-up—Replenish one's drug supply.

righteous dope—Good, high-quality heroin.

run—A sequence of stores targeted by shoplifters.

score—The proceeds from a criminal *hustle;* also, the act of purchasing drugs.

speedball—A combination of heroin and cocaine.

stash—One's supply of heroin.

step on—To *cut.* Each time a quantity of heroin is *stepped on,* its purity is typically reduced by 50 percent.

continued

continued from previous page

strung out—To be totally out of control of one's heroin consumption.

wake-up shot—First shot taken in the morning, immediately after getting out of bed.

works—Needle and syringe ■

Source: Excerpted from Austin S. Iglehart, "Brickin' it and Going to the Pan: Vernacular in the Black Inner-City Heroin Lifestyle." In Bill Hanson et al., *Life With Heroin: Voices From the Inner City.* Lexington, MA: Lexington Books, 1985, p. 111; and Charles E. Faupel, *Shooting Dope: Career Patterns of Hard-Core Heroin Users.* Gainesville, FL: University of Florida Press, 1991, pp. 191–97.

street names provide the basis for a very special identity and attachment to the subculture of heroin use. This name not only symbolizes some physical or biographical feature of an individual, but represents acceptance into a very significant set of social relations. Street heroin users are known to each other primarily by these *monikers,* an identity they do not generally share with those who are not in some way associated with the subculture.

Distinctive Norms, Values, and Ideologies   In addition to the symbolic boundary maintenance mechanisms discussed above, street heroin subcultures can be distinguished from the larger culture by special and often unique norms and values which guide the behavior of subcultural participants. All subcultures of drug use impose the expectation that their members will consume drugs. Some, including the street heroin subculture, also demand some level of criminal or quasi-criminal behavior, an activity commonly referred to as *getting over* (e.g., see Goldstein, 1981). These subcultural norms clearly violate the normative code of most Americans who are not part of such a subculture.

The normative code of the heroin subculture is far more complex than merely demanding the consumption of heroin and engaging in illegal behavior. The subcultural participant is guided rather clearly as to *when* and *under what conditions* it is appropriate to use drugs. It is regarded as highly inappropriate to shoot up in the presence of children or strangers (Faupel, 1991). An offer to "turn on" a young child to heroin is even more strongly sanctioned. There are also commonly understood rules for who makes an appropriate victim or *mark* when engaging in criminal hustles. One can observe a *scale of social distance* that is not so unlike that which can be found in the dominant culture. Contrary to popular belief, heroin addicts prefer not to steal from their own families or close friends to get their copping money. To the contrary, they are much more likely to target large, impersonal department stores if they are a shoplifter, or break into houses in a neighborhood across town if they are a burglar. Because their victims are not personally known to them, it is much easier for them to justify their criminal actions.

Fiddle (1963) has observed that one important element of drug subcultures is an "ideology of justification." This feature is especially pronounced with regard to the criminal activities of street heroin users. Heroin-using criminals justify their actions in many ways, some of which were reported to one of the authors of this book. One such justification might be called the "just desserts" doctrine. Shoplifters frequently use this one, legitimizing their actions against large department stores such as Macy's or Bloomingdales by complaining that these companies have been "ripping off" consumers for years. Hence, they (the companies) are only getting what they deserve. Sykes and Matza (1957) referred to such a justification as a "denial of victim." Another justification could be called the "drop-in-the-bucket doctrine," claiming that the amount of goods that were taken were insignificant in comparison with the large profits realized by the company. This technique, which Sykes and Matza call "denial of injury" plays on the theory that no one was victimized unduly. A related justification which plays on the same theory is that these merchants are insured for their losses anyway, so no one is hurt. Check forgers rationalize their crimes in the same way, claiming that neither the bank nor the individual depositor is victimized because both are insured under the FDIC. A check forger interviewed by one of the authors went so far as to say that he would only forge checks on banks that were insured by the FDIC, and he added that if the individual depositor was stupid enough not to take advantage of getting reimbursed by the FDIC, they deserved to be taken anyway (the "just desserts doctrine" or denial of victim).

In sum, contrary to the popularly believed "dope fiend mythology" (Lindesmith, 1940), drug users do not suffer from an inevitable moral deterioration because of their addiction. Rather, they have adopted an alternative normative code which facilitates their being able to function in the social worlds of which they are a part. These normative codes come complete with ideologies and rationales to justify their behavior in the face of a critical and perhaps hostile cultural environment. The process by which drug users become socialized into this new normative system is discussed in greater detail later in this chapter when we talk about drug-using careers.

Specialized Knowledge and Skills   Many observers of the street scene have noted that heroin users are skilled entrepreneurs who possess highly sophisticated talents and knowledge (Biernacki, 1979; Faupel, 1986, 1987a, 1991; Hanson et al., 1985; and Preble and Casey, 1969). Simply considering the skills and knowledge required for consuming the drug, heroin addicts have to know where to *cop* (purchase) good quality heroin. Unless they are *snorting* (sniffing the drug through their nose), addicts must know how to blend the heroin powder with water and to *cook* the heroin by heating it in a *cooker*, typically a twist-off soda bottle cap. Following this, it is necessary to draw the heroin into a syringe, filtering it for impurities with cotton or even a cigarette filter. Addicts who *mainline* (inject directly into the vein) must also learn how to *tie-up* so as to adequately expose the vein. It is also a challenge for many to learn how to *bang* (inject) themselves properly, being sure to penetrate the vein wall without going all the way through both walls of the vein (in which case, of course, the heroin solution would not be deposited in the vein).

Because of the costly nature of heroin, most addicts have also cultivated criminal skills which are invaluable in helping them to support their habit. (See Chapter 10 for a discussion of the complex relationship between drug use and criminal behavior.) Ethnographers who study heroin addicts have long recognized the skillful and entrepreneurial character of the crimes that they commit (Biernacki, 1979; Goldstein, 1981; Hanson et al., 1985; Preble and Casey, 1969; Sackman et al., 1978; and Waldorf, 1973). Regardless of the type of criminal enterprise, there are certain skills that must be mastered. Each type of crime presents its own challenges, of course; the skills that must be mastered by burglars, of *casing,* and *breaking and entering* without detection are not especially relevant to a prostitute or a check forger. Persons involved in these *hustles* must have developed a keen awareness of the behavior and body language of other people. Prostitutes, for example, must be able to distinguish undercover police officers from would-be *johns.* Similarly, they must be able to size up a *john* quickly to determine if he is a *freak* (one who will make outrageous demands on them, typically of a sado-masochistic nature) or, by contrast, if he will be a rather generous *trick.* Check forgers must be able to present a convincing facade when they present a bank teller with someone else's check, and then be able to quickly read the teller's reaction to this facade. Failure to do either may well result in their arrest.

While most addict-criminals are probably not highly specialized professionals, many if not most street addicts develop a level of expertise that provides a basis for a reasonable income. Gould et al. (1974, p. 52) suggest that:

> . . . the average, middle of the road dope fiend is much more successful than these losers. He usually has one or two hustles which he is fairly good at, but he knows enough about other hustles to be able to boost at Christmas time, work the parking lots in June when the universities are having graduation, and deal a little dope on the side to make ends meet.

This observation suggests that while addict criminals may not be highly specialized professionals, they do tend to gravitate toward some crimes more than others for their criminal income. This reality is what is meant when addicts speak of their *main hustle.* While they may engage in any number of *hustles* from time to time, they tend to fall back on one or two *main hustles* as their primary means of support.

Distinctive Social Organization   Drug subcultures resemble the dominant cultures of which they are a part in that work and other activities are organized and carried out according to broadly defined subcultural expectations. Just as we find specialization of work roles in the legitimate work world, there is a corresponding division of labor in street heroin subculture. As we have seen, addict-criminals tend to develop a *main hustle,* a criminal specialization which allows them to develop sophisticated skills for successfully carrying out their crimes. When this happens, they become identified with their specialties. They become known as a *booster* (shoplifter), an *ounce man* (middle-level drug dealer), or perhaps a *strong-arm man* (armed robber). There are also other identities that street heroin users may acquire. They may be a *tout* or a *steer*, working for a dealer to identify potential customers, advertise the dealer's drugs (touting) and letting them know where they can obtain them (steering). Others may play the part of a *bag man*, physically holding a dealer's drugs. (These individuals are hired by dealers to reduce their risk of getting caught.) Still others may act as *testers* for dealers, injecting small amounts of heroin into their bloodstream to determine the quality of the drug.

Sociologists refer to these "positions" in a social system as *social statuses*. Furthermore, the behavioral expectations that are attached to these positions are called *roles*. How well people perform these roles provides an important basis for social identity, a fact of life in conventional society as well as in drug subcultures. Professors, for example, are evaluated on how well they perform, and as a result get the reputation as being "good" or "bad," "boring" or "interesting", "tough" or "easy." Drug users also occupy statuses within the social system of the drug subculture, and are expected to perform roles that are attached to those statuses (Smeja and Rojek, 1986). Shoplifters, for example, know that when they work in pairs, one member of the team acts as a "lookout" for *floorwalkers* while the other performs that act of theft. Similarly, drug dealers must *cop* quantities of drugs from a wholesale dealer, *cut* these drugs by reducing the concentration of heroin in them, and finally *bag* the drugs for retail distribution. The challenge for the street-level drug dealer is to make as much money as he or she can, while at the same time maintaining a reputation as having, good quality dope (or as they say on the street *righteous dope*). Goldstein et al. (1984) highlight the practical importance of maintaining a good reputation for having good quality heroin in a descriptive study of "trade names" that are used to market heroin in New York City. These authors identified approximately 400 such labels which are used by dealers to identify their products. Some of these "brand names" were *Black Death, Cadillac, Down and Dirty, Feel Like Dynamite, Good Pussy, Pink Panther, Not Responsible, Smoking Joe,* and *Georgia Mud,* among many others. These trade names are employed, according to the authors, as a marketing device. They are a means of communicating to a would-be buyer the dealer who is distributing these drugs, and therefore the quality of the drugs that he or she is purchasing. Dealers get a reputation for having "good righteous dope" or for having "nothing but cut," and the brand names are a convenient name of quality dealers advertising their product. Goldstein et al. (1984) further note that dealers occasionally have to change their trade name because another dealer with lower quality drugs has appropriated it or perhaps a user has purchased the drugs, shot them up, and replaced the contents of the same bag with something other than heroin to resell. If these practices occur on a widespread scale, the dealer's reputation will suffer, and hence it is in his or her interest to change the label as quickly as possible. Similar practices also occur in the legitimate market place, of course, but when they do, it is possible for the wronged party to file suit in court against the person committing the violation for unfair trading practices. Drug dealers do not have such protections.

There is, furthermore, a system of *social stratification* in street heroin subcultures, which provides for different levels of rewards to various statuses in the subculture. Weppner (1973), for example, observed:

> There is a definite multilevel status hierarchy in subculture of addiction which runs from the high-class player, who is admired and emulated, to a garbage junkie, who is on the lowest end of the addict social ladder. The former is an individual who has a very lucrative hustle, such as pimping for a large number of prostitutes. He dresses expensively and may have a large bankroll, a flashy car, and body guards. The latter is the individual who can support his heroin habit only by providing a "shooting gallery" (a place to use drugs) and "works" (the hypodermics to administer them). . . . He is considered to have sunk very low on the status scale. (Weppner, 1973, p. 115).

Weppner's discussion of stratification in the drug subculture suggests an economic base. That is, those addicts who are self-supporting and have lucrative hustles, and who can afford to engage in conspicuous consumption activities (such as buying flashy cars) are accorded greater status in the subculture. Those who do not have these resources are regarded with much greater disdain.

Other researchers have identified hierarchies of drug dealing. One of the early attempts in this area was Preble and Casey's (1969) study of heroin distribution hierarchies in New York City, ranging from the importer at the top of the distribution hierarchy to the juggler at the bottom. Adler (1985) presents a similar hierarchy for marijuana and cocaine dealing. These hierarchies are more restricted to those who engage in the dealing enterprise, but nevertheless demonstrate the ever-present reality of social stratification in drug subcultures.

DRUG-USING CAREERS

When we suggest that drug use and addiction can be understood as **careers,** it almost seems as though we are implying that the activities of drug users are comparable somehow to that of lawyers, doctors, nurses, truck drivers, and other people who work in the legitimate marketplace. In many ways, that is exactly what we are implying. The concept of the "career" was first used by sociologists studying occupations to refer to "the sequence of movement from one position to another in an occupational system by any individual who works in that system" (Becker, 1963:24). The term has also been used by criminologists and other sociologists for many years to understand deviant behavior as well. Goffman (1959, 1961) first introduced this concept to the deviance literature in his discussions of the moral careers of mental patients. Howard Becker (1963) would later extend the application of career to other forms of deviance as well including drug addiction (e.g., see Coombs, 1981; Faupel, 1991; Fiddle, 1976; Rubington, 1967). This section examines career dynamics generally, followed by a special focus on the nature of drug-using careers and especially heroin-using careers.

TYPES OF CAREERS

The concept of "career" is very inclusive, and has been used to examine everything from professional occupational careers such as medicine or law to avocational careers such as volunteer, to deviant careers such as burglary, prostitution, and drug use. Hence, it might be helpful to differentiate between four broad types of careers which can be distinguished on the basis of whether they are *respectable or deviant,* and whether they are *occupational or nonoccupational* in nature.

Respectable vs. Deviant Careers   Respectable careers comprise those activities which are normatively acceptable or even encouraged in the larger culture. In this respect, doctors, lawyers, and other professions are respectable careers. Homemaking, hobbies, and volunteer activities can also be respectable careers. Deviant careers, on the other hand, consist of activities that violate social norms, and consist of criminal behavior patterns as well as noncriminal lifestyles, such as nudism and mental illness, that nevertheless violate commonly accepted standards. These too can be understood as careers (e.g., Bryan, 1966; Faupel, 1991; Goffman, 1959; Wallace, 1965; Weinberg, 1966).

There are important differences between deviant and respectable careers. Luckenbill and Best (1981) point out that because of the deviant (and often illegal) character of deviant careers, these activities must often be carried out in secret or restricted to a small circle of acquaintances who share this lifestyle. Furthermore, the threat of punitive sanctions introduces an additional cost, or potential cost, to these lines of activities, a calculation which does not have to be made by those pursuing respectable careers. Moreover, unlike many respectable careers, deviant careers are not usually carried out in a structured institutional environment. As a result, the sequence of statuses and roles is typically less predictable for those in deviant careers, making it more difficult to measure one's "progress." Unlike the upwardly mobile executive, for example, who measures his or her progress by increased responsibilities and periodic salary increases, this pattern of progression is not usually so clear with deviant careers. Indeed, the stigmatization that often accompanies deviant careers often results in what most outsiders would probably consider *downward* mobility. Drug addicts who become known by local law enforcement agents, for example, may be pressured to become informants. When this happens, it is difficult to maintain quality *connections* (dependable sources of drugs), and the addict may be forced to rely on low quality "street dope," an indication of downward mobility, even in the street culture of hard drug use. On the other hand, having "done time" in a state penitentiary often contributes to the prestige that an individual enjoys on the street. The important feature of deviant careers illustrated here is that there is no clear line of progression in career mobility that most respectable careers enjoy.

Occupational vs. Nonoccupational Careers   We usually think of careers in terms of occupational pursuits, such as doctors, lawyers, nurses, or perhaps truck drivers and machinists. Generally, we might characterize these

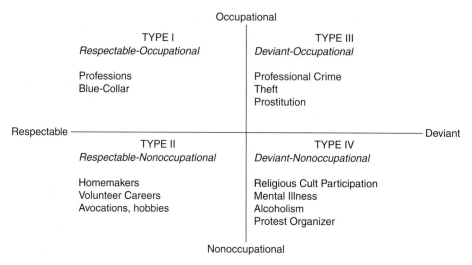

Figure 5.1 Types of Careers

Source: Charles E. Faupel, 1991, *Shooting Dope: Career Patterns of Hard Core Heroin Users*, Gainseville, FL: University of Florida Press, p. 28.

occupational careers as the sequence of statuses, roles, and activities that one engages in for purposes of making a living—what we commonly call *work*. Sociologists have a much broader understanding of career than simply work or professional pursuits. Some 35 years ago, well-known sociologist Everett C. Hughes (1958) was careful to emphasize a broader understanding of career when he talked about homemaking and civic involvement as a career. Hence, we can also speak of *nonoccupational* careers, which include a host of activities around which people meaningfully organize their lives, even though these activities are not a means of livelihood.

Figure 5.1 illustrates four broad types of careers that can be identified on the basis of their normative (deviant vs. respectable) and occupational status. We can see from this figure that it is possible to think in terms of "respectable-occupational" (Type I), "respectable-nonoccupational" (Type II), "deviant-occupational" (Type III) and "deviant-nonoccupational" (Type IV) careers. Included in Figure 5.1 are some specific examples of careers that have been discussed by social scientists that represent each career type.

Drug Use and Career Types

The nature of drug-using careers is dependent upon, among other things, the type of drug that one uses, and how one uses it. Marijuana, for example, is a relatively inexpensive drug which is affordable to a teenager on even a modest allowance. Hence, most individuals who use only marijuana on even a regular basis are probably pursuing Type IV (deviant-nonoccupational) careers. Users of expensive drugs, however, or extremely frequent users of more inexpensive drugs (such as crack cocaine) often find themselves pursuing dual careers as a *drug user* and a *criminal* in order to sustain their habits. This distinction between what Goldman (1981) has called "consumer activities" and "income-generating activities" is important, for it suggests that such heavily involved drug users are typically pursuing multidimensional careers—that of drug consumer and (typically) that of criminal. Importantly, for most of these individuals, criminal profits are not used merely to support a drug habit, although drugs certainly comprise a good share of their consumer budget. Criminal profits are also used to buy nice clothes, cars, and other consumer items. Successful drug-using criminals are, in short, making a living, not unlike those in respectable occupations. As one heroin-using criminal reported to one of the authors, "It was business to me then. My addiction was business. What I had to sell was business. I was very businesslike in manner too. Because it wasn't a game that I was playing." In this respect, many, perhaps most, individuals who use expensive drugs such as heroin or cocaine on a frequent basis are involved occupationally in criminal careers. Agar (1973) captures this quality of heroin careers in the title of his book *Ripping and Running,* a phrase which describes the frenetic pace the heroin-user's criminal lifestyle. Similarly, Biernacki (1979) describes "junkie work" as the criminal hustles which are the basis for the attribution of status in the addict subculture. Indeed Biernacki, and later Faupel (1986, 1991) have found that addicts tend to specialize in a "main hustle" at which they become quite adept in much the same way that individuals pursuing respectable occupational careers tend to specialize in some kind of work. It is, therefore, appropriate to characterize these criminally involved drug users as being engaged in Type III (Deviant-Occupational) careers.

There is, however, another aspect of drug-using careers which relates to the consumer activities of all drug users. These consumer activities consist of those behaviors and reputations that develop around the acquisition and consumption of drugs. Drug users must learn to locate, purchase, and prepare the drugs that they use. They must also learn how to ingest the drug, whether mainlining, snorting, or smoking. Some mainline users even gain respect in the subculture of heroin use for being able to locate and "hit" veins readily. Of course, being able to ingest high-quality drugs and still be able to function, whether it be heroin, cocaine, marijuana, or any other drug, enhances the stature of a drug user in the subculture considerably. These features associated with drug use as a consumer activity predominantly reflect the dynamics of Type IV (Deviant-Nonoccupational) careers.

THE TEMPORAL QUALITY OF DRUG-USING CAREERS

Careers have a temporal quality, which means that they unfold over time and have distinctive characteristics at different periods. Studies of occupational careers, for example, have identified at least three periods, which can broadly be identified as career choice and entry (the early, initial period of careers), career mobility (the period throughout one's occupational lifespan), and career exiting (e.g., retirement).

Drug-using careers have a similar life span, although the terminology is different. Drug users, for example, do not speak of career choice or entry, but rather refer to their early drug-using activities as *turning on*, and will often experiment with several kinds of drugs before settling into their drug of choice. This early period of their careers is, for many, also a time of criminal experimentation until they ultimately settle into their *main hustle*. Having settled into a drug-using and perhaps a criminal lifestyle, these individuals experience many of the same ups and downs that occur in any occupational career, except that these fluctuations are usually much more extreme than that found in most respectable occupational (Type I) careers. More than three decades ago, for example, it was observed that addicts go through a series of periods of abstinence and relapse throughout the course of their careers (Ray, 1961), a pattern that has also been observed by several observers of the drug scene since that time (e.g., Akers et al., 1968; Coombs, 1981; Waldorf, 1971). Similarly, with regard to the criminal activities that sustain expensive drug-using activities, a pattern of frequent "occupational shifts" has been observed (Biernacki, 1979; Fiddle, 1976; James et al., 1976). Indeed, Marsha Rosenbaum, who has studied female drug use very extensively, describes the career of the female addict as "chaotic" (1981). Heroin addicts talk about *getting hooked* (becoming addicted), *jonesing* (withdrawing) developing a *main hustle*, and *getting busted*. This is all to suggest that careers in drug use are subject to conditions contributing to great fluctuation in ability to sustain one's lifestyle, what in conventional careers is referred to as upward and downward mobility.

Finally, while drug users do not usually characterize their leaving the drug scene as "retirement," this waning period is very much a part of most drug-using careers. This aspect of deviant careers has not been widely studied, though there has been some attention to this career phase in the literature (Sommers, Baskin and Fagan, 1994; Sommers, 2001; Waldorf, Reinarman and Murphy, 1991). Charles Winick (1962) described this process among heroin addicts as "maturing out." Waldorf (1983) found that while some addicts do exit their careers through maturing out, there are other patterns of "retirement" as well. Some become converts to religious or other social causes. Still others join the ranks of alcoholics or the mentally ill. There are also many who do not leave the lifestyle completely, but simply scale down their activities considerably, dibbling and dabbling in drugs and crime. Addicted users describe this process as *shaking the monkey*, or *burning out*. To facilitate this process, many enroll in treatment centers, or in some cases seek to voluntarily scale down their drug use and criminal activity.

The temporal character of drug-using careers has been described by several observers of the drug scene. Most of these studies have focused on careers of heroin users. One of the first attempts to define drug use in terms of a career was that of Isidor Chein and his associates in their groundbreaking book, *The Road to H* (1964). This book was a study of black, Puerto Rican, and white teenage heroin users in New York City. While they did not promote the term "career" for the sequence of involvement among the drug users they studied, Chein et al. identified four distinct stages of drug involvement among the teenagers they studied: *experimentation, occasional use, regular use,* and *attempting to quit the habit.* Chein et al. rely primarily on the euphoric effect of the drug and psychological characteristics of the users to explain why some teenagers in their study went on from experimentation to occasional to regular drug use and others did not. Shortly after the publication of *The Road to H,* Earl Rubington (1967) first applied the term "career" to these stages of addiction described earlier by Chein et al. Furthermore, Rubington attempted to understand these levels of drug involvement in the context of the addict subculture and describe some of the cultural contingencies that tend to shape these careers. He notes, for example, that experimentation with drugs is a special rite of passage for adolescents living in inner-city slum neighborhoods where there is a high level of drug use. Furthermore, the role redefinition that occurs after they successfully accomplish this rite of passage effectively blocks off other opportunities in the conventional world, and they are likely to become ever more deeply involved in the world of habitual drug use.

A similar career model has been developed by Coombs (1981), who identifies four distinctive phases to a drug using career: *initiation, escalation, maintenance,* and *discontinuation and renewal.* During the early initiation period, teenagers are motivated to experiment with drugs out of a need for independence from parental authority, a need for adventure, and a need for peer approval. This initiation period is an apprenticeship period during which the young drug user must establish the trust of others in the subculture. Successful initiation opens opportunities in the way of "connections" and criminal hustles that foster the escalation of drug using and criminal activities. The maintenance period, according to Coombs, is the "mature" period of addiction. Whereas during the experimentation and escalation periods, drug use was an exciting challenge, the maintenance period is one in which the addict's activities focus almost exclusively on obtaining supplies of the drug. Stated differently, "the pursuit of drugs is serious business, not fun and games" (Coombs, 1981:380). It is a matter of survival. Finally, one's drug use may be interrupted for any number of reasons ranging from involuntary incarceration or treatment to voluntary abstention. Rarely, however, do addicts discontinue their drug use permanently, according to Coombs. They will resume their consumption after they get out of prison or treatment or after they scale down their habit to more controllable proportions. Only those who have "burned out"—those who have failed, have lost their resources and social standing among their peers—are likely to consider leaving their career permanently. According to Coombs, this is the time in an addict's career when treatment programs can have their most significant impact.

More recently, Faupel (1991) has elaborated a model of heroin-using careers based on two important "contingencies," which he maintains are critical in explaining career patterns of heroin users. According to Faupel, the careers of heroin users are profoundly affected by levels of *drug availability* and *life structure. Drug availability* refers to all of the eventualities that make drug consumption possible. The term thus encompasses more than merely access to dealers who have quantities of the drug to sell, although this is certainly a part of what is meant by availability. In addition, the user must have resources to purchase the drug, whether this be money or various sorts of payment in kind such the trading of sexual services for drugs. It is not surprising therefore, that drug use increases considerably after addicts become adept at criminal behavior, as the proceeds of crime provide the necessary resources to enhance drug availability. Drug availability can also be enhanced through decreased costs, such as when a user "connects" with a wholesale dealer rather than relying on more expensive, retail "street dope."

Life structure refers to the various roles played by drug users which serve to pattern their behavior in a regular and predictable manner. It has been found, for example, the heroin addicts maintain reasonably predictable routines throughout most of their careers as drug users (Beschner and Brower, 1985; Walters, 1985). Many of these roles are conventional in nature, and not very different from those of most nonusers. Many addicts work at conventional jobs, spend time with their families, go grocery shopping, get their children ready for school, etc. In addition, criminally involved addicts structure their days (and nights) through the criminal roles they perform. Shoplifters, for example, frequently establish regular sequences of stores and malls from which they *boost* (steal) during morning and afternoon hours, and *fence* (sell) what they have stolen during late afternoon hours.

Life structure is especially important to drug-using careers because it represents a degree of stability to one's lifestyle. The regularity of events in one's daily life defines one's routines, and allows an individual to maintain control over his or her actions. It is within the daily structure of conventional and criminal routines that heroin addicts *cop* and *shoot* drugs. Drug use is, in effect, "scheduled" as part of one's daily routine. Without such regularity, there is a lack of normative clarity by which to define appropriate actions, especially one's drug use. With large amounts of free, unstructured time on one's hands, the addict does not have a daily routine to "schedule" his or her drug use, and consequently, if the resources are there, he or she is likely to lose control over their drug consumption.

According to Faupel, heroin-using careers are patterned by the intersection of these two contingencies, *drug availability* and *life structure*. Figure 5.2 illustrates these career patterns.

The Occasional User   This period of drug use generally characterizes the beginning user, a period that Coombs (1981) refers to as *initiation*. Levels of drug availability are low due to the fact that at this early point in one's career, wholesale drug "connections" have not yet been established. Also, the beginning user has not yet sufficiently learned a criminal trade to provide a lucrative income to purchase drugs. Early periods of drug-using careers are typically characterized by a comparatively high degree of life structure, according to Faupel. Young novices may be still in school, which occupies a considerable portion of their day. Those who are older when they become involved in

	Life Structure	
Availability	High	Low
High	The stable addict	The freewheeling addict
Low	The occasional user	The street junkie

Figure 5.2 **A Typology of Heroin-Using Career Phases**

Source: Charles E. Faupel, 1991, *Shooting Dope: Career Patterns of Hard Core Heroin Users*, Gainseville, FL: University of Florida Press, p. 47.

drugs may be working at conventional jobs, engaged in domestic responsibilities such as homemaking and child rearing, or involved in any number of avocational interests which occupy their time. These conventional roles provide a strong basis for life structure among many beginning drug users.

Not surprisingly, Faupel found that during this early period of drug-using careers, criminal and drug-using skills were least developed. Interestingly, however, this was also the career period in which drug users most frequently violated the ethical code of the subculture. Novice occasional users frequently turned their nonusing friends on to drugs as one would share a cigarette with a friend. Similarly, this is a time when a young user is most likely to steal money for drugs from his or her family members.

This early period of drug-using careers may last days, weeks, months, or even years. Zinberg (1984) found that there are many heroin users who never move beyond this limited and "controlled" drug use stage. Similarly, Waldorf, Reinarman and Murphy (1991) found that many of their respondents maintained controlled levels of cocaine use for years at a time. For most addicts, however, the limited involvement of occasional users eventually gives way to more systematic and frequent drug use.

The Stable Addict   This career phase is characteristic of the mature, seasoned user, a phase analogous to what Coombs (1981) refers to as *maintenance*. The basic skills necessary to maintain a drug-using lifestyle—knowing how to cop one's drugs, and in the case of heroin users, cooking and injecting, as well as the rudiments of criminal hustling—are learned during the occasional use period. The challenge of the stable addict period, in contrast, is to *maintain* a successful criminal-addict lifestyle. Criminal specialties, or *main hustles* are cultivated during this period which increase the level of one's income, and therefore his or her drug availability. Furthermore, by the time they become stable addicts, most heroin users have developed wholesale copping connections which can supply them with high quality heroin at a reasonable price, a strategy which also increased drug availability through lowered cost.

The stable addict period is also characterized by a comparatively high degree of life structure, although the basis for this structure has changed dramatically. Whereas during the occasional use period, the beginning user was still involved in school, legitimate employment or a myriad of other conventional roles which structured daily routine, the stable addict is immersed in a criminal lifestyle which provides an alternative basis for this life structure. Burglars, for example, typically "case" residential and commercial areas during the day as part of other activities in which they are engaged, and carry out the actual burglary at night. Shoplifters often establish one or more regular "runs," sequences of malls and shopping centers from which they steal. Their fencing, drug copping, and using are all part of a daily routine which is given structure by the patterns of their runs.

Other criminal specialties provide a similar structure, whether it be prostitution, drug dealing, armed robbery, or a combination of two or more such *main hustles*. The importance of criminal specialization during the stable addict career phase, therefore, is measured by both the increased level of drug availability it affords, and by providing a daily structure which allows the addict to maintain some level of control over his or her drug consumption.

The Free-Wheeling Addict   This career phase is characterized by unprecedented levels of drug consumption. Unlike the stable addict period, where drug use may be heavy but always bounded by the structured routines that provide a basis for self-control, the free-wheeling addict has lost control over his or her habit. This period of heroin use may be brought on by any number of factors, such as the divorce or death of a spouse, loss of a job, or even a temporary disruption to one's daily routine. Having developed a tolerance for heroin, the addict is extremely dependent on the external constraints to his or her consumption provided by a highly structured daily routine. When these routines are abandoned, the addict is at the mercy of the physiological cravings that he or she is reminded of almost continuously.

Most commonly, however, the free-wheeling phase of addiction is brought on by the *big sting*, an unusually lucrative *score* from (typically) some criminal action. When this occurs, the addict is not required to maintain a rigorous criminal lifestyle because he or she now has plenty of money to buy drugs without having to worry about getting more. Consequently, the addict who has just hit the *big sting* typically abandons his or her usual criminal routines and enjoys a rather extravagant, leisurely lifestyle. With no rigorous daily routine to gauge their drug consumption, free-wheeling addicts tend to let their habits escalate out of control. In his book, Faupel weaves the story of "Harry," a hard-working burglar who toiled almost daily as a burglar to maintain his heroin habit, as well as pay for gas for his car, clothing, and other incidental expenses. A friend of his dropped by one day with a roll of bills worth several thousand dollars and asked him to join him holding up grocery stores. Harry reports that the money was substantially better, working only a three-day workweek. Harry's drug availability thus increased dramatically with his increased income, and the life structure provided by his daily burglary routines was abandoned. He reported that not only did his heroin use increase astronomically, but he started using cocaine on a regular basis and generally expanded his consumer lifestyle in an uncontrollable fashion. He was, in a phrase, living high off the hog.

The problem is that this free-wheeling phase cannot last forever. The money and the drugs eventually run out. At this point, if the addict has not severed all connections, he or she may return to a stable addict period. Often, however, free-wheeling dynamics set in motion a process of dissociation from fellow-criminals and from wholesale dealers because the free-wheeling addict is not dependent on them for his supply. When this happens, the free-wheeling addict will probably find him or herself faced with the dilemma of the street junkie.

The Street Junkie   This period, characterized by low life structure and low availability, most closely approximates the stereotyped image that most people have of heroin addicts. It is as "street junkies" that addicts are most down and out and desperate for drugs, pathetically unkempt and not able to maintain even the most rudimentary hygienic standards. They literally live a hand-to-mouth—or perhaps more appropriately, a hand-to-arm existence.

This situation may be brought on by either an erosion of life structure, such as the loss of a job, death or divorce of a spouse, or other disruptions which may erode the stable routines of a user. More typically, however, this street junkie career phase is brought on as a result of exhausting one's resources during a free-wheeling phase. Having developed an extremely large tolerance for drugs, and having abandoned criminal hustling routines, it is not unusual for addicts in this situation to find themselves desperate, willing to do nearly anything for a "fix." Because they have probably also severed their wholesale connections, however, they must typically pay top retail "street" prices for their dope, which only exacerbates their situation. Finding themselves in this situation, street junkies often abandon their own ethical codes in search of a bag. Such is the difficult dilemma of the street junkie.

It should be pointed out that the stereotypical image that most Americans have of heroin addicts is that of the street junkie. Faupel maintains that there is good reason for this. It is the street junkie who is most likely to seek out treatment centers, where researchers and the media have most ready access to populations of heroin addicts to do their stories. Similarly, it is the street junkie who is most likely to commit a crime on impulse because of an immediate felt need for dope and, because of this carelessness, is most likely to be caught. Consequently, the image of the heroin addict most visible to criminal justice officials is also that of the street junkie. Faupel cautions, however, that street junkie dynamics are only one small part of heroin-using careers. It is impossible to fully understand the dynamics of heroin addiction, he maintains, without understanding the other three career phases as well.

SUMMARY

This chapter began with a particular set of presuppositions about drug use that are unique to sociology and perhaps a handful of other social sciences such as anthropology. Those presuppositions are that (1) drug use and activities associated with drug use such as criminal behavior can only be understood in the social and cultural context in which these behaviors take place; and (2) when understood in this context, these behaviors are generally not pathological or abnormal, but are quite reasonable and understandable, reflecting a conformity to social and cultural expectations of that cultural context. This is so wherever there are subcultures of drug use that have evolved, as illustrated by the four subcultures that we have examined in this chapter. Indeed, we suggested that in most respects, drug-using lifestyles reflect similar dynamics as conventional lifestyles. Drug users, it was suggested, pursue careers which are defined by contingencies in the addict's cultural environment.

Because illegal drug use is criminal in nature, in some cases sanctioned severely by the criminal justice system, the activities associated with this lifestyle are not part of the cultural mainstream. Drug subcultures provide an alternative cultural and social environment which rewards rather than punishes these deviant behaviors. Furthermore, these subcultures provide valuable boundary maintenance mechanisms in the form of a specialized argot or unique street names which allow the participant in this lifestyle a means of easily distinguishing between those who are and are not a part of the subculture. The drug subculture also provides a complex set of normative prescriptions and proscriptions which guide the behavior of the subcultural participant. Similarly the drug subculture provides a valuable socialization function through the transmission of valuable knowledge and skills which are necessary to function effectively. Finally, not unlike the broader culture of which it is a part, there is a stratification system in the drug subculture which rewards some behaviors and participants more than others.

Illegal drug use is highly deviant in American society and is understood as a pathology to be explained by most professionals and lay persons alike. This chapter has suggested an alternative perspective from which to interpret the lifestyle and behavior of drug users—a perspective that recognizes the rationality and goal-directed character of drug-using/criminal lifestyles that adheres to an alternative set of goals and normative expectations. It may well be that the subcultures that promote such activities are themselves abnormal and even pathological in character; the behavior of *individuals within the context of these subcultures,* however, cannot be regarded as pathological if understood from the social and cultural context in which it takes place. Drug users are, in this respect, not so fundamentally different from the faithful church- or synagogue-goer who engages in ritualistic behavior in response to group norms and expectations.

KEY TERMS

argot

boundary-maintenance
   mechanism

career

drug subculture

moniker

REVIEW QUESTIONS

1. How does the *illegality* or disapproval of certain forms of drug use lead to the formation of drug subcultures? What are the special problems faced by users of illegal drugs, and how do subcultures function to solve them?

2. This chapter presents several lists of answers to the question "What are the characteristics of drug subcultures?" What features do these lists have in common? How do these features contribute to the functioning of the subcultures?

3. Rastafarians and members of the Native American Church argue that the use of drugs, ganja/marijuana and peyote respectively, is sacramental and is linked to their religious belief systems. What roles does using substances play in their religious practices and ceremonies?

4. Why has the American government been more highly critical about the Rastafarian desire for religious freedom to smoke ganja than the Native American Church's spiritual peyote use? What extra social and political hurdles do the Rastas face?

5. There has been a strong media and governmental campaign in recent years to publicize the horrors of club drugs like ecstasy, drugs they claim aren't taken seriously enough by those in the rave scene. Do subcultures such as this one systematically minimize the dangers of drug use?

6. How do the four components of the street heroin subculture collectively serve to protect users from the harsh judgment of outsiders? Can you think of nondrug using deviant subcultures that operate in a similar manner?

7. The typology of careers laid out in Figure 5.1 suggests strongly that drug involvement, both occupational and nonoccupational, follows sequences of steps found in nondeviant careers. What are these stages or periods? However, drug-involved careers also are patterned by factors that mainstream careers don't face. What is the impact of these additional factors?

CRITICAL INQUIRY QUESTIONS

1. This chapter presents an alternative to the prevailing notion that illegal drug use is best understood as a pathology, arguing that much drug involvement has a "rational and goal-directed" character. If our society experienced such a perceptual shift, how might it change our social attitudes toward drug users and, equally importantly, how might antidrug policies enacted by government change?

2. What is the importance of heroin users having a *main hustle?* Compare the skills they acquire to those learned by professional practitioners in a legitimate occupational field of your own choosing. What similarities do you discover?

NOTES

1. Or, as noted by Johnson-Hill (1995), a diet that is consistent with the Deuteronomic and Levitical prohibitions regarding foods such as pork and scaleless fish.

2. The article in the April, 3, 1999 issue of *The Economist* points out the irony that Mexico, a country of key importance in the North American illegal drug trade, has adopted a "hard line" approach to peyote by preventing its harvest and possession.

3. These are actual street names of New York City heroin addicts collected by Edward Preble, long-time street anthropologist doing research in New York City.

OFFICIAL AND UNOFFICIAL DATA SOURCES

CITY/CASE #: _____   CARD 2, cont. ——► CARD 3

(17) OTHER DRUGS: (NON-MEDICAL USE ONLY):	EVER TRY? Age 1st or X=no	EV. 3/WK FOR MO+ Age 1st or X=no	LAST 60 DAYS ACTIVE: FREQUENCY	◄— IF X: AGE AT LAST USE
1. MARIJUANA, hashish				
2. INHALANT (glue, solvents, n.ox.etc)				
3. HALLUCINOGEN (incl. PCP, "THC")				
4. MINOR TRANQUILIZER Valium, Equanil, etc				
5. SEDATIVE (barbit., Quaaludes, etc)				
6. HEROIN				
7. ILLEGAL (not legit!)METHADONE				
8. OTHER Rx-type ANALGESIC (op. or non-opiate)				
9. COCAINE				
10. "LOOK-ALIKE" STIMULANTS				
11. AMPHETAMINES/ "SPEED": Any other non-otc stimulant				
12. OTHER/s (Specify):				

16 17 18 19 20 21 22 23

24 25 26 27 28 29 30 31

32 33 34 35 36 37 38 39

40 41 42 43 44 45 46 47

48 49 50 51 52 53 54 55

56 57 58 59 60 61 62 63

64 65 66 67 68 69 70 71

72 73 74 75 76 77 78 79

CD 3: 3 (AUTO REPEAT)
1 2 3 4 5

6 7 8 9 10 11 12 13

14 15 16 17 18 19 20 21

22 23 24 25 26 27 28 29

30 31 32 33 34 35 36 37

38 39 40 41 42 43 44 45

46 47 48 49

50 51 52 53

54 55

(18) FIRST DRUG TRIED (Circle age)

(19) FIRST USED 3+ TIMES/WEEK FOR AT LEAST A MONTH (Circle age)   d, a:

(20) CLARIFY RELATION OF FREQ's HERE — TO "PREFERRED DRUGS" in S#2. (Or X=not necessary)

WDU/1 - p. 4

We frequently read and hear about estimates of the number of drug users in the United States, or that the prevalence of drug use of a certain type is increasing or declining. You may wonder how such estimates can be made. The task is, in fact, not an easy one. This is, in part, because recreational drug use is largely an illegal activity. People who are involved in illegal behavior are at risk for arrest and are not typically willing to talk about these activities with strangers. Moreover, people are not always willing to admit to their use of drugs that are not illegal but nevertheless might be seen as deviant, such as alcohol or tobacco. Furthermore, unlike other kinds of criminal behavior, we cannot ask the general citizenry if they have ever been a "victim" of drug use. The reason for this is that drug use is a *victimless* crime.[1] While we can estimate the number of burglaries or robberies by asking citizens if they have ever been a victim of such a crime, we cannot estimate the number of drug users, the number of drug purchases, or the number of times a drug is used by asking citizens about victimization. When we say that drug use has no direct victim, we mean simply that the acts of purchasing and using drugs is not forced upon a person by another. These acts require voluntary cooperation between drug dealer and drug user. Hence, it is not reasonable to expect a drug user to say, "Yes, I have been victimized by my drug dealer because he sold me drugs."

This leaves us with two general methods to obtain information about the level of drug use. The first way is through **official statistics,** which we define as *statistics on drug use which are gathered as a function of day to day organizational procedures conducted by the government or other agencies cooperating with the government.* We will be introducing five broad official sources of drug use statistics in this chapter: criminal justice agencies, including the *police* and *correctional institutions;* and noncriminal justice agencies including *hospital emergency rooms, medical examiners,* and *treatment programs.* The other sources that are frequently used in making estimates of the amount of drug use and trends in drug use are **unofficial statistics.** These are *statistics that are gathered by researchers for the express purpose of identifying drug users, learning relevant information about them, and for making estimates of incidence and prevalence.* We will introduce two major unofficial sources of drug-use statistics: the *Monitoring the Future* study and the *National Household Survey.* In addition to these, other unofficial sources of drug use data can be found in *Pulse Check,* the *Community Epidemiology Work Group,* the *Drug Abuse Treatment System Survey* (DATSS), and the *Alcohol and Drug Services Study* (ADSS), which are discussed briefly as well.

SOME IMPORTANT TERMS

If we are to understand and interpret drug statistics appropriately, there are two sets of terms that are often confused and which we must learn to distinguish. These are terms which are drawn from the field of medicine, but have been borrowed by the social sciences, particularly the field of criminology. These terms are found frequently throughout the drug literature, and it is appropriate that we look carefully at them before going on to examine official and unofficial sources of data on drug use.

EPIDEMIOLOGY AND ETIOLOGY

Epidemiology is a term that is derived from two Greek terms ἐπιὀήωος, which means "epidemic;" and λογία which means "discoursing." As the term is commonly used in the medical sciences, it refers to the study of the spread and distribution of diseases. When medical scientists are examining the epidemiology of diseases such as AIDS, they look for how it is distributed across population groups and regions. Epidemiologists learned early on, for example, that the incidence of AIDS was much higher among intravenous drug-using populations and among male homosexuals. This picture may change over time, but it was a "snapshot in time" of the pattern of this disease. The social sciences have used this term as well. While most social scientists no longer see crime and deviance as "pathologies" as they did in the early part of the twentieth century, much of the language from that era, which borrowed heavily from the field of medicine, still exists. Social scientists still talk about the epidemiology of crime, for example, which refers to how crime is patterned. This is, in fact, one of the central questions that criminologists ask: "Where is the rate of crime, or of specific crimes, the highest?" Specifically, the epidemiological profile of crime takes into consideration class, race, gender, occupation, and age, among other factors. These same factors are examined with regard to the epidemiology of drug use. The next chapter examines various dimensions of the epidemiology of drug use including gender, ethnicity and age, as well as various occupations.

   Etiology is often confused with epidemiology by lay people. It is quite different, however. Also derived from the Greek, it refers to the study of causes. Hence, rather than examining how a disease is distributed, etiology concerns itself with what *causes* the disease in the first place. In the case of AIDS, for example, etiologists learned early on that the disease could be traced to the green monkey in Africa. They then began to study the disease at this early point to learn more about its cause. Etiological studies also looked at how it caused human degradation and death by destroying the immune system. This knowledge is often helpful, as it is in the case of the AIDS virus, in searching for cures. This term has been borrowed by the social sciences to refer to the process of identifying the causes of crime and other undesirable social phenomena. The central etiological question addressed by criminologists is "*Why* do people of a particular social class or age group commit more crimes than individuals in other age categories or social classes?" Generally, these etiological factors are addressed by *theories* of crime and drug use. Indeed, because the social sciences are not as exacting as is medical science, most of our etiological explanations for these phenomena remain in the realm of theory, subject to further verification. We have examined some of the major theories for the etiology of drug use (and related behaviors) in Chapter 4.

Prevalence and Incidence

These terms are relevant to both the fields of epidemiology and etiology, but are especially important concepts in the field of epidemiology. They, too, are borrowed from the field of medicine, but are used slightly differently there than in the social sciences. When medical researchers talk about the **prevalence** of a disease, they are referring to *the total number of individuals who have a disease at any given point in time.* **Incidence** refers to *the number of individuals who acquire a disease within a given time period,* typically a year. For example, if in the year 2002 there were 1,000,000 cases of AIDS in the United States, we are talking about a *prevalence* of one million people with AIDS at that time.[2] Let us say that in 2003, there were 1,025,000 people with AIDS; however, 5,000 of the individuals who had AIDS in 2,002 died during that year. That means that there were a total of 30,000 *new cases* of AIDS reported in 2003. This number, 30,000, refers to the *incidence* of AIDS in 2003.[3]

The social sciences use these terms in a slightly different way. Normally, when social scientists talk about *prevalence,* they are referring to the total number of *individuals* who have ever engaged in a particular activity such as crime or drug use.[4] *Incidence,* in the social sciences, refers to the number of *cases* or *events* of a particular phenomenon in a given time period. Survey researchers, for example, will typically ask *how frequently* a respondent has committed a particular crime or used a particular drug. That figure becomes the basis for the *incidence* of crime or drug use. Police statistics present incidence as the number of *arrests* for a particular crime, or the number of crimes that come to the attention of the police in a particular year. As we shall see when we look at some of the official statistics for drug use, incidence may also be represented by the number of emergency room visits that are reported. In sum, prevalence refers to the number of *individuals* who have ever (or within a specified period of time) used drugs, or a particular type of drug. Incidence, on the other hand, refers to *frequency* or *number of times* that drugs have been used over a specified period of time.

Rates

One further concept must be introduced for us to be able to interpret and understand drug use statistics. This is the concept of **rates** of drug use. Very often drug use statistics are reported as simply total numbers of users, or **N's**, which is a straightforward count. Sometimes, they will be reported in terms of *percentages*, which is also straightforward. For example, if, among a sample of 10,000 people, 3,000 admit to having used some sort of illicit substance in the past year, we would say that 30 percent of the sample has used some sort of illicit drug in the last 12 months. A percentage is the number of respondents or cases that fit a category *per one hundred* cases overall.

Rates are similar to percentages, but are not necessarily calculated on a *per 100* basis. *Rate* refers to *the number of drug users per unit of population*. The unit of population may vary, and it is important to know what the unit is before attempting to interpret data. For example, the Uniform Crime Reports, published by the Federal Bureau of Investigation, uses a population unit of 100,000 for its rates; other sources use a unit base of 1,000. If one is not aware of what the unit of population is, they will draw very inaccurate interpretations about the prevalence of drug use!

You may wonder why this is important. It is important for two reasons. First, simply providing an *N* (raw number) does not really give us a clue as to how pervasive drug use, or a particular type of drug use may be. That there are an estimated 500,000 to 1,000,000 heroin addicts in the United States sounds like a great deal. However, when we consider that the entire population of the United States is over 250,000,000 people, the *rate* of heroin use is only 2–4 per 1,000 people. We can see that reporting in rates rather than *N*'s provides a much less dramatic, but more realistic picture of the level of drug use. The rate is even more important, however, when looking at trends in drug use over time. Let us use actual FBI statistics from the Uniform Crime Reports to illustrate our point. The number of heroin/cocaine related drug arrests in 1981 was 72,100. That number increased to 121,966 by the year 1998. That represents a 69 percent increase in the number of heroin and cocaine-related drug arrests. However, the population has also increased during that time. The population in 1981 was just over 229,000,000, while in 1998 it was just over 270,000,000. The rate of heroin/cocaine arrests in 1981 was 31.42 arrests per 100,000 population; in 1998 it was 45.12 arrests per 100,000. The increase in the *rate* of heroin and cocaine arrests was therefore not 69 percent, but rather 43.6 percent.[5] Rates, in effect, take into account shifts in the population base. In so doing, the use of rates provides us with a much better idea if a population is more involved in drugs (or any other behavior for that matter), or whether increased numbers of drug users or arrests is simply a function of more people. We should also note that while the figures employed for this example were for the United States as a whole, we could determine rates for young people aged 10–19; or for men versus women, etc. That is, by identifying our target population of interest, whether it be the population as a whole, or a subpopulation, we can calculate rates of drug use *among that population*.

OFFICIAL DRUG-USE STATISTICS

We have suggested earlier that official statistics are defined as *statistics which are gathered as a function of day-to-day organizational procedures conducted by the government or other agencies cooperating with the government*. Numerous government agencies, such as the National Institute on Drug Abuse, fund special studies on drug use and behaviors related to drug use. The statistics generated by these studies are not what we mean by official statistics, however. Rather, official statistics refer to data that are generated by government and cooperating agencies while doing their normal work routines. For example, when police departments make arrests, these arrests are recorded, and then get compiled by the FBI. Similarly, we will look at emergency room and medical examiner data which are compiled from the charts of emergency rooms and medical examiner reports. We will briefly highlight the nature of data generated from five broad types of agencies:

1. **Uniform Crime Reports (UCR),** reported by local police departments and compiled by the FBI.
2. **Arrestee Drug Abuse Monitoring (ADAM)** program—formerly the *Drug Use Forecasting System* (DUF).
3. **Correctional Data** consist of a myriad of sources, at federal, and local sources, including statistics on probationers.
4. **Drug Abuse Warning Network (DAWN),** comprising data reported by hospital emergency rooms and by medical examiners
5. **Treatment Data** compiled by the Drug and Alcohol Services Information System (DASIS).

UNIFORM CRIME REPORTS

Those of you who have had a course in criminology or juvenile delinquency should be familiar with the *Uniform Crime Reports*. This is a general source of crime statistics gathered from some 17,000 police departments and published by the FBI. The FBI began gathering crime statistics in 1931 in Massachusetts, in response to a legal mandate given the Bureau a year earlier. Reporting by police departments has always been voluntary, and until the 1950s, reporting was not at all systematic, and many police departments failed to report at all. Over the years, with the professionalization of police departments, these statistics have improved substantially in their completeness and usefulness as descriptive tools.

The crimes reported in the *Uniform Crime Reports* fall into two categories, which are simply called "Part I Offenses" and "Part II Offenses." Part I offenses, also known as *index crimes,* consist of eight categories of crime: homicide, aggravated assault, rape, robbery, burglary, grand larceny, motor vehicle theft, and arson. These are considered to be the most serious crimes and form the basis for the general *crime rate,* which is published and broadcast by media when released by the FBI. Certainly, other crimes could be considered as part of the crime rate, and for specific purposes may be used instead of the index crimes. Because the index crimes are considered the most serious, however, when reporting a general crime rate, these form its basis.

Part II offenses consist of 21 additional offenses which are considered less serious than the index crimes. These offenses range from forgery and counterfeiting to juveniles running away from home. A complete list of Part I and Part II offenses are provided in Table 6.1. The categories that

TABLE 6.1	Crimes Reported in the Uniform Crime Reports

Part I Offenses (Index Crimes)
Murder and Non-negligent Manslaughter
Forcible Rape
Robbery
Aggravated Assault
Burglary
Larceny-theft
Motor Vehicle Theft
Arson

Part II Offenses
Other Assault (non-aggravated)
Forgery and Counterfeiting
Fraud
Embezzlement
Stolen property (buying, receiving, possession)
Vandalism
Weapons (carrying, possessing)
Prostitution and Commercialized Vice
Sex Offenses (except forcible rape and prostitution)
Drug Abuse Violations
   Sale/Manufacture
      Heroin/Cocaine and Derivatives
      Marijuana
      Synthetic or Manufactured Drugs
      Other Dangerous Non-narcotic drugs
   Possession
      Heroin/Cocaine and Derivatives
      Marijuana
      Synthetic or Manufactured Drugs
      Other Dangerous Non-narcotic drugs
Gambling
Offenses Against Family and Children
Driving Under the Influence
Liquor Laws
Drunkenness
Disorderly Conduct
Vagrancy
All Other Offenses (except traffic)
Suspicion
Curfew and Loitering Laws
Runaways

will interest us are four crime categories tucked away in the Part II of-fenses: these are *Drug Abuse Violations, Driving Under the Influence, Liquor Laws,* and *Drunkenness.* Drug abuse violations are further divided into two categories: "Sale/Manufacture" and "Possession" When reporting both sale/manufacture and possession offenses, the FBI further distinguishes between four categories: *heroin/cocaine and derivatives, marijuana, synthetic or manufactured drugs,* and *other dangerous non-narcotic drugs.* These cate-gories and subcategories of drug abuse violations are reported only for ar-rests, and in percentages (of all drug abuse violations). No information is provided on rates, or on the total number of each subcategory, though both of these statistics could be derived quite readily if one were interested in doing so.

Incidence of Drug Abuse Violations Reported by the UCR

Table 6.2 provides a snapshot of the number and rate of drug and alcohol arrests in 2000. The FBI reports more than 1 million drug arrests for 2000. Possession-related offenses accounted for 81 percent of the total (not shown). There were estimated to be nearly 1.8 million alcohol arrests, most of which were DUI offenses. Between 1991 and 2000 there was a 49.4 per-cent increase in the number of drug arrests, and a 1.2 percent increase in alcohol arrests.

Evaluation of UCR Data

We must take great care in our interpretation of these statistics. First, we know that the "dark figure" of crime—that portion of the total crimes com-mitted which are not brought to the attention of the police—is very high, and it is particularly high for crimes of this nature. Hence, these data are going to underestimate overall drug use. Moreover, note that these are *arrest*

TABLE 6.2	Drug and Alcohol Arrests, 2000		
Offense	Total N	Rate (per 100,000)	Percent Change in N, 1991–2000
Drug Abuse Violations	1,042,334	572.4	49.4%
DUI Offenses	926,096	508.6	20.2%
Liquor Law Violations	435,672	239.3	13.6%
Drunkenness	423,310	232.5	−27.3%
Total Alcohol	**1,785,078**	**1,191.4**	**1.2%**
Total Drugs and Alcohol	**2,827,412**	**1,887.1**	**22.0%**

Source: Constructed from *Crime in the United States*, 2000, Tables 31 and 32, pp. 219 and 220.

statistics.[6] Typically, for drug sales offenses, there have been several "buys" by undercover police officers before a single arrest is made, because of law enforcement efforts to gain access to higher level dealers. Alcohol statistics do not suffer from these problems, but we know that the dark figure for alcohol violations is also very high. Because of the extremely high dark figure for both drug abuse and alcohol offenses, we must also be wary in interpreting trend data in the Uniform Crime Reports. These statistics suggest a substantial increase in drug arrests, with a slight increase in alcohol arrests. However, this may be merely an artifact of shifting priorities in law enforcement. With a dark figure for these types of crime in excess of 90 percent (meaning that more than 90 percent of these types of crimes committed do not come to the attention of the police), a simple change in law enforcement priority or procedure could easily result in these changes, and they may not represent a fundamental shift in the level of drug use or sales at all.

ARRESTEE DRUG ABUSE MONITORING PROGRAM (ADAM)

The *Arrestee Drug Abuse Monitoring Program* was instituted in 1997. ADAM replaced an earlier data collection initiative called the *Drug Use Forecasting* (DUF) system, established in 1987; however, the basic methodology remained the same. Recent arrestees in selected cities throughout the country are randomly selected and interviewed about their drug use within 48 hours of when they are booked. These interviews are corroborated with urine specimens. Both interviews and urine specimens are voluntary, but in most cities more than 80 percent of the arrestees agree to the interviews, and of those more than 80 percent agree to the urine samples (ADAM, 1999).

Interviews are conducted and drug specimens collected over a two-week period, four times per year. Quarterly collection has an important advantage over annual surveys in that seasonal variations in drug use can be measured. Arrestees are questioned about a variety of areas, including education, living arrangement, criminal behavior, and income sources. The interviews focus most intensively on past and current drug use patterns, however. Urine specimens are then taken to corroborate self-report statements of recent drug use and provide a valuable validity check. Drug-use data are collected for ten categories of drugs: *Amphetamines, Barbiturates, Benzodiazepines* (Valium), *Cocaine, Opiates, PCP, Methadone, Marijuana, Propoxyphene* (Darvon) and *Methaqualone* (Quaaludes and other sedatives).

When the original DUF program was launched, data were collected from 21 cities throughout the country (see Table 6.3). One of these cities (Kansas City, MO) is no longer included in the ADAM program. By the end of 1999, 15 additional cities were added to the program, and currently, still more cities are being added.

TABLE 6.3	Site Cities Participating in the Arrestee Drug Abuse Monitoring Program, 1999

Albuquerque, NM	Houston, TX*	Phoenix, AZ*†
Anchorage, AK	Indianapolis, IN*†	Portland, OR*†
Atlanta, GA	Laredo, TX	Sacramento, CA
Birmingham, AL*†	Las Vegas, NV	St. Louis, MO*†
Chicago, IL*	Los Angeles, CA*†	Salt Lake City, UT
Cleveland, OH*†	Miami, FL*	San Antonio, TX*†
Dallas, TX*	Minneapolis, MN	San Diego, CA*†
Denver, CO†	New Orleans, LA*	San Jose, CA*†
Des Moines, IA	New York, NY*	Seattle, WA
Detroit, MI*	Oklahoma City, OK	Spokane, WA
Fort Lauderdale, FL*	Omaha, NE	Tucson, AZ†
Honolulu, HI	Philadelphia, PA*	Washington, DC*†

* = One of the 21 original sites in the DUF program
† = Sites collecting data from juveniles as well as adults

Prevalence of Drug Use Revealed by ADAM

Figures 6.1 and 6.2 depict changes in drug-use levels among male and female arrestees over the nine-year period from 1990–1999. Utilizing the urine samples of arrestees, these data identify the percentage of arrestees in Los Angeles who tested positive for three specific types of drugs as

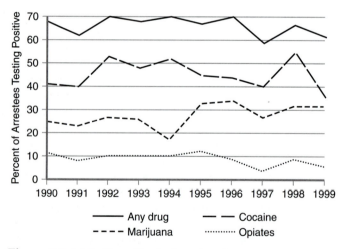

Figure 6.1 Male Drug Use in Los Angeles, 1990–1999

Note: Beginning in 1995, the criteria for marijuana presence was lowered from 100 nanograms to 50 nanograms.

Source: Adapted from National Institute of Justice, *Annual Report on Adult and Juvenile Arrestees*, 1995, 1998, & 1999.

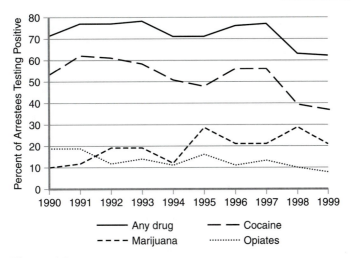

Figure 6.2 **Female Drug Use in Los Angeles, 1990–1999**

Note: Beginning in 1995, the criteria for marijuana presence was lowered from 100 nanograms to 50 nanograms.

Source: Adapted from National Institute of Justice, *Annual Report on Adult and Juvenile Arrestees*, 1995, 1998 and 1999.

well as "any drug." The data will look different for each testing site, of course, but the Los Angeles data provide some sense of the trends among these arrestees.

Overall, between 60 and 80 percent of the men and women arrested had drugs in their system at the time of arrest. Crack cocaine almost certainly accounts for most of this figure. Marijuana and opiates, by contrast, are minimally represented among Los Angeles arrestees. When interpreting these statistics, we must keep in mind that the population that is represented is Los Angeles *arrestees*. Hence, while marijuana is certainly more widely used than cocaine, even among criminals, cocaine is the drug that is present *among those who are arrested*. Because of the extremely high reinforcement potential of cocaine, and especially crack cocaine, users of these drugs are more likely to engage in criminal behavior to get drugs. Perhaps more importantly, users of drugs of this nature may engage in more *desperate* behavior to get their drugs, behavior which is likely to get them in trouble.

Table 6.4 presents the percentage of arrestees with any drugs in their urine according to the offense for which they were arrested. We might hypothesize, for example, that people committing violent crimes are more likely to be on drugs than those who commit property crimes or public order offenses such as prostitution. We might reason that drugs make individuals less rational, or less in control of their behavior, and hence more likely to engage in violent behavior. Property crimes, on the other hand, require more precision and presence of mind. Property offenders, we might thus reason, are less likely to have drugs in their system when arrested.

TABLE 6.4	Percent Positive for Drugs by Offense Category	
Offense	Male	Female
Violent Offenses	47.5	47.3
Robbery	76.3	80.0
Assault	40.1	43.0
Weapons	51.6	100.0
Other Violent Offenses	44.2	58.3
Property Offenses	65.4	70.5
Larceny/Theft	64.8	70.6
Burglary	74.0	75.0
Stolen Vehicle	69.2	77.3
Other Property	53.3	63.2
Drug Offenses	83.0	90.1
Drug Sales	72.5	66.7
Drug Possession	88.5	94.2
Prostitution	25.0	89.5
Other Offenses	62.7	64.9
TOTAL	64.4	71.0

Source: National Institute of Justice, *Annual Report on Adult and Juvenile Arrestees*, 1999.

Table 6.4 presents only very limited support for this idea, however. With the exception of robbery, a *lower* percentage of arrestees for violent crimes than for property crimes tested positive for drugs. The reason for this *may* be, once again, that we are dealing with arrestees. It may well be that our hypothesis is correct, and that most property offenders do, in fact, commit their crimes while "clean," and indeed, the reason these arrestees were arrested in the first place is because they were not of a rational frame of mind to successfully pull off their crime and hence were caught. Such a possibility raises again the limitation of ADAM data in making generalizations to the broader criminal population.

The other interesting observation worthy of note in Table 6.4 is the fact that females are more likely to test positive for drugs for every single crime category except drug sales. We might interpret from these findings that females are more dependent on drugs in the commission of crimes. Insofar as these data are representative of the general criminal population in Los

Angeles, such a proposition would be reasonable. Again, however, because only arrestees are represented here, we must be careful in drawing such conclusions.

Evaluation of ADAM

Because data are collected quarterly, ADAM allows us to track drug use over time. ADAM has other advantages over most official statistics in two important ways. First, data are collected by trained interviewers for purposes of obtaining drug use information. Because most official statistics are merely by-products of official processing of drug users, the information collected on drug use may not be as valid or reliable. Moreover, ADAM has built into it a verification mechanism—urine samples. There is no other data base which is national in scope that uses such a dependable system of validation.

There are also some shortcomings to the ADAM data. Perhaps most significantly, data are collected only on arrestees. Years of street drug research has demonstrated that arrestees may not represent the larger population of drug users (e.g., see Faupel, 1986, 1991). Hence, the findings are generalizable only to those drug users who have been arrested. A second area of weakness, which is being addressed to some extent by the ADAM program, is the fact that data have not been truly national, but have been gathered on a small number of large cities. While these cities have been geographically distributed throughout the country, they are not necessarily reflective of smaller cities, towns, and rural communities. Over the years, ADAM has established sites in more moderate sized cities, which strengthens the data considerably. Moreover, the program has launched an initiative to supplement the urban data collection with rotating "outreach" collections which would include satellite communities and rural areas. The program is also improving its individual sample selection process to ensure probability sampling—a sampling technique that guarantees at least minimal representation from all target groups—which also provides for greater confidence in the generalizability of these data.

An additional feature of the ADAM program, which was added in 1998, is the inclusion of international data. Nine countries were included initially: Australia, Chile, England, the Netherlands, Panama, Scotland, South Africa, the United States, and Uruguay. This international effort is known as I-ADAM, and is the first international drug-abuse prevalence program to generate standardized data on drug abuse.

CORRECTIONAL STATISTICS[7]

There is a small amount of data available on drug use characteristics of state, federal, and local prisoners. Like the Uniform Crime Reports, the reporting of these data by individual states and local jurisdictions is voluntary, though now all states participate to some degree. Data are collected from state and federal prison facilities in each of the 50 states and the District of Columbia by the U.S. Census Bureau. Reports are submitted twice a year—at mid-year and at year end. These data include not only the total count of inmates but also report by several demographic and other categories, including race and ethnicity, sex, and offense type. The Census of Jails (COJ), which involves county and municipal level facilities, is conducted only about once every five years. However, in the intervening years, a less comprehensive Annual Survey of Jails (ASJ) has been conducted since 1982. The ASJ is normally conducted on a smaller sample of the full Census of Jails.

Additionally, every five or six years, the U.S. Census Bureau conducts special surveys in federal, state and local facilities based on scientifically selected samples of the facilities and of inmates housed in them. These special surveys contain detailed information about prisoners not contained in any other source, including information on their current offenses, criminal histories, family and personal backgrounds, and prior drug and alcohol use and treatment. While this information is technically not "official" data, we are considering it here because it so closely parallels the National Prison Survey (NPS) data in methodology and therefore augments it very well.

DRUG ABUSE WARNING NETWORK (DAWN)

Sponsored by the Substance Abuse and Mental Health Services Administration (SAMHSA), the *Drug Abuse Warning Network* (DAWN) represents the first of the noncriminal justice sources for statistics. DAWN collects information from two sources: emergency rooms and medical examiners. DAWN has been collecting information on emergency room and medical examiner records since 1975. DAWN is a valuable data source because it provides information not available through other official sources on health consequences of drug use and abuse. Moreover, DAWN almost certainly taps individuals who do not come to the official attention of the police or other criminal justice agencies.

Emergency Room (ER) Data

The ER data come from a national probability sample of hospitals in the contiguous 48 states. These national data are augmented by a probability sample of hospitals in 21 metropolitan areas. The hospitals eligible to be included in DAWN are nonfederal, short-stay general hospitals that have a 24-hour emergency room. Because probability samples are used, the data are quite representative of cases coming into emergency rooms. The data are collected by nurses and other medically trained personnel after reviewing medical charts for indications that the emergency room visit was related to drug use or abuse. Information in the charts themselves, of course, originate from the attending physicians or other emergency room personnel who have treated the patient.

Cases coming into an emergency room must meet the following five criteria before they are included in the DAWN data base:

- The individual must be at least six years of age.
- The patient must have been treated in the hospital's emergency room.
- The patient's presenting problem was induced by or related to drug use (regardless of when that use occurred).
- The drug in question was illegal, or the use of a legal drug contrary to directions.
- The patient's reason for taking the drug was to satisfy a dependence, a suicide attempt or gesture, or for its psychoactive effects.

The information contained in the emergency room data is the number of "drug mentions" involved in emergency room episodes. Drug mentions are categorized according to type of drug, including cocaine, heroin/morphine, marijuana/hashish, and methamphetamines. This information is presented according to city and geographical area, as well as by various demographic factors such as age, sex, ethnicity, etc.

Medical Examiner Data (ME)

The ME data comprises information on *deaths* attributable to drug abuse. Unlike the emergency room data, the medical examiner portion of DAWN is not drawn from a probability sample, and hence care must be taken when examining these data. Participation in DAWN is voluntary and not all deaths are investigated by a medical examiner, so these data should not be extended to draw conclusions beyond the locations themselves. In 1997, 145 medical examiner facilities in 42 metropolitan areas in the 48 contiguous states submitted reports to DAWN. Within each of the reporting facilities, a designated reporter identifies the cases that meet DAWN guidelines. Those guidelines are:

- The decedent must be between the ages of 6 and 97 years of age.
- The death was drug-induced or drug-related (i.e., drugs were either a direct cause or a contributing factor to the death).
- The death involved use of an illegal drug, or the nonmedical use of a legal drug.
- The reason for taking the substance was for dependence, psychic effect, or suicide.

Any given case may involve multiple mentions. Forms allow for the recording of up to six different types of drugs as well as an alcohol-in-combination entry. Many drug users are polydrug users; hence it is not always possible to determine with precision which drug was primarily responsible for the death. In addition to the drug-related data surrounding the death, ME reports include demographic information about the decedent as well as information about the circumstances of the death.

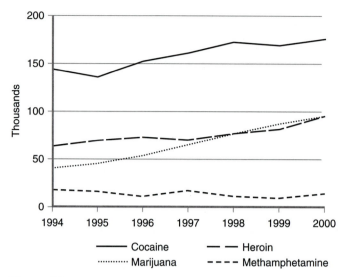

Figure 6.3 **Emergency Room Episodes, 1994–2000**

Source: Substance Abuse and Mental Health Services Administration (2002),
Emergency Department Trends from the Drug Abuse Warning Network, Preliminary
Estimates January–June 2001 with Revised Estimates 1994–2000. DAWN Series D-20,
DHHS Publication No. (SMA) 02-3634, Rockville, MD.

Drug Use Patterns as Revealed by DAWN

Figure 6.3 reveals that during the latter two-thirds of the 1990s the number
of emergency room episodes related to drug use and abuse increased
slightly. It should be noted however, that these years reflect a leveling of a
significant increase that began during the latter 1980s and into early 1990s
(not shown). For example, cocaine episodes increased at an almost alarming rate of more than 70 percent, from 100,000 in 1988 (about 80,000 in 1990)
to more than 170,000 in 1998. This dramatic increase is almost certainly due
to an increased prevalence in crack use (and also an increased purity of cocaine) during the early 1990s. There were far fewer episodes involving marijuana, heroin, and methamphetamines, but the same trend of increasing
rates is evident, particularly among certain age categories, depending on
the drug in question.

The data on marijuana provide an empirical example of what DAWN
data can and cannot tell us. Episodes involving marijuana are lower than
both heroin and cocaine episodes, yet we know from self-report studies that
the prevalence of marijuana *use* is much higher than either heroin or cocaine. We need to be cautious, therefore as we interpret the other data as
well. *These are cases which involve emergency room treatment.* The reason for
the rise might be an increase in the use of a drug; or it may be due to an
increase in the potency of the drugs. Furthermore, it may be due to factors
that have nothing to do with drug use patterns at all, but rather to patterns
of treatment for drug use.

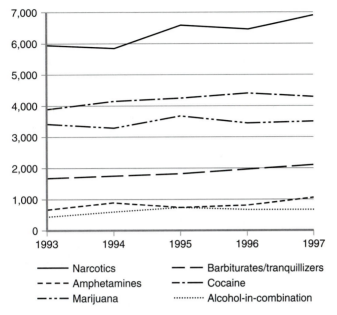

Figure 6.4 Drug-Related Deaths, 1993–1997

Source: Substance Abuse and Mental Health Services Administration, *Drug Abuse Warning Network: Annual Medical Examiner Data, 1996,* July, 1998b; and *Drug Abuse Warning Network: Annual Medical Examiner Data, 1997,* December 1999b. Washington, DC: Department of Health and Human Services.

The medical examiner data present a less dramatic picture. As revealed in Figure 6.4, narcotics-related deaths are clearly the most frequent, and have risen from about 6,000 to 7,000. Next to narcotics, medical examiners see cocaine as the most frequently implicated in death with about 4,000 cocaine-related deaths per year. This number has not increased substantially over the last five years. It is something of a puzzle that while there are substantially more cocaine-related cases seen in the emergency rooms, there are *fewer* deaths attributed to cocaine by medical examiners. One possible explanation is that heroin is much more likely to synergize with a multitude of other drugs than is cocaine. Given that many addicts are poly-drug users, the combination of drugs used with heroin might result in more heroin-related deaths than with cocaine. It is also interesting to note that alcohol, in combination with other drugs is implicated in about 3,500 deaths per year. Alcohol can be particularly toxic when combined with other depressant-type drugs such as narcotics, barbiturates, or tranquilizers. Again, alcohol-related deaths have remained quite constant throughout this period.

Evaluation of DAWN

A major strength of DAWN data is that they provide information not available in any other official source and, for that matter, in any unofficial source. Morbidity and mortality statistics would seem to offer a vital contribution to our understanding of the potential consequences of drug abuse. Additionally, these data are collected annually so that epidemiological trends in emergency room episodes or drug-related deaths can be tracked.

There are some problems associated with the DAWN data as well. First, while they are sometimes interpreted in this way, these data cannot be used as a reliable estimate of drug use prevalence. They are, instead, an indicator of *drug-related health problems.* For example, an increase in the number of emergency room or medical examiner incidents may simply mean that a new drug or drug combination has hit the streets, one that is more potent than that to which local users are accustomed. Indeed, it may mean simply that more users are going to emergency rooms because of successful public relations campaigns in the area. Changing patterns may also reflect changes in procedure at a hospital. For example, if a municipality has instituted a drug-detoxification unit, hospitals may routinely refer incoming drug-related cases there. It has also been suggested that changes to more sophisticated computer equipment may affect (usually increase) drug-related judgments because they are better able to detect and more effectively record drug involvement.

A second area of limitation, related to the above, is that the emergency room data almost certainly underestimate the drug-related problems in a community. Many users experiencing drug overdoses or synergism, or other complications of drug use may choose not to go to the emergency room. Instead, they may consult their pharmacist, local doctor, or a medically experienced friend. Moreover, alcohol, a major drug of abuse, is not included at all in DAWN except as its effect is in combination with other drugs. Yet we know that alcohol is the primary drug implicated in many drunk-driving accidents and violent exchanges resulting in emergency room visits or medical examiner reports. Ignoring alcohol-related incidents or reporting them only in conjunction with other drugs results in a minimization of alcohol's harm as a drug of abuse; it also inappropriately attributes illicit drugs as the cause of ailments or death when the real villain may be the alcohol.

Third, the medical examiner data suffer the additional limitation that reports are often delayed up to six months and more because of the extended time required for the completion of autopsy reports. Medical examiner data are only about 80 percent complete after six months and are not usually fully complete for a full year. Moreover, since 1997, DAWN has not aggregated its medical examiner data making examination of broad trends difficult at best. Trends can be examined for individual cities, however.

DRUG AND ALCOHOL SERVICES INFORMATION SYSTEM (DASIS)

Data collection on drug treatment admissions was first mandated on a national level by the *Drug Abuse Office and Treatment Act* (PL 92-255) in 1972. This act provided federal funding for treatment programs, and with that funding required reporting on clients entering those programs. First reporting efforts were initiated as the Client Oriented Data Acquisition Process (CODAP) in 1973. This program continued for nine years, until 1981, and gathered data from nearly 2,000 federally funded programs which admitted some 200,000 patients over that time.

Mandatory CODAP reporting was terminated in 1981 because of the transferral of funding from the federal to state governments under the Alcohol and Drug Abuse and Mental Health Services Block Grant. The Block Grant program included no reporting requirements, though some states continued to report voluntarily.

In 1988, amendments to the original block grant program were passed which mandated federal data collection on clients receiving substance abuse treatment through programs receiving block grant monies. The Treatment Episode Data Set (TEDS) was established in 1989 in response to this mandate under the auspices of the Substance Abuse and Mental Health Services Administration (SAMHSA). SAMHSA had other treatment services data sets as well. The Drug and Alcohol Services Information System (DASIS) was thus created as a mechanism for integrating these sources of information, and to avoid redundancy. In addition to TEDS, this need for integration resulted in the creation of the National Master Facility Inventory (NMFI), which is a continuously updated and comprehensive listing of all known substance abuse treatment facilities as well as prevention and education facilities identified by the states. NMFI is the core of DASIS. The third component of DASIS is the Uniform Facility Data Set (UFDS), which is an annual survey of the characteristics and utilization of alcoholism and drug abuse treatment facilities. Below, we briefly describe first the UFDS, which is facility-level data, and TEDS, which contains individual client-level data.

Uniform Facility Data Set (UFDS)

The UFDS collects data from state-recognized treatment facilities on facility and client characteristics. Surveys are sent by mail, with a follow-up phone interview for those facilities that did not respond to the mail survey. Numerous questions are asked regarding the facility and the services it provides as well as questions about client characteristics. Unlike TEDS, which tracks admissions over an entire year, the UFDS asks for information as it is pertinent to one specific day. (The 1995 survey, for example, asked questions about facility and client characteristics as they existed on October 2, 1995.) This methodology does not allow for as many detailed questions about client characteristics, though there is information in the UFDS that is not available in TEDS. For example, information is requested on the number of pregnant women in the facility, or for individuals being treated for certain diseases such as tuberculosis.

Treatment Episode Data Set (TEDS)

TEDS compiles data on admissions to treatment programs collected by states as mandated under the revised Substance Abuse Prevention and

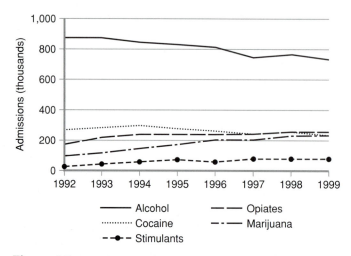

Figure 6.5 **Treatment Facility Admissions, 1992–1999**
Sources: Substance Abuse and Mental Health Services Administration, *Treatment Episode Data Set (TEDS): 1992–1997* and *1994–1999* (1999; 2001). Washington, DC: Department of Health and Human Services.

Treatment Block Grant. A variety of information is collected, including: *type of drug an individual is being admitted for, method of ingestion* (for some drugs), *type of service requested, source of referral, frequency of drug use, age at first use, various demographic information on clients,* and *length of stay and reason for discharge.*

Prevalence of Drug Use According to TEDS.   Figure 6.5 reveals that alcohol is far and away the most frequently treated substance, with some 737,000 admissions in 1999. It is noteworthy, however, that the number of admissions has declined over the years that TEDS data are available, from nearly 900,000 admissions in 1992. The remaining types of drug admissions are much lower, with admissions ranging from about 20,000 to just over 200,000. Treatment facility admissions for these drugs has remained quite steady over time with the exception of marijuana, which has more than doubled over the eight-year period.

The treatment data would seem to contradict the DAWN emergency room data which show a substantial increase in emergency room episodes over the 13-year period from 1988 to 2000. Cocaine witnessed an especially dramatic increase, yet treatment facilities witnessed a slight decline in admissions for cocaine abuse. It may be that cocaine—especially crack—users are not willing to go to treatment facilities and end up in the emergency room instead. Similarly, courts may be less likely to send cocaine and crack users to treatment as part of their sentence, but are more inclined to send them directly to prison. These are inconsistencies that can best be addressed with studies that are specially designed to identify drug users and drug-use patterns. Studies of a more ethnographic nature or which are specially focused on active drug users can intentionally include items which address such anomalies. This is the advantage of *unofficial statistics*, which we examine in the next section.

Evaluation of TEDS.   Because TEDS is based on *treatment admissions*, there are certain limitations inherent to the data. First, not all individuals seek or are referred to treatment; so, like any official data source, generalizations to the general population cannot be made. Indeed, because TEDS is only obtained from treatment programs receiving block grant money, the information contained here may not even be representative of all treatment patients. TEDS patients are more likely to be hardcore users, poorer, and probably court-ordered. It must also be recognized that the unit of analysis is the *admission* and not the individual. An individual may be admitted twice in the same year, for example, which would count as two admissions even though only one person is involved. Finally, there may be variation across states in the reporting of drug treatment episodes that have nothing to do with actual differences in treatment admissions. States vary in their licensure, certification, and accreditation requirements as well as their policies in the disbursement of public funds. In some states, for example, state substance abuse agencies also regulate private agencies and individual practitioners, while in other states private facilities are not so regulated. Those states that do regulate will be more likely to report admissions to private as well as public agencies, while those states that do not so regulate will be reporting only public treatment admissions. Similarly, some states collect data from treatment facilities in prisons, while others do not (Substance Abuse and Mental Health Services Administration, 1999c).

UNOFFICIAL DRUG-USE STATISTICS

Unofficial drug-use statistics are those gathered for the express purpose of identifying drug users, learning relevant information about them, and for making estimates of incidence and prevalence. While government agencies may fund or cooperate with these studies, these are not data which are part of official censuses or other data routinely gathered by these organizations. Two unofficial sources of drug-use data are explored at length in this chapter:

- **Monitoring the Future (MTF)**—an annual survey of high school and college students conducted by the Institute for Social Research at the University of Michigan.
- **National Household Survey on Drug Abuse (NHSDA)**—sponsored by the Substance Abuse and Mental Health Services Administration. This survey conducts interviews with some 70,000 individuals in households across the country.

In addition to these on-going nationally representative initiatives, we will examine more briefly four additional sources of data:

- **Pulse Check**—developed by the Office of National Drug Control Policy. Collects interview data from knowledgeable sources such as police, ethnographers, and treatment providers in 21 metropolitan areas.
- **Community Epidemiology Work Group (CEWG)**—consists of a group of experts from 21 metropolitan areas who report on local indicators of drug use every six months.
- **Drug Abuse Treatment System Survey (DATSS)**—a periodic survey of outpatient substance abuse treatment units.
- **Alcohol and Drug Services Study (ADSS)**—includes information on special treatment populations such as pregnant women, as well as follow-up information on discharged patients.

MONITORING THE FUTURE (MTF)

The Monitoring the Future project began in 1975 at the Survey Research Center of the Institute for Social Research at the University of Michigan. The stated purpose of MTF is ". . . to study changes in the beliefs, attitudes, and behavior of young people in the United States" (Monitoring the Future, 1999a, np). When the project began, it was known as the National High School Senior Survey, and began with senior classes only. The survey was further expanded in 1991 to include nationally representative samples of eighth and tenth graders.

The survey began in 1975 with approximately 16,000 senior students in about 133 schools nationwide. When eighth and tenth graders were added in 1991, a similar sized sample was drawn for each of these cohorts. Today, approximately 50,000 students in about 420 public and private schools are surveyed annually. Additionally, beginning in 1976, a random sample of the senior class has been followed up into their young adult years on a biennial basis to measure changes in use and attitudes for up to 14 additional years.

Data are collected during the spring of each year. A three-stage sampling process is used to insure a nationally representative sample:

- **Stage 1:** The selection of specific geographical areas.
- **Stage 2:** The selection of one or more schools within each of those areas.
- **Stage 3:** The selection of classes within each school.

Students are alerted in advance about the upcoming survey through letters and flyers, and participation is voluntary. The questionnaires are group-administered in classrooms and in some cases larger group formats such as school assemblies. Follow-up questionnaires are mailed to respondents with a small monetary gift of $10 to help ensure higher response rates.

Prevalence of Drug-Use as Measured by MTF

Monitoring the Future reports lifetime, annual, and 30-day prevalence data as the percentage of individuals who report ever using drugs or a particular type of drug. Figure 6.6 provides trend data from 1975–2001 on the number of high school seniors who report having used any of five different types of drugs, including alcohol during the previous month. There is an unmistakable trend in these data. Self-reported drug use seems to have reached a peak in the late 1970s or early 1980s, but then steadily declined over the next ten years. Self-reported drug use reached a low in 1992, and has been increasing since, in some cases, very dramatically, though percentages remain well below the peak years.[8]

Alcohol use has always been high among high school students, with use during the previous month at or about 70 percent throughout the first half of the 1980s, but declining in the late 1980s. The pattern for illicit drug use is slightly different than alcohol. The early 1980s were a peak period in illicit drug use, as revealed by both the combined percentages for "any illicit drug" and for the individual drugs used, except for narcotics use. Furthermore, the illicit drugs witnessed a fairly sharp downward trend in use throughout the 1980s and into the early 1990s, though cocaine and narcotics use has always been low, with less than 7 and 4 percent (respectively) of seniors reporting use of these drugs during the previous month. (Most narcotics use involves drugs other than heroin. Annually (1975–2001), less than 1 percent of the sampled high school seniors reports using heroin in the previous month.)

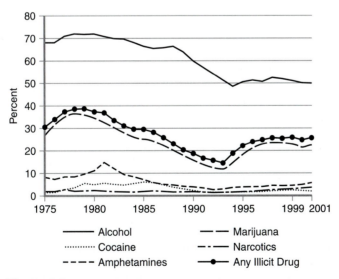

Figure 6.6 **30-day Prevalence of Drug Use for 12th Graders, 1975–2001**

Source: Table 5–3. *Monitoring the Future National Survey Results on Drug Use, 1975–2001. Volume 1: Secondary School Students.* (NIH# 02-5106). 2002.

It is worthwhile pointing out that the data reported by twelfth graders is consistent with the DAWN emergency room data, which shows an increase in incidents throughout the 1990s. This pattern is not so clear in the other official sources of data we have looked at, however. This is not necessarily a reflection on the quality of the data as much as it is of the population of drug users represented in the data. Furthermore, there may be different trends and dynamics in drug *use,* which are reflected in the MTF data, and drug *abuse,* which are reflected in the DAWN data.

Evaluating MTF

Monitoring the Future is one of the most powerful and reliable measures of drug use in the general population of young people. The care given to obtaining random samples provides a strong base for generalizing to the larger population of high school students and young adults. Moreover, because it is done annually and uses more than a single cohort, this project allows for the measurement of four kinds of change:

- Changes over time within a single age cohort (sometimes called "period effects").
- Developmental changes within a cohort over time.
- Differences among class cohorts over the life cycle.
- Changes associated with changing environments (e.g., from high school to college).

One primary limitation to the MTF is that it is restricted to young people, which, of course, is its purpose. Drug-use patterns of individuals much beyond 30 years of age are not measured here.

NATIONAL HOUSEHOLD SURVEY ON DRUG ABUSE (NHSDA)

The National Household Survey on Drug Abuse has been conducted by the federal government since 1971. Between 1971 and 1992, it was conducted on a periodical basis; since 1992, it has been conducted annually under the auspices of the Substance Abuse and Mental Health Services Administration (SAMHSA). Like *Monitoring the Future,* the NHSDA is a self-report measure of drug use among a representative sample of the United States population. Unlike the MTF data, however, the *National Household Survey* attempts to represent all age groups. The survey canvasses residents of households, noninstitutional group living quarters (such as shelters and dormitories) and civilians living on military bases. It does *not* include military personnel, homeless people who are not living in shelters and institutionalized populations such as jails, prisons, and hospitals.

Face-to-face interviews are conducted with a probability sample of household members aged 12 and older. The annual survey includes interviews with approximately 25,000 persons, and in 1999 this number was increased to approximately 70,000 people. The expanded number allows for more accurate estimates of drug-use prevalence at the state level. The survey includes questions on the recency and frequency of drug use, attitudes toward drug use, problems encountered as a result of drug use and treatment needs and experiences. Also included in the survey is information on demographic characteristics of respondents, employment and education information, income, health status, and access to health care and health insurance among others.

Prevalence of Drug Use as Measured by NHSDA

Figure 6.7 presents annual data on use during the previous month for the years 1991–2000. For the most part, overall use changed little during this period. Not surprisingly, alcohol is by far the most frequently used drug. In some ways the figures presented in this table are similar to the *Monitoring the Future* data on high school students during the decade of the 1990s. However, when viewed in context of the data presented in Figure 6.6, an interesting and significant pattern appears. Even though overall use of alcohol and drugs remained stable during this period, use among teenagers appears to have increased during the early 1990s.

It is important not to forget that the *National Household Survey* is a sample of all adults aged 12 and older. It is not examining the same age group over time. Hence, as time passes, and as we move through the period when cohorts of drug users beginning their drug use in the 1960s and then 1970s, more and more people in the population will have used drugs. When reading tables and figures drawn from different populations and using different methodologies, we must examine closely the differences in the populations represented and the methodologies used.

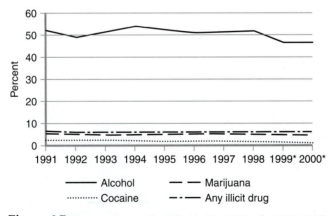

Figure 6.7 Percent Reporting Use in Past Month, 1991–2000

Note: Because of a survey redesign in 1999, NHSDA data for 1991–98 are not directly comparable with figures for 1999–2000.

Source: *1998, 2000 National Household Survey on Drug Abuse* (Summary Findings). Washington, DC: Substance Abuse and Mental Health Services Administration. 1999d; 2001.

Evaluating NHSDA

The NHSDA, like MTF, is a powerful tool in the measurement of drug-use prevalence. Its advantage over the high school survey is that it includes a much broader age range in its sampling procedure. This survey is clearly the most representative survey of the entire United States population, though it does not include institutionalized, military or homeless samples. One criticism that has been leveled against the Household Survey is that it tends to underrepresent reporting of frequent use of heroin and cocaine (Reuter, 1999). This is almost certainly because of the lack of representation of institutionalized (including prison) and homeless individuals in the sample.

OTHER UNOFFICIAL SOURCES OF DRUG USE

In addition to the national representative studies discussed earlier, there are numerous other research initiatives to more fully understand the nature and extent of drug use in the United States. We highlight four of these below.

Pulse Check

The *Pulse Check* report has been published by the Office of National Drug Control Policy (ONDCP) since 1992. Between 1992 and 1996, the ONDCP reported findings on a quarterly basis; since 1996, these data are reported

Unofficial sources of drug use data utilize a variety of strategies, including personal interviews

semiannually. The November 2001 *Pulse Check* included information from the following cities: Baltimore, MD; Billings, MT; Birmingham, AL; Boston, MA; Chicago, IL; Columbia, SC; Denver, CO; Detroit, MI; El Paso, TX; Honolulu, HI; Los Angeles, CA; Memphis, TN; Miami, FL; New Orleans, LA; New York, NY; Philadelphia, PA; Portland, ME; Seattle, WA; Sioux Falls, SD; St. Louis, MO; and Washington, DC. The data in *Pulse Check* are based on conversations and interviews with:

- **Ethnographic and Epidemiological Sources**—*Pulse Check* identifies some of the most well-known ethnographers and epidemiologists as well as sociologists and psychologists working in the drug use area.
- **Law Enforcement Sources**—Key informants from law enforcement agencies at city, county and/or federal levels in each of the 21 cities are interviewed.
- **Treatment Provider Sources**—These sources were selected from the Uniform Facility Data Set (UFDS).

The specific cities and the number of locations from which this information is obtained vary from report to report, but generally there are about a dozen ethnographers and epidemiologists located at various geographical areas across the United States; law enforcement officials from each of the targeted communities geographically distributed across the country; and about 100 treatment programs geographically distributed.

The *Pulse Check* released in November 2001, reports on six drug-use categories: heroin, crack, cocaine, marijuana, methamphetamines, and club drugs.[9] Information that is obtained from the various sources includes the level of use, who is using, method of use, market prices, and so on. Most of the data provided in *Pulse Check* are provided in narrative form, and include information on the level of drug use and drug marketing as perceived by the experts who are interviewed for this reporting program. Table 6.5 provides, in summary form, some of the typical information that is provided in *Pulse Check* by ethnographers and epidemiologists.

The *Pulse Check* data are not as systematic as other sources of data that have been presented earlier; nor are they as precise. Rather, they provide a narrative overview of drug use and drug-using behavior at various points in time that can be quickly assimilated and understood by policy makers and community groups to gain a sense of the nature of drug use in their community and region as compared with others. It is just what it says, a "pulse check." It is not to be used as a full-blown "drug physical." Other data sources are necessary for such information.

The *Pulse Check* reports do, however, draw from data sources not otherwise readily available. The ethnographic data are particularly valuable. **Ethnography** is a research methodology that utilizes researchers' spending time in the natural habitat of the drug user. Rather than relying on captive samples of prisoners or treatment clients, these data are obtained from drug users in their natural settings. Researchers sometimes

TABLE 6.5 *Pulse Check* **Ethnographers and Epidemiologists Report on Drug Use**

	Drug					
	Heroin	Crack	Powder Cocaine	Marijuana	Methamphetamines	Club Drugs[1]
Availability	High/Stable	High/Stable	High/Stable	High/Stable	High in West	Very High
Who's Using/ Change in Users	Increasing among young adults	Younger sellers; females; gangs; suburbs	Young adults; middle class; male; white	Young adults; geographically dispersed	West	Teens, young adults; white, middle class
Prevalent Method of Use	Injection, snorting	Smoking, some injection	Snorting, injecting	Smoking	Smoking, orally, snorting	Tablet form; some snorting and injecting
Drugs in Combination	Cocaine, crack, tranquilizers	Marijuana, heroin	Heroin, oxycontin, marijuana, tranquilizers	Crack, powder cocaine	Marijuana, ecstacy	Marijuana, various club drugs, cocaine
Who's Selling	Gangs, young adolescents	Mostly individuals, some gangs; young adults	Mostly individuals, some gangs; young adults	Varied age, mostly young adults	Young adults	Young adults
Price/Purity	Stable prices and purity ($10–$20/bag)	$100/gram; @ 50% pure	$28–$150/gram; 20–90% pure	$100–$200 oz.; 5–10%	$80–$300/gram; 20–95% pure	$12.50–$45 per tablet

[1]These drugs include: Ecstasy, GHB, ketamine, nitrous oxide, and LSD. Summary items are for ecstasy.

Source: Summarized from Office of National Drug Control Policy, *Pulse Check: Trends in Drug Abuse*, November, 2001 Washington, DC: U.S. Government Printing Office.

interview drug users at length about their drug use and other related behaviors, as well as observe their activity when they are given entree to do so. Valuable information that cannot be obtained even from national self-report surveys such as the *National Household Survey* or *Monitoring the Future* can be obtained. Ethnographers studying drug use are some of the best trained sociologists, psychologists, and other social scientists, seeking to understand drug use *from the perspective of the drug user him or herself.* Hence, while the data are not as systematic and do not lend themselves to generalizations to national-level drug use, they do provide valuable information about drug use not readily available elsewhere. The Drugs and Everyday Life feature provides a first-hand account by Richard Curtis, an experienced ethnographer, of the way ethnographers go about doing their work.

Community Epidemiology Work Group (CEWG)

The Community Epidemiology Work Group is a network of epidemiologists and other researchers who meet every other year to review and discuss trends in drug use and abuse. This group is sponsored by the National Institute on Drug Abuse (NIDA). The CEWG monitors drug use indicators from 21 cities.[10] These researchers base their reports on numerous epidemiological sources, including many of those that we have discussed, including TEDS, DAWN, ADAM, and the UCR, as well as data provided by the Drug Enforcement Agency (DEA), ethnographic sources, focus groups, and other community-based resources. The information available through CEWG is not "new" in the sense of a separate and unique data collection effort; however, researchers in the CEWG do their own unique statistical analyses and interpretations, which provide valuable information and perspectives on drug use in the United States.

Drug Abuse Treatment System Survey (DATSS)

The *Drug Abuse Treatment System Survey* is a periodic survey of outpatient substance abuse treatment units. To date, this survey has been conducted in 1988, 1990, and 1995 by the Survey Research Center of the Institute for Social Research at the University of Michigan, and funded by the National Institute on Drug Abuse. DATSS collected information on types of services delivered, treatment goals, funding sources, and other program-level information. In the 1995 survey, 599 treatment units participated.

Alcohol and Drug Services Study (ADSS)

The *Alcohol and Drug Services Study* is a national survey begun in 1998 as a continuation of two earlier efforts in 1990 called the Drug Services Research Survey (DSRS) and the Services Research Outcomes Study (SROS). The ADSS collects information on treatment capacity and level of utilization,

DRUGS AND EVERYDAY LIFE

An Ethnographer's Self-Portrait

I am an ethnographer specializing in the study of illegal drugs, primarily in New York City neighborhoods. . . . Those who might think I could talk with more authority about crime from the victim's rather than the offender's perspective could not be more wrong. In fact, after more than 20 years of intensive and extensive street-level research in New York city's most dangerous neighborhoods, I have never been harmed or have even really feared for my physical safety except occasionally because of nervous police officers who are surprised to find me in what they consider to be hostile territory, like crack houses or shooting galleries. For the past 10 years I've lived in Brownsville, Brooklyn—Mike Tyson's boyhood neighborhood and the one-time homicide capital of New York city—where my two daughters attend public school and where I've become quite involved in community affairs. My reasons for living in Brownsville are complex. They include my commitment to improving the inner city and my belief that if I want to "talk the talk," I need to "walk the walk." I have never regretted my decision.

What Does an Ethnographer Do?

Ethnographers do many different things. For example, a recent *New York Times* article described how corporations are increasingly turning to ethnographers to better understand how people use their products so that they can devise improvements. The work of an ethnographer—data collection—involves observing individuals over prolonged periods of time and interviewing them about topics of interest. Ethnographers typically study relatively small groups of people, and although we hope that such intensive scrutiny might lead to generalizations that can be applied to other groups across time

and space, that is not always the case. What an ethnographer learns about drug dealing in Harlem or Brooklyn may or may not have relevance to policymakers and public officials outside New York City, except that trends beginning in New York sometimes spread elsewhere.

One might simply say that ethnographers study people's everyday lives. While I do study people's everyday lives, the people I study are involved in illegal activities—typically selling or using drugs. Individuals unfamiliar with the streets or the populations I study often want to know how I actually do the work. First, I am always straightforward about what I am doing with the people I would like to know better. I try never to deceive anyone or misrepresent myself. . . .

. . . Second, I carry no protection while doing research; I rely on the relationships that I develop to ensure my safety. I do not own a gun or carry a knife or any other kind of protection device, and people are generally aware of this. This actually works to my advantage because research subjects are often so concerned about my well-being while I am working in "neighborhood minefields" that they feel obliged to accompany me to ensure my safe passage. On more than one occasion, local "tough guys" who felt it necessary to play bodyguard because they thought I was a walking target for stickup artists were shocked and appalled at how readily I entered crack houses and shooting galleries that even they had been afraid to enter. When they discovered that everyone inside knew me, they were even more surprised. While I do not mean to minimize the dangers involved in this line of work—and there are some if you do not know what you are doing—I have always felt extraordinarily protected by those around me.

continued

continued from previous page

Finally, I try to leave the work in the street when I return home at night. Although I make no secret of my address and telephone number (I am listed in the telephone book), people generally respect my privacy. In emergencies, they know they can call me ∎

Source: Richard Curtis, "The Ethnographic Approach to Studying Drug Crime." Pp. 13–15 in Office of Justice Programs, *Looking at Crime from the Street Level*. Washington, DC: National Institute of Justice, November 1999.

---

and information on pregnant women and injection drug users. Another focus of this initiative will be to collect follow-up information on clients who have been discharged. Interviews are conducted with these individuals to determine current substance use, criminal behavior, employment, and other indicators of treatment success (or failure).

Individual Research Efforts

In addition to the research efforts described throughout this chapter, there are countless researchers from many scientific disciplines who are conducting their own research on drug use. Some of this research is funded by federal agencies such as NIDA and SAMHSA, and some of it is being carried out with the assistance of state, local, and private funds. Findings from these research efforts are reported in various drug-related journals[11] as well as books on the subject.

SUMMARY

This chapter has summarized the major sources of information on drug use and on behavior related to drug use. Similar to more general crime statistics, these data sources can generally be divided into *official drug use statistics* and *unofficial drug use statistics*. Official statistics are defined as *statistics which are gathered as a function of day to day organizational procedures conducted by the government or other agencies cooperating with the government*. These agencies include the police, correctional facilities, treatment facilities, emergency rooms and medical examiners. Unofficial statistics are those *gathered for the express purpose of identifying drug users, learning relevant information about them, and for making estimates of incidence and prevalence*. Two major sources of unofficial statistics are: *Monitoring the Future*, a national survey of eighth, tenth, twelfth, and young adults which is conducted on an annual basis; and the *National Household Survey on Drug Abuse*, which is also a national survey, but of all individuals 12 and older living in a randomly drawn sample of households in the United States. Other sources of information include *Pulse Check*, which includes information from interviews with ethnographers, epidemiologists, police and treatment personnel; and the *Community Epidemiologists Work Group*, a biannual meeting of epidemiologists who report their analyses of statistics gathered through several sources, including many of those studied here. There are also other sources of treatment data which extend the official data available. These include the *Drug Abuse Treatment System Survey* and the *Alcohol and Drug Services Study*. Finally, there are numerous individual research initiatives which produce valuable information.

These sources of data provide varying and even contradictory information. There are several reasons for this. First, and most importantly, they are using different samples—samples which have widely varying drug-use experiences. A national random sample is going to provide very different results than emergency room or treatment samples, for example. Second, the methodologies employed also vary widely. Again, a national random sample will provide a very different profile than will a purposive sample of hardcore street addicts who are the target of many ethnographers. When examining any drug-use data, it is important to carefully consider both the target population and the methodology employed. Far too often, inappropriate conclusions are drawn by policy makers, practitioners, community groups—yes, and even researchers themselves—because they have not carefully considered the implications of these methodological issues.

KEY TERMS

epidemiology	incidence	prevalence
ethnography	N	rate
etiology	official statistics	unofficial statistics

REVIEW QUESTIONS

1. The *epidemiology* of drug use is substantially different from the *etiology* of drug use. What is the focus of each? How are the research questions each would ask different? Finally, how would the data sources each employ differ?

2. Why must estimates of drug use and drug use trends report *rates* rather than raw numbers when presenting data sets? What errors in interpretation could result from a failure to do so?

3. How do the five types of official drug statistics presented in this chapter vary in their data sources? What are the relative strengths and weaknesses of each data source?

4. DAWN (Drug Abuse Warning Network) data assess the extent of drug abuse in the U.S. by charting serious health consequences of abuse rather than more usual criminal justice sources. Does this indicate a federal government commitment to consider drug abuse to be a public health problem. Why or why not?

5. How do unofficial drug use data complement official statistics? In other words, how do they help fill the gaps in our knowledge resulting from reliance on official statistics alone?

6. Compare and contrast the prevalence of American drug use as measured by the two primary unofficial data sources, *Monitoring the Future* and the *National Household Survey*.

CRITICAL INQUIRY QUESTIONS

1. Data sources, both official and unofficial, arguably yield "varying and even contradictory information" because of sampling differences and differences in the questions they ask. How do professionals who desire to understand, predict, and control drug abuse negotiate this minefield? What scientific and ideological interests might guide their choices?

2. During the 1990s, emergency room data showed cocaine and heroin abuse to be on the rise while other data sources, notably treatment center data, showed a modest decline in drug abuse. Speculate on the macrosociological reasons why this contradiction exists.

NOTES

1. This is not to say that there are not victims of drug use. Families of alcoholics and drug users are victims in the sense that a spouse, parent, or child may be abusive. Similarly, the person held up at gunpoint for money to buy drugs is, indeed, a victim of drug use. But this is not the sort of information that we are seeking; rather we are seeking to estimate the number of *drug users*.

2. Prevalence statistics are typically presented as percentages or as rates.

3. Incidence figures are often reported as percentages of the total prevalence from the prior year; i.e., as *percentage increases.*

4. Typically, individuals are asked if they have committed any crimes *within the last 6 months* (or 3 months, or 1 year); or whether they have ever used drugs *within the last 3 months* (or 6 months or year). The term *prevalence* is used to refer either to "lifetime" prevalence, or prevalence for a particular time period.

5. These figures are derived from the following sources: FBI Uniform Crime Reports 1981, 1998; and the U.S. Census Bureau population estimates 1900–1998, n.d.)

6. The FBI does not report these categories in its "Crimes Known to the Police" section for understandable reasons. These are so-called victimless crimes, and are not usually reported to the police, except tantamount to an arrest.

7. Correctional statistics are comprised mainly of the following: National Prisoner Statistics (NPS); Survey of Inmates in State Correctional Facilities (SISCF); Survey of Inmates in Local Jails (SILJ); Census of Jails (COJ); Annual Survey of Jails (ASJ).

8. The exception to this reverse trend is alcohol; however, the wording of the question changed in 1993 to read "more than a few sips." Hence, the drop in alcohol use after 1993 probably reflects the more stringent wording.

9. Prior to the winter, 1998 report, the categories were heroin, cocaine, marijuana, and "emerging drugs."

10. The cities are: Atlanta, Baltimore, Boston, Chicago, Denver, Detroit, Honolulu, Los Angeles, Miami, Minneapolis/St.Paul, Newark, New Orleans, New York, Philadelphia, Phoenix, St. Louis, San Diego, San Francisco, Seattle, Texas,* Washington, D.C.

11. Some of the leading journals in the drug and alcohol field are: *The International Journal of the Addictions; Journal of Drug Issues; Contemporary Drug Problems; Quarterly Journal of Studies on Alcohol; Drug Abuse and Alcoholism Review; Journal of Drug Education; Drugs and Society; Alcoholism; Journal of Health and Social Behavior; Drug and Alcohol Dependence; American Journal of Drug and Alcohol Abuse; Journal of Addictions and Offender Counseling; Chemical Dependencies.*

SOCIAL CORRELATES OF DRUG USE

DEMOGRAPHIC AND OCCUPATIONAL CORRELATES OF DRUG USE

This chapter focuses on two related correlates of drug use. The first, *demographic correlates,* may be a new term for some of you, but it means simply *population categories* which have some relationship to drug use. We will examine three demographic correlates in this chapter, which are identified below. Each of these categories begins with basic statistical information, followed by a discussion of the dynamics of drug use in each of the population categories examined.

The second, related, focus of this chapter examines *occupational correlates* of drug use. This section examines how occupational contexts shape drug-use preferences, and also how those occupations are affected by drug-using participants in them. We are not be exhaustive of all occupational groups that might be prone to various types of drug use here. Rather, we examine a small number of occupations that illustrate how occupational dynamics give rise to substance use and, in many cases, abuse.

DEMOGRAPHIC CORRELATES OF DRUG USE

Demographics are an important part of any understanding of drug use. The fact is that drug use is *not* distributed evenly throughout any society. In the United States, for example, we know that younger people are much more likely to use illicit drugs than are middle-aged or older people. The elderly, by contrast, are much more likely to misuse prescription drugs. Similarly, there is variation in the amount and types of drugs used by different racial and ethnic groups. The demographic variation in drug use goes beyond the frequency and types of drugs used. There are also differences in the way individuals are introduced to drug use, depending on what demographic category they are in, and in the way they manage their drug use over time. In this section we examine the following demographic categories that have received a significant amount of attention in the literature: *sex (and gender), race (and ethnicity),* and *age.*

SEX AND GENDER CORRELATES OF DRUG USE

We begin this section with an examination of drug-use prevalence data for males and females. We make reference to both sex and gender because drug use affects men and women differently both because of physiological differences and because of differences in social expectations. When sociologists use the term *sex,* they are referring to physiological characteristics of men and women. *Gender,* by contrast, refers to differences in the way that men and women are expected to behave, to look, to feel, etc. Gender is *socially* derived, whereas sex is *biologically* or *physiologically* derived.

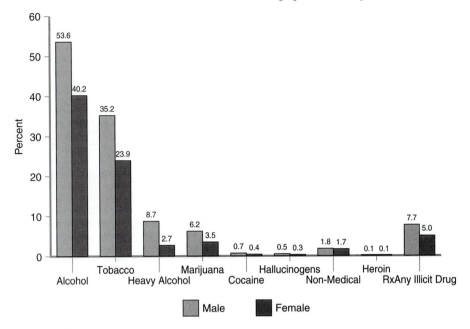

Figure 7.1 Percent of Men and Women Using Drugs in the Last 30 Days, 2000

Source: Adapted from *National Household Survey on Drug Abuse Main Findings, 2000*. Rockville, MD: Substance Abuse and Mental Health Services Administration, 2002.

With regard to likelihood of drug use, Figure 7.1 reveals a clear pattern, namely that males are more likely to use drugs recreationally than are females. This pattern generally holds true for every age group, though younger users, 12–17 years old, are much more equal across gender than are older users (Substance Abuse and Mental Health Services Administration, 2002). This pattern was also found by Lloyd Johnston and his colleagues in their samples of middle school, high school, and college students (Johnston, O'Malley and Bachman, 2000). The pattern is clear: men use more illegal drugs as well as more alcohol and tobacco than do women. This is consistent with our knowledge of deviant behavior in general: men are more often, and more seriously, involved in most deviant behaviors. The exception for the younger age category, however, does raise an important issue about onset of and early socialization into drug use.

Onset and Socialization Into Drug Use Among Males and Females

Data are somewhat mixed as to the age at which men and women are first initiated into drug use. Most early studies of gender differences have suggested that men begin their careers earlier than women (Campbell and Freeland, 1974; Eldred and Washington, 1976; Levy and Doyle, 1974; Moise, Reed and Ryan, 1982). This has not been a universal finding, however, particularly for more expensive drugs such as heroin and cocaine

(Inciardi 1979). Earlier research by Freeland and Campbell (1973) and Bowker (1977) suggests that males are more likely to be "carriers" of marijuana, meaning that they are more likely to introduce females to the drug for the first time. This is most often done in mixed-group settings or two-person settings involving romantic relationships. Similar findings were obtained by Brown and his colleagues regarding initiation into heroin (Brown, Gauvey, Meyers, and Stark, 1971). Moreover, Voss and Clayton (1984) find that transmission of drug use to new users—commonly called "turning someone on" to drugs—typically takes place during the first two years of one's own use—what Voss and Clayton call the "honeymoon period." If, as studies seem to suggest, females are usually turned on by older boys or men, and if the females who are turned on are younger than the men turning them on (which, as we have said, has not been found universally), this might account for why there are as many or more girls using in the 12–17 age group than boys.

The reasons that men and women first begin using drugs is consistent with the patterns of turning on. Research by Brown, Bauvey, Meyers and Stark (1971) reveals that curiosity and the influence of friends and relatives are the two major reasons cited by both males and females for initiation. Females, however, are much more likely to indicate that the influence of others was a major factor than were men. More recent research by Hser, Anglin, and McGlothlin (1987) finds that curiosity was a major reason for initial use of narcotics, though men were more likely to report this as a reason than women. Peer acceptance was also a reason given by men more than women, although women were much more likely to report their spouse's use as a factor in their narcotics initiation. Additionally, the relief of pain was much more a factor for women than for men. Rosenbaum's research (1981b) also cites spousal use as a major factor in women turning on to heroin.

While both women and men report similar motivations for their initial use, namely curiosity or peer pressure, women are much more likely to be drawn into continued drug use because of their reliance on a man. Women are more likely to be living with a spouse or common law partner who is using narcotics than is the case with men (Anglin, Hser, and McGlothlin, 1987). Women also report family problems as a reason for using heroin, probably not so much an escape from these problems, but as an effort to *resolve* them by using with their addicted spouses (Rosenbaum, 1981b). Even more than this, females are much more likely to continue their drug use as a form of self-medication (Inciardi, Lockwood, and Pottieger, 1993). The maladies that women attempt to mask or relieve through drugs are varied, and will be discussed in the next section.

Special Problems Encountered by Drug-Using Women

There is a growing recognition backed by good scientific research that drug-using women encounter problems and issues which are unique to them, and which pose serious consequences. The following problem areas are of particular significance to women: *health issues; domestic issues;* and *stigmatization.*

Health Issues   The use of legal *and* illegal drugs poses potential health risks for both men and women. We do not wish to minimize the risks to men by focusing on health risks to women. Indeed, we focus in more detail on health issues for both men and women in Chapter 8. We focus on women in this section because women face risks that are unique to them, and because many of the health risks that women drug users encounter are generally much more consequential than those faced by their male counterparts. Our examination of women's health issues looks at both how women's health affects their drug use, and how drug use by women affects their health. That is, we will look at health issues as both *antecedent to* (occurring prior to) and *consequences of* drug use (Gomberg and Nirenberg, 1993).

First, examining *antecedent* health variables, an overriding health consideration is that women encounter more physiological "cycles" in ways that affect their well-being and sense of well-being than do men. These cyclical events and life stage markers include pregnancy and childbirth, lactation, menstruation, and menopause. All these physiological events have profound hormonal impacts on women, which often result in depression and stress, leaving many women more predisposed to turn to drugs and alcohol (Gomberg, 1982).

A review of literature by Wilsnack (1984) suggests a high level of sexual dysfunction among alcoholic women, which seems to be antecedent to the onset of drinking problems (Wilsnack, Klassen, and Wilsnack, 1986). Studies have also found higher rates of depression among female alcoholics than men, though it is difficult to determine which is the antecedent condition—alcoholism or depression (Reid, 1998; Hesselbrock, and Hesselbrock, 1993; Schuckit, 1986; Schuckit and Monteiro, 1988). Still another area of potential vulnerability for women is eating disorders. Both clinical and cross-sectional studies have found that women who suffer eating disorders such as bulimia or anorexia nervosa are more likely to use and abuse tobacco, alcohol, and marijuana as well as stimulants, laxatives, and other drugs which are intentionally used to enhance weight loss. As is the case with depression, it is unclear whether there is a common casual factor driving both the eating disorders and the substance use, or whether eating disorders lead to and reinforce drug use. There is evidence to support both hypotheses (Krahn, 1993). One thing is clear, however, and that is that doctors are much more willing to prescribe drugs to women who present health-related symptoms than they do with men, resulting in generations of women becoming addicted to prescription drugs over the past century (Marsh, 1982; Nellis, 1980). According to Nellis and others, there has been an overprescription of drugs to women in American society as physicians have either been less sensitive to physical and/or emotional symptoms presented by women than with men, and/or have been trained to address these symptoms by prescribing tranquilizers and other drugs. There is evidence, however, that this trend may be reversing.

Goode (1999) points out that the number of prescriptions for barbiturates and amphetamines written today is only about 5 to 10 percent of the number written in the 1960s and 1970s.

The health *consequences* of drug and alcohol abuse to women are potentially immense, and are discussed at greater length in Chapter 8. Perhaps the area of greatest concern is complications in pregnancy. Every year, approximately 500,000 infants are born who have been exposed to illicit drugs. There are even more women who use tobacco and alcohol during pregnancy (Reid, 1996). Most drugs that a woman might use or abuse are capable of crossing the placental barrier to affect the fetus and, eventually, the newborn infant. When women abuse drugs and alcohol during pregnancy, they may give birth to infants displaying fetal alcohol syndrome; neonatal addiction; low birth weight, often due to premature delivery; spontaneous abortion; and other symptoms, resulting in a greater likelihood of infant mortality than among infants born of nondrug-using women. (Cuskey, Premkumar, and Sigel, 1972; Finnegan and Fehr, 1980; Little and Wendt, 1993; Rosett, 1980). Additionally, infertility and other forms of sexual dysfunction have been noted in higher rates among women drug users than among nonusers (Lex, 1993).

Other health consequences have also been observed. Women who abuse alcohol more readily develop liver dysfunction than do men, contributing to a 50 to 100 percent higher liver-dysfunction death rate among women than among men (Gomberg and Nirenberg, 1993). A serious health issue that is indirectly related to crack-cocaine use among women is the acquisition of sexually transmitted diseases. So-called "crack whores," who sell themselves sexually for crack, run great risks of acquiring gonorrhea, syphilis, hepatitis, and HIV/AIDS. Female crack users have substantially higher rates of sexually transmitted diseases than do their fellow users who are male (Metsch, McCoy, and Weatherby, 1996).

Domestic Issues   Like health issues, it is not always easy to determine whether the domestic issues that women drug users confront *contribute* to their substance abuse, or are *consequential* to that use. The answer seems to be that it is both. Women who come from troubled domestic backgrounds are more likely to use drugs, often as an attempt to escape from or possibly "fix" a domestic problem; ironically, this very drug use usually exacerbates their domestic crisis. We look first at what we know about how past domestic abuse and other problems contribute to drug abuse. That is followed by a discussion of how patterns of substance abuse by both men and women further complicate patterns of violence and other dysfunction in the family.

It has long been hypothesized that poor family relations contribute to substance abuse and, indeed, delinquency generally. While the research is somewhat divided, it does seem that pathological family dynamics affect girls more than boys. Substance-abusing women consistently report coming from broken homes, sexual abuse, and other unfavorable home environments. Isidor Chein and his colleagues in the now classic *The Road to H* (1964) report that female addicts typically come from homes where the father is absent. Sexual abuse is also a common theme in the biographies of female drug addicts. Cuskey and Wathey (1982) found that more than 30 percent of the female (primarily) heroin addicts in their sample had been sexually abused as children, and nearly 35 percent had been physically abused. Among those who were sexually abused, about one-fourth reported rape as their very first sexual experience. A similar pattern of childhood sexual abuse has been observed among alcoholics (Gomberg and Nirenberg, 1993) and female crack users (Sterk 1999). Finally, both male and female drug abusers typically come from drug-abusing families. Nearly half of the women in Cuskey and Wathey's (1982) study reported alcohol abuse in their families of origin. Familial drug abuse was reported by 50 percent of the black women and 33 percent of the white women in their sample. Drug and alcohol use by parents and other significant adults normatively models this behavior for children who learn to use these behaviors as responses to stressful circumstances.

Domestic relationships and dynamics also are profoundly *affected* by drug use and addiction. Once again, the impact of substance abuse on family life seems to be especially felt by women. Marsha Rosenbaum has studied this issue in her research among women heroin addicts in her 1981 book, *Women on Heroin*. Rosenbaum describes an initial honeymoon period, followed by a process of erosion of stability and structure in the female addict's life. She takes risks which eventually lead to a chaotic lifestyle and becoming overwhelmed by the demands of the heroin lifestyle. What began as a means of *saving* her marriage and family, eventually undermines these relationships and the structure that sustains them (Rosenbaum, 1981a, 1981b, 1981c).

Somewhat different dynamics are reported by observers of the crack scene. Ethnographic reports show that women are much more blatantly and overtly exploited for sex very early into a woman's crack-using career (Inciardi, Lockwood, and Pottieger, 1993; Pettiway, 1997; Sterk, 1999). These reports suggest that women are more likely to experiment with crack-cocaine out of curiosity than out of loyalty to a significant other. Moreover, the pharmacology and economics of crack overtake the user much more quickly than is the case with heroin. Very soon after they begin using, these crack-using women are confronted with the difficult reality that they must find a way to support themselves and their habits. Most do not have a man to depend upon to supply them with the drugs. Crack-addicted women very quickly learn to trade sex for drugs (Inciardi, Lockwood, and Pottieger, 1993).

The domestic consequences and dynamics of alcohol abuse by women more closely resemble that of heroin addicted women than crack-using women. Some women become addicted to alcohol as adolescents, before they ever become involved in a domestic relationship (e.g., see Thompson and Wilsnack, 1984). It is common, however, that female alcoholics become addicted *after* they are married and have established their own homes. Their alcoholism may develop from social drinking, a pattern that is not so unlike Rosenbaum's portrayal of women who become addicted to heroin as a result of wanting to find a way to connect with their spouse. Other women develop a pattern of drinking in response to a sense of isolation from their spouses, and use alcohol as a way of masking loneliness. Regardless of the reason that women begin to use alcohol on a habitual basis, alcohol addiction profoundly affects a woman's relationship with her family. The female alcoholic may be able to mask her addiction for a sustained period of time if she does not have to work outside the home. Her drinking is usually very private and often not observed by others, except perhaps her husband and children. Eventually, however, the female alcoholic experiences a level of "inundation" similar to what Rosenbaum describes among female heroin users. She fails to perform normal domestic duties that results in increased tension between her and her family. Violence is often part of domestic relationships, particularly if her spouse is also a problem drinker (Frieze and Schafer, 1984).

Stigmatization   Substance-abusing women face society's disapproval to an extreme not encountered by men. It is certainly the case that when drugs and alcohol are abused, and when the user loses control over that use as is denoted in addiction, there is a level of stigma regardless if one is a man or a woman. Moreover, the use of *illicit* drugs places the user among the potentially stigmatized, regardless of gender. Beyond the general labeling that is attached to the perpetrators of deviant behavior, however, women who deviate are stigmatized in a manner that is far more scurrilous and destructive than that directed at their male counterparts. Society is much more tolerant of the misadventures of boys and even men than of girls and women. The adolescent boy who deviates is merely "sowing his wild oats"—a luxury that seems to be restricted to boys, and for the most part, middle class boys. Girls engaging in the same behavior are generally cast as "sluts," "whores," "loose," and all manner of sexual stigmatization— regardless of the nature of their indiscretion. Understandably, girls are much more vulnerable to a poor self-concept, which only increases the likelihood of drug and alcohol abuse and indiscriminate sexual activity.

Drug-using women are also stigmatized in a manner that goes far beyond the bounds of what men experience. Rosenbaum describes the nature and the consequences of this differential stigmatization:

> After having been addicted for several years, many women envision a heroin-free life, married to or living with a non-addicted man. . . . But there is an inherent obstacle to such relationships: Never-addicted men are generally not interested in becoming involved with a woman who has been a heroin addict, convicted of a crime, and probably a prostitute. Thus the option for a relationship with a man who is safe in terms of potential addiction or readdiction is reduced for the woman addict. In most cases, she is forced to limit her relationships to either addicted men or ex-addicts, which could lead to recidivism for her.

Men do not suffer the stigma of addiction as severely as women, especially in the area of interpersonal and sexual relationships. Addicted or formerly addicted men often develop relationships with non-addicted women, which is many times considered the road to abstinence for men; this rarely works in the reverse however. The woman who has been an addict seems to fall harder than her male counterpart; she alone is defined as "damaged goods." Differentiated societal mores pertaining to men and women are evident here: The man is seen as having temporarily transgressed, whereas the woman is defined as having permanently fallen (Rosenbaum, 1981, pp. 131–132).

A similar stigmatization takes place in the occupational arena. While both men and women addicts or ex-addicts are stigmatized, the consequences for women are substantially more severe for women. Men, it seems, have an opportunity to redeem themselves through rehabilitation, and are lauded by conventional society for their fortitude in beating their habits. Women are often not so well received. In some cases, she is given the status of a "fallen woman." Part of the rehabilitation process that has been recognized by groups such as AA and others as an important step in the road to recovery, is to share one's experiences with others. What is an important part of recovery and community acceptance for men, however, often results in rejection for women as they attempt to reveal their identities outside of the therapeutic environment. Moreover, society has much higher standards for how women *appear*, and the physical wear and tear that the addicted woman experiences reduces her opportunities for employment and for social acceptance far more so than if she were a man. Her status in the community as an addict is much more difficult to leave behind than it is for her male counterpart. Friedman and Alicea (2001) point out that the use of heroin often begins as a statement of independence for women, an effort to take control of their lives, but as they move further into the heroin world, women heroin users become increasingly exposed to various forms of gender oppression. Indeed, Maher (1997) and Maher and Daly (1996) point out that the crack-using woman not only faces higher levels of discrimination in the conventional employment arena, but encounters reduced economic opportunities within the drug world itself when compared with her male counterparts. She is a member of a *caste*—an *out-caste*, to be sure—from which it is difficult if not impossible to escape.

The stigmatization process does not wait until a woman attempts to go drug-free and live a conventional life. Recent ethnographic evidence that has been reported on crack-addicted women suggests a patriarchal culture that imposes a stigmatizing identity on women far beyond that experienced by heroin-using women. Sterk (1999) reports that the women in her sample of crack users were marginalized *within* the crack subculture. They were, to use a term borrowed from Lofland (1969), "unfit strangers" within the crack subculture itself. Most of these women were not able to maintain steady relationships with noncrack users, and any relationships with male crack users were often strained to the breaking point because of the common practice of trading sex for crack. These women have been referred to as "toss-ups," a term connoting that they are something to be used and then tossed away (Fullilove, Fullilove, Bowser, and Gross, 1990). They have also been pejoratively referred to as "skeezers" and "crack 'hos" (Fullilove and Lown, 1992), "freaks," "base whores," "gut buckets," and "rock monsters" (Metsch, McCoy, and Weatherby, 1996). Crack-using women, perhaps more than any other type of drug user suffer from what Goffman (1963) has referred to as a stigma of "blemishes of individual character."

RACIAL AND ETHNIC CORRELATES OF DRUG USE

Findings from the National Household Survey on Drug Abuse reveal a most startling pattern—startling, at least, for many casual observers of the drug scene: *whites are more likely to use drugs than are either blacks or Hispanics.* Figure 7.2 reveals that for every drug type except tobacco, cocaine and marijuana, there is a larger percentage of whites that currently use than either blacks or Hispanics. This finding clearly defies the commonsense assumptions that many of us make about drug use (especially illicit drug use) being primarily an activity that is engaged in by minority populations.

Hispanic Drug Use Dynamics

The Hispanic population in the United States comprises numerous subpopulations that reflect differences in their countries of origin and, in turn certain distinctive cultural traits (Almog, Anglin, and Fisher, 1993). The

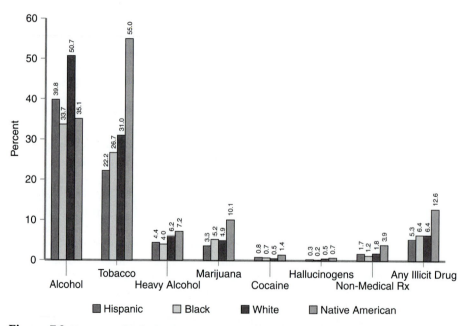

Figure 7.2 **Percent of Ethnic Groups Using Drugs in the Last 30 Days, 2000**

Source: *National Household Survey on Drug Abuse Main Findings, 2000.* Rockville, MD: Substance Abuse and Mental Health Services Administration, 2002.

three dominant Hispanic populations in the United States are those from Mexico, Puerto Rico, and Cuba, in addition to Hispanics immigrating from Central and South America. Mexican Hispanics are located heavily in the Southwest area of the United States and in certain sections of the Midwest; Puerto Ricans are found primarily in New York and other major cities such as Chicago; and Cubans are concentrated largely in Miami and other Florida communities. Generally, Puerto Ricans are most likely to have used drugs within the last 30 days (except for alcohol), while other Hispanic groups have very similar prevalence rates.

Research on the demographics of Hispanic users reveals certain patterns which distinguish them from white users: they have less education, lower rates of employment, more likely to be on welfare, and have higher poverty rates (Anglin, Ryan, Booth, and Hser, 1988; Bourgois, 1995; Bullington, 1977; Chambers, Coskey, and Moffett, 1970). Chicanos are also more likely to have been married and to be living with one or more other persons than are whites (Anglin et al., 1988). These marriage and living arrangements highlight the elevated importance that Hispanics give to family regardless of whether we are observing Chicanos or other Latino groups (Bullington,1977; Moore,1990; Glick,1990; Fitzpatrick,1990). Unfortunately, Hispanic immigrants encounter structural conditions which are disruptive to family life as discovered by Bourgois (1995) among Puerto Ricans and by Page (1990) among Cuban Hispanics.

Drug-use patterns of Hispanics also differ from that of whites. Anglin and his colleagues report that whites are much more likely than Chicanos to have used a variety of drugs, including hallucinogens, amphetamines, cocaine, tranquilizers, PCP, and narcotics other than heroin or street methadone (Anglin et al., 1988). Chicanos, by contrast, more narrowly focus on heroin use, though inhalants and alcohol are also popular drugs of choice (Almog et al., 1993). Alcohol use is also especially prevalent among Puerto Ricans (Singer, Valentin, Baer, and Jia, 1992). Anglin and his associates (1988) find that, except for heroin, Chicano men also tend to become involved in drugs at a later age than whites, a finding also reported by Almog et al. (1993).

It is not possible to fully understand the dynamics of Hispanic drug use apart from the cultural context in which this drug use takes place. Joan Moore (1978, 1991) provides a rich description of life in the barrios of Los Angeles, including drug-using behaviors of the Hispanic youth there. She identifies three cultural traits which are especially relevant to understanding drug use in the barrio: *machismo, personalismo,* and *carnalismo. Machismo* broadly refers to everything from the aggressive supermasculine image for which it is so commonly understood, to the notion of "responsible adult manliness" (1978, p. 77). This translates rather directly to drinking behavior. Singer et al. (1992) report that drinking and masculinity are directly linked among Puerto Rican males, and that refusal to drink may even be interpreted as homosexuality. Research by Hardesty and Black (1999), by contrast finds that Puerto Rican women attach a great deal of importance to motherhood, and that this status is an important lifeline in their attempts to recover from addiction. *Personalismo* refers to the ability to sustain long-lasting loyalties among friends and family, and *carnalismo* refers to the special "blood brother" bond that ties all Chicanos together. Related to the latter two cultural traits is a system of kinship known as *compadrazgo,* that extends responsibility for child rearing beyond immediate blood-family to selected nonblood relatives (Bullington, 1977). These cultural features may account in part for the higher rates of gang membership among Chicano addicts. It also accounts for a different economy of drug use in the barrios. Chicano youth gangs have been an instrumental part of the marketing of heroin and other drugs in the barrios of Los Angeles.

Heroin addicts in the barrio are referred to as **tecatos.** Jorquez (1984) has described the tecato subculture as unique from non-Hispanic heroin subcultures. It has its own history, world view, rituals, and code of conduct. Jorquez suggests that Chicanos typically do not respond as well to mainstream treatment efforts because most treatment programs are not cognizant of these cultural differences. Fitzpatrick (1990) has further pointed out that Puerto Rican families and communities do not generally ostracize their members when they become addicted. They remain connected, which makes it much easier for them to re-enter Puertoriqueño cultural life when they attempt to go drug-free.

African-American Drug Use Dynamics

Empirical research on the cultural dynamics of drug use among African-Americans is surprisingly sparse, though there has been some recent research examining these issues. While there have been numerous studies that included African-Americans as all or part of their samples, and while many of these studies made certain demographic and other comparisons between whites and blacks, these studies did not provide a great deal of information on social or cultural dynamics of drug or alcohol use among African Americans (Herd, 1987; Trimble, Padilla and Bell, 1987). This is quite surprising, given that blacks have been viewed as primary purveyors of drugs and responsible for most drug-related crime. Indeed, many of the early studies of heroin use depicted the typical heroin user as a black, lower class, inner-city male.

Recent research has filled in some of the gaps in our knowledge of the social and cultural dynamics of African-American drug use. An important factor in African-American drug use would appear to be social class, though research directly measuring social class and drug use is extremely sparse. Research by Barr, Farrell, Barnes, and Welte (1993) has demonstrated that social class is particularly significant in determining *level* of substance use among black males. Poor black men are more than five times more likely to use drugs and/or alcohol than poor white men, though differences are minimal for higher income males, a general pattern also reported by Herd (1987) regarding alcohol use. Research has also found a relationship between educational attainment and drug use. Both black and white heroin addicts tend to have dropped out of school (Nurco, Cisin and Balter, 1981);

however, black males with lower educational attainment are much more likely to use drugs than are minimally educated white males (Barr, Farrell, Barnes, and Welte, 1993). These data would suggest that social class seems to be a predominant factor contributing to African-American drug use, though among the lower class, blacks are much more vulnerable to drug use than are whites.

In addition to expensive drugs such as heroin and cocaine, marijuana has been used as part of a more general religious and political statement among some African Americans. Marijuana, or "ganja" is a central ritual element among Rastafarians, who use marijuana in much the same way ritualistically as Christians partake of communion. It is believed that marijuana smoking enhances their spiritual awareness. This religious sect, which traces its origins to the election in 1930 of the Ethiopian black nationalist leader, Ras Tafari, has distinct political overtones challenging the imperialism of the west, a theme that is especially pronounced in the writings of Marcus Garvey, a Jamaican apologist for black culture. Marijuana represents a direct repudiation of the mores of the dominant white culture. Marijuana use by African-Americans is not limited to those who identify with Rastafarianism, of course, but the Rastafarian movement has provided an alternative cultural meaning to marijuana use among blacks that is not available among whites. This culture of drug use is discussed more fully in Chapter 5.

Native American Drug Use Dynamics

Native Americans comprise less than 1 percent of the population in the United States. Yet, there is probably no other ethnic group more notorious for substance abuse—in the form of alcoholism and alcohol abuse. The stereotype of the "drunken Indian" has been reinforced in the media and in our schools. There is a kernel of truth underlying this stereotype. Native Americans rank higher than any other ethnic group with regard to the percentage of their population reporting "heavy" use of alcohol over the past 30 days[1] (Substance Abuse and Mental Health Services Administration, 2002) and (along with Mexican Hispanics) higher rates of alcohol *dependence* than other ethnic groups (Office of Applied Statistics, 1998). These rankings tell only part of the story, however. Native Americans do, indeed, report greater alcohol dependence; however, only 5.6 percent of that population report such dependence, though other studies find higher rates (Heidenreich, 1976). This is a far cry from the stereotype of drunken comportment that is attached to this ethnic group! Moreover, it is also worthwhile pointing out that Native Americans are more likely to report past month use of cigarettes, marijuana, cocaine and most other illicit drugs than all other ethnic groups (See Figure 7.2). Yet, they are not stereotyped according to these dimensions of drug use.

Another area of drug use among Native Americans that we have addressed in Chapter 5, is the use of peyote as part of the religious ritual of the Native American Church. Peyote has been used by Native Americans in religious rituals for centuries without much attention. As the use of peyote in religious rituals spread throughout North America, it took different forms, some of which incorporated Christian elements, while other groups were quite distinctly anti-Christian. Eventually, various of these groups joined together in what was eventually to become the Native American Church, which was incorporated in Oklahoma in 1918. The Native American Church would eventually become incorporated in other states and became an international church in 1954 with the incorporation of the Native American Church of Canada. There are currently an estimated 250,000 people worldwide who practice some form of peyote religion (Anderson, 1996). The acceptance of the Native American Church, and especially the practice of peyotism, has not been well accepted by the American government over the years. Indeed, while the Native American Church has been officially recognized in several states, and the use of peyote is allowed, the drug remains banned in other states, even for religious ceremonial use.

AGE CORRELATES OF DRUG USE

The age distribution of drug use represents an interesting, but very logical pattern. Figure 7.3 portrays the percentage of five major age groups that have used each of five types of drug usage within the past month. The drugs

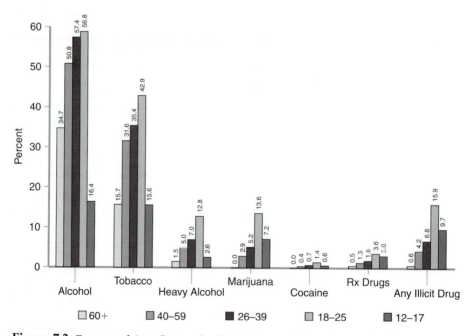

Figure 7.3 **Percent of Age Categories Using Drugs in Last 30 Days, 2000**

Source: Adapted from *National Household Survey on Drug Abuse Main Findings, 2000*. Rockville, MD: Substance Abuse and Mental Health Services Administration, 2002.

examined in this figure are alcohol (and "heavy" alcohol use), tobacco, marijuana, cocaine,[2] and prescription drugs. The age groups represented here correspond roughly to adolescence (12–17), college age (18–25), young adult (26–39), middle age (40–59), and elderly (60 and over).

There is a clear age pattern for all of the drugs represented in Figure 7.3. A significant number of adolescents use these drugs, but adolescence is by no means the highest age group to be using either legal or illegal drugs during the past month. Rather, it is the college age group (18–25) who are most likely to report drug use in the past 30 days (though young adults are slightly more likely to have consumed alcohol). The explanation for this pattern is quite straightforward. While there is a good bit of experimentation with drugs during adolescence, it is during the college years that both experimental and recreational use of most drugs takes place. As people get older their lifestyles change, and the use of both licit and illicit drugs are less and less a part of their lifestyles. There may also be some cohort effects as well. That is, people who are born at one time period may display a different pattern of drug use than those born during a different time period. Examining these trends across age categories does indeed suggest that certain age cohorts are more likely to use than others. Even within age cohorts, however, the pattern of modest levels of adolescent use, expanded college-age use, and gradually diminishing levels of use with increased age remains.

In this section, we will be singling out three specific age groups for closer analysis: *adolescents, college students,* and *the elderly.* We know from research that older people do display certain drug-use and abuse patterns, especially of prescription drugs, that set them apart from the rest of the population. The National Household Survey does not, unfortunately, reflect the misuse of prescription drugs by the elderly since misuse by older persons is usually for medical purposes, even though it is often seriously detrimental to their health.

Drug Use Among Adolescents

Adolescent drug use in the United States has been widely studied empirically since the 1960s, and was originally the sole focus of the *Monitoring the Future* survey conducted by the University of Michigan's Survey Research Center. Recent data from the *Monitoring the Future* survey suggest reason for continued concern regarding adolescent drug use. Figure 7.4 reveals that recent illicit drug use has increased among eighth, tenth, and twelfth graders over the last decade, though it seems to have peaked in the middle of the decade, at least for younger (eighth and tenth grade) users. When more than 10 percent of eighth graders and more than 25 percent of twelfth graders have used illicit drugs in the past month, parents, teachers, and public officials are understandably concerned about teen-age drug use.

Before drawing any final conclusions about levels of adolescent drug use, however, a couple of caveats are in order. First, most of the illicit drug

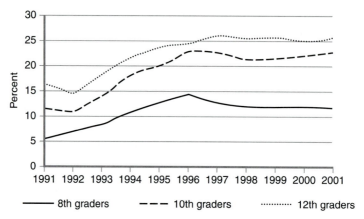

Figure 7.4 Percent of High School Students Using any Illicit Drugs in the Last 30 Days, 1991–2001

Source: Adapted from LD Johnston, PM O'Malley, JG Bachman. (2000). "Trends in Annual and 30-Day Prevalence of Use of Various Drugs for 8th, 10th, 12th Graders, 1991–2001 [On-line]. Available: www.monitoringthefuture.org; accessed April 30, 2002.

use reported by these high school students is marijuana. This is not to suggest that adolescents are not also trying other illicit drugs. Nearly half of the students surveyed reported using other drugs as well. Use of illicit drugs other than marijuana, however, seems to be more sporadic. The second caveat is that even mid-1990 levels of illicit drug use are lower than what was being reported in the mid to late 1970s. In 1979, nearly 39 percent of twelfth graders reported using illicit drugs during the past year; in 2001, only about 26 percent reported such use. There was, in fact, a trend *downward* in teen drug use through the 1980s and early 1990s, a trend which seems to have reversed in the mid-1990s, though possibly leveling off in the last few years.

The trends for alcohol and tobacco are similar to that of illicit drugs. *Monitoring the Future* data reveal that 72 percent of twelfth graders reported the use of alcohol in 1980, but that number declined through the 1980s and 1990s, and in 2001, only about 50 percent of high school seniors report using alcohol in the last 30 days.[3] Tobacco use shows a slightly different trend, at least insofar as cigarettes are concerned. Approximately 30 percent of high school seniors smoked in the previous 30 days during the 1970s, decreasing only slightly through the 1980s, but rising in the 1990s to even higher levels (36.5 percent in 1997) than in the 1970s. There is, furthermore, another tobacco form that appears to be attractive to young people—smokeless tobacco. While cigarettes remain the most common form of tobacco use among teenagers, the National Youth Tobacco Survey, conducted jointly by the American Legacy Foundation and the Centers for Disease Control, found that 4.2 percent of middle school boys and 11.6 percent of high school boys had used smokeless tobacco. The same study also found that *bidis*, imported cigarettes that are pleasantly flavored, are being discovered by younger users. More than 6 percent of high school boys and nearly 4 percent of high school girls reported smoking *bidis* (Centers for Disease Control, 2000).

Drug Use Among College Students

College represents, for many young people, the establishment of their independence from their parents and, indeed, independence from adult authority in many areas of their personal lives. This is also a time when young people are exposed to many new pressures and influences. They are confronted in the classroom with challenges to the belief systems with which they grew up. They are confronted in the dormitories, fraternities, and sororities with lifestyles that are novel and perhaps a bit exciting. It should not be surprising, therefore, that this is a time of greatly expanded drug use for many young adults. Indeed, the National Household Survey reveals that the age group represented by college students—18–25—reports the highest levels of all types of drug use within the past month (see Figure 7.3).

The 1960s left an indelible mark on college campuses for later generations of college students. The country was in turmoil with civil rights unrest and, later in the decade, great disillusionment over the war in Vietnam. College drug-users of the 1960s and 1970s were defined by a distinct posture of protest, and drugs such as marijuana and LSD were a visible part of events such as Woodstock in 1969. Woodstock became a symbol of protest, and part of that symbolism was the open advocacy and use of marijuana and LSD. Experimentation with LSD was facilitated by its endorsement and use by Timothy Leary, a Harvard psychologist who was urging college students to "turn on" to LSD.

Certainly, reports of drug use and especially of the *consequences* of this drug use were greatly exaggerated from time to time. The fact remains, however, that young people *were* turning on to drugs in far greater numbers than ever before. Moreover, these were largely the sons and daughters of middle-class families who were involved in drug use on college campuses at this time. America came to attention when the "cream" of its youth—those from middle-class families—were significantly represented among the ranks of drug users.

Lawmakers responded with haste to send a message to college students that drug use was not acceptable, and that they would be punished accordingly. The real villains sought, however, were the *drug dealers,* who, it was believed, were responsible for turning a generation of young people on to deadly drugs such as marijuana, LSD, and cocaine. The most severe of sentences were reserved for the dealers who, it was believed, were not college students but inner-city entrepreneurs seeking to take advantage of innocent middle class youth (Peterson, 1985). Despite these efforts, college campuses continue to be a context for illicit drug use of various types, including marijuana, hallucinogens, cocaine, methamphetamines, and more recently drugs such as rohypnol.

Most American colleges today are not characterized by protests, as in the 1960s or 1970s, but the effects of these protests, and the drug use that was part of them, remain. College campuses continue to be a place where many middle-class young people first begin experimenting with illegal drugs. However, illicit drug use on college campuses pales in comparison to problematic alcohol consumption. One review of research done on this topic concludes that most studies suggest that between 20 and 25 percent of college students have drinking problems (Berkowitz and Perkins, 1986). One form of problem drinking that is quite common on college campuses is **binge drinking.** Binge drinking is generally defined as five drinks in a single drinking session for men and four for women. A major study of students on 140 college campuses by Henry Wechsler and his associates at Harvard University, found that 44 percent of students reported that they had engaged in binge drinking sometime in the two-week period prior to being interviewed (Wechsler et al., 1994). Durkin, Wolfe and Clark (1999) found that 80 percent of the students in a Maryland college reported binge drinking on at least one occasion during the prior semester.

Binge drinking poses serious consequences for those students who participate, including relationship, academic, and health problems, and for many, eventual alcoholism and problem behaviors associated with chronic heavy drinking. Durkin and Clark (2000) also report that 35 percent of their sample of students on one college campus reported driving a vehicle after a bout of binge drinking; 24 percent became involved in a fight, 23.3 percent engaged in unplanned sexual activity, and 22.4 percent experienced a blackout following binge drinking. These results also suggest that there is a **secondary binge effect** of binge drinking on nondrinking students as well.

These numbers seem staggering, but we must remember that binge drinking is defined in these studies as drinking four (for women) or five (for men) drinks in a single drinking session (Wechsler et al., 1994). Europeans define binge drinking much more stringently. It is said that Italians consider eight drinks in a setting to be *normal* drinking! The fact that 80 percent of a student body drank 4–5 drinks in one session during the past semester is not nearly as dramatic as to suggest that 80 percent engaged in at least one episode of binge drinking. It is precisely the *normality* of drinking four or five drinks in a single setting the some scholars find objectionable about this definition (Dimeff, Kilmer, Baer, and Marlatt, 1995). Moreover, we also know that blood-alcohol content (BAC) depends on body weight. While having four or five drinks may produce some impairment of judgment for some people, there are many who would not be affected by this quantity. The 5/4 threshold is, to be sure, *highly conservative.*

This interpretive caveat is not meant to diminish the potential alcohol-related problems that can occur on college campuses. Driving a car after 4 or 5 drinks *is* enough to make some drinkers illegal drivers and unsafe drivers to those around them. (Midanek et al., 1996; Wechsler, 1998). And we know that many college students drink much more than this threshold level of binge drinking. Indeed, extreme binge drinking can ultimately be fatal, as evidenced by overdose deaths at Massachusetts Institute of Technology and Louisiana State University, as well as on other campuses in recent years (Higson, 1998). Moreover, the data presented in Figure 7.3 suggest also that college-age individuals are much more likely to be involved in "heavy drinking," which is more sustained than is binge drinking. We do suggest, however, that we be cautious when drawing conclusions, and that we not formulate policies and intervention strategies on these relatively rare extreme cases. College students who engage in threshold binge drinking are, in fact, engaging in *normative* behavior; nevertheless, they are easily labeled and stigmatized by zealous intervention efforts, a consequence which may be far more harmful than the drinking behavior itself.

Drug Use Among the Elderly

Drug use among the elderly of our population is of concern, not so much for its *prevalence* in this age group as for its *consequences* and *circumstances of use.*

Consequences of Elderly Drug Use and Abuse   The aging process modifies the way in which the human body responds to drugs and alcohol, including the rate of absorption, how the drug is distributed through the body, and the rate and manner of excretion (Council on Scientific Affairs, 1996). Hence, those who use pharmacological substances in their older years will almost certainly experience effects and consequences very differently from what they might have become accustomed to at an earlier time. Elderly drinkers, for example, generally have higher blood alcohol content due to lower levels of systemic water volume. Heavy drinking is much more likely to affect the intake of food, thus resulting in nutritional deficiencies. Moreover, because elderly users are heavy users of prescription drugs, accounting for more than 30 percent of all prescription drug use (Willcox, Himmelstein, and Woolhander, 1994), they are especially at risk for overdose symptoms resulting from synergism of two or more drugs they may be taking, either legitimately or illegitimately. The results can be disabling or even deadly.

Circumstances of Elderly Drug Use and Abuse   If elderly individuals knowingly and voluntarily used drugs in an inappropriate manner, the consequences of elderly drug abuse might be more easily dismissed. The fact is, however, that many if not most elderly drug abusers are not aware that they engaging in drug abuse. We don't even call it drug abuse. Rather, we refer to it as "overprescription," "inappropriate medication," or "inappropriate drug prescribing." These are terms which tend to minimize the seriousness of this problem. Moreover, elderly drug users are at the mercy of medical professionals who all too often have little time or inclination to respond to their questions or concerns. Because it is easy to prescribe a drug for a particular symptom, elderly patients are often prescribed drugs unnecessarily or even inappropriately. Research by Willcox, Himmelstein and

Woolhandler (1994) revealed that nearly 25 percent of the residents in community living facilities were prescribed drugs that were *contraindicated*, meaning that they were not appropriate for a particular symptom. Indeed, Reid (1998) found that when female patients came in complaining of depression, most physicians don't even inquire about substance use patterns before prescribing sedatives to these women.

The problem is not merely doctors asleep on the job, however. Much of the problem with overprescribing and inappropriate prescribing is a result of the increasing specialization of medicine today. Elderly people are especially likely to be under the care of numerous specialists who each prescribe drugs for particular conditions. The elderly patient may have several pharmacies at which prescriptions are filled, particularly when their specialists may practice in different communities. Unless the patient is alert to all the medications that he or she is taking, it is very easy, indeed likely, that he or she will be prescribed medications that interact with each other to produce adverse effects. This is a problem that could be rectified with a central database, preferably organized on a national level, into which all prescriptions would be entered. Any doctor or pharmacist would only have to access the database to determine whether there were any potential untoward drug interaction effects. At present, however, we have no such program at the national level.

Finally, elderly individuals are also likely to be using over-the-counter medications, in addition to prescribed medications that they may be taking, many of which contain alcohol. Because alcohol synergizes with other depressants, any prescription of sedatives, tranquilizers, or antihistamines to elderly patients could produce severe consequences. Combine this with the fact that many elderly individuals drink alcohol, symptoms of drug overdose are of especially great concern among a population whose bodies do not absorb, distribute, or excrete these chemicals as effectively as do the bodies of younger people.

OCCUPATIONAL CORRELATES OF DRUG USE

The occupation is an important context for understanding drug use in American society for several reasons. First, working people spend a considerable amount of their time at the *workplace*—the geographical locale in which occupational activities are carried out. The workplace is usually a centralized locale where others in the same or similar occupations interact in the production of particular goods or services. Different occupations will bring together different kinds of people to these workplaces. Second, occupations vary in the demands that they impose on those who hold occupational statuses. Some occupations are inherently more stressful than others, for example. Others have unique performance expectations which might be enhanced with the use of certain types of drugs. The occupational subculture of professional sports, for example, at least tacitly supports the use of steroids and other performance-enhancing drugs. These various occupational characteristics may affect the nature and extent of drug use. Third, some occupations and associated workplaces provide *greater access* to certain types of drugs, a particularly important quality of medical occupations. For all of these reasons, occupations are important contexts for understanding the dynamics of drug use in the United States.

Occupations are also important arenas from which to understand drug use because such use may profoundly affect one's performance in the workplace. As early as 1983, then Senator Dan Quayle noted the decrease in productivity in the American labor force, much of which was attributable to drug and alcohol use. Based on data from the Bureau of Labor Statistics, Quayle estimated lost productivity due to drug and alcohol use to be more than $30 billion (Quayle, 1983). Research conducted by the Research Triangle Institute estimated the economic costs of alcohol and drug use to be more than $60 billion in 1983 (Bompey, 1986). Employers are sufficiently concerned about drug abuse to have established Employee Assistance Programs to aid workers who want to go drug free. In some cases, participation in these programs is a requirement if a worker is to keep his or her job. Increasingly, companies are establishing zero-tolerance policies with regard to illegal drugs and are routinely or randomly testing workers for these drugs. We examine these issues in greater detail in Chapters 9 and 13.

The occupations that we will examine in some detail in this chapter are: *the medical profession, the military, sports,* and *law enforcement.* These are not necessarily the *highest* drug using occupations. The entertainment industry, for example, almost certainly has higher levels of drug use than perhaps all of the occupational contexts that we discuss here. Rather, this chapter focuses on occupations (1) for which drug use has been identified as a problem area; (2) for which drug use represents a significant threat to the occupation and/or the welfare of society generally; and (3) which represent the types of occupational dynamics that give rise to drug and alcohol abuse.

DRUG USE AMONG MEDICAL PROFESSIONALS

Drug use in the medical profession is of concern both because of the ease with which medical personnel can obtain drugs, and because of the catastrophic consequences of such use should a health care worker be impaired while carrying out his or her duties. Medical personnel obtain drugs through several means, but most commonly by stealing directly from hospital pharmacies, by falsely prescribing drugs for patients and by diverting them for their own use, and diverting drugs that are legitimately prescribed to patients for their own use. Other tactics used include getting "emergency" drugs from a friendly pharmacist who knows them, or going to their hospital pharmacy and, feigning absentmindedness, informing the pharmacist that they forgot to bring their prescription pad (Winick, 1961).

These practices are especially problematic because hospitals and medical oversight organizations have historically been reluctant to pursue reported cases of illegal drug use (Banta and Tennant, 1989).

The medical profession is beginning to acknowledge and respond to drug use among its members. The pioneering legislation in this area came in the form of a "sick doctor statute" in Florida in 1969, which made it easier to discipline doctors under the medical practice act of Florida. Texas followed with a similar statute in 1971. Prior to these and subsequent acts in other states, physicians had to have committed specified acts of misconduct before being reported. These "sick doctor statutes" identify the inability of a doctor to perform with reasonable skill because of one or more enumerated illnesses (including drug abuse) as grounds for disciplinary action (Council on Mental Health, 1973). Beyond these statutes, Banta and Tennant (1989) report that the Medical Association of Georgia has developed a program for drug-impaired physicians that identifies chemically dependent doctors and monitors their recovery. Other states have implemented similar programs for monitoring physicians.

Patterns of Drug Use Among Medical Personnel

Drug use among physicians was first brought to the attention of sociologists by Charles Winick in his now classic article *Physician Narcotic Addicts* (1961). Here, the reader is informed that there is approximately one addict for every one hundred physicians, a phenomenal rate of addiction compared to the estimated rate of one addict for every 3,000 people in the general population at that time. Other early studies reported similarly high rates of use and addiction among physicians (Modlin and Montes, 1964; Pescor, 1942; Putnam and Ellinwood, 1966). Most physician drug use in these early studies was for purposes of self-medication—primarily narcotics and other depressants (Putnam and Ellinwood, 1966; Valliant, Brighton and McArthur, 1970; Winick, 1961). Early research on drug use by *medical students* also focused heavily on instrumental drug use. Unlike the early studies of physicians, however, which focused primarily on narcotics and depressant use, studies of medical students highlighted the use of stimulants and similar drugs, primarily for the purposes of coping with stress and long hours (Blaine, Lieberman, and Hirsh, 1968; Smith and Blachly, 1966; Watkins, 1970).

A second wave of research on drug use and abuse among medical personnel began in the 1970s, which revealed a new pattern of *recreational* drug use, particularly marijuana use, among physicians and medical students. Marijuana was a visible part of the youth culture during the late 1960s, and it is hardly surprising that this research interest emerged when it did. Lipp and Benson (1972) reported that 25 percent of the physicians in their sample had tried marijuana and 7 percent currently used marijuana. Moreover, most of the physicians in their sample (92 percent) used at least some alcohol. Studies by McAuliffe and his colleagues (1984, 1986) revealed that approximately 30 percent of the physicians surveyed in the New

England area smoked marijuana within the past year, and about 8 percent of these doctors smoked on a regular basis (McAuliffe et al., 1984). This compares with an estimated 13.6 percent of the population in the United States who used marijuana within the past year and just over 9 percent who used currently in 1985 (Substance Abuse and Mental Health Services Administration, 1999).

Research among medical students during this period revealed even greater levels of use. Generally, these studies found that a substantial majority—approximately 70 percent—had at least tried marijuana. Moreover, a sizable minority, between 30 and 45 percent, reported marijuana use within the past year (Mechanick et al., 1973; Rochford, Grant and LaVigne, 1977; Thomas, Luber and Smith, 1977; Conard, et al., 1988; DeWitt et al., 1991; Maddux, Hoppe and Costello, 1986; McAuliffe et al., 1984, 1986). Similar findings were reported by Engs (1982) among medical students in Australia. Alcohol use was also high among medical students during this period, with between 80 and 90 percent reporting that they currently use alcohol. Substantially less numbers of students were tobacco users. Indeed, in almost all cases, both current and lifetime marijuana use is higher among these future physicians than is tobacco use. Other drug use patterns by medical students included cocaine use (Conard et al., 1988; McAuliffe et al., 1984), analgesics of various types, tranquilizers, narcotics, and, increasingly, LSD and other hallucinogens (Baldwin et al., 1991; Maddux, Hoppe, and Costello, 1986; Rochford, Grant, and LaVigne, 1977).

Recent research suggests substantially lower trends among physicians. A recent national study of 9,600 physicians revealed that less than 5 percent used marijuana within the past year, and less than 1 percent had used cocaine, narcotics or amphetamines in the one-month period prior to responding to the survey (Hughes et al., 1992a). Self-reports collected under the auspices of the Substance Abuse and Mental Health Services Administration suggest that only 3.3 percent of the physicians[4] in the sample reported using any illicit drugs in the last year. This figure compares favorably with teachers (9.2 percent), social workers (19.2 percent), and lawyers and judges (19.1 percent) (Hoffman, Brittingham, and Larison, 1996). Nurses, it seems are substantially more likely to use illicit drugs and alcohol than are physicians, according to research conducted under the auspices of the Substance Abuse and Mental Health Services Administration. Among the nurses sampled, 12.1 percent report using illicit drugs during the past year (compared with 3.3 percent of physicians), and 5.5 percent of the nurses reported current (last 30 days) illicit drug use (Hoffman, Brittingham, and Larison, 1996).

Finally, recent research has also investigated differences across *medical specialties* with regard to patterns of drug use. Alcohol use ranks high across *all* medical specialties, with over 90 percent of respondents reporting alcohol use (Hughes et al., 1992b; Hyde and Wolf, 1995). Psychiatry residents tend to have the highest levels of illicit drug use, ranging from 80 percent who have used marijuana to 11 percent who have used barbiturates.

Emergency residents also reported high lifetime use of illegal drugs, particularly marijuana (79.7 percent) and cocaine (38 percent). Surgeons, pediatric and pathology residents, on the other hand, reported the *lowest* levels of illicit drug use (Hughes et al., 1992b).

Explaining Drug Use by Medical Personnel

A variety of reasons have been given for why physicians and other medical personnel self-medicate, and in many cases become addicted to narcotic and depressant drugs. These include overwork, chronic fatigue, physical ailments, marital problems, personality disorders, disillusionment, poor self-concept, and mood enhancement and recreational use (Baldwin et al., 1991; Modlin and Montes, 1964; Winick 1961, 1974). Two competing theories tend to dominate the discussion of why physicians and other medical personnel use drugs, however: *the stress hypothesis* and *the availability hypothesis*.

The **stress hypothesis** posits that physicians are under exceptional occupational stress when compared with most other occupations. Physicians deal with life and death situations, and even a minor slip can result in the death or permanent disabling of a patient. Moreover, hours are long, which not only produces fatigue, but interferes with family obligations, producing role conflict among physicians. Bressler (1976) identifies stress and role conflict as primary factors in physician suicide as well as drug use. Occupational stress is certainly consistent with many of the reasons that physicians give for abusing drugs, and it is also consistent with depressant, and especially narcotic, drug use. The stress hypothesis is also supported by Nancy Stout-Weigand and Roger Trent (1981), who examined drug use and stress among a general sample of physicians, which included general practitioners, anesthesiologists, pathologists, dermatologists, and dentists. When the authors examined levels of drug use by reported stress levels, 23 percent of those who reported high stress levels also reported using drugs, while only 3 percent of "low stress" physicians reported drug use.

The **availability hypothesis** is predicated on the fact that medical personnel have more access to controlled substances than just about any other occupational group. Because drug use is not possible without access to these drugs, it is reasonable to conclude that availability is a primary factor in drug use, abuse, and in some cases, eventual addiction of physicians. Sociologist Charles Winick (1974) has done pioneering descriptive work among nurses, and his findings generally reflect some of the same availability factors that he observed among physicians. Winick writes, for example, that nurses who use drugs often request the night shift—not only because there are fewer people around to monitor their behavior, but also because patients are already sleeping and may not have needed their dosages, making it easy to divert the dosage to their own use. Alternatively, a nurse may give the patient part of the dosage and keep the rest for himself or herself. Still other nurses seek positions in nursing homes where chronic patients receive large dosages of narcotics, and where complaints of pain are not as likely to be investigated. These are fairly elaborate strategies, and nurses who engage in such activities are almost certainly addicted to the drugs that they are using.

It seems likely that availability is a primary factor in the increased *recreational* drug use among medical personnel. Case studies conducted by McAuliffe (1984) reveal that much of the drug use among the health care professionals was for recreational purposes, not functional purposes such as relieving stress. McAuliffe's research is also at least partially supported by research on Quebec physicians, which concluded that it was not possible to identify a single "type" of physician addict. The so-called "therapeutic addict," which has tended to dominate the literature on physician drug abuse, was but one type of addict. Other physicians much more closely resembled the street addict in the nature and purpose of their drug use (Wallot and Lambert, 1984). While numerous variables account for increased recreational use—not the least of which are cultural and philosophical shifts that have occurred over time—it would seem that availability factors may be more important in accounting for increased recreational use than factors related to stress.

DRUG USE IN THE MILITARY

Contemporary concern for drug use among military personnel has its origin in the Vietnam War.[5] It seems that American GIs were sent to Vietnam relatively drug free (drug use primarily limited to alcohol, tobacco, and marijuana) and came back addicted to a pharmacopeia of drugs (Callan and Patterson, 1973; Siegel, 1973). One of the most widely cited studies from the Vietnam era is a 1974 publication by psychiatrist Lee Robins entitled *The Vietnam Drug User Returns*. Robins found that prior to their Vietnam experience, most of the men had used alcohol, and almost half of the soldiers had tried an illicit drug, which was usually marijuana. Only about 1 percent of these individuals had used any narcotic more than a few times, and only 11 percent had even tried narcotic drugs. Prior to Vietnam, these young men were, in short, highly experienced with alcohol and tobacco, less experienced with marijuana, and had almost no experience with the use of other drugs. This changed in Vietnam. Here, they learned to smoke marijuana if they didn't know already (69 percent), and were also turned on to narcotics, primarily opium and heroin (34 and 38 percent respectively). It was not primarily their drug use in Vietnam, however, which caused so much concern among government officials. Approximately half of those who used drugs while in Vietnam continued their drug use after arriving back stateside.

The post-Vietnam years have witnessed increasing attention to the problem of both illicit drug and alcohol use in all the branches of the armed forces. The military pioneered the practice of drug testing, which had begun on a sporadic basis among returning veterans from Vietnam. When a jet fighter crashed into the deck of a nuclear aircraft carrier in 1981, killing 14, injuring 48 others, and doing over two million dollars in damages, the

Department of Defense was prompted to institute mandatory urinalysis in all of the branches of the armed forces (Banta and Tennant, 1989).

There is convincing evidence that the mandatory testing in the military has been effective. Since 1980 the Department of Defense has sponsored seven surveys—the last conducted in 1998—for the purpose of assessing the level of substance abuse among active military personnel. Each of the survey years, between 15,000 and 22,000 active military personnel answered questions about tobacco, alcohol, and illicit drug use, in addition to a host of other questions. Since 1980, the percentage of military personnel using illicit drugs has steadily declined, from 27.6 percent reporting use within the past 30 days in 1980 to only 2.7 percent reporting past 30 day use in 1998 (Bray et al., 1999). This decline reflects a downward trend in drug use in the general population since 1979. Tobacco use also declined significantly, from 34.2 percent who described themselves as heavy smokers in 1980 to 13.4 percent who are heavy smokers 18 years later. Problem alcohol consumption showed a less dramatic decrease, from 20.8 percent of the sample who were heavy drinkers in 1980 to 15.4 percent in 1998.

There are some noteworthy variations across the four branches of the military. The highest rate of illicit drug use initially took place in the Marine Corps, though by 1982 it was the Army that was reporting the highest rates. The lowest rates throughout the 18-year time period are in the Air Force. The Air Force also reports the lowest rate of heavy tobacco and alcohol use during the study period. The heaviest smokers, it seems, are in the Army, and the heaviest drinkers are in the Marine Corps (Bray et al., 1999).

The general decline in tobacco use—and less so with alcohol use—represents a reversal of prior patterns. Historically, smoking and drinking have been encouraged among military personnel, at least informally (Bryant, 1974; Ballweg and Li, 1991). Cigarettes and alcohol were made available at reduced prices, and "happy hours" were frequent on military bases. The Department of Defense changed its posture in the 1980s, instituting mandatory drug testing and establishing policies to improve the health and quality of life of military personnel as a means to improving military readiness generally (Bray and Kroutil, 1995). These policies were accompanied by programs to assist in quitting smoking and drinking, as well as illicit drug use.

There are two competing hypotheses regarding the level of drug use in the military. The first posits that drug, alcohol, and tobacco use will be higher in the military than in the civilian population because of the heightened levels of stress associated with military life. Separation from family for extended tours, frequent relocation, often overseas, and maintaining a level of combat readiness or possible combat experience are all stressors that might predispose one toward higher levels of substance abuse. Alternatively, it is hypothesized that rates of substance abuse should be lower because of the recent military policy of zero tolerance along with programs to assist military personnel in reducing drug, alcohol and tobacco use (Bray, Marsden and Peterson, 1991; Bray, Fairbank, and Marsden, 1999).

Both hypotheses find support in the literature. Prior to the policy shifts of the Department of Defense, military personnel were at least as involved as civilians in illicit drug use, but in the years subsequent to mandatory drug testing, the armed forces samples report substantially less drug use than do household samples of civilians. Zero-tolerance policies do seem to be reversing a previous trend toward greater drug and alcohol use. Nevertheless, Bray, Fairbank and Marsden (1999) report that stress experienced in military life is associated with substance abuse. The specific stress factors tend to be different among women than among men, however. Among men, specific stress factors at work, and the tensions created in their families by military roles tend to be most strongly correlated with substance abuse; women, however, were more likely to use illicit drugs and alcohol as a result of stress created by their minority status as a woman in the predominantly male domain of the military.

"DOPING:"[6] DRUG USE IN SPORTS

The use of drugs by athletes to improve athletic performance, commonly called **doping,** is centuries, indeed millenia old. We are told that gladiators in ancient Rome used stimulants prior to their deadly performances in the Colosseum (Putnam, 1999). Other drugs used during these ancient games included alcohol, psychoactive mushrooms, and strychnine mixed with alcohol to bring about a stimulant effect (Voy, 1991). More recently, canal swimmers in Amsterdam were charged with using drugs in 1865 (Voy, 1991), and in 1886, the first drug-related death in the record of sports was recorded when a bicyclist collapsed after a long-distance race in Europe after taking a "speed ball"—mixture of narcotics and cocaine—which was intended to boost his performance (Putnam, 1999).

There are two broad categories of drugs that are used by athletes. One, **restorative drugs,** are taken to facilitate healing from injuries or to reduce the pain of such injuries. Such drugs are also used to relieve hypertension and sickness. In short, these are drugs which are used to bring an athlete to a state of normalcy as soon as possible. Drugs used in this way include pain killers, tranquilizers, muscle relaxants, anti-inflammatory agents, and in some cases barbiturates. While many of these drugs are banned from use in amateur sports, this type of drug use is not of as much concern to monitoring agencies such as the International Olympic Committee (IOC) and the National Collegiate Athletic Association (NCAA) as are the second, more controversial type of drugs called **additive drugs** (also called *ergogenic aids*). These drugs are taken in order to *enhance athletic performance* (as opposed to bringing an athlete back to normalcy more quickly). A variety of drugs and drug-types are used in this way. The primary drugs in this category are stimulants (amphetamines, methamphetamines, cocaine, etc.) and anabolics. In addition, human beta-blockers (a heart drug) and diuretics are also used by many athletes (Leonard, 1998). Finally, many athletes use drugs *recreationally,* most typically alcohol and marijuana, though a wide variety of other drugs are used in this way as well.

Restorative Drug Use by Athletes

Both professional and amateur athletes misuse restorative drugs. Importantly, most drugs in this category are a legitimate part of the club house pharmacopeia. These drugs are typically used for purposes of alleviating pain due to injury, reducing hypertension or symptoms of various ailments, and speeding the healing process. They are used primarily for the purpose of allowing players to function after illness or injury—in essence, to allow them to function normally under adverse circumstances. Most drugs in this category are not absolutely prohibited when prescribed by a physician; however, there are certain limits and conditions placed on their use. For example, IOC rules allow only local or intra-articular injection of anasthetic drugs, and then only when medically justified. Similarly, most narcotic drugs are prohibited, but certain narcotics such as Darvon and codeine are permitted.

Additive Drug Use by Athletes

The most controversial, and therefore most closely monitored drugs are *additive drugs*. Unlike restorative drugs, these drugs are used for purposes of allowing the athlete to perform beyond what his or her healthy body is capable of doing on its own. Drugs that fall under this category can be divided into four types: *stimulants, anabolics, beta-blockers,* and *diuretics.*

Stimulants   Recall from Chapter 3 that stimulants are those drugs that "stimulate" or accelerate the activities of the central nervous system. Also called *ergogenic* (energy producing) drugs the stimulants include amphetamines, methamphetamines, caffeine,[7] and cocaine. Certain stimulants are permitted for athletes in the form of inhalers for treatment of asthma conditions, but only if there is written notification of this condition by a recognized physician.

There is some disagreement as to how much stimulant drugs actually enhance athletic performance (Schwenck, 1997; Vol, 1991). Clearly, the advantage is small, though as Laties and Weiss (1981) point out, even a 1 percent improvement can provide athletes a significant edge at Olympic Games level of competition. While there are differences of opinion regarding the competitive advantages of stimulants, there is almost no controversy over the fact that stimulants pose potential health risks to athletes. Amphetamines, methamphetamines, and cocaine are particularly potent. Under conditions of athletic performance, when adrenalin production is already stimulated and heart and respiration rates are increased, the use of amphetamines and other stimulant drugs can be potentially lethal. The health hazards of these drugs in the sports arena was sharply driven home in 1986 when two athletes in their prime—Len Bias and Don Rogers—died as a result of cocaine use. Stimulants have been virtually banned from amateur sports, both because of the potential for enhancement—or at least the psychological confidence that they tend to produce—and because of the dangers that they pose to athletes using them (Ray and Ksir, 1999). Nevertheless, stimulants are used frequently in both amateur and professional sports.

Anabolics The term *anabolic* means "building up." The **anabolics,** therefore, are substances that artificially build muscle and body mass and even oxygen levels. There has been a great deal of debate as to whether anabolic drugs are effective in building up muscle mass, though the weight of evidence suggests that they are indeed quite effective (Lombardo, 1990). Anabolics fall into three broad categories: *proteins, steroids,* and *human growth hormones.* Athletes use *anabolic proteins* to increase their stamina in events that require endurance, such as cycling and long-distance running. Artificially injecting these drugs not only provides an unfair competitive advantage, but can be dangerous as well. Athletes who already have naturally high levels of anabolic proteins especially run the risk of their blood thickening and developing clots resulting in shutdown of vital organs. According to Liska (2000) these drugs are suspected in the deaths of some 18 cyclists in Holland and Belgium. Another practice by athletes which produces a similar effect as the anabolic proteins is **blood doping.** Blood doping entails withdrawing amounts of blood (typically about two pints) two to three months prior to an event. This blood is frozen, and by the time of the event, the body has replenished its own blood supply. The athlete will then infuse his system with the red blood cells (that carry the oxygen) of the blood that he or she has earlier withdrawn. The result is an extra supply of oxygen that will sustain the athlete through endurance events. While there is disagreement among sports doctors as to whether this is truly drug use, this practice has been banned by the IOC since 1986 (Voy, 1991).

Anabolic steroids are chemicals produced naturally by our bodies, but are also produced synthetically. Chemically, these artificially produced stereoids closely resemble *testosterone,* the male sex hormone. They are taken for purposes of building body and muscle mass, and to repair muscle damage, albeit at lower dosages. These drugs are used by weight lifters, football players, and other athletes who require muscle strength. While effective in the short run, chronic use of these drugs has serious health consequences. Known consequences include testicular atrophy, male pattern baldness, impotence, elevated cholesterol, increased risk of kidney disease, and heart attack. Women who use anabolic steroids also experience menstrual problems (Liska, 2000). Moreover, psychiatric problems that result from long-term steroid use have also been identified (Katz and Pope, 1990). Both affective (neurotic) and psychotic symptoms were found among athletes while they were on the steroids; these symptoms disappeared during off periods. Symptoms included severe mood swings, aggressiveness, irritability, and other behavioral disorders. The term **roid rage** was coined to describe the increased hostility and aggressiveness among steroid users. Citing various studies, Goldstein (1990) estimates more than 1 million steroid users in the United States, with perhaps as many as 96 percent of professional football players taking this bodybuilding drug. The use of these drugs begins even in high school. More than 6 percent of a national sample of twelfth-grade males admitted to having used steroids (Buckley et al., 1988), and Goldstein estimates that 12 percent of high school football players use steroid drugs.

Human growth hormone (hGH), is also produced naturally in the pituitary gland. Its purpose is to regulate human growth. Individuals whose pituitary gland does not function properly to produce this hormone typically suffer from a condition known as *dwarfism*. The treatment of dwarfism, if caught early enough, is the artificial injection of the hormone. It is widely believed among athletes (though there is controversy in the medical field) that hGH builds muscle mass, and when used in conjunction with anabolic steroids, compounds the effects of the steroids. This is a particularly dangerous practice. Growth hormones cause not only muscle enlargement, but affect nearly every organ of the body. This, combined with the fact that growth hormones tend to reduce the fat protecting vital body organs, make their use especially risky in contact sports such as football. Additionally, in 1984, several fatalities from a latent viral disease called *Creutzfeldt-Jakob* are believed to be a result of use of hGH. This is a fatal neurological disease from a virus that, like the AIDS virus, takes years to incubate (Voy, 1991).

Despite these consequences, athletes are willing to risk their health for the competitive edge that these drugs provide. A 1995 poll of 198 athletes reported in *Sports Illustrated* asked athletes if they would be willing to use performance-enhancing drugs if it were guaranteed that they would not be caught, and that they would win the competition as a result. Only three of the 198 athletes indicated that they would not use the drugs! Furthermore, when asked the same question with the further proviso that they would win every competition over the next five years, but would die from the side effects of these drugs, more than half of the athletes said that they would take the risks and use the drugs (Bamberger and Yaeger, 1997). This is testimony to the seduction of competition and the importance of winning at all costs.

Beta-Blockers   **Beta-blockers** have a depressant-type effect on the central nervous system, and are prescribed by doctors for reducing blood pressure and slowing down the heart rate in patients suffering from conditions associated with high blood pressure. Because these drugs slow the heart rate, they are especially popular among athletes in precision sports such as archery and shooting events. They are relaxants, and more importantly, they provide a longer time between heart beats allowing the athlete more time to aim and shoot between beats (thereby increasing accuracy). These drugs are generally banned for these sports.

Diuretics   **Diuretics** are among the more recent enhancement drugs to hit the sports world, first banned in Olympic competition in 1986 (Voy, 1991). Medically, they are used primarily to treat people with problems in fluid retention. Athletes discovered that they could use these drugs to lose weight in those sports that had imposed weight limitations, such as wrestling and boxing. Another inducement to use these drugs is that they can be used to "mask" other drugs used by athletes. Actually, what most diuretic drugs do is to speed up the process of flushing out drugs of the system, hopefully prior to drug-testing time. Other drugs also act as masking agents by blocking the release of drugs *into* the urine (Liska, 2000). Like other additive drugs, diuretics pose health risks. Because they release fluids and important vitamins and minerals contained in these fluids—particularly potassium—the use of diuretics disturbs the electrolyte balance in the blood. They have also been linked with cardiac arrhythmia and cardiac arrest (Voy, 1991).

Recreational Drug Use by Athletes

Athletes are not immune from recreational drug use. Recent research conducted by the Harvard School of Public Health, which surveyed students at 140 colleges across the United States, has revealed that 61 percent of student athletes report current (past two weeks) binge drinking. This compares with only 43 percent of non- (athlete) involved students. Similarly, 50 percent of sports-involved women (compared with 36 percent of noninvolved women) engaged in binge drinking (Wechsler et al., 1996). Athletes tended to be slightly *less* involved in marijuana and other illicit drug use than were nonathletes, however. Approximately 12 percent of the male athletes (10 percent of female athletes) reported marijuana use, compared with 16 percent of the nonathletes (11 percent of female nonathletes).

Another recreational drug used by athletes is nicotine. While college athletes are less likely to smoke cigarettes, they are more likely to use smokeless tobacco (Wechsler et al., 1996). Schwenck (1997) estimates that smokeless tobacco is used by between 20 and 60 percent of male college athletes, depending on the sport. Baseball players report the highest use of smokeless tobacco. Indeed, 5 to 10 percent of college women athletes use smokeless tobacco, with softball players reporting the highest use.

The frequency and prevalence of drug use by athletes has been debated. Part of the disagreement is a result of different methodologies used to estimate drug use by athletes. Some researchers base their estimates on drug tests. Drug testing generally reveals a very low rate of use, typically 1 to 2 percent of athletes testing positive (Leonard, 1998). These findings are generally confirmed by Yesalis and his colleagues (1990) who look specifically at anabolic steroid use. However, when unannounced tests with no punitive sanctions were conducted, about 50 percent of the athletes tested positive for steroids. Yesalis et al. conjecture that athletes have learned to stop using at the appropriate time prior to testing so as to avoid testing positive. Other researchers use self-report strategies, asking athletes whether they have used drugs (usually within a specified time period). Here again, responses indicate a rather low rate of drug use (Yesalis et al., 1988). A third technique that has been used is to ask athletes their perceptions of the prevalence of drug use in their particular sport. One researcher using this approach reported that, on average, respondents indicated that nearly 30 percent of athletes used steroids (Leonard, 1998).

Drug Policy and Enforcement in Sports

Drug policy in the sports world is a patchwork of rules developed and enforced by various ruling bodies. Each of the ruling bodies varies somewhat in their proscriptions and enforcement, and there are also variations among the particular sports, as to what drugs are allowed and which are permitted. We will discuss some of these variations in this section. The primary distinction that must be made, however, is between *professional* sports and *amateur* sports. Professional sports are, compared with amateur athletics, virtually bereft of drug use policies. A primary reason for this lack are players associations and unions, which fight any attempt at drug screening on the basis of infringement of civil liberties (Wagner, 1987). The result is a patchwork of regulations, specific to each sport in question. The intent of the various drug-control programs in most professional sports is primarily to control recreational street drugs such as marijuana, heroin, and cocaine. The purpose for bans on these drugs is not so much to make a level playing field, as is the case in amateur sports, but rather because it is recognized that professional athletes are role models to a younger generation of admirers. Drug use—particularly illegal street drug use—sends the wrong message to kids. While players will be suspended or even banned for repeated violations if they test positive for drugs, most professional team sports provide employee assistance programs which provide drug counseling for drug-abusing players. Individual sports, such as tennis, may also

Amateur sports are much more prohibitive with regard to drug use than are professional sports

have provision for rehabilitation, but typically require players to pay for their own treatment (Wagner, 1987).

Contrary to professional sports, amateur sports are very highly monitored and tested for drugs. The purpose of drug testing in amateur sports is primarily to ensure a level playing field for all participants, and secondarily to ensure the health and safety of the athletes. Consequently, the range of drugs that are monitored and tested is much broader.

Amateur sports in the United States are governed primarily by two oversight agencies: the National Collegiate Athletic Association (NCAA) and the United States Olympic Committee (USOC), which is a member of International Olympic Committee (IOC).[8] The IOC's list of banned substances falls into five broad categories: stimulants, narcotics, anabolic agents, diuretics, and masking agents. While certain "street drugs" are included in this list, (e.g., heroin and cocaine, but not marijuana), there is no category as such, highlighting the "level playing field" purpose of drug testing by the IOC/USOC. The NCAA did not develop drug-testing legislation until its 1986 convention in New Orleans. There is a great deal of overlap between the NCAA and the IOC in terms of drugs that are screened. One major difference between the two organizations is that the NCAA does include "street drugs" as a special category, which includes heroin and marijuana. This special categorization reflects the NCAA's concern for the health and image of college athletics as well as fairness of athletic competition.

Drug Use Among Law Enforcement Personnel

If the literature on the subject is any indication, it would seem that *the* problematic substance in law enforcement is alcohol. A review of available literature on the subject published in 1986 revealed only two studies that even attempted to assess nonalcohol drug abuse among police officers (Dietrich and Smith, 1986). While there is not a great deal of quantitative data on the prevalence of alcohol use and abuse by police officers, department officials report that as many as 25 percent of police officers have a serious dependence on alcohol (Kroes, 1976). If this is correct, and we define "serious dependence" as alcoholism, alcoholism is significantly higher among police officers than it is in the general population. Other studies tend to confirm Kroes' estimates. A widely cited study in a police trade magazine reports that 40 percent of police officers surveyed drank while on duty (Van Raalte, 1979). Van Raalte also reports instances of off-duty drinking by officers resulting in firearms injuries because of intoxication. Mortality rates for cirrhosis of the liver, another indicator of problem drinking, were found to be substantially higher for police officers than for the general population (Hitz, 1973).

Factors Contributing to High Rates of Alcohol Use by Police

Stress   Stress is perhaps the single most important factor in alcohol use by police officers. A litany of factors have been found to contribute to police stress. Most people assume that law enforcement stress comes primarily from the life and death situations that police officers must face, in some cases on a daily basis. This vulnerability is, indeed, one source of stress among law enforcement personnel. But there are other factors that, taken together, exact a toll on law enforcement more than most occupational fields. These factors include: court scheduling problems; unfavorable court decisions; undesirable assignments; faulty equipment; lack of community support; changing shifts; poor relations with supervisors; boredom; low pay; role conflict; public pressure and scrutiny; peer group pressure; lack of career development opportunities; excessive paperwork; inadequate rewards; distorted press accounts of police incidents; and exposure to human suffering (Blau, 1994; Eisenberg, 1975; Kroes, Margolis, and Hurrell, 1974; Territo and Vetter, 1981). These are but some of the many factors that contribute to police stress. Moreover, these factors are often compounded by the impact that they have on the families of police officers. The officer under stress brings his or her problems and frustrations home and often vents on his or her spouse. Additionally, erratic work schedules and 24-hour on-call availability can produce tremendous stress and conflict within a marital unit. For these reasons, law enforcement as an occupation has the dubious privilege of having one of the highest divorce rates in the country (Territo and Vetter, 1981).

Occupational stress has had severe consequences among law enforcement personnel. In addition to high rates of divorce, numerous researchers have observed excessively high rates of suicide among police officers (Allen, 1986; Arrigo and Garsky, 1997; Bonifacio, 1991; Territo and Vetter, 1981; Wagner and Brzeczek, 1983). Health problems of all sorts have also been reported, including insomnia, memory lapse, heart disease, (Blau, 1994; Territo and Vetter, 1981). An examination of death certificates in Tennessee revealed that police officers were much more likely to die prematurely than individuals in most other occupations (Fell, Richard and Wallace, 1980). It might be expected, then, that alcoholism and other forms of pathological drinking (and other drug use) will also be affected by the high stress levels of law enforcement work. In a review of available literature until that point in time, Dietrich and Smith (1986) conclude that the available evidence suggests that the occupational stressors of police work do, indeed, contribute to greater levels of alcohol consumption. One study in their review by Violante, Marshall and Howe (1985) found that occupational stress was nearly 20 times more powerful in its impact on alcohol use than any of the other variables examined. The use of alcohol as a coping mechanism, of course, only exacerbates many of the problems which led these individuals to become problem drinkers in the first place.

Occupational Subculture   The other set of factors contributing to greater than normal alcohol consumption by police is subcultural in nature. Law enforcement personnel share common experiences which distinguish them from the people around them. They confront potential danger on a daily basis. They confront public criticism more than most occupations. Moreover, many of the stressors that were identified earlier result in a strong sense of subcultural identification among "the men in blue." The subculture of law

DRUGS AND EVERYDAY LIFE

Choir Practice

A vivid illustration of the stresses and strains of big city police work, and of how alcohol consumption is used as a stress reliever by officers, can be found in the novel *The Choirboys* by Joseph Wambaugh (1975). Wambaugh had been a Los Angeles police officer for some 14 years, years where he experienced the violence and strains of police work first hand. During these years he also experienced the "blue curtain" of police fraternalism. To a great extent, the police believe that no one, save another cop, understands what they go through on the job. So when it comes time to "wind down" from work, they turn to each other and to alcohol, often in great quantity.

Wambaugh terms their group bacchanals "choir practices," wherein the officers gather late at night (or early in the morning, depending on one's point of view), in a public park, and sing drunkenly and howl at the moon. It is a catharsis for the choirboys, serving both to relieve stress and enhance fraternal bonds. It is ironic to refer to these officers as choirboys. They shake down liquor store owners for that night's booze, a practice more or less willingly engaged in by the merchants, as long as the cops don't become too greedy and exceed their agreed upon limit of two bottles per store per shift. When drunk—what a surprise—they act in rude and unprofessional ways, getting into fights, having adulterous and indiscriminate sex, acting anything but choirboy-like. Wambaugh's point is that big city officers should no longer be seen as one-dimensional figures of moral authority, but as flawed and fallible people, who generally work hard and play hard, and for whom alcohol abuse is both ingrained in the job and a source of negative consequences for the officers. Among these alcohol-related consequences are divorce, suicide, ill-health, and unrestrained rage. And they aren't just pathologies for the officers in Wambaugh's fictional world, but for all too many flesh and blood policemen and policewomen ■

---

enforcement not only tolerates higher than normal levels of alcohol consumption, but actually encourages it. Drinking is a regular part of off-duty recreational time for many police officers. Dietrich and Smith (1986) also cite literature which suggests that subcultural drinking may be used to test loyalty, trustworthiness, and masculinity. (The police subculture is largely, though not exclusively, a masculine domain.) Refusing to drink is tantamount to rejection of fellow police officers. Moreover, the role that alcohol plays in the intense camaraderie of the subculture of law enforcement often results in a blind eye to alcohol and drug-abuse problems when they occur. Because drinking is such a part of the subculture of policing, fellow officers are often unaware when subculturally induced social drinking slips over into problem drinking. Moreover, loyalty that is developed as part of these recreational activities precludes fellow officers from informing supervisors when they suspect a drinking problem. Finally, the emphasis on masculinity that is so much a part of the police subculture prevents officers with drinking problems from seeking help for their drinking and/or drug-use problem.

SUMMARY

In this chapter, we have examined the question of whether there are certain segments of the population which are more vulnerable to drug use and abuse than others. The answer to the question is that there are. We have seen, for example, that men are generally more likely to use drugs than women. We have also learned, however, that drug-using women face physical and relational complications from their drug use that go far beyond what most men experience. With regard to race, whites are more likely to report drug use than either Hispanics or blacks (with some exceptions, notably heroin and crack). We have also learned, however, that there are cultural, economic, and historical features of not only blacks and Hispanic communities, but other ethnic communities as well, that contribute to unique experiences and problems associated with drug use. Drug use also varies in prevalence and type across different age groups. The motives for use, and the consequences of that use are quite different among adolescents, for example, than among the elderly.

We have also addressed four broadly defined occupations that are known for particular patterns of substance abuse. These are also very critical occupational areas for different reasons. The health professions are especially critical as we entrust our lives to the care of doctors and nurses. Impaired medical personnel can have a profound effect on health care delivery. Our national security is also of vital importance, and anything short of a sober, alert military force should not be acceptable to this society. Ironically, military men and women who serve their country face unique stressors which make them more vulnerable to drug and alcohol abuse. The same irony characterizes law enforcement. Sports is a critical area because sports

figures are so highly emulated and serve as role models for out nation's youngsters.

There are other critical occupational groups which are vulnerable to substance abuse as well. We are increasingly aware of the problems caused by drug abuse in various sectors of the transportation industry, for example. Airline pilots, railroad engineers, bus drivers, and tractor-trailer drivers have all received attention for abuse of alcohol and drugs either in the popular media or in academic circles (e.g., Lund, Preusser, Blomberg, and Williams, 1989; Taggart, 1989). Drug use among employees at critical utilities plants has also been addressed (Osborne and Sokolov, 1989; Crouch et al., 1989). These are all vital occupational areas. We could explore still further: entertainers, college professors, people in the art and literary worlds, and even lumbermen have at some time or another been associated with abnormally high rates of alcohol and drug abuse. Our purpose is not to be exhaustive in our identification and discussion of occupational correlates of drug abuse. Rather, we have identified these four occupational arenas as *representative* of the occupational dynamics that give rise to substance abuse.

This chapter, on the demographic and occupational correlates of drug use, should highlight an important sociological contribution to the study of drug use—namely, that the extent and nature of drug-using behavior varies by *social categories*. While individuals exhibit certain unique drug-using qualities, there are also important similarities, at least broadly speaking, within population and occupational categories. These similarities, and respective differences across categories, suggest that there are *social* as well as individual factors that account for patterns of drug use.

KEY TERMS

additive drug

anabolics

availability hypothesis

beta blockers

binge drinking

blood doping

demographics

diuretics

doping

restorative drug

roid rage

secondary binge effect

stress hypothesis

tecatos

REVIEW QUESTIONS

1. Briefly describe some of the differences in the dynamics of drug use between males and females.

2. What are some of the special problems encountered by drug-using women? Why do you think there are more problems in these areas than for drug-using men?

3. How do patterns of drug use by whites, Hispanics, African Americans, and Native Americans differ? What do you think accounts for the differences in these patterns?

4. Which age category seems to have the highest level of drug consumption as measured by use in the past 30 days?

What is it about this age group that accounts for such higher levels of drug use than other age groups?

5. Briefly describe both the *circumstances* and the *consequences* of drug abuse by the elderly.

6. The authors state that "the occupation is an important context for understanding drug use in American society . . ." Why is the occupation an important context for understanding drug use?

7. Identify two or three reasons why drug use is a significant issue in each of the following occupational contexts: *the medical profession; the military; sports; law enforcement.*

CRITICAL INQUIRY QUESTIONS

1. What are some of the ways in which drug-using women are stigmatized? Why do you think that women who use illicit drugs are stigmatized more than drug-using men? How does this dynamic reflect differential patterns in the treatment of men and women in the larger society?

2. If it is true as the authors suggest that "whites are more likely to use drugs than are either blacks or Hispanics," what do you think accounts for the

stereotype that drug use is primarily concentrated among ethnic minorities?

3. In addition to the occupational contexts discussed in this chapter, identify two or three other occupations or professions in which drug use is a major issue? Discuss the nature of the problem or concern that each of these occupations or professions face with regard to drug use. How are these occupations or professions responding to drug use among their ranks?

NOTES

1. "Heavy use" is defined as drinking five or more drinks on the same occasion on each of five or more days in the past 30 days.

2. Cocaine use does not include crack cocaine. This, and the other drugs included in the prior figures do not have complete data for age categories.

3. In 1993, the *Monitoring the Future* survey asked the question slightly differently, so that alcohol use involved "more than a few sips." Prior to that time, literally *any* use of alcohol was recorded as use. Hence, the percentage will be reduced somewhat. The reduction does not seem to be that much, however. In 1993, the question was posed both ways, and there was only about a three percentage point difference (LD Johnston, PM O'Malley, JG Bachman. (2000). "Footnotes for Table 2–Table 5" [Online]. Available: *http://monitoringthefuture.org/data/ 99data/pr99t2fn.html;* (Accessed November 22, 2000).

4. The category included physicians, dentists, optometrists and podiatrists.

5. There was, of course, drug use and abuse in other wars, including the two world wars, the Korean War, and others. It was the Viet Nam War, however, that drew our attention to the problem of drug use in the military.

6. The term "doping" has an interesting history. It apparently originated in South Africa centuries ago where the term *dop* referred to substances used in religious ceremonies. Over time, an "*e*" was added to form the word *dope*. When the word appeared in the English dictionary, it was defined as a narcotic—an opium mixture used for race horses (Voy, 1991, p. 5). Over time, the term has come to mean different things in America. Among street heroin addicts, for example, the term refers specifically to heroin or other street narcotics (Faupel, 1991). Among athletes, the term has been made into a verb to refer to the process of using any variety of drugs to enhance athletic performance.

7. The NCAA and the IOC prohibit caffeine in excess of 15 and 12 micrograms per millilitre of blood respectively.

8. Lists of specific drugs banned by the International Olympic Committee and by the NCAA can be found at *http://multimedia.olympic.org/pdf/ en_report_22.pdf* and *http://www.ncaa.org/sports_sciences/ drugtesting/banned_list.html* respectively.

HEALTH CORRELATES OF DRUG USE

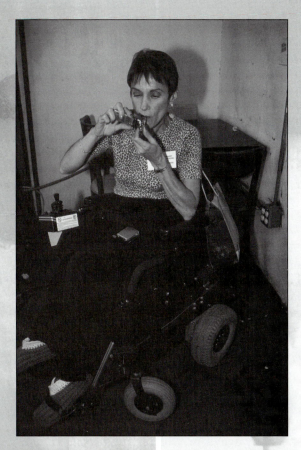

There is possibly no aspect of drug use that is more significant to a community or society than the health consequences of that use. Ultimately, we know that the use of drugs can be fatal if not taken properly. The Drug Abuse Warning Network (DAWN) reports more than 10,000 drug-related deaths in 1998, representing a 5 percent increase since 1995 (Office of Applied Studies, 2000a). Other potentially debilitating health consequences can also result from the careless or inappropriate use of drugs as well. DAWN also reports that in 1999 more than 500,000 emergency room visits were attributable to the abuse of drugs (Office of Applied

Studies, 2000b). While the number of deaths and emergency room visits is but a small fraction of the total number of deaths and emergency room visits due to other causes, these figures establish that drug use is a public health issue. We must recognize, of course, that many of the negative health consequences of illicit drug use are directly related to the legal status of these drugs, and indeed, this factor alone is possibly more debilitating to health than is the pharmacology of the drugs consumed. Because of the illicit nature of IV paraphernalia, for example, IV drug users often rent or borrow needles rather than carry their own for fear of being caught in possession of the prohibited needles. The result has been a rapid spread of AIDS and Hepatitis among IV drug users, a consequence having nothing to do with the pharmacology of the drug in question. We address this issue more fully in this chapter.

There is, furthermore, another side to the health consequences of drug use. Drugs can also be used to *promote* health among the population. We know, of course, that many drugs are routinely used in medicine precisely for this purpose: antibiotics, blood thinners, analgesics, and many others. There is, furthermore, an emerging voice for the use of certain other drugs, such as marijuana, and even heroin and alcohol, as valuable tools in promoting health and well-being.

This chapter examines both types of consequences of drug use as well as some of the health and medical issues associated with these consequences. We begin the chapter with an examination of some of the potentially harmful health consequences of drug use, followed by a discussion of some of the recently emerging issues in the medical use of drugs.

NEGATIVE HEALTH CONSEQUENCES OF DRUG USE

There are many ways in which drugs can seriously affect and jeopardize the health and well-being of the user. We could fill a rather large volume discussing these potentially harmful effects. That is not our purpose in this section. Rather, we want to identify some of the major *factors* that contribute to ill-health among drug users. Within this context we discuss some of the major health consequences associated with the use of chemical substances. The major factors that we are addressing in this section are: *pharmacology of drugs, synergism factors,* and *lifestyle factors* that have implications for the health of the user.

Pharmacology of Drugs

Some ill-health effects of drugs are directly linked to the pharmacology of the drugs themselves. Moreover, certain *types* of drugs are more likely to cause health problems than others. The remainder of this section examines problematic health consequences of the major categories of drugs discussed as part of the taxonomy in Chapter 3.[1] In addition, we address one additional drug category—steroids. While it can be argued that steroids are not psychoactive drugs, and hence beyond the parameters of this book, steroids pose risks that demand our attention given their widespread use especially in the field of sports.

Narcotics

There is perhaps no class of drugs more feared by the general public than are the narcotics. Ironically, the narcotics are among the most benign of drugs when we are talking about their direct health impact pharmacologically. There are many *allegations* about how narcotics ravage the body, but most of these allegations are either exaggerations, confusions with other drug effects, a result of synergism with other drugs, or a result of lifestyle characteristics of those who use narcotic drugs. We discuss synergism and lifestyle characteristics later in this chapter. We do, however, want to discuss one important pharmacological feature of narcotics that can potentially affect the health of the user: the depressant effect that narcotics have on the central nervous system.

Narcotics, like other depressants discussed below, slow down the activity of the central nervous system, which includes respiratory and cardiovascular systems. This quality of the narcotics might potentially put a user in danger of having insufficient oxygen delivered to the brain in an event called a "heroin overdose," or simply "OD," resulting in respiratory and cardiovascular systems virtually shutting down. Overdose is perhaps the most feared consequence of heroin use. There is, however, a great deal of debate as to the risk of overdose. Goode (1999), in the fifth edition of his now almost classic work *Drugs in American Society,* claims that the lethal dose (LD) of heroin is only about 10–15 times higher than the effective dose (ED)–the dose required to notice the effects of heroin (Goode, 1999, p. 315). If this is the case, the potential for overdose is certainly high, if not the "razor thin" difference that Goode suggests. Also, street heroin is more potent today than it was even 20 years ago. Furthermore, given the variable potency that exists on the streets, users often do not know the strength of the heroin that they are shooting.

Unfortunately, Goode does not provide the sources for this claim of a low ED-LD ratio. Other evidence suggests that the risk of overdose is much lower, and indeed, that most so-called overdose deaths are not due to overdose at all. Actually, the evidence *against* overdose being a major factor in what are typically identified as overdose deaths is quite compelling. Studies of overdose deaths tend to find that (1) morphine levels in overdose victims tend to be rather low; and (2) the typical overdose victim is an older, more experienced addict with a higher level of tolerance (Darke, Hall, Weatherburn, and Lind, 1998; Darke and Zador, 1996; Zador, Sunjic, and Darke, 1996). Brecher's (1972) research has revealed that a common practice among medical examiners has been to rule an overdose death in those cases where more precise cause of death cannot be determined if there is circumstantial evidence that a victim has been using drugs or even if he or she is a known drug addict. While Goode maintains a 10–15 ED-LD ratio, other estimates place this at the very conservative end. Various studies suggest a ratio of from 12 at the low end to 50 at the high end (adapted from Brecher, 1972). A more middle-of-the-road, and probably more realistic ratio estimate would be 35–40—meaning that a lethal dose is 35–40 times greater than the effective dose.

The reality of the overdose death, in most cases, is probably death due to synergism, what Brecher has called *Syndrome X*. We know that there are certain drugs that, when used in combination with narcotics, produce a synergistic effect; that is, they produce a depressant effect many times over what the simple additive effect of the two drugs combined. Drugs that produce this effect generally fall into the "depressant" category, and include alcohol, barbiturates, and various tranquilizers. This explanation makes much more sense in light of the fact that reported overdose deaths increased greatly after World War II, and then again in the 1970s. These were periods characterized by higher than normal use of alcohol and other tranquilizing drugs among addicts in the heroin subculture. Some may question the need to distinguish between "overdose" death and death due to synergism. It is important for several reasons. We often make policies based on the assumption that heroin or other narcotics have fantastically destructive powers (while the dangers of other drugs may be inappropriately minimized). This will *not* be good policy. Also, treatment and educational efforts can be much more effective if we understand more completely the dangers associated with drug use patterns.

There are, however, other pharmacologically induced health problems with the use of the narcotics. One such problem is disease of the lung, particularly pneumonia, as a complicating effect of the depressant action of narcotics on the respiratory system. Also, while sudden withdrawal from heroin is not particularly problematic from a health point-of-view for otherwise healthy adults, such rapid termination from heroin use can be fatal to the fetus of a pregnant woman (National Institute on Drug Abuse, 1997). Use of narcotics by pregnant women is thus strongly discouraged, and for those women who are using narcotic drugs, withdrawal should be approached with great care. Still another consequence of narcotics use that has been noted with some concern is a decline in libido and sexual functioning. There is some conflicting evidence surrounding this issue, but the depressant action of the narcotics almost certainly has some impact on sexual functioning, much like alcohol and other depressants. Indeed, some addicts are reported to use heroin purposely to avoid the frustration of sexual arousal.

Depressants

The depressants share many of the same health consequences as the narcotics. Because of the inhibitory effect of these drugs on the central nervous system, depressants such as barbiturates, sedatives, and tranquilizers place the heavy user at potential risk for overdose and even death. Because these drugs have typically been diverted from pharmacies, the dosage is usually clearly indicated, and the user should be aware of the quantity and concentration of the drug that he or she is taking. Unfortunately, if a user is sufficiently under the influence, it may matter little how well that dosages are marked. There is, moreover, the tendency to use depressants with other CNS inhibitors, particularly narcotics and alcohol. When this occurs, depressants synergize and place the user in much greater danger of overdose.

A characteristic feature of non-narcotic depressants, which distinguishes them from the narcotics, is the potentially deadly effect of sudden withdrawal from these drugs. **Delirium tremens** (or "DT's") is the term used to refer to chronic alcoholics who experience sudden withdrawal symptoms, which include tremors, heavy sweating, insomnia, hallucinations, disorientation, and ultimately seizures. While *delirium tremens* is a very rare occurrence even for chronic alcoholics, under extreme conditions these symptoms can be fatal (Moak and Anton, 1999). Other CNS depressants also produce potentially fatal withdrawal effects, though they do not necessarily have all of the effects of alcohol's *delirium tremens* (Brady, Myrick, and Malcolm, 1999).

Still another physiological feature of most of the CNS depressants is their capability to permeate the placental barrier during pregnancy. Regardless of whether the drug is alcohol, barbiturates, tranquilizers, or sedatives, pregnant mothers who consume these drugs run great risk of giving birth to infants who have physiological symptoms of addiction. Moreover, these infants also typically suffer from lower than average birth weight and other physical problems when born (Carroll, 1989).

There is one depressant drug which poses particularly troublesome health risks—alcohol. Alcohol is, ironically, a legal drug for adults in all of the United States though pharmacologically one of the most dangerous of all recreational drugs. There are several health risks posed by alcohol, including liver dysfunction, cardiovascular problems, cancer, neurological problems, complications in pregnancy and accidental death and injury due to lack of motor coordination, among others. We discuss these in the following paragraphs.

Liver Dysfunction   Alcohol directly affects the liver in several ways. One risk is the accumulation of fatty acids that can result in a *fatty liver*. This occurs because the liver burns fatty acids stored in the liver. Alcohol contains a high level of fatty acids, and hence these are used by the liver rather than the body's own fatty acids, resulting in an accumulation of such acids in the liver. If left unattended the cell membranes can rupture, resulting in the death of those liver cells. Another problem that can develop is *alcoholic hepatitis*, which is an inflammation of the liver causing impairment of liver function. This seems to develop where liver cells have died, but it is uncertain as to whether a fatty liver contributes to this condition. The most serious liver problem is *cirrhosis*. There is by now a mountain of evidence that chronic alcohol use causes cirrhosis of the liver. When this happens, healthy liver cells are replaced by nonfunctioning fibrous tissue, resulting in a decrease in blood flow through the liver. The liver can function properly only with an adequate circulation of blood through it. Cirrhosis is the seventh leading cause of death in the United States (Ray and Ksir, 1999).

Cancer and Heart Disease   Additionally, alcohol has been linked to cancer and heart disease. In some cases, excessive alcohol use causes clogged arteries around the heart, known medically as *myocardial infarction*. This is a major cause of heart attacks. A similar symptom observed among alcoholics is the build up of fat in the arteries, thereby limiting blood supplies to the heart. This condition is known as *angina pectoris*. Finally, excessive alcohol use has been linked with *cardiomyopathy*, a disease of the heart muscle itself (Moak and Anton, 1999).

Neurological Dysfunction   Still another physiological consequence of long-term alcohol abuse is brain damage accompanied by psychosis. The name given to this symptom is *Korsakoff's psychosis*. This condition is commonly linked with a lack of thiamine (vitamin B$_1$), a condition known as *Wernicke's disease*. These two conditions are so commonly found together that the condition is usually referred to as **Wernicke-Korsakoff syndrome** (Ray and Ksir, 1999) or simply "wet brain." Because many physicians are not familiar with many of the subtle symptoms of alcoholism, this condition is often underdiagnosed, or misdiagnosed as Alzheimer's or other forms of dementia.

Complications in Pregnancy   Heavy use of alcohol by pregnant mothers can result in **fetal alcohol syndrome** (FAS). This condition, first formally identified in 1973, is recognizable by a number of possible symptoms including an abnormally small head, facial irregularities, heart and genital defects, and severe mental retardation among others (Liska, 2000).[2] According to Ray and Ksir (1999) the three defining characteristics of fetal alcohol syndrome are: (1) growth retardation prior to and/or following birth; (2) abnormal features of the face and head, such as those described above; and (3) CNS abnormalities resulting in mental retardation and abnormal neonatal behavior among other things.

Coordination, Reaction Time, and Motor Vehicle Accidents   Another serious consequence of depressants generally is increased reaction time and loss of coordination. This is a feature of depressant drugs generally that has grave consequences when coupled with driving automobiles and the running of dangerous equipment. The United States Department of Transportation (n.d.) reported that there were 15,786 alcohol-related traffic fatalities in 1999—one every 33 minutes. Alcohol was involved in 38 percent of all traffic fatalities that year. The good news is that this was 1 percent less than the number of alcohol-related traffic deaths in 1998, and 30 percent less than the more than 22,000 alcohol-related fatalities in 1989. It has been estimated that there is eight times the risk for a fatal crash per mile driven if one has a blood alcohol content (BAC) level of 0.10 or higher (Fell, 1987), though Zador (2000), using combined data from the Fatality Analysis Reporting System and the National Roadside Survey of Drivers, estimates that among drivers aged 35 and over, there is more than 11 times the risk for a fatal accident at BAC levels of 0.09. Drivers under 21 with BAC levels of 0.09 are more than 51 times as likely to have a fatal accident than sober adult drivers.[3] It is for this reason that many states have adopted more stringent laws defining the legal level of intoxication. Currently, 16 states have adopted 0.08 as the threshold of intoxication.

Sexual Dysfunction   Still another consequence of chronic alcohol use is a decrease in libido. Contrary to popular opinion, while alcohol may decrease inhibitions and increase "desire," it diminishes sexual functioning. Studies have found that chronic alcohol use results in decreased sperm count and atrophy of the testicles. Shakespeare apparently had it right when he said, "Lechery sir, it provokes and unprovokes; it provokes the desire, but it takes away the performance" (Ray and Ksir, 1999)[4].

Other Medical Problems   Another physiological response to alcohol use which is not commonly recognized is the dilation of peripheral blood vessels. While this is not usually a serious medical condition, it can be fatal under certain circumstances. Under conditions of extreme cold, this response results in the body *feeling* warmer when drinking because the warm blood is flowing closer to the surface of the skin where nerve endings are located. Unfortunately, this takes away the necessary warmth from vital organs, which can be fatal (Ray and Ksir, 1999). Other serious effects of alcohol include stomach ulcers and gastro-intestinal problems generally. This occurs partly due to the direct irritant effect of alcohol on the stomach lining, but primarily because alcohol stimulates the secretion of excess acid (Liska, 2000). Finally, alcohol use has been found to affect hormonal processes. Acute alcohol use sometimes results in low blood sugar levels (hypoglycemia) because of the inhibition of glucose metabolism. Chronic heavy drinking, however, often results in heightened blood sugar levels (hyperglycemia) and can be a major health risk for those individuals predisposed to diabetes (Moak and Anton, 1999).

Stimulants
The principal pharmacological effect of the stimulants is that they accelerate the functioning of the central nervous system. This is not always bad, and

indeed, stimulants are often used intentionally for this purpose, such as when college students consume many cups of coffee while studying for exams or writing papers. This quality of the stimulants becomes problematic to users when the user has a weak or defective cardiovascular system, and/or the drug consumed is in extremely large quantity or great concentration.

The primary health impact of the stimulants, which can be directly attributed to their pharmacology, is the impact that they have on the cardiovascular system. Because stimulants elevate the functioning of the central nervous system, it follows that the cardiovascular system will in some way be affected. Cocaine is particularly powerful in its CNS stimulant effect, though all the stimulants have potentially adverse effects on the heart and circulatory system. Cocaine and methamphetamines have been found to constrict blood vessels bringing blood to the heart, which can trigger chaotic heart rhythms called *ventricular fibrillations*. Moreover, cocaine, along with other stimulants such as amphetamines and nicotine, causes an increase in both heart rate and blood pressure. As a result, users of these stimulants are at highly increased risk for heart diseases and strokes (National Institute on Drug Abuse, 1998a, 1998b, 1999a). It is estimated that about one-fifth of all deaths from heart disease can be directly attributable to smoking cigarettes. Moreover, nicotine use is linked to a greater likelihood of aneurysm (National Institute on Drug Abuse, 1998b). Studies have also found that methamphetamine abuse can result in inflammation of the heart lining itself, placing the user at greater risk for heart disease (National Institute on Drug Abuse, 1998a).

Recent research by Marc Kaufman and his associates (1998) has shed valuable light on the biology and pharmacology of heightened levels of strokes among cocaine users. Using magnetic resonance technology and double-blind comparison groups of individuals receiving cocaine with those receiving a placebo (no cocaine), these researchers found that cocaine users experienced significantly more constriction of cerebral arteries than did the placebo group, and that increased dosages of cocaine produced even greater levels of vasoconstriciton. Moreover, individuals with a history of cocaine use had more constriction than those without, suggesting a cumulative effect of cocaine use on the cardiovascular system. In addition to these findings, the research group found that the experimental (cocaine-using) group also had higher blood pressure and heart rates. Hence, there is not only an increased level of cardiovascular activity and blood pressure, but also a constriction of blood vessels resulting in extreme pressure at certain critical areas. The results can be serious and even deadly, and can occur suddenly and without warning.

Heart disease and other cardiovascular problems are not the only direct pharmacological effects of stimulants. Research by Strickland and his associates (1993) suggests that mental functioning is seriously impaired in cocaine users as a result of vascular constriction in the brain. These researchers reported long-term attention and concentration deficits, memory loss, and other learning deficits among even casual and intermittent cocaine users— even after the cessation of use (in this instance, a minimum of six months).

Another health hazard of the stimulants, particularly powerful stimulants such as cocaine and methamphetamine, is the extreme psychological reaction that they can produce. Schizophrenic-like reactions have been reported, including paranoia, and in the case of methamphetamines, hallucinations and **formication** (delusions of parasites or insects on the skin) have also been observed (Albertson, Derlet, and Van Hoozen, 1999; National Institute on Drug Abuse, 1996a, 1999b).

There are, in addition, potential fetal and neonatal health consequences that may result from stimulant use during pregnancy. Crack and cocaine use have received the most attention, though the research on effects of cocaine use on infants is not at all conclusive. Early studies alleged severe consequences of prenatal cocaine and crack use. According to early studies, infants born to cocaine using mothers tended to have lower birth weight, delivered early, were less responsive to environmental stimuli, and higher than normal incidences of cardio-respiratory problems (Chasnoff, Burns, Schnoll, and Burns, 1985; Chasnoff, Hunt, Kletter, and Kaplan, 1989; MacGregor, Keith, Chasnoff, Rosner, Chisum, Shaw, and Minogue, 1987).

There are various rationale provided for these effects. For example, blood vessels in the placenta become constricted, thereby restricting needed nutrients and oxygen to the fetus, which may result in a low birth-weight infant. If the placenta becomes so damaged by blood vessel constriction caused by heavy cocaine use, much more severe consequences can result, including severe brain damage, or even premature abortion. Moreover, like alcohol and the depressants, stimulants do permeate the placental barrier, and cocaine or crack babies supposedly suffer consequences analogous to infants with *fetal alcohol syndrome*. This syndrome results in low birth weight, incompletely developed internal organs and smaller than normal head size. Cardio-respiratory problems may also develop, depending on what point in her pregnancy a mother was using cocaine. (Brady, Posner, Lang, and Rosati, 1994; Metsch, McCoy, and Weatherby, 1996).

Research after about 1990, however, has found that most of the neonatal impact of prenatal cocaine use disappears when controlling for other lifestyle variables, other drug use, and especially alcohol use (Brown, Bakeman, Coles, Sexson, and Demi, 1998; Neuspiel, Hamel, Hochberg, Greene, and Campbell, 1991; Richardson and Day, 1994; Richardson, Day, and McGauhey, 1993). Many women who use crack or cocaine do not properly care for themselves nutritionally, which also has negative consequences for their fetuses. Similarly, crack-using women especially, often live in older and substandard housing where there may remain lead paint and other environmental hazards (Metsch, McCoy, and Weatherby, 1996). Hence, present research suggests that many of the adverse health consequences of infants previously attributed to mothers' use of cocaine is actually the result of a broader lifestyle that involves poor nutrition, alcohol use, and other unhealthy environmental attributes.

There is perhaps no stimulant—or drug, for that matter—that is more damaging to health than tobacco, though many of the health hazards associated with tobacco use are not directly a result of the stimulant nicotine. In the United States, cigarettes alone cause more than 400,000 deaths per year (Slade, 1999), and the Centers for Disease Control estimate more than 430,000 deaths annually due to all tobacco products. This compares with 100,000–150,000 deaths caused by alcohol and about 25,000 deaths due to all illegal drugs combined (Goode, 1999). It should be stated at the outset that nicotine is a highly toxic substance. A single drop of pure, concentrated nicotine is a fatal dose. To place this in context, there is enough nicotine in a single cigar, if taken in concentrated form, to kill two people (Ray and Ksir, 1999). The reason that smoking a single cigar is not lethal is that the nicotine is diluted enough and is not delivered to the smoker in a short enough time to deliver its fatal blow.

The effects of tobacco smoking go far beyond nicotine, however. It is estimated that cigar and cigarette smoke contain as many as 4,000 chemicals (Liska, 2000), many of which pose health risks to the user. These chemicals include carbon monoxide, carcinogenic tars, and other particulate matter. It is estimated that about 90 percent of tars and other particulate matter remain in the lungs (Carroll, 1989), which greatly increase the risk of cancer for the user. Cancer rates among smokers are approximately twice that of nonsmokers (four times greater among heavy smokers), and cigarette smoking has been linked to about 85 percent of all lung cancer cases (Ray and Ksir, 1999). Other forms of cancer, including cancers of the mouth, larynx, esophagus, stomach, pancreas, cervix, kidney, and bladder are also higher among tobacco users. Moreover, respiratory diseases, such as chronic bronchitis and emphysema are linked to tobacco smoking (National Institute on Drug Abuse, 1998b).

Tobacco smoking also has a deleterious effect on newborns. Nicotine readily permeates the placental barrier, and studies have found that nicotine concentrations in newborn infants have been as much as 15 percent higher than those found in the mother. Nicotine seemingly concentrates in fetal blood, amniotic fluid, and in breast milk, all of which contribute to high concentrations in infants. Also posing a risk, carbon monoxide in tobacco smoke lowers oxygen supply to the fetus (National Institute on Drug Abuse, 1998b). For all these reasons, fetuses of smoking mothers are much more likely to be aborted than those of nonsmoking mothers; and if given live birth, are more likely to be premature and underweight (Ray and Ksir, 1999). There is also heightened risk of Sudden Infant Death Syndrome (SIDS) among infants exposed to tobacco smoke either pre- or postnatally (Slade, 1999; Ray and Ksir, 1999).

Finally, there is a growing body of evidence that smoking poses health risks not only for smokers, but for nonsmokers as well. **Environmental tobacco smoke** (ETS) is believed to cause approximately 3,000 lung cancer deaths annually among nonsmokers, and plays some role in cardiovascular-related deaths of another 40,000 nonsmokers. Asthma sufferers are particularly vulnerable to "passive smoke," and infants in homes where there is smoking are more vulnerable to low birth weight, sudden infant death syndrome, asthma, and other respiratory problems (Aligne and Stoddard, 1997; National Institute on Drug Abuse, 1998b).

Hallucinogens

The hallucinogens have enjoyed both very positive and extremely negative publicity. Proponents of these drugs have claimed that these drugs open the user to existential dimensions not possible otherwise. Opponents have claimed that these drugs, particularly LSD, cause severe flashbacks producing psychotic-like symptoms in the user. Other charges, which have been discussed in Chapter 3, include the allegation that LSD causes genetic damage in users. Both sets of claims are almost certainly greatly exaggerated. Despite the early claims of genetic damage and birth defects, subsequent research under carefully controlled conditions has failed to substantiate these claims (Grinspoon and Bakalar, 1979; Stephens, 1999). The psychological effect of hallucinogens, whether their so-called mind-expansion properties or their ability to produce flashbacks, are subjective effects, which are largely a result of the user's *set* and *setting* (see Chapter 1).

This is not to suggest that hallucinogens pose no direct health concerns. These are very potent drugs, that if taken in excessive dosages can cause very extreme reactions that result in bizarre and dangerous behavior by the user. We have already pointed out in Chapter 3 that LSD is so powerful that dosages are measured in *micrograms,* rather than the standard milligrams. A milligram is 1,000 times stronger than a microgram, which highlights the potency of this particular drug. More recently, other hallucinogens such as ecstasy, have become popular as "club drugs," commonly used at parties, concerts, and other recreational events that attract young people. Recent research sponsored by the National Institute on Drug Abuse has found that MDMA (ecstasy) may indeed cause brain damage. Using Positron Emission Tomography (PET), a brain imaging technique, researchers have discovered that individuals who use ecstasy showed significant reductions in serotonin transporters, which seem to be permanent or at least long-term in their effect. This loss was shown to result in loss of both verbal and visual short-term memory (Bolla, McCann and Ricaurte, 1998; McCann, Mertl, Eligulashvili, and Ricaurte, 1999; Mathias, 1999).

Marijuana

Marijuana is a drug that has had a very checkered history in American pharmacopeia. As we have seen in Chapter 2, it was not until the 1930s that it was made illegal in most states, but only a decade later it was vilified as a scourge on the American landscape. It is therefore quite understandable that there have been numerous allegations about the effects of marijuana, most of which have not stood up to the test of empirical scrutiny. At one time, for example, it was believed that marijuana caused chromosomal damage. Subsequent empirical investigation has failed to support that allegation. Other charges have included that marijuana use causes cerebral atrophy, lowered testosterone levels, and other serious effects. Such charges have not been supported (Goode, 1999). There are, however, physiological and behavioral effects of marijuana that have been substantiated empirically. We turn to these now.

Respiratory Problems   Perhaps most conclusively, marijuana affects the respiratory system of the user. In small to moderate amounts, marijuana has actually been found to benefit certain users, such as those with asthma, by causing the bronchial passageways to enlarge, an effect known as *bronchodilation*. Heavy use, however, has detrimental effects on the user, including inflamation, or narrowing of the bronchial passageways (known as *bronchoconstriction*) (Liska, 2000). Furthermore, Joy, Watson and Benson (1999) report that marijuana smoking (as well as tobacco smoking) causes damage to the lining of the respiratory tract. Chronic marijuana use also significantly reduces capacity of the lungs to function properly.

Cancer   We mentioned in Chapter 3 that marijuana smoke contains some 400 chemicals. The consequences of marijuana smoking, therefore, go beyond that caused by THC, the active ingredient in marijuana. Many of the chemicals found in tobacco are also found in marijuana. Various chemicals in marijuana smoke are also believed to be harmful; indeed, it is estimated that on a per-weight-unit basis, there is as much as four times the amount of tar deposited in the lungs of marijuana smokers than in tobacco smokers. This is partly due to the fact that marijuana cigarettes do not have filters, that marijuana is usually inhaled more deeply than tobacco, and that the marijuana cigarette is smoked more completely than tobacco. On the other hand, it must also be remembered that tobacco is usually rolled much more tightly and that tobacco smokers typically consume many more cigarettes per day than do marijuana smokers (Joy, Watson, and Benson, 1999; Rickert, Robinson, and Rogers, 1982). Epidemiological studies are more difficult because many marijuana smokers are also tobacco smokers (some 50 percent of chronic marijuana smokers are also tobacco smokers—Stephens, 1999), and also because lung cancer takes a long time to develop; since widespread use of marijuana did not begin until the 1960s, there has been difficulty getting large enough samples of users with long-term exposure (Joy, Watson, and Benson, 1999).

Memory Loss   There is also a growing body of evidence that marijuana smoking causes temporary and reversible short-term memory loss. This is especially critical among adolescents because the inability to recall for tests and other school requirements can have serious consequences for labeling and tracking by school officials. We are only recently learning the reason for this short-term loss of memory. It appears that THC suppresses the activity of the neurons in the hippocampus, that part of the brain that is largely responsible for learning and memory. Researchers have discovered that learned behaviors which depend on the hippocampus, deteriorate after sustained marijuana use (Joy, Watson, and Benson, 1999).

Motor Functioning   Motor functioning is also affected by marijuana use. This evidence has been building for the last several decades and is now quite conclusive, though certainly more research needs to be done in this area (Joy, Watson, and Benson, 1999). Much of the evidence is based on laboratory simulations, but street driving and accident evidence also reveals that even a moderate amount of marijuana smoking can quite substantially affect perception and motor coordination (Mathias, 1996; Ray and Ksir, 1999). While marijuana smoking may not cause a lack of coordination like alcohol does, it clearly impairs judgment and hence makes the user a worse driver than one who is sober and straight. This has been reinforced in recent years by investigations of accidents involving marijuana use, including a train accident in Maryland where the engineer was found to have been using marijuana hours earlier.

Addiction   There is growing evidence that marijuana may be addictive. This characteristic of marijuana was rejected for many years, especially by advocates of the legalization of marijuana. We do know, however, that there are withdrawal symptoms associated with heavy marijuana use, including irritability, insomnia, profuse sweating, and GI disturbance. There is also evidence, though disputed, that users develop a tolerance for marijuana. The tolerance seems to be fairly short acting, however, and does not necessarily lead to increased use (Joy, Watson, and Benson, 1999).

Steroids and Human Growth Hormones

These drugs, used primarily by athletes, have very direct and potentially fatal consequences on the user, especially when used in large amounts or over a long period of time. We know that prolonged steroid use can result in testicular atrophy, impotence, kidney disease, and heart attacks. Emotional disorders, including increased aggressiveness and severe mood swings are also linked to steroids (Liska, 2000). The human growth hormone (hGH) also poses health threats. Growth hormones affect most organs of the body in some way. We pointed out in Chapter 7 that recent evidence suggests that the human growth hormone is linked to *Creutzfeldt-Jakob*, a viral disease that, like the AIDS virus, takes years to incubate and can indeed be fatal. Complicating the problems caused by steroids and hGH, athletes often use these drugs in combination. Like so many other drugs, there is a synergism between these drugs which only compounds their effect (Voy, 1991).

SYNERGISTIC EFFECTS

Many of the so-called drug overdoses are really something called *synergism*. **Synergism** can be defined simply as the joint action of two or more drugs that produces an effect that is greater than the sum of the independent effect of the interacting drugs. In some cases, this combined effect is *many times* the sum of the independent drug effects. This effect is not limited to steroids and the human growth hormone. There are innumerable drug combinations that produce synergistic effects, and we will not even attempt to identify them all here. There are, however, a couple of combinations which are particularly relevant to recreational drug use.

One type of drug synergism is that which takes place between CNS depressants. Alcohol and barbiturates, when taken together, produce a powerful multiplier effect that goes far beyond the simple additive effect of the two drugs (Carroll, 1989; Goode, 1999). A similar synergism takes place between narcotics and other CNS depressants. Clinical tests also suggest that opioids may interact with drugs used to treat HIV patients resulting in toxic reactions (Stine and Kosten, 1999). Another common drug combination that results in synergism is cocaine and alcohol. Cocaine is especially dangerous when taken in combination with alcohol because the two drugs synergize to produce something called *cocaethylene,* which has a longer duration in the brain and is more potent and toxic than the simple additive effect of these drugs (National Institute on Drug Abuse, 1999a).

We highlight these synergistic effects because they are most commonly observed among recreational drug users. Mixing of drugs is now commonplace among recreational drug users, and it is often done without any knowledge of just how these drugs interact and what effect that these drug interactions will have. While commonly called "overdose," what is, in fact, taking place is a *dangerous combination* of drugs. While we certainly do not want to downplay the health hazards of individual drugs which might threaten the well-being of the user, greater educational efforts need to be directed toward informing young people (as well as older people who use drugs recreationally or otherwise) of the dramatic consequences of using certain drugs in combination and which drug combinations should be avoided.

DRUG-USING LIFESTYLES AND HEALTH

It is our contention that most of the serious health hazards associated with recreational drug use are a consequence of the *lifestyle milieu* in which these drugs are taken. We do not, hereby, minimize the health hazards that result. Some of them are devastating, indeed fatal, and if Drug Abuse Warning Network (DAWN) emergency room and medical examiner data are any indication, these devastating consequences are affecting more Americans each year (Substance Abuse and Mental Health Services Administration, 1999a, 1999b). Direct pharmacological action does pose certain levels of risk, of course, depending on the drug in question and particularly when volatile combinations of drugs are used together. Even these risks, however, pale in comparison with the risks posed by other features of the lifestyles of many recreational drug users. In this section, we examine three areas of health concern that are primarily lifestyle-generated risks: *infectious diseases, nutrition and hygiene,* and *crime victimization.*

Infectious Diseases

There is perhaps no more deadly risk associated with drug use than that of contracting AIDS. As of June 2000, more than 750,000 cases of AIDS were reported to the Centers for Disease Control. Twenty-five percent of these cases would appear to be a direct result of injection drug use. When sex with injecting drug users are added to the totals, more than 265,000 individuals (more than 35 percent of total cases) have been infected with AIDS either directly or indirectly as a result of IV drug use (Centers for Disease Control and Prevention, 2000a). Even these figures minimize the problem because there are many pediatric cases of AIDS infection that result from pregnant women who have been infected. The Centers for Disease Control and Prevention (2000a) report 8,804 pediatric AIDS cases as of June 2000; 91 percent of these cases are children at risk through their mothers infection or exposure to AIDS.

Drug users contract the HIV virus primarily in one of three ways: (1) through infected needles, which is the mechanism by which most IV drugs users contract the disease; (2) through sexual contact with others who have the disease; and (3) through infected blood acquired in blood transfusions. Intravenous drug users acquire the HIV virus largely through the sharing of needles, a practice common in the subculture of IV drug use. Because needles and syringes are illegal without a prescription in most jurisdictions, these "works" are at a premium. Consequently, there has developed a custom of sharing needles. Often, the individual who bears the risk of holding the needle will be rewarded with a portion of other participants' drugs. Bourgois and his colleagues (1997) have further found that among street addicts in San Francisco, the practice of sharing needles is necessitated by the broader economy of heroin use in that city. Those at the bottom of the underground hierarchy of street heroin users are forced to pool their resources with partners with whom they share their drugs and their works several times a day. While they also make use of needle-sharing programs, these users are dependent on one another to get each other through the day without experiencing major withdrawal symptoms. The camaraderie is a necessity, forced by the economics of the heroin lifestyle.

Some entrepreneurs actually make a business out of renting needles, typically as part of a "shooting gallery" operation where drug addicts can go to buy drugs, rent a set of works, and shoot up away from view of potential undercover law enforcement operatives. The practice of needle-sharing would not be particularly risky if care were taken to sterilize needles between each use. This is seldom the case however. Inciardi and his colleagues (1995) report that between 5 and 15 percent of the syringes tested positive for HIV antibodies, depending on the day of the week tested. Even

DRUGS AND EVERYDAY LIFE

Crack-house Sex

The following observation of activity in a Miami crack-house by James Inciardi and his colleagues illustrates the casual, but risky nature of the sexual exchanges that take place in crack houses:

> There were 16 people in the room. Three men and four women were sitting or lying down by themselves, in various parts of the room. . . . Only two were smoking crack; the others appeared to be resting, or waiting, or watching what was going on elsewhere in the room. In a corner farthest away from the entrance, two men were sitting at opposite ends of a couch. Both were smoking and receiving oral sex from two women. Periodically, one of the women would interrupt her "chicken-heading" to have a hit from the man's crack pipe. In another corner, two women were totally naked, with one straddling the other's face, receiving oral sex. They were "freaking" for crack. That is, they were being paid in crack to perform. Close by, a solitary man was watching them intently, smoking a cigarette with one hand, masturbating with the other. . . .
>
> . . . This scene continued for almost an hour. New customers would come and go— purchase crack, smoke crack, watch sex, engage in sex. Some would just look around and disappear into other rooms. The two men on the couch never spoke to each other, to the women, or to anyone else. . . . The man who was masturbating and watching the two freaking women eventually got up and had vaginal sex with one of them—the one who had been on top, the straddler, the recipient. The other wiped her mouth, lit a cigarette, and watched—disinterested in all the goings-on (Inciardi, Lockwood, and Pottieger, 1993, pp. 70–71) ■

more alarming, they calculated that the average user, frequenting Miami shooting galleries once per day, could expect to test positive for HIV within 22 days. Those users who are careful not to use syringes with any evidence of blood in them could expect to test positive within 44 days. More frequent use of needles would, of course, shorten the time that one could expect to be infected.

The risk for HIV drug users, however, is not confined to the use of infected needles. Because this disease is so prevalent among IV drug users, it is spread readily through sexual relations. One means of income for drug-addicted women as well as men is prostitution. This level of sexual activity increases both the prostitute's risk of contracting the disease from an infected client, as well as her infecting a client. Moreover, many drug-using women will trade sex for drugs, a practice which has become especially common among crack users. Crack, it seems is viewed as an aphrodisiac, promoting sexual desire and intensity on a greater level even than other forms of cocaine. Hence, there is a ready market for sexual favors, and this is nowhere more apparent than in the crack houses themselves. Inciardi and his colleagues describe in very graphic detail the casual and anonymous nature of sexual contact in the crack houses, a phenomenon which seems to be more prevalent than that experienced in other drug subcultures (Inciardi, Lockwood and Pottieger, 1993). An excerpt from their observations is reproduced in the Drugs and Everyday Life feature of this chapter.

In research also conducted in Miami, McCoy, Miles, and Inciardi (1995) describe in more quantitative terms the risk inherent in this type of sex-for-drugs. Female crack users reported more than eight times the number of sexual partners as women who did not use crack, though they were more likely to insist on condom use. Nevertheless, they were nearly twice as likely to test positive for HIV than were noncrack users. Crack-using women were also much more likely to suffer from other forms of sexually transmitted disease, such as syphilis, gonorrhea, genital herpes, and other genital sores.

The good news is that the incidence of HIV and AIDS has been declining over the past several years. Figure 8.1 reveals that the incidence of AIDS cases peaked in 1992–1993 at just under 85,000 cases that year, but has been declining every year since then.[5] Also encouraging are data from the Centers for Disease Control and Prevention (2000a) that injection drug users (IDUs) are comprising a decreasing percentage of all new AIDS cases, from about 30 percent of all new cases in 1997 to 28.6 percentage of all cases in 1999. This means, therefore, that because the incidence of AIDS is decreasing overall, the incidence of IDU cases is indeed dropping. This decline is a testament to the preventive and educational efforts that have been expended in this area. Clearly, these efforts are having an impact, and this very success should justify even more efforts in this area.

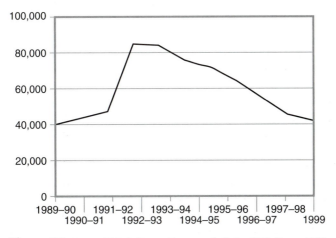

Figure 8.1 New AIDS Cases Reported, July 1989–June 1999

Sources: Centers for Disease Control and Prevention, *HIV/AIDS Surveillance Report*, 2000, Table 2; Centers for Disease Control and Prevention, *HIV/AIDS Surveillance Supplemental Report*, 1999, Table 1.

There are also other infectious diseases that drug users risk contracting and transmitting. Intravenous drug users are especially vulnerable to various forms of hepatitis, some of which are especially toxic, even fatal. Because hepatitis comes in different forms, there is sometimes confusion and misunderstanding regarding this disease. The most common form of hepatitis is Hepatitis A, which is primarily transmitted through water, food, or fecal material. This form of hepatitis normally does not have any long-term serious health consequences, and IV drug users are not much more at risk for this form of hepatitis than the general population. A second type, *Hepatitis B Virus* (HBV), is much more serious, and a form of hepatitis to which IV drug users are especially vulnerable. This is a virus transmitted largely through blood and sexual contact, and can also be transmitted to developing fetuses. HBV attacks the liver, often causing scarring and cirrhosis, causing the death of between 5,000 and 6,000 Americans per year. The Centers for Disease Control and Prevention (2000b) have estimated that there are between 1 and 1.25 million Americans currently affected with this disease with 140,000 to 320,000 new infections each year. The incidence of HBV declined from 1985 to 1993, but has been on the increase among IV drug users since 1993.

Another serious hepatitis strain is *Hepatitis C Virus* (HCV). This virus is also transmitted through blood and sexual contact as well as perinatally. Those groups most at risk are injection drug users, highly active and promiscuous sexual players, health care workers, and infants born to infected women. Like HBV, Hepatitis C attacks the liver, resulting in 8,000 to 10,000 deaths per year. The Centers for Disease Control and Prevention (2000b) estimate that approximately 3.9 million Americans have been infected with HCV, but that the incidence of new cases is only about 36,000 annually (1996 estimates). A final hepatitis virus that affects IV drug users is *Hepatitis D* (HDV), otherwise known as "Delta Hepatitis." This virus depends upon the coexistence of Hepatitis B to replicate itself. When it occurs in conjunction with individuals with *chronic* HBV (known as a *superinfection*), the Delta virus is especially destructive. Long term studies of chronic HBV carriers who acquire HDV in a superinfection suggest that 70–80 percent develop cirrhosis of the liver, compared with 15–30 percent of patients with chronic HBV alone (Centers for Disease Control and Prevention, 2000b).

We want to emphasize that the high prevalence and incidence of these diseases among drug users are only *correlates* of their drug use, not direct consequences. That is, the drugs involved—whether we are talking about heroin, cocaine, crack, or any other drug—do not cause these infectious diseases. Nor do these drugs cause higher rates of other sexually transmitted diseases such as gonorrhea, syphilis, or genital herpes. Rather, these diseases are a consequence of certain aspects of the lifestyles that these drug users lead (Rhodes, 1996). Among heroin and IV cocaine users, for example, acquiring HIV and hepatitis is probably a result of the way in which they administer the drug (intravenously), and the care (or lack of it) that they give to insuring noninfected ("clean") needles. Drug users can substantially reduce their risk of being infected through a number of means: adopting alternative routes of administration (e.g., "snorting" rather than "shooting;"); sterilizing their needles with bleach between each use; turning infected ("dirty") needles in for clean ones where there are needle exchange programs available; and refusing to loan or borrow needles from other addicts. These practices, if widely practiced, would not only reduce individual risks, but curb the spread of these diseases substantially. Other lifestyle features also affect the spread of these diseases. Most significantly is the frequent, and often indiscriminate, sexual practices of some drug users. All of the infectious diseases that we have examined in this section can be transmitted sexually. Once again, reducing sexual activity, maintaining monogamous sexual relationships, and/or taking precautions when engaging in sexual activity are effective preventive measures. Recognition of the lifestyle dynamics of drug users is an important part of understanding the causal complex of the health issues that this population group confronts.

Nutrition and Hygiene

In 1962, the Supreme Court ruled, in *Robinson v. California*, that it was unconstitutional to punish persons merely because they were addicted to narcotics. At least as well known as the decision of the court, is the description of drug addiction presented in the court's opinion:

> To be a confirmed drug addict is to be one of the walking dead. . . . The teeth have rotted out; the appetite is lost and the stomach and intestines don't function properly. The gall bladder becomes inflamed; eyes and skin turn a bilious yellow. In some cases membranes of the nose turn a flaming red; the partition separating the nostrils is eaten away—breathing is difficult. Oxygen in the blood decreases; bronchitis and tuberculosis develop. Good traits of character disappear and bad ones emerge. Sex organs become affected. Veins collapse and livid purplish scars remain. Boils and abscesses plague the skin; gnawing pain racks the body. Nerves snap; vicious twitching develops. Imaginary and fantastic fears blight the mind and sometimes complete insanity results. Often times, too, death comes—much too early in life. . . . Such is the torment of being a drug addict; such is the plague of being one of the walking dead. (U.S. Supreme Court, 1960).

This poignant description, which was intended to describe the heroin addict, paints a portrait of a rather pathetic individual who has worn down his or her body and is fraught with ailments, even impending death. While there are certainly inaccuracies in this description, at least insofar as their application to heroin addiction, the attributes that do apply here have one thing in common: they are all a result of the *lifestyles* that heroin addicts lead, not a result of the pharmacological action of narcotic drugs. Moreover, much of what is described here is a result of a lack of proper nutrition and hygiene.

Many of the negative health effects of illicit drug use are results from lifestyle factors rather than from the direct pharmacological effect of the drugs on their bodies.

Even the most casual observer of the heroin subculture will note that, on average, heroin addicts tend to suffer from weight loss—some even appearing rather emaciated. Heroin addicts participate in a rather frenetic lifestyle, continually looking for a "score" (drug purchase) and trying to "get over" (make money, usually illegally), all the while having to watch their backs to be sure that they are not identified by police or others who would take advantage of them. This lifestyle, commonly called "ripping and running," has been characteristic of post-Harrison Act years—since the recreational use of narcotics was made illegal. A now classic study conducted by Arthur Light and Edward Torrance in Philadelphia in the 1920s addresses the weight-loss issue quite directly. A subsample of 100 heroin/morphine addicts were maintained in a hospital setting on adequate doses of morphine. At the end of the controlled maintenance period, only four of the subjects were grossly underweight—about the percentage that one would find in the general population. Furthermore, 6 of the 100 subjects were obese, and the remaining 90 were within the normal weight range. Yet these subjects had been taking the average of 21 grains of morphine or heroin per day—much more than the typical addict on the street would take. (Light and Torrance, n.d.; cited in Brecher, 1972). This study clearly suggests that it is not the pharmacology of heroin or other narcotics that results in physical deterioration, but rather the peculiar nature of addict lifestyles since the criminalization of narcotics for recreational use.

Other physical problems are also noted in the *Robinson* v. *California* opinion that bear some comment. The scarring and collapsing of veins and jaundiced skin are also reflective of the hygienic conditions that many IV drug users practice their lifestyle. Dirty needles and blunt needles—in short needles that are used far beyond their intended use—cause untold health consequences for addicts, including the spread of infectious diseases, but beyond that the collapsing of veins because of overuse by blunt needles. Jaundiced skin is also related to poor hygiene, often a symptom of hepatitis.

One of the street heroin addicts interviewed by Faupel (1991, p. 111) described the scene at the *crib* (home) of one of her acquaintances in New York City who was a *junkie broad:*

> The baby was all pissy and messy laying in a rag all over the floor. . . . It was ridiculous for anybody to live like that . . . because of her being a woman, she could have got some kind of money some kind of way—if she had to whore, steal it, take it, or rob it—either way, she was supposed to feed those babies she had.

This observation reveals an important truth about the subculture of heroin use, namely that there *is* self-respect among heroin addicts, a fact which is evidenced in the revulsion that this respondent experienced at the sight she saw. The other truth, however, is that when individuals become addicted, especially when they are *desperately addicted*, nutrition and hygiene take on a much lower priority to more urgent needs of securing drugs to appease their hunger for drugs. Over time, this neglect of the physical body takes its toll.

Crime Victimization

Drug users—particularly *illegal* drug users—are more vulnerable to being victimized by crime than most of us. The reason for this is that these are individuals who, by their very act of using illegal drugs, are criminals. That fact brings them into contact with other criminals who might possibly victimize them. The connection between drug use and crime will be addressed in detail in Chapter 10. Much of what we have to say regarding the relationship between criminal offending and drugs has equal relevance to the connection between drug use and crime victimization. Hence, we will not explore that topic exhaustively here. We do, however, want to introduce here research conducted by Paul Goldstein (1985) on the relationship between drug use and violence. Goldstein suggests three models to understand this connection. The first is a **psychopharmacological** model, which suggests that individuals on drugs engage in violent acts because their intoxication induces a loss of rationality and/or control. A second **economic-compulsive** model suggests that people become violent when they are desperate for drugs and do not have the resources to obtain them. At these times, they may engage in violent behavior to extort money for drugs.

Goldstein's third **systemic** model suggests that violence is an intrinsic part of the culture and economy of drug use, a dynamic that Goldstein later found to apply to the crack distribution network as well (Goldstein, Brownstein, Ryan and Bellucci, 1989). It is this connection which we want to highlight in this chapter.

Violence is, to some degree, endemic to the lifestyle associated with illicit drug use. Goldstein (1985, p. 497) identifies several examples of systemic violence associated with the underworld of illicit drug use. Some of these include: disputes over territory between competing drug dealers; robberies of drug dealers in retaliation for perceived past unfair business practices—and typically a violent response by the dealer; punishment for failing to pay a debt; and retaliation against informers. Additionally, Goldstein points out that the AIDS epidemic has introduced still another source of violence, namely falsely representing a set of works to be "clean" or even new, when in fact they have been used by someone who is at risk for AIDS.

Violence is, for a variety of reasons, a risk that individuals take when they choose to become involved in a lifestyle of illegal drug use. Some indication of the health toll that violence takes is revealed by emergency room and medical examiner statistics reported to the Drug Abuse Warning Network. These statistics reveal that 3.7 percent of all drug-related emergency room visits in 1999 were due to injuries of some sort. This represents more than 20,500 emergency room episodes (Office of Applied Statistics, 2000b). Furthermore, medical examiner data reveal that 54.8 percent of all drug related deaths in 1998 were either accidental or unexpected, while another 16 percent were due to suicide (Office of Applied Statistics, 2000a). While not all these deaths are due to systemic violence, data such as these point to violence as a substantial health-risk factor in the subculture and economy of illegal drug use.

One final health risk that is directly connected with the criminal nature of the drug enterprise, and that broadly falls under Goldstein's systemic violence, is the tremendous risks of violence intrinsic to the production of some drugs, particularly methamphetamine. Once the near monopoly of a small number "superlabs" located in Mexico and in the southwestern United States, 237 "superlabs" were seized in 1999 by the DEA in several states, including states on the East Coast. Moreover, in addition to the superlabs, small, amateur clandestine labs have sprung up in virtually every state in the union. More than 7,500 such labs were seized in 1999 (Drug Enforcement Administration, 1999—see Chapter 3). These labs are extremely dangerous— to the operators, to innocent people living in the immediate environment, and to law enforcement. Methamphetamine can be produced with over-the-counter ingredients, but the preparation process can be lethal. Chemicals used are corrosive, toxic, and highly combustible. These chemicals can be particularly deadly, and often explosive when inappropriately mixed. So volatile are the chemicals involved in the manufacture of methamphetamine, that law enforcement personnel are especially trained and provided full-body protective gear before entering a suspected meth lab. They are frequently met with armed resistance, which only exacerbates an already volatile situation (Koch Crime Institute, 1999).

POTENTIAL HEALTH BENEFITS OF DRUGS

In this section, we address three controversies that have arisen in recent years regarding the potential medical benefits of drugs which are normally used only for recreational purposes. The drugs in question are marijuana, which has been proposed as a medical response to several medical conditions; the extended use of stronger narcotics for terminally ill patients; and alcohol in moderate use as a means of enhancing health, particularly the heart and circulatory system.

MEDICAL MARIJUANA

The use of marijuana for medical purposes is not new. The earliest reference to marijuana is found in a pharmacology book written nearly 5,000 years ago by the Chinese emperor Shen Nung, who recommended marijuana for a variety of ailments including gout, rheumatism, malaria, and even constipation and absent-mindedness (Ray, 1978). Other reports of the medical use of marijuana can also be found in ancient Greek writings (Guterman, 2000). Grinspoon (2000) reminds us that marijuana was first recognized by Western medicine in 1839, when W.B. O'Shaughnessy discovered its usefulness as an analgesic, anticonvulsant, and a muscle relaxant. Subsequently, more than 100 articles on the medical use of marijuana were published by American and European medical journals (Grinspoon and Bakalar, 1995). It was touted as being therapeutic for tetanus, neuralgia, rheumatism, and asthma among other conditions. Indeed, marijuana use in the United States was primarily for medical purposes until the 1920s, when alcohol was prohibited and marijuana was sought as a functional alternative to alcohol. Simultaneously, medical interest in the drug was declining. It would be until the 1970s that serious advocacy of marijuana as medicine would reinvigorated (Grinspoon, 2000).

Today, proponents of legalizing medical marijuana point to two specific health areas in which marijuana has been shown to be helpful. First, it has been quite effective in *relieving the nausea associated with chemotherapy among cancer patients*. Cancer patients began experimenting with marijuana in the 1970s as an *antiemetic* drug—for the relief of the side effects of chemotherapy—as an alternative to other conventional medications and generally found it to be much more effective (Grinspoon and Bakalar, 1997; Joy, Watson, and Benson, 1999). There is also some support for the use of marijuana for cancer patients among oncologists. A survey conducted among oncologists in 1994 revealed that while only 12 percent of the physicians reported recommending marijuana to their patients, 30 percent indicated that they would do so if marijuana cigarettes were to be made legal (Schwartz and Sheridan, 1997). An earlier survey by Doblin and Kleiman (1991) reported that 44 percent of oncologists indicated that they had recommended marijuana use to their chemotherapy patients. It is also worthy of note that more than 50 percent of the physicians in the 1994 survey had prescribed Marinol, trade name for dronabinol, a synthetic tetrahydrocannabinol (THC), the primary active ingredient in marijuana (Schwartz and Sheridan, 1997).

Still another potential medical use of marijuana is the stimulation of appetite, particularly among HIV and AIDS patients. Many patients suffering weight loss from AIDS have claimed that marijuana is the most effective and least toxic treatment for the nausea which caused their weight loss (Grinspoon, 2000). The controlled research examining the effect of THC as an appetite stimulant has used dronabinol (Marinol). The research strongly suggests that THC is an effective appetite stimulant (Joy, Watson, and Benson, 1999).

These are by no means the only medical uses that have been claimed for marijuana in recent years. In their 1997 revision of their classic book, *Marijuana: The Forbidden Medicine*, Lester Grinspoon and James Bakalar identify some 30 medical conditions for which patients have found marijuana useful. Included in these symptoms, in addition to the wasting associated with AIDS and the nausea associated with chemotherapy are reducing intra-ocular pressure in glaucoma patients, easing the symptoms of osteo-arthritis, multiple sclerosis, and epilepsy, and relief of chronic pain in various forms (see also Joy, Watson, and Benson, 1999).

There have been efforts to make marijuana legally available for medical purposes. Since the 1960s, the federal government has maintained a marijuana research plot at the University of Mississippi in Oxford, the fruits of which have been used since 1975 in carefully monitored medical cases. This program, which has been termed the Compassionate Investigational New Drug (IND) Program, has been used on an extremely limited basis, however. Among the many thousands of people who would benefit from this program, only 40 individuals throughout the United States have ever been approved. Moreover, only 13 people have actually received the government-cultivated cannabis, and the government has determined that they will not be providing cannabis to any new patients—not even to any of the 40 who have already been approved (Grinspoon and Bakalar, 1993).

Attempts have been made in several states to make marijuana legally available since 1978. By 1991, 34 states had enacted legislation that would formally make marijuana legally available for medical use, and most recently, in 2000, Hawaii was the 35th state to pass such favorable legislation. Most of these laws are grossly ineffective, however, because federal restrictions prevent doctors from prescribing marijuana. Hence, any state statute which includes the word "prescribe" is effectively neutralized by federal law as physicians are unwilling to place themselves at risk for federal sanctions. Furthermore, most of these bills provided no means to legally distribute marijuana, so marijuana patients would have to rely on illegal sources for their drugs (Schmitz, Thomas, and Kampia, 2001).

It was a 1996 referendum in California that represented a major shift in state medical marijuana laws. Underground distribution of marijuana for medical purposes had been going on for years in California. A San Francisco organization called the Cannabis Cultivators Club first opened its doors in 1992, making marijuana available to some 12,000 medical users. City officials essentially turned a deaf ear to what was going on, but in August of 1996, state narcotics agents raided the club and closed it down on marijuana possession charges. This resulted in a backlash by California voters who, with 56 percent of the vote, passed Proposition 215, otherwise known as the Medical Marijuana Initiative. Proposition 215 essentially made it legal to grow, possess, and smoke medical marijuana in California if it was recommended or approved (not "prescribed") by a physician (Rosin, 1997; Schmitz, Thomas, and Kampia, 2001). A similar ballot initiative was passed in Arizona in that same year, and in 1998, three states—Washington, Oregon, and Alaska—voted at the ballots to legalize marijuana for designated medical purposes (Sager, 1999). Maine passed a similar initiative in 1999, followed by Colorado and Nevada in 2000. Hawaii addressed the issue in a different way in 2000, by legislating the removal of criminal penalties for medical marijuana users rather than using a statewide referendum (Schmitz, Thomas, and Kampia, 2001). Figure 8.2 shows the nine states with medical marijuana laws.

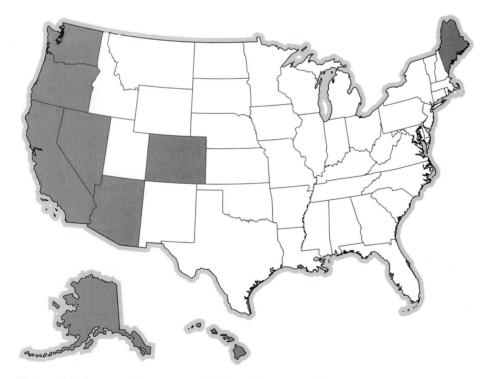

Figure 8.2 **States with strong medical marijuana provisions**
Source: http://www.norml.org; accessed October 3, 2002.

These new state laws do, of course, conflict with federal law that prohibits the possession and distribution of marijuana. Indeed, the federal response to the California referendum was almost immediate: any individual using marijuana, even if recommended by a physician, could face federal prosecution. Moreover, physicians recommending the drug could also be prosecuted as well as lose their drug licenses. Within a few months, the courts ruled that doctors could not be prosecuted, but left open the door to prosecute individual users. The case of *Conant* v. *McCaffrey* filed January 14, 1997, and heard in August of 2000 in Federal District Court, ruled that to prevent doctors from recommending the use of medical marijuana was an abridgement of free speech and therefore was unconstitutional. Federal authorities then began to target distributors, especially larger "clubs," such as the Cannabis Cultivators Club (Sager, 1999) and the Oakland Cannabis Buyers' Cooperative (OCBC). The Justice Department filed suit in January 1998 to close down the operations of these distributors and received a temporary injunction that closed the clubs down. One year later, however, the Ninth Circuit Court of Appeals ruled unanimously that "medical necessity" is a valid defense against federal law provided that the distributor can prove that a patient is seriously ill and that the marijuana is necessary. This was appealed to the Supreme Court by the Justice Department, which ruled in its favor on May 14, 2001. The High Court ruled that the Controlled Substances Act did not recognize medical necessity, except when distributed through government-controlled research projects (United States *v.* Oakland Cannabis Buyers Cooperative et al., 2001). The use of cannabis for medical purposes has, in effect, been rendered illegal throughout the United States on the basis of the federal Controlled Substances Act. The likelihood of federal arrest or prosecution of individual medical users is very small, however. Approximately 99 percent of marijuana arrests in the United States are made by state and local authorities. Hence, in those states that have legalized marijuana for medical purposes, the statistical likelihood of arrest among patients using medical marijuana is only about 1 percent. As Schmitz, Thomas and Kampia (2001, p. 5) state, "(s)imply put, individual medical marijuana users generally are not on the federal government's radar screen."

In sum, there is a long history of medical use of marijuana, a history that is being rediscovered among contemporary Americans with a variety of ailments. There is strong "clinical" evidence that marijuana is an effective antidote to many of these maladies. The federal government has strongly opposed marijuana use for medical purposes and has stubbornly refused to move it from a Schedule I to a Schedule II drug—a designation that indicates a high degree of abuse potential, but nevertheless recognizes medical utility. Increasingly, however, voters and legislators in individual states are recognizing the legitimacy of marijuana under certain medical conditions and are paving the way legally for people to access marijuana. This has created a tension between the federal government and the individual states, a tension that will likely be played out in the courts for some years to come. In contrast to the reticence of the United States to make medical marijuana legally available, Canada legalized marijuana for medical purposes on a national level in legislation introduced on June 14, 2001 (P.C. 2001-1146). We would urge that researchers and policy makers study the impact of this legislation for future policy initiatives in the United States.

Unrestricted Narcotics for Terminally Ill Patients

One of the consequences of advances in medicine is that people not only live longer, but are more likely to die of chronic, rather than acute diseases. Chronic diseases such as cancer often result in rather severe pain toward the end of a patient's life. Studies of outpatients have revealed that anywhere between 12 and 71 percent of dying individuals suffer severe pain in the last week of their life (Pantilat, 1999). Indeed, for some patients, it is the excruciating pain that motivates them to seek suicide (Brown, 1997). Many medical practitioners have decried this situation because they know that they have the ability to alleviate all or at least most of the pain that terminal patients experience through the use of opiates primarily, but also other pain-relieving drugs.

Physicians are hesitant to prescribe massive dosages of narcotics, however, for two reasons. First, there is the fear of shortening the life span of the already terminal patient. Second, many physicians fear that to increase the dosages of narcotic medications will result in patients becoming addicted to these drugs. Finally, related to both of the above concerns, many physicians fear prosecution merely for prescribing these drugs in the large quantities necessary for pain relief because of the scheduling of these drugs (typically Schedule II), which places severe constraints on their use because of their addictive potential. Physicians also fear that they might be charged with assisting in suicide if it is believed that the narcotics they use shorten the lives of their patients. There seems to be a fairly broad consensus among medical practitioners and ethicists about the legitimacy and response to these concerns. We examine each of these concerns in the following paragraphs.

Shortening Life Span

It is commonly believed that narcotics, especially in heavy doses, so depress respiration that their use will prematurely end the life of a terminally ill patient. Extensive clinical evidence suggests that these concerns are unfounded. (Expert Working Group, 1996). Furthermore, controlled research on 238 patients in a hospice unit showed no evidence for hastening of death. Patients who were given marked increases in opiates during their last 48 hours of life showed no significant differences in length of life from admission to the hospice, or in the frequency of unexpected death, from those patients who were given no or only modest increases in opiates (Thorns and Sykes, 2000). The World Health Organization (WHO), has developed an "analgesic ladder" designed to assist physicians in identifying

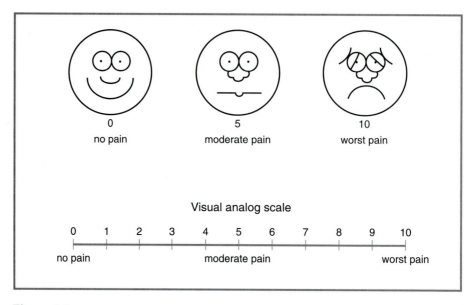

Figure 8.3 Visual Pain Scale

Source: Pantilat, Steven Z. 1999. "Just Say Yes: The Use of Opioids for Managing Pain at the End of Life." *The Western Journal of Medicine*, 171, 4, pp. 257–259.

the appropriate amount of medication to terminally ill patients. This is often used in conjunction with a "visual analog scale" (See Figure 8.3) that has been found to be especially effective in helping patients accurately convey the level of pain that they are experiencing (Pantilat, 1999). Low-level pain often requires little more than acetaminophen or even aspirin. Greater pain requires greater intervention. When opiates are administered with sensitivity to a patient's pain level, medical ethicists agree that there should be no concern with overprescribing narcotics.

Addiction

Many doctors have been reticent to prescribe large dosages of narcotics, especially if these dosages must be maintained over a period of time, because of the potential for creating an addiction among their patients. Practitioners working in palliative care (care of dying patients) respond to this concern in two ways. First, it is argued that medical patients are not as vulnerable to addiction as are street users of narcotic drugs, do not experience the euphoria that a street user experiences, and do not have the same craving for the drug as is experienced by street users (Brown, 1997). The logic of this argument might be a bit suspect in that the craving that street users experience typically come from the *lack* of the drug, a situation that medical patients with prescribed morphine do not typically experience. There is, however, some empirical evidence to back up this claim. Research using data from the Drug Abuse Warning Network reveals that the number of emergency room episodes involving the five opioids most frequently used in treating terminally ill patients[6] *decreased* from 1990 to 1996. This decrease was observed despite the fact that physicians were actually increasing their prescriptions for the use of all these drugs except for meperidine (Joranson, Ryan, Gilson, and Dahl, 2000). The concern over addiction does indeed seem unfounded. Moreover, many wonder why there is a concern regarding addiction, even if the use of these drugs does initiate or increase the level of addiction in patients. These patients are, after all, terminal. Their addiction, if indeed it occurs, allows them to lead useful and productive lives in their last days, an opportunity not available without the narcotics (Pelligrino, 1998).

Concerns About Prosecution

The fact is that most physicians understand that the concern over shortened life span and addiction are not valid reasons to deprive dying patients of pain-reducing narcotics. Most physicians do not prescribe either because they are not alert to the level of pain that a patient is experiencing (Pantilat, 1999), or more likely because they fear that they might be subject to criminal prosecution, especially under the Controlled Substances Act of 1970. Physicians fear criminal prosecution primarily on the grounds that the use of massive amounts of drugs may bring on the early demise of their patients.

This concern is, at one level, valid because a physician who is investigated by law enforcement or by medical examining boards is subject to public degradation that can have potentially catastrophic effects on his or her practice. Nevertheless, the need to provide adequate pain relief, even when it involves exceptionally large doses of narcotics (and in some cases barbiturates) overwhelms the prosecutorial risk, in our assessment. The fact is that the risk of prosecution is substantially limited for at least three reasons. First, as we have discussed earlier, medical evidence is increasingly demonstrating that longevity is not appreciably shortened with the use of pain-killing drugs, and that those who use these drugs do not seek or crave them beyond what is needed to alleviate the pain associated with their medical condition. Second, legislation has been introduced that would protect physicians from prosecution for administering pain-killing drugs. Commonly known as the *Pain Relief Promotion Act of 1999,* this legislation was first introduced in the house by Congressman Henry Hyde (HR-2260) and then in the Senate by Senator Don Nickles (S-1272). The bill clearly states that the dispensing of controlled substances as medically necessary to relieve pain is consistent with the Controlled Substances Act. The bill also calls for education of law enforcement and health professionals on medically accepted means for alleviating pain. The House version of the bill passed with a strong majority in October of 1999; the senate version of the bill had, as of early 2001, been referred to the Senate Committee on Health, Education, Labor, and Pensions (HELP) for further hearings. This legislation, if passed, should leave little reason for fear of prosecution by physicians.

Finally, the administration of pain-relieving medication has long been defended ethically—which has usually translated into a legal defense as well—by a philosophy known as the "Doctrine of Double Effect." This is an old philosophy, dating at least as far back as medieval Catholic theologians, which states that actions are morally permissible, regardless of the consequences of those actions, if it was not the intent of the actor to cause those consequences (Quill, Dresser, and Brock, 1997). The doctrine even allows for those consequences to have been foreseeable by the actor so long as he or she did not intend for those consequences to occur. Hence, when applied to the dispensing of opiates and other pain-relieving medication, *even if* addiction occurs or life is shortened by a physician's actions, the physician is justified in using these medications if his or her intent was to relieve the pain and suffering of the patient and not to cause addiction or death (Quill, 1995). Generally, if an action on the part of a physician leads to a patient's death is to be regarded as morally acceptable under this doctrine, the action must conform to the following legal requirements:

- The medication must have a reasonable chance of reducing suffering or pain.
- The use of medication must be intended *primarily* to reduce pain and *not* to result in death.
- The use of medication cannot be for purposes of producing death as a means of relieving the pain and suffering.
- There must be enough reason to prescribe the increased medication to counterbalance any foreseeable risk of death (Lieberson, 1999).

There is, of course, disagreement among health professionals as well as law enforcement officials as to the appropriateness of the use of this doctrine to the relief of pain in terminally ill patients. These usually come in the "gray areas," such as sedating a person to a level of unconsciousness until their demise (Quill, Dresser, and Brock, 1997). Importantly, however, while recent Supreme Court decisions have upheld the principle of the sanctity of life above patients rights to choose euthenasia,[7] our criminal law has consistently allowed for posing a risk to life if the expected benefits justify the risks. Such a risk is taken, for example, when high-risk surgery is performed to correct a serious medical condition (Quill, Dresser, and Brock, 1997).

For all these reasons, while the law is not crystal clear regarding the potential consequences for a physician administering opiates or sedatives to terminally ill patients, the risk of prosecution to physicians who are conscientious in their response to the pain of the terminally ill should be fairly minimal. There is an increasing effort to educate physicians on how to administer pain-reducing medications in an ethical and legal manner (California Medical Association Foundation, 1999). These efforts should result in a greater use of these medications to reduce the pain and suffering of terminally ill patients.

BENEFITS FROM MODERATE DRINKING

We have discussed at some length, both in this chapter and in Chapter 3, some of the health hazards associated with alcohol consumption. Recent research, however, has revealed that when consumed in moderation, alcohol can actually enhance one's health. It has long been believed that alcohol has health benefits; indeed, its medicinal properties are mentioned in numerous places throughout both the Old and New Testaments. Only recently, however, have carefully designed studies scientifically supported such benefits. We should point out that there is controversy within the scientific community, and especially within the treatment industry regarding the beneficial role that moderate alcohol consumption might have (Moak and Anton, 1999).

It is, of course, important to first define what we mean by *moderate* drinking. Typically, this is defined as a certain number of drinks consumed over a specified period. There is variation, however, in the amount of alcohol contained in different types of drinks, a problem which is especially apparent when examining alcohol consumption cross-culturally (Dufour, 1999). Researchers have been developing more quantitative measures of levels of alcohol consumption (usually measured in the actual amount of alcohol consumed), and have developed equivalency tables for different types of beverages. Beer, for example, contains about 4.5 percent alcohol; wine 12–13 percent; distilled alcohol, 40–45 percent. Hence, if a standard drink contains approximately 0.5 percent alcohol, one 12 oz. can of beer would be about equivalent to a 5 oz. glass of wine or a 1.5 oz. shot of distilled spirits. The question then becomes, what is moderation in drinking? Scholars vary in their assessment, but generally agree that moderation consists of somewhere between one and two standard drinks per day (Dufour, 1999, Klatsky, 1999). Specific studies may use different definitions for moderation, but this definition is useful for purposes of this discussion.

Most of the research in this area has focused on the benefits of moderate drinking in lowering the risk of heart disease. A carefully designed meta-analysis of more than 40 experimental studies on this topic found a clear inverse relationship between moderate drinking and coronary heart disease (Rimm et al., 1999). On the basis of this analysis, it was estimated that 30 grams of ethanol consumption per day should lower one's risk of coronary heart disease by 24.7 percent (Rimm et al., 1999). Research by Michael Thun and his colleagues (1997), which analyzed 46,000 deaths in a prospective study of some 490,000 respondents, found that deaths due to cardiovascular disease were 30–40 percent lower in moderate drinkers than among abstainers.

Several types of heart disease seem to be positively affected by moderate drinking. A large scale study in China, utilizing a sample of more than 18,000 middle-aged men, found that, compared with abstainers, moderate drinkers had a 22 percent lower mortality rate than nondrinkers overall, and that they were 36 percent less likely to die from ischemic heart disease (Yuan and Ross, 97). Most other studies of this type of heart disease also find lower risk among moderate drinkers (Klatsky, 1999). The most common type of heart disease, coronary artery disease (CAD) is also reduced among moderate drinkers (Jackson, Scragg, and Beaglehole, 1991; Rimm et al., 1991; Stampfer et al., 1988). While there remains an open discussion as to why alcohol in moderation lowers CAD, the most common hypothesis is that, in moderation, alcohol raises the level of high-density lipoprotein (HDL), commonly known as "good cholesterol." Several studies have confirmed that this mechanism is indeed operative in lowering CAD (Klatsky, 1999, Rankin, 1994). Other cardiovascular indications for moderate alcohol use include peripheral arterial diseases (PAD), which is a significant cause of death among the elderly (Camargo et al., 1997), strokes (Sacco et al., 1999), heart disease risk among diabetes patients (Senior, 1999), and in reducing mortality among individuals who have already had heart attacks (Muntwyler, Hennekens, Buring and Gaziano, 1998).

While heart disease has been most researched, there is also some evidence that moderate drinking may have certain health benefits in other areas as well. There is now mounting evidence that moderate alcohol consumption may reduce cancer risk. The above-cited study of Chinese men (Yuan and Ross, 1997) found a 15 percent lower cancer death rate among moderate alcohol users relative to lifetime nonusers—a substantive difference, though not statistically significant. Preliminary studies have also suggested possible benefits in reducing Alzheimer's risk (Anonymous, 2000a) and prevention of bone loss in women (Anonymous, 2000b). These findings, while not replicated in carefully controlled studies, are at least suggestive of a range of health benefits of alcohol use in moderation.

SUMMARY

This chapter has set out to identify and describe some of the major health consequences of drug use. We want to emphasize two important things in this summary section. First, the psychoactive drugs *can and often do* pose real health risks to those who use them. Much of the risk, however, is related to factors other than the chemistry of the drugs themselves. Synergism and lifestyle factors account for many of the risks associated with drug use, especially illicit drug use. The recent scourge of AIDS and potentially fatal forms of hepatitis are exacerbated by the lifestyles of crack and IV drug users, a lifestyle which is encouraged by strongly repressive drug policies. Public health demands that we examine closely our drug policies and look for alternative approaches to addressing the

problem of drug use in this country, and indeed, throughout the world.

Second, we want to emphasize that there are also positive health benefits to what might otherwise be considered recreational, or at least inappropriate, drug use. We have examined just three areas—medical marijuana, heavy doses of narcotics for terminally ill patients, and moderate alcohol consumption. The medical community has been very reticent to recognize the medical value of these and certain other drugs. Once again, there is a need to carefully examine both medical practice and culture and legal constraints that would thwart medical practitioners from providing good medical care when it involves drugs which are normally used recreationally. We will examine these issues more thoroughly in Chapters 12 and 15.

KEY TERMS

delirium tremens
economic-compulsive
    violence
environmental tobacco
    smoke (ETS)

fetal alcohol syndrome
formication
psychopharmacological
    violence
synergism

systemic violence
Wernicke-Korsakoff
    syndrome

REVIEW QUESTIONS

1. Discuss what is meant by "drug overdose." What are the physiological causes of overdose from heroin use? Why are the authors skeptical about reports of heroin overdose?

2. What does the term "synergism" mean? Why is it important to recognize that many, if not most, drug

overdoses are, in fact, probably due to synergism?

3. What are some of the direct pharmacological effects of alcohol on the human organism. How do these pharmacological effects compare in number and in nature to the direct pharmacological effects of commonly

identified illegal drugs such as heroin and cocaine?

4. The authors state, "It is our contention that most of the serious health hazards associated with recreational drug use are a consequence of the *lifestyle milieu* in which these drugs are taken." What do the authors mean by this statement? What are some of the specific lifestyle features of drug users that affect health?

5. Why is "crime victimization" identified as a health risk associated with drug use? What are the three types of criminal violence associated with drug use?

6. Why do the authors propose an unrestricted use of narcotics for terminally ill patients? What are the objections to unrestricted narcotics use, and how do the authors respond to these objections?

7. What are some of the health benefits that can accrue from moderate drinking? Do you think these health benefits are sufficient to offset the health risks associated with drinking identified earlier in the chapter?

CRITICAL INQUIRY QUESTIONS

1. If, as the authors maintain, it is the *lifestyle milieu* in which recreational drugs are taken that poses the most serious health risks to users, what does this suggest about how we should respond to recreational drug use? What sorts of policies might be most effective in combating and/or reducing these health risks?

2. "Medical marijuana" has recently emerged as a controversial policy issue in many states. What is the premise for legalizing marijuana for medical purposes. What is *your* position on this controversial issue? Develop a sound rationale for your position.

NOTES

1. We will not be discussing CNS Stabilizers in this chapter. The rather limited health consequences associated with these drugs and their potential for abuse have been discussed in Chapter 3.

2. Less serious than FAS is a condition known as *fetal alcohol effects* (FAE), which consists of low birth rates, spontaneous abortion, and less serious forms or partial features of FAS.

3. The comparison category for risk factors was male drivers aged 21–34. Risk of a fatal accident decreases with age. Hence, for older drivers (35+), the increased risk factor of more than 11 is a conservative figure; for

younger drivers, 16–21, the increased risk factor of more than 51 is slightly exaggerated.

4. William Shakespeare, *Macbeth*, Act 2, Scene 3.

5. We would refer the student to Chapter 4 where we discuss the difference between "incidence" and "prevalence." While the total number of people with the AIDS virus (prevalence) continues to climb, the number of *new cases diagnosed* (incidence) is declining.

6. The five opioids are morphine, fentanyl, oxycodone, hydromorphine and meperidine.

7. See *Vacco* v. *Quill*, 521 U.S. 793 (1997) and *Washington* v. *Glucksberg* 521 U.S. 702 (1997).

DRUGS AND THE ECONOMY

The illicit drug trade is big business. In the United States alone, it has been estimated that Americans spent as much as $140 *billion* per year on illegal drugs during
the height of the crack epidemic in the late 1980s (U.S. House of Representatives,
1988). Today, the figure is probably half that amount due in large part to declines
in cocaine use and availability of cheaper cocaine and heroin (Office of National
Drug Control Policy, 2001, p. 140 and 142). A report by the United Nations (2000)
contends that the amount of acreage used for producing illicit drugs is also
declining. Moreover, legal drugs, such as alcohol and tobacco have a profound

impact on economies in a variety of ways, including tax revenues and retail sales on the one hand, and in health care costs and employer liabilities such as absenteeism on the other. It has been estimated, for example, that health care costs for smoking alone account for as much as 1.1 percent of the gross domestic product in high-income countries and almost that high in low-income countries as well (Lightwood, Collins, Lapsley and Novotny, 2000). It has been suggested that tobacco costs the global economy some $200 billion each year after weighing the economic benefits against costs of health care, premature death, sick leave, etc. (Barnum, 1994). Alcohol costs nearly $150 billion each year to the United States alone (Harwood, Fountain, and Livermore, 1998).

This chapter examines the economy of drug use from a number of perspectives. First, we examine the economic costs and benefits of drug use. We begin with an international perspective, examining the economic impact of the cocaine, heroin and marijuana trade, particularly on those countries which serve as a point of origin for these drugs. Following that discussion, we examine the impact of drug use on the domestic economy. We do this both through a "macro" analysis, examining the large-scale costs of drug use to our economy—costs in health care, worker productivity, and so forth; and through a "micro" analysis, examining the impact of drug use on workers' likelihood of labor force participation, as well as how drug use affects income and wages. A second major section of this chapter examines the *underground economy* of drug use, from cultivation to retail distribution. Finally, the last section examines the dynamics of drug use in the workplace. This section begins by estimating the nature and prevalence of drug use in the workplace, followed by a discussion of workplace conditions that might affect the likelihood of drug use by employees, and finally, how the government and employers are responding to drug use by employees.

AN ECONOMIC COST-BENEFIT ANALYSIS OF DRUGS

It is almost impossible to measure the amount of drug sales on a worldwide basis because of inconsistencies in reporting methodologies. Keh (1997, p. 2), upon reviewing a number of United Nations studies, suggests that the "turnover" in the global illicit drug trade ranges between $100 and $500 billion annually. However, it has been estimated that for some countries, such as Bolivia, coca and cocaine exports alone comprise anywhere from 28 to 53 percent of its *total* exports (United Nations, 1997) and that 10 percent of those employed are working in the illicit drug industry (United Nations, 1994). The importance of the drug trade to the economies of nations is considerable. Clearly, the statement that "the drug business is big business" has enormous political and economic implications. Consequently, recent suggestions that the overall contribution of illicit drug monies to the gross domestic products is declining is viewed with cautious optimism (United Nations, 2000).

The illicit drug trade is not only big business, but, because of its size, has a profound effect on the economies of many drug-producing and drug-using countries. Some of these economic consequences are extremely high—resulting in billions of dollars syphoned out of (or introduced into) countries, huge expenditures on law enforcement and drug treatment, and businesses losing billions of dollars in diminished worker productivity.

An International Perspective

The drug trade is international in scope. At one time or another, nearly all psychoactive drugs have been bought and sold across sovereign borders. Tobacco, caffeine, marijuana, opium and its derivatives, and cocaine have all been traded on the international market. Today, the three categories of illicit substances that contribute the most to the international drug trade, at least as it relates to the United States, are cocaine, narcotics, and marijuana (United Nations, 2000).

International Cocaine Trade

Cocaine derives from the coca plant, which is grown primarily in the highlands of the Andes Mountains, especially in Bolivia, Peru, and Colombia, though it is also grown commercially in Pakistan, Bali, East Asia, and in the Caribbean. Native inhabitants of these areas have been chewing the coca leaf for centuries. Coca has long been part of the economy of these countries and has even been used as a medium of exchange (Brecher, 1972). While chewing of the coca leaf never became popular outside of its native countries, *cocaine,* the active ingredient in the coca leaf did become an international commercial success.

Cocaine-producing countries derive a substantial portion of their gross national product from the sale of the drug. Figure 9.1 reveals that cocaine production and distribution comprise nearly 10 percent of Bolivia's Gross National Product (GNP). Other countries are less dependent, but nevertheless receive sizable income from the sale of cocaine. Some estimates suggest that cocaine may be the largest exported commodity from some cocaine-producing countries (United Nations, 1997). It has been estimated that from the late 1980s until the early 1990s, South American countries alone produced

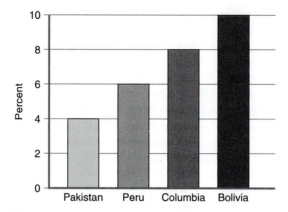

Figure 9.1 **Percentage of GNP Comprised of Cocaine Production and Distribution, Early 1990s**
Source: United Nations, *World Drug Report*, 1997.

in excess of 200,000 metric tons of coca leaf per year (Bureau of International Narcotic Matters, 1990), though recent reports by the Office of National Drug Control Policy (2001, p. 169, 171) show that in the last decade, that amount has been cut by about one-third. To place this figure in some perspective, it should be noted that the weight of coca leaf grown and harvested is not the same as cocaine produced. Less than 1 percent of the coca leaf consists of cocaine, so large amounts of the leaves are required (Inciardi, 2002).

From 1988–1999, the amount of cocaine shipped to the United States is estimated to have dropped by half, from approximately 600 metric tons to approximately 300 metric tons. Furthermore, the average selling price of cocaine has dropped during the same selling period, also by about half (ONDCP, 2001, p. 171). Nonetheless, it is believed that Americans spend tens of billions of dollars a year on cocaine in its various forms. Specifically, in 1998, the total expenditure on cocaine in United States is estimated at $39 billion (Rhodes, Lane, Johnston, and Hozik, 2000).

The impact of cocaine on the economies of producing countries can be measured in other ways as well. A substantial acreage is devoted to cocaine production, particularly in the South American Andes region. A General Accounting Office report estimated that, in 1995, there were approximately 214,000 hectares set aside for cocaine production, primarily in the Andean countries of Bolivia, Ecuador, Columbia, and Peru (General Accounting Office, 1997). The U.S. has fought coca-growing, most notably in Peru, but a "whack-a-mole" phenomenon has seen cultivation soar in Colombia as Peru's contribution declined (ONDCP, 2001, p. 176). The cocaine industry employs many unskilled laborers. As noted earlier, as much as 10 percent of Bolivia's labor force is employed in the production, processing, or distribution of cocaine (United Nations, 1994; 1997). One concern is what to do about coca-growing farmers in the Andes or opium poppy growing farmers in Southwest Asia, whose livelihoods are derived from plants grown for their psychoactivity, and who receive far more for doing so—perhaps four times as much—as for any other crop their land might sustain.

The economic benefits of cocaine are not limited to producing countries. Approximately 75 percent of the global supply of cocaine originates in Colombia, but its distribution and processing is profitable to other countries in South and Central America, as well as in Mexico. For example, cocaine headed to the United States is usually routed through Mexico, where a large-scale distribution network is in place (DEA, 1999). While approximately two-thirds of the cocaine entering the United States does so through the Central American-Mexican corridor, most of the remainder comes through the Caribbean. The geographic position of Colombia is of key importance here, as it is the only South American country that is situated on both the Pacific Ocean and the Caribbean Sea (DEA, 1999).

While there are without question economic benefits to producing countries, there are costs as well. A major cost to these countries is that the drug industry has provided a foothold for organized crime. Powerful organizations, known as **cartels,** often coerce farmers to grow the coca plant by threatening violence or induce farmers to grow the plant by offering extraordinarily high prices for their product. These cartels not only dominate the market in cocaine, but also are involved in money laundering, gun running, and other illegal activities. Civilian governments in South American cocaine-producing countries have become especially vulnerable to threats and control by organized crime groups (United Nations, 1997). Perhaps more problematic in these countries, public officials can easily become corrupted by drug cartels seeking to ensure a favorable and predictable political environment from which they can conduct business (McCaffrey, 1998). Moreover, because funds from illicit drug operations are typically laundered through a series of procedures involving several countries, the integrity of the financial systems of these countries may be seriously compromised. This often results in a loss of confidence in the legitimate economies of these countries, which can have devastating effects on their already fragile economies (United Nations, 1997).

Still another cost to coca-producing countries is the direct impact that billions of dollars pouring in annually will have on their economies' monetary policy. When a country such as Columbia or Bolivia with a modest gross national product experiences *billions* of dollars flowing in annually, it will almost certainly face the risk of excessive inflation (Keh, 1996). Most of this money is controlled by drug lords, but as these resources are introduced into the general economy in the form of purchasing houses, building hotels and resorts, and purchasing other consumer goods, the cost of these goods increases for everyone. Inciardi (1992) points out, for example, that when these funds were introduced, there was a sudden demand for automobiles and other luxury items. For example in 1981, small Chevrolet Chevettes were selling for as high as $25,000 (at that time selling in the United States for about $4,000). Hyperinflation also occurred in real estate, making housing unaffordable for large segments of the population.

The agriculture of these countries is also affected by inflationary increases in the value of land. Because coca production dramatically increases the value of land, many farmers cannot afford to grow conventional crops. There is great pressure to either grow coca, or sell their land at high prices to coca farmers. Farmers in lower-altitude regions, which are not suitable for coca production, are often lured to work in the higher-altitude coca-production areas for higher pay because they cannot earn a sufficient living growing conventional crops (Inciardi, 1992).

International Heroin Trade

On a global level, the countries of Afghanistan, Myanmar (formerly known as Burma), and Laos are the largest producers of opium—followed by the countries of Colombia and Mexico. Virtually all the heroin produced in Colombia and Mexico is destined for the United States. For a number of years, most of the heroin coming into the United States also originated from Southern Asia. This situation, however, changed dramatically in 1993 when Colombian drug organizations expanded into the production and distribution of heroin (DEA, 1999; United Nations, 2000).

The international economy of heroin production and distribution does share an important characteristic with the cocaine economy: the farmers who produce these drugs are very poor and dependent on the income that they derive from poppy production. They are also the most poorly paid. Farmers in Pakistan, for example, realize only about 6 percent of the entire profit from the opium trade emanating from that country; the traffickers, by contrast, lay claim to about 90 percent of the profit. Despite their low position on the production/distribution hierarchy, poppy farmers realize profits of anywhere from 33 to 800 percent more from growing opium than from growing licit crops such as onions, cabbage, wheat, lentils, or other legitimate crops that can be grown in these areas. There is, therefore, great incentive to cultivate opium as a cash crop (United Nations, 1997). The dynamics of the drug trade—from Southwestern Asia poppy growing through Pakistani drug lords to German drug wholesalers and into European drug markets—was captured by the 1989 British television miniseries, "Traffik." The outline of this six-hour masterpiece served as the basis for the popular 2000 movie entitled *Traffic.*

The economic and social costs to heroin-producing countries is very similar to that experienced by countries which produce cocaine. Organized crime is a part of the heroin trade, though it is much more involved in the refinement and distribution stages. The heroin industry is not quite as vertically integrated as are the cocaine cartels. Whereas the cocaine cartels tend to control all stages of the industry—from production to consumer sales—the heroin industry tends to be somewhat more loosely organized (United Nations, 1997). Heroin-producing countries also are vulnerable to political corruption, inflationary economies, and a diversion of agricultural land that could be used for food products into poppy fields.

International Marijuana Trade

In comparison with the illicit trade in cocaine and opiates, information pertaining to marijuana is much more difficult to ascertain. Varieties of the *Cannabis* plant can be found in most countries, be they naturally occurring or cultivated. Because cannabis is the most frequently used illicit drug and can be found in various forms (marijuana, hashish, hashish oil), the sheer size of the marijuana trade makes identifying a single source more difficult. Nonetheless, it appears that Southwest Asia is the leading producer of cannabis resin (hashish), whereas Colombia and Mexico are the leading producers of marijuana (United Nations, 2000).

There is some disagreement as to the extent to which marijuana used in the United States is imported or grown domestically, in part because of changes in the sources over the years. Prior to 1969, Mexico was a primary source for American marijuana. That year, President Nixon launched **Operation Intercept,** a major border initiative which sought to prevent Mexican marijuana from entering the country. While most historians agree that Operation Intercept was a dismal failure in terms of preventing the smuggling of marijuana, it resulted in an increase in domestic production (Brecher, 1972).

Nonetheless, current estimates suggest that approximately 25 percent of marijuana consumed in the United States is grown domestically (United Nations, 2000), California being one of the leading domestic producers (DEA, 2001). The proportion of it coming from Mexico is increasing, however (NNICC, 1998), as well as Colombia (United Nations, 2000). In many instances, those criminal organizations responsible for the transportation of cocaine and heroin from South/Central America through Mexico are also involved in transporting marijuana as well (DEA, 2001). Marijuana is more frequently differentiated by THC content as opposed to country of origin. Generally speaking, marijuana grown in the United States is more potent and is more likely to be grown indoors than that brought in from Mexico (United Nations, 2000).

THE DOMESTIC SCENE—A MACROECONOMIC PERSPECTIVE

The previous sections outline many of the ways in which drugs reach the United States. In this and the following section, we examine some of the costs associated with use and abuse of these substances in the United States. The economic impact of drug use in the United States is difficult to assess, in part because "cost" has been an elusive concept. Our first task should be to identify what is meant by "cost." Perhaps the best way to do so is to elaborate the distinction between *private* costs and *societal* costs. Private costs refer to the immediate costs incurred by the drug consumer in the way of lost wages, cost of drugs, prison time, etc. We will discuss some of these issues next when we talk about the impact of drug use on employment status and other *microeconomic* level costs. Here, however, we are primarily interested in the *societal costs* of drug use. There are, first, the direct economic costs associated with drug use, including higher rates of absenteeism, poor work performance, as well as costs of treatment and enforcement of drug laws. Criminal victimization has also been identified as a cost, though this has been argued to be a "forced transfer" rather than truly a cost from a macro-societal point of view (Marks, 1992).[1] Broader, and more difficult to define costs include health care costs to spouses who are abused; children dependent on welfare because of drug-abusing parents; and health care costs for addicts suffering from complications of AIDS and other drug-related illnesses. Collins and Lapsley have defined the economic costs of drug abuse as ". . . the value of the net resources which in a given year are unavailable to the community for consumption or investment purposes as a result of the effects of past and present drug abuse, plus the intangible costs imposed by this abuse" (Collins and Lapsley, 1996; cited in United Nations, 1997, p. 104).

The cost of drug use in the United States, when cost is defined in terms similar to the definition above, is staggering. Overall, the estimated cost of drug and alcohol abuse in the United States was about $246 billion in 1992, of which more than $148 billion is accounted for by alcohol abuse and $98 billion by illicit drug abuse (Harwood, Fountain, and Livermore, 1998). These figures do not include the economic costs of tobacco use in this country, which were estimated to be $138 billion in 1995 (Horgan, 2001). In this section, we will consider economic costs from a fairly broad perspective. These costs fall into several categories, and we take up each category separately.

Health Care Costs

Table 9.1 provides a breakdown of the costs of drug and alcohol abuse for various years in the 1990s. Slightly more than 10 percent of the overall cost (nearly $29 billion) was taken up by health-related costs. Most of this (nearly $19 billion) was for alcohol abuse, and the remaining (nearly $10 billion) was for drug abuse. Nearly $19 billion went to things like hospitalization due to overdoses, poisoning, drug-induced psychoses, and the like. Also, drug use often contributes to or exacerbates other illnesses or injuries resulting in longer hospital stays, as well as pharmaceutical and ancillary medical expenses such as dental work. Most of these costs were responses to the deleterious *consequences* of drug and alcohol abuse. Tobacco, by contrast, cost the nation proportionately much more for health care, with more than 55 percent of the total costs of smoking, or more than $80 billion per year, going to health care for complications related to smoking. Furthermore, Warner, Hodgson, and Carroll (1999) suggest that the medical costs of smoking may exceed 8 percent of the total cost of medical care in the United States. We would suggest that, compared with illicit drug and even alcohol abuse, this is a very high price to pay for America's addiction to tobacco.

There are some special medical conditions brought on by the substance abuse which should be highlighted. Consider *fetal alcohol syndrome* and the health costs of drug-exposed infants. It has been estimated that there are about 2 fetal alcohol syndrome infants born for every 1,000 births. Estimates of the number of infants *in utero* exposed to illegal drugs vary, but one relatively conservative estimate from a study conducted in California suggests that at least 5 percent of newborns tested positive for

TABLE 9.1	Economic Costs of Alcohol, Drug and Tobacco Abuse in the United States, Selected Years (Millions)			
Economic Costs	Total	Alcohol	Drugs	Tobacco*
Health Care Expenditures		*(1992)*	*(1992)*	*(1995)*
Alcohol and Drug Abuse Services	$9,973	$5,573	$4,400	
Medical Consequences	$18,778	$13,247	$5,531	$80,040
Total, Health Care Expense	*$28,751*	*$18,820*	*$9,931*	*$80,040*
Productivity Effects (Lost Earnings)				
Premature Death	$45,902	$31,327	$14,575	$49,680
Impaired Productivity	$81,901	$67,696	$14,205	$8,280
Institutionalized Populations	$2,990	$1,513	$1,477	
Incarceration	$23,356	$5,449	$17,907	
Crime Careers	$19,198		$19,198	
Victims of Crime	$3,071	$1,012	$2,059	
Total, Productivity Effects	*$176,418*	*$106,997*	*$69,421*	*$57,960*
Other Effects on Society				*(1998)*
Crime	$24,282	$6,312	$17,970	
Social Welfare Administration	$1,020	$683	$337	
Motor Vehicle Crashes	$13,619	$13,619		
Fire Destruction	$1,590	$1,590		$6,950
Total, Other Effects on Society	*$40,511*	*$22,204*	*$18,307*	*$6,950*
Total	*$245,680*	*$148,021*	*$97,659*	*$144,950*

*Tobacco costs are not calculated into the total as they are drawn from sources reflecting different years.
Sources: Harwood, Fountain, and Livermore, 1998 (Analysis by the Lewin Group); Horgan, 2001; Leistikow, Martin, and Milano, 2000).

illegal drugs (Harwood, Fountain, and Livermore, 1998). Harwood and his associates estimate that the cost of treating alcohol and drug-exposed infants is about $2.3 billion. While it is possible to overestimate the costs of *in utero* drug exposure as we did with the so-called "crack baby epidemic" from the late 1980s and early 1990s, health consequences are an objectively real phenomenon (Goode, 1999, pp. 76–77). Cigarette smoking also poses potentially fatal risks for fetuses, and for those fetuses which are not aborted, there is a much higher prevalence of low birth weight infants for smoking mothers. Lightwood, Phibbs and Glantz (1999) estimate that low birth weight infants impose $263 million in additional medical costs each year.

In some ways, the most sobering health consequence of illicit drug use is HIV/AIDS. Currently (as of 2001) between 1 and 1.5 million people in the United States are believed to be infected with HIV. Approximately 36 percent of recent cases are attributable to drug use (one-in-three men, one-in-two women), either directly by using infected needles, or indirectly through sexual contact with an IV drug-using infected person. This represents an increasing proportion, from 27 percent of all new cases in 1987. The costs are staggering, and increasing. In 1985, estimated costs of treating all HIV positive persons were about $630 million (Scitovsky and Rice, 1987). The cost rose dramatically to $10.2 *billion* in 1992 (Hellinger, 1992) and has since leveled off to about $6 to $7 billion dollars, as treatment became less expensive and those with HIV were able to avert AIDS due to powerful drug cocktails that included protease inhibitors (Hellinger and Fleishman, 2000).

In addition to the costly *consequences* of drug and alcohol abuse, there are medical costs associated with *treatment and prevention*. There are more than 11,000 treatment units in the United States which provide various forms of treatment and rehabilitative services to approximately 1 million addicts at any given time. Add to this the various prevention programs aimed primarily at education, and training for staff members, the United States spends in excess of $10 billion per year on treatment and preventive services (ONDCP, 2001:169).

Productivity Losses

The loss in human productivity as a result of drug and alcohol abuse, when stated in monetary terms, without question, is the most costly consequence of widespread substance use. Each year, as a result of premature death, disability, and institutionalization, the American economy is "debited" more than $176 billion (see Table 9.1). It is estimated that in 1992, there were more than 132,000 deaths resulting from drug and alcohol abuse (Harwood, Fountain, and Livermore, 1998). More than 33,000 of these were AIDS cases alone. Other diagnoses include hepatitis B and C, cirrhosis of the liver, and suicide and homicide. Loss of productivity due to premature death among smokers, by contrast, made up 36 percent of the total societal costs of smoking in 1995. Cigarette smoking along accounted for some 2.2 million deaths between 1990 and 1994 (Hargon, 2001).

The monetary cost to premature loss of life is not easily measured. Economists have, however, been able to determine the "cost" of premature death by calculating the wages (including fringe benefits and taxes) that the "average" person would have made during their lifetime, assuming a normal life expectancy. For example, a male who dies at age 35–39, foregoes a calculated $700,000 in lifetime earnings; a female, about $500,000 (Harwood, Fountain, and Livermore, 1998).[2] People who die at a later age have proportionately lower projected lost lifetime earnings. On the basis of these calculations, it is estimated that human productivity losses caused by premature death due to drug and alcohol abuse was just under $46 billion in 1992 (Harwood, Fountain, and Livermore, 1998), and another $50 billion in 1995 due to smoking (Hargon, 2001).

Beyond greater than normal levels of premature mortality, substance abusers also suffer conditions which render them less productive in the workplace. Because of these conditions, which include depression, withdrawal symptoms, overdose symptoms, and physical illnesses of various sorts, persons who are pharmacologically dependent do not perform as well on the job. Economists distinguish between two types of lost productivity caused by drug and alcohol abuse. One type of effect, sometimes called "internal effects" (Harwood, Fountain, and Livermore, 1998), are lower wages, unemployment, and unpaid absences from work experienced by addicts themselves as a result of symptoms and conditions related to their substance abuse. There has been a great deal of research on the impact of substance abuse on wages (Berger and Leigh, 1988; Gill and Michaels, 1992; Kaestner, 1994a,b; Mullahy and Sindelar, 1989, 1993); and labor force participation (Kandel and Davies, 1990; Mullahy and Sindelar, 1991; Register and Williams, 1992). We will be examining these impacts in a later section in this chapter when we discuss the impact of substance abuse on employment. Some economists suggest that internal effects should not be considered as a productivity cost because drug and alcohol users choose to use these substances, and willingly accept the cost of lost wages and lower levels of employment in exchange for the benefits that they experience from the consumption of drugs and alcohol. A second type of effect, sometimes called a "spillover effect," refers to inferior job performance, high rates of absenteeism which are costly to businesses, injuries on and off the job which diminish performance, and the like.

Calculation of lowered productivity costs typically assumes that individuals meeting the criteria for alcoholism or drug addiction will be impaired in their level of productivity in terms of employability, wages, and/or overall earnings. The findings, however, are somewhat mixed. Generally (though with some exceptions), studies examining alcohol and drug *use*—as distinguished from *abuse*—suggest that there is little negative effect on labor force participation or wages and earnings (Berger and Leigh, 1988; Kaestner, 1991; Register and Williams, 1992). Those studies which examine *abuse* of alcohol and other drugs such as marijuana and cocaine, tend to report more negative effects on indicators of economic productivity (Gill and Michaels, 1992; Kandel and Davies, 1990). Harwood, Fountain, and Livermore (1998) confirm that problem drinking and drug abuse negatively affect economic productivity, most significantly when these problem behaviors are initiated early in one's life. Wage rates are similarly affected—early initiates make lower wages than nonusers or later initiates. Females are not as profoundly affected as males, though drug dependence was found to significantly lower their employability. The net effect of impaired productivity caused by alcohol and drug dependence is estimated by Harwood and his associates to be some $82 billion per year (refer to Table 9.1).

In addition to productivity costs due to lowered employability or wages and earnings reduced due to inability to perform, alcoholics and drug addicts who are institutionalized, either in hospitals or residential treatment programs, are removed from the arena of work. Harwood, Thomson, and Nesmith (1994) estimated that in 1991 there were 63,800 clients in long-term residential alcohol and drug treatment programs in the United States on any given day. Add to this nearly nearly 6.9 million days that short-term patients spent in hospitals for drug and alcohol problems, Harwood, Fountain, and Livermore (1998) estimate that at an average of about $25,000 per individual per year, lost productivity due to treatment and hospital institutionalization was about $3 billion. Additionally, drug abusing incarcerated populations represented about 600,000 person-years. The value of this lost labor in the economy was estimated at about $23 billion in 1992 (refer to Table 9.1).

Another productivity cost that is often not considered by most people is the loss of work days by *victims* of drug and alcohol-related crime. The value of time lost is based on the number of victimizations reported in the National Crime Victimization Survey, which estimated 33.6 million victimizations in 1992, averaging about 2.5 days of lost work per crime. Each day of work lost was valued at $133. Calculating only those victimizations which are drug or alcohol-related, Harwood and associates (1998) estimate approximately $3 billion in lost productivity of crime victims.

Finally, researchers have also identified *potential* legitimate activity which is diverted into criminal careers as a productivity cost. Based on an estimated 1.7 million heavy drug users in the United States in 1992, and on the assumption that a significant number of these withdraw from legitimate market activities altogether in pursuit of drug trafficking or predatory crimes, Harwood, Fountain, and Livermore (1998) estimate that there is another $19 billion diverted from legitimate market productivity.

These components—premature death, lowered employability and wages, institutionalization of alcohol and drug addicts in treatment programs, hospitals and prisons, lost work by victims of crimes, and potential legitimate activity which is diverted into criminal careers—are the primary elements that account for lost economic productivity in the United States. As revealed in Table 9.1, this component alone accounts for more than $176 billion in estimated lost economic productivity, and another $58 billion in lost economic productivity due to tobacco use.

Other Effects on Society

We have indicated above that there were an estimated 33.6 million criminal victimizations in 1992, or about one victimization for every six Americans over 12 years of age (Harwood, Fountain, and Livermore, 1998). Victims experience both physical and psychic injury as well as financial loss. There has, of course, been a debate in the literature about the nature of the relationship between drug use and criminal behavior, and particularly around whether alcohol and drug use actually *cause* criminal behavior (see Chapter 11). There is little debate, however, about the observation that drug users are much more heavily involved in crime than nondrug users. With the exception of drug or alcohol-specific laws (e.g., drug possession or DUI) which are by definition drug/alcohol related, percentages range from a low of 2.5 percent to about 30 percent, depending on the type of crime. Based on these estimates, Harwood et al. (1998) estimate about $19 billion in personal injury and property loss to crime.

Society, however also bears the cost of law enforcement, corrections, and other components of the criminal justice system which apprehend and punish drug-related criminals. It is estimated that more than $24 billion were spent in 1992 alone in criminal justice response to alcohol and drug-related crime—primarily to drug-related crimes. Society also bears a heavy cost in providing drug abusers and alcoholics with social services such as disability insurance, Supplemental Security Income (SSI), Temporary Aid to Needy Families (TANF) (formerly known as Aid to Families with Dependent Children—AFDC) and food stamps. Grant and Dawson (1996) estimated that between 6.4 and 13.8 percent of social welfare recipients were heavy drinkers, and between 3.8 and 9.8 percent of those using these services were drug abusers. It is important to point out that these figures are not substantially different than the percentages of alcohol and drug users that we would find in the general population. They do, however, represent a substantial impact on our social welfare system. Harwood, Fountain, and Livermore (1998) estimate that the United States spends more than $1 billion annually on social welfare benefits to drug and alcohol abusers.

Who Pays These Costs?

Victims and their families pay a substantial portion of the costs borne by society for substance abuse. Figure 9.2 reveals that abusers and their households bear 45.1 and 43.9 percent of the costs of alcohol and drug abuse respectively. This is a substantial percentage, and it must be remembered that much of this

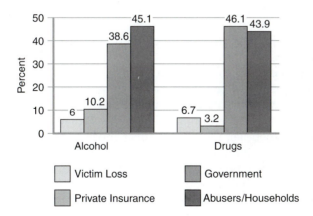

Figure 9.2 **Who Pays for Costs of Drug and Alcohol Abuse?**

Source: Harwood, Fountain, and Livermore, 1998; Analysis by the Lewin Group.

cost burden is borne by innocent spouses and partners and children of the abuser. Moreover, approximately $81.2 billion (nearly 55 percent) of the $148 billion economic burden caused by alcohol abuse is paid for by the nonabusing population. The government bears most of this cost ($57.2 billion), which is, of course, ultimately the American taxpayer. The distribution of drug abuse costs is similar to that of alcohol. Abusers and their families pay about $42.9 billion, or 43.9 percent of the $97.7 billion in economic costs incurred by drug use. The nonabusing population bears more than 56 percent of the costs, with the government once again picking up the largest tab.

THE DOMESTIC SCENE: A MICROECONOMIC PERSPECTIVE

This brief section examines the impact of drug and alcohol use on the economic behavior and productivity of individuals. Research in this area addresses essentially two closely related questions: *Does the use of drugs and alcohol affect labor force participation?* and *Does the use of drugs and alcohol affect income and wages?* The literature is decidedly mixed on both of these questions.

Theoretically, the most straightforward prediction is that drug and alcohol use should affect negatively both labor force participation and wages. Because of the potentially acute intoxicating effect of drugs and alcohol, and longer-term debilitating effects that these substances can have on the human body, we would expect users to be fired more often and more likely to be unemployed. For these reasons, and because alcohol and drug use results in higher rates of absenteeism when workers are employed, we would expect that substance users (and abusers) would report lower wages than nonusers. There is some empirical support for this line of reasoning. Kandel and Davies (1990) found that illicit drug use did adversely affect employment indicators among a subsample of nearly 7,000 males drawn from the National Longitudinal Survey of Youth who were born between 1957 and 1964. The authors found that illicit drug use increased the likelihood of moving between jobs, gaps in employment, and longer terms of unemployment. Each of these, in turn, negatively affected wages. Research by Mullahy and Sindelar (1989, 1991, 1993) among alcoholics in the New Haven, Connecticut, area essentially confirms this view. They did find, however, that the impact of alcoholism varied by gender and by life-cycle dynamics. While alcoholism affects both men and women adversely, women are more severely affected economically as a result of their drinking than are men. Moreover, alcoholism seems to affect those in the prime of their careers most negatively and most significantly. Differences between alcoholics and nonalcoholics were not significant among younger respondents; among older respondents alcoholics actually earned *more* than nonalcoholics.

Mullahy and Sindelar's findings suggest another alternative: Among younger age groups, alcoholics and drug abusers are more likely to have dropped out of school and have thereby established a longer work history than nonusers. This would theoretically result in greater probability of employment and therefore higher wages. Eventually, their lifestyle catches up with them and their nonusing friends overtake them economically. Moreover, in later years, nonusers might retire earlier, thus reflecting lower levels of employment and lower wages than those with a history of substance abuse who must continue working full time much longer. A number of studies support this contention (i.e., Berger and Leigh, 1988; Gill and Michaels, 1992; Kaestner, 1994a,b; Register and Williams, 1992).

THE UNDERGROUND ECONOMY OF ILLICIT DRUGS

Because of the underground nature of the illicit drug economy, it is difficult to describe that economy with a great deal of precision. Furthermore, the nature of the underground economy varies somewhat with different drugs. Hence, we will highlight some of the broad features of this underground economy, as well as draw some comparisons between the illicit drug economy and features of the legitimate economy. Perhaps the best way to describe the underground economy of drugs is to divide it into various "phases" of production and distribution. These phases are *crop cultivation, manufacture, exportation/importation, wholesale distribution,* and *retail distribution* and will be discussed in the sections that follow.

CROP CULTIVATION

The cultivation of illicit drugs—especially opium, coca, and cannabis, the three drug groups that make up most of the illicit drug economy—may take place either legally or illegally. For example, certain strains of cannabis are cultivated in some countries for industrial and nonpsychoactive purposes. Similarly, both opium and coca are used for legitimate medical purposes, and the cultivation of these plants for these purposes is legal. Currently, approximately 12,000 hectares of coca are produced legally in Bolivia (United Nations, 1997). Most of the cultivation of coca or opium poppies, however, is for illicit purposes. These illicit crops produce substantial profit margins, making it difficult for legitimate crops to compete. Moreover, coca can be grown where other crops cannot—on steep slopes with minimal soil fertility. Coca production is also dominated by highly centralized and powerful cartels which exert a great deal of pressure on farmers to produce coca. All of these factors contribute to a strong agricultural production of illicit drugs.

MANUFACTURING

The manufacturing process is a relatively simple procedure for marijuana, especially when compared with the cultivation stage. The leaves and flowering tops of the cannabis plant are stripped and dried, much in the same way that tobacco is "cured." Once fully cured, the dried leaves and flower "buds" are packaged and made ready for distribution.

The manufacture of opium and its derivatives and of coca products is somewhat more complex than that for marijuana. Opium is typically converted into morphine at a refinery local to the farmers who grow the poppy plant. The conversion of morphine to heroin involves a five-stage process to bind the morphine molecule to acetic acid (heroin is diacetyl morphine). Until the 1980s, heroin production was highly centralized, with most of the heroin in the world being refined at either Marseilles, France, or in Hong Kong. More recently, however, heroin manufacture has become more decentralized, with refineries in the growing regions of Southeast and Southwest Asia as well as other parts of the world (Inciardi, 1992).

The production of cocaine also begins in laboratories close to where the coca shrubs are grown. These laboratories soak the coca leaves with a mixture of several chemicals including alcohol, sulfuric acid and benzol. A precipitate is formed with the addition of sodium carbonate, which is then washed with kerosene and chilled. This precipitate is called coca paste, which has up to a 90 percent concentration of cocaine (Inciardi, 1992).

IMPORTATION

There are, essentially, three types of drug importation routes into the United States: *land*, *air*, and *water*. The route that an importer chooses depends upon a number of factors, including the source country, level of technological sophistication available, the drug in question, and the nature of law enforcement surveillance. Importation operations range from small amateur operations that involve individual entrepreneurs going across the border to Mexico to purchase and smuggle in quantities of marijuana, to large bureaucratic organizations which are centrally controlled and exert a tremendous amount of power and control nationally and internationally. Such organizations include the infamous Cali and Medellin Cartels of Colombia, so powerful in the 1980s and early 1990s. These organizations often control production, manufacture, and importation operations. Because of heightened levels of law enforcement at U.S. borders, small entrepreneurial smugglers are increasingly rare.

Importation requires an increasing level of sophistication to outmaneuver Customs' and DEA's highly effective surveillance technology and technique (Adler, 1985; Flynn, 1997). Smugglers now use sophisticated boats and aircraft with state-of-the-art radar and other detection devices. Small, but powerful jet planes are used to quickly fly in and out of small secluded airstrips. Smuggling operations also use commercial vessels to stow away drugs, and provide false labels and documentation. **Mules,** individuals hired especially to take the risk by smuggling drugs on their person, are also used to import illegal drugs. Frequently, these individuals swallow cocaine and heroin in balloons or condoms, or place them in rectal or vaginal cavities to carry across the border and/or through customs.

WHOLESALE DISTRIBUTION

Upon successful entry into the United States, drugs such as heroin and cocaine are typically sold to major wholesalers who may supply an entire region of the country. Most synthetic drugs, such as methamphetamines, MDMA, and LSD are manufactured in the United States and begin their distribution journey at this point. Flynn describes the wholesale organization of the Cali Cartel in New York:

> If a load of cocaine arrives at Kennedy International Airport or at the Port of Newark, one of the 10 to 12 Cali distribution cells in New York receives it. Each cell, made up of 15–20 Colombian employees who earn monthly salaries ranging from $2,000 to $7,500, conducts an average of $25 million of business a month. Each cell is self-contained, with information tightly compartmentalized. Only a handful of managers know all the operatives. The cell has a head, bookkeeper, money handler, cocaine handler, motor pool, and 10 to 15 apartments serving as stash houses (Flynn, 1997, p. 153).

This reflects a very tightly controlled distribution system, and most wholesale drug distribution networks are not this highly centralized or controlled. Adler's (1985) ethnography, for example, describes dealing networks that are much more loose-knit and autonomous than that described by Flynn.

Normally, the heroin or cocaine that a wholesaler receives from an importer is very potent. The wholesaler will usually "step on" or dilute the drugs by adding an adulterant and thereby increasing the volume and hence the profit. Each time these drugs are "stepped on," their volume is typically doubled and their potency thereby diminished by about 50 percent. Moreover, the wholesaler will probably also increase the price per diluted kilogram, which enhances the profitability even more. Figure 9.3 suggests nearly a 1,700 percent added value for cocaine and about a 3,000 percent added value for heroin at this level of distribution.

RETAIL DISTRIBUTION

This level of distribution is very loosely organized. Those at the upper end of retail distribution, sometimes known as *dealers in quantity*, are entrepreneurs

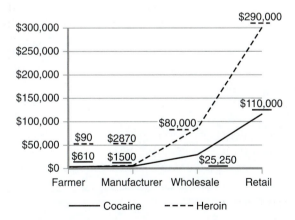

Figure 9.3 Price per Kilogram of Heroin and Cocaine From Farmer to Retail Market

Source: Adapted from United Nations, *World Drug Report*, Table 1, Chapter 4, p. 126, 1997.

who sell for monetary profit. With heroin, these dealers typically deal in *bundles*, a quantity roughly equal to 25 street bags of heroin. Dealers with reputations for good heroin will often sell in concentrations that allow for still another "cut" or dilution, thereby providing the lower level retailer an opportunity for still greater profits. The lower level retailer is often a user as well, thereby earning the name of *juggler*. The modus operandi of the juggler is to buy a quantity of the drug, sell a small amount at a highly inflated price, enough to pay for his own habit and usually a little more for spending money.

Retailing is the most risky enterprise in the entire underground drug economy. The retail distributor is typically selling to users or dealer/users who are very financially unpredictable. Many times a customer will "come up short," without sufficient funds to purchase the quantity of drugs they want. The retail dealer may, of course, refuse to sell to them, but if a user is experiencing a withdrawal, most dealers are not so cold as to send them away sick. So they sell them the drugs with the understanding that they will pay them back at first opportunity. Dealers often never see these individuals again and are cheated out of their money. This often results in violent encounters between dealers and their patrons. The risk does not stop here, however. Drug users and jugglers are often pressured by police for information on their higher-level connections. This is called "flipping an informant." Police on patrol in neighborhoods are quite aware of who the users and street-level dealers are, so that when a decision is made to crack down on drugs in an area, it is very easy for police to gather information on local users and dealers to threaten them with arrest if they do not cooperate. This puts both the

Retail "Street Level" drug distribution is most subject to risk of arrest. Teen-agers are often employed because they are more likely to avoid adjudication as an adult if they are arrested.

lower-level street juggler at risk, but also his or her connection. There is no one in the distribution system of illegal drugs that is more vulnerable to arrest than those at the bottom of the hierarchy. For that reason, teens and preteens are often used, because they will avoid adjudication as an adult if arrested.

This reality reflects a similar pattern in the legitimate social stratification system, of course. Those at the bottom of the hierarchy generally are more prone to health and accident risks in their jobs and least secure in the longevity of their positions. Indeed, the economics of illicit drug distribution reflects in many ways the legitimate economy, and is rooted deeply in it. Robert McBride states,

> . . . heroin use is the end result of certain characteristics of U.S. capitalism that generate both the market for the drug, and the system that supplies it. The demand for heroin is rooted in the class, race, and national conflicts of U.S. society. In turn, the heroin is marketed by an expanding distribution industry which is shaped by the underlying drive of capitalist enterprise to seize market opportunities in the quest for profit (McBride, 1983, p. 147)

The underground economy of illicit drug distribution is especially reflective of our capitalist culture at the retail distribution level. Certain dealers, for example, have developed a reputation for having "righteous dope." They attempt to capitalize on this reputation by developing special "trade names" that will be recognizable to potential customers. Paul Goldstein and his colleagues (1984) examined the street marketing of heroin in New York City. They found that these drugs were being distinctively packaged and labeled as a marketing technique. Dealers sometimes stamp a symbol onto the bag, use specially colored tape to make their drugs stand out, or sometimes simply stamp a number on the bag. Brand names are also used, some of them very colorful. Goldstein and his colleagues were able to identify over 400 "brands" of heroin (see Chapter 5). The proliferation of these "brands" is reflective of broader capitalist economic sectors at early stages in their development, not unlike the relatively unregulated proliferation of internet services and marketing techniques in the early phase of internet development and expansion. As industries develop, control of the industries tends to be concentrated in the hands of a few major corporations—something which may be happening at the top of the illicit drug importation and distribution hierarchy today.

DRUGS IN THE WORKPLACE

We have examined alcohol and drug use patterns in four occupational contexts (Chapter 7). We also examined the economic costs of alcohol and drug abuse, much of which is borne by employers in the form of higher rates of absenteeism and generally lower productivity. Our focus in this section is the work setting itself. This section is divided into three broad subsections: *the nature and prevalence of drug and alcohol use in the work place; working conditions and other factors related to workplace drug and alcohol use;* and *responses to drug use in the workplace.*

The Nature and Prevalence of Drug Use in the Workplace

Most of the information that we have on drug use by employees in the workplace comes from the National Household Survey, which we discussed in Chapter 6. This survey includes questions on level of employment (full-time, part-time or unemployed) as well as occupational sectors in which workers are employed. Additionally, there are limited data available from drug-testing procedures and Employee Assistance Programs (EAPs), though these data are not very systematic.

The typical perception that people have of the alcohol abuser, and especially of those who use illicit drugs, is that of the street user—unemployed, often homeless and without purpose or direction. This picture is greatly distorted. The National Household Survey data reveal that in 1997, more than 70 percent of those who currently used illicit drugs (about 6.3 million people) were employed full time, and another 16.6 percent (1.5 million people) were employed part time. In fact, only 13 percent of current illicit drug users (1.17 million people) were not legitimately employed. Similarly, only 10.2 percent of the heavy alcohol users were unemployed (827,000 people), while more than 77 percent (6.25 million people) report being employed full time (Zhang, Huang, and Brittingham, 1999).[3] Despite the fact that most of the drug and alcohol users in this country are in our workforce, most of the workforce do not use illicit drugs; nor do they heavily consume alcohol. Indeed, current usage levels among full and part-time workers aged 18–49 seems to be decreasing over time for both illicit drugs and heavy alcohol (see Figure 9.4).

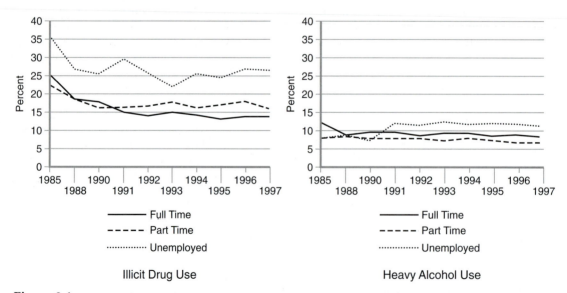

Figure 9.4 **Percent of Labor Force Aged 18–49 Currently Involved in Illicit Drug Use and Heavy Alcohol Use.**

Source: Zhiwei Zhang, Lynn X. Huang and Angela M. Brittingham, *Worker Drug Use and Workplace Policies and Programs: Results from the 1994 and 1997 National Household Survey on Drug Abuse, 1999.*

D R U G S   A N D   E V E R Y D A Y   L I F E

Letters from Nurse Addicts

I was just released from jail today. I have been diverting narcotics from the small hospital that I have worked at for the last 13 yrs. I have been taking narcs for about 2 years now and they finally caught me. It has gotten so bad that I was taking Demerol and injecting up to 300 mgs at a time. I never diverted from my patients or took any narcs while at work. I was deeply respected by all of the people I worked with as well as administration and the doctors I worked very closely with no one, even my family, or my co-workers ever suspected me. I guess I hid my addiction well. Being from a small town where everyone knows and respects me is the hardest thing to deal with. I even made front page news!! My family is very supportive of me. I have a good lawyer, I'm just starting my legal process. I need intense help!! I don't think I will ever be a nurse again. I think part of my problem is that I am extremely burnt out! I am willing to face whatever I need to. I can't live like this anymore. Please . . . what should I do next?
Becky

Hi Becky.
Me too, me too. I'm a nurse anesthetist, and for about two years I was diverting fentanyl. I did take it from my patients, I did take drugs at work, and I was fired from two jobs. I was well liked and well respected at both, until my addiction became so obvious as I spiraled down that my popularity took a big hit, to put it mildly. I thought my secret was a secret, but I think most people knew. I was extremely fortunate not to go to jail, as nobody pressed charges against me, but I was turned in to the board of nursing. I've been in the. . . . peer assistance program for a year and a half now. I had to go through intensive outpatient treatment. I couldn't give controlled meds for the first six months at work, when I finally did go back. It was hard to find a job, but I finally did. I had to work in nursing for the first six months, instead of anesthesia, and then it took me another six months to find a job in anesthesia. Becky, I'm back at my job now, I can do it without taking the drugs, and I will graduate from the peer assistance program and have no restrictions at the end of July, God willing. I remember the shame and humiliation of having everyone know, but now I look back on my addiction as a spiritual wake-up call. I don't think anything less would have got my attention. And I am so grateful that I didn't die! I overdosed so many times, just being alive is a miracle. Here's the thing, my friend, - IT WILL GET BETTER! It will all get a lot better, and all this will be behind you. Many of us here have been in your exact shoes, and we made it through. You will too. Just try to do the next thing in front of you, and know that there is a lot of help available to you. You will have to go through some kind of treatment program, the sooner the better. Your health insurance will probably cover at least some of it. You will have to deal with the board of nursing, might as well do it as soon as possible. Don't rule out nursing in the future, you might want your license, do what you can to preserve it. There are lots of jobs in nursing that do not involve access to controlled drugs.
God bless you. Carol ∎

Letters posted to a discussion group
http://www.voy.com/

It should not be surprising that most of the illicit drug use among workers is marijuana. More than 63 percent of the full-time workers reporting current drug use were using marijuana only; another 14 percent were using marijuana as well as other drugs such as stimulants (including cocaine), tranquilizers, hallucinogens, and heroin. Only about 23 percent of current drug users were *not* using marijuana (Zhang, Huang, and Brittingham, 1999).

RELATIONSHIP BETWEEN WORK CONDITIONS AND DRUG AND ALCOHOL USE

There are some interesting patterns that emerge with regard to the nature of the workplace and its relation to drug and alcohol use. Figure 9.5 reveals an inverse relationship between the size of the workplace and the likelihood of employees using drugs. Whereas 8.6 percent of the employees in small workplaces (with 1–24 employees) reported that they currently used drugs, only 7.6 percent of those in medium-sized workplaces (25–499 employees) and 5.8 percent in large workplaces (500 or more employees) reported illicit drug use in the past 30 days. That pattern is not quite so clear for heavy alcohol use. Only 7 percent of those in small businesses report heavy use; 8.3 percent of those employed in medium-sized settings report heavy alcohol consumption within the last 30 days, and in very large settings, only 7.4 percent reported heavy use (Zhang, Huang, and Brittingham, 1999).

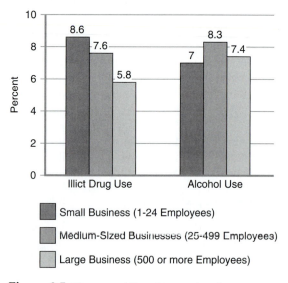

Figure 9.5 Percent of Employees Aged 18–49 Currently Using by Size of Workplace

Source: Zhiwei Zhang, Lynn X. Huang and Angela M. Brittingham, *Worker Drug Use and Workplace Policies and Programs: Results from the 1994 and 1997 National Household Survey on Drug Abuse, 1999.*

The likelihood of drug and alcohol use also seems to vary by the type of occupation. Chapter 7 discussed four occupational areas and the dynamics that seem to be involved in substance abuse in these work settings. In addition to these four areas, drug and alcohol use seem to be particularly high among those in the food preparation industry, including waiters, waitresses, and bartenders. Data from 1997 reveal that among these workers, 18.7 percent reported drug use within the last 30 days and 15 percent reported using alcohol heavily (Zhang, Huang, and Brittingham, 1999). Construction workers also have higher than average rates of drug and heavy alcohol consumption. Generally, blue-collar workers tend to have higher rates of drug use than do white collar workers (Gleason, Veum, and Pergamit, 1991).

Research has focused on the relationship between a number of psychological factors potentially related to substance use and abuse in the workplace, such as job satisfaction (Seeman and Anderson, 1983; Seeman, Seeman, and Budros, 1988), job stress (Cooper, Russell, and Frone, 1990; Martin and Roman, 1996b; Pearlin and Radabaugh, 1976; Roman, 1978), and a sense of powerlessness in relation to work (Martin and Roman, 1996a). A second line of inquiry, based on the social learning perspective, suggests that alcohol and drug use may be influenced by co-workers, especially where there may be attitudes that are tolerant of or even encourage use may exist (Ames and James, 1990; Cahalan, 1970; Martin and Roman, 1996a). The results of most of these studies have been either mixed or inconclusive.

Due in part to the disparate findings of many of the studies that have examined the role of the workplace on alcohol and/or drug use, it has been suggested that drug and alcohol use are much more a function of the *workforce*. That is, characteristics of the employee—as opposed to the workplace—are better predictors of substance use and abuse. Using data from the National Longitudinal Survey of Youth, Mensch and Kandel (1988) examined both job characteristics (such as supervisor support and physical demands of the job) and workforce characteristics (such as marital status, education, race, etc.) for their effect on alcohol, tobacco, marijuana, and cocaine use. They found that job characteristics had very little explanatory power among the subjects in their sample. Certain of the individual characteristics did significantly predict drug use, however. Mensch and Kandel characterize the significant variables as those which suggest ". . . a lack of conformity or attachment to social institutions" (p. 181). These individual characteristics included having dropped out of school, having participated in delinquent activity, and being unmarried. Three other studies by Gleason, Veum, and Pergamit (1991), Hollinger (1988) and Steffy and Laker (1991) also found that demographic variables such as age, sex, and race more strongly predicted substance abuse among workers than did workplace characteristics. Consistent with findings of alcohol and drug use in general, younger workers, men, and whites are the categories most likely to be involved in drug and alcohol use.

RESPONSE TO SUBSTANCE USE IN THE WORKPLACE

Historically, the response of most workplaces to drug and alcohol use by workers has been to ignore it as a problem. Until the 1970s, substance use and abuse has been seen as a problem of individuals, with little recognition or concern about company responsibility or response to drug problems in the workplace, except to terminate the employment of individuals who posed problems because of substance abuse. Scanlon (1991) points out that early responses were largely to alcohol use, and that prohibitionist organizations were strong influences in motivating industry to respond harshly to alcohol use. While there were some therapeutic programs in place even in the 1940s, such as the Occupational Alcoholism Program (OAP), industry response was largely punitive in the sense of terminating employees who abused drugs and alcohol. The last 30 years has witnessed increased attention to this issue by both small and large businesses because of the adverse economic impact of drug and alcohol-impaired individuals. This recent response represents both an extension of older punitive approaches and emerging therapeutic understandings of drug and alcohol abuse. Specifically, workplaces are adopting one or both of two responses to drug use among their employees: *drug testing* and *employee assistance programs*. Both drug testing and employee assistance programs are related to an important piece of legislation known as the *Drug-Free Workplace Act of 1988*. We begin with a brief discussion of that legislation.

Drug-Free Workplace Act of 1988

In 1986, Congress passed the Omnibus Drug Act (ODA), which authorized $1.7 million for drug enforcement and education efforts. This Act was enacted and signed into law in response to the growing concern with drug use in the United States. Other laws would follow, and in 1988, President Reagan signed into law an addition to the ODA called the Anti-Drug Abuse Act of 1988. Part of this Act, known as the **Drug-Free Workplace Act of 1988 (DWFA),** applied to drug use in the workplace. This Act requires both federal contractors and grantees (such as universities receiving federal funds) to certify that they will provide a drug-free work place. Private employers are not affected by the requirements of the DWFA, though many private employers subscribe to its principles.

A drug-free workplace is defined under these regulations as one in which employees are prohibited from manufacturing, distributing, dispensing, possessing, or using controlled substances (Scanlon, 1991). Compliance with the Act requires that employers:

- Certify that they will maintain a drug-free workplace.
- Inform employees of the prohibition of drug-related activities at the workplace.
- Establish a drug-free awareness program, informing employees of the dangers of drug use at the workplace, and of sanctions that might be applied against them.

- Communicate to employees that they must inform the employer of any criminal conviction for a violation of a drug statute involving an incident at work.
- Report such convictions to the federal contracting or granting agency.
- Take appropriate personnel action against the employee, or require the employee to participate satisfactorily in a drug rehabilitation program.
- Make a good faith effort to provide a drug-free workplace by implementing the above activities (Legal Action Center, 1989; as quoted in Scanlon, 1991).

These provisions of the DFWA do not require the establishment of either drug testing or employee assistance programs. Clearly, however, these provisions provide an important legal incentive for both drug testing and employee assistance programs among federally subsidized workplaces. Moreover, the legislation has raised awareness of the importance and value of the drug-free workplace generally. Companies have come to be aware of the tremendous costs associated with addicted and intoxicated workers. While it is difficult to assess how much the DFWA has directly affected awareness of the need for detection and prevention/treatment programs in the private sector, or simply confirmed an awareness already there, it was almost certainly a catalyst for these programs, as they have sprung up like dandelions since the passage of this legislation.

Currently, the federal government's comprehensive drug-free workplace program is in place in more than 120 agencies, and covers in excess of 1.8 million workers. It has been quite successful, according to those in the government who are monitoring the program. In 1997, just 0.5 percent of the more than 80,000 federal workers tested, had positive drug test results for illegal drugs. This compared with positive test rates in the private sector of approximately 5 percent of the 4 million tests done the same year. (SAMHSA, 1999). According to the Drug Test Index, reported semi-annually, the national rate of positive drug tests in the private sector has declined considerably over the years, from a high of 13.6 percent in 1988 to a low of 4.7 percent for the first half of 2000 (SAMHSA, 2001).

Drug Testing

Drug testing in workplaces is almost totally limited to testing for *illicit,* substances such as marijuana, cocaine, etc, though alcohol testing may be included as well. These tests are conducted either as *pre-employment screening* of potential employees prior to hire; or *postemployment* periodic testing of employees. Postemployment tests may either be given *with cause,* such as following an industrial accident, or *randomly* as a deterrence mechanism.

Drug testing has increased quite dramatically over the past 20 years. Hartwell, Steele, French and Rodman (1996) have noted that participation in drug-testing programs increased from 18 percent of Fortune 500 companies in 1985 to 40 percent in 1991, representing more than a 100 percent increase in six years. Other studies report even higher levels of participation (Harris and Heft, 1992). There are certain patterns that can be observed in what types of companies are more likely to utilize drug testing. First, testing programs are much more common among larger companies. Hayghe (1991) found that in 1990 only 2.6 percent of companies with 1 to 49 employees had drug-testing programs in place, while 45.9 percent of companies with 250 employees or more had such programs. Implementation of drug testing programs also tends to vary by type of industry. Those industries involved in manufacturing, mining, communications, public utilities and transportation report the highest rates of participation. Retail trade and service industries, such as banks, and insurance companies are least likely to implement such programs (Hartwell, Steele, French, and Rodman, 1996). Drug testing as a preventive response to drug use is discussed in some detail in Chapter 13.

Employee Assistance Programs

Employee Assistance Programs (EAPs) are, essentially, confidential, employer-financed programs to assist employees who are afflicted with any of a variety of psychological problems, including drug and alcohol abuse. Not only are the workers *afflicted,* but the workplaces are substantially *affected* by drug and alcohol abuse. As we have noted elsewhere, drug abuse is a social problem with enormous consequences, and one arena where the consequences are felt acutely is in the American workplace, where drug abusers in the workforce have greater absenteeism and tardiness, have more erratic work histories, use several times more sick benefits than normal, have greater injuries on the job (and file a higher percentage of worker's compensation claims), and experience reduced productivity (SAMHSA, 1991; 1999a).

Clearly, there are a number of potentially devastating economic ramifications of drug abuse, consequences that give workplaces a powerful incentive to help valued employees overcome their drug and alcohol abuse. The move away from punitive responses to employee drug and alcohol dependence and toward treating the issue constructively as a health concern, which is what Employee Assistance Programs do, emerged in the 1970s and spread rapidly during the 1980s. By 1990, there were more than 20,000 EAP's in place in companies of various types throughout the country (Scanlon, 1991). Most EAP's are located in the company's human resources or personnel departments. Others may be located in the medical department or even the executive offices (Backer, 1989). Like drug-testing programs, EAP's are much more prevalent in larger organizations. Fifty-two percent of workplaces with greater than 750 workers have them, compared with 15 percent of workplaces with 50–99 employees. Overall, just under one-third of all American employees work for a company with an EAP (SAMHSA, 1999a).

There is an increasing accumulation of evidence that EAP's are effective, both in terms of individual outcome measures (reduction in levels of drug and alcohol abuse, decreased absences, etc.), and in terms of cost-benefit analysis to the employer. Blum and Roman (1995), in an overview of studies conducted since the 1970s, conclude that problems related to employee drug and alcohol abuse are reduced considerably in companies with EAP programs. Moreover, the overall savings to these employers is substantial, with savings-to-investment ratios ranging from 1.5:1 to 15:1. Federal government assessments report that EAP's have assisted in positive drug tests being cut by 50 percent or so in the last decade, though they also credit drug-testing programs (SAMHSA, 2001).

SUMMARY

We have, in this chapter, attempted simply to sketch some of the broad economic dimensions of illicit drugs. At the macroeconomic level, the cultivation, production, and distribution of illicit drugs has profound effects on the broader economies of those countries involved. The cultivation of drugs such as cocaine, heroin, and marijuana preempts the growing of other agricultural products because they take up both land and labor resources that could be used in other agricultural pursuits. We have also seen that the high levels of money coming into certain drug-producing countries, while making a few people very wealthy, has produced higher than normal levels of inflation that negatively affect citizens of those countries.

Drugs have an economic impact not only on producing nations, but also on consuming nations. Drug and alcohol consumption have had an impact on the American economy by way of higher levels of absenteeism and lowered levels of productivity. There is some contradictory evidence regarding the impact of drug and alcohol consumption on family economics, in terms of labor force participation and wage earnings, but the evidence does seems to suggest that families are also negatively affected economically in these ways. Certainly, families are affected economically in that money that could otherwise go to buying food, clothing, and other necessities is instead being spent on drugs, alcohol, and tobacco. Our interpretation of the wage and labor force data further suggests that users of drugs and alcohol leave school and enter the labor force earlier, and remain in the labor force when nonusers are able to retire.

The underground, illicit drug industry further reflects, in many ways, the broader economic dynamics of the host society—particularly in relation to capitalism. There is an importation and distribution hierarchy that resembles the distribution of other goods and services. At the retail level, the drug trade tends to resemble newly developing entrepreneurial areas. Competition—along with risk—is great, but so is the potential for profit. Higher-level distribution patterns, by contrast, more closely resemble more mature capitalistic sectors. There is more control exerted by a relatively small number of actors, resulting in fewer risks. And because of the greater level of monopolistic control, profits are guaranteed. There are certainly ways in which the economy of illicit drugs is different from the larger economy. The very fact that these drugs are illegal introduces an element not present in the legitimate economy. Drug dealers at all levels must take into consideration the risks and costs associated with running an illegitimate enterprise. There is the risk of arrest and incarceration; the risk that comes with dealing with individuals who work in the marginal sectors of society, such as greater levels of unpredictability; and the risk of violence, as these illicit entrepreneurs do not have access to courts to enforce agreements and contracts. Despite these differences, however, the similarities are instructive. Understanding the illicit drug economy as a reflection of the larger economy helps to demystify what takes place in the world of drug importers, distributors, and street dealers.

Finally, drug use profoundly affects the workplace in ways that go beyond productivity and wages. Research on drug use in the workplace has revealed several factors that seem to be related to drug use, including size of the workplace, type of occupation, and factors such as job stress, worker morale, and alienation or powerlessness experienced by workers. Some have suggested, on the other hand, that it is the quality of the *workforce* not the *workplace* that determines the likelihood of drug use—factors such as age, marital status, education, and race. Regardless of the reasons for drug use in the workplace, employers have responded to this situation, attempting to curtail employee drug use. They have done this through adopting drug-free workplace principles, drug testing, and through employee assistance programs. While the effectiveness of these programs has been debated, evidence does seem to suggest at least marginal, if not substantial effectiveness of these initiatives.

KEY TERMS

cartel
Drug-Free Workplace Act
 of 1988 (DWFA)

employee assistance
 program (EAP)
mules

Operation Intercept

REVIEW QUESTIONS

1. Obtain a flat map of the world. Using different colors, trace the route of cocaine and heroin into the United States. Identify those locations which represent various steps in the manufacturing process.

2. What was "Operation Intercept," and what did it teach us about international control of drugs?

3. What are the major domestic costs of drug use in the United States? Why is it valuable to distinguish between "private costs" and "societal costs" when talking about domestic costs?

4. Briefly describe each stage of the production and distribution of illicit drugs, focusing especially on heroin, cocaine, and marijuana. What are some of the problems and/or challenges at each stage?

5. Do you think that drug and alcohol use in the workplace is more a result of characteristics of the *workplace* or of the *workforce*? Explain your answer by (1) identifying what is meant by each of the above; and (2) providing comparative evidence supporting your position.

6. What effect do you think the *Drug-Free Workplace Act of 1988* will have on drug use in the workplace? Provide a rationale for your answer.

7. Two responses that employers have had to drug use in the work place is *drug testing* and *employee assistance programs*. What is the difference between these two approaches in terms of (1) their philosophy; and (2) their goals? Do you think these two approaches are incompatible? Why or why not?

CRITICAL THINKING QUESTIONS

1. The international drug trade provides a lucrative source of income for many farmers in developing countries. International drug-control efforts seriously threaten that income. Carefully consider the costs and benefits of such international drug-control efforts. On the basis of this analysis, what is your position on the advisability of international drug-control efforts? What sort of policy might you suggest?

2. Assume that you are the CEO of a mid-sized business, employing about 150 people. It has come to your attention that some of your employees might have drug and/or alcohol problems. You have noticed that your absenteeism rates seem to be a little higher than normal, which would be consistent with these reports. How would you respond to these reports? Answer this question by identifying the specific steps that you would take, and explain *why* you would take each of these steps.

NOTES

1. The reason that crime and victimization is not considered a cost from a macrosocietal view is that the money or value of goods remains in circulation within the society (unless taken out of the country, of course). Hence, while there is certainly a cost to the individual victim, society at large still has the money/goods in circulation. Indeed, Preble and Casey (1969) have suggested that crimes by drug addicts serves as something of an underground welfare system, as stolen goods are made available to low income people for prices that they can afford.

2. The calculation of forgone wages, and productivity costs due to premature mortality uses a rather complex set of assumptions and procedures known as the "human capital approach." If you are interested in learning more about how productivity loss is calculated, you might consult one or more of the following sources: Harwood, Fountain, and Livermore, 1998; Heien and Pittman, 1989; Hodgson and Meiners, 1982.

3. It must be remembered, of course, that the National Household Survey will miss most homeless and all institutionalized populations. This figure, therefore, underestimates the percentage of unemployed drug users. Nevertheless, it is also clear that illicit drug users are heavily represented in the nation's workforce.

DRUGS AND CRIME

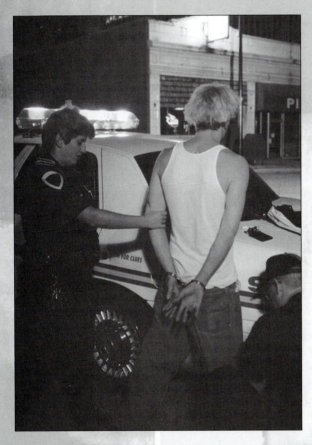

Perhaps the greatest fear that many people have of illegal drugs is the association that these substances have with other forms of criminal behavior. These fears are continually reinforced in the media where addicts are depicted as being hopelessly enslaved to expensive and violence-causing drugs. In the minds of many Americans, crime is almost an inevitable consequence of drug use, and to be a drug addict is tantamount to being a criminal. The following quote from a San Francisco journalist captures the fear that many people

have of the causal relationship between drug use
and crime:

> He's after that money; he needs it to buy heroin. And
> he'll take it from you if you are his nearest and dearest
> friend, even if he has to kill you to do it (quoted in Silver
> and Aldrich, 1979:42).

More recently, allegations of the causal relationship between
illegal drug use and crime have reached almost a feverish
pitch as the media, lawmakers, educators, clergy, criminal
justice personnel, treatment specialists, and others widely
concur that drug use and related criminal behavior rank as
one of the leading problems in the country today. Democrats
and Republicans have both sought to maintain a high moral
ground on this issue throughout the 1980s, 1990s and into
the new millennium. On the seriousness of drugs and crime
in the United States, Al Gore and George W. Bush found
themselves strangely in agreement, even though they stood
miles apart on most ideological and political issues. There is
hardly a day or week that passes that one or more major
newspapers or magazines do not offer commentary suggesting or at least implying that drugs are the cause of
much crime in American society today. Former Senator
Alfonse D'Amato of New York has referred to drug addicts
as "walking crime machines," proposing the death penalty
for drug kingpins (United States Senate, 1984).

This chapter examines the substance behind the allegations regarding the role of drug use in criminal behavior. We
begin with an historical overview of how the relationship between drugs and crime was viewed, and how these views
contributed to the drug policies that are in place today. This
discussion is followed by a section that describes three
broad theoretical connections between drug use and crime:
drugs cause crime, crime causes drug use, and *"common
cause" or subcultural explanations*. Finally, the chapter concludes with an examination of the empirical evidence regarding the relationship between drug use and crime.

HISTORICALLY UNDERSTANDING DRUG
USE AND CRIME

The concern over drugs and crime is not unique to this
generation, nor, for that matter, to the twentieth century. During the early seventeenth century in England,

King James I was especially anxious to rid his country of tobacco. His strategy, not unlike what would be used centuries later, was to identify tobacco with evil foreigners who represented a threat to a civilized way of life. While not specifically suggesting that tobacco use causes crime, the implications are clear. According to the King, tobacco smoking belongs to:

> that sort of costumes, which having their original from base corruption and barbarity, doe in like sort, make their first entry into a Countrey, by an inconsiderate and childish affectation of Noveltie. . . . For Tobacco . . . was first found out by some of the barbarous Indians, to be a Preservative, or Antidot against the Pockes, a filthy disease, whereunto these barbarous people are (as all men know) very much subject, . . . so that as from them was first brought into Christendome, that most detestable disease, so from them likewise was brought this use of Tobacco, as a stinking and unsavourie Antidot, for so corrupted and execrable a Maladie, the stinking Suf-fumigation whereof they yet use against that disease, making so one canker or venime to eat out another. . . . Shall we . . . that have bene so long civill and wealthy in Peace, famous and invincible in Warre, fortunate in both, . . . shall we, I say, without blushing, abase ourselves so farre, as to imitate these beastly Indians?. . . . Why doe we not as well imitate them in walking naked as they doe?. . . . yea, why do we not denie God and adore the Devill as they doe? (Quoted in Corti, 1931:77).

Marijuana was another drug that was associated with antisocial behavior from time to time. There is the legend of an eleventh century Persian religious cult known as the "Assassins" who committed murder for political reasons. Marco Polo is credited with first spreading the legend of this group who used marijuana and, as the legend developed over history, committed murder and barbarous crimes after using the drug. The tales of this cult were later popularized in Alexander Dumas' nineteenth century work, *The Count of Monte Crisco*. In 1931, Dr. A.E. Fossier wrote of this group, "this diabolical, fanatical, cruel and murderous tribe . . . under the influence of hashish . . . would madly rush at their enemies and ruthlessly massacre everyone within their grasp" (Fossier, 1931:247; cited in Grinspoon, 1971). In retrospect, Grinspoon (1971) points out that these tales were greatly exaggerated and the causal link between the drug and murders committed was not suggested until much later.

Alcohol has also been regarded as an evil menace causing a variety of types of crime and other social ills. The temperance movements of the nineteenth and early twentieth centuries played on and often exaggerated these tragedies. These reform efforts sought to vilify alcohol, producing books and tracts which depicted it as a curse on civilized society. One such publication, *The Curse of Drink: Or Stories of Hell's Commerce*, edited by nineteenth-century prohibitionist Elton Shaw in 1909, is filled with tales of murder, debauchery, abuse, and neglect brought on by the use of alcohol.

These early concerns over the potential criminal character and effect of using drugs notwithstanding, the concern over drugs and crime as we know it today is uniquely a twentieth and twenty-first century phenomenon. Never before has crime been so intricately related to drug use in the minds of policy makers, practitioners, and the general public as it has in the last 70 or so years. One of the earliest twentieth-century moral crusaders to fight drug use on this basis was a celebrated Navy captain, Richard Pearson Hobson who, as we have seen in Chapter 2, led military-like crusades against alcohol and later narcotics use. Hobson's voice was not as one crying in the wilderness. He touched a sensitive nerve in the consciousness of a morally receptive twentieth-century American society. Shortly after his moral crusading against narcotics, the Bureau of Narcotics was formed within the Department of Treasury in 1930, under the leadership of Harry B. Anslinger. Anslinger launched a major antimarijuana campaign in the 1930s that depicted marijuana as "the Devil's Weed" and the "assassin of youth," causing violent and irrational behavior. Perhaps no other antidrug campaign prior to that time or since has played so loose with the facts in its attempts to create a moral climate of intolerance toward marijuana. The Bureau of Narcotics leaked several stories of alleged criminal incidences involving marijuana. The following story cited by Anslinger and Tompkins (1953:23–24) and later by Grinspoon (1971:21–22) is an example of the type of information that was being released by the Bureau:

> Del Rio, Texas. 1940. One Eleutero G. while allegedly under the influence of marijuana, shot to death two women and then committed suicide by literally slicing himself to bits about the abdomen, heart, and throat, in a manner which indicated that he was bereft of all reasoning. . . . It was the opinion of the doctor who saw G. just before he died that no one could so mutilate himself unless he was unable to feel "shock" and the only thing he knew that would produce such a condition, to such a degree, is marijuana.

Perhaps most remembered in the drug education campaign of the 1930s was the movie *Reefer Madness,* which was produced as a documentary for purposes of warning parents of the evils of marijuana. The story is of a young man, Billy, raised in an upstanding family in the community, and doing well in school until he is introduced to the killer drug, **marijuana.** His performance in school declines precipitously, and he becomes unfaithful to his girlfriend. While high on marijuana Billy is seduced by another marijuana user. During their love-making interlude, he hears his girlfriend's voice. He dashes out only to find her being seduced by another older marijuana user in the room. A fight ensues, a gun goes off and accidentally kills his girlfriend. Billy, who has himself been knocked unconscious, wakes up to find a gun in his hand and (he thinks) responsible for his girlfriend's murder. In point of fact, he has been framed and is later exonerated. The moral that the movie is attempting to convey, however, is that marijuana is a killer drug that leads inevitably to a life of crime and debauchery.

By the 1940s there was a growing literature that depicted marijuana and other illegal drug users as morally degenerate, sexually violent, and criminally aggressive (Inciardi, 1981). These stereotypes, which one social scientist writing at that time referred to as the "dope fiend mythology" (Lindesmith, 1940), became so firmly entrenched by this time that they went virtually unquestioned by academicians and policy makers for the next three decades and beyond, in spite of a growing amount of evidence to the contrary (White and Gorman, 2000).

By the late 1960s, however, marijuana was no longer depicted in terms of "reefer madness." Indeed, rather than exciting the baser passions as was believed earlier, it was now understood to cause lethargy and laziness, a phenomenon commonly referred to as the "amotivational syndrome." The drug that was targeted for its role in causing crime was once again heroin. The person most responsible for launching this new "war on drugs" in the 1960s was the governor of New York, Nelson Rockefeller. Rockefeller had been elected governor in 1958, but soon set his sights for the presidency. He lost his bid for the Republican nomination in 1964 to Barry Goldwater. Concerned with his image of being too "liberal" a Republican, Rockefeller recognized the need to court the more conservative wing of the Republican party, while at the same time not alienate the party's moderate-to-liberal constituency. He quickly seized upon the issue of drugs and crime, capitalizing on public opinion polls, which were showing a growing concern of the American people toward drug use and crime (Epstein, 1977). Rockefeller worked diligently to establish a connection between drug use and crime in the mind of the American public, and to do so, he used some of the same strategies and vivid imagery of Richard Hobson years earlier. Rather than to argue a physiological basis for this connection as Hobson had done, however, Rockefeller suggested that as the user became physiologically dependent on drugs, he or she would be inevitably compelled to steal and commit other crimes to pay for this habit. Rockefeller cultivated what Epstein (1977:268) has described as a "vocabulary of fear" to launch "an all-out war on drugs and addiction." Capitalizing on growing public sentiment, Rockefeller rushed a law through the legislature providing for the involuntary confinement of drug addicts for up to five years for treatment, regardless of whether they were guilty of any crime. In this, which has been described as "the nation's toughest drug law" (Joint Committee on New York Drug Law Evaluation, 1978) Rockefeller succeeded not only in appealing to both conservative and liberal elements in the Republican party, but also firmly re-established the link between drug use and crime at the policy level.

Rockefeller's "war on drugs" took on national proportions under the Nixon administration. Edward Jay Epstein's (1977) book *Agency of Fear* chronicles the extended effort of the Nixon administration to wage this war on several fronts. During the 1970s the federal government undertook several initiatives to stop the flow of drugs into this country as well as to stop the distribution of drugs within our borders as part of an unprecedented "war on crime." So fully institutionalized was the presumption that drug use caused criminal behavior that these policies were being implemented in the absence of a strong body of empirical evidence for such a causal relationship. Indeed, when one study that was commissioned by the National Institute on Drug Abuse (Research Triangle Institute, 1976) failed to find conclusive evidence that drug use caused crime, the National Institute on Drug Abuse (NIDA) refused to publish it (Clayton, 1981).

The concern over drugs and crime has reached such a feverish pitch in the last decade that billions of dollars are being expended each year to fight this perceived menace. Correspondingly, there has been a monumental amount of research conducted by many social scientists around the country attempting to more fully understand the nature of the relationship between drug use and criminal behavior. While there are some common areas of agreement, these studies have also produced many contradictory findings. The remainder of this chapter examines what we know and don't know about the relationship between drug use and crime. We do this by, first, re-viewing the theoretical and conceptual linkages between drug use and crime. We then review several empirical studies that examine this rela-tionship. As we shall see, the relationship between drug use and crime is much more complex than the common-sense assumption that "drug use causes crime."

THEORETICALLY UNDERSTANDING DRUG USE AND CRIME

It is generally accepted that drug users commit far more than their fair share of crime if by "drug users" we mean regular users of expensive drugs such as heroin and cocaine. We must qualify this statement in two ways, however. First, not *all* drug users commit more than their fair share of crime. Many users of illegal drugs are otherwise law-abiding citizens. They use drugs on an occasional basis and do not let their drug use get out of control. These week-end "chippers" are what Norman Zinberg (1984) calls "controlled users." Second, even among those drug users who are involved in other types of criminal activity, it is not necessarily the case that drug use *causes* crime as is commonly assumed. Stated in more scientific terms, a **correlation** be-tween these two sets of behaviors (i.e., where there is one there is usually the other), does not imply **causality** (that one causes the other to occur). White and Gorman (2000) point out that there are three possible ways in which we might conceive of the relationship between drug use and crime: (1) drug use causes crime; (2) crime causes drug abuse; and (3) both drug use and crime share common causes. This section broadly discusses these possible ways that drug use and crime might be related. Following this discussion, we look closely at several studies that examine this relationship empirically.

DRUG USE CAUSES CRIME

It is most commonly believed that illegal drug use somehow "causes" criminal behavior. As we have discussed, this belief has predominated throughout much of the twentieth century. This view has certainly not waned in the latter part of the twentieth century, as evidenced by the testimony of Senator D'Amato earlier. Generally, explanations for how drug use causes criminal behavior fall into two broad categories which we refer to as "pharmacological" and "economic" explanations respectively.

Pharmacological Explanations

Pharmacological explanations suggest that criminal behavior is a direct effect of a drug's chemical qualities on the human organism. Understood in this way, a drug may cause a person to think, and therefore act irrationally. Alternatively, drugs may lower one's ability to engage in self-control resulting in impulsive criminal acts. The early moral entrepreneurs, such as Richard Pearson Hobson and Harry Anslinger whom we discussed in previous chapters, generally adhered to this explanation for the drugs–crime connection. While these views are generally not accepted today by most serious observers in regard to either heroin or marijuana, the pharmacological explanation continues to be used to explain aggression associated with some types of drugs. Jeffrey Fagan (1990), in an extensive review of theoretical and empirical studies examining the relationship between drug intoxication and aggression, finds that certain drugs such as alcohol, barbiturates, cocaine, amphetamines, and PCP tend to be more strongly related to aggressive behavior than other drugs such as marijuana and heroin. Fagan (1990) suggests, however, that the link should not be viewed at face value as causal, as numerous variables mediate this association.

Several specific explanations have been offered for the aggressive behaviors that tend to accompany the use of these drugs. Studies conducted by medical and biological scientists tend to focus on neurological, hormonal, and/or genetic factors which are triggered by certain types of drugs. Some studies, for example, have sought to identify specific neural pathways and stimulus thresholds that provoke aggression (Moyer, 1976). Other researchers have found a relationship between alcohol use and reduced testosterone levels (Cicero, 1983). Schuckitt (1988) found that prolonged use of anabolic steroids result in decreased levels of testosterone and also reported feelings of aggressiveness and irritability. Still other studies (Maccoby and Jacklin, 1974) have suggested that there may be a genetic predisposition toward aggressiveness.

Another pharmacological explanation for drug use causing crime emerges primarily from psychology. This "psycho-pharmacological" perspective suggests that the use of certain drugs causes psychological impairment that, in turn, leads to violent and/or criminal behavior. Credited with formulating the first comprehensive psycho-pharmacological causal relationship between drug use and aggression was Abe Wikler, a pharmacologist and psychiatrist who worked for many years at the Federal Narcotics hospital in Lexington, Kentucky (Mayfield, 1983). Wikler compared the actions of alcohol and the opiates on human behavior using controlled experiments at the hospital. He found that opiates tend to reduce the "primary drives," such as sex, hunger, and aggression. Alcohol, on the other hand, not only intensifies these drives, but also reduces the "secondary drives" which serve to constrain the expression of primary drives (Wikler, 1952). This explanation, and variations on it, later came to be known as the **disinhibition hypothesis** which is probably the most popular of the pharmacological explanations for aggressiveness associated with alcohol. The disinhibition hypothesis suggests that drug intoxication affects central nervous system functions that presumably control or inhibit aggression. Under the influence of such drugs, normal constraints and inhibitions on behavior are removed, resulting in antisocial behavior. This explanation has been most often used in relation to alcohol to explain both violence (e.g., see Collins, 1983) and antisocial sexual behaviors (Langevin et al., 1988; Reinarman and Critchlow-Leigh, 1987).

Other psycho-pharmacological explanations suggest that certain kinds of drugs activate underlying pathologies causing heightened states of anxiety and even paranoia (Kramer, 1983; Mayfield, 1983). Still others point to an impairment of cognitive abilities while intoxicated (Pernanen, 1976). If this is the case, drug intoxication may reduce one's ability to engage in coping strategies in situations which may be deemed threatening (Collins, 1983). Also, if drug intoxication reduces one's ability to function cognitively, communication is less effective, and other people's behavior, which is normally rational and understandable, might now be perceived as arbitrary and even irrational. These perceptual misunderstandings might understandably lead to aggressive behavior (Pernanen, 1981).

Evaluation of Pharmacological Explanations   Pharmacological explanations for a causal connection between drug use and antisocial behavior are intuitively appealing. They are direct, and can be corroborated by casual observation that people who are under the influence of drugs often act in an aggressive or otherwise antisocial manner. There are a number of problems with these explanations, however, which merit careful review. First, it is important to recognize that these explanations are generally restricted to a limited number of drugs, typically alcohol and other depressants such as barbiturates, certain stimulants such as cocaine, amphetamines, and more recently crack, and a few other drugs such as phencyclidine (PCP) (Goldstein, 1985). These explanations are not generally applied to drugs such as marijuana, heroin, sedatives, and tranquilizers, or many of the hallucinogens. Furthermore, pharmacological explanations are generally applicable only to crimes of violence which are usually of an expressive nature; i.e., crimes which are not oriented toward some ulterior end such as making money.

Beyond this general caveat, pharmacological explanations also suffer in that, despite their popularity, the causal mechanisms that trigger violent behavior remain elusive. White and Gorman (2000) point out that it is not well understood how alcohol and other drugs act on the nervous and endocrine systems to produce aggressiveness. Perhaps this should not be surprising, for as Mayfield (1983) points out, we do not even know the precise biological mechanisms by which alcohol causes drunkenness!

Most extensively criticized, perhaps, is the disinhibition hypothesis. Ironically, it is also perhaps the most widely accepted explanation, at least among the general public. Despite the popularity of this explanation, there has yet to be any scientific research which biologically and pharmacologically accounts for such disinhibition (Woods and Mayfield, 1983; Fagan, 1990). As noted by Sutherland, Cressey, and Luckenbill (1992, p. 145), some individuals may become aggressive or act violently, just as others are likely to "sing, exchange dirty stories, or cry." In this regard, it has been suggested that disinhibition effects may be socially learned rather than pharmacologically induced (see Taylor, 1983). According to proponents of this "learned disinhibition" hypothesis, persons who consume large amounts of alcohol may simply behave consistently with their expectation that intoxication will result in disinhibition, and in turn aggression and otherwise disapproved sexual behavior. Related to this, others point out that normative expectations for behavior are relaxed for intoxicated persons. There is a disavowal of responsibility while under the influence of alcohol which, within reasonable limits, is regarded as socially acceptable. According to this perspective, drinking may be an excuse to engage in otherwise antisocial behavior (Collins, 1983; Fagan, 1990). There is, finally, a philosophical premise underlying the disinhibition hypothesis which is debatable. Since inhibitions are learned constraints which are suppressed under the influence of alcohol (or other drugs), one's behavior while intoxicated betrays a rather savage, antisocial human nature lurking behind the inhibitory constraints of culture. This understanding of human nature may well be correct, and it is not limited to those who hold to the disinhibition hypothesis; it is, for example, a central part of Freudian theory. We raise this issue because it is important to be aware of the philosophical assumptions that undergird explanations such as this.

In sum, while pharmacological explanations have a broad-based appeal and provide important clues about the relationship between some types of drug use and some types of criminal behavior, these explanations are less than complete. Social scientists point out that the pharmacology of drug use takes place within a social context which may profoundly affect the way in which drugs and human behavior interact. As Mayfield (1983:142) points out, "we . . . see the 'maudlin drunk,' the 'amorous drunk,' the 'gregarious drunk,' the 'belligerent drunk.'" If chemistry alone is responsible for antisocial behavior, we should expect to find a much more predictable response to such intoxication. Hence, we must look beyond these immediate pharmacological and biological mechanisms if we are to understand the drugs–crime connection.

Economic Explanations

It is possible that drug use may cause criminal behavior in a less direct way. Perhaps drug intoxication does not produce irrational or aggressive states pharmacologically, but rather, users of these drugs commit crimes to pay for an expensive habit. This explanation, which Goldstein (1985) calls the "economic-compulsive" model, is premised on two important assumptions:

(1) illegal drugs are *expensive;* and (2) illegal drugs are *addicting.* It is important to note that both of these premises are directed toward *illegal* drugs. It is not true, of course, that all illegal drugs are expensive. Marijuana, for example, is relatively cheap, as are LSD and many illegally used prescription drugs such as Valium. Hence, those arguing that the causal linkage between drug use and crime is an economic one are generally referring to more expensive drugs such as heroin and cocaine.

The problematic character of these drugs is not just that they are expensive, however. They are also addicting, or at least strongly reinforcing. It is assumed (though not well documented empirically) that once users of drugs like heroin and cocaine become dependent on these substances, they will not be able to control their need for these drugs. As Collins et al. (1985) describe it, these dependencies create an "inelastic demand." Furthermore, because these drugs are addictive, the user develops an increasing tolerance for the drug requiring even greater amounts of the drug with each use in order to experience the same effect. This spiral of addiction to drugs which are already expensive thus makes it necessary for the user to engage in crime just to feed his or her habit. These two factors—the expensive nature of the drugs and their addictive qualities—are a sure recipe for crime according to advocates of this perspective. This is why Goldstein (1985) has called this the "economic-compulsive" model.

Evaluation of Economic Explanations   The economic model has fueled the policy agendas of the last three presidential administrations, and indeed, there have been some empirical studies, which we describe in more detail in the section on empirical research on drugs and crime below, that provide some support for such a model (Anglin and Speckart, 1986, 1988; Anglin and Perrochet, 1998; Ball et al., 1981, 1982, 1983; Speckart and Anglin, 1986). The series of studies conducted by John Ball and his associates was especially instrumental in the shaping of public policy, as it was formally reviewed in the senate hearings on alcoholism and drug abuse (United States Senate, 1984). Despite the important character of these studies, it would be premature to conclude that drug use causes crime in the fashion that they suggest. In the first place, these studies were based on either arrestees or, in the case of the Anglin and Speckart studies, of methadone patients. We must be careful about making generalizations from captive samples such as this, as these individuals are not necessarily representative of the addict population at large. They are in trouble, or are having difficulty coping with their habit which is why they were arrested or entered a methadone maintenance program in the first place. Chaiken and Chaiken (1985) found, for example, that among incarcerated offenders, those who are arrested frequently are either emotionally disturbed and inept offenders who commit very few crimes but get caught nearly every time they do; or they are frequent users of drugs who commit crimes frequently, but get caught because they do not carefully plan their crime to avoid detection. These studies do point to one important truth, namely that people who use drugs with great frequency are more likely to be arrested than people who do not use frequently. We should not infer from this, however, that high frequency drug use causes the behavior that results in arrest. People who use drugs less frequently may commit just as many crimes, but may also be more careful in how they commit these crimes.

It is also important not to confuse correlation with causation. The Ball et al. and the Anglin and Speckart research do demonstrate a *correlation* between drug use and criminal behavior among the addicts in their samples. It is quite logical to assume from such data that drug use causes the criminal behavior. It is just as plausible, however, to conclude that crime "causes" the drug use. This does not mean that people feel some overwhelming compulsion to use drugs as a result of committing crime. However, as we shall describe below, it is possible that crime is functionally related to subsequent use of drugs in a more or less causal way. Alternatively, it is possible that both drug use and crime are the result of still other factors in the environment of the criminal addict. This possibility is discussed in greater detail in the section entitled "Common Cause and Subcultural Explanations." The point we want to make here is that while it *intuitively* makes sense to infer that drug use causes crime when higher levels of drug use are accompanied by greater criminal activity, such judgments are premature. The relationship between drug use and criminal behavior is much more complex than this, and most research fails to demonstrate a clear, unambiguous causal relationship between drug use and crime. (See Chaiken and Chaiken, 1991 and Hunt, 1991 for recent reviews of this literature.) Hence, we now examine other ways in which the relationship between drug use and criminal behavior might be interpreted.

CRIME CAUSES DRUGS

Empirical research on the drugs–crime connection conducted by social scientists over the past four decades has led many observers of the drug scene to re-evaluate the assumption that drug use causes criminal behavior. Studies conducted since the 1950s have quite consistently found that initial involvement in criminal activities begins substantially prior to experimentation with drugs for most users (Chaiken and Chaiken, 1982; Greenberg and Adler, 1974; Inciardi, 1979). Moreover, while increased levels of crime tended to accompany higher levels of expensive drug consumption, research by Faupel (1991) suggests that changes in the levels of drug use were typically *preceded* by increased criminal activity as measured by criminal income. This suggests that the demand for drugs is quite *elastic* depending on the resources available, in contrast to the commonly held inelastic demand model (see Collins et al., 1985; Fields and Walters, 1985). If this is the case, it does indeed make sense to suggest that perhaps crime "causes" drug use in some way.

The ethnographic evidence suggests one way in which crime may, in a sense, cause drug use. Several researchers have reported that various types of drugs may actually be used to *facilitate* the commission of crimes

(Faupel, 1991; Goldstein, 1979) or that certain drugs are often used to celebrate a particularly successful criminal *score* (Faupel, 1991; Walters, 1985). Goldstein (1979) reports, for example, that it is common for prostitutes to turn to alcohol or other drugs as a means of coping with the sometimes harsh demands of their trade. Faupel (1991) also reports that drugs are used for quite functional reasons in committing other crimes. Armed robbers sometimes use alcohol and barbiturates to place them in a more belligerent frame of mind. Others reported taking amphetamines to provide the necessary energy to sustain an active criminal lifestyle. Most of the addicts interviewed by Faupel also used heroin at one or more times in their careers to help them in the commission of their crimes.

These data suggest that, insofar as there is a causal relationship between drug use and crime, it may be opposite the expected direction. As experienced by the addicts in the respective studies of Goldstein and Faupel, drugs are often used to support and maintain a criminal lifestyle, not vice versa. At the same time, the proceeds of crime are also used to pay for the drugs that these addicts consume. These studies reflect a growing body of literature suggesting a *reciprocal* relationship between drug use and crime.

"COMMON-CAUSE" AND SUBCULTURAL EXPLANATIONS

Social scientists are increasingly of the opinion that it does not make sense to speak in simple causal terms when describing the relationship between drug use and criminal behavior. Both behaviors, they argue, are inextricably interwoven with the broader subculture of which these activities are a part. That is, crime cannot be understood simply as a response to a drug craving; nor can drug use be understood simply as an accessory to crime. These are mutually supportive activities, and both are linked with other features of a drug-using subculture which values and encourages criminal behavior and drug use. The relationship between drug use and crime is, in this sense **spurious.**

A spurious relationship is one in which there is the appearance that there is a causal relationship between two variables, but where both variables are related in the same way to a third variable. The result is a *correlation* between the two variables in question which appears to be causal in nature. Observers of the drug scene take note of the fact that most drug-using criminals begin committing crimes at an earlier age than they begin using drugs, or at least expensive drugs such as heroin or cocaine that are purported to cause crime because of their addictive and costly nature. Rather than to interpret this sequence to mean that crime causes drug use, however, the common-cause explanation understands both drug use and criminal behavior to be products of a cultural system which promotes and rewards these behaviors. Studies have found, for example, that many factors such as delinquent peers, which are strongly related to delinquency are also related to drug and alcohol use (Elliot et al., 1989; Goode, 1972; White et al., 1987, 1999). Other variants of this common-cause model hold that drug use and criminal or delinquent behavior are merely coincidental, that they serve similar functions for individuals who engage in them, or that both behaviors are manifestations of a single, underlying attribute or characteristic. A growing body of research supports the notion for serious offenders in particular.

Jessor and Jessor (1977) suggest that both delinquency and drug use are two of a number of nonconforming expressions of independence from adult authority figures that function to assist youth in identifying with delinquent peer groups. The authors refer to the recurring, persistent presence of delinquent behaviors as a **problem behavior syndrome,** which includes alcohol/drug use, delinquency, and being sexually active (Donovan and Jessor, 1985). Subsequent research provides support for this argument, finding that these various dimensions of unconventional behavior reflect a more general dynamic at work, that being the need for peer acceptance (Donovan, Jessor, and Costa, 1988). In that regard, Huizinga and Jakob-Chien (1998) show in particular that drug use among these juveniles is associated with serious delinquency.

Other research, not necessarily based upon the Jessor findings, clarifies a number of elements associated with this relationship among serious offenders. Osgood, Johnston, O'Malley, and Bachman (1988) propose that the simultaneous occurrence of drug use and delinquency/crime illustrates the phenomenon referred to as "generality of deviance." Their research suggests that behaviors such as alcohol/drug use, delinquency, sexual promiscuity, poor school performance, etc., are all reflections of this single attribute. The authors contend that the debate over whether drug use precedes delinquency or vice versa is irrelevant for these offenders because both activities tend to be mutually reinforcing. Similarly, Gottfredson and Hirschi's (1990) influential work proposes that substance use and other manifestations of deviant/delinquent behavior are characteristics of persons who possess low self-control. Finally, Terrie Moffitt (1993; 1997) provides a compelling argument that delinquency and drug use during adolescence reflects the desire to mimic adult behaviors. Moffitt distinguishes between adolescence-limited delinquency and "life-course persistent" offending. For the former, experimentation with drug use, delinquency, and sexual activity is in some ways a natural occurrence from the transition from childhood to adult status. As these youths enter adulthood, delinquent behavior decreases substantially or altogether because these individuals begin taking adult roles and responsibilities. On the other hand, life-course persistent offenders exhibit antisocial behavior at early ages and continue into and throughout adulthood.

Still others have identified a more general subcultural context promoting both drug use and criminal behavior. Street drug subcultures tend to encourage both drug use and crime in a number of ways. (See also, Chapter 5, on drug using careers.) In the first place, these subcultures provide a network of friends and associates who possess drugs or have means of obtaining drugs. It is thus quite natural for young people with acquaintances who use drugs to eventually experiment themselves. Moreover, it is often these same acquaintances that introduce the would-be drug user to a criminal lifestyle. Life history data obtained by Faupel (1991) reveal that early experimentation with delinquency and crime is usually pursued with others who are often experimenting with drugs and crime themselves.

Drug subcultures not only provide a network of drug-using and criminal acquaintances, but with them a vehicle for transmitting the necessary knowledge for successfully maintaining a criminal and drug-using lifestyle (Biernacki, 1979; Faupel, 1986, 1987a, 1991; Gould et al., 1974; Sackman et al., 1978). The ability to acquire a sufficient income to support a drug habit requires some degree of criminal sophistication, whether one's crime is shoplifting, prostitution, burglary, robbery, or any of a number of crimes that users of expensive drugs rely on for income.

Still another important component of subcultures of drug use and crime is a stratification system that confers status and prestige on those who can acquire and consume large amounts of drugs, and who demonstrate a mastery of the skills described above (Biernacki, 1979; Faupel, 1991; Rosenbaum, 1981). Accompanying this system of stratification is a set of norms which define appropriate means for pursuing criminal and drug-using activities (Faupel, 1987b, 1991; Hanson et al., 1985; Sutter, 1969). Together, the normative and stratification dynamics operative in drug-using subcultures serve to encourage drug use and crime among subcultural participants.

Evaluation of "Common Cause" and Subcultural Explanations   Common cause and subcultural explanations are similar in that both types of explanations identify extraneous variables which affect both drug use and criminal behavior. Drug-using criminals do not exist in a vacuum, but live their lives in a broader social context that affects their behavior, including both use of drugs and commission of crime, in profound ways. Common-cause explanations point to dynamics such as the need for peer acceptance or establishing independence from adult authority figures. The subcultural perspective understands the drugs–crime connection in the context of a broader cultural and interactional framework which defines and encourages both sets of activities. Seen in this way, it does not make sense to speak of "cause" when considering the relationship between drug use and crime. Goode (1972) summarizes the "subcultural" position on the relationship between marijuana use and crime, an observation that might be applied to other types of drug use as well:

> We are led overwhelmingly to the conclusion that *marijuana users tend to be somewhat more likely to commit crimes solely because they are part of a drug-using subculture;* the actual properties of marijuana appear to be completely unassociated with criminal behavior. Anyone (*whether he uses marijuana or not*) who makes friends and becomes involved with others who use drugs—especially others who use drugs in addition to and aside from marijuana—stands a higher likelihood of committing offenses, simply because this segment of the population tends to be more lax about obeying the law. It is merely because marijuana users tend to associate with others who are part of this subculture that their crime rate is somewhat higher. In other words, the marijuana–crime relationship—in terms of the causal or effects model—*is completely spurious* (Goode, 1972:451; emphasis in the original).

Drug users are involved in various types of crimes. It has not been firmly established, however, that drug use causes *crime.*

Common cause and subcultural explanations are both profoundly *sociological* in their understanding of the relationship between drug use and crime. They are sociological because they implicitly recognize the broader social context in which these behaviors occur. This is not to suggest that there are not causal mechanisms which link crime with drug use. These mechanisms, however, cannot offer a complete explanation for the correlation that we see between drug use and criminal behavior.

EMPIRICALLY UNDERSTANDING DRUG USE AND CRIME

The relationship between drug use and criminal activity has been extensively studied by social scientists, indeed perhaps more so than any other topic in the field. Furthermore, this is a relationship about which there is very little consensus, as we have seen in the previous section. The purpose of this section is to examine more closely the empirical evidence regarding the drugs–crime connection. This review does not attempt to be exhaustive of all the literature, as there are literally hundreds of studies that have examined this question (see Austin and Lettieri, 1977; Gandossy et al., 1980; Greenberg and Adler, 1974; and Speckart and Anglin, 1986b for more extensive reviews of this literature). Rather, we discuss a small number of studies which represent the variety of methodologies used and results obtained by social scientists doing research in this area. Broadly speaking, two types of data have been used: official data, obtained from criminal justice records; and self-reported data obtained directly from drug users.

Empirical Evidence from Official Sources

Official sources of data on drug use and crime include primarily prison and arrest statistics. Data from each of these sources is discussed next.

Prison Statistics

The most widely distributed data on drug use and crime using prison statistics are disseminated by the Bureau of Justice Statistics, a division of the National Institute of Justice in Washington, D.C. These data are drawn from thousands of inmates in state prisons and local jails who are sampled in such a way as to be representative of the population of jail and prison inmates in the United States. These inmates are then interviewed regarding their drug use history. Some 80 percent of both male and female inmates in state prisons have used drugs on at least one occasion, and about 70 percent have used on a regular basis at some point in their lives. The data further reveal that about half had used during the month prior to the offense for which they were incarcerated (Mumola, 1999). These percentages are substantially higher than that for the general population, where 47.6 percent of those aged 18–34 (the highest drug-using age group) reported that they had ever used illicit drugs in their lifetimes, and only 11.7 percent reported any such use during the past month (Office of Applied Statistics, 1999). It is also worthwhile to also point out that approximately half of the state prison inmates reported that they were under the influence of drugs at the time they committed the offense for which they were incarcerated.

These data make it clear that incarcerated offender populations have much higher rates of drug use than does the general population. Statistics such as these suggest, preliminarily at least, that drug use may play some sort of role in criminal behavior. Indeed, the finding that approximately one-half of the inmates sampled reported that they were under the influence of drugs at the time they committed their offense provides some support for the pharmacological explanation discussed above. Care must be taken in the interpretation of these data, however. As we have emphasized in the previous section, the fact that incarcerated offenders report higher rates of drug use than does the general population does not necessarily mean that the use of these drugs *caused* the user to commit the crimes in question.

Arrest Statistics

In Chapter 6, we introduced *The Arrestee Drug Abuse Monitoring Program (ADAM)*. You will recall that sampled arrestees participate on a voluntary basis, providing a urine sample and agreeing to an interview with an ADAM staff person. The urinalysis provides objective evidence as to whether or not one has been using drugs within one to two days prior to his or her arrest, in the case of most drugs, and within a month prior to arrest in the case of PCP or marijuana. In addition, the interviews ask arrestees about their prior use of drugs, means of administration, etc. (Wish and Gropper, 1990).

ADAM data reveal that there is a high percentage of drug positives for all offense types, although some offense types are more highly represented than others. Offenses claiming the highest percentage of drug positives are drug offenses and property crimes, typically about 80 percent and 70 percent respectively. Drug positives are less represented among violent offenders, though in most cities more than half of violent arrestees did test positive (Arresteee Drug Abuse Monitoring Program, 2000).

The high percentage of arrestees testing positive for drugs—regardless of the offense for which they are arrested—further confirms that there is a strong correlation between criminal behavior and drug use. Again, however, we must be cautious in how we interpret these data. ADAM results are often misinterpreted as providing evidence for the link between drug use and crime. The urine-test results simply do not provide the definitive evidence necessary to draw a conclusion about the role of drug use on crime. The drug use may have occurred prior to the crime, after the crime, just before arrest, or even after arrest while in detention. The test, therefore, indicates nothing about whether the drugs, or the need for drugs, was a motive for the crime. In addition, the test results say nothing about whether the arrestee was a chronic user or a casual experimenter. The results do indicate the types of drugs recently used by arrestees in a jurisdiction and changes in use trends (Wish and Gropper, 1990:369). Hence, while these data are dramatic, and are often used as the strongest evidence yet for the causal role of drug use and addiction in criminality, other approaches are required to more adequately assess the drugs-crime relationship.

EMPIRICAL EVIDENCE FROM SELF-REPORTS

In an effort to more precisely measure the relationship between drug use and crime, research efforts have come to increasingly rely on self-report methodologies. While there are recognized problems with underreporting and other potential sources of bias, there is a general consensus among researchers using this method that it is possible to mitigate most sources of bias through careful choice of interviewers, developing validity checks within questionnaires (typically by asking the same question in different ways and locations in the interview), and comparing results with findings from other researchers as well as with official data (called *triangulation*). These safeguards, which have been developed over several decades of self-report studies, have provided reasonable assurance to all but the most skeptical that the advantages of self-report methodologies in allowing for more detailed and directly focused data far outweigh the potential disadvantages that may occur as a result of potential underreporting or misleading reporting.

Numerous specific self-report methodologies have evolved to examine the relationship between drug use and crime. Three broad types of methodologies are described here, which we refer to as *sequence studies, longitudinal studies,* and *ethnographic studies.* The differences between these methodologies are not always sharply defined, and some individual studies may appropriately be considered under more than one of these categories.

Sequence Studies

Studies that use what we have called the "sequence" methodology examine the sequence of initiation into drug use versus criminal activity. Respondents are asked to indicate when they first began using drugs and when they first committed a crime. The logic behind this kind of questioning is that if drug-using criminals began using drugs before they committed their first crime, there is a stronger basis for drawing a causal connection between the two behaviors. If, on the other hand, one's first crime is committed prior to the time they first began using drugs, the common-sense assumption that drug use causes crime must be re-examined. In either event, by ascertaining the sequence of initiation into drug use and crime, researchers have been able to move beyond simply establishing a correlation between drug use and crime. Establishing that one set of activities occurs before or after the other provides at least a rudimentary basis for drawing some conclusions about the causal relationship between drug use and crime.

One of the most extensive studies utilizing self-report data from "street" respondents (respondents who are not incarcerated or in treatment) was conducted by James Inciardi over a several year period beginning in the 1970s. Inciardi and his colleagues interviewed street heroin addicts in several major cities throughout the country. These street addicts were asked a series of questions regarding their drug-using and criminal histories. They were asked how old they were when they first began using each of a list of some 20 different drugs, including alcohol. In addition, they were asked to indicate how old they were when they committed their first criminal offense, as well as when they began to use drugs and commit crimes on a regular basis.

Table 10.1 presents the median ages at which the street addicts from Inciardi's Miami sample began to commit crimes and to use various drugs. Table 10.1 reveals that the only drug use that preceded the first crime committed by the addicts in Inciardi's sample was alcohol and, for women, marijuana. Other types of drug use, however, which are more expensive and usually suspected in criminal behavior, did not begin until some two to four years following the first crime committed by these addicts.

It should be pointed out that these data were collected prior to the introduction of crack cocaine. Inciardi and his colleagues did, however, do follow-up studies among crack users (Inciardi and Pottieger, 1994; McCoy, Inciardi, Metsch, Pottieger, and Saum, 1995). Their findings nearly mirrored the sequence found in the earlier study among heroin users, except that the

TABLE 10.1	Sequence of Initial Drug Use and Crime Among 353 Active Heroin Users and 198 Crack Users			
	Median Age			
	1970s Heroin Study		**1990s Crack Study**	
Activity	**Males (N = 236)**	**Females (N = 117)**	**Males (N = 114)**	**Females (N = 84)**
First Alcohol Use	12.8	13.8	10.0	10.0
First Alcohol Intoxication	13.3	13.9	—	—
First Crime	15.1	15.9	14.0	14.0
First Illicit Drug Use	15.2	15.2	14.0	14.0
First Marijuana Use	15.5	15.4	14.0	14.0
First Arrest	17.2	18.3	15.0	15.0
First Barbiturate Use (pill)	17.5	17.0	15.0	15.0
First Heroin Use	18.7	18.2	17.0	16.5
First Continuous Heroin Use	19.2	18.4	—	—
First Cocaine Use	19.7	18.7	16.0	16.0
First Crack Use	—	—	21.0	20.0

Sources: Adapted from James A. Inciardi, "Heroin Use and Street Crime." *Crime and Delinquency,* July 1979; James A. Inciardi and Anne E. Pottieger, "Crack-Cocaine Use and Street Crime," *Journal of Drugs,* Winter/Spring 1994; and H. Virginia McCoy, James A. Inciardi, Lisa R. Metsch, Anne Pottieger, and Christine A. Saum, "Women, Crack and Crime: Gender Comparisons of Criminal Activity Among Crack Cocaine Users," *Contemporary Drug Problems,* Fall 1995.

ages for all initiation experiences of the crack users were one to three years earlier than the 1970s heroin users. These findings are also reported in Table 10.1.

Inciardi's findings raise some perplexing questions about the drugs–crime connection. Insofar as these data are valid, and we have no reason to believe that they are not, they preclude any simplistic causal explanation which says that involvement with drugs directly "causes" one to begin committing crimes. Indeed, these data provide stronger support for the idea that involvement in criminal activities has a causal effect on eventual drug-using behavior.

Another study using a slightly different methodology for establishing the sequence of initiation into drug use and crime was conducted by Jan and Marcia Chaiken in the early 1980s for the RAND Corporation (Chaiken and Chaiken, 1982). The Chaikens surveyed some 2,200 male inmates in Michigan, California, and Texas prisons. They found, first, that 35 percent of their respondents reported that they had never used drugs. Among those who were drug users, however, their data suggest that the onset of crime is just as likely to precede first drug use as vice versa. Just over 20 percent of the drug-using sample (10 percent of the total sample) reported that their drug use began prior to their first crime, while more than 26 percent (12.5 percent of the total sample) reported that they began committing crimes in an earlier measurement period than they began using drugs. More than 52 percent (25 percent of the total sample) reported that they began using drugs and crime about the same time.

Chaiken and Chaiken's findings further call into question both the pharmacological and economically based drugs-cause-crime hypotheses. While approximately 20 percent of their sample reported earlier drug use involvement, the overwhelming majority of these inmates began their drug-using behavior either coterminously with or substantially after they began engaging in criminal activities. Moreover, when inmates were further asked about their motivations for committing crimes, only 26 percent of those using "hard" or expensive drugs cited a need for money for drugs as one of the primary reasons for their first crime. Indeed, less than half (46 percent) indicated that needing money for drugs was an important or very important reason for later criminal activity, and only 2 percent cited their drug involvement as the only important motive for later criminal activity.

One final study examining the sequence of initiation into drug use and crime using still a different methodology is the National Youth Survey, an extensive study of more than 1,700 youth who were aged 11–17 in 1976, and were interviewed seven different times over a ten-year period. Approximately each year, these youth were queried regarding their participation in minor (nonindex) crimes, major (index) crimes, alcohol use, marijuana use, and polydrug use. These responses were then compared from one year to the next to determine the sequence of initiation into each of these sets of behaviors.

Results from these surveys have been extensively reported by Delbert Elliot and colleagues (1989). They report a substantial history of criminal behavior before the onset of drug use for most of the youth in their sample. Among those youth for whom it was possible to ascertain a temporal ordering (a temporal ordering was not ascertainable if the first reporting of both sets of behaviors occurred in the same interview period), these researchers found the following:

Involvement in Minor (Nonindex) Offenses:

- Preceded first alcohol use in 63 percent of the cases.
- Preceded first marijuana use in 93 percent of the cases.
- Preceded first polydrug use in 99 percent of the cases.

Involvement in Major (Index) Offenses:

- Followed first marijuana use 63 percent of the cases.
- Preceded polydrug use in 67 percent of the cases.

Collectively, studies which focus on the sequence of initiation into drug using and criminal behavior provide quite convincing empirical evidence that criminal behavior on the part of drug users cannot be understood in the simple cause-effect explanations that have commonly been forwarded. These data provide no evidence whatsoever that young people somehow get seduced into using drugs, develop a habit, and are then forced to commit crimes to pay for that habit. The only types of drug use that precede criminal behavior in the biographies of most drug-using criminals are alcohol and marijuana. Neither of these are the sorts of expensive and addictive drugs that are depicted as having the power over addicts to cause them to engage in criminal activities. Studies examining the sequence of drug use and crime initiation clearly and consistently call for a rejection of this rather simplistic understanding of the relationship between drug use and criminal behavior. As we shall see, however, the casual relationship between drug use and crime may be understood in more complex terms than the sequence studies are able to address.

Longitudinal Studies

Partly in response to the implications suggested by findings such as those described above, a number of researchers have argued that it is not sufficient to merely determine the sequence of initiation into drug use and criminal behavior. Rather, they argue, it is necessary to examine the relationship between drug use and crime over time throughout the careers of addict criminals. These researchers correctly point out that while it may be the case that the onset of criminal behavior patterns precede experimentation with drugs, or at least expensive drugs, it may well be that over the course of their careers, as addicts develop more sizable habits, the tolerance that they develop for these drugs makes a criminal lifestyle increasingly mandatory. Hence, while the hypothesis that drug use causes crime is necessarily rejected as applied to the early, experimental stage of drug-using and criminal careers, this hypothesis may have more plausibility when considered with respect to the overall careers of addicts. Studies examining the relationship between drug use and crime over a more extended period of time— that which we call "longitudinal studies"—generally attempt to identify periods at various times in an addict's biography wherein levels of drug use and crime are compared. This section examines three such studies, each of which utilizes a slightly different methodology to ascertain the relationship between drug use and crime over time.

A widely cited series of studies was conducted by David Nurco, John Ball, and their associates among arrested addicts, initially in the Baltimore area (Ball et al., 1981, 1982, 1983) and later extended to New York City (Nurco et al., 1988; Hanlon et al., 1990). The research team interviewed addicts in these areas extensively about their history of drug use and crime over their lifetimes. Specifically, these researchers identified biographical periods when the addicts in their sample were "at risk;" meaning that they were not in prison or in an institutional setting. They found that, on average, these addicts were on opiates 61.6 percent of the time they were at risk (Ball et al., 1981). Addicts were closely questioned regarding levels of crime during times that they were addicted (which they defined as using regularly over a period of at least a month) and during times when they were not addicted. Rather than calculate the total number of criminal events, the researchers simply recorded the number of *days* that one or more criminal events took place. In this way, their study sought to compare the regularity with which criminal activity took place during addicted and nonaddicted periods.

Their results are quite remarkable, given the findings of the studies described in the section above: the number of crime days per year at risk was substantially higher during periods of addiction. Indeed, they were more than six-times as likely to have committed a crime on any given day while they were addicted. These data thus strongly suggest that, while drug use may not precede crime in terms of the sequence of initiation, criminal activity picks up dramatically when addicts are using expensive drugs on a daily basis.

A slightly different methodology was employed by Anglin and Speckart as they attempted to gauge the relationship between drug use and crime over time among methadone patients in California (Anglin and Speckart, 1986, 1988; Anglin and Yih-Ing Hser, 1987; Speckart and Anglin, 1986a). These researchers attempted to identify critical points in time in the biographies of 671 male addicts they interviewed, including when narcotic drugs were first tried; the onset of addiction (as defined by the first time narcotics were used daily for a period of at least 30 days); and the termination of addiction. They then queried their respondents regarding the number of arrests during each of these periods, as well as the percentage of their time involved in property crime, the average number of crime days (see Ball et al., described earlier), and the average number of crime dollars for each period (Anglin and Speckart, 1988). Similar to the Ball and Nurco research, Anglin and Speckart found that the addicts in their sample were substantially more involved in crime when they were using narcotics on a daily basis, whether measured by percentage of time spent on crime, crime days, or criminal income.

These findings reinforce the Baltimore and New York City findings of Ball, Nurco, and their colleagues. While there is certainly evidence for pre-addiction criminality, there is a substantial increase in criminal activity after the onset of addiction. Regardless of the measure of criminality employed, these differences are dramatic and significant. Anglin and Speckart concur with the conclusion by Ball et al. that there is a monotonic and causal relationship between narcotics use and criminal behavior.

While the Baltimore/New York City and California research discussed earlier was under way, Bruce Johnson and his associates were devising a rather novel strategy in New York City (Johnson et al., 1985). Their methodology was unique in that they did not question addicts regarding their drug use and criminal behavior over their entire career as the two studies discussed above had done. Rather, the Johnson et al. team interviewed several cohorts of addicts who were using varying levels of drugs at the time of interview. These New York City addicts were interviewed daily for a period of five days, followed by weekly interviews over the next four weeks. During each session, respondents were asked to relate specifically what crimes they had committed and what drugs they had used *that day* or *during the preceding week*. Similarly, they were asked to indicate whether they used any of a list of drugs each day/week they were interviewed. In this way, the Johnson et al. team was able to avoid the problems of respondents' not being able to remember crime and drug use from months or even years earlier. The sample was then divided into three "user-groups," based on the frequency of their heroin use: "irregular users" who used heroin two or less days per week; "regular users" who used three, four, or five days per week; and "daily users" who used six or seven days per week. The level of criminal activity for the three groups was then compared.

The findings of Johnson et al. are not quite as dramatic as those reported by the Ball and Nurco team or by the Anglin and Speckart research, but the trends are nevertheless consistent with the Baltimore and California studies. Table 10.2 compares both the average number of crimes committed,

TABLE 10.2	**Average Number of Crimes per Year and Average Annual Criminal Income of Street Addicts in New York City**

Average Number of Crimes

| | Heroin User Group | | |
Type of Activity	Irregular	Regular	Daily
Nondrug Crimes[a]	116	162	209
Drug Business Crimes[b]	245	823	880
Miscellaneous Drug Activity[c]	95	177	283
Minor Crimes (noncash)[d]	59	54	76
Total	515	1,217	1,447

Average Annual Income

Nondrug Crime Income[a]	$2,885	$5,719	$8,540
Drug Business Income[b]	$1,566	$1,402	$2,752
Miscellaneous Drug Income[c]	$1,417	$3,965	$7,418
Minor Crime Income (noncash)[d]	$136	$117	$110
Total Criminal Income	$6,004	$11,203	$18,820

[a]Includes robbery, burglary, shoplifting (for resale), "other larcenies," forgery, con games, prostitution, pimping, and "other illegal."
[b]Includes drug sales, steering and touting (for money), copping (for money).
[c]Includes drug thefts, steering and touting (for drugs), copping (for drugs), avoided expenditures for drugs.
[d]Includes shoplifting (for own use) and fare evasion.
Source: Adapted from Bruce D. Johnson, Paul J. Goldstein, Edward Preble, James Schmeidler, Douglas S. Lipton, Barry Spunt and Thomas Miller, *Taking Care of Business: The Economics of Crime by Heroin Abusers*. Lexington, MA: Lexington Books, 1985. Tables 7-2 and 7-4, pp. 77 and 81.

and the average dollar value of these crimes across the three user-groups. Overall, daily users were committing nearly three times the number of crimes than were irregular users. Furthermore, the average annual criminal income of daily users was more than three times that of the irregular users.

Johnson et al. also discovered that heroin addicts are much less criminally involved, at least in the traditional sense, than is commonly believed. Rather, they rely on a number of quasi-criminal activities to enhance their access to drugs. The addicts in their study reported that much of their income derived from such activities as *touting* and *steering* (directing potential customers to fellow dealers), renting their works, *hitting* (injecting) less-experienced users, and *testing* drugs for local dealers. Typically, they would be remunerated for these services with heroin or other drugs rather than with cash. Hence, by interviewing addicts on a daily and weekly basis regarding their drug-using and criminal activities, Johnson and his colleagues have demonstrated that addicts are able to maintain a drug-using lifestyle in many ways, including but not limited to predatory criminal activities.

The longitudinal studies that we have reviewed here portray a dramatically different picture of the relationship between drug use and criminal behavior than did the earlier studies which sought to establish the sequence of initiation into drug use and criminal behavior. How do we account for these findings which seem so diametrically opposed? First, we must recognize that the "sequence" studies and the longitudinal studies are, in fact, measuring two very different phenomena. Studies using the sequence methodology seek only to determine patterns of initiation into drug use and crime. Any statement of the causal relationship between these two activities is limited to whether or not drug use plays a role in an individual becoming involved in crime in the first place. The answer is that it does not. The longitudinal studies, on the other hand, seek to determine whether, once addicted, *greater levels* of criminal activity are required in order to maintain a drug-using lifestyle than would be the case if the addict were not using drugs, or using them so extensively. The answer is that increased levels of drug use are clearly accompanied by increased levels of criminal behavior.

Despite their greater level of methodological sophistication, however, the longitudinal studies fail to definitively establish causality. That is, while they demonstrate that higher levels of criminal activity correspond to periods of daily use or addiction, such an analysis remains correlational in nature. These studies fail to demonstrate which came first, for example, an increase in the level of drug use, or an increase in the level of criminal activity. Again, it is *assumed* that addicts increase their criminal involvement in response to the demands of their addiction. However, as we have demonstrated in the theoretical discussion earlier, it is also plausible to suggest that the level of one's drug consumption increases only after one's income (typically acquired through criminal means) expands sufficiently to support such a habit. In order to adequately assess the relationship between drug use and crime over time, methodologies that are more sensitive to the temporal dynamics of addict careers, such as those employed by more qualitatively oriented ethnographers, are necessary.

Ethnographic Studies

Beginning in the late 1960s a number of researchers began to seriously question many of the common-sense notions about drug addicts and addiction, such as the idea that drug addicts suffered from "addiction-prone personalities," or that they were "retreatists" and "double failures" who preferred to drop out of society rather than to compete in it. These researchers argued that it was necessary to attempt to understand the world of drug addiction from the perspective of the addict him or herself. In order to gain this subjective understanding, it was necessary to utilize a methodology that allowed the addict to frame the issues, in essence, to permit the respondent to "do the talking." Most ethnographic accounts have not focused specifically on the relationship between drug use and criminal behavior as we have discussed it here. Rather, the general lifestyle dynamics of drug users are described, including both criminal and drug-using activities. Among the first to describe the lifestyles of street drug users was an urban anthropologist by the name of Edward Preble (Preble and Casey, 1969). In this groundbreaking article, Preble and Casey depict the lifestyles of heroin addicts in rather revolutionary terms. They maintain that the heroin addict is not a sick, pathological individual suffering from an addictive personality, or who is a retreatist or double failure who "drops out" because he is not able to succeed in the conventional world of work. In their view, the heroin addict is a skillful entrepreneur who successfully meets the challenges of a lifestyle of addiction:

> Heroin use today by lower class, primarily minority group, persons does not provide for them a euphoric escape from the psychological and social problems which derive from ghetto life. On the contrary, it provides a motivation and rationale for the pursuit of a meaningful life, albeit a socially deviant one. The activities these individuals engage in and the relationships they have in the course of their quest for heroin are far more important than the minimal analgesic and euphoric effects of the small amount of heroin available to them. If they can be said to be addicted, it is not so much to heroin as to the entire career of a heroin user. The heroin user is, in a way, like the compulsively hard-working business executive whose ostensible goal is the acquisition of money, but whose real satisfaction is in meeting the inordinate challenge he creates for himself (Preble and Casey, 1969:21).

The insights that Preble and Casey provided were soon echoed by other ethnographers (Biernacki, 1979; Hanson et al., 1985; Rosenbaum, 1981; Sackman et al., 1978; Sutter, 1969). These studies portray street heroin users as highly skilled entrepreneurs, actively engaged in a meaningful criminal lifestyle. This character of addict criminality is depicted by the street term "main hustle," which implies a criminal specialization of sorts, whereby addicts develop the requisite skills and expertise to maintain a successful criminal lifestyle. While much of the proceeds of these crimes is spent on

DRUGS AND EVERYDAY LIFE

Manny's Story on Drug Use and Crime

Robbery worked for me for such a long time for two basic reasons. First, I was lucky. God must take care of dope fiends. Because for almost two solid years, while on a constant heroin run that cost on the average of $150 per day to maintain, I pulled off robberies almost daily. Seldom a week went by without at least one or two major robberies. In all this time I was only busted once—at the end of the run. The sun shines on the just and the unjust; I believe it!

Second, robbery worked for me because it is a swift, and relatively sure, method of criminal endeavor. I mean, in between fixes and noddings I could venture forth from my apartment, meet my partners, pull the caper off, and return to my pad—sometimes within fifteen minutes! New York is wall-to-wall people, sidewalks are crowded with folks doing their thing. It is a simple matter to step out four or five blocks, step in to one of a thousand or so neighborhood shops, score, and go home. People don't have the slightest idea how simple it is. . . . Other times we'd just walk out the door, find a likely place that had cash, hit it, and hole up for a few hours until the local cops changed shifts. When nobody is killed on a robbery, shift change at the station house usually kills the investigation. They got so many unsolved robberies in downtown New York they could paper the county with them. Sometimes people don't even report it when they're hit,

especially if they don't carry insurance or haven't paid it up.

After we'd been together for a while I turned my friends onto robbing connections and bookies. I figured, what the hell. The bookie's money is just as good as the grocer's. And I knew where a thousand nag parlors and numbers shops were located. Sometimes there's more money in cigar stores and shoeshine joints than in the local bank. And they bend easy. They don't want to get blown away for mere money. You can always score money in the underworld, but you only live once regardless of your game. Bookies don't like to get hit, but what can they do if they can't kill you? Can they call the cops? No. Can they spend a a lot of time looking for you if they don't know who you are? No. So they usually just mark it off and go on taking care of business. . . .

. . . Yes, it's a kick! You know, it's really a choice thrill to pull off a caper against the other underworld operator. It's like a game. It doesn't do violence to the "underworld code of honor" either, the way I figure it. It's like legitimate competition, sort of like manifest destiny or the survival of the fittest" ∎

Source: Excerpted from Richard P. Rettig, Manual J. Torres and Gerald R. Garrett, *Manny: A Criminal-Addict's Story*. Boston: Houghton Mifflin Company, 1977, pp. 59–61.

drugs, the ethnographic evidence strongly suggests that throughout much of their careers at least, criminal addicts are not driven to crime by their habits as the drugs-cause-crime hypothesis might suggest. Quite to the contrary, criminal involvement provides its own rewards in the way of a sense of accomplishment and increased stature in the subculture when one is successful in his or her criminal endeavors.

There have been a small number of ethnographic studies which have directly examined the relationship between drug use and crime. All these studies reveal that this relationship is much more complex than either "drugs-cause-crime" or the "crime-causes-drugs," or for that matter, that both drug use and crime are somehow "caused" by a common set of variables. A 1976 study of 30 recently institutionalized addicts in New York State by Smith and Stephens examined the sequence of (1) "scoring" (making money, typically through criminal means); (2) levels of drug use; and (3) subsequent criminal activity during their last month on the street (prior to their institutionalization). The authors found a total of 28 different patterns among their respondents, although most criminal/drug-using events fell into one of three patterns. The first, and most common pattern was that of an "average" score, "average" drug use, and "average" levels of subsequent criminal activity. This was the most "routine" pattern as illustrated by the following recollection of one of their respondents whom they called "Ron:"

> I was workin' seven hours everyday . . . over at this numbers hole. . . . I used to get a quarter and stretch it out over three days . . . that was enough to keep me right (i.e., to avoid withdrawal symptoms). Everyday it was pretty much the same routine. The hours were regular . . . I'd tighten up in the morning and be over there by 11 A.M., before the first drop, and stay there until 2 P.M. Then I'd leave . . . take care of myself again and be back by 5 P.M. and stay there until 9 P.M. . . . I come back later for an hour or so and then I'm finished for the day. I had enough to use what I needed if I didn't get greedy, which I didn't . . . and I had some change in my pocket too . . . to get some good shoes and things (Smith and Stephens, 1976:161).

A second dominant pattern was a "high" score, "high" drug use, followed by "low" or no criminal activity. Here, the proceeds of their scoring were so high that addicts were able to cease their criminal activity for a period of time before resuming normal "average" hustling routines. Finally, a third pattern depicts a "low" score, "low" to "average" levels of drug use, followed by "average" hustling activity. Respondents reporting this pattern generally experienced difficulty scoring, which resulted in their having to scale down their drug consumption. Because they did not have access to large amounts of drugs, they immediately commenced engaging in subsequent hustling activity.

Smith and Stephen's findings suggest first, that there is not a monotonic relationship between drug use and crime, as suggested by Anglin and Speckart. Quite to the contrary, the relationship between drug use and crime is very elastic. Indeed, Smith and Stephens go on to point out that these sequences are also affected by numerous confounding factors. Second, these findings suggest that levels of drug consumption are largely a function of available resources ("scores"), which are usually derived from criminal activities. Furthermore, when these resources are more limited, the level of drug consumption decreases accordingly. Their research thus suggests that drug use is much more elastic, and that drug users are much more capable of adjusting to lower amounts of drugs than characterized by the longitudinal studies discussed above. In this way, drug use is portrayed to be primarily a function of the level of criminal activity rather than vice versa.

Research conducted by Goldstein (1979) examining prostitution and drug use also presents a complex portrayal of the drugs–crime connection. With regard to initiation into drug use and prostitution, Goldstein found instances where drug use preceded prostitution, other instances where prostitution preceded drug use, and still others where initiation into both drug use and prostitution occurred at about the same time. Beyond the sequential relationship between drug use and prostitution, however, Goldstein finds that drug use may be related to prostitution in a number of ways. First, drug use may be *economically* related to prostitution, when women turn to prostitution to support a drug habit. Second, there may be a *psychoactive* relationship between these two behaviors, as when girls or women find themselves providing sexual services while they are in an altered state of consciousness. Third, drug use may be *functionally* related to prostitution, when, as a prostitute, women find that the use of drugs actually facilitates their prostitution. Finally, there may be a *subcultural relationship* between drug use and prostitution, when women in a drug-using subculture respond to peer pressure to engage in prostitution (or vice versa).

One final study that directly examines the relationship between drug use and criminal behavior from an ethnographic perspective is that of Faupel (1991). Similar to the earlier ethnographies, this research portrays a complex and dynamic relationship between drug use and criminal behavior. Faupel's research utilizes the conceptual framework of the career to understand various aspects of the lifestyles of heroin users, and the reader is referred to Chapter 5 for a more detailed discussion of the career framework employed in this study. Faupel maintains that the relationship between drug use and crime is variable over the course of an addict's career. Four career "phases" are identified as they relate to levels of drug availability and life structure. During the early, "occasional use" period of their careers, when drug availability is low and life structure is high, the use of drugs and criminal behavior have no causal connection with each other whatsoever. Insofar as they are related, they are both a product of a common subcultural experience. In terms of the theoretical models presented earlier in this chapter, therefore, the "common cause" or "subcultural" explanation best explains this early period of initiation into drugs and crime. As addicts move into the "stable addict" phase of their careers, drug availability increases, and both heroin and other drug consumption and criminal activity escalates dramatically. Faupel maintains, however, that this escalation of the criminal lifestyle is not in any way caused by heightened addiction. Indeed, it is quite the other way around. As young heroin-using criminals become more adept at crime, they make more money, which provides them the basis for increased drug consumption. One of the respondents in that study explained this relationship as follows:

> The better I got at crime the more money I made; the more money I made, the more drugs I used. I think that most people that get high, the reason it goes to the extent that it goes—that it becomes such a high degree of money—is because they make the money like that. I'm saying if the money wasn't available to them like that, they wouldn't be into drugs as deep as they were" (Faupel, 1991:73).

The "free-wheeling" phase of addiction, where addicts indulge in seemingly uncontrolled, hedonistic drug consumption, is also usually brought on by criminal activities, often in the form of the "big sting." This occurs when an addict makes a criminal score so big that they do not have to resort to their usual criminal routines for a period of time. Hence, with seemingly unlimited resources, and no need to engage in the daily routines of hustling, addicts easily let their habits get out of control. When this occurs, they develop a rather high tolerance for heroin that will eventually necessitate further criminal involvement. Importantly, however, the free-wheeling period itself comes about, typically, because of the unusual success that one has enjoyed as a criminal. Hence, both the stable addict and free-wheeling addict phases of addiction are most accurately characterized as "crime causes drug use."

It is when addicts reach the last "street junkie" phase of their addiction that they become desperate for drugs. Having developed a tolerance for heroin as "free-wheeling" addicts, and eventually running out of the money that permitted that level of drug use, street junkies must rely on whatever means they have available to supply them with their next fix. This is the period in an addict's career when he or she will commit desperate acts for drugs, often violating their own subcultural code of ethics, and often getting them arrested. This is the only period of an addict's career, Faupel maintains, that we can truthfully say that "drugs cause crime."

Faupel's research, like earlier ethnographies, therefore cautions us not to be overly simplistic in our understanding of the relationship between drug use and criminal behavior. This relationship is a much more complicated and dynamic one, that changes over the career of an addict.

SUMMARY

It is commonly assumed in American society that drug use causes users to commit crimes. This idea is not an entirely new one, with casual references to crime and other antisocial behavior resulting from the use of one form of drug or another appearing well prior to this century. The pervasiveness of this belief, and its reflection in public policy decisions, however, is uniquely a twentieth-century phenomenon. In this respect, compared with earlier times, twentieth-century America truly has had a "drug bugaboo."

The scholarly literature addressing the relationship between drug use and crime typically falls into three theoretically distinct categories. That literature which suggests that "drugs cause crime" is usually stated either in terms of the *pharmacological*, or psychoactive effect that drugs have on users, limiting their ability to think clearly or to control their impulses; or in terms of the *economic* demands placed on users as a result of being addicted to expensive drugs such as heroin or cocaine. A second theoretical argument is that "crime causes drugs," which suggests that only as individuals become involved in delinquent and criminal lifestyles, do they begin to participate in drug-using activities. Finally, it has been suggested that both drug use and criminal behavior are the result of a "common cause," typically involvement in a subculture which rewards these behaviors.

Social scientists have been empirically examining the relationship between drug use and crime for several decades. A number of research methodologies have been employed, including both the use of prison and arrest statistics and self-reports of drug use and crime. This research provides no conclusive evidence about *the* relationship between drug use and crime—it is much more complex than that. Studies of arrestees and prison inmates reveal that these populations are much more likely to have used drugs than the population as a whole. Interestingly, however, research that attempts to establish the sequence of initiation into drug use and crime almost invariably finds that delinquent and criminal behavior commence prior to initiation into serious drug use. Hence, in terms of *initiation* into drug use and crime, these studies, combined with the ethnographic research that has been conducted over the past 20 years, fails to support the idea that young people get hooked on drugs which forces them into a life of crime which they might otherwise avoid. Generally, the empirical research supports the idea that both drug use and crime are initiated through common subcultural associations.

The issue of initiation into drug use and crime tells only part of the story, however. We can also ask, is there a causal relationship between drug use and crime after one becomes initially involved in these behaviors? Longitudinal studies, which compare levels of criminal behavior during periods of addiction or daily use with periods of more infrequent or no use, provide very clear and convincing evidence that addicts are much more criminally active when they are using drugs on a daily basis. These studies conclude from this that as the level of one's drug consumption increases, drug use plays a causal role in criminal behavior. This interpretation has been questioned by ethnographers researching this question, however. While they agree that both drug use and crime might increase over the career of an addict, this does not necessarily mean that the increased drug use *caused* the increases in crime. Indeed, Faupel's (1991) research suggests that, in fact, throughout much of an addict's career, it is increased criminal income which facilitates increased drug use. Only when an addict has developed an uncontrollable tolerance and is without a stable means of supporting such a level of drug use, as a "street junkie," does his or her addiction actually "cause" them to commit acts of crime.

Taken as a whole, then, the empirical literature fails to exclusively support *any* of the theoretical positions described earlier in this chapter. Rather each of these descriptions accurately describes the drugs–crime connection in different ways and at different times in an addict's career. This literature further suggests that it is not possible to explain *the* relationship between drug use and crime, because there are several ways in which these two sets of behaviors are related. It might rather be appropriate to describe the relationship between *initiation into drug use and criminal behavior;* or between the *escalation of drug use and crime;* or perhaps even between the *maintenance of drug-using and criminal lifestyles.* In sum the empirical research, when taken collectively, suggests that we must move beyond a simple cause and effect understanding of the relationship between drug use and criminal behavior.

KEY TERMS

causality
correlation
disinhibition hypothesis

problem behavior
    syndrome
spurious relationship

REVIEW QUESTIONS

1. The authors open this chapter by stating that *"perhaps the greatest fear that many people have of illegal drugs is the association that these substances have with other forms of criminal behavior."* What do the authors mean by this statement? What are the perceptions that most people have regarding the association between illegal drug use and crime?

2. How have people understood the relationship between drug use and crime in prior generations and centuries? What were some of the drugs most feared? What sorts of behaviors were these drugs alleged to cause?

3. What are the two ways in which drug use might cause crime? To what types of drugs might these explanations apply?

4. How could one seriously argue that "crime causes drug use?"

5. What are some of the "common causes" of drug use and crime?

6. Describe the difference between "sequence studies" and "longitudinal studies." What can longitudinal studies tell us that sequence studies cannot?

7. How do ethnographic studies help to illuminate the causal connection between drug use and crime?

CRITICAL THINKING QUESTIONS

1. What lessons does our experience with *Reefer Madness* have for us with regard to how we should respond to allegations about the consequences of drug use?

2. Perhaps the most commonly cited reason for the "war on drugs" is that drug use causes criminal behavior. Based on the information in this chapter, what sort of a "war" on drugs would you devise in response to the connection that seems to exist between illegal drug use and criminal behavior?

SOCIETAL RESPONSES OF DRUG USE

LEGAL RESPONSES TO DRUG PROBLEMS: PROHIBITION, LEGALIZATION, AND DECRIMINALIZATION

This chapter takes a close look at the possible legal responses to drug use and abuse in the United States. As the title of this chapter suggests, there are three policy alternatives that have been discussed by scholars and researchers, policy makers, politicians, practitioners, and social commentators. These options include prohibition (or criminalization), legalization, and decriminalization. Each of these approaches to the drug problem is addressed in detail in this chapter, as well as a newly emerging, fourth policy option called "harm reduction." Despite the fact that, as the authors of this book, we have our own policy preferences, the purpose of this chapter is not to convince the reader of the advisability of one policy option over the others. Rather, we seek to discuss each of these approaches as objectively as possible, review historical experience with each, and consider the advantages and disadvantages offered by policies of prohibition, legalization, and decriminalization respectively. At the end of the chapter, and in Chapter 14, we offer our own suggestions for workable drug policies for the twenty-first century.

THE IMPORTANCE OF POLICY TO UNDERSTANDING DRUG USE IN AMERICA

You may wonder why it is important to understand these larger policy options in the first place. After all, drugs may be quite harmful to the individuals who abuse them, as well as to those around them, and to do anything other than to prohibit these dangerous substances seems not to make sense. Besides, how does understanding these larger policy questions contribute to our knowledge about why people use drugs in the first place, what kinds of people use drugs, the relationship between drug use and crime, and a host of other issues that we have already addressed in earlier chapters of this book? We contend that *all* these aspects of drug use in American society are affected by the legal and political climate in which these drugs are used.

Let us take just one set of examples that illustrate how such broad drug policies affect many aspects of drug use. Tobacco is a drug that has enjoyed widespread popularity throughout much of the twentieth century, and to this day is a legal drug in all state jurisdictions, restricted only to minors and by local ordinances prohibiting smoking in certain public places. Even then, the penalties for smoking where prohibited is minimal, despite the fact that tobacco is one of the most harmful recreational drugs used today. Because of its legal status, however, tobacco is not *perceived* to be a dangerous drug as is heroin, for example. Furthermore, because tobacco is a legal drug, it is a drug of choice across a broad spectrum of the population, including upper-, middle-, and lower-class individuals, men and women, young and old, blacks and whites. Narcotics such as heroin, on the other hand, were used more often by lower class, minority males between 18 and 35 years old throughout most of the twentieth century. This is no coincidence. This segment of the population has comparatively little stake in the conventional social order. Most do not own their own homes. Many do not have jobs, and if they are employed, it is not a high-paying professional position that offers them standing in the community at large. It is not surprising that this is the segment of the population most likely to use prohibited narcotics, which act to dull the pains of existence. Furthermore, this is the segment of the population most likely to be involved in street crime, and hence we can observe at least an apparent link between drug use and crime among those who use illegal drugs (see Chapter 10 for a lengthy discussion on this issue). This linkage is not reported among users of tobacco. Similarly, there is no "subculture" of tobacco users such as that found among heroin users. As we have seen, the highly prohibited nature of heroin is fertile ground for the development of a heroin subculture (see Chapter 5).

We are arguing, in short, that we are concerned about policy issues because we cannot fully understand all of the other aspects of drug use without knowing something about the legal and social context in which these drugs are used. Hence, in the sections that follow, we look at four broad policy approaches to drugs. The first three—*prohibition, legalization,* and *decriminalization*—have dominated discussions and debates among policy makers and practitioners throughout the twentieth century. *Harm reduction,* the final approach discussed, is a relative newcomer to the formal debate, advocating strategies that would minimize the harm resulting from drug use and society's reaction to that use.

Prohibition

Prohibition refers to a policy of "criminalization," whereby the production, manufacture, growing, sale, and/or possession of drugs are violations of one or more criminal statutes. This is the policy response to most substances that are commonly considered "drugs," including marijuana (in most states), heroin, cocaine, crack, methamphetamine, etc. Drugs that fall under a policy of prohibition, while different in their pharmacological effect, share one important feature in common: they are illegal, and those who use these drugs are potentially criminals. The primary agency of societal response to drug use under a policy of prohibition is the criminal justice system.

Mark Kleiman (1985) identifies five levels of enforcement of prohibition statutes. One approach is to reduce the amount of illegal drugs produced in the first place, a strategy known as **source reduction.** This involves a number of possible strategies, depending on the drug in question. In the case of heroin and cocaine and other drugs that are not grown or manufactured domestically, this policy involves working with other governments in eradicating drug crops. Drugs that are grown or manufactured domestically, are "source reduced" by gathering intelligence information, making arrests, and confiscating or destroying the drugs and/or drug manufacturing equipment. There is a certain logic to source reduction. Drug marketing, like most marketing strategies, is typically organized in a hierarchal, pyramid fashion, with a smaller number of actors at the top. Because there are fewer people involved at the top end of the pyramid, enforcement actions should be most effective here. However, in the case of the international drug trade, such as with heroin or cocaine, such action involves imposing on sovereign governments. In many cases, the cultivation of the poppy plant is a staple agricultural export, with many farmers growing it. One strategy of the U.S. government has been to implement crop substitution programs so as to provide an alternative source of income for local farmers. These programs have met with only limited success (Kaplan, 1983). Recent experience from Peru and Colombia suggests that the reason for resistance to course substitution by local farmers is a combination of rising prices for cocaine and the globalization of agricultural markets, which diminishes the demand for food from local farmers (Garcia, 1999; Lama, 2000). One success story is Pakistan, which, by the Pakistani governments estimates, reduced the number of hectares of poppy production from about 32,000 in 1980 to only 29 in 1999. This resulted in a decrease in opium production from about 800 tons to only 17 tons respectively. It would appear that one factor in the alleged success of Pakistan's crop substitution program is that it was accompanied by a host of other incentives and infrastructure improvements such as the building of roads to markets, the electrification of rural areas, the development of more schools and the provision of health services to rural areas (Anti-Narcotics Force, n.d.). Historically, drug crop production often pops up in a neighboring country (e.g. Afghanistan instead of Pakistan) and thus negates the effectiveness of source reduction.

A second strategy, border **interdiction** seeks to prevent illegal drugs from entering the United States after leaving the borders of producing nations. Like source reduction, interdiction is usually accomplished at the federal law enforcement level. The primary agencies involved in border intervention are the U.S. Coast Guard (at sea) and the U.S. Customs Service (at ports of entry), though other agencies such as the Immigration and Naturalization Service, the FBI, and the DEA become involved from time to time. A recent statement by the Customs Service claims seizures of more than 4,000 pounds of narcotics and $1.2 million in drug money on a typical day (Hall, 2000). For its part, the U.S. Coast Guard reported 103,000 pounds of cocaine and 102,000 pounds of marijuana seized in 1997 (U.S. Coast Guard, n.d.). The sheer volume of traffic entering the United States makes drug interdiction an extremely difficult operation. The U.S. Customs Service reports that on the Texas border alone, more than 14 million pedestrians, 34.5 million cars and trucks, and nearly 125,000 buses entering the United States from Mexico were processed by the service in 2000 (U.S. Customs, 2000). On a typical day, the Customs Service examines more than 1.3 million people coming into the United States (Hall, 2000). While their

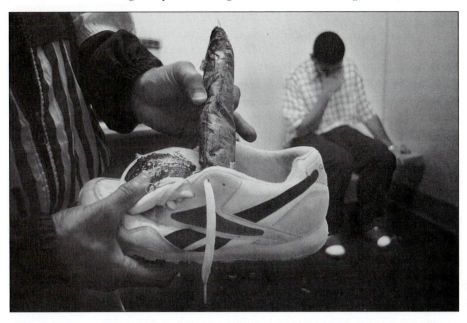

Drug interdiction involves the detainment and search of suspected drug traffickers entering the country.

seizures are impressive, these figures should make obvious the difficult challenge of stemming the flow of drugs into the United States.

A third level of enforcement is *disruption of distribution networks* of illegal substances. This strategy is targeted at high level domestic trafficking operations, and is typically carried out by the DEA and FBI. At the state and local level, comprising the fourth and fifth levels of law enforcement, agencies focus on targeting *wholesalers* (middle-level dealers in charge of large distribution rings in a city or region) and *street dealers*. In 1998, 1,559,100 drug abuse violation arrests were reported in the Uniform Crime Reports, representing nearly a 20 percent increase from 10 years earlier, and nearly 200 percent from 1980.

Street level enforcement uses a variety of tactics. One tactic involves using undercover operatives over a sustained period of time in order to eventually get to high level dealers controlling large distribution rings. The theory behind this approach is that by closing down a major distribution ring, the supply of drugs is seriously curtailed in a given area. There are problems, however. This approach is much more vulnerable to the possibility of police corruption. It is also extremely time consuming, and months or even years of undercover work may ultimately result in nothing to show for it. Moreover, even if a major operation were shut down, it is very likely that either new or existing organizations would fill the drug vacuum (Kleiman and Smith, 1990).

Because of the difficulties in going after the heads of major distribution rings, many law enforcement agencies are focusing more on street-level retail markets. Strategies vary. In some cases, merely flooding a drug-infested area with uniformed police officers can cut down on the amount of illegal drug dealing that takes place there. Police departments have long used informants to make drug buys, which are later prosecuted on the strength of their informants' testimony in court. Needless to say, problems with the truthfulness of informants and their believability in court has limited the effectiveness of this enforcement strategy. More recently, many departments have gone to a strategy known as "buy-busts," where undercover operatives or informants buy drugs from local dealers using marked money. Officers who are directly in the vicinity make an immediate arrest. This strategy is more effective because there is usually an officer who witnesses the transaction, and the marked money, which is seized at the time of the arrest verifies the officer's testimony. Still another strategy that is being used is to establish police "mini-stations" in high drug-dealing areas. This provides a greater presence of law enforcement in these areas, which is hypothesized to have a deterrent effect.

Retail level enforcement, or what Kleiman and Smith (1990) call "street sweeping" is not without problems. Perhaps most problematic is that there is great potential for abuses of authority—harassing innocent citizens, brutality in making arrests, and even the planting of evidence in order to make a bust. Moreover, because of the high demand for drugs, successful "sweeps" in one area typically result in drug operations emerging in nearby neighborhoods. This has been referred to as the "pop-up" phenomenon: suppression in one area is followed by distribution networks popping up in other areas.

Source reduction, interdiction, and street-level enforcement are all *supply-side strategies* (see Chapter 14). "Supply-side" refers to the fact that these are efforts to curtail the *supply* of drugs. Supply-side strategies have been the principal weapons of the prohibitionist policy throughout the twentieth century. In addition to these supply-side strategies, prohibitionist policies also make use of *demand-side strategies* (see Chapter 14). These strategies attempt to reduce the *demand* for drugs and include treatment and drug education programs, which may either be ordered by the courts or as an alternative to a prison sentence. These strategies are discussed in Chapters 12 and 13.

ADVANTAGES OF PROHIBITION

Prohibition has at least two important advantages over the other policy alternatives. First, it results in fewer people using substances that may be potentially very harmful to them and those around them. Second, and related to the first point, such a policy sends an important symbolic message about virtues valued by Americans, virtues such as sobriety and self-control. We examine each of these advantages in this section.

Limits the Number of Users

The rhetoric and the debate over legalization often obscures the fact that policies of prohibition do, in fact, limit the number of people who use a particular drug (Goldstein and Kalant, 1990; Inciardi and Saum, 1996). Our experience with alcohol has demonstrated the repressive effect that a policy of prohibition can have on drug use. Currently, two of every three Americans consume alcohol at a social cost that is twice that of all other illegal drug use combined. And, as Goldstein and Kalant (1990) correctly point out, many illegal drugs *are* potentially dangerous, and hence any policy that reduces the potential number of users is, on the face of it, virtuous. Citing evidence from the National Household Survey on Drug Abuse, Kleber (1994) suggests that, indeed, prohibition strategies *are* working to reduce the level of drug use in this country.

Opponents of prohibitionist policies claim that while criminalization of drugs may reduce the overall number of users and quantity of drugs consumed, these policies accomplish this at great costs to health, social well-being, and civil liberties (Nadelmann, 1988). The prohibition of alcohol, for example, while substantially lowering levels of alcohol use, gave rise to certain other social problems such extending the domain of organized crime. These concerns, which are discussed more fully below, are true, and for that reason, sober consideration of alternative policies are very important as we look to the future. Nevertheless, because of the potentially destructive effect that drug use can have on users and those around them, the advantage of reducing overall levels of drug use must not be ignored as we consider future drug policy. James Jacobs (1990, p. 41) has noted,

> The drug-legalization movement is urging us to consider the transformation of American society from an alcohol culture to a poly-drug culture in which a wide range of psychoactive drugs . . . would instantly be made the legal equivalents of alcohol. These drugs would become as widely available as alcohol and would spawn commercial industries promoting and celebrating their use. It would be as if the United States had decided to multiply its alcohol experience many times over with dozens of new drugs. The impacts of such a revolution would surely be felt in every niche of our society and culture.

This is a sobering observation that weighs in heavily as we consider the relative value of a policy of prohibition over other policy alternatives.

Reinforces Values of Sobriety and Self-Control

The second advantage of a prohibitionist policy, which is closely related to the first, is that such a policy reinforces the moral value that our culture places on sobriety and self-control. We are not talking here merely about the instrumental effect of the law on public attitudes toward drug use (which would hopefully result in fewer people using less drugs). There is, in all likelihood, a connection between public law, attitudes toward the behavior which is the object of the law, and compliance. Tyler (1990) notes that people obey the law for a variety of reasons. It may be that they simply fear the consequences of getting caught. Moreover, it may be that they accept the legitimacy of the law's authority, whether or not they believe the behavior is wrong. Or they may obey the law because of the pressure of family and peer groups whose relationship they value. Finally, many people obey the law because the law reflects their own sense of morality. Our prohibitionist drug policies perform an important *symbolic* function, the function of reinforcing deeply held values and traditional virtues that have served our society quite well over the years. Gusfield (1967) states that such laws express support for one set of norms over others. They give legitimacy to one way of life over another. Gusfield was talking about the prohibition of alcohol, but there is a valuable principle to be learned regarding nonalcohol drug laws as well. They provide a normative and institutional support structure for behaviors and lifestyles which society says that it values. The other side of that coin, of course, is that these laws lose their symbolic value and perhaps even their ability to substantially curtail behavior if they do not reflect dominant social values. Insofar as the symbolic function of prohibitionist drug laws are concerned, therefore, it would seem that an important task of social scientists and policy makers alike is to accurately assess the values and the beliefs that Americans hold with regard to the use of recreational drugs.

DISADVANTAGES OF PROHIBITION

There have been numerous critiques of American prohibitionist drug policies. Among the most often cited is a pair of articles authored by a leading advocate of drug policy reform, Ethan Nadelmann (1988, 1989). In addition to his contention that prohibitionist policies have failed, Nadelmann argues that there are serious social and economic costs to these policies which must be carefully weighed.

Costs to the Taxpayer

Nadelmann (1988) notes that between 1981 and 1987, federal expenditures for the enforcement of drug laws more than tripled, from less than a billion dollars per year to approximately 3 billion. That figure has increased to 16 billion in 1997 (Wenner and Nadelmann, 1997). The drug law enforcement agencies have received massive budgetary increases over the past 20 years. The Drug Enforcement Administration has increased its budget from $74.9 million in 1973 to more than $1.4 *billion* in 1999—a nearly 20-fold increase. Other drug enforcement agencies such as the FBI, the U.S. Marshal's Service, Coast Guard, and the U.S. Custom's Service also received hefty increases. Nadelmann (1988) estimated that the total expenditure for drug law enforcement in the United States in 1987 to be 10 billion dollars. By the mid-1990s, this figure doubled, to more than $20 billion annually (Nadelmann, 1995). In addition to the increase in budgetary allocations, the amount of effort that state and local police devote to drug enforcement has also been increasing over the years. In New York City, drug law violations accounted for more than 40 percent of all felony arrests in 1987, up from 25 percent in 1985 (Nadelmann, 1988). By 1990, drug law violations accounted for nearly 50 percent of all new commitments to state prisons in some of the more urban states such as New Jersey, New York, California and Pennsylvania (Nadelmann, 1995); and more than 60 percent of all federal prisoners are incarcerated for drug law violations (Nadelmann, 1994).

These statistics do not reveal the totality of the financial burden to American taxpayers. Due to increased arrests, court dockets become clogged creating a need for more judges, prosecutors, and in many cases more courts, including special "drug courts." Many of the defendants in these cases also require the use of public defenders, again at great cost to taxpayers. Moreover, the demand for new prisons because of prison overcrowding is at an all-time high. All of these are direct economic costs to taxpayers. Advocates of legalization argue that not only could these costs be reduced greatly if drug were to be legalized, but the government could actually reap great economic benefits through the tax revenues that could be collected from the sale of these substances. We will address this issue more fully below.

Costs in Increased Crime

We have discussed in Chapter 10 the relationship between drug use and crime. As we have seen, this relationship is a complex one that defies simple cause-effect analyses. Critics of America's prohibitionist policies reject the simplistic assumption that drugs intrinsically cause criminal and violent behavior through some sort of pharmacological mechanism. If this assumption were correct, reducing the level of drug use would automatically reduce the level of crime and violence in the United States. Critics of prohibition do, however, fall back on an equally simplistic understanding of the relationship between drug use and crime when they argue that prohibitionist policies inflate the price of drugs, thus requiring those addicted to these drugs to commit crimes to sustain their drug habits. Nadelmann (1988, p. 17) notes, for example:

> . . . many illicit-drug users commit crimes such as robbery and burglary, as well as drug dealing, prostitution, and numbers running, to earn enough money to purchase the relatively high-priced illicit drugs. Unlike the millions of alcoholics who can support their habits for relatively modest amounts, many cocaine and heroin addicts spend hundreds and even thousands of dollars a week. If the drugs to which they are addicted were significantly cheaper—which would be the case if they were legalized—the number of crimes committed by drug addicts to pay for their habits would, in all likelihood, decline dramatically.

We have seen in Chapter 10, however, that drug users do not necessarily engage in higher levels of crime because of an increase in either the level of their use or in the price of their drugs. Most addicts begin their criminal careers before they become involved in expensive drugs, and frequently expand their criminal activity before their drug consumption picks up. Furthermore, it is not uncommon for drug users to lower their drug consumption at least temporarily to accommodate to lower levels of availability. In short, drug consumption is not as *inelastic* as Nadelmann's argument implies, but varies greatly both up and down as drugs become more or less available.

There are two connections between drug use and crime, however, which *are* directly linked to prohibitionist policies. The first of these is definitional, namely, the buying, selling, and possessing of illegal substances themselves.

Because these activities are defined as criminal under prohibitionist policies, these policies can be said to literally cause the crime. This is not to say that the policies cause the *behavior* (i.e., buying or selling of drugs); but the buying or selling of drugs is a *crime* directly because of the policy. Hence, by criminalizing drugs, we automatically increase the level of crime in a society. This is significant, because much of the taxpayer expenditure for drug-related crimes is precisely for these crimes by definition. As a result, the criminal justice system is required to process drug offenders, placing a heavy burden on overloaded courts and correctional systems.

A second linkage directly resulting from prohibitionist policies is what Goldstein (1985) referred to as *systemic* violence, resulting from the operation of illegal drug markets. Systemic criminal acts involve such things as disputes over territories between rival drug dealers; punishment for failing to come good on a debt; retaliation for selling adulterated drugs; the intimidation or elimination of informers; or the robbery of dealers who may have sold "short" (less than the full amount) or diluted drugs. All these are crimes virtually unheard of in legitimate markets. The reason is because there are other legal courses of action that parties can take if they have been treated unjustly in a financial transaction. One can file suit in a small claims court, notify the Better Business Bureau, or seek legal injunctions on competitors violating franchise boundaries. None of these mechanisms is available to dealers and consumers of illegal drugs (or any other illegal product or service) *precisely because they are illegal.* While these sorts of crime do not comprise even close to a majority of all drug-related crimes, they are not insignificant. These crimes are a true "cost" of our current "war on drugs" in that they are directly a result of prohibitionist drug policy.

Costs of Corruption

Police officers responsible for narcotics law enforcement are particularly vulnerable to corruption. This is so for a couple of reasons. First, violation of narcotics laws, particularly when it involves large amounts of expensive drugs such as heroin and cocaine, carries with it very severe sanctions. Drug dealers have a large incentive to bribe narcotics officers handsomely to look the other way. Second, because of the high profit margins that drug dealers enjoy, they can afford to pay off officials who might stand in their way. Finally, both drug dealing and bribery are offenses which are covert, with little incentive to report the crime. Therefore, narcotics officials can be "on the take" with virtual impunity (Barnett, 1987; Nadelmann, 1988). Even most idealistic individuals are corruptible given the amounts of money that are involved.

Costs to Public Health

The prohibition of drugs poses certain public health risks both to addicts and to the rest of society. Prohibitionist policies create risks to users and addicts in several ways. First, because possession of drugs with intent to deliver is a serious offense, distributors and manufacturers are motivated to produce and distribute drugs which are highly concentrated, taking up less bulk thereby reducing the visibility of their trafficking (Nadelmann, 1995). It has been argued that this factor is largely accountable for the shift from less potent opium smoking to more potent and potentially toxic injectable drugs. Furthermore, because prohibitionist policies effectively render the government impotent to regulate and monitor drug quality, addicts really do not know what they are getting in terms of the purity and potency of street drugs; drug concentration and potential contaminants are not consistent. In addition, many states also prohibit the possession of needles and syringes which are the "works" required to inject drugs. This has resulted in an addict using the same needles over and over again, and also to "needle sharing" with other addicts. Indeed, entrepreneurial drug dealers have learned that they can make a good profit on renting needles, often as part of a larger "shooting gallery" operation where addicts come to get out of sight of the police while they inject their drugs (Inciardi et al., 1995; Murphy and Waldorf, 1991). This phenomenon has led to widespread hepatitis-B among IV drug users, and more recently, the spread of HIV (Human Immuno-suppressant Virus) leading to Acquired Immuno-Deficiency Syndrome (AIDS). The spread of HIV and AIDS could be dramatically curtailed among IV drug users with the ready availability and utilization of clean works.

The public health threat is not limited to current addicts. Sexual partners of infected addicts are directly exposed to hepatitis and HIV, and to a lesser extent children and others living in their household might also be affected. The public health is also threatened through the crimes, particularly violent crimes, that addicts might perpetrate against them. Still another health casualty of prohibition policies are those who have legitimate medical needs that Schedule I drugs might provide. The medical benefits of marijuana are increasingly accepted by individual medical practitioners, if not by major medical associations such as the American Cancer Society (Schwartz and Sheridan, 1997). Yet, in most places, patients cannot obtain these drugs legally. Terminal patients often have difficulty obtaining adequate prescriptions for morphine and other narcotic analgesics because of fears by doctors that they will be perceived as feeding an addiction. While it is technically legal to prescribe these drugs in such situations, our prohibitionist attitude creates an atmosphere of suspicion upon doctors who prescribe large amounts of narcotics to their patients. Cocaine is also an effective anesthetic in dealing with acute pain yet is effectively precluded under current policy.

Good drug education is another casualty of our current policies. There is a wealth of public health information that is not made available to would-be drug users. Drug education programs are limited in the kinds of information they can convey under a policy of prohibition. The only acceptable content is "abstain." There are those who are reached by these messages, and we do not dispute that our current drug education programs may be effective in convincing *some youngsters* not to use drugs. Those young people who choose to experiment with drugs despite this admonition, however, have no authoritative guidelines for "responsible" experimentation. Such individuals are left with nothing but the informal knowledge and wisdom of peers as they embark on their pharmacological journeys. This is, of course, a controversial issue because many believe that such information may actually encourage or at least lend symbolic support to drug use as a way of life (refer to earlier discussion). These concerns are part of the balancing act required in identifying what sort of drug policy we want for the twenty-first century.

Costs to Civil Liberties

Critics of prohibition suggest that the assault on civil liberties may be the greatest cost associated with prohibition (Nadelmann, 1988, 1989; Wisotsky, 1986). The use of wiretapping and other forms of technological surveillance, compulsory drug testing, and forcible entering of suspected drug dealers' homes are some of the many ways in which the privacy of citizens is threatened. Police are pressured to make busts, which results in unreasonable searches and seizures of innocent persons and their homes (Barnett, 1987). More than 73 percent of the 1,186 court authorized wiretaps in 1997 were for suspected narcotics violations—a percentage that has been creeping up through the years (Bureau of Justice Statistics, 1997, p. 376). Wisotsky (1986), in an especially probing look at drug legislation, identifies many of the sources of attack on civil liberties. Among these include the Comprehensive Crime Control Act of 1984, which effectively denied bail to drug defendants on a finding by a judge that the defendant posed a danger to the community—a finding that could be applied even to drug dealing. There has also been a loosening of the exclusionary rule for drug cases. Wisotsky discusses how search and seizure procedures have been interpreted to get around otherwise constrictive exclusionary rule requirements:

> The law does not regard the dog's sniffing as the equivalent of a search on the theory that the odor of contraband is an exterior olfactory clue in the public domain. As a result of this theory, no right of privacy is invaded by the sniff, so the police do not need a search warrant or even probable cause to use the dog on a citizen. If the dog alerts, moreover, that fulfills the probable cause requirement, and the police may then search the driver or vehicle for drugs (Wisotsky, 1986, p. 128).

The prohibitionist war on drugs has challenged heretofore protected liberties in other ways as well. Recently, we have witnessed an increase in the use of "profiling," the practice of selectively detaining automobiles and drivers who fit a "profile" of a typical drug runner. This is a proactive law enforcement effort that attempts to more systematically interdict shipments of drugs enroute to their destinations after they have entered this country. Unfortunately, the typical "profile" involves being black and male, a fact that has resulted in an observation that it is not safe to be "driving while black" (a word play on the charge "driving while intoxicated"). One writer has charged that this practice has resulted in "the Fourth Amendment's death on the highway" (Harris, 1998). Most of those stopped because of profiling have no contraband in their possession, resulting in great numbers of innocent citizens—disproportionately those of color—being inconvenienced and subjected to the humiliating experience of being detained for possible drug law violations.

DRUGS AND EVERYDAY LIFE

Two Pertinent Policy Debates

Drug Profiling

Drug profiling, more commonly known as "racial profiling" is one of the more aggressive strategies that has been implemented in the war on drugs. Profiling is a practice that targets *potential* drug traffickers moving drugs from one geographical area to another. Law enforcement personnel look for certain profile characteristics of drivers, especially along certain interstate highways, which are consistent with profiles that have been developed of "typical" drug couriers. The initial profile issued by the Florida Department of Highway Safety and Motor Vehicles, for example, alerted officers to watch for rental cars, overly scrupulous observance of traffic laws, drivers who do not "fit the vehicle," excessive jewelry, etc. An additional criterion was ethnicity (Harris, 1999). This criterion, while no longer formally identified, is believed to still be a major criterion for identification of potential drug couriers—a contention that has been at the heart of a major debate over the discriminatory use of this method of drug enforcement.

Beginnings   The practice of profiling began in the early 1970s when DEA agent Paul Markonni was assigned drug surveillance duty at the Detroit Metropolitan Airport. He developed a list of primarily behavioral attributes, such as nervousness, paying for airplane tickets with cash, dubious destinations, etc. Markonni's profile was soon adopted at airports across the country. Profiling along the nation's highways did not systematically begin, however, until 1984, when the DEA launched "Operation Pipeline," a nationwide interdiction program that focuses on private automobiles. State police agencies in New Mexico and New Jersey had already established their own highway interdiction programs with huge payoffs in terms of drug

seizures. The DEA's program nationalized these efforts. A second, corollary effort called "Operation Convoy" was launched in 1990. Operation Convoy has the same goals as Operation Pipeline, but focuses on commercial vehicles, such as 18-wheel trucks. (Drug Enforcement Administration, n.d.).

Procedure and Legal Issues   When a law enforcement officer identifies a vehicle and/or driver who fits the "profile," he or she must have a "pretext" for stopping a motorist. This pretext is usually a minor violation such as a speeding violation, not wearing a seatbelt, wavering over the centerline, etc. Such pretexts provide an officer an opportunity to examine a vehicle and its occupants more closely. If, upon closer examination, the officer finds probable cause for a full search, he or she may do so. The use of these pretexts has been at the heart of the legal debate, because, it is argued, they are selectively used against ethnic minorities.

The legal basis for such pretext stops goes all the way back to 1968 when the Supreme Court ruled, in *Terry* v. *Ohio* that search and seizure was legal without probable cause. The contraints imposed by the *Terry* ruling were somewhat restrictive, but over time, the courts have become ever more lax in their interpretation of this ruling (Harris, 1994). A more recent Supreme Court ruling, which bears directly on the issue of pretext stops is *Whren* v. *United States*. The Supreme Court unanimously agreed in *Whren* that when an officer witnesses a traffic offense, nothing more is necessary to establish probable cause for a stop. While *Whren* did not justify further intrusion, it did allow law enforcement to make traffic stops on the most minor of offenses, thereby allowing officers to detain a suspect and acquire further information which might constitute probable cause for vehicle

continued

continued from previous page

searches. *Whren* was followed shortly by two other Supreme Court Cases: *Ohio v. Robinette* and *Maryland v. Wilson*. These two cases, together, established the legitimacy of voluntary searches and involuntary searches of the person of the driver following a routine traffic stop (Harris, 1998).

These cases provide the legal grounds for pretext stopping, which is absolutely central to Operations Pipeline and Convoy. The practice has raised a firestorm of legal controversy, however, regarding both the Fourth and Fourteenth Amendments. The Fourth Amendment's protections against unreasonable searches and seizures should be clear. The Fourteenth Amendment's guarantees against denying any person equal protection under the law is underscored by studies showing an overwhelming percentage of traffic searches being of vehicles driven by minorities, despite evidence that nonminorities are at least as likely to be involved in targeted activities (Harris, 1999). The Justice Department defends these activities, not only on legal grounds, but as a practical matter, reporting nearly 125,000 kilograms of cocaine seizures alone since 1986.

The Future of Drug Profiling   Operation Pipeline has been a highly effective law enforcement tool against the traffic in drugs. As long as drug use remains such a high issue of concern among Americans, profiling and pretext traffic stops are likely to continue. Recent Gallup Poll information suggest that while both blacks and whites disapprove of the idea of racial profiling (making stops on the basis of race as the primary profile element), there is a sharp divide between these two groups as to their approval rating of state and local police. Even among blacks, however, more than 50 percent report high approval of law enforcement (Gallup, 2000). The courts have established a firm legal footing for this practice, though the racially based pretext stops are likely to be challenged even more strongly in the coming years as concern over racial discrimination is becoming more widespread. This problem has

been especially highlighted in New Jersey in recent years where, in a state that is 74 percent white, blacks and Hispanics accounted for more than 77 percent of highway searches, typically accompanied by aggressive treatment (Martello, 1999).

Asset Forfeiture

A relatively recent tool used by both federal and state governments in their war against drugs is the forfeiture of assets related to drug enterprises. Assets that can be seized fall into four broad categories:

- *Contraband*—illegal substances themselves, such as drugs or illegal firearms
- *Derivative contraband*—conveyances used for transporting contraband, including airplanes, boats, and road vehicles
- *Direct proceeds*—typically cash, but could include other material goods that are exchanged for drugs
- *Derivative proceeds*—those goods which are purchased by direct proceeds, including stocks, real estate and other items of real value

Seizure of assets falling into the above categories can be accomplished either through *criminal* or *civil* proceedings. Criminal proceedings require that the party first be found guilty in a court of law; civil proceedings require much less burden of proof, merely a preponderance of evidence that a defendant acquired the property during or shortly after the commission of an offense and that there is no other likely source for the property other than a criminal violation (Abadinsky, 1993).

Legal Basis for Forfeiture   The legal grounds for the forfeiture of assets are found in a series of six statutes that date to 1970:

- *Controlled Substances Act (CSA), 1970*—This act, which was part of the Comprehensive Drug Abuse and Control Act of 1970, provides for the forfeiture of assets that are directly involved in the drug trade—vehicles,

continued

continued from previous page

equipment, and raw materials (substance, and materials used to manufacture it) (Evans, 1996).

- *Racketeer Influenced and Corrupt Organizations Act (RICO), 1970*—A very broadly defined act that was originally targeted to combat organized crime. RICO references 24 federal and 8 state felony crimes, and stipulates that anyone who has been found guilty of two or more of these crimes within a 10-year period has undertaken a "pattern" of racketeering. Dombrink and Meeker, 1985, 1986) Once racketeering is established, forfeiture of assets is possible under the Comprehensive Forfeiture Act (below).

- *Continuing Criminal Enterprise Act (CCE), 1970*—A counterpart to RICO, focuses specifically on patterned violation of federal drug statutes. Once such a pattern is established, substantial prison sentences, fines, and forfeiture of profits obtained in the enterprise can be invoked (Dombrink and Meeker, 1985, 1986).

- *Bank Secrecy Act (BSA), 1970*—Requires banks and other financial institutions to keep records and report on all monetary transactions of $10,000 or more. This makes it easier to identify profits for forfeiture (Evans, 1996).

- *Comprehensive Forfeiture Act (CFA), 1984*— Clearly established that an individual's gains from racketeering were forfeitable, and specified that real property could be forfeited. Also amended the CSA to include all felony drug offenses (Presidents Commission on Organized Crime, 1986).

- *Money Laundering Control Act (MLCA), 1986*—Included a provision for both criminal and civil forfeiture proceedings (Evans, 1996).

Taken together, these statutes provide very broad powers to prosecute drug distribution activities as *organized enterprises* of illegal

activity, and in so doing, the statutes are able to seriously affect the profitability of these enterprises by forfeiting the profits of these activities. There are, however, concerns over the use of these statutes which must also be weighted.

Concerns About Forfeiture Procedures   The power of the government to seize assets comes as a mixed blessing at best. While these statutes have allowed federal and state governments to seriously affect drug distribution enterprises, this ability also comes at great costs socially. All that is needed is "probable cause" to begin forfeiture proceedings—the same level of evidence required to make a simple arrest (Dombrink and Meeker, 1986). Because eligible assets now include proceeds and derivative proceeds from stated illegal acts, there is a great deal of incentive for local law enforcement to initiate these procedures. Asset forfeiture is, for many law enforcement agencies, a lucrative way of enhancing funding for their departments without the political costs associated with budgetary and tax increases (Abadinsky, 1993).

Most alarming, however, is the potential victimization of innocent third parties. A child who uses a parent's car to make a drug deal, for example, is putting his parents at risk for losing their car—even if they did not know what their car was being used for. Similarly, a grandmother runs the risk of having her home seized if she provides haven for her grandson who is dealing drugs—even if she is not aware of his activities. Once forfeited, the burden of proof is on the individual whose assets have been seized to prove his or her innocence. How does one prove their lack of knowledge in these cases? It is, in fact, difficult to do so, and the only recourse is to hire attorneys to fight the forfeitures in court. Most individuals do not have the resources to prove their innocence without creating great hardship for themselves and their families. The effect is a presumption of *guilt* rather than innocence ∎

Prohibitionist policies have also created costs to our civil liberties through the Comprehensive Forfeiture Act (CFA) that allows officials to seize all assets related to a drug enterprise, including contraband, tools to facilitate transport and promotion of contraband (e.g., automobiles and aircraft), and both direct and indirect proceeds of drug enterprises. The intent of these statutes is to make it truly costly for drug dealers and distributors to operate. Normally, assets seized are cash and automobiles, but personal items and even homes have been seized under the CFA alleging them as indirect proceeds. These assets are normally retained by local law enforcement agencies, which provides an incentive for departments to seize property with only a minimal level of evidence that these are contraband or proceeds of drug trafficking. There have been numerous allegations of innocent third parties having their property seized under this statute. Once the property is seized, it then becomes the responsibility of the alleged conspirator to prove his or her innocence in order to get their property returned. Clearly, this is a reversal of the normal presumption of innocence.

Eric Sterling, President of the Criminal Justice Policy Foundation, broadly charges that the war on drugs challenges civil liberties. In remarks delivered before the Colorado Bar Association, Sterling charged that the war on drugs has eroded the Thirteenth and Fourteenth Amendments as well all the first ten Amendments that comprise the Bill of Rights (Sterling, 1990). Some of his arguments might seem a slight stretch, but there is an eerie discomfort with the truth of what Sterling is saying, namely that constitutionally guaranteed rights and liberties are taking second place to our massive concern with repressing drug use and distribution.

There are clearly benefits to maintaining a policy of prohibition. Some of these are real, measurable benefits, such as minimizing the number of people who use potentially dangerous substances. There are also significant benefits which cannot be directly measured, for example, the benefit of an unequivocal statement regarding the value that our culture places on sobriety and drug-free lifestyles. There are, however, sobering costs to what many have called the great American "experiment" with drug prohibition. These costs are not trivial; they challenge some of our core values of privacy, health, and even law and order itself. These costs demand a sober look at alternatives to our current policies of prohibition. We turn to those alternatives now.

LEGALIZATION

The second major policy alternative is **legalization.** Legalization involves the lifting of all criminal and civil prohibitions and sanctions. Legalized drugs become commodities that are available in the legitimate marketplace, whether through prescription, through private or state-run specialty outlets, or generally over the counter. Legalization is often presented as synonymous with decriminalization, but these are two very distinct policy approaches and we keep them separate here. (A discussion of decriminalization follows the assessment of legalization.)

Legalization itself is not a unitary policy option. Indeed, one of the criticisms of legalization is that it is not always clear what advocates of this policy option mean by the term. The impetus for legalization comes primarily from two sources: civil libertarians and public health advocates. We have recently seen a number of high-profile political and public figures advocate a policy of legalization. Each has their own personal reasons, of course, but their *reasoning* is generally out of concern for *either* civil liberties *or* public health (usually not both). We see, on the one hand, figures such as conservative talk show host William Buckley and conservative economist Milton Friedman advocate a policy of legalization based largely on civil libertarian grounds. Their concern is with the inappropriate interference of government into the affairs of private citizens. Others, such as George Schultz, former Secretary of State under Ronald Reagan, Baltimore Mayor Curt Schmoke, and Gary Johnson, current governor of New Mexico, have advocated a policy of legalization because it allows for *greater* government control in the way of quality oversight to help ensure that the public health is not as jeapordized. Legalization is a policy position which clearly unites people with very different political and social goals. It should come as no surprise, that the kind of legalization policy proposed by these two groups will be very different. Hence, it is worthwhile, before discussing the benefits and costs of legalization, to briefly describe some of the models that have been put forth. It should be noted that all models that have been seriously proposed would allow access only to adults. These approaches to legalization are *laissez faire model*, *limited distribution model*, and *medical model* respectively.

LAISSEZ FAIRE MODEL

This is the most extreme of all models proposed for legalization. This approach to drug legalization most closely resembles the way in which tobacco is distributed today. Drugs would be available through a variety of outlets, including drug stores, grocery stores, vending machines in restaurants, etc. Minors would be prohibited from purchasing drugs, but if our experience with the sale of tobacco products is any indication, this prohibition would be almost impossible to enforce.

The *laissez faire* model is the one most strongly advocated by civil libertarians. These voices base their position on their understanding of human nature and of the founding political principles of the United States. Civil libertarians generally believe that human beings are blessed with the gift of free choice and rational decision making. Indeed, they point out that our criminal justice system itself is based on this understanding of human nature. The notion of *mens rea*, for example, implies the freedom to choose between right and wrong. Steven Wisotsky, who argues primarily from a civil libertarian base, suggests that the current direction of prohibitionist drug policies totally ignores this premise:

> The impasse in the War on Drugs thus finds its anchor in this unexamined, unconscious denigration of the human capacity for responsible choice and self-control in the matter of drugs and consciousness. Ironically, that meta-conception violates the fundamental moral premise of our political, economic, and legal systems: that the individual is competent to order his life, to vote, to manage his own affairs and be responsible for whatever results he produces in life (Wisotsky, 1988, p. 201).

This understanding of human nature is closely linked with a *laissez faire* political philosophy that is committed to preserving the freedom of individual choice. An architect of this philosophy was John Stuart Mill, whose position on this issue was nearly absolute:

> The only purpose for which power can be rightfully exercised over any member of a civilized community, against his will, is to prevent harm to others. His own good, either physical or moral, is not a sufficient warrant. He cannot rightfully be compelled to do or forebear because it will be better for him to do, because it will make him happier, because, in the opinions of others, to do so would be wise, or even right (Mill, 1956, p. 13; cited in Kaplan, 1983, pp. 103–104).

The *laissez faire* model, in its most pure and uncompromising form, proposes no restriction on the sale and availability of any form of substance, with the exception of restricting access to children. The model is one of unrestrained, free-market capitalism. While philosophically compelling to some, it is a model that is not taken seriously by most practitioners and lobbyists who are working to take practical steps toward legalization, or at least away from current repressive prohibitionist policies.

LIMITED DISTRIBUTION MODEL

This model is a variant of the *laissez faire* model. Like *laissez faire* advocates, proponents of limited access advocate free access to mind-altering substances for those legitimately entitled to such access, namely adults who are not impaired in their ability to make rational decisions. The major difference between those who advocate *laissez faire* and those who advocate limited access is in the concern and emphasis placed on preventing *unwarranted* access to drugs, particularly in limiting access to children. For this reason, limited access advocates propose carefully regulated sales either through government outlets (similar to state run alcohol stores), or through private outlets with special licenses and subject to close government regulation and monitoring. The closest model that we have to a limited distribution approach are state-run liquor stores and gambling enterprises (Jacobs, 1990). Jacobs points out that there is very little difference between these operations and private retail outlets except that prices are higher, hours are shorter, and (in the case of gambling) the odds are stacked more favorably for the house. It is questionable how effective a limited distribution model would be in limiting access to objectionable sectors of the population.

MEDICAL MODEL

This model is the most restrictive of the three legalization models. Essentially, a medical maintenance approach to legalization calls for the legalized distribution of drugs to either (1) persons with medical conditions which could benefit medically from currently prohibited drugs; and/or (2) current addicts for purposes of eliminating withdrawal symptoms. Most proponents of the medical model focus on the legal distribution of maintenance dosages to addicts. Since we have discussed the medical use of certain drugs, particularly marijuana, in Chapter 8, our focus here will be on medical maintenance. Proponents of this model call for drugs to be distributed through physicians or medical clinics, and addicts would be monitored in much the same way as a patient receiving any other kind of medication. They would be required to come into the clinic or doctor's office where they would be questioned and perhaps provide urine and/or blood samples before having their prescriptions continued.

Proponents of medical maintenance look to the British model for maintaining addicts. When the Harrison Act was passed in the United States in 1914, the British passed a similar act, the Dangerous Drugs Act, which essentially limited the distribution of narcotic drugs to physicians and other medical personnel such as pharmacists. The Harrison Act stated that narcotics could be supplied to patients only "if in the practice of his profession;" the British allowed physicians to dispense "So far only as is necessary for the practice of his profession" (cited in Kaplan, 1983, p. 156). These qualifying phrases are responsible for the differences in how the British and American systems evolved. In the United States, Supreme Court decisions subsequent to the Harrison Act effectively ruled that the prescription of narcotics to addicts for purposes of maintenance was *not* in accord with "in the practice of his profession." Hence, by the mid-1920s, addict maintenance was illegal except for the use of morphine at the Federal Public Health Service Hospitals in Lexington, Fort Worth, and other select clinics across the country. Britain, however, never interpreted its legislation in the same restrictive sense, and physicians were free to prescribe heroin and other narcotics to addicts that came through their offices. In effect, Great Britain approached the issue of addiction as primarily a *medical* problem requiring medical solutions, while the United States approached it primarily as a *criminal* matter.

The British model worked well throughout much of the twentieth century. Among social scientists, an early American proponent of the British model was Edwin Schur, who noted in 1965 that addiction in Great Britain was "remarkably benign" (p. 154). Schur went on to say that there were less than a thousand addicts in all of Britain, and that there was almost no illicit trafficking in narcotics because addicts were not only able to obtain them legally, but could purchase them at very low cost because these drugs are subsidized under the National Health Service. These early reports have led to a great deal of support for a similar system in the United States. Critics and other observers have pointed out, however, that since the time that Schur was writing, the situation has changed dramatically in Britain. Indeed, Britain has all but abandoned this system of narcotics distribution. When it began, those who were being treated in the British clinics and doctor's offices were primarily middle-class addicts who became addicted while being treated for pain. However, as awareness of the availability of heroin in Britain became more widely known, it attracted more individuals who were committed to the use of heroin for pleasure, and it was not long before doctors and clinics were overwhelmed with requests for narcotics, much of which was later diverted to other subcultural users (Kaplan, 1983). Kaplan points out that between 1961 and 1969, the number of addicts in Britain increased by at least 500 percent, and more importantly, the *kind* of addict changed from the primarily middle class, medically induced addict to younger, less stable addict. The results of these changes were severe restrictions on heroin distribution, and the withdrawal of power from most private physicians from prescribing heroin at all (Kaplan, 1983). The British model did not, according to critics, work in Britain and we should not expect it to work here either. Moreover, Jacobs (1990) points out that even if it were an effective policy here, its effectiveness is restricted to heroin and the narcotics. Control of drugs such as cocaine and crack, LSD, methamphetamines, marijuana, and many other drugs of concern would not benefit from such a model. These are recreational drugs usually taken for the pleasure of effect rather than avoidance of withdrawal symptoms, because they are not "addicting" in the classical sense of producing physical tolerance. There is no "maintenance dose" for most of these drugs, and it is not even appropriate to talk about "medical maintenance" for anything other than narcotics, according to Jacobs.

Advantages of Legalization

Most of the benefits of legalization are legalization advocates' answers to the *costs* of prohibition. The advantages of legalization are generally stated in terms of *economic benefits, moral benefits*, and *public health benefits*.

Economic Benefits

Advocates of legalization point to the dramatically escalating economic costs of a prohibitionist policy which is, by most standards, not working very well. We have already discussed the 16-fold increase in taxpayer dollars being spent on supply-side efforts to curb the availability of drugs in this country—an increase from about $1 billion per year in 1981 to about

$16 billion annually in 1997 (Wenner and Nadelmann, 1997). This is money that could be used much more productively, according to legalization advocates such as Nadelmann (1988). Beyond the money that is saved, a policy of legalization also allows for *taxation* of drugs, in much the same way that alcohol and tobacco are taxed today. Hence, rather than spending billions of dollars annually to curtail drug importation and distribution, federal, state, and local governments could be the beneficiary of stronger tax bases. Treatment and drug-education programs could be the beneficiary of much of this money, thereby focusing on *demand reduction* and recognizing drug use and addiction as a medical issue requiring education and treatment rather than punishment.

Moral Benefits

We use the term "moral benefits" in its broadest sense to refer to the answers legalization provides to the moral dilemmas posed by prohibition. One of the dilemmas that we have already discussed is the widespread corruption that we observe among police officers in narcotics units. Legalization should reduce the level of police corruption considerably. In the first place, the underground market that creates the need for corrupt officials, should be substantially reduced. Moreover, legal drug enterprises do not require corruption of officials to operate profitably. The expectation of legalization proponents is that for both of these reasons, corruption would not be a major issue if drugs were made legal.

Another moral dilemma created by our current system of prohibition is the *hypocrisy* of a policy that heavily penalizes the possession and use of some drugs (e.g., marijuana) while other drugs that are by just about any standard more socially and personally harmful (e.g., alcohol and tobacco) are permitted and even promoted. Such an inconsistent policy sends out mixed and confusing messages to children and young people. There comes a time for many, if not most, young people watching their parents use alcohol, tobacco, and prescription drugs, to reject the legal distinction as an irelevant *moral* distinction in the choices that they make.

This reality suggests another difficulty with current policy that could at least potentially be answered by legalization; that is the inability to reach young people who have already made the decision to use drugs. Drug education must be an "all or nothing" proposition under a policy of prohibition. "Drugs are bad. You shouldn't use them. Here are the reasons why." That is the only message that can be communicated. Ethan Nadelmann states with regard to current marijuana policies,

> It's still impossible . . . for any government official to speak out publicly about
> the difference between responsible and irresponsible use of marijuana, as they
> would with alcohol. All marijuana use is defined as drug abuse—notwithstanding
> extensive evidence that most marijuana users suffer little if any harm. That
> position may be intellectually and scientifically indefensible, but those in
> government regard it as politically and legally obligatory (Nadelmann, 1997,
> p. 51)

Young people who experiment with drugs and discover that the effects prophesied did not take place are likely to reject any future efforts to educate them by anyone in authority. Moreover, for those who have already rejected this message, there are no moral or practical guidelines for their drug use. If we were to legalize drugs, educators would have a much wider variety of options for reaching current users. We are using such an approach with alcohol with messages such as "Friends don't let friends drive drunk." The message is that *if you are going to drink,* at least don't drink and drive. The opportunity for moral and practical influence greatly expands when drugs are legalized.

The other "moral benefit" of a policy of legalization is the potential restoration of civil liberties that have been seriously imperiled by our expanding war on drugs. These threats have been discussed at length in the earlier section on prohibition. While it is anticipated that legalization will not eradicate entirely the underground market for drugs, and hence will not completely eliminate the need for repressive law enforcement strategies, such a policy should certainly *reduce* the threats to civil liberties that we now experience.

Public Health Benefits

The public health benefits to a policy of legalization come in several forms. First, only through a policy of legalization can the government truly regulate the quality of drugs distributed. Many of the toxic reactions to drugs are the result of either wide variations in the purity of the drug distributed, or the use of toxic materials to dilute the drugs. Marijuana, for example, can be laced with "angel dust" (PCP) and other potent substances like embalming fluid (a combination known as "fry"). If the user is unaware of this, severe reactions could result (Nadelmann, 1989). Similarly, while heroin is usually diluted with milk sugar and perhaps quinine—both inert substances—dealers have been known to "cut" their drugs with strychnine and even rat poisoning which can produce toxic and even fatal effects. Additionally, legalization provides a much firmer basis for the distribution of clean needles, thereby substantially reducing the risk of contracting the HIV and hepatitis viruses. The Lindesmith Center (1997) reports that approximately 36 percent of all AIDS cases in the United States and a majority of cases of HIV-infected heterosexuals, children, and infants are believed to have been contracted through illegal IV drug use. A third public health benefit provided by a policy of legalization is that access to certain drugs for medical uses will be enhanced. While certainly, it is possible to make exceptions to general prohibition policies for medical use of certain drugs such as marijuana as a treatment for glaucoma or nausea related to chemotherapy for cancer, the reality is that there is great resistance to these exceptions. It is difficult for glaucoma or cancer patients to gain legal access to marijuana. It is virtually impossible to access cocaine for anaesthetic purposes, and doctors are extremely hesitant to prescribe narcotic medications for at-home pain relief even though such drugs are often called for. We will address these issues later in this chapter, but suffice it to acknowledge here, a general policy of legalization would provide avenues for medical treatment not now easily available. A final benefit of legalization, which is more indirect, is that it squarely defines addiction as a *medical* issue, and provides the political base to support a stronger effort at treatment and drug education. While both drug treatment and drug education have been given some attention under our current prohibition policy, there are serious constraints on their effectiveness. The United States has never *seriously* waged a treatment and education campaign, at least not with the same degree of commitment that we have waged supply-side efforts of law enforcement.

DISADVANTAGES OF LEGALIZATION

Opponents of legalization have challenged the proposed benefits of legalization, and have identified additional problems with a policy of legalization as set forth by legalization champions. Other than government officials such as former drug czars William Bennett and General Barry McCaffrey and current drug czar John Walters, there has been perhaps no more outspoken critic of legalization than James A. Inciardi, Director of the University of Delaware's Center for Drug and Alcohol Studies. Inciardi has identified numerous problem areas with drug legalization that we highlight here.

Insufficient Development of Legalization Proposals

Perhaps the greatest criticism that Inciardi and others level at legalization advocates such as Ethan Nadelmann is that they have not really provided us with meaningful legalization proposals at all (Inciardi and McBride, 1989, 1990; Jacobs, 1990). These critics point to many areas of insufficient policy development in the legalization agenda. First, it is not clear as to whether *all* or just *some* drugs should be legalized; and if just some, *which* drugs should be made legal? What potency limits should be established? What about minimum age limits? What type of distribution model should be established—a *laissez faire*, limited access, or medical maintenance model? Where could the drugs be sold—in supermarkets? For on-premises uses such as alcohol is in bars? What about cultivation, and where would it take place? Should advertising be permitted? These are but a few of the questions that need to be answered in a well-conceived proposal for legalization. In the absence of these details, legalization is not worthy of serious policy consideration according to critics.

Increased Use and Public Health Costs

It is almost certain that legalization would result in an increase in the use of those drugs legalized. While some advocates of legalization have

questioned this likelihood, both our historical experience with alcohol prohibition (and its lifting) and the logic of classical economics would affirm
this assumption. Even a massive increase in drug consumption would not
be of particular concern if drugs were, in fact, benign substances that did
no harm to the user or those around him or her. However, not even the
most ardent supporters of legalization make the claim that drugs are completely harmless. Even marijuana, once considered virtually harmless, especially when compared with tobacco, is now recognized as containing
hundreds of chemicals, many of which have unknown or potentially serious
health effects. Cocaine, thought in the late 1970s to be benign and nonaddictive, is now known to have a physiological basis for addiction, albeit a
different basis than the narcotics. We also know that cocaine is potentially
dangerous to those with heart conditions, and is especially toxic when
combined with alcohol.

Given the potential harm that is caused by these drugs, we must
ask ourselves if we are willing to put more citizens at risk by legalizing
them, since critics rightfully note that the numbers of users would climb
postlegalization. More specifically, we must ask ourselves if the public
health *benefits* described earlier, outweigh the public health *costs* of many
times more people being exposed to the physiological and psychic risks
that these drugs pose. This is an important question, because while
legalization advocates claim that we are losing the war on drugs, the
best survey research indicates that overall drug use has actually *declined*
since the 1970s, and has leveled off after a slight rise in the 1990s among
high school students. While there are some exceptions to this pattern,
most notably a sharp rise in the use of the drug ecstasy since the late
1990s (Johnston, O'Malley an Bachman, 2000), it would seem that if current prohibition policies have not eliminated drug use, they have at least
contained it.

Costs of Going Against Public Opinion

This argument against legalization closely parallels the position that prohibition sends an important symbolic message about the value of sobriety.
The fact is, legalization opponents claim, the American people do not want
to see drugs legalized. Even marijuana, the most tolerated of currently illegal drugs, has little support for nonmedical legalization. Recent Gallup
Poll data indicate that 69 percent of Americans oppose the legalization of
marijuana. Opposition to legalization varies directly with age, with only
54 percent of 18–29 year olds opposing, and 85 percent of those over 65
years of age opposing legalization of marijuana (Moore, 1999). It should
also be pointed out that there is strong *support* for legalization of marijuana for medical purposes when prescribed by physicians. We will address that issue shortly. These findings by the Gallup organization generally reflect other polls on this issue as well (Inciardi, 1990). While those
who oppose prohibition on the basis of civil liberties, public health, or
moral arguments will not be impressed with public opinion as the basis

for policy, the practical problems of implementing a policy that is contrary to what more than two-thirds of the population believes desirable are immense.

DECRIMINALIZATION

Decriminalization is a policy alternative that is similar to legalization, but with some very important differences. Many people understand decriminalization as some sort of "compromise" policy, half-way between prohibition and legalization. This is perhaps the reason that marijuana has been decriminalized, but not legalized, in a number of states. Legislators are more willing to take this seeming half-way step than to legalize. This conception of decriminalization as something "just short" of legalization could not be further from the truth, however. Decriminalization is, in fact, a third policy option that, while similar to legalization, is unique.

Decriminalization is a policy that *removes criminal sanctions* from the activity in question. In the case of drugs, that activity which is targeted for removal of criminal sanctions is usually the possession of small amounts of a drug. This does not mean that the activity in question is *legal*. In most states that have decriminalized marijuana, possession of even small amounts of marijuana is still a violation of the law—but not the *criminal* law.[1] Typically, such possession is regarded as a civil infraction—much like going over the speed limit—and is subject to civil penalties, usually fines, but no jail time or other restriction of liberty can be meted out.

Decriminalization of marijuana has been established as policy in eleven states (true as of late 2002). Alaska, which had once decriminalized the drug, has recriminalized it; however, individuals can grow up to 25 marijuana plants under Alaska's right to privacy act (see Table 11.1). This policy option did not come to pass suddenly or without precedent, however. Starting in the mid-1960s, individual states began to reduce the criminal penalties for marijuana possession such that by 1972, simple possession of less than an ounce of marijuana was classified as a misdemeanor in all but eight states (Bonnie, 1980). Currently, all 50 states have either reduced the charges for possession of small amounts of marijuana to a misdemeanor, or have decriminalized such possession. Also in 1972, the National Commission on Marijuana and Drug Abuse (which was created by the same legislation that enacted the Controlled Substances Act of 1970) issued the first of two reports, entitled *Marihuana: A Signal of Misunderstanding*. This report called for a drastic change in policy regarding possession and "casual distribution" (not for profit) of marijuana. The Commission called on federal and state governments to remove these low-level offenses from the list of criminal offenses, though the *public* possession and use could result in fines (National Commission on Marihuana and Drug Abuse, 1972). States soon responded. Oregon was the first state

TABLE 11.1	States that Have Decriminalized Marijuana	
State	**Quantity Involved**	**Penalty**
**Alaska	0–8 ounces	90 days; $1,000 fine
*California	0–1 ounce (28.5 grams)	$100 fine
Colorado	0–1 ounce	$100 fine
Maine	0–2.5 ounce	$200–$400 fine
*Minnesota	0–1.5 ounce (42.5 grams)	$100 fine; drug education
*Mississippi	0–1 ounce (30 grams)	$100–$250 fine
Nebraska	0–1 ounce	$100 fine; drug education
*Nevada	Any amount (if over 21 yrs.)	$600
New York	0–1 oz. (25 grams)	$100
*North Carolina	0–1/2 ounce	30 days suspended
Ohio	0–3½ ounces (100 grams)	$100
*Oregon	0–1 ounce	$500–$1000 fine

*States that maintain misdemeanor status on possession for personal use, but which do not arrest or suspend sentences for cooperative defendants.

**Alaska recently recriminalized marijuana; however, individuals can grow up to 25 marijuana plants under that state's right to privacy act.

Source: National Organization for the Reform of Marijuana Laws, 2002. http://www.norml.org/index.cfm [Accessed October 28, 2002].

to decriminalize in 1973, with a statute stating that unlawful possession of one ounce or less of marijuana was a "violation" and punishable by not more than $100. Other states followed suit. These states, and the penalties associated with the use and possession of small quantities of marijuana are listed in Table 11.1.

The impact of decriminalization on levels of drug use has been closely monitored over the past 25 years. According to Thies and Register (1993) marijuana use in Oregon did increase from about 24 percent prevalence (of 18 to 29 year olds) in 1974 to 30 percent prevalence in 1977. Similar increases were reported following decriminalization in California (Cuskey, Berger and Richardson, 1978). It should be pointed out, however, that the prevalence of marijuana use was increasing nationwide during this period of time. Cross-cultural research by Trebach (1987) suggests a slight *decline* in drug use in Holland following decriminalization there. While cross-cultural data must be interpreted with great care, it seems safe to conclude, considering the growing body of data from the United States, that the impact of decriminalization of marijuana on the prevalence of use will be minimal at most. What is not so certain, however, is the impact of decriminalization of other drugs, such as heroin or cocaine, on the prevalence of their use. Marijuana is a drug that is already quite widely available, even in those jurisdictions where it is criminally prohibited. We would not expect decriminalization to have as much of an impact where a substance is already relatively easy to obtain. Drugs such as heroin, cocaine, crack, and many other substances that have much more restricted distribution would likely experience a substantial increase in prevalence.

ADVANTAGES OF DECRIMINALIZATION OVER LEGALIZATION

When compared with prohibition policies, decriminalization carries with it many of the advantages and disadvantages of legalization. There are, however, some unique benefits and costs to this policy option that distinguish it from legalization. Let us look first at some of the advantages.

Stronger Base of Public Support

The very fact that several states have decriminalized marijuana is suggestive of the fact that the public is much more willing to endorse a policy of decriminalization over one of legalization. Moreover, all 50 states have reduced simple marijuana possession to a misdemeanor—again suggesting that there is public support for constraining criminal law in this area.

Maintains Stronger Symbolic Message

Many drug policy experts are much more comfortable with a decriminalization model because, in their view, it does not represent wholesale support, symbolically, of drug use. Rather, it is a recognition that for certain drugs, particularly marijuana, harsh criminal offenses are doing more harm than good, and indeed, more harm than moderate drug use itself. Hence, while not *endorsing* the use of these drugs, decriminalization is believed to lessen the damaging consequences of that drug use.

Maintains Criminal Sanctions for Trafficking

This advantage over legalization is the counterpart to maintaining a stronger symbolic message. Those who believe that marijuana use is potentially very destructive argue that there must be mechanisms in place to severely punish large-scale traffickers. Decriminalization allows for such punitive action.

DISADVANTAGES OF DECRIMINALIZATION OVER LEGALIZATION

While decriminalization is politically advantageous over legalization, given the mood of the country with regard to drugs and drug use, there are nevertheless several ways in which decriminalization is not as attractive an alternative to drug prohibition.

Public Health Disadvantages

All the public health costs associated with prohibition essentially remain under policies of decriminalization. Because decriminalized drugs are not made legal, there are no mechanisms by which the government can systematically monitor or regulate the production and quality of these substances. Users are still at the mercy of an underground market, and the questionable ethics associated with that method of distribution.

Crime and Corruption Disadvantages

Decriminalization will probably not have much impact on the level of crime and corruption. High-level dealers of decriminalized drugs remain subject to major penalties and continue to have incentive to corrupt public officials. The cost of decriminalized drugs is also governed by illegal market dynamics, so to the extent that there is an economic link between drug use and crime, this link remains where drugs are decriminalized.

Limited Cost Savings

Decriminalization does indeed represent some cost savings to law enforcement, in that enforcement efforts can focus on major dealers and distributors. Courtroom dockets are not as deadlocked with casual users, and prisons may be less overcrowded. Decriminalization does not, however, allow for the public treasury to recoup the costs associated with the distribution of these substances in the form of taxation. Hence, decriminalization continues to be a *drain* on public funds rather than a source of renewal.

Still a Criminal Justice Model

Many advocates of legalization urge the movement toward a *medical model* of drug addiction. The argument is that addiction is a disease and should be treated in the same way as alcoholism. It is impossible to fully embrace a medical model of addiction with a policy of decriminalization. Indeed, decriminalization does not move us any closer to medicalizing addiction than does a policy of prohibition, except perhaps to make the electorate more accepting of the use of otherwise illegal drugs for special medical purposes.

Limited Applicability

Decriminalization has been reasonably successful in the states which have decriminalized marijuana. Studies have shown that there has not been a substantial rise in the prevalence of marijuana use in thse states (Thies and Register, 1993). This does not mean, however, that decriminalization is a viable policy option for most illegal drugs today. Due to the highly reinforcing effect of some drugs such as heroin and cocaine, and the hysteria associated with so many illegal drugs, a policy of decriminalization of *any* amount of these drugs will likely result in quite different consequences than has our experience with marijuana. Under a policy of marijuana decriminalization, for example, an individual may be more likely to experiment a few times than would otherwise be the case, and may even go on to use occasionally. If the same increase in levels of experimentation with more dependency-producing substances such as cocaine or heroin were to take place, it is likely that decriminalization would produce a substantial population of addicts who would develop habits that would require them to become involved in drug sales to sustain their consumption levels. These newly created addicts would be forced to deal in higher-level volume than would be acceptable under most decriminalization statutes. Hence, even if decriminalization is a workable policy option for marijuana, it cannot be simply transposed to other drugs.

HARM REDUCTION: AN ALTERNATIVE FRAMEWORK FROM WHICH TO APPROACH DRUG POLICY

The concept of **harm reduction** as a formalized approach to drug policy evolved in the late 1980s, though many of the strategies embodied in harm reduction were being implemented in the underground drug culture and literature of the 1960s and 1970s. Recreational users and addicts were informed through comic books and other media how to avoid the pitfalls associated with the use of a variety of drugs (Nadelmann, McNeely, and Drucker, 1997). Harm reduction was promoted as a serious policy approach initially by European countries and Australia, though many policy experts in the United States were watching closely (Nadelmann, 1998; Nadelmann, McNeely, and Drucker, 1997).

Harm reduction generally shifts the goal of drug policy from that of eliminating drug use, or even lowering drug use (which is the goal of current policy), to reducing the harm that is caused by both drug use and drug policies (Massing, 1999). Clearly, abstinence and reduced levels of drug use on a societal basis are laudable goals and should be pursued whenever it is possible to do so without risking greater harm to the user and/or to society in the process. Our current policies of prohibition, however, themselves pose risks. Harm reduction proponents advocate a weighing of the risks of drug use against the policies which attempt to curtail this use. Harm reduction, in its essence, embodies President Jimmy Carter's challenge to congress in 1977: "Penalties against drug use should not be more damaging to an individual than the use of the drug itself. Nowhere is this more clear than in the laws against possession of marijuana in private for personal use" (Carter, 1977). The harm-reduction approach is grounded in the supposition that drug use will never be totally eliminated, and that we can expect recreational drug use to remain a part of society indefinitely.

TABLE 11.2	Level of Intervention in a Harm-Reduction Approach	
Level of Intervention	**Definition**	**Policy Responses**
Primary Prevention	Prevention of drug use where feasible, and especially of addiction	Marijuana decriminalization Drug education Medical legalization
Secondary Prevention	Limiting severity, and consequences to community, of drug addiction	Needle exchange programs Drug zones
Tertiary Prevention	Limiting consequences of addiction to user	Treatment

Source: Adapted from Ethan Nadelmann, Jennifer McNeely and Ernest Drucker, "International Perspectives," 1997, Table 4.1.

Harm-reduction strategists identify several approaches to harm reduction. Nadelmann, McNeely and Drucker (1997) offer what is perhaps the most systematic approach to a harm-reduction strategy. They conceptualize three levels of prevention, highlighted in Table 11.2, each with its own specific strategies:

PRIMARY PREVENTION

Primary prevention strategies focus on discouraging drug use where possible. Among those who have already chosen to use drugs, primary prevention efforts are directed at warding off addiction. While abstinence might be viewed as an ideal, it is but one of several approaches to avoiding the problems currently associated with drug use. At the primary level of prevention, harm reductionists would seek to encourage *responsible* patterns of drug use—limiting drug use to occasional or recreational levels if possible or at least manageable levels of more frequent use. A major component of a harm-reductionist strategy is to eliminate the necessity of purchasing drugs in the illegal market place. Users who are forced to become involved with the illegal subculture of drug use run much higher risks of addiction as they become more and more immersed in this subculture. Risk of addiction is enhanced because, as friendship patterns develop in these subcultures, there are greater pressures to conform to the drug-using lifestyles of peers. Access to drugs is also enhanced through contacts with dealers and wholesalers. Furthermore, the public labeling and degradation of identity that results from being arrested, tried, and punished helps to set in motion a process that makes one vulnerable to addiction. According to labeling and symbolic interactionist theorists, the public labeling of one as a deviant only reinforces the deviant self-concept, and we tend to act in a way that is consistent with our self-identity.

There are, of course, other social and public health problems associated with the illegal drug market such as uncertain quality of drugs, crime, and infectious diseases that harm reductionists would seek to avoid. Hence, a major harm-reduction proposal is to decriminalize, if not legalize, certain drugs which have lower potential for addiction. Marijuana is the drug most targeted for decriminalization or legalization, but other drugs are candidates as well. The legalizing of marijuana for medical purposes has been especially targeted in recent years as more and more physicians are recognizing and speaking out on the potential benefits of marijuana in the treatment of glaucoma, nausea due to chemotherapy in cancer patients, and the "wasting syndrome" common among AIDS patients.

Another strategy, which is not always identified as part of a primary prevention strategy (but is consistent with it) is a focus on drug education. Current education efforts are not sufficient to reach those who have already chosen to use drugs. The only message that is contained in D.A.R.E., Partnership for a Drug-Free America, and other educational initiatives in the United States is "abstinence." Harm-reduction educational efforts would focus on putting safety first by providing information such as: what kind of drug combinations to avoid because of synergism and other interactive effects; subjective effects to expect, and what sorts of behaviors to avoid while using these drugs; hygienic practices that ensure safer drug use; and how to pace one's drug use and cope with symptoms of withdrawal. This is all information that drug users need to avoid the pitfalls of addiction and the harmful consequences of use and addiction should addiction occur. Much of this information is, indeed, an important part of "secondary" prevention efforts.

SECONDARY PREVENTION

Secondary prevention is directed primarily at those individuals who might already be characterized as "addicted." At the secondary level, harm-reduction policies would seek to reduce the length and severity of addiction and drug-related disorders. Many of the education elements that were suggested above under *primary prevention* are also aimed at minimizing the severity of drug addiction to addicted individuals. These educational efforts often go hand-in-hand with needle-exchange programs, which are also a central part of secondary prevention efforts. Needle-exchange programs were seriously considered only after the recognition of the seriousness of the AIDS epidemic among IV drug users (Singer, Irizarry and Schensul, 1991). These programs seek to reduce the spread of AIDS and hepatitis by providing addicts with clean and sterile needles so that they do not have to rely on infected needles. Moreover, most of these programs require that addicts turn in used needles before they are given additional clean needles. This requirement helps to minimize the prevalence of dirty needles available to addict users (Singer, Irizarry, and Schensul, 1991). Needle-exchange programs also typically provide condoms to addicts to help reduce the spread of AIDS among IV drug users through sexual contact. Many needle-exchange programs also provide educational materials to addicts, including instructions on how to sterilize needles using bleach, information about safer sexual practices, and assistance in linking addicts with needed medical services. Some of these programs are quite aggressive in their efforts to reach addicts, using vans and buses to get the word out, while others operate as drop-in centers (Nadelmann, McNeely, and Drucker, 1997).

Another strategy that has been employed with mixed success primarily in European cities, is the provision of specially zoned areas for drug users to congregate and not be subject to harassment or risk of arrest from police. The principle behind this idea is the same as that which governs red light districts and pornography shops in large cities: containment within a delimited area so as to avoid the spread of these unwanted activities in other commercial and residential areas. The first well-known designated drug locale was in Zurich, Switzerland's Platzspitz (commonly known as "Needle Park"). Needle Park was deemed a success early on, as heroin addicts and other drug users did indeed congregate here rather than in various isolated pockets throughout the city. The enthusiasm waned, however, as Needle Park soon became a haven for thousands of outsiders who would flock to Zurich, creating a strain on the system and threatening surrounding neighborhoods. Needle Park was eventually shut down (Nadelmann, McNeely, and Drucker, 1997). While the efficacy of special "zones" for addicts to congregate continues to be debated, this concept has been replaced with a more restricted proposal of "safe spaces" for addicts. These safe spaces consist of small centers where drug users can go to get clean needles, condoms, obtain basic medical care, and even "get off" in a hygienic environment. These are policies, according to harm-reduction strategists that are consistent with other policing practices in the United States as well as Europe which seek to contain other marginal behavior, including sex, drinking, and gambling establishments (Nadelmann, McNeely, and Drucker, 1997).

TERTIARY PREVENTION

Tertiary prevention is directed primarily at full-blown addicts, and seeks to minimize the medical and social consequences of their addiction to themselves and to others with whom they might have contact. The distinction between secondary and tertiary intervention efforts is by no means sharply delineated. Much of what is identified as "secondary prevention" is clearly aimed at reducing the spread of AIDS and containing crime— clearly efforts to reduce social and medical consequences. As articulated by Nadelmann and his colleagues, however, *tertiary prevention* is reserved primarily for greater access to treatment, particularly drug maintenance treatment. There are essentially two maintenance models: the "British model" and Methadone maintenance, which is the model adopted in the United

States. The British model authorized physicians to prescribe maintenance dosages of heroin to addicts, and was implemented from the 1920s to the 1960s, at which time there was concern about the number of addicts who were being prescribed heroin. At that time, the British government went to a government-sponsored clinic system of distribution of heroin. Almost from the beginning of narcotics prohibition in the United States, the use of heroin for addict maintenance was ruled illegal, though addicts were given dosages of morphine in the U.S. Public Health Hospitals in Lexington and Fort Worth, primarily as a means of gradual withdrawal. The 1960s, however, witnessed the development of methadone, which was soon adopted as a maintenance treatment modality (see Chapter 12). Methadone maintenance is the most widely used form of drug treatment for hard-core heroin addicts in the United States today.

Harm-reduction strategists such as Nadelmann and others urge the proliferation of methadone maintenance as a means of reducing higher-risk drug injection. Rather than limit methadone distribution to government-controlled clinics, harm reductionists urge the integration of methadone maintenance into mainstream medical practice so that private physicians could prescribe methadone to their addicted patients. Such a policy would increase the availability of noninjectable drugs (methadone is usually taken orally), thereby reducing the necessity of relying on illegal, perhaps toxic, injectable heroin. Moreover, because of an expansion in the potential number of methadone providers, such a system is more effective in linking addicts with other needed medical services (Nadelmann, McNeely, and Drucker, 1997).

HARM REDUCTION: A VIABLE APPROACH?

Contrary to what is popularly believed, many if not most harm reductionists are not favorable to legalization for one reason or another. While harm reduction has indeed been embraced by most legalization advocates, it is also believed by many staunch prohibitionists to represent workable solutions to some of the most serious costs to prohibition policies. These harm-reduction strategies are believed by many (though certainly not all) prohibition advocates to be workable within a more general prohibitionist framework (Nadelmann, 1998). Indeed, insofar as illicit drug use continues to be a politically charged issue—which, by all indications, it will continue to be—harm reduction can be effective *only if* it can work within a prohibitionist framework. Despite the initial rush to decriminalize marijuana in the 1970s, there has been no corresponding enthusiasm on the part of the state and federal legislatures toward either *legalization* or further *decriminalization*. Insofar as harm reduction strategies are politically or publicly linked with a policy of legalization or decriminalization, it is highly unlikely that they will ever be adopted on a widespread basis in the United States. It is perhaps somewhat foreboding that the Office of National Drug Control Policy opposes the use of needle exchange programs, a harm-reduction approach that holds potential to curtail the spread of AIDS—a death sentence—among IV drug users (Office of National Drug Control Policy, 1992). It would seem that until harm reduction can be articulated in terms that do not diminish the goals of prohibition—reduced drug use—its adoption in the United States will be limited. Harm reduction is, however, a policy alternative that will overshadow both legalization and decriminalization. Indeed, it already has, as evidenced by the fact that such ardent legalization advocates as Ethan Nadelmann now insist on a self-identity of "harm reductionist" (Nadelmann, personal communication). Harm reduction does appear to offer a potential meeting ground for old prohibitionists and old legalization advocates to develop a sound drug policy agenda for the twenty-first century. Some potential agenda items are discussed more fully in Chapter 14.

SUMMARY

In this chapter we have endeavored to provide a balanced assessment of the major policy options that involve legal responses to American drug problems. Prohibitionist approaches, legalization proposals, and decriminalization models all have consequences and implications, benefits and costs, which should be taken into consideration by anyone planning drug strategy. Drug policy makers in this country have often been unwilling to be thoughtful, which has resulted in a collection of policies that are at times contradictory and ineffective. Political expediency and moral entrepreneurship, rather than a sober and balanced approach have led to the implementation of policies that at times do more harm than good. "Harm reduction" often gets crowded out. Public opinion on a host of "legal response" issues is similarly swayed by ideas and beliefs that, while popular, are not grounded in empirical research on policy alternatives. In Chapter 14, we make sense of the considerable drug policy knowledge that exists.

KEY TERMS

decriminalization
harm reduction
interdiction

legalization
primary prevention
prohibition

secondary prevention
source reduction
tertiary prevention

REVIEW QUESTIONS

1. Why is a study of drug policy critical to understanding drug use?

2. Identify the five-tier strategy of prohibition. What are the problems encountered at each of these levels of prohibition?

3. What are the advantages of prohibition over legalization and/or decriminalization? What are its disadvantages?

4. What is the difference between legalization and decriminalization? What might specific policies of decriminalization and legalization look like?

5. The authors stated in this chapter that the impetus for legalization comes generally from two sources: civil libertarians and public health advocates. How do these two advocates differ in their vision of what a good legalization policy might look like? Which of the three models of legalization do each of these advocates generally favor?

6. What distinguishes a policy of harm reduction from the other three policy options discussed in this chapter? Do you believe a harm-reduction policy orientation is superior or inferior to prohibition?

7. Distinguish between primary, secondary, and tertiary policy strategies. Which of these strategies do you think should receive the greatest emphasis in our response to drug use and addiction?

CRITICAL THOUGHT QUESTIONS

1. Develop a case for either prohibition, legalization, or decriminalization. Be sure to consider all of the costs and benefits of each policy orientation, and then make the case for why the policy you choose is superior.

2. If you were asked by your governor to write a drug policy based on principles of harm reduction for your state, what would that policy look like? Identify as many components as possible, and provide a rationale for each of those components based on harm reduction principles.

NOTE

1. Some states, which are considered to have decriminalized small amounts of marijuana, technically maintain criminal statutes. Enforcement of these statutes, however, is conducted as though it were a civil offense, by imposing fines rather than jail time.

THERAPEUTIC RESPONSES TO DRUG PROBLEMS: DRUG TREATMENT

This chapter addresses varied approaches to the treatment of drug addiction. While there are a number of treatment philosophies, the concept of "treatment" implies at least two things which all therapeutic approaches have in common. First, it assumes that excessive drug use is itself a problem, and moreover that it is an individual problem in need of correction. Second, regardless of approach, treatment implies that these problems can, in fact, be corrected. These presuppositions might seem to be obvious to anyone even casually familiar with drug use as a social issue. However, as we have pointed out early in this book, there is no universal agreement that drug use—even high levels of drug use—necessarily represents an individual problem. As we discussed in Chapter 11, many scholars and observers of the drug scene suggest that the "problem" is society's punitive response toward drug use not the use of drugs themselves. Furthermore, it has not always been assumed that drug abuse and addiction are treatable. As recently as the 1960s it was widely believed, even by professionals in the field, that "once an addict always an addict." As the phrase was interpreted then, there was a sense of hopelessness for the abuser who had gone too far down the scale. Today, it more often is taken to mean that while the biochemical alterations caused by addiction remain, the individual does not have to be an active, using addict.

The discussion that follows must be understood with these considerations in mind. We begin by briefly sketching the history of drug treatment efforts in the United States. This section is followed by a discussion of the major treatment "modalities," or approaches to treatment, and the philosophies which undergird these treatment efforts. We will then discuss the effectiveness of treatment, and finally, we identify some of the major issues in treatment today.

HISTORY OF TREATMENT FOR DRUG ADDICTION

Early societal responses to both drug and alcohol abuse were moralistic and mostly punitive. The drug user—one who used pharmacological substances which were socially disapproved—was viewed as morally depraved. This was at least partially the response of the twentieth-century prohibitionist movement to the user of alcohol as well, who was characterized as a "drunkard" or a "sot." At least one author of the time referred to the sale of alcoholic beverages as "hell's commerce" (Shaw, 1910). By the early twentieth century, moralistic rhetoric began to wane. Drug addicts and alcoholics were increasingly seen as redeemable, and a treatment industry began to emerge. It should be noted that the treatment of drug abuse in the United States, until recent years, was oriented primarily to alcohol and narcotics abuse. Alternative treatment methodologies for other types of drugs would eventually come, but the dominant treatment methods have been shaped by efforts to treat alcohol and narcotics addiction. It is also important to point out that treatment for alcohol and narcotics addiction followed separate paths. Researchers and practitioners working in these treatment fields remained largely segregated, resulting in separate but parallel research and programmatic efforts at treatment.

HISTORY OF ALCOHOL TREATMENT

While early responses to alcohol abuse were heavily moralistic in nature, there was also the recognition that the alcoholic suffered from a malady, a "disease" that was beyond his or her control and which required treatment. An early proponent of what would eventually be understood as a "disease model" of alcoholism was Dr. Benjamin Rush, who saw chronic inebriation as an addiction. Indeed, Schneider (1978) suggests that the early prohibitionist movement in the nineteenth century explicitly recognized inebriety as a disease. There were also "inebriates' institutions" in the nineteenth century, which were intended to remove the alcoholic and alcohol abuser from jails and from lunatic asylums so that their problems could be more effectively addressed (Baumohl, 1986). These institutions and the treatment effort they represented did not last long. Baumohl suggests that they were all but extinct by the time of Prohibition in 1920.

Alcoholics Anonymous

In 1935, soon after the end of national alcohol prohibition, two alcoholics by the name of Bill Wilson and Bob Smith met in Akron, Ohio, to offer support to each other in their desire to achieve and maintain sobriety. This would later be recognized as the very first Alcoholics Anonymous meeting, the start of a spiritually based self-help form of alcohol treatment that in its history has helped millions live sober lives. As it developed, Alcoholics Anonymous drew heavily from two ideological sources. First, AA accepted the idea that alcoholism was a disease over which the alcoholic had no control. This medical understanding of alcoholism was combined with a spiritual focus, specifically Christian teaching regarding sinful humanity, the necessity of confession of sin and the redemption of sinful humanity through the power of God. Especially influential was a movement formed in the 1920s known as the Oxford Group, which held to conservative Christian teaching, but which rejected the institutional character of religion. This group met in homes and hotels rather than in churches and cathedrals, had no organized board of officers, and called itself an "organism" rather than an "organization." Bill W. and Doctor Bob, as they are widely known in the AA fellowship, attended meetings of the Oxford Group and based their 12 steps on the tenets of this movement. While AA has been criticized for its distinctly Christian roots, it has been praised by many for its role in saving millions of lives. In June of 1999, *Time* magazine named Bill W. one of its 20 "heroes and icons" of the twentieth century, a group chosen because they "articulate the longings of the last 100 years, exemplify courage selflessness, exuberance, superhuman ability and amazing grace." (*Time,* June 14, 1999). The program of Alcoholics Anonymous received similar end-of-the-century recognition.

E. M. Jellinek and the Yale Research Group

Also shortly after the repeal of Prohibition, the Research Council on Problems of Alcohol was formed at Yale University. This council was made up of physicians and scientists interested in identifying the causes of alcoholism. The Council pushed the concept of alcoholism as a disease and invited Elvin M. Jellinek to direct a multidisciplinary Yale Center for Alcohol Studies. Jellinek published numerous articles promoting the idea of alcoholism as a disease, culminating in his book, *The Disease Concept of Alcoholism,* in 1960. Here, Jellinek proposed a four-stage progression of alcoholism, which he identified as *alpha, beta, delta,* and *gamma* alcoholism. Gamma alcoholism is characterized by an increased tolerance to alcohol, adaptation of cell metabolism, withdrawal symptoms, and an inability to control how much one drinks at any given time, despite obvious physiological consequences including cirrhosis of the liver (Schneider, 1978). The disease model of alcoholism was officially endorsed by the World Health Organization in 1951 and by the American Medical Association in 1956. The American Psychiatric Association also formally promoted this idea in 1965 following Jellinek's influential work, and by the late 1970s, the DSMIIR listed "alcohol dependence syndrome" as a treatable psychological illness (Hobbs, 1998).

The successful promotion of alcoholism as a disease resulted in the establishment of a very profitable treatment industry for alcoholism. These efforts began with simple **detoxification,** a term drawn from medicine which refers to the process of getting rid of toxins (poisons) in the body. Alcohol and other chemical substances are viewed as poisons that have accumulated in the body which need to be purged. Treatment efforts have since expanded in complexity. Residential programs such as the Betty Ford Foundation in California and Hazeldon in Minnesota and Florida draw heavily from the disease model of addiction.

HISTORY OF NARCOTICS TREATMENT

Early Treatment Efforts

Addiction to opium and other narcotics was also interpreted through a moral lens prior to the twentieth century. By the 1890s, the physiological basis for opiate addiction was being recognized, though by no means fully understood, by the medical profession. The primary debate regarding proper treatment at this time was whether sudden, rapid, or gradual withdrawal from opium and morphine was the most effective (Terry and Pellens, 1928). Any treatment effort for narcotics at this time was simply a detoxification effort, the debate simply being around the best method of detoxifying. "Cure" was equated with a drug-free blood system, regardless of how short-lived that condition might be. There was a great deal of experimentation at this time, as some experts recommended withdrawal over the course of a year or more, while others recommended sudden withdrawal over a matter of days. Drugs used to help patients withdraw gradually also varied. It was believed in the latter nineteenth century that cocaine was effective as a cure for narcotics addiction. When heroin was introduced by Bayer Pharmaceuticals in 1898, it was believed to be nonaddictive and was advocated as a method of withdrawal and as a cure for morphine dependency (Lipton and Maranda, 1983). With the passage of the Harrison Narcotics Act in 1914, this debate ended as the Act was considered by most medical professionals to mean that supplying narcotics to addicts was illegal. Local health departments responded in 1920 by providing maintenance dosages of narcotics to addicts—a measure which was, interestingly enough, initially endorsed by the Treasury Department. This endorsement did not last long, however. Abuses led the government to shut down the maintenance programs, closing the last program in 1924.

Establishment of Narcotics Institutions

Serious treatment efforts for narcotics addicts did not begin until the establishment of the Federal Public Health Service Hospitals—commonly known as "narcotics farms"—in the 1930s. Like the inebriates' institutions before them, these hospitals represented an effort to separate narcotics addicts from the general federal prison population for purposes of treatment and treatment experimentation. Voluntary "walk-ins" were also treated in these institutions, but most patients were court-ordered to the facilities. Treatment consisted primarily of gradually weaning patients from heroin with decreasing dosages of morphine, though later methadone was used. The hospitals closed within four decades after they started, another experiment in drug treatment coming to an end when the Lexington, Kentucky, hospital was transformed into a minimum-security federal prison in 1973. The federal hospitals did provide researchers with a great deal of data on narcotics addiction and its treatment, much of which continues to be cited today.

"Synanon" and the Therapeutic Community

There was very little in the way of treatment innovation for narcotics or other drugs until 1958 when a former alcoholic by the name of Charles Dederich founded a program in California that he called "Synanon."[1] Synanon represented a new approach to drug treatment that used an environment insulated from outside influences, 24 hours a day, and emphasized confrontation and shock therapy to break down the addict's psychological defenses. Additionally, these programs provided educational and vocational opportunities. This approach was more generally referred to as a *therapeutic community*, and Synanon's model was replicated throughout the country starting in the early 1960s.[2] The therapeutic community was and still is a rather controversial treatment modality, but continues to find wide-spread support for not only treatment of addiction to narcotic drugs, but other forms of drug addiction as well.

Methadone Maintenance

A major breakthrough in treatment for narcotics addiction came in 1965 when Drs. Vincent Dole and Marie Nyswander introduced the first meth-adone clinic in New York City. Methadone, a synthetic narcotic that could be used to forestall an addict's physiological craving for heroin, had been synthesized in the 1940s but was not recognized as an approach to ad-diction treatment until Dole and Nyswander's pioneering efforts. Initially, the goal of the methadone clinics was to gradually detoxify heroin ad-dicts with decreasing dosages of methadone, much in the way that mor-phine had been used earlier. Over time, the goals and purpose of the meth-adone clinics have evolved, and proponents of this treatment approach generally acknowledge that most addicts treated with methadone will re-main dependent on narcotics, and they now advocate continued *mainte-nance* of addicts on methadone. By the 1970s, **methadone maintenance** was accepted as a major mode of treatment for narcotics addiction, an appeal due largely to the fact that it is relatively inexpensive and that there are very quick and observable results in terms of lowered levels of criminal activity.

Criminal Justice-Related Programs

The 1960s also witnessed another innovation in drug treatment—linking drug treatment with the criminal justice system. In 1961, the state of California established the California Civil Addict Program, which repre-sented the first major effort at involuntary commitment of (primarily) narcotics addicts for treatment. Essentially a diversion program, one which presented an alternative to incarceration, it was administered by the California Department of Corrections, and through which addicts would serve their time in treatment rather than prison. A similar program was es-tablished in New York, though it was short-lived. The federal government also established a civil commitment program, authorized by the Narcotic Addict Rehabilitation Act of 1966. This, too, was a rather short-lived effort. The 1960s also witnessed the introduction of treatment programs within state and federal prisons. These programs were based on a general thera-peutic community model and were very popular throughout the 1970s (Anglin and Hser, 1990).

Since the 1960s the general trend in drug treatment has been (1) to rec-ognize the differences among individual addicts—particularly males and females—and the necessity of a multiple treatment approach to address the variety of individual treatment needs; and (2) to broaden the scope of treat-ment to address addiction to drugs other than narcotics and alcohol, the two types of drugs that were the object of earlier treatment efforts. The

Many treatment programs utilize group therapy techniques, often led by ex-addicts.

section that follows identifies the major treatment modalities in place today, approaches which include the programs that we have already discussed in this historical overview.

MAJOR TREATMENT MODALITIES

The literature of drug abuse treatment identifies broad **treatment modalities** or general approaches to treatment, representing fundamentally different strategies for treating drug addiction. We identify four general types, representing the broad range of treatment options as: *medical/pharmacological approaches, residential drug-free programs, out-patient drug-free programs,* and *self-help programs.* Specific treatment programs may integrate two or more of the approaches above; indeed, these integrated efforts are often among the most successful.

MEDICAL/PHARMACOLOGICAL APPROACHES

There are two basic types of pharmacological approaches to treatment for drug addiction. The first of these comprise *programs of drug substitution,* either to maintain the addict or to gradually withdraw the addict from dependence on the drug. There have been numerous efforts throughout history to treat substance abuse with the use of alternative drugs which are believed to be either less addicting and/or less harmful to the user. Indeed, as we have already pointed out, heroin was initially proposed as a substitute for morphine addiction because it was believed to be less addictive.

We now know, of course, that this was not the case! The most widely recognized programs of this type are *methadone maintenance or methadone detoxification*. The second type of pharmacological approach involves using antagonists, which either block the effect of the addict's drug of choice or produce highly uncomfortable countereffects.

Methadone Maintenance

Because methadone is a synthetic narcotic (see Chapter 3), its use in drug treatment is limited to narcotics addiction. Methadone programs today are driven by two broad, and somewhat contradictory, philosophies that Graff and Ball (1976) call the "metabolic" and "psychotherapeutic" models. The *metabolic* model understands drug addiction as a metabolic disease resulting from a biochemical deficit or imbalance. As a consequence, those who adhere to this model do not believe that the addict is capable of functioning without narcotics or a narcotics substitute. Eventual abstinence is not a realistic goal, and long-term maintenance on methadone is assumed. While certain forms of psychotherapy and other therapeutic initiatives are seen as useful, they are but ancillary to the central form of treatment, namely the daily dosage of methadone. The *psychotherapeutic* model, by contrast, understands drug addiction primarily to be a psychiatric or emotional disorder. Rather than being ancillary, psychotherapy is understood to be the primary method of treatment, and methadone is used only for stabilizing the addict so that he or she can more effectively benefit from the psychotherapy. The ultimate goal of treatment for those adhering to the psychotherapeutic model is abstinence. Hubbard et al. (1989), in their comprehensive study of treatment programs in the United States, note that while there is an increasing trend toward a psychotherapeutic model, most programs are still of the metabolic variety.

The treatment experience of an addict in methadone maintenance is highly variable, depending on the treatment philosophy of the program, how bureaucratically it is structured, the adequacy of funding, and a host of other factors. Since retention in the methadone program is an important component of success, the nature of the addict's treatment experience is highly relevant. Methadone maintenance, whether short or long term, is a central feature of all methadone programs. The federal government defines maintenance as the continuous administration of methadone for a period of at least 21 days (U.S. Department of Health and Human Services, 1980). Methadone is advantageous over other narcotics because it has a longer effective dose, ranging from 24 to 36 hours, and it is taken orally. This allows for a daily dispensing of the drug, rather than having to dispense several times per day. The addict is initially assessed with regard to his or her tolerance during what Lowinson and Millman (1979) call the "induction phase." This is done over a several day period, gradually bringing the addict up to a maintenance level dosage. During this period, the addict may also be assessed for psychotherapeutic and other rehabilitative needs, and an individualized treatment plan ideally is developed (Hubbard et al., 1979). Most methadone programs are out-patient in nature, meaning that in the "maintenance phase" the addict comes into the clinic on a daily, or sometimes weekly basis to obtain their daily or weekly allotment of methadone. There is a great deal of controversy surrounding weekly "take-home" dosages, as there is potential for **diversion**—selling of unused weekly dosages underground (Inciardi, 1977). All the clinics in the Hubbard et al. study allowed at least some of their patients take-home dosages of methadone after they had been in the program for a specified length of time.

Programs vary greatly in size and structure. Hubbard et al. (1989) found in their national study of treatment effectiveness that the average clinic serves 260 patients; more recent estimates point to numbers closer to half that size (Lindesmith Center, 1997). Some clinics are linked with larger hospitals, while others are free-standing and supported by community social service organizations. The larger programs typically have various types of counseling services available, though they are often understaffed. Lowinson and Millman (1979) recommend that educational services, family therapy, vocational rehabilitation, job training, and legal services, as well as general psychotherapeutic services, be made available to methadone patients. Clearly, the dynamics of addiction (and the sources of potential relapse) are tied into a host of roles and statuses which the addict occupies. The addict is subject to urinalysis to detect heroin use, which is prohibited while on methadone maintenance. A successful urinalysis would be defined as test results that are methadone positive and morphine negative (heroin is also known as diacetyl morphine and breaks down into morphine in the bloodstream).

Methadone maintenance is the most widespread form of government-supported treatment for narcotics addiction in the United States today, with approximately two of every ten heroin addicts enrolled in a methadone program. As of 1995, there were approximately 750 methadone clinics throughout the United States treating about 115,000 patients at any given time. More than half of these patients are in New York and California—about 40,000 in New York State and another 20,000 in California. (Institute of Medicine, 1995; Lindesmith Center, 1997). Advocates for methadone maintenance such as the National Alliance of Methadone Advocates or NAMA (www.methadone.org) and the Lindesmith Center (www.soros.org/lindesmith/) claim that it is effective at reducing illicit and unhealthy drug use, drug-related crime, and death and disease. They would like to see government restrictions on its use lifted, and greater funding of methadone programs, so that more heroin abusers (and by extension, society as a whole) can benefit from access to methadone. They also advocate doctors' being able to prescribe methadone for individual patients, something not currently permitted, and for pharmacies to carry methadone, which they view as a life-preserving drug. One last area of advocacy involves the destigmatization of methadone treatment centers and their clients. Planning for methadone clinics frequently suffers from the NIMBY ("not in my back yard") phenomenon, where neighborhoods either deny that narcotics addiction is a problem in their locale or where they attempt to block them because of fears that the clientele will be a threat to the area. Such fears, advocates say, prevent an important solution to a serious public health problem.

Two new drugs, approved by the FDA in late 2002 are similar to methadone but do not have some of the drawbacks commonly associated with methadone maintenance. These recently-approved drugs, Subutex and Suboxone (with the narcotic antagonist naloxone), do not produce a high yet seem to satisfy drug cravings. While methadone is only available at federally licensed clinics or treatment centers, these drugs, as a result of the Drug Addiction Treatment Act of 2000, may be obtained at a doctor's office. Additional benefits are that empirical studies have found them effective at reducing illegal narcotics use, they have a lower potential for overdose and withdrawal symptoms than does methadone, and they need to be taken less often than methadone. Additionally, addicts would have more control over treating their addiction, they would face less stigmatization, thus encouraging addicts to seek help and to comply with their treatment plans. Some experts project that the debate over drug decriminalization will be affected if heroin addiction becomes recognized as a "treatable medical condition" rather than as a "dangerous social menace" (Markel, 2002).

Smoking Reduction Efforts

Another area where drug substitution has been effective is in smoking reduction efforts. Today, there are about 46 million smokers in the United States, of whom more than 70 percent want to quit according to the Centers for Disease Control (Lewis, 1999; Nordenberg, 1997). Each year, approximately 17 million smokers try to stop, according to the American Cancer Society, but only about 1.3 million or 8 percent of them succeed for any appreciable period of time (Lewis, 1999). It is this high failure rate that led former U.S. Surgeon General C. Everett Koop to declare that "nicotine was more addicting than heroin." Various nicotine substitution products have been approved and marketed widely to assist smokers in quitting. These products come in four different forms: chewing gum, transdermal patches, nasal sprays, and inhalers. These products deliver decreasing doses of nicotine into the bloodstream, thus easing withdrawal symptoms when smokers attempt to quit, but do not contain the harmful tars and carbon monoxide which are responsible for some of the most serious health consequences of cigarette smoking. Studies on the effectiveness of these replacement products are promising, though they are not effective for everyone.

Chemical Antagonists

Chemical **antagonists** are drugs that either block the effects of an addictive substance or produce highly unpleasant side effects if the addictive substance is used. These are not drug substitutes, though methadone has been called a narcotic antagonist. While the use of methadone does block any further effect of heroin or morphine use, methadone is a synthetic narcotic and as such, it is a substitute for heroin, morphine, or other narcotics. Two narcotic antagonists that have been used in the treatment of narcotics addiction are *cyclazocine* and *naltrexone* (also called *Trexone*). These drugs are not themselves addicting, and actually induce a withdrawal syndrome. However, if these antagonists are taken after one has already withdrawn and is no longer physically dependent on narcotics, the antagonists work to prevent euphoria and dependence in the future should the recovering addict take these drugs, thereby serving as an effective behavior modification agent (Resnick, Schuyten-Resnick and Washton, 1979; Julius, 1976). Another class of narcotic antagonists (e.g., naloxone, better known as narcan) are used to induce rapid reversal of opiate overdoses. The federal government has promoted research on narcotic antagonists, especially naltrexone. There is not a strong, unequivocal body of research that suggests its effectiveness. Antagonists do seem to reduce the craving for the drug in the period immediately following detoxification, but once the antagonist is discontinued, craving for narcotics is once again experienced. This reinforces the ideas stressed in Chapter 5 that addiction is much broader than a physical dependence.

A second drug that we have classified as a chemical antagonist is *Antabuse*® (generic name, Disulfiram). Unlike the narcotic antagonists, however, which simply block the effects of narcotic drugs, *Antabuse*® produces a heightened sensitivity to alcohol that results in a highly unpleasant, often severe reaction if alcohol is taken when antabuse is still in the system. Some of the symptoms include flushing, throbbing in the head and neck, difficulty in breathing, nausea and vomiting, chest pains, heart palpitation, vertigo, blurred vision, and others (Internet Mental Health, nd). While Antabuse has been used for many years in the treatment of alcoholism and shows some promise, Doweiko (1990) points out several drawbacks to its use. First, the interaction effects can be extremely severe, requiring emergency hospitalization. Second, antabuse does not take effect immediately, taking up to 30 minutes to react to the presence of alcohol. Because of this delayed effect, it has been suggested that it is of limited aversive conditioning value. Third, the drug must be administered on a daily or nearly daily basis for optimal effect; effectiveness would be highly affected by a patient's willingness to continue using the drug. Finally, because *Antabuse*® does not recognize the source of the alcohol, use of over-the-counter products containing alcohol will produce the same untoward side effects as beverage alcohol. For all of these reasons, *Antabuse*® has not been a major treatment approach in alcoholism.

RESIDENTIAL TREATMENT PROGRAMS

Residential treatment programs are, by definition, drug-free programs, except where short-term chemical substitution is required for gradual withdrawal from certain drugs. Generally, participants in residential treatment have been detoxified and stabilized medically before admission. Residential programs involve 24-hour care. These programs vary on the length of stay recommended, though higher success rates are generally correlated with longer stays.

Therapeutic Communities

The **therapeutic community** (TC) is a fairly broad term that encompasses some 500 treatment programs across the United States (DeLeon, 1985.) As we mentioned, the genesis of residential treatment is generally traced to a California program founded in 1958 by Charles Dederich called *Synanon*. Treatment in the TC is governed by a treatment philosophy that mandates a comprehensive change in an addict's lifestyle—a *resocialization* process. Physical dependency is but the first of many lifestyle problems that have to be addressed if the addict is to live successfully in the outside world. The goal of the TC is, therefore, not only the cessation of drug use, but also seeing that the addict leads a productive life with legitimate employment, healthy family and social relationships, and an absence of criminal activity. TCs vary in the details of their approach to treatment. TCs modeled after Synanon tend to be long-term programs—at least 15 months in length. These programs are typically divided into three phases: *residential, re-entry,* and *aftercare*. Each phase has its own goals and processes, which we briefly describe below. Modified TCs also exist which are not as comprehensive and usually involve a shorter duration. These programs do not place as much emphasis on the re-entry or aftercare elements of treatment. (Hubbard et al., 1989)

Accomplishment of program goals involves a variety of therapy approaches, including confrontation and encounter therapy, educational opportunities, aid in job placement, and more. The heart of the therapeutic community, however, is the group therapy sessions, which are led by former drug abusers and often confrontational in nature. During the *residential phase,* addicts are confronted with their former destructive way of life and challenged to change their focus. These confrontations, sometimes called "haircuts,"[3] can be harrowing, almost brutal, to the addict being confronted. Yablonsky (1965, p. 241) describes this process as it was practiced in Synanon: "This form of verbal attack employs ridicule, hyperbole, and direct verbal onslaught. . . . An important goal of the 'haircut' method is to change the criminal tough guy pose. The self-image held by newcomers is viciously attacked and punctured in the 'haircut.'" These verbal attacks are designed to bring a resident to a breaking point, at which time the group is also there to encourage and build them up in their efforts to embody positive values and lifestyles.

As individuals progress through the program, they are gradually given more and more responsibilities. At some point in the program, usually after at least 12 months, the addict is considered ready for *reentry*. This phase involves spending time outside of the program, usually working a full- or part-time legitimate job. The recovering addict is still tied very closely to the program during this phase. Hawkins (1979) points out that a central task of the reintegration phase of treatment is to assist the addict in developing meaningful bonds with individuals and institutions in conventional society. *Aftercare* is the logical extension of re-entry. During this phase, the addict is formally "graduated" from the program. The program remains available to him or her, however, as a resource when encountering difficult terrain. Occasional counseling sessions or job placement services may be necessary. The program is available to the recovering addict for these purposes. These last two stages, reentry and aftercare, have received much less emphasis by treatment programs, but some attempts have been made to foster reintegration into the local community.

The Minnesota Model

The **Minnesota Model** is discussed here to represent comprehensive, though usually shorter term, approaches to drug addiction and especially alcoholism. Minnesota had long been a leader in alcohol intervention programs, and by the early 1980s the state had more than 3,800 beds and 1,000 outpatient slots for alcoholics (Laundergan, 1982). The formal name for this model is called *The Minnesota Model for Chemical Dependence Intervention and Treatment,* which had its beginnings in the late 1940s. The model was based on the 12 steps of Alcoholics Anonymous, which were applied initially in two small treatment programs—Pioneer House (in 1948) and Hazelden (in 1949). Over time, addictions professionals were added, treatment wards were unlocked allowing freedom of activity for patients, and lectures and group and individual therapy sessions were added to the program. Today, "Minnesota" style programs have a mix of professional and nonprofessional staff persons; among the professional personnel are medical practitioners, psychiatrists, psychologists, clergy, and social workers.

The Minnesota Model is best represented by Hazelden facilities located in Minnesota and Florida, which hold to the philosophy that alcoholism and drug addiction are progressive and incurable medical diseases, which can be arrested through treatment. Treatment at Hazelden is an approximately 30-day program involving a variety of therapeutic approaches (though many addicts are referred subsequently to extended care residential facilities). Initially, most patients go through detoxification. This is not regarded as a primary therapy so much as a prelude to group and individual therapy strategies. Early in the treatment process, the patient is exposed to group therapy, where he or she is confronted by others with the nature of their condition. About one-third of the way through the program, the patient is exposed to the 12 steps of AA (or Narcotics Anonymous), and overcoming the patient's resistance to attending such groups is given a lot of attention. Participation in 12-step programs is seen as essential for successful long-term recovery. The more the patient embraces the 12-step way of life voluntarily, the greater the chance of success (Miller and Hoffman, 1995; McCrady and Delaney, 1995). The spiritual dimension of recovery is highly emphasized, and clergy are a visible part of Hazelden's program (Laundergan, 1982). Aftercare is also emphasized, and the facility is available at any time to graduates of the program. Hazelden and the Minnesota

Model have been replicated and/or adapted by numerous programs throughout the country. Perhaps the most well-known, for its celebrity connections, is the Betty Ford Center in Rancho Mirage, California (now with a second center in Irving, Texas, as well).

OUT-PATIENT DRUG-FREE PROGRAMS

This category of programs is comprised of a host of local treatment facilities, which generally provide either chemical detoxification services or individual and group therapy counseling or both. Both of these types of services are included in comprehensive residential programs such as Hazelden and the Betty Ford Center as discussed earlier. *Detoxification* is a central component of these programs. The process of detoxification varies, depending on the substance involved. Detoxification from narcotics is generally accomplished without the use of drugs, and is often done "cold turkey"—that is suddenly, over a period of a few days. Other drugs, such as alcohol, barbiturates, and most tranquilizers may require a more gradual process, as there is a risk of seizures and other medical complications. Detoxification as a formal treatment process is done under the watchful eye of a physician, though of course many addicts detoxify on their own. Detoxification addresses only one's physiological dependence on a drug. Insofar as drug addiction involves psychological and social components, the long-term prospects for an addict who has been through detoxification without any further treatment is not very bright. Indeed, many addicts go through detoxification, not so much to assist them in leading a drug-free life as to lower the level of their dependence on heroin, alcohol, or other drugs and thereby lessen the financial or health burdens of their addiction.

Individual, family, and *group therapy* programs are what we usually think of when we talk about out-patient drug-free treatment. In some cases, programs are little more than "crisis centers" where individuals call or drop in to get them through acutely distressful situations. Other programs range from informal drop-in "rap centers," which typically use peer relationships along with other structured and unstructured activities to help refocus youth and younger adult addicts, to highly professional counseling centers (Kleber and Slobetz, 1979). Behavior and family therapy are common therapeutic strategies. In their treatment typology, Cole and James (1975) identify two broad approaches to out-patient drug-free treatment: "change-oriented" and "adaptive." Change-oriented approaches seek a more comprehensive identity transformation similar to the resocialization process that takes place in therapeutic communities. Adaptive approaches, by contrast, are a much less radical approach and seek to lessen the dependence of an individual on alcohol or drugs so that they can function more effectively in their lives. Hubbard et al. (1989) found that among the out-patient drug-free programs in their study, about half were change-oriented. Most used individual counseling rather than group counseling strategies. Because most out-patient drug-free programs are very small and locally governed, often with only the most meager record keeping, there has been very little research conducted on the effectiveness of these programs.

SELF-HELP GROUPS

The model that most self-help groups pattern themselves after is Alcoholics Anonymous (AA), which was started in 1935 in Akron, Ohio, by two alcoholics, Bill W. and Bob S. The truncation of their last names is significant, as Alcoholics Anonymous and those programs that borrow their philosophies from AA emphasize anonymity. Meetings often close with the admonition that "Who you see here, what you hear here, when you leave here, let it stay here." Twelve-step groups are fundamentally spiritually oriented, and their primary principle is that the alcoholic or drug addict is powerless over his or her addictive disease, and dependent upon God (or one's "Higher Power") for the resources to maintain sobriety. Addiction is regarded as a disease that has spiritual as well as physical and psychological dimensions. Sobriety, rather than controlled drinking is the goal of AA, because it is believed that alcoholism is a permanent disease requiring continual and daily awareness of one's dependence on God. Self-examination and accountability to others are also fundamental principles of AA, as are making amends for the wrongs done to others, and being ready to assist other alcoholics along the "12-step" path.

Today, there are more than one million members of AA worldwide. A general survey of the United States population revealed that about 9 percent of American adults have been to at least one AA meeting (Room and Greenfield, 1993). Over the years, the basic structure and content of AA meetings have not changed much, though the membership has changed substantially. Whereas members were at one time primarily comprised of middle-class white males, females and various ethnic groups are now quite highly represented (McElrath, 1998). The AA model has also been adapted and applied to populations using other substances, as well as those experiencing nondrug addictions such as gambling, overeating, and compulsive sexuality. There are now chapters of Narcotics Anonymous, Cocaine Anonymous, and Marijuana Anonymous (Miller, Gold and Pottash, 1989).

What sets AA and its clones apart from the treatment approaches we have discussed thus far is its explicit acknowledgment of a spiritual dimension to addiction and recovery. While recognizing physiological, psychological, and social dimensions to substance abuse, the spiritual dimension is a separate, though inextricable part of all of the above. Morever, the nature of our spiritual selves is such that we recognize that we are part of a larger cosmic order than what is empirically observed and that we are dependent upon the Creator of that order. It is for this reason that, even

DRUGS AND EVERYDAY LIFE

If I Just Don't Drink

I'm Judy and I'm an alcoholic. I am a 50 plus married lady and married 30 years. I have had a long drinking career. I have a twin brother who has been sober 19 years now. My uncle was 18 years sober in AA when he died of lung cancer. My father had a drinking problem, which I can see now as I look back, and mother was a social drinker who kept us all in line.

I started in my teens. I usually drank to get high. I found that I always ran around with older men because I thought they were more exciting and I could get served easier. I managed to drink my way out of college and decided I was in love. So I got married. That marriage lasted 3 years. After that I was on my own and off and running. Being high allowed me to feel pretty, thin and funny, the life of the party.

There were lots of men because I always thought the next one would be perfect. I had many blackouts and ended up in a lot of places I did not want to be. When I look back now I thank God that AIDS was not around then. My men friends started to get worried about me and decided to fix me up and get me married off. Did I forget to say I had lots of men who were just friends? They were safer than women were.

Into my life came my second husband (hopefully the last). He was a doll and in the beginning tried to keep me in line, but the drinking was pretty much out of control. Over the years I worked as a legal secretary and when the booze called, I would quit my job. My husband was supporting me, thank you very much. I discovered I was unable to have children. So, being the perfect alcoholic I felt justified drinking whenever I wanted.

After all, no one understood what I was going through.

It was a long and hairy period in my life. My husband became my enabler. He didn't understand what alcoholism was and that I simply could not just stop. For the large majority of this time I was able to be the caretaker of the family. I always managed to stay sober during family crises. My brother got sober. I just assumed the men in my family were weak and could not drink like I could. I buried my father and mother and continued on.

Finally on December 23, 1990 I got sick and tired of being sick and tired and stumbled into the rooms of Alcoholics Anonymous. I was scared to death! Didn't know I could say no! So I followed all the directions and suggestions that were given to me. I was sober but I had so many things; I felt I hadn't lost much. I still had the house, the car, and a husband. Then I realized I had lost me. I had robbed myself of an education and decent job.

Today by the grace of God and this wonderful fellowship, I have gone back to school to learn computers. Although I am still very much a novice, I have a nice part-time job. I try to work the steps each day. I am working on accepting my husband, who is getting old—75 years—and cranky. For so many years he accepted me, warts and all, without question and for that I am grateful. I have a great sponsor, the best home groups, and many friends in the program.

IF I JUST DON'T DRINK, GO TO MEETINGS, AND TRUST MY HIGHER POWER, I should be all right one day at a time ■

Source: http://www.anonymousone.com/stories.htm

with the broader, revised wording that describes this Higher Power (or a "God of one's understanding"), some atheists and agnostics have a difficult time with the precepts of the AA model (Horowtiz, 2000). The importance of the spiritual dimension has been long-recognized in the medical profession, however, and recently the academic literature on drug addiction and treatment has recognized its importance (Green, Fullilove, and Fullilove, 1995), though others interpret what goes on in AA meetings strictly in clinical psychological terms (Khantzian and Mack, 1994).

EFFECTIVENESS OF DRUG TREATMENT

When evaluating the effectiveness of drug treatment programs, there are several things that we need to keep in mind. First, many if not most drug addicts eventually quit on their own. Referring to narcotics addiction, Winick (1962) has called this "maturing out" of addiction. Waldorf refers to the same process as the "natural recovery" from addiction (Waldorf, 1983; Waldorf and Biernacki, 1981). However labeled, when it comes to heroin addiction, most addicts seem to cease or at least seriously curtail their drug use by the time they reach their middle-age years. It has therefore been suggested that those who seek treatment (or are compelled to seek treatment) may be the hardest to reach cases (Goode, 1993). Furthermore, many addicts seeking treatment are not even attempting to go drug free; they want to lower their tolerance to a drug so that their habit will not be as costly, or so that they may slow down the rat race of their lives temporarily (Faupel, 1981). Effectiveness statistics must be interpreted in light of these realities. On the other hand, addicts who *are* ready to exit the drug-using lifestyle may seek treatment to assist them in this process. Many of these are individuals who would probably be successful in a "natural recovery" anyway, and it is not clear how much one's lifestyle change can be credited to the treatment program itself or to other factors working in an addict's life to motivate him or her to quit using drugs. For all these reasons, we must always qualify our assessment of treatment effectiveness.

INDICATORS OF TREATMENT EFFECTIVENESS

Historically, studies have used three indicators to assess the effectiveness of drug treatment. These indicators are: (1) abstention from (or reduced) drug use; (2) abstention from (or reduced) crime; and (3) employment and/or other indicators of mainstream success such as enrollment in school or conventional domestic roles (Sells, 1979). Multiple indicators such as these are used because it is recognized that drug use is multifaceted both in its cause and in its effects. An effective treatment program designed for hard-core drug addicts should address at least these fundamental areas: *reduced drug use, reduced crime,* and *increased conventional productivity.*

Assessment of treatment effectiveness is not an easy task, and there are a number of methodological considerations which affect this assessment. Such considerations include:

- Is total abstinence from drug use (or crime) necessary to consider a program successful, or are we willing to consider *reduced* drug use (or crime) an indicator of success?
- For *how long following treatment* must a client be drug free (or reduced in usage) to be considered successful?
- What point in an abuser's addictive career *prior to starting treatment* do we use as the comparison point for evaluating treatment effectiveness?
- Where reduction in criminal activity is used as a measure, how is it measured: Arrests? Charges? Convictions? Self-reported behavior?
- How is productive conventional activity measured? Is it appropriate to use the same measures for everyone and if not, on what basis do we compare levels of productive behavior? For example, many drug addicts have regular jobs, but underperform because of active drug abuse. This is substantially different from the addict who has never had steady legitimate work.

Studies of treatment effectiveness have not been consistent on any of these dimensions and for that reason, it is difficult to assess how effective treatment has been (Faupel, 1981). There are, however, some general statements that can be made on treatment effectiveness.

Data on Treatment Effectiveness

Despite the methodological difficulties in measuring treatment effectiveness, numerous independent efforts have been made to assess the effectiveness of treatment. Three efforts are particularly important for what they tell us about treatment effectiveness: the *Drug Abuse Reporting Program (DARP);* the *Treatment Outcome Prospective Study (TOPS);* and the *Drug Abuse Treatment Outcome Studies (DATOS).* We will briefly examine each of these sources of information with regard to what they tell us about the effectiveness of the various treatment modalities.

Drug Abuse Reporting Program (DARP)

DARP was the earliest attempt to collect data on treatment effectiveness on a national level. Data were collected on some 44,000 addicts entering treatment between 1969 and 1972. A total of 52 federally funded agencies were represented in the study, comprising 139 separate treatment programs. DARP collected data on clients entering methadone maintenance, therapeutic communities, out-patient drug-free programs, and simple detoxification programs. Clients were followed up over the next 12 years to determine treatment effectiveness. The evidence suggests that treatment does have a positive impact on drug use and criminal behavior. While nearly 75 percent of the sample reported one or more relapses in opiate use in the 12 years they were studied, only 41 percent reported a continuous relapse for two years or more. Moreover, 75 percent of the sample had not used daily for at least a year (61 percent had not used at all for the past year). Arrest rates, which were used as a measure of criminality, also declined by about 50 percent following treatment (Simpson and Sells, 1990), and employment improved following treatment (Simpson, Joe and Bracy, 1982).

Treatment Outcomes Prospective Study (TOPS)

This national study conducted by Hubbard and his associates (1989) collected data from more than 11,000 clients admitted to treatment between 1979 and 1981. A total of 41 treatment programs in 10 cities are represented in these data. The TOPS data comprises methadone maintenance programs, therapeutic communities, and out-patient drug-free programs. The data from TOPS are summarized below and in Figures 12.1 through 12.3.

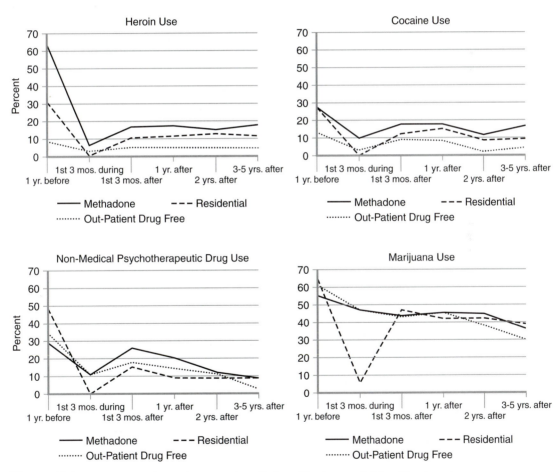

Figure 12.1 Prevalence of Regular Drug Use Before, During, and After Treatment

Source: Robert Hubbard et al., *Drug Treatment: A National Study of Effectiveness*. Chapel Hill, NC: University of North Carolina Press, 1989. Figures 5.1–5.4.

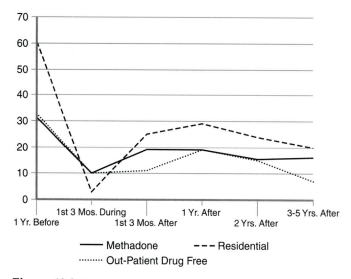

Figure 12.2 Prevalence of Predatory Crime Before, During, and After Treatment

Source: Robert Hubbard et al., *Drug Treatment: A National Study of Effectiveness.*
Chapel Hill, NC: University of North Carolina Press, 1989. Figure 6.1.

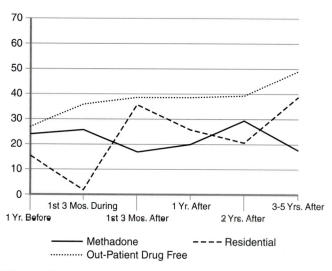

Figure 12.3 Prevalence of Full-Time Employment Before, During, and After Treatment

Source: Robert Hubbard et al., *Drug Treatment: A National Study of Effectiveness.* Chapel Hill, NC: University of North Carolina Press, 1989. Figure 6.2.

Impact on Drug Use   Figure 12.1 reveals that all types of drug use decreased while in, and following, treatment. It should be noted that these data are referring to the percentage of treatment clients in the sample who reported engaging in *regular* (daily or weekly) drug use. *Abstinence* data are far less dramatic. Among the four types of drug use examined here, cocaine seems to be least responsive to treatment, while heroin and nonmedical psychotherapeutic drug use were most strongly affected. Hubbard et al. (1989) further found that cocaine was least affected by such factors as time spent in treatment and treatment services offered. The reasons for this are unclear. It may be that because cocaine's intense psychoactive effect is so positively reinforcing, it represents a greater seduction than other types of drugs.

With regard to treatment modality, methadone maintenance had a stronger impact on heroin use, while residential treatment and out patient drug-free programs more strongly impacted other types of drug use. Methadone maintenance explicitly focuses on opiate use and this result should not be surprising. Therapeutic communities also are geared toward narcotics use; however, the treatment methodology is not as narrowly focused and is effective for other types of addiction as well. The lower level of effectiveness of residential communities for heroin use is no doubt due to a higher drop-out rate among TC clients. Hubbard et al.'s research found, consistent with many other studies, that the length of time spent in treatment is among the strongest predictors of reduced drug use following treatment. De Leon, Wexler and Jainchill (1982) found that among those who *graduated* from Phoenix House, a leading therapeutic community, 75 percent remained abstinent through five years of follow-up observation, while among dropouts from the program, only 31 percent remained drug-free.

While there are certainly differences in treatment effectiveness across modalities and across drug-use types, there is reason for optimism regarding treatment effectiveness. While caution must be exercised when interpreting data such as these for reasons that we have suggested earlier, drug treatment efforts do appear to be effective. Improvements in treatment outcome will almost surely come as treatment professionals learn to identify the best kind of treatment for specific patient needs, and as they find ways to keep patients in treatment for longer periods of time.

Impact on Crime   Clients in all the modalities examined by Hubbard et al. reduced the level of their criminal involvement while in and following treatment. The most significant drop was among those enrolled in residential treatment programs. Prior to treatment, 60 percent were involved in at least one predatory crime; only 20 percent of residential clients were known to have engaged in a predatory crime in the 3–5-year period following treatment. Both methadone maintenance and out-patient drug-free programs contributed to substantially reduced criminal activity among their clients. These generally positive findings are consistent with what other researchers have found as well (De Leon, Wexler, and Jainchill, 1982; Faupel, 1981; Hser, Anglin, and Chou, 1988). One thing that must be remembered when interpreting data such as these is that addicts often enter treatment when their drug use and/or criminal behavior is escalating, and therefore the baseline in these studies may be atypically high. Hence, we should expect to see such a reduction—a reduction which may occur eventually even without treatment (Faupel, 1981, 1991).

Impact on Legitimate Employment   The impact of drug treatment on productive, legitimate employment is less clear than the other indicators of treatment success. Methadone clients were *less likely* to be employed full time three to five years after treatment than they were prior to entering the treatment program. Both out-patient drug-free programs and residential programs saw more of their clients obtaining full-time employment following treatment. This difference among the treatment modalities may be due to the fact that legitimate employment is more likely to be a part of the treatment goals in these modalities, or in the case of out-patient drug-free programs, clients may be more likely from the ranks of the employed but because of their drug abuse problems were temporarily unemployed at the time of their entry intro treatment. Studies of treatment effectiveness in improving employment are not as common as those examining reduction in drug use and crime, but Hubbard et al's findings do find support in other literature as well (McLellan et al., 1982; Simpson et al., 1978).

Drug Abuse Treatment Outcome Studies (DATOS)

This, the most recent series of national studies, was launched in 1990. The treatment modalities included in these studies include methadone maintenance, long-term residential programs, such as therapeutic communities, short-term inpatient programs, and out-patient drug-free programs. More than 10,000 clients in 96 treatment programs, located in 11 U.S. cities were sampled initially. A one-year follow-up study of just under 3,000 clients conducted by Hubbard et al. (1997) found an overall 50 percent reduction in daily and/or weekly cocaine use as reported by the clients in the sample, across all types of treatment. Self-reported criminal activity also decreased by approximately 50 percent. These clients also reported about a 10 percent increase in employment. Another study by Hser, Anglin and Fletcher (1998) compares the relative effectiveness of the various treatment modalities with regard to drug use. The authors found that patients with a less severe drug-use history were attracted to the out-patient drug-free programs, while clients with high rates of narcotics use were better suited for methadone. Clients in all the modalities in the study reduced the level of their drug use. Overall, there was at least a 50 percent reduction in drug use one year following entry into treatment. Methadone maintenance was less effective among heroin users who were using on a less-than-daily basis, and did little for the cocaine-using populations.

Out-patient drug-free programs were less effective among heroin users. Residential programs were particularly effective in reducing levels of heroin use. Cocaine users were less affected by any of the treatment modalities than were heroin users.

SUMMARY OF TREATMENT EFFECTIVENESS

Because of the methodological differences in research efforts examining treatment effectiveness, there is quite wide variation in the reporting of treatment outcomes. Moreover, we must be careful that we do not incorrectly assume a causal relationship between treatment efforts and positive changes in indicators of treatment success. As we have suggested, it may well be the case that many individuals entering treatment were ready to change their lifestyles and would have eventually reduced their drug use, reduced their criminal participation, and would have found employment regardless of treatment participation. However, while the *degree* of effectiveness varies from study to study, the *fact* of improved lifestyle during and following treatment is nearly universally found across the research done on this issue. This very fact is important and should be noted by policy makers when making funding decisions. Treatment shows great promise in our efforts to reduce drug use and untoward behaviors associated with it, yet is relatively underfunded by government.

CONTEMPORARY ISSUES IN TREATMENT

As treatment for drug addiction has evolved, several issues or treatment alternatives have emerged which bear on the effectiveness of treatment. We address five of these issues below: *compulsory and court-ordered treatment, including prison-based treatment programs; gender issues in treatment; community reintegration after treatment; the "British Model" of drug treatment; and rapid opiate detoxification.*

COMPULSORY TREATMENT AND PRISON-BASED PROGRAMS

Compulsory treatment refers to the nonvoluntary participation of addicts in treatment programs. It is not a special type of treatment modality, and indeed, nonvoluntary and voluntary clients are often treated within the same programs. The term "compulsory treatment" refers to required drug treatment and a variety of legal and quasi-legal incentives for such treatment. It might refer to a probation officer's recommendation to enter treatment; a judge's order to enter treatment as a condition of probation; the option provided by a judge of entering treatment as an alternative to prison; or a mandatory treatment program while in prison. Moreover, a variety of terms have been used, often interchangeably, to refer to this process: coercion, mandated treatment, involuntary treatment, legal pressure, and criminal justice referral are all terms that have been used (Anglin, Prendergast, and Farabee, 1998). Leukenfeld and Tims (1990) have suggested that the term "compulsory treatment" replace the variety of terms now used to refer to this process of commitment in order to capture the variety of forms that it takes.

Compulsory treatment is based on the philosophy that most drug addicts are not intrinsically motivated to seek treatment, or to stay in treatment once being admitted, and hence must be forced to do so for their own benefit but especially the benefit of the community. Those opposed to compulsory treatment argue that effective rehabilitation requires that the addict be committed to change, a commitment that cannot generally be externally imposed. If this is the case, compulsory treatment would not be particularly effective, and might even be counterproductive as addicts forced to undergo treatment would resist and undermine treatment procedure and goals (Hartjen, Mitchell, and Washburn, 1981). Others opposed to compulsory treatment have raised both ethical and constitutional issues regarding involuntary commitment of drug abusers (Platt et al., 1988; Rosenthal, 1988). Because of these concerns, researchers and policy experts have been especially interested in whether or not such efforts to induce treatment have been effective. To the extent that coerced clients are as effectively rehabilitated as voluntary clients, compulsory treatment is justifiable, it is claimed, on the grounds that more addicts can be reached.

Compulsory treatment is not a new concept in our response to drug abuse in American society. Earlier in this chapter we learned that Congress authorized the establishment of the U.S. Public Health Service Hospitals, which were hardly "hospitals" at all, but were alternative forms of incarceration specifically designed for narcotics addicts (Inciardi, 1988). California instituted a large-scale civil commitment program in 1961 which provided for compulsory treatment of addicts for up to seven years without being convicted of a criminal offense. This program was followed by a similar program in New York in 1966, and the Narcotic Addict Rehabilitation Act of 1966 (NARA) which provided for compulsory treatment of addicts *charged* with nonviolent federal offenses; treatment instead of imprisonment for addicts *convicted* of federal crimes; and voluntary commitment of addicts (Inciardi, 1988).

More recently in 1972, a program entitled Treatment Alternatives to Street Crime (TASC) was established. Under this program, nonviolent offenders with drug or alcohol addiction were referred to community-based treatment programs as an alternative or supplement to other criminal justice procedures. TASC clients were monitored for compliance with individually tailored treatment plans, which ultimately entailed goals of abstinence and improved social functioning and employment. (Cook and Weinman, 1988). It was hoped that early forced intervention will prevent more serious crime later. By 1988, TASC programs were established in 18 states (Tonry and

Wilson, 1990). Other states have implemented similar programs over the past two decades.

Studies that have been conducted on the effectiveness of compulsory treatment have had mixed results, but are generally optimistic. An early evaluation of the California Civil Addict program found a substantial reduction in crime and drug use as well as an increase in employment during the treatment period. Post-treatment indicators were not as dramatic, but were, nevertheless, promising (McGlothlin, Anglin and Wilson, 1977).

Hubbard et al's (1989) analysis shows some interesting differences between criminal justice referrals and voluntary treatment clients. Those referred by the criminal justice system tended to stay longer in treatment than voluntary referrals, a factor that has been associated with treatment success (Anglin and Hser, 1990; De Leon, 1988, Simpson and Friend, 1988). There is simply more time to apply therapeutic techniques (and perhaps to overcome client resistance as well). Criminal justice clients did indeed do better with regard to lowered levels of drug use. Those clients in the Treatment Alternatives to Street Crime (TASC) programs were particularly affected by treatment. It seems that the interruption of drug-use patterns early in one's career, which the TASC program seeks to do, is instrumental in long-term drug reduction. Predatory criminal behavior, however, was not substantially lower among criminal justice referrals than among voluntary entrants, and CJ referrals actually performed more poorly with regard to employment following treatment. Care must be taken in the interpretation of this finding, however, because their involvement in the criminal justice system might suggest that these individuals were less employable to begin with.

There is also evidence that compulsory treatment is efficacious for the treatment of alcohol abuse. Rosenberg and Liftik (1976) found that convicted drunk drivers who were required to attend a treatment clinic as a condition of probation had much better and longer attendance rates than voluntary admissions. Using a much larger base of 1,055 subjects collected through the Washington State Alcoholism Monitoring System, Dunham and Mauss (1982) found that not only did involuntary patients stay in treatment longer, but were more successful in maintaining abstinence than were voluntary patients—indeed, court-ordered referrals were more than twice as likely to remain abstinent as were voluntary referrals.

Criminally involved, hard-core drug abusers are at the core of many of the social pathologies found in our society. Linking drug treatment with criminal justice services makes sense, because we are able to hold addicts accountable for their criminality while at the same time offer the same addicts support for changing their behavior and their lifestyles. For nonviolent offenders, this can occur as an alternative to prison. For serious offenders, drug treatment will need to be provided while they are incarcerated, a separate, though related issue in substance abuse treatment to which we now turn.

The last couple of decades has witnessed a movement to locate treatment programs in prisons. This has been a controversial issue in part because of the high cost of such programs and also because of the perceptions that many people have that these and other rehabilitation programs should not be the responsibility of the taxpayer. This is a short-sighted point of view, as most criminals with drug-abusing histories will eventually be returned to the community. Relieved of their compulsive substance abuse, they are a substantially reduced threat to those very same taxpayers. Most prison-based treatment programs model themselves after community-based therapeutic communities. Most of these treatment programs are isolated from the rest of the prison population, providing a 24-hour treatment environment. Typically, treatment staff are themselves former addicts, such as is found in community-based TCs.

Studies of prison-based programs in New York and Oregon by Wexler et al. (1988) and Field (1992) respectively, demonstrated that there was an inverse relationship between how long prisoner-clients were in these programs and their recidivism rates. Indeed, Andrews et al. (1991) report that at least 40 percent of the carefully designed evaluation studies report positive effects of prison-based rehabilitation programs generally (both drug and nondrug programs). Their own meta-analysis of the literature in this area revealed that the effectiveness of prison-based treatment was dependent upon the appropriateness of treatment for the specific needs of the client.

Compulsory treatment does, on balance, seem to have a positive impact on post-treatment outcomes. The fact that clients can be coerced to stay in treatment for a longer period of time is almost certainly the primary reason for this positive outcome. Compulsory clients may not be as motivated to engage the treatment process, at least initially, which might mute the effect of forced treatment. A motivated client would seem to be the best candidate for treatment success. Even clients who are not motivated initially, however, may learn the motivation in the process of treatment. Just as we have suggested that drug use is a learned behavior, so one can learn to live a drug and crime-free lifestyle. Hence, even court-ordered treatment entrants may learn to accept the value of being drug-free, and may participate as willingly as voluntary participants. Moreover, we must be careful not to assume that all compulsory clients are necessarily nonwilling—and that all voluntary clients are necessarily willing. That is, while compulsory clients are required to enter a treatment program by the criminal justice system, some or even many may be ready for such an experience (Anglin, Prendergast, and Farabee, 1998). For some, especially those early in their criminal and drug-using careers such as TASC clients, the criminal justice encounter may be the attention-getter that is necessary to motivate them to change their lives. On the other hand, so-called voluntary clients may be under threat of eviction or loss of a spouse if they do not enter treatment (Maddux, 1988). Such an entry is hardly willing even though technically considered voluntary. One thing we do know—compulsory clients are usually in treatment for a substantially longer period of time, and this time spent in a therapeutic environment has been demonstrated to be effective in producing a changed lifestyle, particularly in reducing the level of drug use.

GENDER ISSUES IN TREATMENT

Until the 1970s, there was almost no attention given to treatment for women addicts. Virtually all of the research on drug treatment—and drug addiction generally for that matter—was conducted among male addicts. It was widely and mistakenly believed that knowledge gained in studying male addicts would apply to women as well. Research supported by the National Institute on Drug Abuse, as part of their initiative "Drug Addiction Research and the Health of Women," shows that "gender differences play a role from the very earliest opportunity to use drugs, that women and men tend to abuse different drugs, that the effects of drugs are different for women and men, and that *some approaches to treatment are more successful for women than for men.*" (NIDA 2000; our emphasis).

In 1973, the First National Conference on Women and Drug Concerns was held in Washington, DC, where women raised concerns about the need to understand women as a special drug-using and treatment group. This conference was soon followed by special programs for women's concerns established by the National Institute on Drug Abuse and in 1976, Public Law 94-371 was passed giving priority consideration to prevention and treatment programs for women (Beschner and Thompson, 1981). A 1989 study by Stevens, Arbiter and Glider, however, revealed that more than 10 years after the 1976 legislation, only 35 treatment programs across the United States were identified as having any special services for women.

While female addicts share many of the circumstances, experiences and needs of their male counterparts, there are also treatment needs that are unique to women. Numerous problems specific to women or more often encountered by women in treatment or seeking treatment have been noted in the literature over the past 25 years. We address some of the major issues that have been raised in this section.

Lack of Child Care Facilities

Rosenbaum and Murphy (1981), Laign (1987) and others have identified the lack of child care facilities as the leading obstacle to women entering treatment. Beschner and Thompson (1981) find in their review of the studies conducted on women in treatment that anywhere from 67 to 73 percent of the women in treatment have dependent children. A more recent study by Hanke and Faupel (1993) found that 75 percent of the women in New York treatment facilities reported at least one child and that 50 percent reported having two or more children. Faupel and Hanke (1993) further found that while 67 percent of the women who have ever been in treatment had at least one child, 98 percent of the women who have *never* been in treatment have one or more children. While these data are not conclusive, it is suggestive that many women may be deterred from seeking treatment because of a lack of child care facilities.

Counseling Needs

Because most treatment programs are oriented toward men, or have grown out of male-oriented models, women entering treatment are likely to encounter a male-dominated treatment process. Male domination manifests itself in a variety of ways. Residential programs, particularly therapeutic communities, frequently use ex-addicts as counselors. They are typically male. Male counselors are often counterproductive in treating addicted women, who have been physically and/or sexually abused by men (Gil-Rivas, Fiorentine, Anglin, and Taylor, 1997). Also, residential treatment programs typically use confrontive therapy, such as the "haircut" discussed earlier in this chapter. This can be a very effective approach in breaking down the "tough guy" image that men often present, but can be devastating to a woman addict who already suffers from emotional, physical, and/or sexual abuse at the hands of men (Cuskey, Berger and Densen-Gerber, 1977; Reed, 1987). Reed (1987) suggests that these tactics that have been found effective in confronting men with what they have long denied, may cause women who have developed a "learned helplessness" to feel even more out of control.

Still another way in which the counseling needs of women fail to be met in traditional programs is the ratio of male to female clients in these programs. While many programs have separated men and women for therapy purposes, there remain many mixed-sex programs. Where this occurs, males usually dominate. Reed (1987) reports that most women in treatment were in programs with anywhere from a 2:1 to a 10:1 ratio of men to women. Research by Hanke and Faupel (1993) was less dramatic, but still found that a majority of women (57.3 percent) reported that they were in the minority to men in the treatment programs of which they were a part. Residential programs were particularly dominated by men, with 64 percent of the women in these programs reporting that less than half of the residents were women. Research from a variety of fields has demonstrated that men are more outspoken and assertive than women in mixed group settings. Such domination by men makes it likely that the women in these programs may not be able to fully address their issues and concerns, at least not in group therapy sessions.

Sexism

Friedman and Alicea (2001) in a recent study of women in methadone treatment programs identified sexism as a major obstacle encountered by women seeking treatment. Counselors regarded these women as poor mothers, and those on the outside—family and friends—did as well. The demeaning interactions they encounter discourage many women from seeking treatment, opting to try to get by as best they can on their own. Cuskey et al. (1977) also point out that treatment staff often view women as inherently "sicker" than men; that whereas men's problems are primarily centered around lack of motivation and/or skills training, women are believed to have more deep-set problems. Consequently, many of the services available to men such as job training skills and the like are not offered to women because it is believed that they either could not benefit from them due to other psychological problems, or because job skills are not necessary for women (the assumption being that they will be supported by a man). While NIDA supported research (NIDA, 2000) does back up the notion that women treatment clients often have a greater range of other problems (e.g., physical ill health, physical and sexual abuse, history of attempted suicide), that should not be used to exclude them from a full range of programs that might benefit them.

Unique Physical Needs of Women

Women coming into treatment often have physical symptoms or needs that are unique. Studies have found that women are more likely than men to cite physical symptoms a motivators for treatment (Beschner and Thompson, 1981). Many women entering treatment have prostituted themselves for drug money, and bring with them many physical problems, including gynecological and urinary infections, venereal disease and AIDS. Pregnant women pose particular needs and concerns, and the number of women seeking treatment who are pregnant is not insignificant. Pregnancy is often a motivator to seek treatment, as these women do not want to give birth to addicted children. Many treatment programs will not admit pregnant women at all (Cuskey et al., 1977; Karan, 1989). Those that do often do not have pre- or postnatal care.

COMMUNITY REINTEGRATION

Perhaps the most neglected aspect of drug treatment has been follow-up services designed to assist clients in maintaining a drug free lifestyle after the structured environment of treatment. Following treatment, addicts face the difficult challenge of integrating into a community which, for many, is rather foreign. Many addicts have lived their lives on the streets in inner-city areas, have relied on criminal activities to support their habits and lifestyles, and have developed friendship networks that are primarily comprised of other addicts. This is the *setting* of their addiction. If treatment is to be successful in the long term, a change of setting will almost certainly be required. Former addicts seeking to live a drug and crime free lifestyle need legitimate employment. They also need friendship networks that are supportive of a conventional lifestyle. Broken family relationships need repair. If such a supportive community is not available to recovering addicts, the only recourse for many is to return to the streets from whence they came, with all of the influences and triggers that led them into a lifestyle of drug use and crime in the first place. Treatment programs of a number of different types warn against the "people, places, and things" that will lead one back to abusing drugs. Steering clear of them may require not only changing one's attitude but one's latitude as well.

The word that is used to describe the shift in *setting* from the nonconventional and drug-using milieu of the streets to a more conventional context is called *reintegration*. This is probably a misnomer, because at least for many recovering addicts, this will be the first time they have ever been a part of a conventional community. Reintegration is quite typically initiated by placing the addict in a **halfway house.** Halfway houses are transitional living facilities which serve as a "bridge" between the treatment program and the conventional community. Here, the addict lives with other addicts in a therapeutic environment with some, though not all, of the structure of the treatment program, and is encouraged to seek work and build relationships in conventional society. Several problems have been identified with halfway houses. Perhaps most problematic is that communities are resistant to hosting them. Ideally, halfway houses should be located in communities which are free of drugs and crime and which might be a catalyst for helping integrate the former addicts into conventional society. These are the very neighborhoods which are most resistant to halfway houses, however (Davidson, 1981; Dembo, Ciarlo, and Taylor, 1983). Residents in these communities do not understand addiction and have a fear of the unknown, the same NIMBY mentality mentioned with methadone clinics. There is also fear of a reduction of property values as a result of such facilities moving in (Dembo, Ciarlo, and Taylor, 1983).

Employment is a major need of recovering drug addicts. A two-year demonstration study funded by the Special Action Office for Drug Abuse Prevention found that employment was an important part of post-treatment success (National Institute on Drug Abuse, 1977). Unfortunately, many employers are hesitant to hire ex-drug users, understandable in light of their often shaky work history while using drugs. Some efforts have been made to facilitate work opportunities for recovering addicts. Wolkstein (1979) for example, describes some early efforts made in the establishment of government subsidized employment opportunities for ex-addicts. This, of course, is but a temporary solution. Another program established in New York City is an employment agency specializing in the placement of ex-addicts (Wolkstein, 1979). Related to employment, many addicts need vocational and educational skills before they can even begin work. Educational institutions can be very intimidating to ex-addicts. Problems in school were often catalysts for them becoming involved in drugs and crime in the first place. Programs that encourage and help to facilitate educational pursuits are needed. One such program that was established a couple of decades ago is the "Miniversity" program, jointly run by Daytop Village (a large residential treatment program in New York City) and the City University of New York. While still in treatment, Daytop clients could take courses and earn credits toward an undergraduate degree at CUNY (Faupel, 1985). Another program in Washington State placed qualified addicts in federal and state prisons who wished to pursue college degrees, on the same floors in college dormitories, but where they were also able to interact with other students in the dorm (Hawkins, 1979).

There are other important points of reintegration as well. Families of addicts may be seriously strained or broken due to the addiction. Friendship networks need to be established, whether informally, or formally through organizations such as churches and synagogues, neighborhood associations, family counseling, and others. Some of these organizations are also resistant to helping recovering addicts, or may not be especially knowledgeable about how to do so. The common theme in all of the obstacles to reintegration is the need to educate the community regarding the nature of addiction and the positive contribution that recovering addicts can make to an organization, neighborhood, or community. The obstacles to successful reintegration lie not just with the addict or with the aftercare component of treatment programs. They especially lie within us as residents and members of would-be host communities and all of the social service groups contained therein. The unspoken skepticism of most Americans regarding the rehabilitative potential of recovering addicts too often results in a self-fulfilling prophecy. That is, we generally expect that recovering addicts will relapse or underperform, yet it is our very resistance to community reintegration that most likely brings about such a result.

THE "BRITISH METHOD:" HEROIN MAINTENANCE

Since the years immediately following the Harrison Narcotics Act of 1914, and reinforced more recently by the Comprehensive Drug Abuse Prevention and Control Act of 1970 (both discussed in Chapter 2), heroin maintenance has been precluded legally in the United States. Heroin is a Schedule I drug, which means that it has no officially recognized medical utility, and hence is illegal for all medical purposes in this country. That includes use for relief of severe or chronic pain and for purposes of keeping addicts comfortable. In addition, after 90 years of antiheroin sentiment, and a raft of media messages that heroin may just be the devil incarnate, Americans are not likely to be open to a discussion of heroin as legitimate medicine. Yet *heroin maintenance*—widely known as the **"British method"** or the "British system"—is used in several European countries, and its efficacy and desirability as a treatment modality for heroin addiction in this country has been debated for 30 years or more, particularly in the 1970s.

The British are credited by name because they were the first to use heroin maintenance as part of drug-abuse policy. Starting in the 1960s, addicts who had tried to kick their heroin habits by other means and were unsuccessful could register with the government and the National Health Service, and could have heroin prescribed for them.[4] As with other NHS programs, the heroin was provided free of charge, in amounts geared to the level of the addict's habit. Thus it was fairly unprofitable for them to divert their heroin to the black market, a major concern of those who challenge such a plan (Kaplan, 1983, pp. 158–183). The focus of the heroin maintenance policy is not a punitive one, designed to stamp out drug abuse, but rather is on public health and is designed to mitigate the damage that drug abuse does (Nadelmann, 1995). [We discuss such an approach under the rubric of "harm reduction" in Chapter 14.] One of the reasons why heroin maintenance might reduce the consequences of heroin addiction is that the heroin being provided is legal (and free or inexpensive) and is of known purity. Hence, the addict would not have to worry about being arrested, would not have to steal to afford his drug of choice, and would unlikely suffer a drug overdose. It should also be mentioned that heroin, when administered under healthful conditions, is a relatively benign drug meaning that it doesn't damage the body's ability to function as many other drugs, including pharmaceuticals, can do. Most of the deaths associated with heroin arise from its illegality not its toxicity (Goode, 1999, p. 326).

The popularity of heroin maintenance as an alternative drug-abuse treatment policy rose in the early 1990s in some circles with the realization that new cases of HIV and hepatitis infection were increasingly being found in IV drug using populations. Concern about public health led the governments of Switzerland, the Netherlands, and Denmark to offer legal heroin to addicts (Nadelmann, 1995; Sheldon, 1997). The Swiss experience since 1994 is quite instructive. They sell heroin at state-run clinics to addicts who meet rigid qualifications—at least two consecutive years of active addiction, plus criminal records or health problems (other than addiction), or both. Addicts come to the clinic one to three times a day, pay 15 Swiss francs each time (about $10), and inject on site under antiseptic conditions. The addicts are also enrolled in free comprehensive health, social, and psychological services. The program is monitored by the World Health Organization of the United Nations (Nadelmann, 1995).

The results are convincing. From 1994 to 1997, crimes the addicts committed decreased 90 percent, new HIV and hepatitis infections dropped to almost zero, and the number who were employed jumped from 30 percent to 60 percent. It is easy to see why some government officials proclaimed it a huge success. Others, however, who believe that abstinence is the only true success in drug policy disagreed. They proposed a constitutional amendment that would disallow heroin (and a host of other drugs) to be used medically. This was rejected by Swiss voters in the fall of 1997 (Sheldon, 1997). Nadelmann (1995) concludes that however much sense this approach makes to the British, the Swiss, the Dutch, and to scientific researchers, the United States is a long way from giving it serious consideration as a policy alternative. American drug policy will not consider it, because we are locked into a drug-war mentality. We, your textbook authors, would welcome open discussion of heroin maintenance, as an example of "thinking outside the drug-war box."

RAPID OPIATE DETOXIFICATION

We mentioned previously that the detoxification process is often a necessary first stage in overcoming drug addiction. It allows the addicts, typically over five to seven days, to cleanse themselves of the drug(s) in their system, which reduces physiological drug craving and allows them to benefit from therapy groups and other modes of treatment. **Rapid opiate detoxification** shortens the detoxification process and the discomfort it produces in the addict. It was developed by European physicians in the 1980s, and refined by an Israeli physician, Dr. Andre Waissman, in the early 1990s. Under heavy sedation or general anesthesia, the opiate receptors in the patient's brain are blocked by a drug like naltrexone, while other medications speed up the reactions to the rapid drug withdrawal. The result is that the patient awakens without having experienced withdrawal symptoms (Cucchia, et al. 1998). Depending on the method and drugs that are employed, the process can take as little as four to six hours (called ultrarapid detox) or 12 to 24 hours. The addict is then prescribed naltrexone, a narcotic antagonist, to reduce the likelihood of postprocedure relapse. Its appeal to addicts is pretty easy to see, though it might not be the "cure" they believe it to be.

Rapid detoxification has its critics in the medical, scientific, and legal fields. Some question its effectiveness, claiming relapse rates of 80 percent within six months of detox (Cucchia, et al., 1998). Also, patients have died soon after having the procedure, seven patients (over four years) in one physician's outpatient practice alone. The doctor in question, Lance L. Gooberman, himself a recovering drug addict, argues that they had underlying heart conditions that he and others had not detected. In response, many in the medical community assert that the procedure is too stressful for the bodies of addicts ravaged by years of drug abuse (Marshall, 2001; Associated Press, 2000). Gooberman was prohibited from performing the procedure for an 18-month period (during which he claimed $2.7 million in lost revenue), and faces losing his medical license altogether. Mark Herr, the director of New Jersey's Division of Consumer Affairs, which oversees the State Board of Medicine, said: "We just want to make sure these 'cutting-edge treatments' aren't cutting off life." (Associated Press, 2000). It is important to note, that while the procedure has been approved for use by the American Society of Addiction Medicine, experts agree that more research is needed. The National Institute on Drug Abuse (NIDA), is currently conducting a three-year national study comparing rapid detoxification with two methods of slower detoxification, the results to be published in 2004 (Associated Press, 2000).

SUMMARY

Drug treatment programs, also known as therapeutic approaches to the problem of drug dependency, use a variety of methods or treatment modalities to help those who are dependent on legal or illegal drugs and no longer desire to be. The drug(s) people are dependent on, their physical and mental health, their commitment to change, and their financial resources and support systems all influence which type of treatment they might seek. Drug treatment assumes that addiction is a medical illness or condition capable of being arrested, if not outright cured. Most experts contend that addiction affects one physically and emotionally (and perhaps spiritually as well). Therefore, the most effective drug-treatment programs are comprehensive and multifaceted, including some combination of the following: detoxification and medical stabilization, drug counseling and drug education, individual and group therapy, and aftercare planning, including relapse prevention and help with a support network.

Drug treatment works. For many addicts, therapeutic intervention, the application of an appropriate treatment modality at the right time allows them to give up a habit and a way of life that is self-destructive and harmful to others. This doesn't mean that treatment is any kind of a guaranteed cure for drug dependency; frankly, it is unsuccessful for many and is unnecessary for others. We are aware, and have argued in this chapter, that claims of success, particularly from treatment programs themselves, need to be examined with a critical eye. We are likewise cognizant of the fact that some researchers claim a failure rate of 70–90 percent. Those seeking drug treatment are more likely to be hard-core abusers, who have been unsuccessful at stopping on their own and who have not been helped by the criminal justice system's punitiveness. These hard-core abusers consume a disproportionate amount of illegal drugs, and their impact on our social institutions—the family, the economy, health care, and criminal justice among them—is enormous. Anything that can ameliorate these considerable consequences is worth considering. We argue that treatment works because we choose to focus on those it helps, to whatever degree it helps, regardless of the particular form the treatment takes. We are not alone in this position. Our federal government concurs, though as we have noted, actual *funding* for drug treatment has lagged behind spending on law enforcement. Consider the following from statement from the Office of National Drug Control Policy (essentially, the "drug czar's" office): ". . . numerous studies support the logic and rationale of providing treatment for drug users. The research reveals that the societal costs of untreated addiction, such as violence, crime, poor health, and family breakup far exceed the costs of providing treatment." (ONDCP, 2001). We concur—drug rehabilitation can be costly, but we believe that *not* treating hard-core drug and alcohol dependency can end up costing our society much more. Russell W. Peterson, a former governor of Delaware, calls our current emphasis on imprisonment over treatment for the addicted "an immoral offense that threatens our way of life." He writes that we have two options: to continue our bankrupt strategy or to invest enough in drug treatment to ensure decent lives for as many as we can help (Peterson, 2000).

KEY TERMS

antagonist

British Method

compulsory treatment

detoxification

diversion

halfway house

methadone maintenance

Minnesota Model

rapid opiate detoxification

therapeutic community
  (TC)

treatment modalities

REVIEW QUESTIONS

1. What are the two assumptions that advocates of drug treatment make, regardless of their approach to treatment? Do you agree with these assumptions?

2. Early understandings of alcoholism and drug addiction by treatment specialists was that these were quite literally diseases that involved toxins that needed to be detoxified. In what ways do current treatment efforts reflect this "disease model" of addiction? In what ways have treatment efforts today departed from this model?

3. Compare and contrast medical/ pharmacological approaches to drug treatment with the other approaches discussed in this chapter. Which of these general approaches do you think holds the greatest potential for successful treatment? Why?

4. Some have suggested that the therapeutic community (TC) is more *sociological* in its approach to understanding addiction and treatment than any other type of treatment. What is the basis for this claim?

5. Empirically, what are the measures of treatment effectiveness? Do you agree that these are appropriate measures? Are these measures consistent with what you would consider to be the proper goals of treatment (see Critical Thought Question 1)?

6. What might be some ways that treatment programs could be made more "female friendly?"

7. The "British Method," at least in earlier years, made heroin easily available to addicts through physicians and clinics. The rationale for this approach is that addiction is a disease and that insofar as there is no "cure," physicians should be free to treat the symptoms of that disease (withdrawal distress). The United States rejected this model, but uses methadone, which is also a narcotic that some have argued is much more troublesome than heroin in terms of its effects on users. The rationale for rejecting the British Method is that heroin use is a crime, therefore it would be improper to prescribe heroin to addicts. Which approach do you think makes more sense? Why?

CRITICAL THOUGHT QUESTIONS

1. There is a major divide that separates drug-treatment specialists regarding the purpose and goals of treatment, resulting in further differences of opinion regarding proper techniques for accomplishing these goals. There are those who argue that the purpose and goals of treatment should be to make the drug addict completely drug free, and that treatment should consist of drug-free methods of accomplishing this task. Others argue that treatment should facilitate the addict's effective functioning in society, not necessarily to make an individual drug-free. Reflect on this philosophical divide and articulate what you think should be the proper goals and techniques of drug treatment.

2. Alcoholic's Anonymous (and its counterpart Narcotics Anonymous) are widely acclaimed self-help groups for addicts that base their efforts heavily on spiritual restoration. What role do you think spirituality and faith have in recovery from addiction?

NOTES

1. The word "synanon" originated with one of the early residents of the program. Attempting to say two words in the same breath—symposium and seminar—he managed to come out with a badly garbled rendition that sounded like "synanon." From this point forward the organization was known as "Synanon" (capital S) and the group seminars known as "synanons" (small s). The history of this group is more fully described in Yablonsky (1965).

2. Some of the more well-known therapeutic communities include Phoenix House, Odyssey House, and Daytop Village, all in New York City, and Gateway Foundation in Chicago.

3. The "haircut" is usually a systematic verbal attack on an individual by others in the group in response to misbehavior or exemplifying inappropriate attitudes. This process received its name in the original Synanon community, however, to refer to actual haircuts, whereby individuals in the group would participate in chopping the hair of the wayward resident as a symbol of their disapproval (Yablonsky, 1965).

4. The British amended this system in 1968, setting up heroin-maintenance clinics as part of the National Health Service. Private patients, with the financial means, may still go to their own physicians for prescriptions of heroin.

PREVENTIVE RESPONSES TO DRUG PROBLEMS: DRUG EDUCATION AND DRUG TESTING

The third mode of societal response to the problem of drug abuse in America is prevention. Unlike drug treatment, which addresses the problem of drug abuse *after* it has affected individuals, the two responses considered in this chapter—drug education and drug testing—generally attempt to intervene *prior* to the development of a drug-abuse problem. Preemptive responses are fairly recent newcomers in society's arsenal of responses to drug use. This is surprising, given the recognition in medicine that it is better to prevent a disease than to treat it once it has already occurred. It is all the more surprising given that treatment efforts to date have not had a consistent track record. Federal spending on prevention efforts, which are usually identified as drug education efforts, is up some 48 percent since 1996, though they still comprise less than 14 percent of the federal drug budget, about the same as what it was in 1991 (Office of National Drug Control Policy, 1992, 1999).

Drug prevention is a "demand-side" response to the problems associated with drug use. Both drug testing and drug education represent efforts to reduce the number of individuals who use drugs and/or the amount of drugs that people use. As we have suggested in Chapter 11, practitioners and policy makers often distinguish between *primary, secondary,* and *tertiary* prevention strategies. *Primary prevention* is geared toward preventing the initial, or at least chronic, use of drugs by individuals, which is the goal of most drug-education programs. *Secondary prevention* focuses on early identification of drug use and intervention prior to the development of major drug-related problems and full-blown addiction. Most drug testing is conducted with this purpose in mind. *Tertiary prevention* is directed at those who are already addicted, and while this is referred to as a prevention strategy, it actually focuses on rehabilitation (Bukoski, 1991). The major tertiary prevention is drug treatment, which was addressed in Chapter 12.

DRUG EDUCATION

Drug education has a fairly long history in the United States, even though it has only recently been emphasized in drug policy strategies. Perhaps the earliest drug-education programs emerged from the prohibitionist movement and the efforts of the Women's Christian Temperance Union (WCTU) to eradicate alcohol and the problems it caused from the face of the American landscape (Bordin, 1981). Early efforts at drug education were profoundly ideological in nature, often making exaggerated claims that would eventually fail to hold up to empirical investigation. Perhaps the most well-known early education effort was the film *Teach Your Children,* which was originally produced as a drug-education film in 1936 by the Federal Bureau of Narcotics. It was later released under the title *Reefer Madness*. The film depicts an upstanding, middle-class high school boy getting turned on to marijuana and becoming a sexually aggressive, rather crazed, and violent person, who is eventually charged with a murder he did not commit. The information presented here is clearly exaggerated, but was widely believed at the time. The problem with this kind of information, of course, is that when claims about the effects of these drugs do not materialize, the credibility of the message and the messenger is compromised. This can have unfortunate consequences. Marsha Rosenbaum quotes a heroin addict who, when asked how she became addicted to heroin, replied,

> When I was in high school they had these so-called drug education classes. They told us if we used marijuana we would become addicted. They told us if we used heroin we would become addicted. Well, we all tried marijuana and found we did not become addicted. We figured the entire message must be b.s. So I tried heroin, used it again and again, got strung out, and here I am (Rosenbaum, 1999, p. 1)

When "drug education" is mentioned today, what immediately comes to mind for most people are high-profile programs such as DARE (Drug Abuse Resistance Education) or the many commercials sponsored by the Partnership for a Drug Free America. These are, indeed, drug-education programs, but they represent a narrow sliver of the broad spectrum of approaches to drug education in the United States today.

Through the years, there have been numerous approaches to classifying drug-education programs. Perhaps the most helpful typologies are those which characterize the *nature of the message communicated* to the audience. Ellickson (1995), among others, distinguishes between the *informational model*, *affective model*, and *social influence model*, a typology that we have found most useful for our discussion. After discussing each of these models and their effectiveness, we will examine an emerging approach that falls under the more general approach to drug policy, *harm reduction.*

INFORMATIONAL MODEL

The **informational model** is probably most familiar to baby boomers who went through public schools in the 1960s and early 1970s. This traditional approach is designed simply to convey factual information about the nature of drugs and what drugs can do to the human body in the short and long term. Drugs and their effects were always presented in negative terms, and the consequences of drug use were often exaggerated. Typical of these programs was the use of "scare tactics" with a method of presentation that allowed little opportunity for student interaction or engagement.

Informational programs are typically implemented through the schools, but other media are also used, especially the public media of communication. Among the first organizations to provide drug educational material through this medium were the American Cancer Society and the American Heart Association. These organizations targeted cigarette smoking. Studies of the effectiveness of these campaigns suggest that they were quite successful in reducing smoking (Flay, 1997; Pisani, 1995). Alcohol has also been the target of mass media advertising. The object of this advertising has not been so much abstinence as responsible drinking, and especially not driving if drinking. These ads have been sponsored by Mothers Against Drunk Driving, the Ad Council, and by beer companies themselves (Pisani, 1995). Jacobs (1989) points out that these educational attempts have been less than effective in changing behavior, namely drunk driving. There are numerous reasons for this, including the fact that there are strong prodrinking messages that are also sent out over the airwaves, and also that the transfer of *knowledge* to *behavior* is often difficult when it comes to drinking and driving.

Perhaps the most visible antidrug information to be disseminated through the mass media, however, is that sponsored by the Partnership for a Drug-Free America. The Partnership, was conceived in 1986 by Phil Joanou, chairman of the Dailey Advertising Agency. It is a nonprofit, private sector coalition consisting of representatives from advertising, public relations firms, and media companies (Pisani, 1995). Since 1998, the organization has worked in close partnership with the National Office on Drug Control Policy (NODCP). The messages were initially directed primarily at preteens who had not yet begun to experiment with drugs, and they were powerful in their content. Very few will forget the "this is your brain on drugs" message sponsored by the Partnership. More recently, the Partnership has also been targeting parents and caregivers. Research conducted by the Gordon S. Black Corporation, examining drug attitudes and behavior from 1987 to 1992 suggests that the advertising campaign of the Partnership for a Drug-Free America may have had some impact, though many variables may have intervened in producing a downward trend in use, and it should also be noted that there have been fluctuations in drug use since (Pisani, 1995).

One other type of informational program that has found widespread acceptance is what has commonly been called "drunk driving schools." Based upon a model developed in Phoenix, Arizona, in response to the high number of drunk-driving-related fatalities in that area, these classes designed for DUI arrestees, provide extensive information on things such as how driving skills deteriorate at various BAC levels; the fallacy that alcohol effects can be counteracted with coffee or cold water; and the penalties for driving under the influence. These educational courses also include sessions which are more reflective in nature, such as keeping diaries, and life activities inventories which address issues of personal and social adjustment (Jacobs, 1989).

Effectiveness of Information-Based Programs

Evaluation studies of the impact of informational drug education programs have generally produced disappointing results. A review of the evaluations of the drinking/driving schools by Jacobs (1989) revealed that the recidivism rate for individuals graduating from these schools was about the same as a control group which received no education. School-based programs do not fare much better. Meta-analyses—which analyze the results of studies which have already been conducted—of studies of school-based programs reveal that while these programs may be quite effective in affecting the *attitudes* of youth toward drugs, they are not especially effective in changing their *behavior* (Tobler, 1986; Tobler and Stratton, 1997; White and Pitts, 1998). Moreover, Tobler (1986) found that "knowledge only" programs (i.e., information-based programs) were inferior to other programs, particularly those that involve peer resistance. Information-based programs are highly didactic in nature and allow for very little interaction. She also found that multimodal programs were more effective than single modalities. In her 1997 follow-up to this study, conducted with Howard Stratton, Tobler found that "interactive" programs were much more effective than "noninteractive" programs. Finally, of 62 evaluations included in their review, White and Pitts (1998) found only 18 studies that suggested program effectiveness, but of those, only two provided verification for absence of drug use; the remaining 16 were based on self-reports.

The conclusion that we draw from these evaluations is that information-oriented drug education programs are not effective for deterring drug use. It is generally acknowledged that these programs are quite effective in increasing levels of knowledge about drugs and their effects, and even that they have an impact on attitudes about drug use. Knowledge and attitudes do not, however, automatically translate into desired behavior. One might speculate that the reason for such ineffectiveness is the greatly exaggerated claims about drugs and the damage that they do. We know that these claims have damaged the credibility of authorities who make these claims, as evidenced by the quotation by the heroin addict that was included at the beginning of this section. If this were the only problem, it would easily be solved—we would simply cease making exaggerated claims. The more fundamental problem with information-based programs is that there is no mechanism to translate *cognitive changes* into *behavioral changes*. Because of the failures of information-based programs, practitioners have sought to develop other approaches to drug education which address emotional and behavioral levels as well as cognitive levels of understanding.

AFFECTIVE MODEL

Programs using the **affective model** seek to improve communication skills, decision-making ability and self-assertion, all of which are believed to underlie a predisposition toward drug abuse (Ellickson, 1995; Kim, 1981). The affective model emerged in the early 1970s in response to a growing recognition that there were certain "risk factors" that were associated with vulnerability to drug use. Such risk factors include everything from genetic and congenital conditions to personality characteristics to socioeconomic conditions of one's family and neighborhood (Gerstein and Green, 1993). It is, of course, impossible to address all of these predispositions in a drug-education program, but there are factors that can be addressed. A widely used curriculum using the affective model is *Reconnecting Youth: A Peer Group Approach to Building Life Skills* (Eggert, Nicholas, and Owen, 1995.). This curriculum, oriented to high school students, was first developed in 1984 and seeks to enhance self-esteem, teach students decision-making skills, and develop communication skills. These are all factors that, when absent, are believed to predispose young people to drug use and abuse, as well as other maladies such as depression and suicide. Students who are poor academic achievers are targeted for the program, which is a semester-long, daily curriculum that is interactional in nature. In addition, there are social activities that seek to build positive friendships and develop positive attitudes toward school. It is believed that by developing social, communication, and decision-making skills, all of which should result in enhanced self-esteem, many at-risk students will be prevented from becoming drug abusers. The logic behind this program is a direct application of the principles of social control theory, which suggest that drug use and other forms of delinquency are the result of a lack of social bonds connecting young people with conventional society. These activities can be prevented through programs which establish strong social and emotional bonds between children and parents, teachers, and other conventional adults. Furthermore, positive social bonds provide young people with a favorable attitude toward school and other conventional institutions, which in turn, make drug use and other antisocial behavior less appealing. (For more discussion of social control and its implications for drug use and abuse, see Chapter 4.)

Another program which also draws upon social control theory is Preparing Parents for the Drug Free Years (PDFY). This program focuses especially on the establishment of positive bonds within the family, which include opportunities for involvement in family activities, development of skills to accomplish tasks and solve problems, and a healthy system of rewards and punishments within the family (Haggerty, Kosterman, Cagalano, and Hawkins, 1999). Unlike the *Reconnecting Youth* program, PDFY targets families with children in grades 4 through 8. Moreover, this program targets the *parents and guardians* of children in this age range rather than the children themselves. The idea is to train parents to proactively develop bonds with their children, thereby insulating their children from the pull toward drug abuse. Parents are typically invited to participate in five one-hour sessions which address issues such as setting clear expectations regarding drug and alcohol use, learning how to identify risk factors associated with drug use, managing family conflict, and establishing family bonds. PDFY was piloted during the mid-1980s in 10 public schools in Seattle, Washington. Other field tests were conducted with a health maintenance organization and in a program involving the broadcast media. Since its inception, PDFY has been implemented in more than 30 states and in Canada, training more than 120,000 families (Haggerty et al., 1999).

Effectiveness of Affective Programs

Affective programs have shown some promise, although the effectiveness of these programs is not altogether clear. An early study of a drug-intervention program, known as Ombudsman, targeted to students in grades 5–9, revealed that students in this program developed more positive attitudes toward their teachers than did the control group. The study also found that students' attitudes toward drug use was affected in the intended direction (Kim, 1981). The author cautions, however, that these effects are not substantial, and that they are stronger in the lower grades than in among older students. An evaluation of the *Reconnecting Youth* program conducted by the developers of the program showed a favorable impact (Eggert, Seyl, and Nicholas, 1990; Eggert and Herting, 1991). Controlling for other factors, the researchers found that participation in the program significantly reduced drug use among these high school participants. Results of the parent education program (PDFY) are also promising. Most of the evaluation research on this program was conducted in rural Iowa communities. The results of these studies include the following:

- Parents who participate in the PDFY curriculum demonstrated better general child management and intervention-specific behaviors than did the control group (Kosterman et al., 2001; Spoth and Redmond, 1995, 1996a).
- Mothers tend to implement and generalize intervention behaviors more readily than fathers (Kosterman et al., 2001; Spoth and Redmond, 1995, 1996a).
- Alcohol and drug use were significantly more delayed among children of program participants than among children of a control group (Park et al., 2000; Spoth, Reyes, Redmond, and Shin, 1999).
- There are numerous barriers to parental participation in the PDFY program, including logistic problems, time factors and family member influences (Spoth and Cleve, 1996b).

The results of these evaluations are certainly promising. Most of these studies, however, have been conducted by those who have been instrumental in developing or implementing the programs, and we must keep this in mind when assessing their results. Moreover, there are limitations to these studies. The PDFY evaluations, for example, were conducted among primarily rural families. There are many conditions and pressures in urban areas toward drug use which may not be as present or powerful in rural areas. Moreover, we do not have evidence for the long-term impact of these programs. These evaluations usually are not carried out more than one year, though some have followed up for as long as three years. It must also be remembered that these programs have a broader focus than simply reduction in drug use, though this is certainly a central goal. *Reconnecting Youth* also has as its stated goals reduction in depressive episodes and suicides among youth. Hence, a fair evaluation of these programs must also consider these goals as well.

SOCIAL-INFLUENCE MODEL
The **social-influence model** is the most recent, and according to some—though it has its critics—the most promising approach to drug education (Ellickson, 1995). This model, sometimes referred to as *drug-resistance*

education, seeks to prepare young people to resist the pressures by peers toward drug use. Adolescents are particularly vulnerable to peer pressures, and smoking, drinking and other forms of drug use are often perceived as avenues to peer acceptance. The theoretical bases for the social influence model are drawn from social inoculation theory, developed by William McGuire (1964), and social learning theory, particularly as it was developed by Albert Bandura (1977). Inoculation theory argues that as one is confronted by persuasive arguments and pressures toward a particular activity, he or she becomes "inoculated" against the effect of those pressures. This idea views peer pressure as a cultural equivalent of "germs;" hence, if we expose a young person to a weaker and more protected "dose" of these "germs" (persuasive arguments), "antibodies" (resistance) to the real world pressures should develop. Social learning theory, as developed by Bandura, stresses the importance of imitation and reinforcement of preferred behavior. Hence, by presenting young people with the arguments for using drugs, typically in a simulated situation, and then modeling how one might resist that pressure and positively reinforcing proper responses to that pressure, young people should be better equipped to resist the pressure to use drugs.

Some of the earliest attempts to use the social influence model were employed in the 1970s to prevent smoking among junior high youth (Evans et al., 1978; Hurd et al., 1980; McAlister, Perry, and Maccoby, 1979; Murray, Johnson, Luepker, and Mittelmark, 1984). These programs were aimed at seventh graders because it was believed that up until that age, most young people do not face serious pressures to smoke. The earliest of these studies were conducted by Richard Evans and his associates in Houston area schools. Evans exposed students to nonsmoking peers on film, and also provided information about short-term health hazards of smoking. The Houston research found a significantly later onset of smoking among those students exposed to the smoking information than among a control group not exposed to this information. Later, researchers at the Harvard University School of Public Health and the Stanford University Heart Prevention Program began delivering the same messages, but using older, live role models, and also introducing role playing to help build resistance. This research also found significantly lower rates of smoking among students exposed to older role models than among the control group. After the academic year program, nearly 10 percent of the control sample reported smoking within the past week, whereas only 5.6 percent of the experimental group reported smoking behavior. (McAlister, Perry, and Maccoby, 1979). Minnesota researchers presented factual information as well as using both same-age peer opinion leaders and adult (teacher) leaders who led student discussions in response to films depicting short-term consequences of smoking. This research also demonstrated a significant effect of antismoking education on smoking behavior. Two components of this education had a particularly strong deterrent effect: an emphasis on immediate consequences of smoking (especially social consequences); and a personalization of the course materials by using peer role models and role playing (Hurd et al., 1980; Murray et al., 1984).

With the success of smoking-resistance education programs, the model was soon applied to other programs as well. Project SMART (Self-Management and Resistance Training) began as a demonstration project at the University of Southern California. This study targeted the three so-called "gateway drugs"—tobacco, alcohol, and marijuana—among seventh graders. The study used interactive instructional techniques for resisting peer and media influences as well as parental pressures and role modeling to use these drugs. Both affective and social influence strategies were employed. Results generally favored the social-influence model over the affective model in delaying the onset of use of these drugs. A similar project, ALERT (Adolescent Learning Experiences in Resistance Training), headed by Phyllis Ellickson at the RAND Corporation targeted seventh and eighth graders. This program addresses beliefs about the consequences of drug use and develops drug-resistance strategies for students at this vulnerable age. Students are taught a variety of ways to "say no" and provided opportunities to practice identifying the internal and external pressures toward drug use (Ellickson, 1995). Other programs of a similar nature include Project STAR in the Midwest, and AMPS (Alcohol Misuse Prevention Study) focusing specifically on alcohol misuse (Ellickson, 1995).

The most well-known drug-resistance education effort, project DARE (Drug Abuse Resistance Education) was implemented jointly by the Los Angeles Police Department and the Los Angeles public school system in 1983. By the mid-1990s DARE was being implemented in more than 7,000 schools across the United States. Between 1989 and 1994, the percentage of school districts in the United States implementing the DARE curriculum rose from 20 percent to 62 percent (Bureau of Justice Assistance, 1995). The DARE program is targeted primarily to grades 5 and 6, but includes components that are used throughout K–12, as well as special education and parent components (Bureau of Justice Assistance, 1995). DARE differs from all of the other social-influence curricula in that materials are presented primarily by police officers rather than by teachers (though teachers are often involved in ancillary educational activities). The curriculum is typically divided into 17 one-hour lessons, which are delivered one day each week of a semester. The curriculum is quite typically integrated into a school's curriculum as part of health, science, social studies, or other subject areas as appropriate. The primary focus in these sessions is on peer pressure resistance—teaching students to recognize peer pressure and suggesting alternative ways to resist that pressure. It is believed that using police officers to deliver the content of the DARE curriculum lends credibility to that content. Other actors are also used as well, however, including teachers and older high-school students as role models (Clayton, Cattarello, Day, and Walden, 1991).

D R U G S   A N D   E V E R Y D A Y   L I F E

Project DARE: Ineffective Scientifically, Popular Ideologically

For many, if not most of you, your first exposure to drug education in any form was Project DARE, which you initially encountered in elementary school. We know this because of DARE's amazing success at being selected as the drug education program of choice in 75 percent of school districts nationwide (and in 54 other countries around the world) as of 2001 (Zernike, 2001:A1). You met the police officers who came into your classroom; you wore the T-shirts with the red DARE logo; your parents drove you around in cars festooned with DARE bumper stickers, paying for gas with their DARE affinity credit. As one expert noted, "it was the only game in town."

Project DARE, which stands for Drug Abuse Resistance Education, was created in 1983 by the Los Angeles Police Department, in response to, among other things, the moral entrepreneurship of then-First Lady Nancy Reagan and her "Just Say No" campaign. Indeed, much of what DARE does is to teach young students that drugs are dangerous and teach them the eight ways to say "No." Self-esteem building is also part of the curriculum. At very simple levels it contains an informational component, an affective component, and a peer-resistance component. Through the 1980s and 1990s DARE solidified its position as the drug-education program politicians love to fund, perhaps because elected officials like rhetorical campaigns that make complex issues seem easily manageable. From the beginning, the simplistic nature of the program drew criticism from a wide range of experts who pointed out flaws in the program's intention and in its design (Cohn, 2001). Indeed, more than 30 research studies which evaluated the program largely agreed that the program was ineffective in changing student drug-using behavior and in improving peer resistance (Zernike, 2001). The

most comprehensive of these studies, by Clayton and associates (1996), concluded that "it was clear . . . DARE has no sustained effects on adolescent drug use." Indeed, as we mention elsewhere, adolescent drug use had gone up during much of the 1990s. Critics of the program gained momentum. By the year 2000, several cities had jettisoned the program, including Salt Lake City, where it had been in place for a decade, but whose mayor declared it a "poor substitute" for effective drug education and "a complete fraud on the American people." (Janofsky, 2000). The surgeon general, who is the country's chief medical officer, and the National Academy of Sciences, likewise gave DARE a thumbs-down. Of greatest consequence was the decision of the Department of Education, distributor of $500 million of the $2 billion dollars in federal drug education grants, to ban schools from using its money on the DARE program because it lacked scientific proof (Zernike, 2001; Cohn, 2001). For their part, DARE and its supporters in government and law enforcement, had responded consistently that the program had no flaws, accomplished its goals, and that its critics represented disgruntled groups bent on decriminalizing drug use (Zernike, 2001).

So it came as somewhat of a public relations surprise when the head of DARE admitted in February of 2001, that his program has not been sufficiently effective, and that DARE had been reinventing itself for two years with the help of a $13.7 million grant from the Robert Wood Johnson Foundation (Cohn, 2001; Zernike, 2001). In short, they were acknowledging the validity of long-leveled criticisms and of research studies showing the program to be an ineffectual failure. But they were being given another opportunity by politicians who felt that it would be cheaper to fix the broken DARE than to start up a program that could achieve the 75 percent

continued

continued from previous page

penetration that DARE had achieved. The "new and improved" DARE focuses on an older cohort of students, and largely replaces lecturing by police officers with discussion groups and role-playing that will hopefully lead the students themselves to conclude that they do not need to use drugs or give in to peer pressure to do so. Currently, both the old and the new DARE programs are being used, with the curricula to be evaluated side-by-side through surveying middle-school and high-school students, grades 7 through 11 ∎

Evaluation of Social-Influence Programs

Prevention programs using the social-influence model have been shown to be comparatively more effective than either the information or affective models discussed earlier. Early studies of the impact of social influence models for deterring smoking have shown a significant deterrent effect as measured by the amount of time until the onset of smoking (Arkin et al., 1981; Evans et al., 1978; Hurd et al., 1980; Murray, Luepker, Johnson, and Mittelmark, 1984). All these studies also found that stressing *short-term physiological consequences* was more effective than focusing on long-term consequences of smoking. Project SMART data collected by William Hansen and his colleagues at the University of Southern California revealed that the social-influence programs were also much more effective in delaying the onset of marijuana, tobacco, and alcohol use than were affective programs. Indeed, they found that students in the affective programs had an earlier onset than controls (Hansen et al., 1988). Project ALERT, also targeting tobacco, alcohol, and marijuana, substantially affected tobacco and marijuana use, though its impact on alcohol use was much more limited (Ellickson, Bell, and Harrison, 1993). Finally, meta-analyses of existing research on drug-education programs of all three types alone and in combination reveal that social-influence programs produce the highest effects on subjects' knowledge, attitudes, drug use, and life skills (Tobler, 1992). Peer-based programs were found to be nearly three times more effective in delaying or reducing drug use than were the affective programs, and some *13 times* more effective than information-only programs (Tobler, 1992).

The one exception to this pattern, ironically, is the DARE program. One study, consisting of an evaluation of results in 36 Illinois schools revealed that DARE had no effect on subsequent tobacco or alcohol use as compared with a control group (other drug use was not tested), though some very short-term effects were noted (Ennett et al., 1994). Other studies found a similar pattern of a short-lived impact on drug use. Examining the impact of DARE programs in Lexington, Kentucky schools over a five-year period, University of Kentucky researchers found no appreciable difference between DARE and control students (Clayton, Cattarello and Johnstone, 1996). Similar findings were reported by Lynam and his colleagues (1999) who followed DARE students over a ten-year period. A meta-analysis of eight studies by

Nancy Tobler and her colleagues found that, unlike other social influence programs, DARE made virtually no significant impact on subsequent drug use. While knowledge of and attitudes about drugs were favorably affected, drug *use* was not (Ennett, Tobler, Ringwalt, and Flewelling, 1994).

Are social-influence (otherwise called "resistance education") programs effective? The evidence is, to be sure, mixed. Project DARE has consistently failed to demonstrate any appreciable impact on drug use. Other programs have been more promising, particularly when compared with information-only and affective-only curricula. Gorman (1998) makes the case that *none* of the drug-education efforts have been substantially effective and that our efforts at drug education have continued despite the negative evidence only because such programs are compatible with prevailing political and ideological winds. Other reports, such as *In Their Own Voices,* (Brown et al., 1995) based on the experience of students and teachers in California's drug-education programs, have also raised serious questions about how effective these programs are. While there is clear evidence of some level of effectiveness, critics have challenged abstinence-only approaches generally.

HARM-REDUCTION MODEL

The admittedly modest effectiveness of social influence programs, though more favorable than information and affective models, has led some scholars to suggest an alternative approach to drug education. Critics of existing drug-education efforts point to several questionable assumptions underlying all of these efforts: (1) abstinence for all adolescents is a realistic goal; (2) drug *use* is synonymous with drug *abuse*; (3) the "stepping stone" theory, that one form of drug use inevitably leads to another; (4) understanding the risks associated with drugs will automatically deter young people from experimenting; and (5) children are not able to make responsible decisions about drug use on their own (Rosenbaum, 1996). These critics further observe that despite decades of drug education efforts, drug use has not appreciably declined among our nation's youth. Hence, they are calling for a more "reality-based" approach (Rosenbaum, 1999) based on principles of harm reduction, and generally known as a harm-reduction model.

Harm-reduction as an approach to substance abuse is not at all new in practice, though it has not always been recognized as a formal policy approach until quite recently. With regard to drug education, harm-reduction strategies have targeted alcohol use for about 30 years, with messages encouraging "responsible" alcohol use among adults. Responsible alcohol use involves things such as using designated drivers; maintaining awareness of how much alcohol one is consuming, facilitated by the proliferation of "standard serving" information; pacing one's drinking; finding alternative ways to cope with problems; and finding recreational activities other than drinking alcohol, to name just a few (Riley, 1993).

Harm reduction as a specific approach to *drug education* began to get notice in the 1980s. One attempt by Andrew Weil and Winifred Rosen in

1983 was taken off the shelves of drug-education curricula almost as soon as it was introduced. This text, *From Chocolate to Morphine: Everything You Need to Know About Mind-Altering Drugs,* provided comprehensive, objective information to students about the nature of drugs and stressed achieving *nonabusive* relationships to drugs if any relationship was to be achieved (Rosenbaum, 1996). An earlier attempt by David Duncan in 1972 was successful in reducing adverse reactions to "huffing" in a southwestern urban locale. Duncan and his colleagues developed the harm-reduction program, which encouraged abstinence, but also provided information about how to engage in these activities safely if they were going to do it (Duncan et al., 1994). Despite its success, this program was not widely disseminated. More recently, other model programs have been developed, including a British-based program, *Harm Reduction Drug Education* (HRDE), which advertises itself as a "secondary" prevention approach in that its goal is not to *prevent* drug use per se, but rather to recognize the reality of drug use and attempt to prevent the abuse of drugs. This program has received only limited support in the United Kingdom (Rosenbaum, 1996). A second program was developed in the United States in 1982 by Sandee Burbank, an Oregon mother who was dissatisfied with the nature of drug education in the schools in Oregon. This program, *Mothers Against Misuse and Abuse* (MAMA) addresses the potential abuses of licit and illicit drugs and seeks to provide factual information about these drugs. MAMA's primary approach is to present factual information through the use of pamphlets and other written materials. Other organizations that sponsor a harm-reduction approach include The Center for Educational Research and Development in Berkeley, California, The Harm Reduction Coalition in New York, and DrugEdNet in Melbourne, Australia.

According to Rosenbaum (1996, 1999), a harm-reduction approach to drug education, which Rosenbaum refers to as "safety first," is based on four assumptions. First, "drugs" include both legal and illegal substances which can be abused. Legal drugs can be dangerous when used inappropriately, and illegal drugs can be used comparatively safely under appropriate conditions. Second, harm-reduction education recognizes that abstinence is not realistic for all young people. Third, the *use* of drugs, does not necessarily constitute *abuse*. Drugs *can* be used in a responsible manner according to harm reductionists. Finally, the *context* of drug use is a primary factor in safe drug use. The context includes both the psychological state of the user (drug "set") and the social context of use (drug "setting"). Based on these assumptions, harm-reduction education has a number of specific goals (Rosenbaum, 1996, 1999):

- Provide objective factual information about legal and illegal substances. Such information should include facts about the physiological effects of drugs as well as risks and benefits. Presentation of this material must distinguish between real and imagined dangers of drugs.

- Incorporate the experiences of the youths themselves. Because children are often the "experts" in certain aspects of drug use, their experiences should be a part of any drug education program.
- Incorporate role models into drug education materials. Rosenbaum suggests using older peers who have used, but not abused, drugs as role models.

The harm-reduction model is not generally accepted by government or schools because it departs from the abstinence-only mind set attached to illicit drugs. This is understandable. It is difficult to advocate *responsible* use of illegal drugs. Indeed, we must ask, is *any* illicit drug use responsible, given the potential social consequences? It is one thing to advocate responsible alcohol use, for example, which is a legal substance and one is not likely to be arrested for possession of it. Otherwise responsible use of illicit drugs such as marijuana, cocaine, or heroin, however, can have very serious consequences that can destroy the life of the user in today's repressive prohibitionist social and legal environment. The required context for an effective harm-reduction approach to drug education, it would seem, is a broad drug-control policy that is built upon principles of harm-reduction.

DRUG TESTING

Drug testing can take many forms ranging from crude observational techniques such as looking for needle tracks or pupil constriction as an indicator of narcotics use to sophisticated blood and hair analyses. Drug testing has been used for a variety of purposes, including reducing drunk driving, ensuring fair competition in athletic events, cutting down on drug use in the military, and screening potential employees for drug use prior to hire as well as testing current employees for drug use. Professionals in this field frequently distinguish between *drug testing* and *drug screening*. **Drug screening** is a less precise process that involves a qualitative analysis of a sample to determine whether particular drugs are present. Drug testing is a more precise process which involves a quantitative analysis of body tissue or fluids to determine with greater precision the concentration of a particular substance in an individual (Montagne, Pugh, and Fink, 1988a). These two processes have broadly similar goals, and indeed frequently use the same technology. Hence, we do not distinguish between drug testing and drug screening here, and use the term drug testing to refer to both.

HISTORY AND PREVALENCE OF DRUG TESTING

Drug testing has been conducted in one form or another in the United States since at least the nineteenth century through observational techniques such as slurred speech in the case of alcohol intoxication to constricted pupils among narcotics users (Ackerman, 1991). Drug testing as we understand it today, however, is a distinctly twentieth-century phenomenon. We will

Drug testing has taken on an increasing role in the war against drugs, in numerous organizational contexts. It is not without controversy.

examine the history of drug testing in the United States as it came to be used in an ever expanding number of social contexts.

Drug Testing in Law Enforcement and the Criminal Justice System

The first bio-chemical testing for drugs took place in the 1920s in response to concern over alcohol intoxication. Any manufacture or distribution of alcohol was prohibited under the Eighteenth Amendment, and intoxication certainly implied the manufacture and distribution of alcohol. Because alcohol is metabolized rather quickly, and expired through the lungs, the only ways to test for the presence of alcohol is in the blood or on one's breath. Some police departments made use of kits that provided a rather crude analysis for the presence of alcohol in the blood of motorists suspected of driving under the influence of alcohol. The technology to analyze breath, a far less invasive form of testing, was developed in the 1930s, a technology commonly referred to as "breathalysers" (Ackerman, 1991; Montagne, Pugh, and Fink, 1988a).

Drug testing of arrestees began on a systematic basis in 1987 with the establishment of the Drug Use Forecasting System (DUF), which in 1997 evolved into the Arrestee Drug Abuse Monitoring System (ADAM) (see Chapter 6). Interviews are conducted and drug specimens collected over a two-week period, four times per year. Urine specimens provide a valuable validity check on self-reported drug use, and are used to confirm 10 categories of drugs: *Amphetamines, Barbiturates, Benzodiazepines* (Valium), *Cocaine,*

Opiates, PCP, Methadone, Marijuana, Propoxyphene (Darvon) and *Methaqualone* (Quaaludes and other sedatives).

In addition to law enforcement, other criminal justice agencies, such as correctional institutions, also test for drugs. The Federal Bureau of Prisons routinely inspects for a wide variety of prescription as well as recreational drugs. Because prescription drugs are closely controlled in the prison system, these drugs are screened to detect illicit use (Willette, 1986). Postconviction testing of parolees, probationers and others on community release is also frequently conducted. Some jurisdictions utilize an "intensive supervision probation" (ISP), involving a reduction in caseloads for probation officers so as to enable them to maintain closer surveillance of clients, including testing for the use of drugs (Mieczkowski and Lersch, 1997).

Finally, it should also be pointed out that drug testing of criminal justice *personnel* is increasingly commonplace. While not without controversy, the practice has been upheld as constitutional by the United States Supreme Court in several rulings including *Policeman's Benevolent Association* v. *Washington Township* (1988), *Guiney* v. *Roach* (1989), and *National Treasury Employee's Union* v. *von Raab* (1989) (Walsh and Trumble, 1991).

Drug Testing in Sports

Drug testing in sports began in the 1930s, though at this time, it was not human athletes who were being tested. The testing, rather, was for race horses suspected of having been given morphine which was known as a performance enhancer. The method used to test the horses involved injecting mice with the saliva from the horse. If the mouse's tail became rigid, this meant that the horse tested positive and was disqualified from the race (Ackerman, 1995).

Drug testing among human athletes did not begin until the 1960s, when the International Olympic Committee (IOC) began screening the urine of Olympic athletes. The impetus for the Olympic Committee's testing program was the death of a cyclist who had been using amphetamines to enhance his performance (Zemper, 1991). The IOC did not comprehensively test Olympic athletes until the 1972 games, however; the primary reason for testing at this time was to ensure an even playing field among all of the amateur athletes participating. Committee officials were particularly concerned about the use of stimulants, but in 1976, the IOC began testing for anabolic steroids, which were recognized as performance enhancers (Montagne, Pugh, and Fink, 1988a). Other drugs would also be banned because of concern for the safety and health of the athletes (Ackerman, 1995). Collegiate sports were not systematically subjected to testing until 1986, when the National Collegiate Athletic Association (NCAA) first developed and implemented a drug-testing policy. Drugs banned by the NCAA are similar to those banned by the IOC, with some noteworthy differences.

Professional sports have been much slower to adopt drug testing, particularly mandatory testing. The major reason for this is a strong resistance on the part of players' unions. Nevertheless, drug testing does occur in professional sports albeit in a rather patchwork fashion. Some sports, such as tennis, have provisions for mandatory testing. Others, such as football, provide for testing with cause; that is, if a player demonstrates behavior that might suggest that he is on drugs, that individual player can be tested. Insofar as drug testing does take place in professional sports, the purpose is not so much to promote fair competition as to provide positive role models for youngsters who follow these sports (Wagner, 1987). Chapter 7 provides more information on drug use and control of drug use in sports.

Drug Testing in the Military

Drug use among military personnel has been recognized as a problem at least since the Civil War, when thousands of soldiers became addicted to morphine, which was indiscriminately used as an analgesic for war wounds and for dysentery. The frequency of soldiers returning home addicted from this and subsequent wars was substantial, and addiction to morphine came to be known as "soldier's disease" (Ray and Ksir, 1999). It was not until soldiers began returning home from the Vietnam war addicted to heroin that the government became concerned enough to begin testing for drug use. The military drug testing effort was only sporadic, however, until the early 1980s. The Pentagon conducted a survey of some 20,000 military personnel in 1980, finding that 27 percent of Navy personnel under 25 reported using drugs (Ackerman, 1995). Then, in 1981 a tragic crash of a jet fighter on the deck of the nuclear aircraft carrier *Nimitz* killed 14 people and injured 48 others. Six of the deck crew who were killed were found to have used illegal drugs within the past 30 days (Ackerman, 1995; Banta and Tennant, 1989). This led the Department of Defense to institute mandatory urinalysis in all branches of the armed forces. The Navy conducts the most extensive drug-testing program, screening for amphetamines, barbiturates, cocaine, marijuana, opiates, and PCP. The Navy's testing program has become a model for rigorous procedures to insure valid and reliable results, performing some 1.8 million uranalyses annually, with only a handful of reversals of disciplinary action because of faulty reports (Ackerman, 1991).

Drug Testing in the Workplace

Problems with alcohol abuse in the workplace were recognized by nineteenth-century industrialists who hired investigators to probe the off-work drinking habits of their employees (Hanson, 1993). The toll that drug and alcohol abuse were taking in the American workplace has been widely recognized since the 1960s. Pre-employment drug screening was being recommended by the early 1970s as a response to the cost of drug abuse in accidents and absenteeism. Estimated costs to employers for drug and alcohol-related accidents alone reached $135 billion in 1988 (Ackerman, 1995).

Private industry did not begin to test for drug use among its employees until the 1980s, following the lead of the United States military. Among the first in the private sector to initiate testing programs were the transportation and utilities industries. Task forces were organized among companies in these industrial sectors as early as 1982 to look into testing employees for drug use, though some companies, such as Greyhound, had already been testing by that time (Walsh and Trumble, 1991). Then in 1983, the National Transportation Safety Board issued a report implicating alcohol or drugs in seven train accidents involving several fatalities and more than $17 million in property damage between June 1982 and May 1983. This resulted in more routine testing in the public transportation industry and in other public safety-related industries.

A major impetus for drug testing in the workplace was the signing of Executive Order #12564 on September 15, 1986, by Ronald Reagan. This Order established the goal of a Drug-Free Federal Workforce. Less than one year later, in July 1987, Congress enacted legislation implementing the executive order and effectively established drug-testing procedures in the agencies of the federal government (National Institute on Drug Abuse, 1989). While this legislation mandated testing for federal agencies only, private-sector companies were not long in developing their own workplace testing policies.

Workplace drug testing today generally takes one of three forms: (1) applicant screening; (2) random testing of current employees; and (3) reasonable suspicion testing. Additionally, larger firms with Employee Assistance Programs (EAP's) may require drug testing as a follow-up to counseling or rehabilitation services.

Drug testing is now quite routine among many large corporations and even smaller businesses. Hartwell and his colleagues (1996) reported that more than 48 percent of workplaces, representing 62 percent of America's workforce, test for drug use. Among smaller work sites (50–99 employees), 40.2 percent reported testing, while 70.9 percent of employers with more than 1,000 workers tested for drug use. The prevalence of drug testing also varies by type of business. At the high end, 72.8 percent of communications and transportation industry work sites reported testing, while only 22.6 percent of worksites in the finance and insurance fields required drug testing of their employees. Finally, region of country seems to affect the likelihood of drug testing. Employers in the South were most likely to test (56.3 percent), while workplaces in the Northeast were least likely (33.3 percent). Workers are less likely to be tested for alcohol use than for drug use, with only 23 percent of work sites reporting alcohol testing programs. This is certainly a statement of the level of concern that exists over illegal drug use in light of the fact that alcohol is far more prevalent and alcohol-related accidents far more numerous than drug impairment in the workplace. Finally, it should be pointed out that not all places of employment test *all* their employees, nor do they all test on a regular basis. Only 23.6 percent of the worksites in the Hartwell et al., study reported that they tested all employees, and 14 percent reported testing only applicants. Moreover, only 13.7 percent of the businesses surveyed tested on a regular basis; most of the worksites with testing programs test on a random basis (Hartwell et al., 1996).

DEVELOPMENT OF DRUG-TESTING TECHNOLOGY

Laboratory testing was first introduced in the 1920s in the form of crude analysis of blood samples for alcohol intoxication (Ackerman, 1991). Breathalyzers replaced blood testing in the 1930s as a less invasive detection technique. Use of breathalyzers was not widespread, however, until the 1960s when growing concerns about highway safety resulted in the passage of the National Highway Safety Act in 1966. This statute provided for alcohol testing, and has been a standard weapon in the arsenal of law enforcement since (Ackerman, 1995).

Testing for drugs other than alcohol would not take place until the 1950s. At that time, an observational test, the nalorphine pupil test, emerged as a standard technique to detect narcotics use by parolees. This test used a narcotics antagonist, nalorphine, which produced different chemical reactions in people who had recently used narcotics than in those who had not (Motagne, Pugh, and Fink, 1988a). Most noticeably, it caused the pupils of individuals under the influence of narcotics to increase in size. Studies have indicated, however, that this test has a high rate of both false negatives and false positives (DeAngelis, 1976). Urinalysis is the most common means of drug testing today, and actually dates to ancient times when Hippocrates recommended examining urine to help make medical diagnoses (Ackerman, 1991). This was a visual test only, of course, and it wasn't until the nineteenth century, with the advent of the microscope that urinalysis came to be a standard diagnostic aid. Urinalysis would not be used as a means of testing for drug use, however, until the middle of the twentieth century. The discussion that follows examines five broad types of testing, a typology based on the bodily source of evidence: *breath tests, blood tests, urinalysis, saliva tests,* and *hair analysis*.

Breath Tests

Breath tests are used exclusively for testing for alcohol intoxication. There is a direct relationship between the concentration of alcohol in the blood with the concentration of alcohol in the breath—a ratio of 2100 to 1. That is, 2100 milliliters of breathed air contain an equivalent amount of alcohol as one milliliter of blood (Freudenrich, 2000). Hence, breath tests can produce a reliable reading of blood alcohol content BAC, and have the advantage of being less invasive and a more cost effective alternative to blood testing for alcohol concentrations. There are actually three types of devices to determine alcohol levels in breath. The most commonly used method is *gas chromatography,* commonly known as the *Breathalyzer*. While actually a proprietary name for a specific breath-testing device, the *Breathalyzer* has become virtually synonymous with breath tests generally. A second device for measuring alcohol on the breath is called an *Intoxilyzer,* also a proprietary name, which uses infrared spectroscopy to identify types of molecules on the basis of how they absorb infrared light (Freudenrich, 2000). Finally, *fuel cell detectors* use two platinum electrodes with an acid electrolyte material that measures electrical current produced by oxidized alcohol molecules (Freudenrich, 2000). This technology has an advantage over the other two in that it can be manufactured as a portable unit (Montagne, Pugh, and Fink, 1988a).

Blood, Urine, and Saliva Tests

Testing for drugs in blood, urine, and saliva utilizes the same basic techniques, regardless of the medium used. Before discussing the techniques, however, we would like to point out some things regarding each of these fluid sources. First, testing for drugs in the blood stream has disadvantages which have made it a very unpopular means of drug testing. Extracting samples of blood is highly invasive, and when less-invasive techniques were developed, they became very popular. Use of blood samples also heightens the risk to test administrators of contracting HIV/AIDS and other communicable diseases. Finally, evidence of drugs in the bloodstream is temporary, and hence is not of great use for determining *past* drug use. Blood tests are, however, considered the most reliable for detection of *current* evidence of drug use, and are often used in accident investigations, or in some cases, taken in conjunction with urine samples for purposes of confirmation if a urine sample comes back positive (Potter and Orfali, 1990). Urine is by far the most common of these three mediums for drug detection today. It is relatively noninvasive and has an advantage over blood specimens because drug concentrations remain in urine for an extended period of time, resulting in greater concentrations and allowing for assessing past as well as current drug use. Urine sampling, also known as *urinalysis,* is limited, however, in that it cannot measure current levels of toxicity or concentration and thereby cannot assess whether one is currently impaired as a result of drug use. Urinalysis as a method for determining whether drug use was the cause of an accident, for example, is quite unreliable. Finally, saliva has been used with increasing frequency in recent years. This medium is generally considered even less invasive than urinalysis, and has the advantage of providing more current readings on drug intoxication than does urine. Moreover, saliva maybe used to test for the presence of most drugs.

Testing for drugs in blood, urine, and saliva is conducted using one of two broad types of methods. The first, *chromatography,* is the oldest laboratory method of drug detection. The basic principle behind chromatography is that different chemicals have varying affinities for other chemicals. Generally, the process involves forcing sample material (blood, urine, saliva) that is mixed with other liquids or gases through a medium that separates the individual parts of the sample material at different rates. Because the sample material contains potentially several chemicals, each with their own unique level of affinity and style of interaction with the medium, they will separate at different times/places in this process. A detection technique is then used to determine the concentrations of each chemical (drug) present after the separation process.

A significant development in the technology of drug detection came in the 1970s with the introduction of *immunoassays,* the second method used to separate and measure the presence of drugs in bodily fluids. Immunoassays utilize antibodies produced by animals injected with antigens consisting of drug-protein compounds. These antibodies are specific to particular drugs which will attach to them when exposed in urine or blood media (DeAngelis, 1976). Several immunoassay techniques have been developed, but the most widely used is the enzyme multiplied immunotechnique (EMIT). The immunoassays, and particularly the EMIT test, are very popular because they are inexpensive to administer and provide very quick results. They are limited, however, in that they are prone to *cross-reactivity*, meaning that the antibodies of the immunoassay will sometimes interact with substances chemically similar to the drug that the test was designed to measure (Montagne, Pugh, and Fink, 1988a). Hence, when positive results are found using these methods, reputable testing centers will usually use more precise techniques such as sophisticated chromatography procedures to verify them.

Hair Analysis

A relatively recent development in drug-testing technology is hair analysis. The principle behind this technique is that the hair follicle absorbs the drug from the bloodstream and deposits it in the hair as it grows. Hence, by analyzing hair at different points of growth, it is possible to identify approximately *when* drugs were used and even the level of use at that time, as strands of hair lock in the record of drug use and can be read much in the same way as the rings on a tree provide evidence as to its age (Holden, 1990; Montagne, Pugh, and Fink, 1988a). Normally, hair to be analyzed is taken from the head, which normally grows at a rate of about 1 to 1.3 centimeters per month, so hair that is 12 centimeters long will provide a record of drug use for between 9 and 12 months. The test used to determine the presence of drugs in the hair is normally radioimmunoassay (RIA), with gas chromotography/mass spectronamy (GC/MS) used to confirm RIA results (Fay, 1991; Holden, 1990).

Hair analysis has the advantage of preserving the evidence of drug use for a much longer period of time than is possible through the other techniques, thereby allowing investigators to go back months and perhaps even years in determining the presence of drugs. The pioneer of this method, Werner Baumgartner was able to analyze a lock of hair that once belonged to the poet John Keats, and found evidence of opiates preserved there. More importantly, however, because hair keeps a permanent record of drug use, as well as other trace metals, it is possible to trace prior drug use in *living* individuals to a time many months earlier (in contrast to urine, which maintains a record of most drugs for only about 72 hours). There is, however, a downside to this technology. Some have suggested that RIA has not yet proven itself accurate for hair analysis (Holden, 1990). Moreover, unlike urinalysis, hair analysis does not allow for precise time-frame identification for drug use. Where it is necessary to identify whether drugs were used on a particular day or even a narrow window of days, hair analysis does not offer a necessary level of precision to make such determinations (Fay, 1991).

EFFECTIVENESS OF DRUG TESTING

It is difficult at this point in time to assess the effectiveness of drug-testing programs. For one thing, organizations have various goals when doing drug testing and screening. Hanson (1993) identifies various goals of drug testing:

- Identification of drug users in an organization.
- Deterrence of potential drug abuse.
- Improvement of worker morale.
- Increased productivity.
- Decreased workplace accidents.
- Overall cost-effectiveness.

Hence rather than asking *"Is* drug testing effective," we might better ask *"How* is drug testing effective?" Even the answer to that question remains somewhat elusive, however, because there is not a great deal of good, systematic information regarding effectiveness at this time (Krauthamer, 1998; Maltby, 1999). Nevertheless, there is some scattered research which has attempted to answer this question.

Identification of Drug Users

Hanson (1993) attempts to evaluate the effectiveness of drug testing for identifying users by comparing national epidemiological data with results of testing programs. The 1988 National Household Survey on Drug Abuse estimated that about 8 percent of full-time employees reported drug use within the past 30 days (Kopstein and Gfroerer, 1991). Studies conducted of workplace drug use of employees and applicants revealed by drug tests reveal similar percentages (Bureau of Labor Statistics, 1989; Zwerling, Ryan, and Orav, 1990). The fact that there appears to be consistency between anonymous self-report data and drug-testing data would suggest that this goal of drug testing may be effectively met.

Deterrence

There have been a small number of studies which have examined trends in positive drug tests over time, which is an indicator of the deterrent effect of drug-testing programs. A national study of postal employees suggests that drug prevalence among applicants was somewhat lower than that for the general population. While other factors may account for some of this difference, researchers suggest that awareness of preemployment drug testing probably had some deterrent effect (Normand, Salyards, and Mahoney, 1990). Lange et al. (1994) more rigorously tested for the deterrent effect by comparing applicants testing positive *prior* to instituting a drug testing program with applicants two years *following* the establishment of a drug screening program. Applicants for employment at a major teaching hospital (Johns Hopkins) were tested over a two-month period in 1989 so as to provide a baseline aggregate indicator of positive drug tests. A drug-screening program was then established. The original data were compared with applicants who applied two years later, during the same two-month window.

Those testing positive had decreased from 10.8 percent of the applicants to 5.8 percent—nearly a 50 percent decrease.

The deterrent effect of drug screening has also been tested with military personnel. The military has a dual policy of mandatory random drug testing and zero tolerance. Mehay and Pacula (1999) found that prior to the implementation of mandatory drug testing by the military in 1981, rates of drug use by military personnel corresponded closely with that of civilian personnel, as revealed by self-reports. Ten years after mandatory testing was introduced, drug use decreased from 27.6 percent (1980) to only 3.4 percent in 1992—a rate significantly below that of the civilian workforce.

Researchers examining and reviewing the data on the deterrent effect of drug testing urge caution in our interpretation of these data. As drug testing is being increasingly conducted on a more random basis, for example (as opposed to testing for cause or suspicion), the larger general samples alone will reduce the percentages testing positive (Hanson, 1993). Others suggest that declining rates in firms that test for drug use is simply reflective of an overall decline in drug use in the general population (Maltby, 1999). Despite these cautions, the evidence does seem to indicate that drug testing may have at least some deterrent effect.

Impact on Worker Morale

There is great concern that drug testing will negatively affect worker morale (Maltby, 1999). These concerns are not taken lightly by employers because low morale inevitably affects worker productivity, absenteeism, accident rates, etc. The impact on morale is not entirely clear, but research conducted on this issue suggests that this should not be an overwhelming concern to employers if such testing is conducted appropriately. LeRoy (1991) found that most unionized workers (76.6 percent) generally favored drug testing as long as the tests are carefully controlled for privacy. Coombs and Coombs (1991) examined the attitudes of college athletes toward mandatory drug testing. Most of the 500 athletes they interviewed were not greatly affected by drug testing and did not report strong opinions one way or the other. Some, however, reported embarrassment and being anxious about false positives. Others found the experience quite interesting and reported positive benefits such as acquiring new information and even finding the drug test to be a socially acceptable way of refusing drugs in social situations. Several recommendations were made for improving the procedure, including a better orientation about what to expect, more comfortable test settings, and more rigorous testing standards.

Impact on Productivity

There is an intuitive argument that could be made regarding the effectiveness of drug testing on productivity. On the one hand, one might argue that drug users are more likely to be less attentive, have higher rates of absenteeism, and hence be overall less productive than nondrug users. Moreover, it might be argued that highly productive workers prefer to work in companies that weed out drug users, resulting in a self-selection process whereby companies that test for drug use get the best and most productive employees. This argument is based on the premise that drug use impairs functioning and productivity, an assumption which has not been well documented in the literature. It can be argued, on the other hand, that drug tests are time consuming (as well as expensive to conduct) and distract workers from performing their jobs as effectively. Moreover, when workers are fired because of positive tests, and replacements hired, there is a learning curve that lowers the overall level of productivity in a company. Finally, insofar as there are morale problems associated with drug testing, it is plausible that workers might act in a passive-aggressive manner by maintaining lower levels of productivity.

There is some minimal support for the idea that drug testing might improve productivity. The research by Zwerling, Ryan, and Orav (1990) revealed an absentee rate higher among those who tested positive for marijuana or cocaine than among those who tested negative. These authors note, however, that the differences are not as great as one might expect. Moreover, recent research by Shepard and Clifton (1998) challenges the assumption that drug testing should result in higher levels of productivity. Examining 63 companies in the computer and communications fields, Shepard and Clifton compared net sales divided by the number of employees—a proxy measure for productivity—of companies that test for drug use with companies that do not. The authors also examined the impact of pre-employment drug testing and random employee drug testing independently. They found that companies which tested for drug use had *lower* levels of productivity than did those companies which did not test. These findings were achieved for both companies that utilized preemployment screening and random testing. More research needs to be done in this area—research that uses various measures of productivity as well as a variety of organizational settings. The limited research that we do have, however, does not indicate a strong positive effect on productivity.

Impact on Accident Rates

Drug testing has been imposed on certain industries precisely because of safety concerns associated with drug use on the job. High-profile accidents in which drugs are allegedly involved often result in a clamor for drug testing of employees in positions that involve public safety—industries such as public transportation, law enforcement, and medicine. The evidence is not at all clear, however, as to how effective drug testing is in reducing accidents. Research in Houston by Fay (1996) reveals that worker compensation claims decreased by more than 63 percent over a four-year period studied among companies that utilized both pre-employment screening and random drug testing—significantly more than the 19 percent reduction over the same period among companies that did not utilize these testing procedures. Fay also found a significant reduction in the *amount* of compensation payment in companies that tested whereas companies that did not test experienced an *increase* in compensation payments over the same period. Similarly, Zwerling, Ryan, and Orav (1990) found that both accidents and injuries on the job by postal employees were higher among those testing positive for drugs, suggesting that if drug testing *does* deter drug use, accident rates might go down as a result of testing. Other research, however, is less conclusive. Recent research by Swena and Gaines (1999) among commercial truck drivers suggest that the number of accident fatalities per 100 million miles declined significantly in the first two years following the establishment of a random drug testing program for interstate carriers in 1989. After the first two years, however, the impact was negligible. There would appear to be a waning of the impact of drug testing on accidents—or at least fatal accidents—over time. Once again, more research is needed which examines various types of industries using a variety of measures in order to fully assess the effectiveness of drug-testing programs for increasing worker and public safety.

Cost Effectiveness

When asked, most managers who utilize drug testing believe that their programs are cost effective (American Management Association, 1992). Yet, millions of dollars are spent to identify a relatively small number of drugs users in workplaces across America. While drug testing does appear to be effective in identifying and weeding out drug users as potential employees, and seems to have something of a deterrent effect, companies must ask the question whether the overall benefits outweigh the burdensome cost of testing. The answer is probably dependent on the level of drug use in a particular area or potential employee pool. Zwerling, Ryan, and Orav (1992) report that drug screening would have saved the Postal Service in Boston $162 per applicant hired. They note, however, that this benefit is based on the fact that 12 percent of the applicant pool tested positive for drugs. Moreover, their cost-benefit analysis is based on a cost of $49 per urine sample screened. Others have suggested a much lower rate of drug use in the population. Anglin and Westland (1989) report that only about 1 or 2 percent of drug samples sent to commercial testing laboratories in California test positive. Under such conditions, drug testing is *not* cost effective. Furthermore, drug testing may cost much more than the $49 per sample assumed by Zwerling and his associates, again limiting the cost-effectiveness of drug. It would seem, based on the evidence that we have, that drug testing is only marginally cost effective at best, at least from a financial point of view.

Controversies Surrounding Drug Testing

Drug testing has not been without controversy. The major objections to drug testing have been reliability and constitutionality of the tests. We discuss these issues below.

Reliability of Drug Testing

A major concern that critics of drug-testing programs have is the potential for false positives in drug testing. The most popular test used, the EMIT test discussed earlier, has great potential for false positives. All immunoassay techniques hold the potential for false positives because of *cross-reactivity*, which occurs when the antibodies which detect certain drugs interact with chemicals that are similar to the drug that the antibody was designed to detect (Montagne, Pugh, and Fink, 1988a). The problem, of course, is that these drugs which interact with the antibodies may not be illegal substances. The consequences can be devastating, including losing a job or failing to be employed, being disqualified from sporting events, or even arrest.

Because of problems with cross-reactivity, most organizations which test or screen for drug use will follow up on all positive tests with more sophisticated tests before making any final judgments or taking any action against individuals who test positive. Typically, this will be done with a chromatography technique such as gas chromatography, which has a much greater level of *specificity* in distinguishing between various types of drugs. The problem, of course, is that not all companies do confirmatory analyses, though more and more companies are recognizing that such confirmatory tests are advisable for legal purposes (Montagne, Pugh, and Fink, 1988b).

There remains, however, one further problem, namely, that most drug-testing techniques do not measure *current level* of drug use or impairment but rather simply provide evidence of drug use in the past (Faley, Kleiman, and Wall, 1988). Hair analysis is capable of storing information for a year or longer depending on the length of hair strands available. Urine and saliva samples also provide evidence of past drug use which, in most cases, takes place during off-hours. Many have argued that it is not appropriate in most cases to be infringing on the private activities of individuals (see below). Beyond this argument, however, when such tests are used for "cause," such as determining the cause of an accident, they are used inappropriately, and reputations can be inappropriately harmed as a result. Only blood tests (and breath tests for alcohol use) can provide information about immediate levels of toxicity (Potter and Orfali, 1990), and there is evidence that the courts recognize the advantages of blood tests over urine tests (Faley, Kleiman, and Wall, 1988).

Constitutionality of Drug Testing

Perhaps the major objection raised to programs of involuntary drug testing is that they represent a violation of the Fourth Amendment, which guarantees the right of people against unreasonable search and seizure of one's person. It is argued that drug testing represents a most invasive practice—the extrapolation and examination of bodily fluids. This procedure, according to critics, is even more invasive than searching one's home, which is typically the focus of the Fourth Amendment protections. The practice was so reprehensible to some that as early as 1972, drug testing came to be dubbed "chemical McCarthyism" (Lundberg, 1972). Moreover, in order to ensure that urine is not switched or otherwise tampered with, the process of collecting urine itself can be invasive, involving monitors to ensure against cheating.

Drug testing certainly involves search and seizure—the seizing of body fluids for purposes of searching for illegal substances. The Constitutional questions are (1) does this practice involves *unreasonable* search and seizure?; and if it does (2) *who* is restricted from engaging in drug testing? Supreme Court rulings as well as numerous lower court rulings have generally recognized that *mandatory* drug testing programs that test *without cause* do constitute unreasonable search and seizure. Testing for cause or because of suspicious behavior, however, has generally not been regarded as unreasonable (Montagne, Pugh, and Fink, 1988b). Furthermore, the courts must balance the rights of individuals to be free from unreasonable search and seizure with the safety and well-being of the community. Hence, the courts have generally upheld the constitutionality of mandatory drug testing where the safety and well-being of the public is at stake (Ackerman, 1991; 1995). That is, mandatory drug testing, even without suspicion is not considered unreasonable when the state has a *compelling interest* to do so. Two Supreme Court cases, decided together in 1989, were especially instrumental in defining the compelling interest argument. The first was *Skinner* v. *Railroad Labor Executive's Association (NLEA)*. The Federal Railroad Administration (FRA) had established regulations requiring the testing of train employees involved in train accidents. The high court upheld the constitutionality of these regulations, even though any given individual was not under suspicion, because safety on the nation's railroads constituted a compelling interest justifying a departure from normal probable cause requirements. The second case was the *National Treasury Employee's Union (NTEU)* v. *Von Raab*. This case involved slightly different circumstances. In 1986, the U.S. Custom's Service under the direction of Commissioner William Von Raab, implemented a drug testing program for employees who either carry firearms, are involved in drug interception at the borders, or are in high-level positions which involve access to classified information. Even though public safety was not directly an issue here, the court concluded that a compelling interest of the government was at stake, that being minimizing the drug trade. Hence, normal search and seizure precautions were not necessary. A third case decided in 1995, *Vernonia School District* v. *Acton*, extended this exception to high-school athletes on the basis of ensuring the safety of minors under governmental supervision.

A major distinction that has been recognized by the courts, however, is that between the private sector and the public sector organizations. All of the cases cited above involve government agencies or organizations. Mandatory drug testing by private employers is generally not considered a violation of the Fourth Amendment because such testing does not constitute *governmental* search or seizure. The problem, however, is that the distinction between public- and private-sector employment is not always clear. Public utilities which are regulated by the federal government, for example, may be subject to constitutional restraints even if they are privately owned as we saw in *Skinner* v. *RLEA*. Similarly, private companies which are contracted with the federal government may be subject to the same constraints as public organizations (Ackerman, 1995; Montagne, Pugh, and Fink, 1988b).

The Fourth Amendment is not the only constitutional basis for objecting to drug testing. The Fifth Amendment, which protects a defendant against self-incrimination, has also been argued as a constitutional basis for the illegality of drug testing. The logic behind this argument is that by making urine or other bodily fluids available for testing, positive test results are a form of self-incrimination. The courts have generally rejected this reasoning, however, maintaining that the Fifth Amendment applies to testimonial evidence, not to physical evidence (Montagne, Pugh, and Fink, 1988b).

Finally, the opponents of drug testing have invoked the Fourteenth Amendment in challenging the legality of the practice. Section 1 of the Fourteenth Amendment states that the government shall not ". . . *deprive any person of life, liberty, or property, without due process of law; nor deny to any person within its jurisdiction the equal protection of the laws.*" There are two challenges contained here, what are commonly called the "due process clause" and the "equal protection clause." Due process is not clearly defined in the constitution, and the courts are left to define its meaning within the context of the cases that it hears. Due process in cases of drug testing involves, at a minimum, confirmatory testing and maintaining an appropriate chain of custody for information (Ackerman, 1985; Montagne, Pugh, and Fink, 1988b).

The equal protection clause has been used to challenge refusal of employment to methadone patients because most methadone patients in the jurisdiction in question (New York) were either black or Hispanic. The court agreed with this line of argument in the 1979 case *New York City Transit Authority* v. *Beazer,* finding that the Transit Authority violated the equal protection clause of the Fourteenth Amendment. The other way in which the equal protection clause has been invoked has been to define drug and alcohol dependency as a handicap. While the language of the Federal Vocational Rehabilitation Act of 1973 does not specifically identify drug addiction or alcoholism as a disability, subsequent court cases tended to interpret the act as though *past* drug addiction was protected as a disability (Bompey, 1986). More recently, the Americans with Disabilities Act of 1990 specifies that individuals with a *past history of addiction* (not casual use or current addiction) are protected under the Act. While this does not necessarily affect drug testing, organizations are constrained in how they can respond to positive tests.

The constitutionality of drug testing will continue to be challenged. The organization taking the lead in this area is the American Civil Liberties Union (ACLU). Indeed, numerous cases are being challenged as of this writing, including cases of public schools that have made drug testing mandatory for all students (American Civil Liberties Union, 2001a,b), and a Michigan law requiring welfare recipients to undergo drug testing (American Civil Liberties Union, 2000).

SUMMARY

This chapter has addressed two types of societal response to drug use, which have one important characteristic in common—they are both preemptive efforts to prevent drug use and/or drug abuse. Beyond that important characteristic, drug education and drug testing have relatively little in common. Drug education is oriented primarily to the prevention of drug *use;* drug-testing targets current drug users in order to prevent *abuse.* Drug education typically targets younger people 10 years old and even younger; drug testing typically targets older youth and adults. The context for most drug education is in the school; drug testing is carried out in a variety of environments, but probably most commonly in the work place. Finally, while not a stated objective, drug testing is often used in a punitive way—loss of one's job, failure to get a job, removal from athletic competition, or even arrest if one tests positive. Drug education is purely preventive in its focus.

There is, furthermore, a great deal of controversy over *how* to implement these policies. Very few people would dispute the value of good drug education programs. What constitutes good drug education, however, is widely disputed. Scholars and practitioners not only disagree on the kinds of content that should be included in drug-education programs, but even on what the goals of drug education should be. Ostensibly the goal for most drug educators is to prevent drug use. Yet, when effectiveness of drug-education programs are measured, drug-using behavior is often a very minor part of the outcome measures. Highlighted instead in many of the evaluation studies are change of attitude and level of knowledge. These are hardly indicators of behavior. Moreover, there is a growing body of researchers and practitioners who suggest that abstinence is not a realistic goal, and that we may be doing more harm than good by putting all of our emphasis there. Rather, harm reductionists argue that we need to provide reliable information to young people (and parents and other adults) about the effects of drugs so that people can make responsible choices about drugs.

Drug testing also is laden with controversy. There are, of course, the technological and cost issues that cause debate among drug experts, but beyond these there are the fundamental questions: *Should we be testing for drugs in (school, work, sports, etc.)? What should we do with the results of drug tests? What do we want to accomplish by testing?* These are fundamental questions that need answers. Otherwise, as is the case with so many areas, our *ability* to test with ever-increasing precision will result in more and more motivation to do so, even at the expense of precious and long-held cultural values, particularly the sacred respect of one's privacy.

KEY TERMS

affective model

drug education

drug screening

drug testing

informational model

social influence model (drug resistance education)

REVIEW QUESTIONS

1. Briefly describe the major features of the informational, affective, and social-influence models of drug education, and highlight the philosophical premise behind each. Based on these features, which approach do you think *should* be most effective?

2. Why do you think DARE, a social-influence model program, has been so ineffective while other social-influence model educational programs have been comparatively effective in accomplishing their goals?

3. What are the central elements of a harm-reduction model with regard to drug education? Is a harm-reduction approach incompatible with any of the other approaches to drug education?

4. What does "drug testing" mean? Do you think there is value in maintaining a distinction between "drug testing" and "drug screening?"

5. Provide one or two scenarios under which each of the following would be most appropriate as a drug testing procedure: *breath tests, urinalysis, blood analysis,* and *hair analysis.* Provide a brief rationale for each.

6. What are the goals of drug testing? Do you believe these are appropriate goals? How effective is drug testing in accomplishing these goals?

CRITICAL THOUGHT QUESTIONS

1. Harm reduction, as an approach to drug education questions the assumptions made by existing drug-education efforts. Carefully consider the assumptions identified as questionable by harm reduction strategists. Utilizing your knowledge of the sociology of drug use gleaned thus far in this course, engage in a dialogue with the harm reductionists on these points.

2. Drug testing has been challenged on both practical and constitutional grounds. Consider the legitimacy of these challenges. After careful consideration, answer the question, "Under what conditions, if at all, should drug testing take place?"

DRUG POLICY FOR THE TWENTY-FIRST CENTURY

Throughout this text, we have attempted to represent fairly issues related to the study of psychoactive drugs from a range of perspectives so that you, the student, will have the broad base of information necessary to think critically about drugs in American society. This chapter, by contrast, is much more partisan in nature; we are using it as a platform to develop recommendations on some of the major social and political issues in drug policy that have been raised throughout this text, and particularly in Chapters 11 through 13. Following a brief discussion of harm reduction, which is our guiding philosophy in this chapter, we review and evaluate both supply-side and demand-side policies, providing recommendations based on these evaluations. The final section of this chapter examines several key areas of policy consideration, namely drug legalization, legalization of medical marijuana, needle exchange, drug testing, drug education, and drug treatment.

OUR GUIDING PHILOSOPHY

We urge policy-makers, practitioners, and the general public, including you, the student, to take a reflective and critical look at our current drug policies and their implementation. The philosophical position from which we will be articulating policy suggestions throughout this chapter is two-pronged. First, we urge that policies and practices be primarily *empirically* based. This does not mean that we do not see a place for moral argument or even consideration of tradition in our drug policies for the twenty-first century; we just mean that such policies should be reinforced by *good* empirical evidence. Good empirical evidence is methodologically sound, based on the systematic collection and analysis of data, and is not selected simply because it backs up an *a priori* theoretical position. When active or proposed policies lack solid support, we need to reevaluate either our empirical evidence, or the basis for the moral positions and/or traditions which guide our thinking. It is not helpful to maintain policies which are strongly dissonant with the weight of empirical evidence simply because "it has always been this way." We concur with Ethan Nadelmann (1998, p. 111) when he writes that "U.S. drug policy . . . has preferred rhetoric to reality, and moralism to pragmatism."

Second, we are guided by an ethic of *reduction of harm*. Reduction of harm is a philosophical position which states that drug policies should be aimed at reducing the many costs—to physical health and emotional well-being, to social relationships and roles, to economic stability—associated with drug abuse. Harm reduction has been advocated by many drug policy reformers including Nadelmann, the Director of the Drug Policy Alliance; he calls it "commonsense drug policy". Robert Westermeyer (n.d.) suggests that the harm-reduction approach to drug abuse and other addictive behaviors rests on three central tenets: (1) that drug behaviors should be seen as a continuum from high risk to minimal risk, rather than an all-or-nothing phenomenon; (2) changing addictive behavior should be approached in a step-wise fashion, with abstinence being the final step; and (3) that sobriety may not be everybody's goal. What Westermeyer is saying, first, is that we must not be content to simply see drug use as "dangerous," but that there are varying levels of involvement, different types of drugs which represent different levels of danger, different modes of ingestion some of which are more risky than others, and differing lifestyle factors, all of which result in a continuum of risk. We must recognize this continuum, identify high risk drug-using behaviors, and make them our highest priorities in our drug policies. We must recognize, for example, that occasional recreational use of drugs is very different from highly addictive drug use, which is much more destructive of health and social relationships. Second, it is not realistic to expect that we can "cure" drug addiction by some magic "bullet." Addiction is a complex process in its development, and the "undoing" of addiction is also a complex process taking place one step at a time. Finally, Westermeyer suggests that it is important to recognize that abstinence is not for everyone. This means a couple of different things, which may be seen by some as controversial. He is strongly suggesting that we don't set as our goal the eradication of all drug use; it isn't going to happen. Some compulsive drug users are going to be unable to stop using, "choosing" drug involvement over sobriety. More controversial, certainly, is the interpretation that people should be able to choose to experience subjective drug effects which they define as pleasurable. We recognize that some forms of chemically altered consciousness are allowed by our society, moderate recreational drinking being the most obvious example. And as stipulated elsewhere in this text, there are other, currently illegal drugs such as marijuana, that may be used in a similar manner. We don't endorse the notion, though, that there is a generalized right in our society to recreational intoxication. We feel the philosophical basis of harm reduction is compelling, yet acknowledge that there is room for disagreement among observers of the drug scene as to what policies and practices best accomplish this purpose. Indeed, the authors of this text have a couple of differences among us in policy emphases, though they are admittedly few and not terribly significant.

SUPPLY-SIDE AND DEMAND-SIDE POLICIES

A QUICK REVIEW

Drug scholars and policy makers distinguish between "supply-side" and "demand-side" strategies for addressing problems associated with drug use and abuse in American society. **Supply side** strategies are those that are directed at curtailing supplies of drugs that might otherwise be made available to users in the population. **Demand side** policies, by contrast, focus on reducing the need or demand that users or potential users have for drugs. Primary supply-side strategies employed by the United States include:

- *Source reduction*—works toward eliminating supplies of drugs where they are grown or manufactured. This often involved international politics, working with other governments to provide incentives for farmers not to produce the raw materials for drugs, or to employ sanctions against those who continue to do so.
- *Border interdiction*—involves the interception of supplies of drugs moving from growers and manufacturers to dealers after they leave other countries and before they enter the United States. These activities often take place directly at the borders, on the high seas, or in coastal waterways, but may also be carried out in rural, uninhabited areas where planes with drugs land and dispose of their cargo.
- *Curtailing domestic distribution*—endeavors to break the supply chains between drug suppliers in this country, as drugs move from the hands of large-scale importers to local street dealers. These strategies are carried out by federal, state, and local officials, depending on the size of the operation and whether or not drugs are being transported across state lines.

There is an additional supply-side strategy which is fundamentally at variance with the above approaches currently used—this strategy is to *change the legal definition* of drugs. Changing the legal definition involves either *legalizing* or *decriminalizing* drugs. Legalization and decriminalization policy proposals vary, ranging from a carte blanche, *laissez faire* approach, to focusing on very selective drugs and conditions for changing the legal status of a particular drug. A very selective approach would be, for example, the legalization of marijuana for medical purposes. Legalization and decriminalization are normally not considered a supply-side drug strategy because the results and the purposes of these policy approaches are so fundamentally different from other supply-side strategies. Changing the legal definition of drugs generally makes drugs *more* accessible rather than less accessible. Because they are policy alternatives which affect the supply of available drugs, we feel it is appropriate to consider them supply-side strategies. And they are strategies that work well with demand-side approaches to which we now turn our attention.

Demand-side strategies include two basic approaches, often used in conjunction with one another. These approaches are drug treatment and drug education, which were discussed in Chapters 12 and 13 respectively. Each of these strategies comprise a number of approaches and philosophies to reducing the demand for illegal drugs. Drug education seeks to target young people *before* they begin using drugs, or drug users of all ages before they become abusers of or, addicted to, habit-forming drugs. One approach to education appeals to the powerful emotion of fear, depicting the potential consequences of drug use in the most extreme form. This has been the approach taken by the Partnership for a Drug-Free America, recently working together with the Office of National Drug Control Policy. We believe that this is of limited usefulness, working only with the very youngest of targeted audiences, and then only for a few years at best. Other approaches, such as the Drug Abuse Resistance Education program (DARE) target the reality of peer pressure in the lives of adolescents, and teach children how to resist the pressure to use drugs. We discussed the general ineffectiveness and unrealistic goals of this approach in Chapter 12. Other programs are primarily informative, providing basic information about drugs and how they affect the human body. This approach is more common in health education courses that are a part of a school's general curriculum. We feel that drug education must provide information that is:

- Of age-appropriate intention, complexity, and depth; for example, simple moral messages are acceptable for six year olds but not for preteen and older students;
- Based on knowledge that is current and empirically derived, presenting drug risks honestly and without exaggeration (or minimization, for that matter);
- Aimed at reducing the harm done by drug abuse in our society; appropriately-informed students will usually avoid drug use or, if not, will generally be safer drug consumers.

Treatment programs, by contrast, intervene in the demand cycle *after* an individual has already become addicted to drugs and is living a drug-dependent lifestyle. These programs have varied, and sometimes competing, philosophies about how best to go about treatment, which makes sense because drug dependency is not a one-size-fits-all phenomenon. The long-term, chronic addict who has gone through many attempts at "getting clean" only to relapse repeatedly, is a different, and more difficult case, than an addict whose life has not yet begun to revolve totally around the phenomenon of addiction. Methadone maintenance, perhaps appropriate for the former but certainly not for the latter, understands addiction to be a function of biochemical alteration of basic brain functioning, one that demands a chemical solution. Other modalities, grounded more firmly in the social sciences, understand addiction as primarily a social and psychological process. Therapeutic communities, group and individual therapy, and self-help groups address individual and environmental factors within the addict's control. These groups adopt abstinence as their goal and encourage a drug-free lifestyle. Certainly, the recent addict would be more appropriately placed here, though we wish to stress that many people who decide to stop abusing drugs and suffering consequences are able to do so without formal drug treatment. There are, in addition, approaches to treatment that are spiritually based. These are primarily self-help groups such as Alcoholics Anonymous—and its counterparts targeting other substances and compulsive behaviors—which have no membership fees and advocate a drug-free lifestyle (though AA remains tolerant of caffeine and nicotine use). Literally millions of Americans, and many others around the world, have achieved and maintained sobriety within these fellowships. We endorse them unreservedly, particularly for addicts who are willing to seek spiritual solutions to their addiction.

While these demand-side approaches to the problem of drug use and addiction vary widely in their philosophies and approaches, they share in common a commitment to reducing the level of marketplace demand (American's "hunger") for illicit substances. A market for illegal drugs will surely be met by suppliers who will go to great lengths to maximize their profits. We believe that short of transforming our society into a police state, no level of law enforcement will effectively curtail the supply of illegal drugs to a demanding market.

EVALUATING SUPPLY- AND DEMAND-SIDE POLICIES

An assessment of the worthiness of prohibitionist-based supply-side strategies depends a great deal on one's political and ideological point of view. There is little doubt that these policies have curtailed the availability and consumption of recreational drugs above what would be the case if drugs were allowed to be freely distributed. This is particularly true for experimental or social-recreational users. While some have argued that prohibitionist policies have produced a "forbidden fruit" mentality that ultimately creates a *greater* demand for drugs (e.g., Friedman, 1972), we feel the evidence is strong that prohibitionist policies do curtail the overall level of drug use. If there was one positive consequence of our national experiment with alcohol prohibition, it was that the number of alcohol users and the amount of alcohol consumed was reduced. Ray and Ksir (1999) report, for example, that alcohol-related deaths and hospital admissions declined during the period immediately following the enactment of prohibition, and while the decade of the 1920s saw these numbers increase gradually, they never reached the level of the pre-prohibition period. Solid research has shown that when supplies of an addict's drug of choice are temporarily unavailable, he or she is very likely to enter a period of abstinence from drug abuse. (Faupel, 1991)

Prohibition had many social and economic costs which must be considered as well. We know that more people drank alcohol that was illegally produced and distributed ("moonshine") than ever before, a supply which was potentially tainted and hence more dangerous. There were also great economic costs incurred. Alcohol taxes, which were a significant source of income prior to prohibition, were eliminated. Law enforcement was also greatly expanded at all levels of government. Ray (1978) also notes that during the statewide prohibition efforts leading up to the Eighteenth Amendment, more than 100,000 licensed drinking establishments were closed, representing a major economic cost to communities. There are similar economic costs associated with prohibition of other recreational drugs.

The costs of Prohibition extend far beyond economic costs, however. We pointed out in Chapter 11 that prohibitionist policies have created or at least expanded the context for law enforcement corruption, as police officers face great temptation to either extort money and drugs from drug dealers and other criminals, or to accept bribes as payoff for nonenforcement. There is no way to fully quantify this cost to society, because it goes far beyond the value of the money or drugs changing hands. Police and criminal justice corruption deeply affects the morale of a department and undermines the credibility of the criminal justice system itself. Consider, also, the legacy of Prohibition as a breeding ground for organized crime. *Someone* had to provide for our nation's considerable thirst for alcohol that didn't disappear when legal channels dried up. When the Twenty-first Amendment ended our experiment with Prohibition, many criminal syndicates went looking for other lucrative markets, including the illegal drug market, which today generates tens of billions of dollars in underground profits.

There are also public health costs that can be attributed directly to prohibitionist drug policies. We have discussed several health consequences of prohibitionist policies in Chapter 11, but of urgent concern at this time is the rapid spread of HIV/AIDS among the injectable drug using population. Around one-third of HIV positive men and boys, and one-half of HIV positive women and girls contracted the disease through drug abuse (ONDCP, 2001:164). The spread of this deadly disease, as well as hepatitis and other diseases spread through contaminated needles could be curtailed substantially by lifting criminal sanctions for possession of hypodermic needles and syringes. Not only the drug user may be infected by dirty needles, but spouses and others with whom an infected person has intimate relations as well. Moreover, public health departments and other educational resources are limited by governments in the material that they can distribute, materials that could provide valuable information on how to protect one's self from acquiring HIV, from overdosing, from increasing the harm done by drug abuse. Such materials are incompatible with a "zero tolerance" policy of prohibition. Finally, we have also identified civil liberties costs that are attached to prohibitionist policies. Wiretaps, surveillance and mandatory drug testing are all intrusions into the private lives of individuals. Americans have so far been willing to sacrifice privacy rights in order to help reach the goal of drug-free neighborhoods and workplaces. This does represent a cost, however, which has questionable returns given the impossibility of the goals these prohibitionist practices have intended to accomplish.

Unfortunately, demand-side strategies have not been unequivically effective either. Most evaluations conducted of drug-education programs have not had encouraging results. The effectiveness of drug treatment is highly variable across treatment modalities, due in part to the fact that the various modalities define their goals differently. The goal of drug-free treatment programs is nothing less than a lifestyle of abstinence, and in some cases success is further defined as having productive employment and a cessation from criminal activity. Methadone maintenance, by contrast, seeks only to eliminate *illegal* drug use, while providing addicts with a safer and legal alternative drug, methadone. Because of cross-dependence, heroin addicts can satisfy their craving for heroin without having to acquire substances through illegal sources and, ideally, not having to pay for it through illegally acquired income. Methadone maintenance has been reasonably successful from the standpoint of its own success criteria, most notably that addicts remain heroin (morphine) free and test methadone positive instead, and this success has led harm-reduction strategists to tout methadone maintenance as a major thrust of their policy promotion package (Nadelmann, McNeely, and Drucker, 1997).

Supply-side policies rest on three fundamental premises regarding drug use. The first assumption is that availability of drugs in communities and neighborhoods creates addicts. The lure of drugs is so overwhelming that children and teenagers will be drawn to experiment, and once experimenting, have a great likelihood of becoming addicts. Second, addiction to drugs creates an *inelastic demand* for drugs. That is, the addict *requires* the addicting drug, in amounts that typically increase as tolerance for the drug sets in. Third, because the demand for the drug is inelastic, and illegal drugs such as heroin are very costly, addicts will be forced to commit crimes to support their habits. Consequently, supply-side theorizing goes, the very *availability* of drugs is the critical factor in determining the extensiveness of addiction and the antisocial behavior associated with it. Most supply-side policies are focused on *reducing* levels of availability so that, in the most optimistic scenario, it will be impossible for addicts to get drugs and will then result in a reduced demand for drugs. Interestingly, drug legalization also accepts the same presuppositions as prohibitionist strategies, but argues that by making drugs legal, addicts (with inelastic needs and demands for drugs) can purchase drugs that will be both cheaper and less harmful to one's health, thereby eliminating the need to commit crime for drug purchases. Levels of drug use will remain high, but without the ancillary social costs attached.

Decades of research seriously challenge the assumptions upon which supply-side intervention strategies are based. The first assumption, that the availability of drugs reliably creates a population of addicts is highly questionable. Addict populations certainly develop where there are drugs available. This is hardly surprising. Yet we saw in Chapter 7 that addiction among health professionals—doctors, nurses, and medical students—is not substantially higher than in the general population, and in the case of physicians, it is actually *lower*. Clearly, availability alone cannot account for the high rates of drug involvement in inner cities and other high-drug-use locales. Moreover, the assumption that once an individual begins using drugs on an occasional basis he or she will necessarily progress to addiction has not been supported by research. We know that there are many people who use drugs like heroin and cocaine on an occasional basis for years without becoming addicted. While availability is certainly an important variable in levels of drug use, there is no automatic or inevitable connection between levels of availability and addiction. The second assumption, that addiction produces an inelastic demand for drugs, is also questionable. The fact is that addicts frequently reduce their level of drug use, sometimes voluntarily, sometimes involuntarily. During "panics," periods when drugs are not as accessible, most users simply lower their consumption and/or turn to other legal or illegal drugs during these periods. Heroin users report that they will cut down on their level of heroin consumption during times when they have to abort their normal criminal activities because of police surveillance (Faupel, 1991). Periods of incarceration or forced treatment represent involuntary periods of elasticity in an addict's level of use. The empirical reality is that even once one is addicted, drugs do not act on individuals as though they were marionettes on strings. Drug addicts, like consumers of other goods, make choices, including the choice to lower the level of their use in many cases. Insofar as levels of drug consumption are *elastic*, it is also questionable to assume that drug use or addiction "causes" crime and other antisocial behavior. Indeed, as we have discussed in Chapter 10, it is often the case that criminal activity is a precursor to increased drug use. In short, the assumptions on which supply-side proposals are predicated are questionable in our view. Our concerns are reinforced by the limited success of a war on drugs that has escalated to a level where we spend many billions of dollars per year, yet drug supplies remain plentiful, with purity levels quite high and costs to the addict lower than they were a decade or more ago.

Demand-side policies begin with a fundamentally different premise, namely that demand drives supply, rather than vice versa. That is, where there is a demand for a product—a drug-hungry market, for example—suppliers will respond to that demand. This is a totally different starting point from supply-side strategies which assume that supplies create the demand. If it is the case that demand for drugs fuels the illicit drug industry, then it makes sense to address problems associated with drug use—crime, drug abuse, health problems, etc.—by attempting to curtail the demand for these drugs. Demand-side approaches also bring to the table different assumptions about the nature of addiction. Rather than addiction creating an *inelastic* demand, these approaches recognize that individuals largely *choose* to use drugs. Choices are also made following addiction, including the choice to forgo food for drugs, to commit crime, etc. Drug addicts can also choose to use alternative drugs or engage in alternative behaviors that do not involve the use of drugs. Indeed, the two demand-side approaches—drug treatment and drug education—emphasize these alternative behavior choices. Proponents of these approaches suggest that only by assisting young people in finding modes of expression other than beginning drug use in the first place through various educational approaches, and/or helping current users to quit using drugs through treatment, can we significantly address the problem of drug abuse. Demand-side proponents argue

that demand for drugs is not often created by peddlers of dope who se-
duce teenagers and capture them in a web of addiction for life. Rather, drug
abuse cycles can be stopped through educational and treatment efforts, providing addicts and would-be addicts the tools to exercise their choice to
resist drug use today and in the future.

Unfortunately, drug education and drug treatment programs have not
had much more success in realizing their goals than have supply-side strategies. Some approaches have proven more effective than others, especially
if they are tailored appropriately to the needs of the individual student or
client. We have been cautious in our critique of drug education and drug
treatment, however, because we believe that our society has not made a
strong commitment to demand-side policies. Despite promises that things
will be otherwise, relatively minuscule amounts of federal dollars are spent
on drug education and treatment efforts as compared with the massive
amounts of funding to law enforcement organizations for supply-side initiatives. It is our considered opinion that the equation needs to be reordered,
with the bulk of our financial resources steered away from law enforcement
programs and committed to demand-side policies. We recognize that drug
supplies are not going to dry up permanently, no matter how hard we try,
and that as long as there are supplies of drugs available, education and
treatment efforts will lose significant numbers of people to the seduction
of instant gratification through mind altering drugs. As long as we continue to view the phenomena of drug abuse and addiction as primarily
criminal justice problems, rather than public health issues, progress will be
modest at best and will come at great social and economic cost.

SPECIFIC POLICY ISSUES AND RECOMMENDATIONS

As we recommend specific policy options, we remind the reader that our
discussion is governed by principles of *harm reduction.* This means that we
are not governed by the lofty yet unreachable goal of zero drug use in
American society. Only political rhetoricians, those trying to convey their
"toughness" on the subject for their own political gain, promise the utterly
unattainable. We do believe, however, that it is a reasonable goal to *reduce*
the level of drug use. Ultimately, however, from a harm reduction standpoint we are committed to *reducing the harm* caused by drugs and drug use.
Drug use reduction and harm reduction are related, but not necessarily
identical goals.

DRUG LEGALIZATION
Drug legalization and decriminalization are both *supply-side* policy recommendations that are promoted out of concern for the social and personal harm that has been caused by the strong prohibitionist policies of the
twentieth (and early twenty-first) century. We have discussed the costs of

prohibition both in Chapter 11 and earlier in this chapter. Most serious scholars concur that drug policy in the United States since the Harrison Narcotics Act of 1914 has resulted in extremely heavy economic, health, and civil liberties costs for individuals and for our society as a whole. Proponents of legalization, however, must demonstrate convincingly that the consequences of abandoning prohibition would be *less* costly before any serious-minded legislature will entertain such a proposal. This is certainly understandable. Beyond empirical evidence that is convincing, many decades of ideological resistance to altering our drug policy course must also be overcome. It is very difficult to gather the necessary evidence in support of either legalization or decriminalization given the prohibitionist legal milieu in which we find ourselves. Much of the literature has been highly speculative, making theoretical arguments for or against legalization or decriminalization. Advocates of decriminalization, for example, typically argue that decriminalization of marijuana should cause, at most, a small increase in the number of users and frequency of marijuana use, since we are near a "saturation point" for marijuana use. This should be counteracted, they say, by individuals abandoning alcohol, cocaine, and other more harmful forms of drug use for marijuana, which they contend has less serious consequences. Opponents of altering marijuana policy generally predict a considerable increase in marijuana and other types of drug use, arguing that decriminalization symbolizes public acceptance of drug use (Thies and Register, 1993). Who's right?

The growing body of empirical evidence in this area suggests that decriminalization has *not* resulted in significant increases in marijuana and illegal drug use as opponents of decriminalization have claimed. Research among high-school seniors conducted at the University of Michigan reveals, for example, that while marijuana consumption was slightly higher in states that decriminalized marijuana relative to nearby states, this was the case prior to decriminalization as well (Institute for Social Research, 1981). An early review of the literature by Walter Cuskey and his associates (1978) also found only modest levels of increase in marijuana use following decriminalization in Oregon and California. Thies and Register (1993), using more sophisticated econometric techniques, also conclude that decriminalization has not resulted in a significant increase in marijuana or other drug use. Clearly, the lifting of criminal sanctions has not had the drastically negative consequences that opponents project. The *advantages* of decriminalization are less certain, though there is evidence that decriminalization has allowed law enforcement to focus more resources on other, more serious forms of drug use and crime.

Decriminalization does not allow for government regulation or taxing of marijuana commerce, which is a potential benefit of legalization (but also a source of concern for those who don't want the drug trade regulated according to government whim). We do not know what untoward effects legalization would have on drug use, but the best evidence that we have based on decriminalization research casts serious doubts on the claims made by prohibitionists. There are, moreover, compelling arguments for legalization of drugs from both a public health and an economic standpoint. Only by legalizing drugs can there be effective regulation of drug quality which should ameliorate public health problems such as inadvertent drug overdoses and other health problems associated with variable purity of street drug samples. Such regulation would be costly, of course, but these costs could be more than off-set with tax revenues generated from the sale of formerly illegal drugs. Legalization of drugs would, additionally, provide more options for treatment and drug education, demand-side strategies for reducing drug use. If drug education didn't have to preach pure abstinence, as is currently the arrangement most often under a prohibitionist orientation, we might reach experimenting teenagers, or those on the invitational edge of use, more effectively. These individuals need an educational approach that provides important and valuable information about how drugs might affect them, about drug interaction effects, and about how to avoid contracting HIV and other contagious diseases. Drug treatment programs might also benefit from legalized drugs, by gradually taking poly-drug users off of currently illegal drugs, using presumably safer substitutes in the detoxification process.

Despite these potential advantages, we are not advocating full legalization of all psychoactive drugs at this time. What we are calling for, as a necessary precondition to significant policy change, is open and honest dialog between scholars, practitioners, and politicians. A climate that would foster this does not currently exist and will not as long as we allow ideologically based rhetoric, absent of scientific backing, to predominate. Drug policy is highly politicized, with distrust causing erosion of the common-sensical middle ground. Our first goal in developing workable solutions is to break the impasse that we have experienced in the rhetoric and practice of the drug war. Almost certainly, conflict-management teams will be a necessary part of these dialogues to help partisans get past caricatures of distrust.

We are hopeful that such dialogue would promote creative alternatives to be given thoughtful consideration, and that implementation strategies and teams responsible for overseeing such strategies would be supported. Such strategies must include working with states and localities who wish to develop creative responses to problems of drug abuse in their jurisdictions. The "one size fits all" national drug control policy simply hasn't worked. The activists' maxim that we should "think globally, but act locally" makes sense here. Currently, the federal government's attempts to squelch any efforts by states or localities to legalize Schedule I drugs for any purposes, including medical ones, are shortsighted and divisive. The Drug Enforcement Administration and the Office of National Drug Control Policy threaten those who challenge the established orthodoxy with loss of federal funding or with using the federal courts to override state initiatives. In short, we are challenging the long-held notion that the national fathers know best. Alternative policies which have been proposed by scholars and experts on the front lines of drug abuse prevention—which might range from decriminalization or legalization of certain drugs to limited legalization for medical purposes—need to be carefully researched and evaluated, however politically unpopular that might prove to be. Would these policies result in greater levels of drug use? Do they decrease or increase the economic, social, and/or public health costs? Such research should be part of a broad assessment process, the results of which would be shared with states and localities, and indeed the federal government itself, prior to adopting these policies. It is critical that any change in existing policy be made only on the basis of good objective empirical research. To obtain such data, pilot programs must be implemented in "real life" situations, with jurisdictional limits and a prescribed probationary period.

Legalization of Medical Marijuana

As of the end of 2002, nine states, all in the West except Maine, have effectively legalized marijuana for medical purposes, among them reducing nausea associated with chemotherapy in cancer patients, to help prevent weight loss among AIDS patients, and to relieve intraocular pressure among glaucoma patients. The federal government has been quick to react to the state laws, attempting to target doctors who recommend marijuana to their patients. The federal government has also targeted individual users and the "clubs" that distribute marijuana to authorized medical patients. We saw this in the recent decision in *United States* v. *Oakland Cannabis Buyers Cooperative, et al.,* (U.S. Supreme Court, 2001), where a locally hailed program that provided truly ill individuals an opportunity to purchase medicinal marijuana, with the support of California voters and local law enforcement officials, was declared in violation of federal law. The government's attempts to close down the cannabis collectives is being challenged in both the state and federal courts. Yet in other situations, the federal government has been frustrated in their attempt to negate these state laws by the Supreme Court in such cases as *Conant* v. *McCaffrey* which ruled that to prevent doctors from recommending the use of medical marijuana was an abridgement of free speech and therefore unconstitutional.

It is precisely this combative approach to grassroots policy which is detrimental to effective drug policy. Oncologists, physicians who specialize in the diagnosis and treatment of cancer and tumors, are strongly, though not universally, supportive of the use of marijuana to reduce the nausea associated with cancer chemotherapy. There is also broad-based support in the medical community (but not officially by the American Medical Association) for the medicalization of marijuana for AIDS and glaucoma patients. This is clearly a public health issue, not a criminal justice issue, a distinction that gets buried by antidrug hysteria. Physicians should be the primary consultants for federal as well as state and local policy regarding the use of marijuana to treat medical conditions. There is a sufficiently long history of the use of marijuana medically to evaluate the social and economic impact of those policies. A federal response of tolerance and a willingness to study the impact of these state initiatives should be implemented. Coordinating federal policy with state policies, would provide strong guidelines for other states which might be wanting to move in the direction of making marijuana medically available to patients who need it.

LEGALIZATION OF NEEDLES/NEEDLE EXCHANGE

Making needles legally available through what is broadly referred to as **needle exchange,** is another variant of the legalization theme. Such a policy does not imply nor require the legalization of drugs of any form and hence lacks an important feature of supply-side policies, namely, addressing the level of availability of drugs in a given area. Neither advocates nor opponents of the legalization of needles suggest that they will significantly affect the availability of heroin or other injectable drugs. Indeed, these programs may be more likely to affect demand in that there are often treatment referral and educational services built in to many current needle-exchange programs which, if successful, may lower the demand for injectable drugs. On the other hand, if opponents of these programs are correct that legalizing needles sends a moral message that drug use is an acceptable behavior, the demand for these drugs may increase slightly.

The controversy surrounding the legalization of needles seems to revolve around the moral message that such a policy would send, and the supposition that there would occur a subsequent increase in drug use because of greater access to needles (Burack and Bangsberg, 1998). Research by Gostin, Lazzarini, Jones, and Flaherty (1997) reveals that every state in the Union and the District of Columbia have laws that restrict legal access to needles and syringes. There has been substantial resistance to needle-exchange programs in various localities throughout the country (Singer, Irizarry, and Schensul, 1991). Legislating against needle exchanges accords greater weight to the moralizers' position than to genuine public health concerns. This is unfortunate, because, as we have noted elsewhere, a substantial proportion of new HIV infections result from the sharing or use of tainted paraphernalia. The empirical evidence is clear and quite unequivocal. Wherever access to clean needles has been legitimized, the frequency of needle sharing has declined and the spread of HIV and AIDS slowed down. A metastudy commissioned by the Centers for Disease Control to evaluate the impact of needle exchange programs in California concluded that 10 of 14 credible studies documented a reduction in the frequency of needle sharing among IDUs (Lurie et al., 1994). Research by Watters (1994) in San Francisco revealed a 47 percent reduction in needle sharing after the introduction of a needle exchange program there. Similarly, Broadhead, Van Hulst, and Heckathorn (1999) reported a 118 percent increase in the reuse and sharing of dirty needles following the closing of a needle-exchange program in Connecticut. Similar results have been reported elsewhere in the United States and around the world (Burack and Bangsberg, 1998). These behavioral changes have had an impact on the spread of HIV and AIDS.

Harm reductionists strongly advocate making clean needles legally available, either over-the-counter or at specially designated needle exchange facilities.

Research by Des Jarlais and his colleagues (1996) in New York City found that IDUs who did not avail themselves of needle-exchange programs were 3.3 times more likely to test positive for the HIV virus. Studies of Hepatitis B transmission have also documented a downward trend following the introduction of needle-exchange programs (Burack and Bangsberg, 1998). We would also point out that those studies which addressed the issue found little or no increase in drug use in those locales that established needle-exchange programs (Burack and Bangsberg, 1998).

The empirical evidence regarding the public health benefits of legally available syringes is overwhelming. The appropriate question is not *whether* we should make clean needles and syringes available to injecting drug users, but rather *how* that process should take place. There are two models: one is a *laissez faire* model, which would make needles and syringes available over the counter at local pharmacies. This model has certain advantages. First, needles will be more readily available to addicts wherever they might be; rather than having to drive across town to a needle-exchange program and risk being discouraged in the process and using a dirty needle, an addict in withdrawal distress could more easily access sterile equipment through this model. A second advantage is that such a model might be less likely to create a "needle park" syndrome, a gathering place for addicts that might be undesirable for residents of local neighborhoods. The second model is more restricted and is embodied in the needle exchange programs that exist today (where they are allowed to operate). These programs typically operate on a "one-for-one" basis, at least until an addict has established a dependable track record. One-for-one means that an addict is given one clean needle and syringe for every dirty needle and syringe turned in. This model has a number of advantages. First, it allows for a system of monitoring the distribution of needles specifically to addicts. Second, and perhaps most importantly, this model has a built-in mechanism for getting dirty needles off the street, thus affecting nonenrolled addicts or nonusers who might accidently wound themselves. Finally, needle-exchange programs provide a valuable educational and referral forum. Many needle-exchange programs have educational materials available on how to avoid HIV transmission both through needles and unprotected sex. Knowledgeable counselors are also available at some to answer questions that clients might have. Addicts who want assistance in getting off drugs can also get referrals to methadone or other treatment programs as well. A third model, one used effectively in Amsterdam, is to proactively bring the clean needles and counseling to the addicts, through the use of mobile public health vans.

We strongly recommend, as a first step, that states establish enabling legislation that would (1) remove all criminal penalties for possessing needles and syringes; and (2) establish principles for the establishment of needle-exchange programs. Many such programs are already in place with very promising results and providing a model for other states and localities to follow. Moreover, while there are certain advantages to a laissez faire model, a more cautious policy and implementation, one that allows us to more easily evaluate the consequences, seems in order at this time. The restricted model embodied by needle-exchange programs is also less likely to send symbolic messages encouraging drug use. Access to needles would be more difficult than in the laissez faire model, and such access would be made available in a public health setting, either by clinic or van, not in a free market setting. Needle access is an urgent public health issue not a criminal justice issue; indeed, it is not even primarily a moral issue, except insofar as it saves lives. It should not be politicized. Bi-partisan support of such programs in both state and federal legislatures is long overdue.

DRUG TESTING

Drug testing has been a controversial policy primarily because of the protections against unreasonable searches and seizures afforded by the Fourth Amendment to the Constitution. The Fourth Amendment states:

> The right of the people to be secure in their persons, houses, papers, and effects, against unreasonable searches and seizures, shall not be violated, and no Warrants shall issue, but upon probable cause, supported by Oath or affirmation, and particularly describing the place to be searched, and the persons or things to be seized.

Opponents of drug testing contend that it involves an invasion of the body itself in extracting bodily fluids for purposes of testing for the presence of illegal substances, and hence violates the principle of being secure in one's person, especially when there is no particular reason to suspect the individual of illegality. Such a practice, they argue, is considerably more invasive than other practices which are prohibited on the basis of the Fourth Amendment. Indeed, some nine states have provisions in their constitutions that make drug testing illegal except when there is a compelling interest of the state to conduct such testing. Federal government employees, with the exception of the military and certain other critical positions such as the secret service, are protected against random drug testing. The private sector, however, has embraced occupational drug screening and testing much more readily.

Like other policy proposals, we evaluate drug testing policies from a "harm reduction" perspective. There are both costs and benefits associated with drug testing and screening programs. The potential costs of drug testing are (1) invading one's person; (2) violating one's right to private conduct, particularly that which doesn't affect public roles; and (3) the potential for false positives stemming from imprecise measurement. We have already addressed the constitutional basis for privacy concerns. Privacy, and the right to be secure in our households (and indeed our own bodies), is a fundamental tenet of American values and justice. This is a right that should not be trampled upon for anything less than compelling interests of the collective. Moreover, as we have discussed in Chapter 13, the most common (EMIT) test procedure that is used to test for drugs in urine is known to have a high rate of false positives. While many employers will routinely subject positive reports to other tests, not all employers do. Consequently, not only are the privacy rights of individuals violated by drug tests, but they may unjustly lose their jobs and means of livelihood.

Before dismissing drug testing as a violation of personal and civil rights, however, we must also recognize that there are important benefits that this procedure provides. We know that alcohol and drug abuse account for a great deal of absenteeism and workplace accidents (see Chapter 9). Workers under the influence of drugs not only threaten their own safety and company productivity, but may also threaten the safety of other workers as well. Indeed, in certain situations, the well-being of the collective may very well be in jeopardy when users report to work with drugs or alcohol in their system, or use such substances in the workplace. Clearly, a workforce with even a small percentage of people under the influence of drugs and alcohol poses a potential risk to safety and productivity.

Our search for a responsible policy on drug testing must acknowledge both costs and benefits. The policy that has been evolving in this country over the past several years, both statutorily and through case law, has in fact analyzed costs and benefits. Current policy distinguishes between *random* testing and testing *for cause*. Random testing means that *all* employees or organizational members (or those in certain occupational categories) are subject to testing at the discretion of the organization. Testing for cause means that an individual can be tested only if it can be demonstrated that there is reasonable cause to do so—typically erratic behavior or other performance-related observations. The guiding principle here is the search and seizure clause of the Fourth Amendment which states that unreasonable searches shall not be made and that such searches require that probable cause be established. This is an important principle, though it is subject to certain exemptions.

First, existing policy distinguishes between high risk or highly sensitive occupations and those which do not pose such a risk to collective welfare (e.g., *Skinner* v. *Railway Labor Executives' Association*, 1989; *National Treasury Employees Union* v. *Von Raab*, 1989). These two cases, one involving testing of transportation employees, the other of Secret Service personnel, explicitly recognize the special nature of these occupations and the overriding public interest that is served by testing employees in these strategic occupations. The court has ruled that testing of employees in such occupations is inherently reasonable because of the compelling interest that the state has in ensuring a drug-free workforce in these occupations. Many lives depend upon the good clear judgment of transportation personnel, and in the case of the military, Secret Service, and similar organizations, national security is potentially at stake. This is sound policy and is not only constitutionally justified, as interpreted by the Supreme Court, but is also consistent with harm-reduction principles.

A second distinction that is apparent in existing policy is the distinction between public and private organizations. Public organizations, particularly federal government agencies and organizations which are funded by the federal government, must adhere to a strict interpretation of the Fourth Amendment, and are not allowed to conduct drug testing without cause except in the high-risk occupations discussed above. Private companies, however, are given much more latitude in drug testing. Private employers routinely administer periodic mandatory random testing. The motive is usually stated in commercial terms—drug-using employees have higher absentee rates and perform less well on the job. Commercial interests have never been recognized by the courts as a compelling interest to justify exemption from Constitutional provisions. We feel strongly that there is no *defensible* reason why the protections of the Fourth Amendment should be extended only to public employees. The provisions and protections of the Constitution should not be denied private employees any more than they should be denied racial minorities or women. If indeed, the Supreme Court has found that random drug testing for federal and public employees violates the intent of the Constitution, then indeed, random testing of private employees violates it as well. While private employers find drug testing to be a valuable tool in weeding out bad employees, such intrusive mechanisms should be challenged. Abadinsky (1993) maintains that good job performance monitoring can accomplish the same goals more effectively and with less chance for inappropriate dismissal than the use of drug tests. With the exception of those occupations that are strategic in terms of responsibility for the safety of citizens and national security—occupations such as airline pilots, air traffic control operators, the military, etc.—random drug testing poses a far greater risk to the public well being than the good that it sets out to achieve. We recommend, therefore, that the restrictions currently applied to public workers also be applied to the private sector.

Drug Education

Research has failed to demonstrate that drug education has had a great impact on drug use in the United States, though it certainly does show that some approaches are more effective than others. Generally, the research findings have been disappointing to drug education advocates, but do not necessarily imply that all drug education is futile. Drug education, *as it has been implemented,* has been expensive and ineffective. Furthermore, the stated goals of many education programs have been misguided or overly ambitious. We need more sophisticated empirical research and we need a willingness to reconsider what would make for effective education programs. There are several approaches to drug education, which we have discussed in Chapter 13. Our purpose here is not to repeat that discussion, nor to evaluate the effectiveness of individual approaches to drug education. Rather, we want to comment on the importance of drug education generally, and to discuss possible directions for future educational efforts.

We must recognize that different types of educational approaches are more effective for some individuals but less effective for others. There are age-appropriate pedagogies, but also approaches which have differential appeal and effectiveness depending on gender, race, and social class. Furthermore, regular users of drugs should be targeted with different approaches than nonusers or those who are just experimenting. Such users have already made the decision to use drugs and adopt attendant lifestyles. They need information as to how to avoid or minimize the risks associated with drug use. This need not conflict with or undermine an abstinence message, but simply recognizes that there will be those who choose not to abstain.

We urge that drug-education efforts be developed and coordinated more systematically than they have in the past. Rather than the piecemeal efforts that have been developed by various types of agencies and within professional niches, a streamlined strategy analogous to what takes place in general education should be pursued. Professional drug educators should be leading, developing and implementing the nation's drug education program, with input from psychologists, sociologists, criminal justice specialists, and public health personnel. Moreover, drug education should be fully integrated as part of the curriculum throughout the K–12 experience, rather than something which is artificially inserted just for the sake of "doing something." Finally, we suggest as part of the nation's drug education program, that the nature and effect of drug use be presented in a realistic fashion. Scare tactics which involve greatly exaggerated claims of what drugs might do to the user have no place in any educational curriculum. Drug education, like any other education, must be about providing students with *accurate* information, and engaging them to integrate that information into their cognitive, emotional, moral, and behavioral lifestyles. It seems to us that the use of dramatic and exaggerated claims about the hazards of drug use by groups such as the Partnership for a Drug Free America represents a rather desperate response to circumvent empirical data and go directly to emotional appeal. This is a response which holds potential for great *harm* as young people learn for themselves—either through their own experience or through the testimony of peers—that these claims are exaggerated if not completely manufactured. This discovery results in cynicism toward all representations made by authority figures, including teachers, parents, pastors, counselors, and others. Credibility then gets bestowed upon peers who, in many cases, use and abuse drugs with no moral compass or normative parameters to constrain their behavior. Our nation's drug education program must be, above all, *credible* to the population that we are attempting to reach.

DRUG TREATMENT

Drug treatment is a demand-side strategy to reduce the level of drug use among current users. As we have seen in Chapter 12, there are a variety of treatment types, or *modalities*, with accompanying differences in philosophies about the nature of addiction and treatment. We will not be debating the philosophical premises of treatment approaches here, though we will be making suggestions about improving our treatment efforts.

Supply-side advocates frequently point to the high recidivism and relapse rates of clients in treatment programs as evidence of the failure of drug treatment, and of demand-side policies generally. This is surely a "the glass is half-empty response," which carries with it an unrealistic expectation of what success means in the battle against drug dependency. In truth, if those who relapse after treatment are given second and third opportunities to stay abstinent, the success rate grows. This does take patience as well as a greater commitment to funding drug treatment. The fact is, the amount of public money spent on treatment has been a pittance as compared with that spent on law enforcement and other supply-side approaches to drug reduction. The federal government spends twice as much on supply-side strategies as on demand-side strategies (Sourcebook, 1999). State and local governments, in most cases, are even more one-sided in their funding of law enforcement over treatment efforts. To say that treatment has failed is, in our view, premature. Drug treatment explicitly recognizes drug addiction as a public health problem rather than a criminal justice issue. While the strong arm of the law no doubt plays a role in deterring would-be drug offenders, drug addiction is much more complex than merely the rational choice to use drugs—which is the philosophical premise of our criminal justice system. Addiction is an intricate web of physical, psychological and, indeed, social pathologies which cry for a strong public health response.

Such a response will require commitment from two sets of actors. The first are the potential source of funding of treatment programs. The core of such funding, we contend, must be the federal government itself, followed by state government, local government and private funding sources—in that order. Some of the best treatment available today is funded by private sources—typically by clients themselves, or third-party insurance underwriters. Dependence upon for-profit treatment denies this opportunity to many who most need it. While private treatment still has a place for those who can afford it and prefer the greater privacy, anonymity and other benefits that these facilities may have to offer, public treatment facilities should not be inferior in quality or availability for those who cannot afford the luxury of private treatment.

The second set of actors is the professional drug and alcohol treatment community itself. Treatment approaches vary, of course. As we have seen in Chapter 12, the various modalities are born out of deeply differing philosophies about the nature and causes of addiction, as well as differences in the definition of success. These differences of perspective should not be a cause of cynicism, however. They represent different perspectives on the proverbial elephant—or perhaps we should say proverbial monkey-on-the-back. The cynicism will likely continue, however, as long as treatment professionals continue fighting among themselves about which approach is superior. The time has come to move beyond the parochialism of defending turf, to working together toward a comprehensive drug-treatment strategy in the United States. This effort must involve treatment professionals from all of the leading modalities coming to the table and working toward strong public health policy in this area. There is a certain beauty and self-contained logic in ideological purity. The fact is, however, that while methadone maintenance, for example, has demonstrated itself to be very effective in keeping heroin addicts off heroin, and even helping them to build productive lives, they are still dependent on a powerful drug which limits their potential. Therapeutic communities provide certain tools and strategies, not available in most methadone clinics to help the addict go drug free. On the other hand, laudable as the goals of the therapeutic community and other drug-free programs are, most addicts are not ready for the rigors and challenges imposed by these programs. Drop-out rates are high, even among those who do work up the nerve to walk through their doors. Methadone maintenance provides an opportunity to lead a reasonably productive life for those addicts who are not willing or able—or at least not *yet* willing or able—to confront the issues that have led to their continued addiction. Both types of programs have an important role to play in a coordinated and comprehensive treatment strategy, as do out-patient drug-free programs and chemically based disincentives.

SUMMARY

We have expressed serious reservations with the past and current direction of American drug policy. The "war on drugs" has been counterproductive and overheated rhetorically. Built on questionable assumptions about drugs and drug users, and oriented toward absolutely unreachable goals, it has made the costs to our society of "the drug problem" *worse*. Our hopes for the *future* of drug policy, one that we feel is sane and which is likely to produce demonstrable benefit moving forward, have been expressed in this chapter. The issues discussed herein are not exhaustive. More specific policy concerns such as using racial profiling to make drug arrests, habitual offender statutes which saddle repeat drug offenders with ridiculously long sentences, and the use of highly sophisticated, but privacy-trampling surveillance equipment are also important areas for public drug debate that must be addressed in a realistic fashion in the years ahead. The policy areas that we have addressed here, however, are some of the *pivotal* policy concerns. These are pivotal concerns, both in the sense of their importance and urgency for our time, and also in the sense that how we respond to these concerns will almost certainly be an indicator of how we respond to other drug policy issues in the future.

The perspective from which we must evaluate drug policy in the twenty-first century is, in our view, harm reduction. Policies which would, on balance, reduce the overall level of harm to individuals and society should be pursued; those policies which would not reduce or which may even increase levels of harm should be abandoned. Also to be abandoned is the oft-stated goal to have a "drug-free America by the year _____." Erich

Goode (1999, p. 413) captures this well: "The only realistic approach to the drug problem is to develop methods not to eliminate drug use or even reduce it drastically, but to live with it and make sure that drug users do not seriously harm themselves and others." Harm reduction is a broad concept whose benefits will not always be easy to quantify. It strives to improve individual and public health, reduce the economic cost of our expensive "war," and to reverse civil liberties that have been trampled. Establishing good drug policy for the twenty-first century will require two types of evaluation, neither of which will be an easy task. First, it will be necessary to *assess the costs* of current policies, and the *cost reduction* of proposed policies. This is the task of the social sciences. It is a monumental task that involves the quantification of a reality that is not always easily quantifiable. It also involves the ability to make correct assumptions about how policies may change behavior. This is not at all a simple matter, which is why we have suggested earlier that we need to take advantage of jurisdictions that have made small-scale policy changes and evaluate the impact of those changes. Social scientists have been attempting to make good reasoned assessments of the impacts of current and potential drug policies, and have come to very different conclusions. This work must continue until we arrive at a sufficient consensus to make sound policy recommendations to our policy makers.

The second task that must be accomplished is quite out of the range of social scientists; that is to *rank the areas of harm*. Because of the multifaceted nature of harm reduction, reducing harm in one of area may increase risks and potential harm in other areas. For example, a policy of legalization might reduce economic costs, civil liberties costs, and even perhaps individual and public health costs, but such a policy might well exacerbate domestic conflicts and moral dilemmas in our culture. Similarly, needle-exchange programs will greatly reduce the risks of HIV and hepatitis but would increase economic costs to taxpayers over current prohibition policies by way of the needles themselves, potentially increasing criminal activity at least in certain areas (assuming that drugs themselves are not legalized) because addicts feel comfortable in using greater quantities of drugs and therefore step up the level of their criminal activity in anticipation of increased drug use. Some of these questions, of course, require good measurement, but we must also make evaluative decisions about what kinds of costs to individuals and to society are of greatest priority for harm reduction. This is a question that must be addressed by moral philosophers and others who might construct arguments about the societal good and is, as such, beyond the scope of this text. It is, however, work that must be done as we develop the architecture for drug policy in the coming century.

KEY TERMS

demand-side policies   needle exchange   supply-side policies

REVIEW QUESTIONS

1. In the "Our Guiding Philosophy" section, the authors argue for drug policies and programs to be based on good empirical evidence rather than rhetoric or politics or morality alone. Why? Why do you think that policy has not often been based on quality research to date?

2. How are the goals of drug policies based on an "ethic of harm-reduction" fundamentally different from those of a "War on Drugs"?

3. What are the assumptions made by "supply-side" drug strategies, and how do they differ from those of "demand-side" strategies? How has empirical research challenged some of these assumptions?

4. In your estimation, why have government policies at all levels emphasized supply-side solutions to drug abuse as a social problem? Why do Faupel, Horowitz, and Weaver recommend that greater emphasis be placed on demand-side policies?

5. What significant changes—potentially beneficial and potentially destructive— would a policy of national drug legalization likely bring about? Why do the authors not advocate legalization as a workable option at this time?

6. Assess the relevance to drug policy of the maxim: "Think globally (or nationally), but act locally."

7. What evidence is presented to support the contention that drug policy to date has made drug problems *worse* rather than better?

CRITICAL THOUGHT QUESTION

1. How have your own experiences as a recipient of drug-education efforts shaped your personal position on drug use for you and your peers? If you found it to be a positive experience, what, in particular, worked for you? If you found it ineffective (or worse), what do you wish you had been taught? Consider both the approach used and the specific messages imparted to you.

GLOSSARY

A

addictive personality Term used to describe the notion that addiction is more likely to occur among persons having an inadequate personality. This concept is unsupported by most research.

additive drug Drugs used to enhance performance, typically athletic performance, beyond levels considered to exceed normal limitations of the body.

affective model Modality of drug education, based on the assumption that some individuals possess an underlying predisposition to drug abuse, that seeks to improve communication skills, decision-making, and self assertion—all of which are believed to be related to this predisposition.

amotivational syndrome Alleged personality changes associated with marijuana use, such as laziness and decreased motivation.

anabolics Substances that artificially build muscle and body mass.

antagonist Drug that blocks the effect of another drug or causes uncomfortable side effects if a particular drug is used.

antagonistic effect Process through which one drug cancels the effect of another.

Anti-Drug Abuse Act of 1988 Broad legislation dealing with various aspects of drug and alcohol use which served to increase the penalties associated with various substance-related activities among other provisions.

argot Nonstandard or specialized language associated with a particular group or subculture which serves distinguish that group from the outside world.

availability hypothesis Notion that persons having easy access to drugs are more likely to use them (e.g., physicians and pharmacists).

B

beta blockers Often used as a treatment for hypertension, substances that are designed to lower blood pressure and the heart rate.

binge drinking Defined by Wechsler as the consumption of five or more alcoholic drinks on one occasion for men, and four or more drinks on one occasion for women.

blood-alcohol content (BAC) The concentration of alcohol in the blood, measured in grams of alcohol per 100 milliliters of blood.

blood doping   Introduction of red blood cells into the blood supply for the purpose of increasing endurance by increasing the oxygen-carrying capacity of the circulatory system.

boundary-maintenance mechanism   Various ways in which members of a group (in-group) can distinguish themselves from nonmembers (out-groups).

British Method   Controversial treatment modality whereby registered narcotic addicts are dispensed heroin via a legal prescription.

C

career   A sequence of activities around which an individual organizes some aspect of his or her life, including drug use and/or criminal behavior.

cartel   Term for drug trafficking organizations operating primarily out of Central and South American countries.

causality   Term denoting the relationship between two variables in which one variable causes the other to occur (e.g., the claim that drug use causes crime).

chronic effect   Effects of drug use that accumulate over time as one continues to use or abuse a particular substance.

CNS Stabilizers   Category of drugs that stabilize mood and/or behavior.

compulsory treatment   Nonvoluntary participation in drug treatment, often court-ordered.

Controlled Substances Act   Sweeping legislation passed in 1970 that superceded U.S. drug laws following the Harrison Act and also provided a classification scheme (schedules) of drug categories.

correlation   An association (not necessarily causal) between two variables.

D

decriminalization   Policy that removes criminal sanctions associated with an activity or behavior (as opposed to removing all restrictions, or legalization).

delirium tremens   Severe withdrawal symptoms associated with alcoholism, such as hallucinations, disorientation, or seizures that can, in extreme circumstances, result in death.

demand-side strategies   Refers to a variety of programs and efforts, including treatment and education, that serve to reduce the demand for drugs.

demographics   Characteristics used to distinguish individuals from one another, such as age, gender, race or ethnicity, socioeconomic status, etc. Of particular importance is how behavior such as drug use differs across one or more of these categories.

depressants   Substances that slow the actions of the central nervous system and the physiological processes dependent on it, such as respiration, heart rate, and reaction time.

detoxification   Refers to the processes through which the body rids itself of poisonous (toxic) substances; applied to drugs and alcohol, the process of ridding the body of the physical presence of drugs.

differential reinforcement   According to Akers' social learning theory, the balance of actual or anticipated rewards and/or punishments associated with past, present, and future behavior.

disinhibition hypothesis   Notion that alcohol or drug use interferes with a person's internal control mechanisms of the central nervous system, or that use affects the recognition of external controls (i.e., possibility of arrest), resulting in antisocial behavior.

diuretics   Substances that have the effect of flushing liquids out of the body.

diversion   Refers to the underground sale (by the user) of drugs obtained by a legal prescription.

doping   The use of drugs to improve athletic performance.

dose   The amount of a substance taken on one occasion.

double failure   According to differential opportunity theory, a person who is unable to achieve "success" through legitimate or illegitimate means.

drug   A substance that, once ingested, may alter the structure or functioning of a person; sociologically, a drug is something that has been defined by society, or certain segments of society, as a drug.

drug abuse   The use of a substance or substances in such a way that it leads to unintended (and usually negative) personal, interpersonal, or social consequences.

drug addiction   Condition characterized by the physical need for a drug, commonly accompanied by physical symptoms when the drug is withdrawn.

drug dependence   Condition characterized by the physical, psychological, or behavioral need for a drug.

drug education   Broad term referring to measures to prevent and/or reduce drug use by providing information on, among other things, the impact and negative consequences of use.

Drug-Free Workplace Act of 1988   Federal law requiring that federal contractors and grantees implement policies providing for a drug-free workplace.

drug interaction   Effect of one drug on another when both are consumed.

drug schedules   Classification criteria outlined in the Controlled Substances Act of 1970, which categorizes drugs based on the characteristics of medical use and potential for abuse.

drug screening   Qualitative analysis of a blood or urine sample to identify the presence of a drug.

drug subculture   Groups which are a part of the cultural mainstream and often share many of the values and goals of the cultural mainstream, but nevertheless maintain a distinctive lifestyle which is integrated around the use of illegal drugs.

drug testing   Analysis of body tissue or bodily fluids to determine the concentration of a particular substance.

drug use   Use of any chemical substance that act acts like a drug or that is believed to act like a drug.

E

economic-compulsive violence   That violence occurring when an individual engages in violence in an attempt to secure drugs or money to purchase them.

effective dose   Dose most often appropriate for the effect one wishes to achieve.

employee assistance program (EAP)   Confidential, employer-financed programs and services designed to address a number of issues related to productivity in the workplace, including alcohol and drug use.

endorphin   An opiate produced in the body that functions as a neurotransmitter.

environmental tobacco smoke   Refers to when nonsmokers inhale air having traces or large amounts of tobacco smoke; also called *passive smoke*.

epidemiology   From medicine, the study of the spread and distribution of diseases; used in social sciences to refer to study of spread and distribution of social phenomenon such as drug use and crime.

ethnography   Research methodology that utilizes researchers spending time in the natural habitat of the subjects they are studying.

etiology   Refers to the study of the causal factors associated with a phenomenon.

F

fetal alcohol syndrome   Refers to a number of birth defects that are attributed to the children of women who consumed alcohol while pregnant.

formication   A delusion or hallucination associated with stimulant use, characterized by the belief that insects, reptiles, or spiders are crawling on or under the skin.

functional alternative   The substitution of one drug for a similar drug in terms of action and/or effect.

G

gateway drug   Drug that is believed to lead to the use of other, more dangerous or addictive substances.

H

halfway house   Transitional living facilities that serve as a "bridge" between residential drug treatment programs and reintegration into the community.

hallucinogens   Substances that produce extreme subjective effects in users, such as physical distortion of reality, often resembling hallucinations.

harm reduction   Drug policy approach that focuses on reducing the harm or negative consequences associated with drug use.

Harrison Narcotics Act of 1914   Legislation that in effect criminalized the nonmedical use of narcotics and cocaine.

I

idiosyncratic effect   Sensitivity to the effect of one drug is greatly enhanced by the presence of another.

incidence   From a social science perspective, refers to the frequency of engaging in an activity or behavior (i.e., How many times have you . . . ?).

informational model   Drug education philosophy that provides information which emphasizes various negative consequences of alcohol or drug use.

interdiction   Law-enforcement measures designed to prevent illegal drugs from entering their intended destination, typically at the borders of a country.

intoxication   Behavioral and mental dysfunction caused by the effect of alcohol or drug use on the central nervous system.

L

legalization   Refers to the removal of all criminal and civil penalties associated with an activity or behavior.

lethal dose   Amount of a drug that results in death.

M

Marihuana Tax Act of 1937   Federal legislation that placed severe restrictions on the cultivation, sale, and distribution (and ultimately the possession) of marijuana.

methadone maintenance   Treatment program for narcotic abuse whereby methadone, a synthetic narcotic, is substituted for heroin.

Minnesota Model   Treatment modality originating in Minnesota based on the assumptions that addiction is a disease that can be maintained through counseling and therapy.

moniker   Slang term or nickname used to refer to someone who is a member of a subculture.

moral entrepreneur   Individuals or groups who argue that they are the ones who should define the reality of drugs and their users.

mules   Individuals who smuggle illegal drugs by concealing them on or in the body itself.

N

N(n)   Statistical symbol used to denote the size of a population (N) or sample (n) under study.

narcotic   Natural derivative of the opium poppy or a synthetic substance that is, chemically speaking, similar to it. These highly addictive substances produce euphoric and/or analgesic effects.

National Prohibition (Volstead) Act   Legislation paving the way for passage of the Eighteenth Amendment to the U.S. Constitution, which prohibited the manufacture, sale, and distribution of alcohol. The twenty-first Amendment (ratified in 1933) repealed prohibition.

needle exchange   Harm reduction programs in which persons who inject cocaine or heroin are allowed to exchange used hypodermic needles for unused ones in an attempt to reduce the spread of HIV and other communicable diseases.

neurotransmitter   Chemical mechanism through which impulses are transmitted from one nerve cell to another.

O

objective drug effect   Drug effects which are the result of being under the influence of a substance and which can be measured reliably.

official statistics   Data on drug use which are gathered as a function of the day-to-day organizational procedures conducted by the government or other agencies cooperating with the government.

operant conditioning   The reinforcement of behavior resulting from actual or perceived rewards associated with engaging in that behavior.

Operation Intercept   1969 initiative of the Nixon administration that sought to curb trafficking of marijuana into the United States from Mexico. Considered by most to be a failure, this operation had the effect of increasing domestic production of marijuana.

P

patent medicine   Medications, tonics, or elixirs containing alcohol, cocaine, morphine, or cannabis that were readily available in the nineteenth century at medicine shows or over the counter.

pharmacology   Study of how drugs affect the structure and function of the body.

potency   Strength of a particular drug.

prevalence   From a social science perspective, refers to the number of individuals who have engaged in a particular activity or behavior, such as crime or drug use (i.e., Have you ever . . . ?).

primary deviance   According to Lemert, those norm violations that are often inadvertent, not the result of a deviant self concept.

primary prevention   Policies and preventive efforts designed to discourage the onset of drug use.

problem behavior syndrome   Used to describe the notion that among persistent juvenile delinquents, various forms of nonconformity (i.e., delinquency, drug use, being sexually active) are expressions of an underlying characteristic.

prohibition   Term reflecting the ideal of abstinence as it relates to alcohol or drug use; also refers to general policy initiatives also known as "criminalization", whereby the production, manufacture, growing, sale, and/or possession of drugs are violations of one or more criminal statutes.

Prohibition (Volstead Act)   Term synonymous with the period between 1920 and 1933, during which time the manufacture, sale, and distribution of alcohol was prohibited in the U.S.

psychedelic   Term originating in the 1960s to more positively characterize the use and effects of hallucinogenic drugs.

psychoactive drug   Substances that affect the thoughts, perceptions, mood, and behavior via their impact on the central nervous system.

psychopharmacological violence   Situation in which an individual engages in violent behavior as a consequence of being under the influence of a drug.

Pure Food and Drug Act of 1906   Broad legislation that placed a number of restrictions on the production and distribution of both food and drugs. Of key importance is the requirement that ingredients be listed.

purity   Percentage of a substance consisting of the drug itself.

R

rapid opiate detoxification   Controversial treatment program utilizing the use of various drugs to accelerate detoxification and withdrawal from narcotic addiction.

rate   Refers to the number or frequency per unit of population; e.g., Uniform Crime Reports on a per 100,000 population, so the rate is calculated as ((number/population)*100,000).

restorative drug   Refers to drugs that are used to accelerate the recuperation of the body from injuries or to reduce pain accompanying them.

retreatist   According to Merton's anomie theory, an individual who rejects both the goals of society and the accepted means of achieving them; drug addicts generally fall into this category.

roid rage   Term used to describe increased aggressiveness and hostility which is associated with use of anabolic steroids.

route of administration   Method through which drugs are introduced into the body.

S

secondary binge effect   Consequences of binge drinking that affect persons other than the user (e.g., unwanted sexual advances by someone who has been binge drinking or being involved in an automobile accident caused by someone who has been binge drinking).

secondary deviance   Violations of norms which are in response to the consequences of primary deviance. Secondary deviance reflects ones' self-identification as deviant.

secondary prevention   Policies and measures intended to reduce the severity of consequences associated with drug use after it has been initiated.

serotonin   Neurotransmitter involved in regulating a number of basic yet important bodily functions, including mood.

set   Psychological state of the individual at the time of drug use, including one's expectations or emotional mood.

setting   The environment in which drug use occurs.

social construction   Process through which reality is influenced as a consequence of individuals interacting with one another and with social groups or organizations; in the case of drugs and drug use, the process that leads the public at any given point in time to label a substance as a drug, or drug use as a problem behavior.

social influence model   Educational philosophy that seeks to build resistance peer pressure to use drugs through various means; also called *drug resistance education*.

source reduction   Refers to a number of strategies designed to reduce the amount of illegal drugs produced, including crop eradication, confiscation, seizure of equipment, etc.

spurious relationship   When the believed relationship between two variables can be explained by the presence of a third variable.

stigma   A deviant identity associated with some type of discrediting behavior.

stimulant   Category of drugs that stimulate or increase the action of the central nervous system.

stress hypothesis   Refers to the notion that alcohol and drugs are utilized as a means of dealing with excessive stress, particularly that which is related to employment.

subjective drug effect   Drug effects which cannot be measured on a consistent scale, and are grounded in the experiential reality of the user.

supply-side strategies   Refers to a variety of efforts designed to curtail, control, or regulate the available supply of drugs.

synapse   The microscopic space between two neurons, across which electrical impulses are transmitted by neurotransmitters.

synergism (synergistic effect)   The joint action of two or more drugs that produces an effect that is greater than the sum of the independent effect of the interacting drugs.

synesthesia   Effect of hallucinogen use characterized as a "blending" of the senses (e.g., hearing or smelling colors, etc.).

systemic violence   Violence that is related to the nature of the illicit drug trade and culture.

T

taxonomy   Classification or categorization based on some attribute or characteristic of the object under consideration.

tecatos   Slang term used to refer to an addict associated with the Hispanic heroin subculture.

temperance   Philosophical position that alcohol should be used in moderation.

tertiary prevention   Aimed at individuals who are already addicted, policies and interventions designed to minimize the medical and social consequences of addiction for addicts themselves, and for others around the addict (i.e., family, co-workers, etc.).

therapeutic community (TC)   Comprehensive, residential-based treatment program that emphasizes confrontation followed by resocialization.

therapeutic dose   Amount of a drug necessary to achieve an intended medical effect.

tolerance   Resistance to the effect of a drug that develops over time, which results in greater amounts being necessary to achieve a particular result.

treatment modalities   Term used to describe broad or general approaches to treatment of alcohol or drug abuse/addiction.

U

unofficial statistics   Data that are gathered by researchers for the purpose of identifying drug users, learning relevant information about them, and for making estimates of incidence and prevalence of use.

W

Wernicke-Korsakoff Syndrome   Brain damage attributed to excessive alcohol consumption, believed to be related to the way in which alcohol interferes with the absorption of vitamins, particularly thiamine.

References

Chapter 1

Becker, Howard S. 1963. *Outsiders: Studies in the Sociology of Deviance*. New York: The Free Press.

Berger, Peter L. 1963. *Invitation to Sociology: A Humanistic Perspective*. Garden City, NY: Anchor Books.

Brecher, Edward M., et. Al. 1972. *Licit and Illicit Drugs*. Boston: Little, Brown.

Duster, Troy. 1970. *The Legislation of Morality: Law, Drugs, and Moral Judgment*. New York: Free Press.

Fromme, Kim and Julie Wendel. 1995. "Beliefs About the Effects of Alcohol on Involvement in Coercive and Consenting Sexual Activity," *Journal of Applied Social Psychology 25(23)*, pp. 2099–2117.

Fuqua, Paul. 1978. *Drug Abuse: Investigation and Control*. New York: McGraw-Hill.

Gladwell, Malcolm. 2001. "Java Man: How Caffeine Created the Modern World," *The New Yorker* (July 30), pp. 76–80.

Goode, Erich. 1975. "Marijuana and the Politics of Reality," pp. 170–181 in Frank R. Scarpitti and Paul T. McFarlane, *Deviance: Action, Reaction, Interaction*. Boston: Addison-Wesley.

_____. 1990. "The American Drug Panic of the 1980's: Social Construction or Objective Threat?" *The International Journal of the Addictions*. 25(9), pp. 1083–1098.

_____. 1999. *Drugs in American Society* (5th edition). New York: McGraw-Hill College.

Grinspoon, Lester and James B. Bakalar. 1976. *Cocaine: A Drug and Its Social Evolution*. New York: Basic Books.

Gusfield, Joseph R. 1963. *Symbolic Crusade: Status Politics and the American Temperance Movement*. Urbana: University of Illinois Press.

Inciardi, James A. *1992. The War on Drugs II*. Mountain View, CA: Mayfield.

Inciardi, James A. and Karen McElrath. 1998. *The American Drug Scene* (Second Edition). Los Angeles: Roxbury.

_____. 2001. *The American Drug Scene* (Third ed.). Los Angeles: Roxbury.

Inciardi, James A. and Robert A. Rothman. 1990. *Sociology: Principles and Applications*. New York: Harcourt, Brace, Jovanovich.

Jenkins, Philip. 2001. "The 'Ice Age': Social Construction of a Drug Panic," Inciardi and McElrath, *The American Drug Scene* (Third Edition). Los Angeles: Roxbury.

Klam, Matthew. 2001. "Experiencing Ecstasy," *New York Times Magazine* (January 21), pp. 38–43, 64, 68, 72, 78, 79.

Leshner, Alan I. 1999. "Science-Based Views of Drug Addiction and Its Treatment," *The Journal of the American Medical Association* (October 13), pp. 1320–21.

Lindesmith, Alfred R. 1938. "A Sociological Theory of Drug Addiction," *The American Journal of Sociology* (Volume 43), pp. 593–613.

McAuliffe, William E. and Robert A. Gordon. 1974. "A Test of Lindesmith's Theory of Addiction: The Frequency of Euphoria Among Long-Term Addicts," *The American Journal of Sociology* (Volume 79), pp. 795–840.

McGraw, Seamus. 2001. "The Most Dangerous Drug to Hit Small-town America Since Crack Cocaine?" *Spin Magazine* (June), pp. 107–114.

Mills, James. 1987. *The Underground Empire: Where Crime and Governments Embrace*. New York: Dell.

Musto, David F. 1987. *The American Disease: Origins of Narcotics Control* (expanded edition). New Haven, CT: Yale University Press.

_____. 2001. "They Inhaled." *New York Times Book Review* (August 12), pp. 16.

Nadelmann, Ethan A. 1989. "Drug Prohibition in the United States: Costs, Consequences, and Alternatives" in *Science* (September 1), pp. 939–947.

National Center for Health Statistics. 2001. "Fastats on Alcohol Use." Accessed October 3, 2001. *http://www.cdc.gov/nchs/fastats/alcohol.htm.*

Office of National Drug Control Strategy. 2002. *National Drug Control Strategy: 2002 Annual Report.* Washington, D.C.: U.S. Government Printing Office.

Parker, Robert Nash. 1995. *Alcohol and Homicide: A Deadly Combination of Two American Traditions.* Albany, NY: State University of New York Press.

Reinarman, Craig. 2000. "The Social Construction of Drug Scares," in Patricia A. Adler and Peter Adler (eds.), *Constructions of Deviance: Social Power, Context, and Interaction* (3rd ed.). Belmont, CA: Wadsworth/Thomson, pp. 147–158.

Substance Abuse and Mental Health Services Administration (SAMHSA). 2000. *Preliminary Results from the 1999 National Household Survey on Drug Abuse.* Rockville, MD: SAMHSA.

Tough, Paul. 2001. "The Alchemy of OxyContin," *New York Times Magazine* (July 29), pp. 32–37, 52, 62, 63.

Waldman, Hilary. 2001. "Patients Fear Limits on Painkiller," *The News Journal* (Wilmington, Delaware; August 20), pp. E3

Weil, Andrew T. 1972. *The Natural Mind: A New Way of Looking at Drugs and the Higher Consciousness.* Boston: Houghton-Mifflin.

Weiner, Tim. 2001. "In Tijuana, a New Kind of Drug Peril," *New York Times* (August 14), pp. A9.

Chapter 2

Anslinger, Harry J. and Courtney Ryley Cooper. 1937. "Marihuana: Assassin of Youth." *American Magazine.* 124, pp. 19, 150–153.

Becker, Howard S. 1963. *Outsiders: Studies in the Sociology of Deviance.* New York: The Free Press.

Berger, Peter. 1963. *Invitation to Sociology: A Humanistic Perspective.* Garden City, NY: Anchor Books.

Black, J.R. 1889. "Advantages of substituting the morphia habit for the incurably alcoholic." *Cincinnati Lancet-Clinic.*

Bonnie, Richard J. and Charles H. Whitebread. 1970. "The Forbidden Fruit and the Tree of Knowledge: An Inquiry into the Legal History of American Marijuana Prohibition." *Virginia Law Review* 56 Available online: *http://www.drugtext.org/reports/vlr/vlrtoc.htm* (Accessed July 15, 2002).

Booth, Martin. 1998. *Opium: A History.* New York: St. Martin's Press.

Brecher, Edward M. 1972. *Licit and Illicit Drugs.* Boston: Little, Brown and Company.

Bureau of Justice Statistics. 1992. *Drugs, Crime, and the Criminal Justice System: A National Report from the Bureau of Justice Statistics.* Washington, D.C.: USGPO.

Bureau of Narcotics. 1932. *Traffic in Opium and Other Dangerous Drugs for the Year Ended December 31, 1931.* Washington, DC: U.S. Treasury Department.

_____. 1936. *Traffic in Opium and Other Dangerous Drugs for the Year Ended December 31, 1935.* Washington, DC: U.S. Treasury Department.

_____. 1937. *Traffic in Opium and Other Dangerous Drugs for the Year Ended December 31, 1936.* Washington, DC: U.S. Treasury Department.

Capehart, Tom. 1998. "Outlook for U.S. Tobacco." Economic Research Service. Washington, D.C.: U.S. Department of Agriculture.

Cowan, Richard. 1986. "How the Narcs Created Crack." *National Review* (December 5), pp. 30–31.

Crothers, T.D. 1902. *Morphinism and Narcomanias from Other Drugs.* Philadelphia: W.B. Saunders & Co.

Darrow, Clarence and Victor Yarros. 1927. *The Prohibition Mania: A Reply to Professor Irving Fisher and Others.* New York: Boni and Liveright.

Drug Enforcement Administration. 1996. *Drugs of Abuse.* Washington, D.C.: USGPO.

_____. 1999. *DEA Briefing Book.* Washington, D.C.: USGPO.

Epstein, Edward Jay. 1977. *Agency of Fear: Opiates and Political Power in America.* New York: G.P. Putnam's Sons.

Goode, Erich. 1993. *Drugs in American Society* (4th ed.). New York: McGraw-Hill.

Ihde, Aaron J. 1982. "Food Controls Under the 1906 Act." pp. 40–50 in James Harvey Young (ed.), *The Early Years of Federal Food and Drug Control*. Madison, WI: American Institute of the History of Pharmacy.

Jones, Ernest. 1953. *The Life and Work of Sigmund Freud: Volume 1—The Formative Years and the Great Discoveries, 1856–1900*. New York: Basic Books.

Kleber, Herbert D. 1994. "Our Current Approach to Drug Abuse: Progress, Problems, Proposals." *New England Journal of Medicine* 330(5), pp. 361–365.

Leavitt, Fred. 1995. *Drugs and Behavior*. (3rd ed.). Thousand Oaks, CA: Sage.

Lender, Mark Edward and James Kirby Martin. 1987. *Drinking in America: A History* (Revised and Expanded Edition). New York: The Free Press.

Lindesmith, Alfred. 1965. *The Addict and the Law*. Bloomington, IN: Indiana University Press.

McDowell, David M., and Henry I. Spitz. 1999. *Substance Abuse: From Principles to Practice*. Philadelphia: Taylor and Francis.

Merlin, Mark David. 1984. *On the Trail of the Opium Poppy*. Rutherford, NJ: Fairleigh Dickinson University Press.

Musto, David. 1973. *The American Disease: Origins of Narcotics Control*. New Yaven: Yale University Press.

———. 1999. *The American Disease: Origins of Narcotics Control* (3rd ed.). New Yaven: Yale University Press.

Pillard, Richard Colestock. 1970. "Marijuana." *New England Journal of Medicine* 283, 6 (August 6), pp. 294–303.

Ray, Oakley. 1978. *Drugs, Society and Human Behavior* (2nd ed.). St. Louis: Mosby.

Santayana, George. 1905. *Life of Reason, Reason in Common Sense*. Scribner's.

Scott, James Maurice. 1969. *The White Poppy*. New York: Funk and Wagnalls.

Shaw, Elton. 1909. *The Curse of Drink; or Stories of Hell's Commerce*. (Privately published by Elton Shaw).

Shulgin, Alexander T. 1992. *Controlled Substances: A Chemical and Legal Guide to Federal Drug Laws*. Berkeley, CA: Ronin Publishing.

Terry, Charles E. and Mildred Pellens. 1928. *The Opium Problem*. New York: Committee on Drug Addictions, Bureau of Social Hygiene, Inc.

Thornton, Mark. 1991. *Alcohol Prohibition Was a Failure*. Policy Analysis No. 157 (July 17). Washington, DC: The Cato Institute.

United States Congress. 1914. Public Law No. 223, 63rd Congress, December 17.

United States Supreme Court. 1916. *U. S. v. Jin Fuey Moy*, 241 U.S. 394.

———. 1919. *Webb et al. v. U.S.*, 249 U.S. 96.

———. 1920. *Jin Fuey Moy v. U.S.*, 254 U.S. 189.

———. 1922. *U.S. v. Behrman*, 258 U.S. 280.

———. 1925. *Linder v. U.S.*, 268 U.S. 5.

———. 1962. *Robinson v. California*, 370 U.S. 660.

Warburton, Clark. 1932. *The Economic Result of Prohibition*. New York: Columbia University Press.

Winger, Gail, Frederick G. Hofmann, and James H. Woods. 1992. *A Handbook on Drug and Alcohol Abuse: the Biomedical Aspects*. (3rd ed.). New York: Oxford University Press.

Young, James Harvey. 1961. *The Toadstool Millionaires: A Social History of Patent Medicines in America Before Federal Regulation*. Princeton, NJ: Princeton University Press.

Chapter 3

Albertson, Timothy E., Robert W. Derlet and Brent E. Van Hoozen. 1999. "Methamphetamine and the Expanding Complications of Amphetamines." *The Western Journal of Medicine* 170, pp. 214–219.

American Cancer Society. n.d. "American Cancer Society Hosts 23rd Great American Smoke out." web: *http://www2.cancer.org/gas/* Accessed December 10, 1999.

Andrews, George and Simon Vinkenoog (eds.). 1967. *The Book of Grass: An Anthology of Indian Hemp*. New York: Grove Press.

Anslinger, Harry J. and William F. Tompkins. 1953. *The Traffic in Narcotics*. New York: Funk and Wagnalls.

Baldessarini, Ross J., Leonardo Tondo, John Hennen and Adele C. Viguera. 2002. "Is Lithium Still Worth Using? An Update of Selected Resent Research. *Harvard Review of Psychiatry* 10, pp. 59–75.

Baldessarini, Ross J. and Leonardo Tondo. 2001. "Long-Term Lithium for Bipolar Disorder." *The American Journal of Psychiatry* 158, p. 1740.

_____. 2000. "Does Lithium Treatment Still Work? Evidence of Stable Responses Over Three Decades." *Archives of General Psychiatry* 57, pp. 187–190.

Baldessarini, Ross J., Leonardo Tondo and John Hennen. 1999. "Effects of Lithium Treatment and Its Discontinuation on Suicidal Behavior in Bipolar Manic-Depressive Disorders." *Journal of Clinical Psychiatry* 60, pp. 77–84.

Barbey, J.J. and S.P. Roose. 1998. "SSRI Safety in Overdose." *Journal of Clinical Psychiatry* 59 (Supplement), pp. 42–48.

Becker, Howard S. 1967. "History, Culture and Subjective Experiences: An Exploration of the Social Bases of Drug-Induced Experiences." *Journal of Health and Social Behavior* 8; pp. 163–176.

Biederman, J., T. Wilens, E. Mick, T. Spencer and S.V. Faraone. 1999. "Pharmacotherapy of Attention-Deficit/Hyperactivity Disorder Reduces Risk for Substance Use Disorder." *Pediatrics* 104, p. e20.

Birmingham, Karen. 2001. "Dark Clouds over Toronto Psychiatry Research." *Nature Medicine* 7, p. 643. Available online: *http://www.pssg.org/jick.htm* (Accessed June 27, 2002).

Black, J.R. 1889. "Advantages of Substituting the Morphia Habit for the Incurably Alcoholic." *Cincinnati Lancet-Clinic.*

Booth, Martin. 1998. *Opium: A History.* New York: St. Martin's Press.

Bourguignon, Robert. n.d. "Problems with Prozac." Available online: *http://www.camtech.net.au/malam/reports/prozac.htm.* (Accessed June 26, 2002).

Boyce, P. and F. Judd. 1999. "The Place for the Tricyclic Antidepressants in the Treatment of Depression." *Australian and New Zealand Journal of Psychiatry* 33, pp. 323–327.

Boyce, S.S. 1900. *Hemp, A Practical Treatise on the Culture of Hemp for Seed and Fiber with a Sketch of the History and Nature of the Hemp Plant.* New York: Orange Judd.

Brady, Kathleen T., Hugh Myrick and Robert Malcolm. 1999. "Sedative-Hypnotic and Anxiolytic Agents." Pp. 95–104 in Barbara S. McCrady and Esizabeth E. Epstein (eds.), *Addictions: A Comprehensive Guidebook.* New York: Oxford University Press.

Brecher, Edward M. 1972. *Licit and Illicit Drugs.* Boston: Little, Brown and Company.

Bromfield, Richard. 1996. "Is Ritalin Overprescribed?—Yes." American Council on Science and Health, *Priorities in Health* 8. Available online: *http://www.acsh.org/publications/priorities/0803/pcyes.html* (Accessed June 27, 2002).

Bureau of Justice Statistics. 1992. *Drugs, Crime, and the Criminal Justice System: A National Report from the Bureau of Justice Statistics.* Washington, D.C.: USGPO.

Canadian Association of University Teachers. 2001. "Academic Freedom in Jeopardy at Toronto." *CAUT-ACPPU Bulletin* 48. Available online: *http://www.caut.ca/english/bulletin/2001_may/default.asp* (Accessed June 27, 2002).

Capehart, Tom. 1998. "Outlook for U.S. Tobacco." Economic Research Service. Washington, D.C.: U.S. Department of Agriculture.

Carroll, Charles R. 1989. *Drugs in Modern Society* (2nd ed.). Dubuque, IA: William C. Brown.

Centers for Disease Control. 1994. "Preventing Tobacco Use Among Young People: Report of the Surgeon General." Atlanta, GA: Centers for Disease Control.

_____. 2000a. "Tobacco Use Among Middle and High School Students—United States, 1999." *The Journal of the American Medical Association* 283, pp. 1134–1142.

_____. 2000b. "Targeting Tobacco Use: The Nation's Leading Cause of Death." Atlanta, GA: Centers for Disease Control. Available online: *www.cdc.gov/tobacco/oshaag.pdf* (Accessed October 9, 2000).

Cohen, Maimon M., Michelle J. Marinello and Nathan Back. 1967. "Chromosomal Damage in Human Leukocytes Induced by Lysergic Acid Diethylamide." *Science.* 155; pp. 1417–1419.

Crothers, T.D. 1902. *Morphinism and Narcomanias from Other Drugs.* Philadelphia: W.B. Saunders & Co.

Centers for Disease Control. n.d. "History of the 1964 Surgeon General's Report on Smoking and Health. web: *http://www.cdc.gov/tobacco/30yrsgen htm*

Chein, Isidor, Donald L. Gerard, Robert S. Lee and Eva Rosenfeld. 1964. *The Road to H: Narcotics, Juvenile Delinquency and Social Policy.* New York: Basic Books.

Cherek, Don R., Ralph Spiga and J.L. Steinberg. "Effects of Secobarbital on Human Aggressive and Non-aggressive Responding." *Drug and Alcohol Dependence.* 24, pp. 21–29.

Chitwood, Dale D., James E. Rivers, and James A. Inciardi. 1996. *The American Pipe Dream: Crack Cocaine and the Inner City.* Fort Worth: Harcourt Brace.

Consumer Reports. 1993. "High Anxiety." *Consumer Reports.* Yonkers, NY: Consumer's Union of U.S., Inc.

de Ropp, Robert S. 1957. *Drugs and the Mind.* New York: St. Martin's Press, (MacMillan).

Drug Abuse Warning Network. 2000. *Annual Medical Examiner Data, 1998.* Rockville, MD: Substance Abuse and Mental Health Services Administration.

Drug Enforcement Administration. 1997. *Drugs of Abuse*. Washington, D.C.: USGPO.

———. 1999. *DEA Briefing Book*. Washington, D.C.: USGPO.

———. nd. *Drugs of Concern*. Available online: *http://www.usdoj.gov/dea/concern/ rohypnol.htm* (Accessed: March 19, 2002).

Epstein, Edward Jay. 1977. *Agency of Fear: Opiates and Political Power in America*. New York: G.P. Putnam's Sons.

Fagan, Jeffrey. 1990. "Intoxication and Aggression." Pp. 241–320 in Michael Tonry and James Q. Wilson (eds.), *Drugs and Crime*. Chicago: University of Chicago Press.

Frontline. 1998. "Inside the Tobacco Deal." PBSOnline: *http://www.pbs.org/wgbh/pages/frontline/shows/ settlement/etc/synopsis.html*

Gable, R.S. 1993. "Toward a Comprehensive Overview of Dependence Potential and Acute Toxicity of Psychoactive Substances used Nonmedically." *American Journal of Drug and Alcohol Abuse* 19, pp. 263–281.

Goldstein, Paul, Douglas S. Lipton, Edward Preble, Ira Sobel, Tom Miller, William Abbot, William Paige, and Franklin Soto. 1984. "The Marketing of Street Heroin in New York City." *Journal of Drug Issues* 3, Summer, pp. 553–556.

Goode, Erich 1999. *Drugs in American Society* (5ᵗʰ ed.). New York: McGraw-Hill.

Grinspoon, Lester and James B. Bakalar. 1979. *Psychedelic Drugs Reconsidered*. New York: Basic Books.

———. 1994. "The War on Drugs: A Peace Proposal." *New England Journal of Medicine* 330, 5, pp. 357–360.

———. 1997. *Marijuana: The Forbidden Medicine*. New Haven, CT: Yale University Press.

Grinspoon, Lester and Peter Hedblom. 1975. *The Speed Culture: Amphetamine Use and Abuse in America*. Cambridge, MA: Harvard University Press.

Healey, David. 2000. "Emergence of Antidepressant Induced Suicidality." *Primary Care Psychiatry* 6, pp. 23–28.

Inciardi, James A. 1992. *The War on Drugs II*. Mountain View, CA: Mayfield Publishing Co.

———. 1979. "Heroin Use and Street Crime." *Crime and Delinquency* 25, 335–346.

———. 1977a. "The Changing Life of Mickey Finn: Some Notes on Chloral Hydrate Down Through the Ages. *Journal of Popular Culture*, 11, 3, pp. 591–596.

———. 1977b. *Methadone Diversion: Experiences and Issues*. NIDA Research Monograph. Rockville, MD: National Institute on Drug Abuse.

Inciardi, James A., Dorothy Lockwood and Anne E. Pottieger. 1993. *Women and Crack-Cocaine*. New York: MacMillan Publishing Co.

Ioannou, C. 1992. "Media Coverage Versus Fluoxetine as the Cause of Suicidal Ideation." *American Journal of Psychiatry* 149, p. 572.

Jacobs, Barry. 1987. "How hallucinogenic drugs work." *American Scientist* 75, 4.

Jick, Susan S., Alan D. Dean and Hershel Jick. 1995. "Antidepressants and Suicide." *British Medical Journal* 310, pp. 215–218.

Johnston, Lloyd D. 1973. *Drugs and American Youth*. Ann Arbor, MI: Institute for Survey Research.

Johnston, Lloyd D., Patrick M. O'Malley, and Jerald G. Bachman. 2002. *Monitoring the Future National Results on Adolescent Drug Use: Overview of Key Findings*. Bethesda MD: National Institute on Drug Abuse.

Johnston, Lloyd D., Patrick M. O'Malley, and Jerald G. Bachman. 1999 (Dec.). "Drug trends in 1999 are mixed." University of Michigan News and Information Services: Ann Arbor, MI. Available online: *www.monitoringthefuture.org;* (Accessed December 20, 1999).

———.1998. *National Survey Results on Drug Use from the Monitoring the Future Study, 1975–1997. Volume I: Secondary School Students*. (NIH Publication No. 98-4345). Rockville, MD: National Institute on Drug Abuse.

Joy, Janet E., Stanley J. Watson Jr. and John A. Benson Jr. 1999. *Marijuana and Medicine: Assessing the Science Base*. Washington, DC: National Academy Press.

Kandel, Denise B. 1975. "Stages in Adolescent Involvement in Drug Use." *Science* 190 (November 28), pp. 912–914.

Kandel, Denise B. and K. Yamaguchi. 1993. "From Beer to Crack: Developmental Patterns of Drug Involvement." *American Journal of Public Health* 83, pp. 851–855.

Kandel, Denise B., K. Yamaguchi and K. Chen. 1992. "Stages of Progression in Drug Involvement from Adolescence to Adulthood: Further Evidence for the Gateway Theory." *Journal of Studies on Alcohol* 53, pp. 447–457.

Kleber, Herbert D. 1994. "Our Current Approach to Drug Abuse: Progress, Problems, Proposals." *New England Journal of Medicine* 330(5), pp. 361–365.

Kranzler, Henry R. and Raymond F. Anton. 1994. "Implications of Recent Neuropsychopharmacologic Research Understanding the Etiology and Development of Alcoholism." *Journal of Consulting and Clinical Psychology* 62, pp. 1116–1126.

Leavitt, Fred. 1995. *Drugs and Behavior*. (3rd ed.). Thousand Oaks, CA: Sage.

Light, Arthur B. and Edward G. Torrance. n.d. (1929 or 1930). *Opium Addiction*. Chicago: American Medical Association.

Lingeman, Richard R. 1974. *Drugs from A to Z: A Dictionary*. New York: McGraw-Hill.

Lipton, Douglas S. and Michael J. Maranda. 1983. "Detoxification from Heroin Dependency: An Overview of Method and Effectiveness." *Advances in Alcohol and Substance Abuse* 2, pp. 31–55.

Liska, Ken. 2000. *Drugs and the Human Body* (6th ed.). New York: MacMillan Publishing Co.

Matchan, Don C. 1977. *We Mind if You Smoke*. New York: Pyramid Books.

Mathias, Robert. 1999. "'Ecstasy' Damages the Brain and Impairs Memory in Humans." NIDA Notes, 14, 4. Rockville, MD: National Institute on Drug Abuse.

McDowell, David M., and Henry I. Spitz. 1999. *Substance Abuse: From Principles to Practice*. Philadelphia: Taylor and Francis.

McGlothlin, William H. and David O. Arnold. 1971. "LSD Revisited-a Ten-Year Follow-up of Medical LSD Use." *Archives of General Psychiatry* 24, pp. 35–49.

Mechanic, David and David A. Rochefort. 1990. "Deinstitutionalization: An Appraisal of Reform." *Annual Review of Sociology* 16, pp. 301–327.

Meyer, H. 1954. *Old English Coffee Houses*. Emmaus, PA: The Rodale Press.

Moak, Darlene H. and Raymond F. Anton. 1999. "Alcohol." Pp. 75–94 in Barbara S. McCrady and Esizabeth E. Epstein (eds.), *Addictions: A Comprehensive Guidebook*. New York: Oxford University Press.

Mortimer, W. Golden. 1901. *Peru: History of Coca: "The Divine Plant" of the Incas with an Introductory Account of the Anean Indians of Today*. New York: J.H. Vail.

National Alliance for the Mentally Ill. n.d., *Access to Effective Medications: A Critical Link to Mental Illness Recovery*. Available online: *http://www.nami.org/update/ 000709b.html* (Accessed September 26, 2000).

National Clearinghouse for Smoking and Health. 1969. *Use of Tobacco*. Washington, D.C.: U.S. Department of Health, Education and Welfare.

National Drug Intelligence Center. 2001. *Information Bulletin: OxyContin Diversion and Abuse*. Document No. 2001-L0424-001 (July). Washington, DC: U.S. Government Printing Office.

National Institute on Drug Abuse. 1999. "Cocaine abuse and addiction." NIDA Research Report Series, NCADI # PHD813. Rockville, MD: National Institute on Drug Abuse.

———. 1998. "Nicotine Addiction." National Institute on Drug Abuse Research Report Series NCADI # PHD762. Rockville, MD: National Institute on Drug Abuse.

———. 1996. "Facts About Marijuana and Marijuana Abuse." NIDA Notes, 11, 2. Available online: *http://www.nida.nih.gov/NIDA_Notes/NNVol11N2/MarijuanaTearoff.html*. (Accessed December 21, 1999).

———. 1990. "Overview of the 1990 National Household Survey on Drug Abuse." Rockville, MD: National Institute on Drug Abuse.

———. n.d.a. "Nationwide Trends." NIDA Infofax, #13567. Washington, D.C.: United States Government Printing Office. Available online: *http://165.112.78.61/Infofax/nationtrends.html* (Accessed August 18, 2001).

———. n.d.b. "Methylphenidate (Ritalin)." NIDA Infofax, #13555. Washington, D.C.: United States Government Printing Office. Available online: *http://www.nida.nih.gov/Infofax/ritalin.html* (Accessed June 14, 2002).

Nellis, Muriel. 1980. *The Female Fix*. New York: Penguin Books.

Nyswander, Marie. 1956. *The Drug Addict as a Patient*. New York: Grune and Stratton.

Office of National Drug Control Policy. 1998. *Pulse Check: National Trends in Drug Abuse, Summer 1998*. Washington, DC: U.S. Government Printing Office.

Platt, Jerome J. 1975. "'Addiction-Proneness' and Personality in Heroin Addicts." *Journal of Abnormal Psychology*. 84, 3, pp. 303–306.

Pletscher, A. "The Discovery of Antidepressants: A Winding Path." *Experientia* 47, pp. 4–8.

Preble, Edward A. and Babriel V. Laury. 1967. "Plastic Cement: The Ten Cent Hallucinogen." *International Journal of the Addictions*, 2, 2 (Fall), pp. 271–281.

Ray, Oakley. 1978. *Drugs, Society and Human Behavior* (2nd ed.). St. Louis: Mosby.

Ray, Oakley, and Charles Ksir. 1999. *Drugs, Society and Human Behavior* (8th ed.). St. Louis: Mosby.

Reinarman, Craig and Harry G. Levine. 1997. *Crack in America: Demon Drugs and Social Justice*. Berkeley: University of California Press.

Russell, M.A. Hamilton. 1971. "Cigarette Smoking: Natural History of a Dependence Disorder." *British Journal of Medical Psychology*, 44.

Sabbatini, Renato M.E. n.d. "The History of Shock Therapy in Psychiatry." Available Online: *http://www.epub.org.br/cm/n04/historia/shock_i.htm* (Accessed June 20, 2002).

Scott, James Maurice. 1969. *The White Poppy*. New York: Funk and Wagnalls.

Shulgin, Alexander T. 1992. *Controlled Substances: A Chemical and Legal Guide to Federal Drug Laws*. Berkeley, CA: Ronin Publishing.

Siegel, Harvey and James Inciardi. 1995. "A brief history of alcohol." Pp. 45–49 in James A. Inciardi and Karen McElrath (eds.) *The American Drug Scene*. Los Angeles: Roxbury Publishing Co.

Spencer, T., J. Biederman, T. Wilens, M. Harding, D. O'Donnell and S. Griffin. 1996. "Pharmacotherapy of Attention-Deficit Hyperactivity Disorder Across the Life Cycle." *Journal of the American Academy of Child and Adolescent Psychiatry* 35, pp. 409–432.

Stephens, Robert S. 1999. "Cannabis and Hallucinogens." Pp. 121–140 in Barbara S. McCrady and Elizabeth E. Epstein (eds.), *Addictions: A Comprehensive Guidebook*. New York: Oxford University Press.

Stine, Susan M. and Thomas R. Kosten. 1999. "Opioids." Pp. 141–161 in Barbara S. McCrady and Elizabeth E. Epstein (eds.), *Addictions: A Comprehensive Guidebook*. New York: Oxford University Press.

Stoll, W.A. 1947. "Lysergsäure-Diäthylamide, ein Phantastikum aus der Mutterkorngruppe." *Swiss Archives of Neurology and Psychiatry, 60*.

Surgeon General of the United States. 1964. *Smoking and Health: Report of the Advisory Committee to the Surgeon General of the Public Health Service*. Washington, D.C.: U.S. Government Printing Office.

Teicher, Martin H., Carol Glod and Jonathan O. Cole. 1990. "Emergence of Intense Suicidal Preoccupation During Fluoxetine Treatment." *American Journal of Psychiatry* 147, pp. 207–210.

Tondo, Leonardo, John Hennen and Ross J. Baldessarini. 2001. "Lower Suicide Risk with Long-Term Lithium Treatment in Major Affective Illness: A Meta-Analysis." *Acta Psychiatrica Scandinavica* 104, pp. 163–172.

Volkow, Nora D., Gene-Jack Wang, Joanna S. Fowler, Samuel J. Gatley, Jean Logan, Yu-Shin Ding, Robert Hitzemann, and Naomi Pappas. 1998. "Dopamine Transporter Occupancies in the Human Brain Induced by Therapeutic Doses of Oral Methylphenidate." *The American Journal of Psychiatry* 155, pp. 1325–1331.

Weaver, Michael F. and Sidney H. Schnoll. 1999. "Stimulants: Amphetamines and Cocaine." Pp. 105–120 in Barbara S. McCrady and Esizabeth E. Epstein (eds.), *Addictions: A Comprehensive Guidebook*. New York: Oxford University Press.

Weiner, Jerry. 1996. "Is Ritalin Overprescribed?—No." American Council on Science and Health, *Priorities in Health* 8. Available online: *http://www.acsh.org/publications/priorities/0803/pcno.html* (Accessed June 28, 2002).

Williams College Neuroscience. 1998. "Synaptic Transmission: A Four-Step Process." Available online: *http://www.williams.edu/imput/synapse/index.html* (Accessed June 25, 2002).

Winger, Gail, Frederick G. Hofmann, and James H. Woods. 1992. *A Handbook on Drug and Alcohol Abuse: the Biomedical Aspects*. (3rd ed.). New York: Oxford University Press.

Zinberg, Norman E. 1984. *Drug Set and Setting: The Basis for Controlled Intoxicant Use*. New Haven, CT: Yale University Press.

Zuckoff, Mitchell. 2000. "Prozac Data was Kept From Trial, Suit Says." *Boston Globe*, June 8, p. A01.

Chapter 4

Adler, Israel and Denise B. Kandel. 1981. "Cross-Cultural Perspectives on Developmental Stages in Adolescent Drug Use. *Journal of Studies on Alcohol* 42, pp. 701–715.

Agar, Michael N. 1973. *Ripping and Running: A Formal Ethnography of Urban Heroin Addicts*. New York: Academic Press.

Agnew, Robert and David Peterson. 1989. "Leisure and Delinquency." *Social Problems* 36, pp. 332–348.

Akers, Ronald L. 1969. *Deviant Behavior: A Social-Learning Approach*. Belmont, CA: Wadsworth.

———. 1992. *Drugs, Alcohol, and Society: Social Structure, Process and Policy*. Belmont, CA: Wadsworth.

Akers, Ronald L., Robert L. Burgess and Weldon Johnson. 1968. "Opiate Use, Addiction, and Relapse. *Social Problems* 15, pp. 459–469.

Akers, Ronald L. and John K. Cochran. 1985. "Adolescent Marijuana Use: A Test of Three Theories of Deviant Behavior." *Deviant Behavior* 6, pp. 323–346.

Akers, Ronald L., Marvin D. Krohn, Lonn Lanza-Kaduce and Marcia Radosevich. 1979. "Social Learning and Deviant Behavior: A Specific Test of a General Theory." *American Sociological Review* 44 (August), pp. 636–655.

Akers, Ronald L., Anthony J. La Greca, John K. Cochran and Christine Sellers. 1989. "Social Learning and Alcohol Behavior Among the Elderly." *Sociological Quarterly* 30, pp. 625–663.

Bandura, Albert. 1969. *Principles of Behavior Modification.* 1969. New York: Holt, Rinehart and Winston.

Becker, Howard. 1963. *Outsiders: Studies in the Sociology of Deviance.* New York: Free Press.

———. 1967. "History, Culture and Subjective Experience: An Exploration of the Social Bases of Drug-Induced Experiences." *Journal of Health and Social Behavior* 8, pp. 163–176.

Biernacki, Patrick. 1979. "Junkie Work, 'Hustles' and Social Status Among Heroin Addicts." *Journal of Drug Issues* 9, pp. 535–551.

Burkett, Steven R. and Bruce O. Warren. 1987. "Religiosity, Peer Associations, and Adolescent Marijuana Use: A Panel Study of Underlying Causal Structures." *Criminology* 25, pp. 109–131.

Chein, Isidor, Donald L. Gerard, Robert S. Lee and Eva Rosenfeld. 1964. *The Road To H: Narcotics, Delinquency and Social Policy.* New York: Basic Books.

Cloward, Richard and Lloyd Ohlin. 1960. *Delinquency and Opportunity.* New York: Free Press.

Cohen, Albert K. 1955. *Delinquent Boys: The Culture of the Gang.* New York: The Free Press.

Cox, W. Miles. 1985. "Personality Correlates of Substance Abuse." Pp. 209–246 in Mark Galizeo and Stephen A. Maisto (eds.), *Determinants of Substance Abuse: Biological, Psychological and Environmental Factors.* New York: Plenum Press.

Crowley, Thomas J. 1981. "The Reinforcers for Drug Abuse: Why People Take Drugs." Pp. 367–381 in Howard Shaffer, Milton Earl Burglass (eds.), *Classic Contributions in the Addictions.* New York: Brunner/Mazel.

Currie, Elliott. 1985. *Confronting Crime: An American Challenge.* New York: Pantheon Books.

———. 1993. *Reckoning: Drugs, the Cities, and the American Future.* New York: Farrar, Straus, and Giroux.

Dembo, Richard, Gary Grandon, Lawrence La Voie, James Schmeidler and William Burgos. 1986. "Parents and Drugs Revisited: Some Further Evidence in Support of Social Learning Theory." *Criminology* 24, pp. 85–104.

Dole, Vincent P., "Addictive Behavior." *Scientific American.* 243 (December), pp. 138–154.

Dole, Vincent P., Marie E. Nyswander and Alan Warner. 1968. "Successful Treatment of 750 Narcotics Addicts." *Journal of the American Medical Association.* 206 (December 16), pp. 2708–2711.

Dull, R. Thomas. 1983. "An Empirical Examination of the Anomie Theory of Drug Use." *Journal of Drug Issues* 13, pp. 49–62.

———. 1985. "Friends' Use and Adult Drug and Drinking Behavior: A Further Test of Differential Association Theory." *The Journal of Criminal Law and Criminology* 74, pp. 1608–1619.

Durkin, Keith F., Timothy W. Wolfe and Gregory Clark. 1999. "Social Bond Theory and Binge Drinking Among College Students: A Multivariate Analysis." *College Student Journal* 33, pp. 450–162.

Epstein, Edward Jay. 1977. *Agency of Fear: Opiates and Political Power in America.* New York: G.P. Putnam's Sons.

Faupel, Charles E. 1991. *Shooting Dope: Career Patterns of Hard-Core Heroin Users.* Gainesville, FL: University of Florida Press.

Finestone, Harold. 1957. "Cats, Kicks and Color." *Social Problems* 5 (July), pp. 3–13.

Fishbein, Diana H. and Susan E. Pease. 1990. "Neurological Links Between Substance Abuse and Crime." Pp. 218–243 in Lee Ellis and Harry Hoffman (eds.) *Crime in Biological, Social and Moral Contexts.* New York: Praeger Publishers.

Gawin, Frank H. 1991. "Cocaine Addiction: Psychology and Neurophysiology. *Science* 251 (March 29), pp. 1580–1586.

Gendreau, Paul and L.P. Gendreau. 1970. "The Addiction-Prone Personality: A Study of Canadian Heroin Addicts." *Canadian Journal of Behavioral Science.* 2, pp. 18–25.

Goffman, Erving. 1963. *Stigma; Notes on the Management of Spoiled Identity.* Englewood Cliffs, N.J., Prentice-Hall.

Goode, Erich. 1970. *The Marijuana Smokers.* New York: Basic Books.

Greenspan, Stanley I. 1978. "Substance Abuse: An Understanding from Psychoanalytic Developmental and Learning Theory Perspectives." Pp. 73–87 in Jack D. Blaine and Demetrious A. Julius (eds.), *Psychodynamics of Drug Dependence.* Rockville, MD: National Institute on Drug Abuse.

Gusfield, Joseph. 1963. *Symbolic Crusade: Status Politics and the American Temperance Movement.* Urbana, IL: University of Illinois Press.

Hill, H.E., C.A. Haertzen and H. Davis. 1962. "An MMPI Factor Analytic Study of Alcoholics, Narcotic Addicts and Criminals." *Quarterly Journal of Studies on Alcohol.* 23, pp. 411–431.

Hill, H.E., C.A. Haertzen, and R. Glazer. 1960. "Personality Characteristics of Narcotic Addicts as Indicated by the MMPI." *Journal of General Psychology,* 62, pp. 127–139.

Hirschi, Travis. 1969. *Causes of Delinquency.* Berkeley, CA: University of California Press.

Johnson, Bruce D. 1973. *Marijuana Users and Drug Subcultures.* New York: Wiley.

_____. 1980. "Toward a Theory of Drug Subcultures." Pp. 110–119 in Dan J. Lettieri, Molly Sayers and Helen Wallenstein Pearson, *Theories on Drug Abuse: Selected Contemporary Perspectives.* Rockville, MD: National Institute on Drug Abuse.

Junger-Tas, Josine. 1992. "An Empirical Test of Social Control Theory." *Journal of Quantitative Criminology* 8, pp. 18–29.

Kandel, Denise. 1973. "Adolescent Marijuana Use: Role of Parents and Peers." *Science* 181 (September 14), pp. 1067–1070.

_____. 1975. "Stages in Adolescent Involvement in Drug Use." *Science* 190, pp. 912–914.

_____. 1980. "Developmental Stages in Adolescent Drug Involvement." Pp. 120–127 in Dan J. Lettieri, Mollie Sayers and Helen Wallenstein Pearson (eds.), *Theories on Drug Abuse: Selected Contemporary Perspectives.* Rockville, MD: National Institute on Drug Abuse.

Kandel, Denise and Mark Davies. 1991. "Friendship Networks, Intimacy, and Illicit Drug use in Young Adulthood: A Comparison of Two Competing Theories." *Criminology* 29 (August), pp. 441–469.

Khantzian, Edward J., John E. Mack and Alan F. Schatzbert. 1974. "Heroin Use as an Attempt to Cope: Clinical Observations." *American Journal of Psychiatry* 131 (Feb), pp. 160–164.

Kolb, Lawrence. 1925. "Drug Addiction and its Relation to Crime." *Mental Hygiene* 9, pp. 74–89.

Krohn, Marvin D., Ronald L Akers, Marcia J. Radosevich and Lonn Lanza Kaduce. 1982. "Norm Qualities and Adolescent Drinking and Drug Behavior: The Effects of Norm Quality and Reference Group on Using and Abusing Alcohol and Marijuana." *Journal of Drug Issues* (Fall), pp. 343–359.

Krohn, Marvin D., Lonn Lanza Kaduce and Ronald L. Akers. 1984. "Community Context and Theories of Deviant Behavior: An Examination of Social Learning and Social Bonding Theories." *The Sociological Quarterly* 25 (Summer), pp. 353–371.

Krohn, Marvin D., William F. Skinner, James L. Massey and Ronald L. Akers. 1985. "Social Learning Theory and Adolescent Cigarette Smoking." *Social Problems* 32, pp. 455 473.

Lemert, Edwin. 1951. *Social Pathology.* New York: McGraw-Hill.

Levinthal, Charles F. 1988. *Messengers of Paradise: Opiates and the Brain.* New York: Doubleday.

Lindesmith, Alfred R. 1938. "A Sociological Theory of Drug Addiction." *American Journal of Sociology* 43, pp. 593–613.

Lindesmith, Alfred R. and John H. Gagnon. "Anomie and Drug Addiction." Pp. 158–188 in Marshall B. Clinard (ed.), *Anomie and Deviant Behavior.* New York: The Free Press.

Logue, A.W., 1986. *The Psychology of Eating and Drinking.* New York: W.H. Freeman and Company.

Marcos, Anastasios C., Stephen J. Bahr and Richard E. Johnson. 1986. "Test of a bonding/Association Theory of Adolescent Drug Use." *Social Forces* 65 (September), pp. 135–161.

McAuliffe, William E. 1975. "A Second Look at First Effects: The Subjective Effects of Opiates on Nonaddicts." *Journal of Drug Issues* 5 (Fall), pp. 369–399.

McAuliffe, William E. and Robert A. Gordon. 1980. "Reinforcement and the Combination of Effects: Summary of a Theory of Opiate Addiction." Pp. 137–141 in Dan J. Lettieri, Molly Sayers and Helen Wallenstein Pearson, *Theories on Drug Abuse: Selected Contemporary Perspectives.* Rockville, MD: National Institute on Drug Abuse.

Merton, Robert K. 1938 "Social Structure and Anomie." *American Sociological Review* 3, pp. 672–682.

Nakken, Craig. 1988. *The Addictive Personality: Understanding Compulsion in Our Lives.* San Francisco: Harper and Row.

O'Donnell, John A. 1967. "The Rise and Decline of a Subculture." *Social Problems* 15 (Summer), pp. 73–84.

Peterson, Ruth. 1985. "Discriminatory Decision Making at the Legislative Level. *Law and Human Behavior.* 9, pp. 243–269

Platt, Jerome J. and Christina Labate. 1976. *Heroin Addiction: Theory, Research and Treatment.* New York: John Wiley and Sons.

Preble, Edward and John J. Casey. 1969. "Taking Care of Business—The Heroin User's Life on the Street." *The International Journal of the Addictions* 4 (March), pp. 1–24.

Raskin, H.A., T.A. Petty and M. Warren. 1957. "A Suggested Approach to the Problem of Narcotic Addiction." *American Journal of Psychiatry* 113, pp. 1089–1094.

Savitt, Robert A. 1963. "Psychoanalytic Studies on Addiction: Ego Structure in Narcotic Addiction." *Psychoanalytic Quarterly*. 32, pp. 42–57

Schuckit, Marc. 1983. "The Genetics of Alcoholism." Pp. 31–46 in Boris Tabakoff, Patricia B. Sutker and Carrie L. Randall (eds.), *Medical and Social Aspects of Alcohol Abuse*. New York: Plenum Press.

Schuckit, Marc. 1985. "Genetics and the Risk for Alcoholism." *Journal of the American Medical Association*. 254, 18 (November 8), pp. 2614–2617.

Schur, Edwin M. 1971. *Labeling Deviant Behavior: Its Sociological Implications*. New York: Harper and Row.

———. 1973. *Radical Nonintervention: Rethinking the Delinquency Problem*. Englewood Cliffs, NJ: Prentice-Hall.

Sellers, Christine S. and L. Thomas Winfree. 1990. "Differential Associations and Definitions: A Panel Study of Youthful Drinking Behavior." *The International Journal of the Addictions* 25, pp. 755–771.

Shaw, Clifford and Henry McKay. 1972. *Juvenile Delinquency and Urban Areas* (Rev. Ed.). Chicago: University of Chicago Press.

Sher, Kenneth J. 1991. *Children of Alcoholics*. Chicago: University of Chicago Press.

Sunderwirth, Stanley G. 1985. "Biological Mechanisms: Neurotransmission and Addiction." Pp. 11–19 in Harvey B. Milkman and Howard J. Shaffer (eds.) *The Addictions: Multidisciplinary Perspectives and Treatments*. Lexington, MA: D.C. Heath.

Sutherland, Edwin. 1939. *Principles of Criminology*. Philadelphia: Lippincott.

Sykes, Gresham and David Matza. 1957. "Techniques of Neutralization: A Theory of Delinquency." *American Sociological Review* 22, pp. 664–670.

Tarter, Ralph E. 1988. "Are there Inherited Behavioral Traits that Predispose to Substance Abuse?" *Journal of Counseling and Clinical Psychology*. 56, pp. 189–196.

Tarter, Ralph E., Arthur I. Alterman, and Kathleen L. Edwards. 1985. "Vulnerability to Alcoholism in Men: A Behavior-Genetic Perspective." *Journal of Studies on Alcohol*. 46, pp. 329–356.

Terenius, Lars. 1993. "Opiate Receptors–the Historical Breakthrough in Drug Research." Pp. 13–25 in S. Wonnacott and G.G. Lunt (eds.), *Neurochemistry of Drug Dependence*. London: Portland Press.

Van Voorhis, Patricia, Francis Cullen, Richard Mathers and Connie Chenoweth Garner. 1988. "The Impact of Family Structure and Quality on Delinquency: A Comparative Assessment of Structural and Functional Factors." *Criminology* 26 (May), pp. 235–261.

Vesell, E.S.. 1975. "Ethanol Metabolism: Regulation by Genetic Factors in Normal Volunteers Under a Controlled Environment and the Effect of Chronic Ethanol Administration." *Annals of the New York Academy of Sciences* 197, pp. 79–88.

Weil, Andrew, 1986. *The Natural Mind: An Investigation of Drugs and the Higher Consciousness*. Boston: Houghton-Mifflin.

Wikler, Abraham. 1981. "Dynamics of Drug Dependence: Implications of a Conditioning Theory for Research and Treatment." Pp. 352–366 in Howard Shaffer, Milton Earl Burglass (eds.), *Classic Contributions in the Addictions*. New York: Brunner/Mazel.

Winick, Charles. 1974. "A Sociological Theory of the Genesis of Drug Dependence." Pp. 3–13 in Charles Winick (ed.), *Sociological Aspects of Drug Dependence*. Cleveland, OH: CRC Press.

Wolfgang, Marvin E. and Franco Ferracuti. 1967. *The Subculture of Violence*. London: Tavistock.

Wurmser, Leon. 1978. "Mr Pecksniff's Horse? (Psychodynamics in Compulsive Drug Use)." Pp. 36–72 in Jack D. Blaine and Demetrious A. Julius (eds.), *Psychodynamics of Drug Dependence*. Rockville, MD: National Institute on Drug Abuse.

———. 1981. "Psychoanalytic Considerations of the Etiology of Compulsive Drug Use." Pp. 133–153 in Howard Shaffer, Milton Earl Burglass (eds.), *Classic Contributions in the Addictions*. New York: Brunner/Mazel.

Chapter 5

Adler, Patricia A. 1985. *Wheeling and Dealing: An Ethnography of an Upper-Level Drug Dealing and Smuggling Community*. New York: Columbia University Press.

Agar, Michael. 1973. *Ripping and Running: A Formal Ethnography of Urban Heroin Addicts*. New York: Seminar Press.

Akers, Ronald L., Robert L. Burgess, and Weldon T. Johnson. 1968. "Opiate Use, Addiction and Relapse." *Social Problems* 15,4 (Spring), pp. 459–469.

Anderson, Edward F. 1996. *Peyote: The Divine Cactus*. Tucson, AZ: The University of Arizona Press.

Becker, Howard S. 1953. Becoming a marijuana user." *American Journal of Sociology* 59, pp. 235–242.

_____. 1963. *Outsiders: Studies in the Sociology of Deviance*. Glencoe, IL: Free Press.

_____. 1967. "History, Culture and Subjective Experience: An Exploration of the Social Bases of Drug-Induced Experiences." *Journal of Health and Social Behavior* 8, pp. 163–176.

Biernacki, Patrick. 1979. "Junkie Work, 'Hustles' and Social Status Among Heroin Addicts." *Journal of Drug Issues* 9, pp. 535–551.

Brecher, Edward M. 1972. *Licit and Illicit Drugs*. Boston: Little-Brown.

Breiner, Laurence A. 1985/1986. "The English Bible in Jamaican Rastafarianism." *Journal of Religious Thought* 42(2), pp. 30–43.

Bryan, James H. 1966. "Occupational Ideologies and Individual Attitudes of Call Girls." *Social Problems* 13,4 (Spring), pp. 441–50.

Campbell, Horace. 1980. "Rastafari: Culture of Resistance." *Race & Class* 22, pp. 1–22.

Castro, Russel A. 2001. "Drug Use, Cultures, and Subcultures." Pp. 294–296 in Clifton Bryant (ed.), *Encyclopedia of Criminology and Deviant Behavior, Vol. 4*. Philadelphia, PA: Taylor and Francis.

Chein, Isidor, Donald L. Gerard, Robert S. Lee, and Eva Rosenfeld. 1964. *The Road to H: Narcotics, Juvenile Delinquency and Social Policy*. New York: Basic Books.

Cohen, Alfred. 1955. *Delinquent Boys*. Glencoe, IL: Free Press.

Comerford, Mary, Dale D. Chitwood, James A. Inciardi, and David K. Griffin. 1996. "Inner City Crack Houses." Pp. 15–32 in Dale D. Chitwood, James E. Rivers and James A. Inciardi (eds.), *The American Pipe Dream: Crack Cocaine and the Inner City*. Fort Worth, TX: Harcourt-Brace.

Coombs, Robert H. 1981. "Drug Abuse as Career." *Journal of Drug Issues* 11 (Fall), pp. 369–387.

Drug Enforcement Administration. 2000. *Drug Intelligence Brief: An Overview of Club Drugs*. Washington, D.C.: U.S.D.O.J.

Economist. 1999. "A Field Full of Buttons." *The Economist* 351(8113), pp. 27

Edmonds, Ennis F. 1998. "The Structure and Ethos of Rastafari." Pp. 349–360 in *Chanting Down Babylon: The Rastafari Reader*, edited by N.S. Murrell, W.D. Spencer, and A.A. McFarlane. Philadelphia: Temple University Press.

Faupel, Charles E. 1986. "Heroin Use, Street Crime and the 'Main Hustle': Implications for the Validity of Official Crime Data." *Deviant Behavior* 7, pp. 31–45.

_____. 1987a. "Heroin Use and Criminal Careers." *Qualitative Sociology* 10,2, pp. 115–131.

_____. 1991. *Shooting Dope: Career Patterns of Hard-Core Heroin Users*. Gainesville, FL: University of Florida Press.

Fiddle, Seymore. 1963. "The Addict Culture and Movement into and out of Hospitals." Pp. 3154–62 in U.S. Senate Judiciary Committee Hearings. Washington, DC: U.S. Government Printing Office.

_____. 1976. "Sequences in Addiction." *Addictive Diseases: An International Journal* 2,4, pp. 553–568.

Goffman, Erving. 1959. "The Moral Career of the Mental Patient." *Psychiatry* 22, pp. 123–142.

Goldman, Fred. 1981. "Drug Abuse, Crime and Economics: The Dismal Limits of Social Choice." Pp. 155–182 in James A. Inciardi (ed.) *The Drugs-Crime Connection*. Beverly Hills, CA: Sage Publications.

Goldstein, Paul. 1981. "Getting Over: Economic Alternatives to Predatory Street Crime Among Street Drug Users." Pp. 67–84 in James A. Inciardi (ed.), *The Drugs-Crime Connection*. Beverly Hills, CA: Sage Publications.

Goldstein, Paul, Douglas S. Lipton, Edward Preble, Ira Sobel, Tom Miller, William Abbot, William Paige, and Franklin Soto. 1984. "The Marketing of Street Heroin in New York City." *Journal of Drug Issues* 3 (Summer), pp. 553–566.

Golub, Andrew and Bruce D. Johnson. 2001. "The Rise of Marijuana as the Drug of Choice Among Youthful Adult Arrestees." *National Institute of Justice, Research in Brief* (June). Washington, DC: National Institute of Justice.

_____. 1999. "Cohort Changes in Illegal Drug Use Among Arrestees in Manhattan: From the Heroin Injection Generation to the Blunts Generation." *Substance Use & Misuse* 34, pp. 1733–1763.

Goode, Erich. 1970. *The Marijuana Smokers*. New York: Basic Books.

Gordon, Milton C. 1947. "The Concept of the Sub-culture and Its Application." *Social Forces* 26 (October), pp. 40–42.

Gould, Leroy, Andrew L. Walker, Lansing E. Crane and Charles W. Lidz. 1974. Connections: *Notes from the Heroin World*. New Haven, CT: Yale University Press.

Grinspoon, Lester, and James B. Bakalar. 1979. *Psychedelic Drugs Reconsidered*. New York: Basic Books.

Hanson, Bill, George Beschner, James W. Walters and Elliot Bovelle. 1985. *Life with Heroin: Voices From the Inner City*. Lexington, MA: Lexington Books.

Harris, Mervyn. 1973. *The Dilly Boys*. Rockville, MD: New Perspectives.

Hayano, David M. 1982. *Poker Faces: The Life and Work of Professional Card Players*. Berkeley, CA: University of California Press.

Hepner, Randal L. 1998. "Chanting Down Babylon in the Belly of the Beast: The Rastafarian Movement in the Metropolitan United States." Pp. 99–216 in *Chanting Down Babylon: The Rastafari Reader*, edited by N.S. Murrell, W.D. Spencer, and A.A. McFarlane. Philadelphia: Temple University Press.

Iglehart, Austin S. 1985. "Brickin' It and Going to the Pan: Vernacular in the Black Inner-City Heroin Lifestyle." Pp. 111–133 in Bill Hanson et al., *Life With Heroin: Voices From the Inner City*. Lexington, MA: Lexington Books.

Inciardi, James A. 1975. *Careers in Crime*. Chicago: Rand-McNally Publishing Co.

Institute for Substance Abuse Research. 1990. *Drugs of Abuse Digest: A Prevention Guide for the Family, School and Workplace*. (6th ed.). Vero Beach FL: ISAR.

Irwin, John. 1980. *Prisons in Turmoil*. Boston: Little, Brown and Company.

James, Jennifer, Cathleen T. Gosho, and Robin Watson. 1976. "The Relationship Between Female Criminality and Drug Use." Pp. 441–455 in Research Triangle Institute (ed.), *Drug Use and Crime: Report of the Panel on Drug Use and Criminal Behavior*. National Technical Information Service Publication No. PB-259–167. Springfield, VA: U.S. Department of Commerce.

Johnson, Bruce D. 1973. *Marijuana Users and Drug Subcultures*. New York: Wiley.

Johnson-Hill, Jack A. 1995. *I-Sight: The World of Rastafari: An Interpretive Sociological Account of Rastafarian Ethics*. Metuchen NJ: Scarecrow Press.

Julien, Robert M. 2001. *A Primer of Drug Action: A Concise Nontechnical Guide to the Actions, Uses, and Side Effects of Psychoactive Drugs*. Revised ed. New York: W.H. Freeman and Company.

Kitzinger, Sheila. 1969. "Protest and Mysticism: The Rastafari Cult of Jamaica." *Journal for the Scientific Study of Religion* 8, pp. 240–262.

Kiyaani, Mike, and Thomas J. Csordas. 1997. "On the Peyote Road: Worlds of the Shaman." *Natural History* 106(2), pp. 48–50.

Lanternari, Vittorio. 1965. *The Religions of the Oppressed*, New York: Mentor Books.

Lawrence, Jeffrey T. 1990. "The War on Drugs and Denominational Preferences: Farewell to Strict Scrutiny Analysis." *Brigham Young University Law Journal* 1990(3), pp. 1083–1105.

Lewis, Linden. 1989. "Living in the Heart of Babylon: Rastafari in the USA." *Bulletin of Eastern Caribbean Affairs* 15(1), pp. 20–30.

Lewis, William F. 1993. *Soul Rebels: The Rastafari*. Prospect Heights, IL: Waveland Press.

Lewis, Rupert. 1998. "Marcus Garvey and the Early Rastafarians: Continuity and Discontinuity." Pp. 145–158 in *Chanting Down Babylon: The Rastafari Reader*, edited by N.S. Murrell, W.D. Spencer, and A.A. McFarlane. Philadelphia: Temple University Press.

Lindesmith, Alfred R. 1940. "'Dope Fiend' Mythology". *Journal of Criminal Law and Criminology* 31, pp. 199–208.

Lindesmith, Alfred R. 1965. *The Addict and the Law*. Bloomington, IN: Indiana University Press.

Liska, Ken. 2000. *Drugs and the Human Body: With Implications for Society*. 6th ed. Upper Saddle River NJ: Prentice-Hall.

Luckenbill, David F., and Joel Best. 1981. "Careers in Deviance and Respectability: the Analogy's Limitations." *Social Problems* 29,2 (December), pp. 197–206.

Marshall, Donnie R. 2001. DEA Congressional Testimony, Senate Caucus on International Narcotics Contol, March 21.

Murrell, Nathaniel Samuel. 1998. "Introduction: The Rastafari Phenomenon." Pp. 1–19 in *Chanting Down Babylon: The Rastafari Reader*, edited by N.S. Murrell, W.D. Spencer, and A.A. McFarlane. Philadelphia: Temple University Press.

Murrell, Nathaniel Samuel, and Burchell K. Taylor. 1998. "Rastafari's Messianic Ideology and Caribbean Theology of Liberation." Pp. 390–411 in *Chanting Down Babylon: The Rastafari Reader*, edited by N.S. Murrell, W.D. Spencer, and A.A. McFarlane. Philadelphia: Temple University Press.

National Drug Intelligence Center. 2001. *Raves*. U.S. Department of Justice Information Bulletin. Washington, D.C.: USDOJ.

National Institute on Drug Abuse. 1999. *NIDA Notes* 14(6). Bethesda, MD: National Institute of Health.

O'Donnell, John A. 1967. "The Rise and Decline of a Subculture." *Social Problems* 15,1 (Summer), pp. 73–84.

Peregoy, Robert M., Walter R. Echo-Hawk, and James Botsford. 1995. "Congress Overturns Supreme Court's Peyote Ruling." *NARF Legal Review* 20(1), pp. 1, 6–25.

Preble, Edward and John H. Casey Jr. 1969. "Taking Care of Business—the Heroin User's Life on the Street." *International Journal of the Addictions* 4,1, pp. 1–24.

Ray, Oakley, and Charles Ksir. 1999. *Drugs, Society, and Human Behavior.* (8th ed.). Boston: McGraw-Hill.

Rosenbaum, Marsha. 1981. *Women on Heroin.* New Brunswick, NJ: Rutgers University Press.

Rubington, Earl. 1967. "Drug Addiction as a Deviant Career." *International Journal of the Addictions* 2,1, pp. 3–20.

Sackman, Bertram, M. Maxine Sackman and G.G. DeAngelis. 1978. "Heroin Addiction as an Occupation: Traditional Addicts and Heroin Addicted Poly-drug Users." *International Journal of the Addictions* 13, pp. 427–441.

Savisinsky, Neil J. 1998. "African Dimensions of the Jamaican Rastafarian Movement." Pp. 125–145 in *Chanting Down Babylon: The Rastafari Reader,* edited by N.S. Murrell, W.D. Spencer, and A.A. McFarlane. Philadelphia: Temple University Press.

Smeja, Carol M. and Dean G. Rojek. 1986. "Youthful Drug Use and Drug Subcultures." *The International Journal of the Addictions* 21(9–10), pp. 1031–50.

Sommers, Ira B. 2001. "Criminal Careers." Pp. 155–158 in Clifton D. Bryant (ed.), *Encyclopedia of Criminology and Deviant Behavior,* Vol. 2. Philadelphia, PA: Taylor and Francis.

Sommers, Ira B., Deborah Baskin, and Jeffrey Fagan. 1994. "Getting Out of the Life: Crime Desistance by Female Street Offenders." *Deviant Behavior* 15, pp. 125–150.

Sutherland, Edwin H. 1939. *Principles of Criminology* (3rd ed.). Philadelphia: Lippincott.

Sykes, Gresham M., and David Matza. 1957. "Techniques of Neutralization: A Theory of Delinquency." *American Sociological Review* 22, pp. 664–670.

Taylor, Timothy B. 1984. "Soul Rebels: The Rastafarians and the Free Exercise Clause." *Georgetown Law Journal* 72, pp. 1605–1635.

Waldorf, Dan. 1971. "Life Without Heroin: Some Social Adjustments During Long-Term Periods of Voluntary Abstention." *Social Problems* 18, pp. 228–243.

———.1973. *Careers in Dope.* Englewood Cliffs, NJ: Prentice-Hall.

Waldorf, Dan, Craig Reinarman and Sheigla Murphy. 1991. *Cocaine Changes: The Experience of Using and Quitting.* Philadelphia, PA: Temple University Press.

Wallace, Samuel. 1965. *Skid Row as a Way of Life.* Totowa, NJ: Bedminster Press.

Weinberg, Martin S. 1966. "Becoming a Nudist." *Psychiatry: Journal for the Study of Interpersonal Processes* 29,1 (February), pp. 15–24.

Weir, Erica. 2000. "Raves: A Review of the Culture, the Drugs, and the Prevention of Harm." *Canadian Medical Association Journal* 67(2), pp. 1843–1848.

Weppner, Robert S. 1973. "An Anthropological View of the Street Addict's World." *Human Organization* 32,2 (Summer), pp. 111–121.

Zellner, William W. 2001. *Extraordinary Groups: An Examination of Unconventional Lifestyles.* New York: Worth Publishers.

Zinberg, Norman E. 1984. *Drug Set and Setting: The Basis for Controlled Intoxicant Use.* New Haven, CT: Yale University Press.

Chapter 6

ADAM. 2000. *1999 Annual Report on Drug Use Among Adult and Juvenile Arrestees.* Washington, DC: National Institute of Justice.

ADAM. 1999. *1998 Annual Report on Drug Use Among Adult and Juvenile Arrestees.* Washington, DC: National Institute of Justice.

Curtis, Richard. 1999 (November). "The Ethnographic Approach to Studying Drug Crime." Pp. 13–15 in Office of Justice Programs, *Looking at Crime from the Street Level.* Washington, DC: National Institute of Justice.

Faupel, Charles E. 1986. "Heroin Use, Street Crime, and the 'Main Hustle:' Implications for the Validity of Official Crime Data." *Deviant Behavior* 7, pp. 31–45.

———. 1991. *Shooting Dope: Career Patterns of Hard Core Heroin Users.* Gainesville, FL: University of Florida Press.

Federal Bureau of Investigation. 1981. *Crime in the United States.* Washington D.C.: U.S. Government Printing Office.

———. 2001. *Crime in the United States.* Washington D.C.: U.S. Government Printing Office. Available online: *http://www.fbi.gov/ucr.htm* (Accessed July 3, 2002).

Golub, Andrew Lang and Bruce D. Johnson. 1997. "Crack's Decline: Some Surprises Across U.S. Cities." National Institute of Justice, Research in Brief (July). Washington, DC: U.S. Department of Justice.

Johnston, L.D., P.M. O'Malley, J.G. Bachman. 2002. *Monitoring the Future National Survey Results On Drug Use, 1975–2001. Volume 1: Secondary School Students.* (NIH Publication No. 02-5106). Bethesda, MD: NIDA.

Monitoring the Future. 1999a. *Purpose and Design.* Ann Arbor, MI: University of Michigan [Online] Available *http://monitoringthefuture.org/purpose.html* accessed January 13, 2000.

Monitoring The Future 1999b. *Table 2: Long-Term Trends in Lifetime Prevalence of Use of Various Drugs for Twelfth Graders.* Ann Arbor, MI: University of Michigan Available online: *http://monitoringthefuture.org/data/data.html* (Accessed January 14, 2000).

National Institute of Justice. 1995. *Drug Use Forecasting 1994: Annual Report on Adult and Juvenile Arrestees.* Washington, DC: United States Department of Justice.

———. 1998. *ADAM: 1997 Annual Report on Adult and Juvenile Arrestees.* Washington, DC: United States Department of Justice.

———. 1999. *ADAM: 1998 Annual Report on Adult and Juvenile Arrestees.* Washington, DC: United States Department of Justice.

Office of National Drug Control Policy. 1998. *Pulse Check: National Trends in Drug Abuse.* (Winter) Washington, DC: U.S. Government Printing Office.

Reuter, Peter. 1999. "Drug Use Measures: What are They Really Telling Us?" *National Institute of Justice Journal* (April), pp. 12–19.

Substance Abuse and Mental Health Services Administration. 2001. *Emergency Department Trends from the Drug Abuse Warning Network, Preliminary Estimates January–June 2001 with Revised Estimates 1994–2000.* Washington, DC: Department of Health and Human Services.

———. 2001b. *Treatment Episode Data Set (TEDS): 1994–1999.* Washington, DC: Department of Health and Human Services.

———. 1998a. *Mid-Year 1997 Preliminary Emergency Department Data from the Drug Abuse Warning Network* (September). Washington, DC: Department of Health and Human Services.

———. 1998b. *Drug Abuse Warning Network: Annual Medical Examiner Data, 1996* (July). Washington, DC: Department of Health and Human Services.

———. 1999a. *Year End 1998 Emergency Department Data from the Drug Abuse Warning Network* (December). Washington, DC: Department of Health and Human Services.

———. 1999b. *Drug Abuse Warning Network: Annual Medical Examiner Data, 1997* (December). Washington, DC: Department of Health and Human Services.

———. 1999c. *Treatment Episode Data Set (TEDS): 1992–1997.* (August). Washington, DC: Department of Health and Human Services.

———. 2001. *2000 National Household Survey on Drug Abuse.* Washington, D.C.: Substance Abuse and Mental Health Services Administration.

———. 1999d. *1998 National Household Survey on Drug Abuse.* Washington, DC: Substance Abuse and Mental Health Services Administration.

United States Census Bureau. n.d. "Historical National Population Estimates: July 1, 1900 to July 1, 1998." Washington, D.C.: U.S. Government Printing Office Available online: *http://www.census.gov/population/estimates/nation/popclockest.txt.* (Accessed December 29, 1999).

Chapter 7

Allen, Scott H. 1986. "Suicide and Indirect Self-Destruction Behavior Among Police." Pp. 413–417 in James T. Reese and Harvey A. Goldstein (eds.), *Psychological Services for Law Enforcement.* Washington, DC: National Symposium on Police Psychological Services, FBI Academy, Quantico, VA.

Almog, Yishai J., M. Douglas Anglin and Dennis G. Fisher. 1993. "Alcohol and Heroin Use Patterns of Narcotics Addicts: Gender and Ethnic Differences." *American Journal of Drug and Alcohol Abuse* 19, pp. 219–238.

Anderson, Edward F. 1996. *Peyote: The Divine Cactus.* Tucson, AZ: The University of Arizona Press.

Anglin, M. Douglas, Timothy M. Ryan, Mary W. Booth and Yih-Ing Hser. 1988. "Ethnic Differences in Narcotics Addiction I: Characteristics of Chicano and Anglo Methadone Maintenance Clients." *The International Journal of the Addictions* 23, pp. 125–149.

Anglin, M. Douglas, Yih-Ing Hser and W.H. McGlothlin. 1987. "Sex Differences in Addict Careers 2: Becoming Addicted." *American Journal of Drug and Alcohol Abuse* 13, pp. 59–71.

Arrigo, Bruce A. and Karyn Garsky. 1997. "Police Suicide: A Glimpse Behind the Badge." Pp. 609–626 in Roger G. Dunham and Geoffrey P. Alpert (eds.), *Critical Issues in Policing: Contemporary Readings*. Prospect Heights, IL: Waveland Press, Inc.

Ballweg, John A. and Li Li. 1991. "Trends in Substance Use by U.S. Military Personnel." *Armed Forces & Society* 17, pp. 601–618.

Bamberger, Michael and Don Yaeger. 1997. "Over the Edge." *Sports Illustrated* 86 (15) (April 14), p. 60.

Banta, William F. and Forest Tenant. 1989. *Complete Handbook for Combating Substance Abuse in the Workplace*. Lexington, MA: Lexington Books.

Barr, Kellie E.M., Michael P. Farrell, Grace M. Barnes and John W. Welte. "Race, Class, and Gender Differences in Substance Abuse: Evidence of Middle-Class/Underclass Polarization Among Black Males." *Social Problems* 40, pp. 314–327.

Berkowitz, Alan D. and H. Wesley Perkins. 1986. "Problem Drinking Among College Students: A Review of Recent Research." *Journal of American College Health* 35, pp. 21–28.

Blaine, Jack D., Carl M. Lieberman and Joseph Hirsh. 1968. "Preliminary Observations on Patterns of Drug Consumption Among Medical Students." *The International Journal of the Addictions* 3, pp. 389–396.

Blau, Theodore H. 1994. *Psychological Services for Law Enforcement*. New York: John Wiley and Sons, Inc.

Bompey, Stuart. 1986. "Drugs in the Workplace: From the Batter's Box to the Boardroom." *Journal of Occupational Medicine* 28, pp. 825–832.

Bonifacio, Philip. 1991. *The Psychological Effects of Police Work: A Psychodynamic Approach*. New York: Plenum Press.

Bourgois, Phillippe. 1995. *In Search of Respect: Selling Crack in El Barrio*. Cambridge, England: Cambridge University Press.

Bowker, Lee. 1977. *Drug Use Among American Women, Old and Young: Sexual Oppression and Other Themes*. San Francisco: R & E Research Associates, Inc.

Bray, Robert M., John A. Fairbank and Mary Ellen Marsden. 1999. "Stress and Substance Abuse Among Military Women and Men." *American Journal of Drug and Alcohol Abuse* 25, pp. 239–251.

Bray, Robert M., Mary Ellen Marsden and Michael R. Peterson. 1991. "Standardized Comparisons of the Use of Alcohol, Drugs, and Cigarettes Among Military Personnel and Civilians." *American Journal of Public Health* 81, pp. 865–869.

Bray, Robert M. and Larry A. Kroutil. 1995. "Trends in Alcohol, Illicit Drug and Cigarette use Among U.S. Military Personnel: 1980–1992." *Armed Forces & Society* 21, pp. 271–283.

Bray, Robert M., Rebecca P. Sanchez, Miriam L. Ornstein, Danielle Lentine, Amy A. Vincus, Tracy U. Baird, June A. Walker, Sara C. Wheeless, L. Lynn Guess, Larry A. Kroutil, Vincent G. Iannacchione. 1999. Highlights 1998 Department of Defense Survey of Health Related Behaviors Among Military Personnel. Available online: *http://www.tricare.osd.mil/analysis/surveys/98survey/survey.html* (Accessed June 20, 2000).

Bressler, Bernard. 1976. "Suicide and Drug Abuse in the Medical Community." *Suicide and Life Threatening Behavior*. 6, pp. 169–178.

Brown, Barry S., Susan K. Gauvey, Marilyn B. Meyers and Steven D. Stark. 1971. "In Their Own Words: Addicts' Reasons for Initiating and Withdrawing from Heroin." *The International Journal of The Addictions* 6, pp. 635–645.

Bryant, Clifton D. 1974. "Olive-Drab Drunks and GI Junkies: Alcohol and Narcotic Addiction in the U.S. Military." Pp. 129–145 in Clifton D. Bryant (ed.), *Deviant Behavior: Occupational and Organizational Bases*. Chicago: Rand-McNally.

Buckley, William E., Charles E. Yesalis, K.E. Freidl, William A. Anderson, A.L. Streit, and James E. Wright. 1988. "Estimated Prevalence of Anabolic Steroid Use among Male High School Seniors." *Journal of the American Medical Association* 260, pp. 3441–3445.

Bullington, Bruce. 1977. *Heroin Use in the Barrio*. Lexington, MA: D.C. Heath.

Callan, John P. and Carroll D. Patterson. 1973. "Patterns of Drug Use Among Military Inductees." *American Journal of Psychiatry* 130, pp. 260–264.

Campbell, Richard S. and Jeffrey B. Freeland. 1974. "Patterns of Female Drug Use." *International Journal of the Addictions* 9, pp. 289–300.

Carey, James J. 1968. *The College Drug Scene*. Englewood Cliffs, NJ: Prentice-Hall.

Centers for Disease Control. 2000. "Tobacco Use Among Middle and High School Students—United States, 1999. *The Journal of the American Medical Association*, 283, p. 1134.

Chambers, Carl D., Walter Cuskey and Arthur D. Moffett. 1970. "Mexican American Opiate Addicts. In John C. Ball and Carl D. Chambers (eds.), *The Epidemiology of Opiate Addiction in the United States.* Springfield, IL: Charles C. Thomas.

Chein, Isidor, Donald L. Gerard, Robert S. Lee and Eva Rosenfeld. 1964. *The Road to H: Narcotics, Delinquency, and Social Policy.* New York: Basic Books.

Cockerham, William C., Morris A. Forslund and Rolland M. Raboin. 1976. "Drug Use Among White and American Indian High School Youth." *The International Journal of the Addictions* 11, pp. 209–220.

Conard, Scott, Patrick Hughes, DeWitt C. Baldwin, Karl E. Achenbach and David V. Sheehan. 1988. "Substance Use by Fourth-Year Students at 13 U.S. Medical Schools." *Journal of Medical Education* 63, pp. 747–758.

———. 1989. "Cocaine Use by Senior Medical Students." *American Journal of Psychiatry* 146, pp. 382–383.

Council on Mental Health. 1973. "The Sick Physician: Impairment by Psychiatric Disorders, Including Alcoholism and Drug Dependence." *Journal of the American Medical Association* 223, pp. 684–687.

Council on Scientific Affairs. 1996. "Alcoholism in the Elderly." *Journal of the American Medical Association* 275, pp. 797–801.

Crouch, Dennis J., Douglas O. Webb, Lynn V. Peterson, Paul F. Buller and Douglas E. Rollins. 1989. "A Critical Evaluation of the Utah Power and Light Company's Substance Abuse Management Program: Absenteeism, Accidents and Costs." Pp. 169–193 in Steven W. Gust and J. Michael Walsh (eds.), *Drugs in the Workplace: Research and Evaluation Data.* NIDA Research Monograph 91. Rockville, MD: National Institute on Drug Abuse.

Cuskey, Walter R., T. Premkumar and Lois Sigel. 1972. "Survey of Opiate Addiction Among Females in the United States Between 1850 and 1970." *Public Health Reviews* 1, pp. 6–39.

Cuskey, Walter R. and Richard B. Wathey. 1982. *Female Addiction.* Lexington, MA: D.C. Heath.

DeWitt, C. Baldwin Jr., Patrick H. Hughes, Scott E. Conard, Carla L. Storr and David V. Sheehan. 1991. "Substance Use Among Senior Medical Students: A Survey of 23 Medical Schools." *Journal of the American Medical Association* 265, pp. 2074–2078.

Dietrich, Joseph F. and Janette Smith. 1986. "The Nonmedical Use of Drugs Including Alcohol Among Police Personnel: A Critical Literature Review." *Journal of Police Science and Administration* 14, pp. 300–306.

Dimeff, Linda A., J. Kilmer, John S. Baer, and Alan G. Marlatt. 1995. "Binge Drinking in College" (letter). *Journal of the American Medical Association* 273, pp. 1903–1904.

Durkin, Keith F. and Gregory A. Clark. 2000. *Binge Drinking in a Sample of University Students: Prevalence, Consequences and Correlates.* Lake Charles, LA: McNeese Community Coalition to Prevent Underage Drinking.

Durkin, Keith F., Timothy W. Wolfe and Gregory Clark. 1999. "Social Bond Theory and Binge Drinking Among College Students: A Multivariate Analysis." *College Student Journal* 33, pp. 450–462.

Eisenberg, T. 1975. "Labor Management Relations and Psychological Stress." *Police Chief* 42, pp. 54–58.

Eldred, C.A. and M.M. Washington. 1976. "Interpersonal Relationships in Heroin Use by Men and Women and Their Role in Treatment Outcome." *International Journal of the Addictions* 11, pp. 117–130.

Engs, Ruth. 1982. "Drinking Patterns and Attitudes Toward Alcoholism of Australian Human-Service Students." *Journal of Studies on Alcohol* 43, pp. 517–531.

Faupel, Charles E. 1991. *Shooting Dope: Career Patterns of Hard Core Heroin Users.* Gainesville, FL: University of Florida Press.

Fell, Ronald D., Wayne C. Richard and William L. Wallace. 1980. "Psychological Job Stress and the Police Officer." *Journal of Police Science and Administration.* 8, pp. 139–144.

Finnegan, Loretta P. and Kevin O'Brien Fehr. 1980. "The Effects of Opiates, Sedative-Hypnotics, Amphetamines, Cannabis, and Other Psychoactive Drugs on the Fetus and Newborn." Pp. 653–723 in Oriana Josseau Kalant (ed.), *Alcohol and Drug Problems in Women.* Volume 5 in the series *Research Advances in Alcohol and Drug Problems.* New York: Plenum Press.

Fitzpatrick, Joseph P. 1990. "Drugs and Puerto Ricans in New York City." Pp. 103–126 in Ronald Glick and Joan Moore (eds.), *Drugs in Hispanic Communities.* New Brunswick, NJ: Rutgers University Press.

Freeland, Jeffrey B. and Richard S. Campbell. 1973. "The Social Context of First Marijuana Use." *The International Journal of the Addictions* 8, pp. 317–324.

Friedman, Jennifer and Marixsa Alicea. 2001. *Surviving Heroin: Interviews with Women in Methadone Clinics.* Gainesville, FL: University Presses of Florida.

Frieze, Irene Hanson and Patricia Cooney Schafer. 1984. "Alcohol Use and Marital Violence: Female and Male Differences in Reactions to Alcohol." Pp. 260–279 in Sharon C. Wilsnack and Linda J. Beckman (eds.), *Alcohol Problems in Women: Antecedents, Consequences and Intervention*. New York: Guilford Press.

Fullilove, R.E., Mindy Thompson Fullilove, B.P. Bowser, and S.A. Gross. 1990. "Risk of Sexually Transmitted Diseases Among Black Adolescent Crack Users in Oakland and San Francisco, California." *Journal of the American Medical Association* 263, pp. 851–855.

Fullilove, Mindy Thompson and Anne Lown. 1992. "Crack 'hos and Skeezers: Traumatic Experiences of Women Crack Users." *Journal of Sex Research* 29, pp. 275–287.

Glick, Ronald. 1990. "Survival Income and Status: Drug Dealing in the Chicago Puerto Rican Community." Pp. 77–101 in Ronald Glick and Joan Moore (eds.), *Drugs in Hispanic Communities*. New Brunswick, NJ: Rutgers University Press.

Goffman, Erving. 1963. *Stigma: Notes on the Management of Spoiled Identity*. Englewood Cliffs, NJ: Prentice-Hall.

Goldstein, G. S., E. R. Oetting, Ruth Edwards and Velma Garcia-Mason. 1979. "Drug Use Among Native American Young Adults." *The International Journal of the Addictions* 14, pp. 855–860.

Goldstein, Paul J. 1990. "Anabolic Steroids: An Ethnographic Approach." Pp. 74–96 in Geraline C. Lin and Lynda Erinoff (eds.), *Anabolic Steroid Abuse*. NIDA Research Monograph Series #102. Rockville, MD: National Institute on Drug Abuse.

Gomberg, Edith S. Lisansky. 1982. "Historical and Political Perspective: Women and Drug Use." *Journal of Social Issues* 38, pp. 9–23.

Gomberg, Edith S. Lisansky and Ted D. Nirenberg. 1993. "Antecedents and Consequences." Pp. 118–141 in Edith S. Lisansky Gomberg and Ted D. Nirenberg (eds.), *Women and Substance Abuse*. Norwood, NJ: Ablex Publishing.

Goode, Erich. 1999. *Drugs in American Society* (5th ed.). New York: McGraw-Hill.

Grant, Bridget F. and Deborah A. Dawson. 1996. "Alcohol and Drug Use, Abuse, and Dependence Among Welfare Recipients." *American Journal of Public Health* 86, pp. 1450–1454.

Hardesty, Monica and Timothy Black. 1999. "Mothering Through Addiction: A Survival Strategy Among Puerto Rican Addicts." *Qualitative Health Research* 9, pp. 602–619.

Heidenreich, C. Adrian. 1976. "Alcohol and Drug Use and Abuse Among Indian Americans: A Review of Issues and Sources." *Journal of Drug Issues* 6, pp. 256–272.

Herd, Denise. 1987. "Rethinking Black Drinking." *British Journal of Addiction* 82, pp. 219–223.

Hesselbrock, Michie N. and Victor M. Hesselbrock. 1993. "Depression and Antisocial Personality in Alcoholism: Gender Comparison." Pp. 142–161 in Edith S. Lisansky Gomberg and Ted D. Nirenberg (eds.), *Women and Substance Abuse*. Norwood, NJ: Ablex Publishing.

Higson, Ralph W. 1998. "College Age Drinking Problems." *Public Health Reports* 113, 1, pp. 52–54.

Hitz, D. 1973. "Drunken Sailors and Others: drinking Problems in Specific Occupations." *Quarterly Journal of Studies on Alcohol* 34, pp. 496–505.

Hoffman, John P., Angela Brittingham, and Cindy Larison. 1996. *Drug Use Among U.S. Workers: Prevalence and Trends by Occupation and Industry Categories*. Rockville, MD: Substance Abuse and Mental Health Services Administration.

Hser, Yih-Ing, M. Douglas Anglin and William McGlothlin. 1987. "Sex Differences in Addict Careers 1: Initiation of Use." *American Journal of Drug and Alcohol Abuse* 13, pp. 33–57.

Hughes, Patrick H., Nancy Brandenburg, DeWitt C. Waldwin Jr., Carla L. Storr, Dristine M. Williams, James C. Anthony and David V. Sheehan. 1992a. "Prevalence of Substance use Among U.S. Physicians. *Journal of the American Medical Association* 267, pp. 2333–2339.

Hughes, Patrick H., DeWitt C. Baldwin Jr., David V. Sheehan, Scott Conard and Carla Storr. 1992b. "Resident Physician Substance Use, by Specialty." *American Journal of Psychiatry* 149, pp. 1348–1354.

Hyde, Gordon L., and James Wolf. 1995. "Alcohol and Drug Use by Surgery Residents." *Journal of the American College of Surgeons* 181, pp. 1–5.

Inciardi, James A. 1979. "Heroin Use and Street Crime." *Crime and Delinquency* 25, pp. 335–346.

Inciardi, James A., Dorothy Lockwood and Anne E. Pottieger. 1993. *Women and Crack-Cocaine*. New York: Macmillan Publishing Co.

International Olympic Committee. 2000. *Olympic Movement Anti-Doping Code, Appendix A: Prohibited Classes of Substances and Prohibited Methods*, 1st April, 2000. Available online: *http://www.nodoping.org/pos_anti_dop_code_e.html* (Accessed June 27, 2000).

Johnston, Lloyd D., Patrick M. O'Malley, and Jerald G. Bachman. 2000. *The Monitoring the Future National Results on Adolescent Drug Use: Overview of Key Findings*. Rockville, MD: National Institute on Drug Abuse.

Jorquez, Jaime S. 1984. "Heroin Use in the Barrio: Solving the Problem of Relapse or Keeping the Tecato Gusano Asleep." *American Journal of Drug and Alcohol Abuse* 10, pp. 63–75.

Krahn, Dean D. 1993. "The Relationship of Eating Disorders and Substance Abuse." Pp. 286–313 in Edith S. Lisansky Gomberg and Ted D. Nirenberg (eds.), *Women and Substance Abuse*. Norwood, NJ: Ablex Publishing.

Kroes, William H. 1976. *Society's Victims—The Police: An Analysis of Job Stress in Policing*. Springfield, IL: Charles C. Thomas.

Kroes, William H., Margolis, B.L., and Hurrell, J.J. 1974. "Job Stress in Policemen." *Journal of Police Science and Administration* 2, pp. 145–155.

Laties, Victor G. and Bernard Weiss. 1981. "The Amphetamine Margin in Sports." *Federation Proceedings* 40, pp. 2689–2692.

Leonard, Wilbert Marcellus II. 1998. *A Sociological Perspective of Sport*. Boston: Allyn and Bacon.

Levy, Stephen J., and Kathleen M. Doyle. 1976. "Attitudes to Women in a Drug Treatment Program." *Journal of Drug Issues* 4, pp. 423–434.

Lex, Barbara W. 1993. "Women and Illicit Drugs: Marijuana, Heroin and Cocaine." Pp. 162–190 in Edith S. Lisansky Gomberg and Ted D. Nirenberg (eds.), *Women and Substance Abuse*. Norwood, NJ: Ablex Publishing.

Lipp, Martin R. and Samuel G. Benson. 1972. "Physician Use of Marijuana, Alcohol and Tobacco." *American Journal of Psychiatry*. 129, pp. 612–616.

Liska, Ken. 2000. *Drugs in the Human Body: With Implications for Society* (6th ed.). Upper Saddle River, NJ: Prentice-Hall.

Little, Ruth E., and Judith K. Wendt. 1993. "The Effects of Maternal Drinking in the Reproductive Period: An Epidemiologic Review." Pp. 191–213 in Edith S. Lisansky Gomberg and Ted D. Nirenberg (eds.), *Women and Substance Abuse*. Norwood, NJ: Ablex Publishing.

Lofland, John. 1969. *Deviance and Identity*. Englewood Cliffs, NJ: Prentice-Hall.

Lombardo, John A. 1990. "Anabolic-Androgenic Steroids." Pp. 60–73 in Geraline C. Lin and Lynda Erinoff (eds.), *Anabolic Steroid Abuse*. NIDA Research Monograph Series #102. Rockville, MD: National Institute on Drug Abuse.

Lund, Adrian K., David F. Preusser, Richard D. Blomberg and Allan F. Williams. 1989. "Drug Use by Tractor-Trailer Drivers." Pp. 47–67 in Steven W. Gust and J. Michael Walsh (eds.), *Drugs in the Workplace: Research and Evaluation Data*. NIDA Research Monograph 91. Rockville, MD: National Institute on Drug Abuse.

Maddux, James F., Sue K. Hoppe, and Raymond M. Costello. 1986. "Psychoactive Substance Use Among Medical Students." *American Journal of Psychiatry* 143, pp. 187–191.

Maher, Lisa. 1997. *Sexed Work: Gender, Race and Resistance in a Brooklyn Drug Market*. Oxford: Clarendon Press.

Maher, Lisa and Kathleen Daly. 1996. "Women in the Street-Level Drug Economy: Continuity or Change?" *Criminology* 34, 4, pp. 465–490.

Mandel, Jerry and Harvey W. Feldman. 1986. "The Social History of Teenage Drug Use." Pp. 19–42 in George Beschner and Alfred S. Friedman (eds.), *Teen Drug Use*. Lexington, MA: Lexington Books.

Marsh, Jeanne C. 1982. "Public Issues and Private Problems: Women and Drug Use." *Journal of Social Issues* 38, pp. 153–165.

McAuliffe, William E. 1984. "Nontherapeutic Opiate Addiction in Health Professionals: A New Form of Impairment." *American Journal of Drug and Alcohol Abuse* 10, pp. 1–22.

McAuliffe, William E., Mary Rohman, Paul Fishman, Rob Friedman, Henry Wechsler, Stephen H. Soboroff and David Toth. 1984. "Psychoactive Drug Use by Young and Future Physicians." *Journal of Health and Social Behavior*, 25, pp. 34–54.

McAuliffe, William E., Mary Rohman, Susan Santangelo, Barry Feldman, Elizabeth Magnuson, Arthur Sobol and Loel Weissman. 1986. "Psychoactive Drug Use Among Practicing Physicians and Medical Students." *The New England Journal of Medicine* 315, pp. 805–810.

Mechanick, Philip, James Mintz, John Gallagher, Gary Lapid, Richard Rubin and John Good. 1973. "Nonmedical Drug Use Among Medical Students." *Archives of General Psychiatry* 29, pp. 48–50.

Metsch, Lisa R., H. Virginia McCoy and Norman L. Weatherby. 1996. "Women and Crack." Pp. 71–88 in Dale Chitwood, James E. Rivers and James A. Inciardi (eds.), *The American Pipe Dream: Crack Cocaine and the Inner City*. Fort Worth: Harcourt Brace.

Midanik, Lorraine T., Theresa W. Tam, Thomas K. Greenfield and Raul Caetano. 1996. "Risk Functions for Alcohol-Related Problems in a 1988 U.S. National Sample." *Addiction* 91, pp. 1427–1437.

Modlin, H.C., and A. Montes. 1964. "Narcotics Addiction in Physicians." *American Journal of Psychiatry* 121, pp. 358–363.

Moise, Rebecca, Beth G. Reed and Virginia Ryan. 1982. "Issues in the Treatment of Heroin-Addicted Women: A Comparison of Men and Women Entering Two Types of Drug Abuse Programs." *International Journal of the Addictions* 17, pp. 109–139.

Moore, Joan. 1978. *Homeboys: Gangs, Drugs and Prison in the Barrios of Los Angeles.* Philadelphia, PA: Temple University Press.

———. 1990. "Mexican American Women Addicts: The Influence of Family Background." Pp. 127–153 in Ronald Glick and Joan Moore (eds.), *Drugs in Hispanic Communities.* New Brunswick, NJ: Rutgers University Press.

———. 1991. *Going Down to the Barrio: Homeboys and Homegirls in Change.* Philadelphia, PA: Temple University Press.

National Center on Addiction and Substance Abuse. 1998. "1998 CASA National Survey of Teens, Teachers and Principals." New York: Columbia University.

National Collegiate Athletic Association. 2000. "NCAA Banned Drug Classes, 2000–2001" Available online: *http://www.ncaa.org/sports_sciences/drugtesting/banned_list.html* (Accessed June 27, 2000).

Nellis, Muriel. 1980. *The Female Fix.* New York: Penguin Books.

Nurco, David N., Ira H. Cisin, and Mitchell B. Balter. 1981. "Addict Careers. II. The First Ten Years." *The International Journal of the Addictions* 16, pp. 1327–1356.

Oetting, E. R., Ruth Edwards, Goldstein, G. S. and Velma Garcia-Mason. 1980. "Drug Use Among Adolescents of Five Southwestern Native American Tribes." *The International Journal of the Addictions* 15, pp. 439–445.

Office of Applied Studies. 1998. *Prevalence of Substance Use Among Racial and Ethnic Subgroups in the United States, 1991–1993.* Rockville, MD: Substance Abuse and Mental Health Services Administration.

Osborne, Carl E. and Jacque J. Sokolov. 1989. "Drug Use Trends in a Nuclear Power Company: Cumulative Data From an Ongoing Testing Program." Pp. 69–80 in Steven W. Gust and J. Michael Walsh (eds.), *Drugs in the Workplace: Research and Evaluation Data.* NIDA Research Monograph 91. Rockville, MD: National Institute on Drug Abuse.

Page, J. Bryan. 1990. "Streetside Drug Use Among Cuban Drug Users in Miami." Pp. 167–191 in Ronald Glick and Joan Moore (eds.), *Drugs in Hispanic Communities.* New Brunswick, NJ: Rutgers University Press.

Pescor, Michael J. 1942. "Physician Drug Addicts." *Diseases of the Nervous System* 3, pp. 2–3.

Peterson, Ruth D. 1985. "Discriminatory Decision Making at the Legislative Level: An Analysis of the Comprehensive Drug Abuse Prevention and Control Act of 1970." *Law and Human Behavior* 9, pp. 243–269.

Pettiway, Leon E. 1997. *Workin' It: Women Living Through Drugs and Crime.* Philadelphia, PA: Temple University Press.

Poplar. Jimmie F. 1969. "Characteristics of Nurse Addicts." *American Journal of Nursing* 69, pp. 117–119.

Putnam, Douglas T. 1999. *Controversies of the Sports World.* Westport, CT: Greenwood Press.

Putnam, Peter L. and Everett H. Ellinwood Jr. 1966. "Narcotic Addiction Among Physicians: A Ten-Year Follow-Up." *American Journal of Psychiatry* 122, pp. 745–748.

Quayle, Dan. 1983. "American Productivity: the Devastating Effect of Alcoholism and Drug Abuse." *American Psychologist* (April), pp. 454–458.

Reid, Jeanne. 1998. *Under the Rug: Substance Abuse and the Mature Woman.* New York: Center on Addiction and Substance Abuse, Columbia University.

———. 1996. *Substance Abuse and the American Woman.* New York: The National Center on Addiction and Substance Abuse, Columbia University.

Robins, Lee N. 1974. *The Viet Nam Drug User Returns.* Special Action Office for Drug Abuse Prevention Monograph, Series A, Number 2. Washington, DC: U.S. Government Printing Office.

Rochford, Joseph, Igor Grant and Gregory LaVigne. 1977. "Medical Students and Drugs: Further Neuropsychological and Use Pattern Considerations." *The International Journal of the Addictions* 12, pp. 1057–1065.

Rosenbaum, Marsha. 1981a. *Women on Heroin.* New Brunswick, NJ: Rutgers University Press.

———. 1981b. "Sex Roles Among Deviants: The Woman Addict." *The International Journal of the Addictions* 16, pp. 859–877.

————. 1981c. "Women Addicts' Experience of the Heroin World: Risk, Chaos, and Inundation." *Urban Life* 10, pp. 65–91.

Rosett, Henry L. 1980. "The Effects of Alcohol on the Fetus and Offspring." Pp. 595–652 in Oriana Josseau Kalant (ed.), *Alcohol and Drug Problems in Women*. Volume 5 in the series *Research Advances in Alcohol and Drug Problems*. New York: Plenum Press.

Schuckit, Mark A. 1986. "Genetic and Clinical Implications of Alcoholism and Affective Disorder." *American Journal of Psychiatry* 143, pp. 140–147.

Schuckit, Mark A. and Maristela G. Monteiro. 1988. "Alcoholism, Anxiety and Depression." *British Journal of Addiction* 83, pp. 1373–1380.

Schwenck, Thomas L. 1997. "Psychoactive Drugs and Athletic Performance." *The Physician and Sportsmedicine* 25, pp. 32–46.

Siegel, MAJ Arthur, MC. 1973. "The Heroin Crisis Among U.S. Forces in Southeast Asia." *Journal of the American Medical Association*, 223, pp. 1258–1261.

Singer, Merrill, Freddie Valentin, Hans Baer and Zhongke Jia. 1992. "Why Does Juan Barcia Have a Drinking Problem? The Perspective of Critical Medical Anthropology." *Medical Anthropology* 14, pp. 77–108.

Smith, Stanley N. and Paul H. Blachly. 1966. "Amphetamine Usage by Medical Students." *Journal of Medical Education* 41, pp. 167–170.

Sterk, Claire E. 1999. *Fast Lives: Women Who Use Crack Cocaine*. Philadelphia, PA: Temple University Press.

Stout-Weigand, Nancy and Roger B. Trent. 1981. "Physician Drug Use: Availability or Occupational Stress?" *The International Journal of the Addictions* 16, pp. 317–330.

Substance Abuse and Mental Health Services Administration. 1999a. *National Household Survey on Drug Abuse Main Findings, 1997*. Rockville, MD: Substance Abuse and Mental Health Services Administration.

Substance Abuse and Mental Health Services Administration. 1999b. *1998 National Household Survey on Drug Abuse*. Washington, DC: Substance Abuse and Mental Health Services Administration.

Substance Abuse and Mental Health Services Administration. 2002. *National Household Survey on Drug Abuse Main Findings, 2000*. Rockville, MD: Substance Abuse and Mental Health Services Administration.

Taggart, Robert W. 1989. "Results of the Drug Testing Program at Southern Pacific Railroad." Pp. 97–108 in Steven W. Gust and J. Michael Walsh (eds.), *Drugs in the Workplace: Research and Evaluation Data*. NIDA Research Monograph 91. Rockville, MD: National Institute on Drug Abuse.

Territo, Leonard and Harold J. Vetter. 1981. "Stress and Police Personnel." *Journal of Police Science and Administration* 9, pp. 195–208.

Thomas, R. Buckland, Shula Avni Luber and Jackson A. Smith. 1977. "A Survey of Alcohol and Drug Use in Medical Students." *Diseases of the Nervous System* 38, pp. 41–43.

Thompson, Kevin M. and Richard W. Wilsnack. 1984. "Drinking and Drinking Problems Among Female Adolescents: Patterns and Influences." Pp. 37–65 in Sharon C. Wilsnack and Linda J. Beckman (eds.), *Alcohol Problems in Women: Antecedents, Consequences and Intervention*. New York: Guilford Press.

Trimble, Joseph E., Amado M. Padilla and Catherine S. Bell. 1987. *Drug Abuse Among Ethnic Minorities*. Rockville, MD: National Institute on Drug Abuse.

Valliant, George E., J.R. Brighton and C. McArthur. 1970. "Physicians Use of Mood Altering Drugs: A 20-Year Follow-up Report." *New England Journal of Medicine* 272, 7, pp. 365–370.

Van Raalte, R.C. 1979. "Alcohol as a Problem Among Officers." *The Police Chief* 44, pp. 38–40.

Violante, John M., James R. Marshall and Barbara Howe. 1985. "Stress, Coping and Alcohol Use: The Police Connection." *Journal of Police Science and Administration* 13, pp. 106–110.

Voy, Robert (with Kirk D. Deeter). 1991. *Drugs, Sport and Politics*. Champaign, IL: Leisure Press.

Wagner, Jon C. 1987. "Substance-Abuse Policies and Guidelines in Amateur and Professional Athletics." *American Journal of Hospital Pharmacy* 44, pp. 305–310.

Wagner, Marcia and Richard J. Brzeczek. 1983. "Alcoholism and Suicide: A Fatal Connection." *FBI Law Enforcement Bulletin* 52(8), pp. 8–15.

Wallot, Hubert and Jean Lambert. 1984. "Characteristics of Physician Addicts." *American Journal of Drug and Alcohol Abuse* 10, pp. 53–62.

Wambaugh, Joseph. 1975. *The Choirboys*. New York: Delacorte Press.

Watkins, Charles. 1970. "Use of Amphetamine by Medical Students." *Southern Medical Journal* 63, pp. 923–929.

Wechsler, Henry and S. Bryn Austin. 1998. "Binge Drinking: The Five/Four Measure." 1998. *Journal of Studies on Alcohol* 59, pp. 122–124.

Wechsler, Henry, Andrea E. Davenport, George W. Dowdall, Susan J. Grossman and Sophia I. Zanakos. 1996. "Binge Drinking, Tobacco, and Illicit Drug Use and Involvement in College Athletics." *Journal of American College Health* 44, pp. 1–6.

Wechsler, Henry, Andrea E. Davenport, George W. Dowdall, Barbara Moeykens and Sonia Castillo. 1994. "Health and Behavioral Consequences of Binge Drinking in College: A National Survey of Students at 140 Campuses." *Journal of the American Medical Association* 272, pp. 1672–1677.

Willcox, Sharon M., David U. Himmelstein and Steffie Woolhandler. 1994. "Inappropriate Drug Prescribing for the Community-Dwelling Elderly." *Journal of the American Medical Association* 272, pp. 292–296.

Wilsnack, Sharon C. 1984. "Drinking, Sexuality and Sexual Dysfunctions in Women." Pp. 189–227 in Sharon C. Wislnack and Linda J. Beckman, *Alcohol Problems in Women: Antecedents, Consequences, and Intervention.* New York: Guilford Press.

Wilsnack, Richard W., Albert D. Klassen and Sharon C. Wilsnack. 1986. "Retrospective Analysis of Lifetime Changes in Women's Drinking Behavior." *Advances in Alcohol and Substance Abuse* 5, pp. 9–28.

Winick, Charles. 1961. "Physician Narcotic Addicts." *Social Problems* 9, 174–186.

———. 1974. "Drug Dependence Among Nurses." Pp. 155–165 in Charles Winick (ed.), *Sociological Aspects of Drug Dependence.* Cleveland, OH: CRC Press.

Yesalis, Charles E., R.T. Herrick, William E. Buckley, K.E. Friedl, D. Brannon, and James E. Wright. 1988. "Self-Reported Use of Anabolic-Angrogenic Steroids by Elite Power Lifters." *Physiological Sports Medicine.* 16, pp. 91–100

Yesalis, Charles E., William A. Anderson, William E. Buckley and James E. Wright. 1990a. "Incidence of the Nonmedical Use of Anabolic-Androgenic Steroids." Pp. 97–112 in Geraline C. Lin and Lynda Erinoff (eds.), *Anabolic Steroid Abuse.* NIDA Research Monograph Series #102. Rockville, MD: National Institute on Drug Abuse.

Yesalis, Charles E., J.R. Vicary, Wiliam.E. Buckley, A.L. Streit, D.L. Katz and James E. Wright. 1990b. "Indications of Psychological Dependence Among Anabolic-Androgenic Steroid Abusers." Pp. 196–214 in Geraline C. Lin and Lynda Erinoff (eds.), *Anabolic Steroid Abuse.* NIDA Research Monograph Series #102. Rockville, MD: National Institute on Drug Abuse.

Chapter 8

Albertson, Timothy E., Robert W. Derlet and Brent E. Van Hoozen. 1999. "Methamphetamine and the Expanding Complications of Amphetamines." *The Western Journal of Medicine* 170, pp. 214–219.

Aligne, C. Andrew and Jeffrey J. Stoddard. 1997. "Tobacco and Children: An Economic Evaluation of the Medical Effects of Parental Smoking." *Archives of Pediatric and Adolescent Medicine* 151, pp. 648–653.

Anonymous. 2000a. "Drinking Could Reduce Alzheimer's Risk." *Alcoholism and Drug Abuse Weekly,* 12 (July 31), p. 8.

———. 2000b. "Moderate Drinking Prevents Bone Loss in Older Women." *Better Nutrition,* 62, 12 (December), p. 20.

Bolla, K.I., U.D. McCann and Ricaurte, G.A. 1998. "Memory Impairment in Abstinent MDMA ("Ecstasy") Users." *Neurology,* 51, pp. 1532–1537.

Bourgois, Phillippe, Mark Lettiere and James Quesada. 1997. "Social Misery and the Sanctions of Substance Abuse: Confronting HIV Risk Among Homeless Heroin Addicts in San Francisco." *Social Problems* 44, pp. 155–173.

Brady, Joanne P., Marc Posner, Cynthia Lang and Michael J. Rosati. *Risk and Reality: The Implications of Prenatal Exposure to Alcohol and Other Drugs.* Available online: *http://aspe.os.dhhs.gov/hsp/cyp/drugkids.htm* (Accessed August 21, 2000).

Brady, Kathleen T., Hugh Myrick and Robert Malcolm. 1999. "Sedative-Hypnotic and Anxiolytic Agents." Pp. 95–104 in Barbara S. McCrady and Elizabeth E. Epstein (eds.), *Addictions: A Comprehensive Guidebook.* New York: Oxford University Press.

Brecher, Edward M. 1972. *Licit and Illicit Drugs.* Boston: Little, Brown and Company.

Brown, Edwin W. 1997. "Why Suffer from Chronic Pain?" *Medical Update* 21, 2, pp. 1–2.

Brown, Josephine V., Roger Bakeman, Claire D. Coles, William R. Sexson and Alice S. Demi. 1998. "Maternal Drug Use During Pregnancy: Are Preterm and Full-Term Infants Affected Differently?" *Developmental Psychology,* 34, pp. 540–554.

California Medical Association Foundation. 1999. "California Initiative Attempts to Reassure Physicians Who Prescribe Opioids." *Alcoholism and Drug Abuse Weekly,* 11, 7 (February 15), p. 1.

Camargo, Carlos A. Jr., Meir J. Stampfer, Robert J. Glynn, J. Michael Gaziano, JoAnn E. Manson, Samuel Z. Goldhaber and Charles H. Hennekens. 1997. "Prospective Study of Moderate Alcohol Consumption and Risk of Peripheral Arterial Disease in U.S. Male Physicians." *Circulation* 95, pp. 577–580.

Centers for Disease Control and Prevention. 2000a. *HIV/AIDS Surveillance Report* 12, 1. Rockville, MD: Centers for Disease Control and Prevention.

———. 2000b. *Viral Hepatitis.* Available online: *http://www.cdc.gov/ncidod/diseases/hepatitis/index.htm* (Accessed February 8, 2001).

———. 1999. *HIV/AIDS Surveillance Supplemental Report.* 6, 1. Atlanta, GA Centers for Disease Control and Prevention.

Chasnoff, Ira J., William .J. Burns, Sidney H. Schnoll and Kayreen A. Burns. 1985. "Cocaine Use in Pregnancy." *New England Journal of Medicine* 313, pp. 666–669.

Chasnoff, Ira J., Carl E. Hunt, Ron Kletter, and David Kaplan. 1989. "Prenatal Cocaine Exposure is Associated with Respiratory Pattern Abnormalities." *American Journal of Diseases of Children* 143, pp. 583–587.

Darke, Shane, Wayne Hall, Don Weatherburn and Bronwyn Lind. 1998. "Fluctuations in Heroin Purity and the Incidence of Fatal Heroin Overdose." *Drug and Alcohol Dependence* 54, pp. 155–161.

Darke, Shane and Deborah Zador. 1996. "Fatal Heroin 'Overdose': A Review" *Addiction* 91, pp. 1765–1772.

Doblin, R. and M.A.R. Kleiman. 1991. "Marihuana as Anti-emetic Medicine: A Survey of Oncologists' Attitudes and Experiences." *Journal of Clinical Oncology.* 9, pp. 1275–1290.

Drug Enforcement Administration. 1999. *DEA Briefing Book.* Washington, D.C.: USGPO.

Dufour, Mary C., "What is Moderate Drinking?" *Alcohol Health and Research World,* 23, 1, pp. 5–14.

Expert Working Group of the European Association for Palliative Care. 1996. "Morphine in Cancer Pain: Modes of Administration." *British Medical Journal,* 312, pp. 823–826.

Faupel, Charles E. 1991. *Shooting Dope: Career Patterns of Hard-Core Heroin Users.* Gainesville, FL: University of Florida Press.

Fell, J.C. 1987. "Alcohol Involvement Rates in Fatal Crashes: A Focus on Young Drivers and Female Drivers." *Proceedings of the 31st Annual Conference of the American Association for Automotive Medicine,* pp. 23–42. Washington, DC: Center for Statistics and Analysis.

Goldstein, Paul. 1985. "The Drugs/violence Nexus: A Tripartite Conceptual Framework." *Journal of Drug Issues* (Fall): 493–506.

Goldstein, Paul, Henry H. Brownstein, Patrick J. Ryan and Patricia A. Bellucci. 1989. "Crack and Homicide in New York City, 1988: A Conceptually Based Event Analysis." *Contemporary Drug Problems* 16, pp. 651–687.

Goode, Erich. 1999. *Drugs in American Society* (5th ed.). New York: McGraw-Hill.

Grinspoon, Lester. 2000. "Wither Medical Marijuana?" *Contemporary Drug Problems* 27 (Spring), pp. 3–15.

Grinspoon, Lester and James B. Bakalar. 1997. *Marijuana: The Forbidden Medicine.* (Revised and expanded edition). New Haven: Yale University Press.

Grinspoon, Lester and James B. Bakalar. 1995. "Marihuana as Medicine: A Plea for Reconsideration." *Journal of the American Medical Association* 273, no. 23, pp. 1875–1876.

Grinspoon, Lester and James B. Bakalar. 1993. *Marijuana: The Forbidden Medicine.* New Haven: Yale University Press.

Guterman, Lila. 2000. "The Dope on Medical Marijuana." *Chronical of Higher Education,* Vol. 46, Issue 39 (June 2), p. A21.

Inciardi, James A., J. Ryan Page, Duane C. McBride, Dale D. Chitwood, Clyde B. McCoy and H. Virginia McCoy. 1995. "The Risk of Exposure to HIV-Contaminated Nedles and Syringes in Shooting Galleries." Pp. 277–283 in James A. Inciardi and Karen McElrath (eds.), *The American Drug Scene: An Anthology.* Los Angeles, CA: Roxbury Publishing Co.

Inciardi, James A., Dorothy Lockwood and Anne E. Pottieger. 1993. *Women and Crack-Cocaine.* New York: Macmillan Publishing Co.

Jackson, Rodney, Robert Scragg and Robert Beaglehole. 1991. "Alcohol Consumption and Risk of Coronary Heart Disease." *British Medical Journal* 303 (July 27), pp. 211–216.

Joranson, David E., Karen M. Ryan, Aaron M. Gilson and June L. Dahl. 2000. "Trends in Medical Use and Abuse of Opioid Analgesics." *The Journal of the American Medical Association* 283, 13 (April 5), pp. 1710–1714.

Joy, Janet E., Stanley J. Watson Jr. and John A. Benson Jr. 1999. *Marijuana and Medicine: Assessing the Science Base.* Washington, DC: National Academy Press.

Kaufman, Marc J., Johathan M. Levin, Marjorie H. Ross, Nicholas Lange, Stephanie L. Rose, Thellea J. Kukes, Jack H. Mendelson, Scott E. Lukas, Bruce M. Cohen and Perry F. Renshaw. 1998. "Cocaine-Induced Cerebral Vasoconstriction Detected in Humans with Magnetic Resonance Angiography." *Journal of the American Medical Association* 279, 5 (February 4), pp. 376–380.

Klatsky, Arthur L. 1999. "Moderate Drinking and Reduced Risk of Heart Disease." *Alcohol Health and Research World*, 23, 1, pp. 15–22.

Koch Crime Institute. 1999. "Manufacturing of Methamphetamine." Available Online: *http://www.kci.org/meth_info/making_meth.htm* (Accessed April 9, 2002).

Lieberson, Alan D. 1999. *Treatment of Pain and Suffering in the Terminally Ill.* Available online: *http://www.preciouslegacy.com/chap11.html* (Accessed March 14, 2001).

Liska, Ken. 2000. *Drugs and the Human Body: With Implications for Society* (6th ed.). Upper Saddle River, NJ: Prentice-Hall.

MacGregor, Scott N., Louis G. Keith, Ira J. Chasnoff, Marvin A. Rosner, Gay M. Chisum, Patricia Shaw and John P. Minogue. 1987. "Cocaine Use During Pregnancy: Adverse Prenatal Outcome." *American Journal of Obstetrics and Gynecology* 157, pp. 686–690.

Mathias, Robert. 1999. "'Ecstasy' Damages the Brain and Impairs Memory in Humans." *NIDA Notes*, 14. Rockville, MD: National Institute on Drug Abuse.

———. 1996. "Marijuana Impairs Driving Related Skills and Workplace Performance." *NIDA Notes*, 11, 1 (January/February).

McCann, U.D., M. Mertl, V. Eligulashvili and G.A. Ricaurte. 1999. "Cognitive Performance in (+/−) 3,4-methylenedioxymethamphetamine (MDMA, "ecstasy") users: a controlled study." *Psychopharmacology*, 143, pp. 417–425.

McCoy, H. Virginia, Christine Miles and James A. Inciardi. 1995. "Survival Sex: Inner-City Women and Crack-Cocaine." Pp. 172–177 in James A. Inciardi and Karen McElrath (eds.), *The American Drug Scene: An Anthology.* Los Angeles, CA: Roxbury Publishing Co.

Metsch, Lisa R., H. Virginia McCoy and Norman L. Weatherby. 1996. "Women and Crack." Pp. 71–88 in Dale D. Chitwood, James E. Rivers and James A. Inciardi (eds.), *The American Pipe Dream: Crack Cocaine and the Inner City.* Fort Worth, TX: Harcourt Brace College Publishers.

Moak, Darlene H. and Raymond F. Anton. 1999. "Alcohol." Pp. 75–94 in Barbara S. McCrady and Esizabeth E. Epstein (eds.), *Addictions: A Comprehensive Guidebook.* New York: Oxford University Press.

Muntwyler, Jorg, Charles H. Henekens, Julle E. Buring and J. Michael Gaziano. 1998. "Mortality and Lithe to Moderate Alcohol Consumption After Myocardial Infarction." *The Lancet* 352 (December 12), p. 1882.

National Institute on Drug Abuse. 1996a. "Facts About Methamphetamine." From NIDA Notes 11, 5 (December). Rockville, MD: National Institute on Drug Abuse. Available online: *http://165.112.78.61/NIDA_Notes/NNVol11N5/Tearoff.html* (Accessed January 15, 2001).

———. 1996b. "Facts about marijuana and marijuana abuse." NIDA Notes, 11, 2. Available online: *http://www.nida.nih.gov/NIDA_Notes/NNVol11N2/MarijuanaTearoff.html* (Accessed December 21, 1999).

National Institute on Drug Abuse. 1997. *Heroin Abuse and Addiction.* NIDA Research Report Series, NIH Publication # 00-4165. Rockville, MD: National Institute on Drug Abuse.

National Institute on Drug Abuse. 1998a. *Methamphetamine Abuse and Addiction.* NIDA Research Report Series, NIH Publication # 98-4210. Rockville, MD: National Institute on Drug Abuse.

National Institute on Drug Abuse. 1998b. *Nicotine Addiction.* NIDA Research Report Series, NIH Publication # 98-4342. Rockville, MD: National Institute on Drug Abuse.

National Institute on Drug Abuse. 1999a. *Cocaine Abuse and Addiction.* NIDA Research Report Series, NIH Publication # 99-4342. Rockville, MD: National Institute on Drug Abuse.

National Institute on Drug Abuse. 1999b. "Crack and Cocaine." From NIDA Infofax #13546. Rockville, MD: National Institute on Drug Abuse. Available online: *http://www.nida.nih.gov/Infofax/cocaine.html* (Accessed January 15, 2001).

Neuspiel, D.R., S.C. Hamel, E. Hochberg, J. Greene and D. Campbell. 1991. "Maternal Cocaine Use and Infant Behavior." *Neurotoxicology and Teratology* 13, pp. 229–233.

Office of Applied Studies. 2000a. *Drug Abuse Warning Network: Medical Examiner Data, 1998*. Rockville, MD: Department of Health and Human Services.

Office of Applied Studies. 2000b. *Year-End 1999 Emergency Department Data from the Drug Abuse Warning Network*. Rockville, MD: Department of Health and Human Services.

Pantilat, Steven Z. 1999. "Just Say Yes: The Use of Opioids for Managing Pain at the End of Life." *The Western Journal of Medicine*, 171, 4, pp. 257–259.

Pellegrino, Edmund D. 1998. "Emerging Ethical Issues in Palliative Care." *The Journal of the American Medical Association* 279, 19 (May 20), pp. 1521–1522.

Quill, Timothy E. 1995. "You Promised Me I Wouldn't Die Like This! A Bad Death as a Medical Emergency." *Archives of Internal Medicine*, 155, 12 (June 26), pp. 1250–1254.

Quill, Timothy E., Rebecca Dresser and Dan W. Brock. 1997. "The Rule of Double Effect—A Critique of Its Role in End-of-Life Decision Making." *The New England Journal of Medicine* 337, 24 (December 11), pp. 1768–1771.

Rankin, James G. 1994. "Biological Mechanisms at Moderate Levels of Alcohol Consumption That May Affect Coronary Heart Disease." *Contemporary Drug Problems* 21, pp. 45–57.

Ray, Oakley. 1978. *Drugs, Society and Human Behavior* (2nd ed.). St. Louis: The C.V. Mosby Company.

Rhodes, Tim. 1996. "Culture, Drugs and Unsafe Sex: Confusion About Causation." *Addiction* 91, pp. 753–758.

Richardson, Gale A. and Nancy L. Day. 1994. "Detrimental Effects of Prenatal Cocaine Exposure: Illusion or Reality?" *Journal of the American Academy of Child and Adolescent Psychiatry* 33, pp. 28–34.

Richardson, Gale A., Nancy L. Day and Peggy J. McGauhey. 1993. "The Impact of Prenatal Marijuana and Cocaine Use on the Infant and Child." *Clinical Obstetrics and Gynecology* 36, pp. 302–318.

Rickert, William S., Jack Robinson and Byron Rogers. 1982. "A Comparison of Tar, Carbon Monoxide and pH Levels in Smoke from Marihuana and Tobacco Cigarettes." *Canadian Journal of Public Health*, 73; pp. 386–391.

Rimm. Eric B., Edward L. Giovannucci, Walter C. Willett, Graham A. Colditz, Alberto Ascherio, Bernard Rosner and Meir J. Stampfer. "Prospective Study of Alcohol Consumption and Risk of Coronary Disease in Men." *The Lancet* 338 (August 24), pp. 464–468.

Rimm, Eric B., Paige Williams, Kerry Fosher, Michael Criqui, and Meir J. Stampfer. 1999. "Moderate Alcohol Intake and Lower Risk of Coronary Heart Disease: Meta-Analysis of Effects on Lipids and haemostatic Factors." *British Medical Journal* 319 (December 11), pp. 1523–1528.

Rosin, Hanna. 1997. "The Return of Pot." *The New Republic* 216, 7, pp. 18–24.

Sacco, R.L., M. Elkind, B. Boden-Albala, I.F. Lin, D.E. Kargman, W.A. Hauser, S. Shea and M.C. Paik. 1999. "The Protective Effect of Moderate Alcohol Consumption on Ischemic Stroke." *Journal of the American Medical Association* 281 (January 6), pp. 53–60.

Sager, Ryan H. 1999. "Grass Roots." *National Review* 51, 21 (November 8), pp. 30–31.

Schmitz, Richard, Chuck Thomas and Robert Kampia. 2001. *State-by-State Medical Marijuana Laws: How to Remove the Threat of Arrest:* Washington, DC: Marijuana Policy Project.

Schwartz, Richard H. and Michael J. Sheridan. 1997. "Marijuana to Prevent Nausea and Vomiting in Cancer Patients: A Survey of Clinical Oncologists." *Southern Medical Journal*, 90,2 (February), pp. 167–172.

Senior, Kathryn. 1999. "Moderate Drinking Reduces Coronary Heart Disease Risk in Diabetes." *The Lancet* 354 (July 24), p. 311.

Slade, John. 1999. "Nicotine." Pp. 162–170 in Barbara S. McCrady and Elizabeth E. Epstein (eds.), *Addictions: A Comprehensive Guidebook*. New York: Oxford University Press.

Stampfer, Meir J., Graham A. Colditz, Walter C. Willett, Frank E. Speizer and Charles H. Hennekens. 1988. "A Prospective Study of Moderate Alcohol Consumption and the Risk of Coronary Disease and Stroke in Women." *The New England Journal of Medicine* 319 (August 4), pp. 267–273.

Stephens, Robert S. 1999. "Cannabis and Hallucinogens." Pp. 121–140 in Barbara S. McCrady and Esizabeth E. Epstein (eds.), *Addictions: A Comprehensive Guidebook*. New York: Oxford University Press.

Stine, Susan M. and Thomas R. Kosten. 1999. "Opioids." Pp. 141–161 in Barbara S. McCrady and Esizabeth E. Epstein (eds.), *Addictions: A Comprehensive Guidebook*. New York: Oxford University Press.

Strickland, T.L., I. Mena, J. Villaneuva-Meyer, B.L. Miller, J. Cummings, C.M. Mehringer, P. Satz and H. Myers. 1993. "Cerebral Perfusion and Neuropsychological consequences of Chronic Cocaine Use." *Journal of Neuropsychiatry and Clinical Neurosciences* 5, pp. 419–427.

Substance Abuse and Mental Health Services Administration. 1999a. *Year End 1998 Emergency Department Data from the Drug Abuse Warning Network* (December). Washington, DC: Department of Health and Human Services.

Substance Abuse and Mental Health Services Administration. 1999b. *Drug Abuse Warning Network: Annual Medical Examiner Data, 1997* (December). Washington, DC: Department of Health and Human Services.

Thorns, Andrew and Nigel Sykes. 2000. "Opioid Use in Last Week of Life and Implications for End-of-Life Decision-Making." *The Lancet* 356, pp. 398–399.

Thun, Michael J., Richard Peto, Alan D. Lopez, Jane H. Monaco, S. Jane Henley, Clark W. Heath and Richard Doll. 1997. "Alcohol Consumption and Mortality Among Middle-Aged and Elderly U.S. Adults." *The New England Journal of Medicine* 337 (December 11), pp. 1705–1714.

United States Department of Transportation. n.d. *Traffic Safety Facts 1999: Alcohol.* Washington, DC: National Center for Statistics and Analysis.

U.S. Supreme Court. 1960. *Robinson v. California*, 370 U.S. 660.

_____. 2001. *United States v. Oakland Cannabis Buyers Cooperative et al.* #00151.

Voy, Robert (with Kirk D. Deeter). 1991. *Drugs, Sport and Politics.* Champaign, IL: Leisure Press.

Yuan, Jian-Min and Ronald K. Ross. 1997. "Follow up Study of Moderate Alcohol Intake and Mortality Among Middle Aged Men in Shanghai, China." *British Medical Journal*, 314 (January 4), pp. 18–23.

Zador, Deborah, Sandra Sunjic and Shane Darke. 1996. "Heroin-Related Deaths in New South Wales, 1992: Toxicological Findings and Circumstances." *Medical Journal of Australia* 164 (Feb 19), pp. 204–207.

Zador, Paul L., Sheila A. Krawchuk, and Ropbert B. Voas. 2000. "Alcohol-Related risk of Driver Fatalities and Driver Involvement in Fatal Crashes in Relation to Driver Age and Gender: An Update Using 1996 Data." *Journal of Studies on Alcohol*, 61, pp. 387–395.

Chapter 9

Adler, Patricia A. 1985. *Wheeling and Dealing: An Ethnography of an Upper-Level Drug Dealing and Smuggling Community.* New York: Columbia University Press.

Ames, Genevieve and Craig Janes. 1990. "Drinking, Social Networks, and the Workplace: Results of an Environmentally Focused Study." Pp. 95–111 in Paul M. Roman (ed.), *Alcohol Problem Intervention in the Workplace: Employee Assistance Programs and Strategic Alternatives.* New York: Quorum Books.

Backer, Thomas E. 1989. "Drug Abuse Services and EAP's: Preliminary Report on a National Study." Pp. 224–244 in Steven W. Gust and J. Michael Walsh (eds.), *Drugs in the Workplace: Research and Evaluation Data.* NIDA Research Monograph 91. Rockville, MD: National Institute on Drug Abuse.

Barnum, Howard. 1994. "The Economic Burden of the Global Trade in Tobacco." *Tobacco Control* 3, pp. 358–361.

Berger, Mark C. and J. Paul Leigh. 1988. "The Effect of Alcohol Use on Wages." *Applied Economics*, 20, pp. 1343–1351.

Blum, Terry C. and Paul M. Roman. 1995. *Cost-Effectiveness and Preventive Implications of Employee Assistance Programs.* Rockville, MD: Substance Abuse and Mental Health Services Administration.

Bostic v. MCLendon. 1986. 650 F. Supp. 1507 (N.D. Ga.).

Brady, John C. II. 1985. *Substance Abuse and Treatment in Silicon Valley—A Cost Analysis, July.* Milpatas, CA: Psychology Management Systems.

Brecher, Edward. 1972. *Licit and Illicit Drugs.* Boston: Little, Brown and Company.

Browne Miller, Angela. 1991. *Working Dazed: Why Drugs Pervade the Workplace and What Can Be Done About It.* New York: Plenum Press.

Bureau of International Narcotic Matters. 1990. *International Narcotics Control Strategy Report.* Washington, DC: Department of State.

Bureau of Justice Statistics. 1992. *Drugs, Crime, and the Justice System.* Washington, DC: U.S. Department of Justice.

Cahalan, Don. 1970. *Problem Drinkers: A National Survey.* San Francisco: Jossey-Bass.

Collins, D.L. and H.M. Lapsley. 1992. *The Social Costs of Drug Abuse in Australia in 1998 and 1992.* Report prepared for the Commonwealth Department of Human Services and Health, Canberra, Australia.

Cooper, M. Lynne, Marcia Russell and Michael R. Frone. 1990. "Work Stress and Alcohol Effects: A Test of Stress-Induced Drinking." *Journal of Health and Social Behavior* 31, pp. 260–276.

Drug Enforcement Administration. 2001. *Drug Trafficking in the United States.* Washington DC: USGPO.

_____. 1999. *DEA Briefing Book.* Washington DC: USGPO.

Faley, Robert H., Lawrence S. Kleiman and Patricia S. Wall. 1988. "Drug Testing in the Public and Private-Sector Workplaces: Technical and Legal Issues." *Journal of Business and Psychology* 3, pp. 154–186.

Fillmore, Kaye Middleton. 1990. "Occupational Drinking Subcultures: An Exploratory Epidemiological Study." Pp. 77–94 in Paul M. Roman (ed.), *Alcohol Problem Intervention in the Workplace: Employee Assistance Programs and Strategic Alternatives.* New York: Quorum Books.

Flynn, Stephen. 1997. "Worldwide Drug Scourge: The Expanding Trade in Illicit Drugs." Pp. 147–157 in Larry K. Gaines and Peter B. Kraska (eds.), *Drugs, Crime and Justice: Contemporary Perspectives.* Prospect Heights, IL: Waveland Press. (Originally "Worldwide Drug Scourge: The Expanding Trade in Illicit Drugs." *The Brookings Review* 11,1, pp. 6–11 (1993).

General Accounting Office. 1997. *Drug Control: Song-Standing Problems Hinder U.S. International Efforts.* Washington, DC: U.S. Government Printing Office.

Gill, Andrew M. and Robert J. Michaels. 1992. "Does Drug Use Lower Wages?" *Industrial and Labor Relations Review* 45, pp. 419–434.

Gleason, Philip M., Jonathan R. Veum and Michael R. Pergamit. 1991. "Drug and Alcohol Use at Work: A Survey of Young Workers." *Monthly Labor Review* (August), pp. 3–7.

Goldstein, Paul J., Douglas S. Lipton, Edward Preble, Ira Sobel, Tom Miller, William Abbott, William Paige and Franklin Soto. 1984. "The Marketing of Street Heroin in New York City." *Journal of Drug Issues* 14, pp. 553–566.

Goode, Erich. 1999. *Drugs in American Society* (5th ed.). New York: McGraw-Hill College.

Grant, Bridget F. and Deborah A. Dawson. 1996. "Alcohol and Drug Use, Abuse, and Dependence Among Welfare Recipients." *American Journal of Public Health* 86, pp. 1450–1454.

Harris, Michael M. and Laura L. Heft. 1992. "Alcohol and Drug Use in the Workplace: Issues, Controversies, and Directions for Future Research." *Journal of Management* 18, pp. 239–266.

Hartwell, Tyler D. 1996. "Aiding Troubled Employees: Prevalence, Cost, and Characteristics of Employee Assistance Programs in the United States." *American Journal of Public Health* 86, 6, pp. 804–808.

Hartwell, Tyler D., Paul D. Steele, Michael T. French and Nathaniel F. Rodman. 1996. "Prevalence of Drug Testing in the Workplace." *Monthly Labor Review* 119 (November), pp. 35–42.

Harwood, Henrick, M. Thomson and T. Nesmith. 1994. *Healthcare Reform and Substance Abuse Treatment: The Cost of Financing Under Alternative Approaches.* Fairfax, VA: Lewin-VHI.

Harwood, Henrick, Douglas Fountain and Gina Livermore. 1998. *The Economic Costs of Alcohol and Drug Abuse in the United States—1992.* Washington, DC: National Institute on Drug Abuse.

Hayghe, Howard V., 1991. "Anti-Drug Programs in the Workplace: Are They Here to Stay?" *Monthly Labor Review* 114 (April), pp. 26–29.

Heien, Dale M. and David J. Pittman. 1989. "The Economic Costs of Alcohol Abuse: An Assessment of Current Methods and Estimates. *Journal of Studies on Alcohol* 50, pp. 567–579.

Hodgson, Thomas A. and Mark R. Meiners. 1982. "Cost-of-Illness Methodology: A Guide to Current Practices and Procedures. *Milbank Memorial Fund Quarterly* 60, pp. 429–462.

Horgan, Constance. 2001. *Substance Abuse: the Nation's Number One Health Problem.* Waltham, MA: The Schneider Institute for Health Policy.

Hellinger, Fred J. 1992. "Forecasts of the Costs of Medical Care for Persons with HIV: 1992–1995. *Inquiry* 29, p. 356.

Hellinger, Fred J. and John A. Fleishman. 2000. "The National Cost of Treating HIV Disease." *Journal of Acquired Immune Deficiency Syndromes,* Volume 24, pp. 182–188.

Hollinger, Richard C. 1988. "Working Under the Influence (WUI): Correlates of Employees' Use of Alcohol and Other Drugs." *Journal of Applied Behavioral Science* 24, pp. 439–454.

Inciardi, James A. 1992. *The War on Drugs II.* Mountain View, CA: Mayfield Publishing Co.

Kaestner, Robert. 1991. "The Effects of Illicit Drug Use on the Wages of Young Adults." *Journal of Labor Economics* 8, pp. 318–412.

———.1994a. "New Estimates of the Effect of Marijuana and cocaine Use on Wages." *Industrial and Labor Relations Review* 47, pp. 454–470.

———. 1994b. "The Effect of Illicit Drug Use on the Labor Supply of Young Adults." *The Journal of Human Resources* 29, pp. 126–155.

Kandel, Denise B. and Mark Davies. 1990. "Labor Force Experiences of a National Sample of Young Adult Men: The Role of Drug Involvement." *Youth and Society* 21, pp. 411–445.

Keh, Douglas I. 1996. *Drug Money in a Changing World: Economic Reform And Criminal Finance.* UNDCP Technical Series #4. Vienna: UN Office for Drug Control and Crime Prevention.

Legal Action Center. 1989. "The Drug-Free Workplace Act: Background Materials." New York: Legal Action Center.

Leistikow, Bruce N., Daniel C. Martin and Christina E. Milano. 2000. "Fire Injuries, Disasters, and Costs from Cigarettes and Cigarette Lights: A Global Overview." *Preventive Medicine* 31, pp. 91–99.

Lightwood, James, David Collins, helen Lapsley and Thomas E. Novotny. 2000. "Estimating the Costs of Tobacco Use." Pp. 63–103 in Jha Prabhat and Frank Chaloupka (eds.), *Tobacco Control in Developing Countries*. Oxford, England: Oxford University Press.

Lightwood, James M., Ciaran S. Phibbs and Stanton A. Glantz. 1999. "Short-Term Health and Economic Benefits of Smoking Cessation: Low Birth Weight." *Pediatrics* 104, pp. 1312–1320.

Lund, Adrian K., David F. Preusser, Richard D. Blomberg and Allan F. Williams. 1988. "Drug Use by Tractor-Trailer Drivers. *Journal of Forensic Sciences* 33, pp. 648–661.

Marks, Robert E. 1992. "The Costs of Australian Drug Policy." *Journal of Drug Issues* 22, pp. 535–547.

Martin, Jack K. and Paul M. Roman. 1996a. "Job Stress, Drinking Networks, and Social Support at Work: A Comprehensive Model of Employees' Problem Drinking Behaviors." *Sociological Quarterly* 37, pp. 579–599.

_____. 1996b. "Job Satisfaction, Job Reward Characteristics, and Employees' Problem Drinking Behaviors." *Work and Occupations* 23, pp. 4–25.

McCaffrey, Barry. 1998. "Illegal Drugs: A common Threat to the Global Community. Available online: *http://www.whitehousedrugpolicy.gov/news/commentary/unchron.html* (Accessed July 27, 2000).

McBride, Robert. 1983. "Business as Usual: Heroin Distribution in the United States." *Journal of Drug Issues,* 13, pp. 147–166.

Mensch, Barbara S. and Denise B. Kandel. 1988. "Do Job Conditions Influence the Use of Drugs?" *Journal of Health and Social Behavior* 29, pp. 169–184.

Miller, Ted R., Mark A. Cohen and Shelli B. Rossman. 1993. "Victim Costs of Violent Crime and Resulting Injuries." *Health Affairs* 12, pp. 186–197.

Mullahy, John and Jody Sindelar. 1989. "Life-Cycle Effects of Alcoholism on Education, Earnings, and Occupation. *Inquiry* 26, pp. 272–282.

_____. 1991. "Gender Differences in Labor Market Effects of Alcoholism." *American Economic Review* 81, pp. 161–165.

_____. 1993. "Alcoholism, Work, and Income. *Journal of Labor Economics* 11, pp. 494–520.

National Narcotics Intelligence Consumers Committee. 1998. *The NNIC Report 1997.* DEA-98036. Washington DC: Drug Enforcement Administration.

Office of National Drug Control Policy. 2001. *National Drug Control Strategy: 2001 Annual Report.* ONDCP.

Pearlin, Leonard I. and Clarice W. Radabaugh. 1976. "Economic Strains and the Coping Function of Alcohol." *American Journal of Sociology* 82, pp. 652–663.

Preble, Edward and John J. Casey. 1969. "Taking Care of Business—the Heroin User's Life on the Street." *International Journal of the Addictions* 4, pp. 1–24.

Register, Charles A. and Donald R. Williams. 1992. "Labor Market Effects of Marijuana and Cocaine Use Among Young Men." *Industrial and Labor Relations Review* 45, pp. 435–448.

Rhodes, William, Mary Lane, Patrick Johnston, and Lynne Hozik. 2000. *What America's Users Spend on Illegal Drugs 1988–1998.* Office of National Drug Control Policy. Cambridge MA: ABT Associates.

Roman, Paul M. 1978. "Possible Effects of Using Alcohol to Control Distress: A Reanalysis of Pearlin and Radabaugh's Data." *American Journal of Sociology* 83, pp. 987–991.

SAMHSA. 1991. *How Drug Abuse Takes Profit Out of Business. How Drug Treatment Helps Put It Back.* U.S. Department of Health and Human Services (PHD574).

_____. 1999a. *An Analysis of Worker Drug Use and Workplace Policies and Programs, 1997.* U.S. Department of Health and Human Services (PHD627).

_____. 1999b. *Annual Survey of Federal Agency Drug Free Workplace, 1997.* Rockville, MD.: U.S. Department of Health and Human Services.

_____. 2001. *Drug Abuse and Workforce Demographics.* Rockville, MD: U.S. Department of Health and Human Services.

Scanlon, Walter F. 1991. *Alcoholism and Drug Abuse in the Workplace: Managing Care and Costs Through Employee Assistance Programs* (2nd ed.). New York: Praeger Publishing.

Scitovsky, Anne A. and Dorothy P. Rice. 1987. "Estimates of the direct and Indirect Costs of Acquired Immunodeficiency Syndrome in the United States, 1985, 1986, 1991. *Public Health Reports* 102(1), p. 5.

Seeman, Melvin and Carolyn S. Anderson. 1983. "Alienation and Alcohol: The Role of Work, Mastery, and Community in Drinking Behavior." *American Sociological Review* 48, pp. 60–77.

Seeman, Melvin, Alice Z. Seeman and Art Budros. 1988. "Powerlessness, Work, and Community: A Longitudinal Study of Alienation and Alcohol Use." *Journal of Health and Social Behavior* 29, pp. 185–198.

Skinner v. *Railway Labor Executive Association*. 1989. 109 S. Ct. 1402.

Steffy, Brian D. and D.R. Lake. 1991. "Workplace and Personal Stresses Antecedent to Employees' Alcohol Use." *Journal of Social Behavior and Personality*, 6, pp. 115–126.

United Nations. 2000. *World Drug Report*.

———. 1997. *World Drug Report*.

U.S. House of Representatives. 1988. *Fact Sheet: The Human Costs of Drug Trafficking and Abuse*. Select Committee on Narcotics Abuse and Control (August). Washington, DC: U.S. Government Printing Office.

Warner, Kenneth E., thomas A. Hodgson and Caitlin E. Carroll. 1999. "Medical costs of Smoking in the United States: Estimates, Their Validity, and Their Implications." *Tobacco Control* 8, pp. 290–300.

Zhang, Zhiwei, Lynn X. Huang, and Angela M. Brittingham. 1999. *Worker Drug Use and Workplace Policies and Programs: Results from the 1994 and 1997 National Household Survey on Drug Abuse*. Substance Abuse and Mental Health Services Administration, Analytic Series A-11. Rockville, MD: Substance Abuse and Mental Health Services Administration.

Chapter 10

Anglin, M. Douglas and Yih-Ing Hser. 1987. "Addicted Women and Crime." *Criminology* 25,2, pp. 359–397.

Anglin, M. Douglas, and Brian Perrochet. 1998. "Drug Use and Crime: A Historical Review of Research Conducted by the UCLA Drug Abuse Research Center." *Substance Use and Misuse* 33,9, pp. 1871–1914.

Anglin, M. Douglas and George Speckart. 1986. "Narcotics Use, Property Crime, and Dealing: Structural Dynamics across the Addiction Career." *Journal of Quantitative Criminology*. 2, pp. 355–375.

———. 1988. "Narcotics Use and Crime: A Multisample, Multimethod Analysis." *Criminology* 26,2, pp. 197–233.

Anslinger, Harry J. and William F. Tompkins. 1953. *The Traffic in Narcotics*. New York: Funk and Wagnalls.

Anslinger, Harry J. and Courtney Ryley Cooper. 1937. "Marijuana: Assassin of Youth." *American Magazine* 124 (July), pp. 19–20, 150–153.

Arrestee Drug Abuse Monitoring Program. 2000. *1999 Annual Report on Drug Use Among Adult and Juvenile Arrestees*. Washington, DC: National Institute of Justice.

Austin, Gregory A., and Dan J. Lettieri. 1976. *Drugs and Crime: The Relationship of Drug Use and Concomitant Criminal Behavior*. National Institute on Drug Abuse, Research Issues #17. Rockville, MD: National Institute on Drug Abuse.

Ball, John C., Lawrence Rosen, John A. Flueck, and David N. Nurco. 1981. "The Criminality of Heroin Addicts: When Addicted and When Off Opiates." Pp. 39–65 in James A. Inciardi (ed.) *The Drugs-Crime Connection*. Beverly Hills, CA: Sage Publications.

———. 1982. "Lifetime criminality of heroin addicts in the United States." *Journal of Drug Issues* 3, pp. 225–239.

Ball, John C., John W. Shaffer, and David N. Nurco. 1983. "The Day-to-Day Criminality of Heroin Addicts in Baltimore: A Study in the Continuity of Offense Rates." *Drug and Alcohol Dependence* 12,1, pp. 119–142.

Biernacki, Patrick. 1979. "Junkie Work, 'Hustles' and Social Status among Heroin Addicts." *Journal of Drug Issues* 9, pp. 535–551.

Brecher, Edward. 1972. *Licit and Illicit Drugs*. Boston: Little-Brown.

Chaiken, Jan M. and Marcia R. Chaiken. 1982. *Varieties of Criminal Behavior*. Santa Monica, CA: Rand.

———. 1990. "Drugs and Predatory Crime." Pp. 203–239 in Michael Tonry and James Q. Wilson (eds.), *Drugs and Crime*. Chicago: University of Chicago Press.

Chaiken, Marcia R. and Jan M. Chaiken. 1985. "Who Gets Caught Doing Crime?" Discussion Paper. Washington, D.C.: Bureau of Justice Statistics.

Cicero, Theodore J. 1983. "Behavioral Significance of Drug-Induced Alterations of Reproductive Endocrinology in the Male." Pp. 203–226 in E. Gottheil, K.A. Druley, T.E. Skoloda, and H.M Waxman (eds.), *Alcohol, Drug Abuse and Aggression*. Springfield, IL: Charles C. Thomas.

Clayton, Richard. 1981. "Federal Drugs-Crime Research: Setting the Agenda." Pp. 17–38 in James A. Inciardi (ed.), *The Drugs-Crime Connection*. Beverly Hills, CA: Sage Publications.

Collins, James J. Jr. 1983. "Alcohol Use and Expressive Interpersonal Violence: A Proposed Explanatory Model." Pp. 5–25 in E. Gottheil, K.A. Druley, T.E. Skoloda, and H.M Waxman (eds.), *Alcohol, Drug Abuse and Aggression*. Springfield, IL: Charles C. Thomas.

Collins, James J., Robert L. Hubbard, and J. Valley Rachal. 1985. "Expensive Drug Use and Illegal Income: A Test of Explanatory Hypotheses." *Criminology* 23, pp. 743–764.

Corti, Count Egon Ceasar. 1931. *A History of Smoking*. London: George C. Harrap and Company.

Donovan, J.E., and R. Jessor. 1985. "Structure of Problem Behavior in Adolescence and Young Adulthood." *Journal of Consulting and Clinical Psychology* 53, pp. 890–904.

Donovan, J.E., R. Jessor, and F.M. Costa. 1988. "Syndrome of Problem Behavior in Preadolescence." *Journal of Consulting and Clinical Psychology* 56, pp. 762–765.

Elliott, Delbert S., David Huizinga and Scott Menard. 1989. *Multiple Problem Youth: Delinquency, Substance Use and Mental Health Problems*. New York: Springer-Verlag.

Epstein, Edward Jay. 1977. *Agency of Fear: Opiates and Political Power in America*. New York: G.P. Putnam's Sons.

Fagan, Jeffrey. 1990. "Intoxication and Aggression." Pp. 241–320 in Michael Tonry and James Q. Wilson (eds.), *Drugs and Crime*. Chicago: The University of Chicago Press.

Farrington, David P. 1995. "The Development of Offending and Antisocial Behavior from Childhood: Key Findings from the Cambridge Study in Delinquent Development." *Journal of Child Psychology and Psychiatry* 360(6), pp. 929–964.

Faupel, Charles E. 1986. "Heroin Use, Street Crime, and the 'Main Hustle:' Implications for the Validity of Official Crime Data." *Deviant Behavior* 7, pp. 31–45.

———. 1987a. "Heroin Use and Criminal Careers." *Qualitative Sociology* 10,2 (Summer), pp. 115–131.

———. 1987b. "Drug Availability, Life Structure and Situational Ethics of Heroin Addicts." *Urban Life* 15,3(January), pp. 395–419.

———. 1991. *Shooting Dope: Career Patterns of Hard-Core Heroin Users*. Gainesville, FL: University of Florida Press.

Fishbein, Diana H. and Susan E. Pease. 1990. "Neurological Links Between Substance Abuse and Crime." Pp. 218–243 in Lee Ellis and Harry Hoffman (eds.), *Crime in Social, Biological and Moral Contexts*. New York: Praeger.

Fossier, A.E. 1931. "The Marijuana Menace." New Orleans Medical Surgical Journal 84.

Gandossy, Robert P., Jay R. Williams, Jo Cohen and Henrick J. Harwood. 1980. *Drugs and Crime: A Survey and Analysis of the Literature*. Washington, D.C.: National Institute of Justice.

Goldstein, Paul J. 1979. *Prostitution and Drugs*. Lexington, MA: Lexington Books.

———. 1985. "The Drugs/Violence Nexus: A Tripartite Conceptual Framework." *Journal of Drug Issues* (Fall), pp. 493–506.

———. 1997. "The Relationship between Drugs and Violence in the United States of America." *World Drug Report: United Nations International Drug Control Program*. Oxford: Oxford University Press.

Goode, Erich. 1972. "Excerpts from Marijuana Use and Crime." Pp. 447–453 in National Commission of Marijuana and Drug Abuse, *Marijuana: A Signal of Misunderstanding*. Appendix, Vol. 1. Washington, D.C.: U.S. Government Printing Office.

Gottfredson, M.R., and T. Hirschi. 1990. *A General Theory of Crime*. Stanford, CA: Stanford University Press.

Gould, Leroy G., Andrew L. Walker, Lansing E. Crane, and Charles W. Lidz. 1974. *Connections: Notes from the Heroin World*. New Haven, CT: Yale University Press.

Greenberg, Stephanie and Freda Adler. 1974. "Crime and Addiction: An Empirical Analysis of the Literature, 1920–1973." *Contemporary Drug Problems* 3, pp. 221–270.

Grinspoon, Lester. 1971. *Marijuana Reconsidered*. Cambridge, MA: Harvard University Press.

Hanlon, Thomas E., David N. Nurco, Timothy W. Kinlock and Karen R. Duszynski. 1990. "Trends in Criminal Activity and Drug Use Over An Addiction Career." *Journal of Drug Issues* 16, pp. 223–238.

Hanson, Bill, George Beschner, James W. Walters, and Elliot Bovelle. 1985. *Life With Heroin: Voices from the Inner City*. Lexington, MA: Lexington Books.

Huizinga, David, and Cynthia Jakob-Chien. 1998. "The Contemporaneous Co-Occurrence of Serious and Violent Juvenile Offending and Other Problem Behaviors. Pp. 47–67 in *Serious and Violent Juvenile Offenders: Risk Factors and Successful Interventions*, edited by R. Loeber and D. Farrington. Thousand Oaks, CA: Sage.

Hunt, Dana. 1990. "Drugs and Consensual Crimes: Drug Dealing and Prostitution." Pp. 159–202 in Michael Tonry and James Q. Wilson (eds.) *Drugs and Crime*. Chicago: University of Chicago Press.

Inciardi, James A. 1979. "Heroin Use and Street Crime." *Crime and Delinquency* 25 (July), pp. 335–346.
_____. 1981. "Introduction." Pp 7–16 in James A. Inciardi (ed.), *The Drugs-Crime Connection*. Beverly Hills, CA: Sage Publications.

Inciardi, James A., and Anne E. Pottieger. 1994. "Crack-Cocaine Use and Street Crime." *Journal of Drug Issues* 24, pp. 273–292.

Jessor, Richard and Shirley Jessor. 1977. *Problem Behavior and Psychosocial Development—A Longitudinal Study of Youth*. New York: Academic Press.

Johnson, Bruce D., Paul J. Goldstein, Edward Preble, James Schmeidler, Douglas S. Liptom, Barry Spunt and Thomas Miller. 1985. *Taking Care of Business: The Economics of Crime by Heroin Abusers*. Lexington, MA: Lexington Books.

Joint Committee on New York Drug Law Evaluation. 1978. *The Nation's Toughest Drug Law: Evaluating the New York Experience*. Washington, D.C.: United States Department of Justice.

Kramer, Mark S. 1983. "Pharmacotherapy for Violent Behavior." In E. Gottheil, K.A. Druley, T.E. Skoloda, and H.M Waxman (eds.), *Alcohol, Drug Abuse and Aggression*. Springfield, IL: Charles C. Thomas.

Langevin, R., J. Bain, G. Wortzman, S. Hucker, R. Dickey and P. Wright. 1988. "Sexual Sadism: Brain, Blood and Behavior." *Annals of the New York Academy of Sciences*. 528, pp. L163–171.

Lindesmith, Alfred R. 1940. "'Dope Fiend' Mythology." *Journal of Criminal Law and Criminology* 31 (July/August), pp. 199–208.

Maccoby, E.E. and J.N. Jacklin. 1974. *The Psychology of Sex Differences*. Palo Alto, CA: Stanford University Press.

Mayfield, Demmie. 1983. "Substance Abuse and Aggression: A Psychopharmacological Perspective." Pp. 139–149 in E. Gottheil, K.A. Druley, T.E. Skoloda, and H.M Waxman (eds.), *Alcohol, Drug Abuse and Aggression*. Springfield, IL: Charles C. Thomas.

McCoy, H. Virginia, James A. Inciardi, Lisa R. Metsch, Anne E Pottieger and Christine A. Saum. 1995. "Women, Crack, and Crime: Gender Comparisons of Criminal Activity Among Crack Cocaine Users." *Contemporary Drug Problems* 22, pp. 435–451.

Mendelson, Jack H. and Nancy K. Mello. 1974. "Alcohol, Aggression and Androgens." In S.H. Frazier (ed.), *Aggression*. Baltimore: Williams & Wilkins.

Moffitt, Terrie E. 1993. "Adolescence-Limited and Life-Course-Persistent Antisocial Behavior: A Developmental Taxonomy." *Psychological Review* 100(4), pp. 674–701.
_____. 1997. "Adolescence-Limited and Life-Course-Persistent Offending: A Pair of Complementary Theories. Pp. 11–54 in *Developmental Theories of Crime and Delinquency*, edited by T.P. Thornberry. New Brunswick, NJ: Transaction Press.

Moyer, Kenneth E. 1976. *The Psychobiology of Aggression*. New York: Harper and Row.

Mumola, Christopher J. 1999. *Substance Abuse and Treatment, State and Federal Prisoners, 1997*. Washington, DC: Bureau of Justice Statistics.

Nurco, David N., Thomas E. Hanlon, Timothy W. Kinlock, and Karen R. Duszynski. 1988. "Differential Criminal Patterns of Narcotic Addicts over an Addiction Career." *Criminology* 26,3 (August), pp. 407–423.

Office of Applied Statistics. 1999. *National Household Survey on Drug Abuse, 1997: Main Findings*. Rockville, MD: Substance Abuse and Mental Health Services Administration.

Osgood, D.W., L.D. Johnston, P.M. O'Malley, and J.G. Bachman. 1988. "The Generality of Deviance in Late Adolescence and Early Adulthood." *American Sociological Review* 53, pp. 81–93.

Pernanon, K. 1976. "Alcohol and Crimes of Violence." In B. Kissin and H. Begleiter (eds.), *The Biology of Alcoholism: Social Aspects of Alcoholism* (vol. 4). New York: Plenum.
_____. 1981. "Theoretical Aspects of the Relationship Between Alcohol Use and Crime." In James J. Collins Jr. (ed.), *Drinking and Crime: Perspectives on the Relationship between Alcohol Consumption and Criminal Behavior*. New York: Guilford.

Preble, Edward, and John J. Casey Jr. 1969. "Taking Care of Business—the Heroin User's Life on the Street." *The International Journal of the Addictions* 4,1 (March), pp. 1–24.

Reinarman, C. and B.C. Critchlow-Leigh. 1987. "Culture, Cognition and Disinhibition: Notes on Sexuality and Alcohol in the Age of AIDS." *Contemporary Drug Problems* 14, pp. 435–460.

Research Triangle Institute. 1976. *Drug Use and Crime: Report of the Panel on Drug Use and Criminal Behavior*. Research Triangle Park, NC: Research Triangle Institute.

Rettig, Richard P., Manual J. Torres and Gerald R. Garrett. 1977. *Manny: A Criminal-Addict's Story*. Boston: Houghton Mifflin Company.

Rosenbaum, Marsha. 1981. *Women on Heroin*. New Brunswick, NJ: Rutgers University Press.

Sackman, Bertram, M. Maxine Sackman, and G.G. DeAngelis. 1978. "Heroin Addiction as an Occupation: Traditional Addicts and Heroin Addicted Poly-drug Users." *International Journal of the Addictions* 13, pp. 427–441.

Schuckitt, M.A. 1988. "Weight Lifter's Folly: The Abuse of Anabolic Steroids." *Drug Abuse and Alcoholism Newsletter* 17, pp. 8.

Shaw, Elton. 1909. *The Curse of Drink or Stories of Hell's Commerce.* (Privately published by Elton Shaw).

Silver, G. and M. Aldrich. 1979. *The Dope Chronicles: 1850–1950.* New York: Harper and Row.

Smith, R.B. and Richard C. Stephens. 1976. "Drug Use and 'Hustling': A Study of Their Interrelationships." *Criminology* 14,2 (August), pp. 155–176.

Speckart, George and M. Douglas Anglin. 1986. "Narcotics Use and Crime: A Causal Modeling Approach." *Journal of Quantitative Criminology* 2, pp. 3–28.

———. 1986b. "Narcotics Use and Crime: An Overview of Recent Research Advances." *Contemporary Drug Problems* 13, pp. 741–769.

Sutherland, Edwin H., Donald R. Cressey, and David F. Luckenbill. 1992. *Principles of Criminology.* 11th ed. Dix Hills, NY: General Hill.

Sutter, Alan G. 1969. "Worlds of Drug Use on the Street Scene." Pp. 802–829 in Donald R. Cressey and David A. Ward (eds.), *Delinquency, Crime and Social Process.* New York: Harper and Row.

Taylor, Stuart P. 1983. "Alcohol and Human Physical Aggression." Pp. 280–291 in E. Gottheil, K.A. Druley, T.E. Skoloda, and H.M Waxman (eds.), *Alcohol, Drug Abuse and Aggression.* Springfield, IL: Charles C. Thomas.

United States Senate. 1984. *Impact of Drugs on Crime, 1984.* Hearing before the Subcommittee on Alcoholism and Drug Abuse of the Committee on Labor and Human Resources, May 10, 1984. Washington, D.C.: U.S. Government Printing Office.

Walters, James M. 1985. "Taking Care of Business' Updated: A Fresh Look at the Daily Routine of the Heroin User." Pp. 31–48 in Bill Hanson, George Beschner, James M. Walters and Elliot Bovelle (eds.), *Life with Heroin: Voices from the Inner City.* Lexington, MA: Lexington Books.

Watters, John K., Craig Reinarman, and Jeffrey Fagan. 1985. "Causality, Context, and Contingency: Relationships Between Drug Abuse and Delinquency." *Contemporary Drug Problems* 12,3, pp. 351–373.

White, Helene Raskin, and D.M. Gorman. 2000. "Dynamics of the Drug-Crime Relationship." Pp. 151–218 in *The Nature of Crime: Continuity and Change. Criminal Justice 2000,* Volume 1. NCJ 182408. Washington, D.C.: U.S. Department of Justice.

White, Helene Raskin, Rolf Loeber, Magda Stouthamer-Loeber, and David P. Farrington. 1999. "Developmental Associations between Substance Use and Violence." *Development and Psychopathology* 11, pp. 785–803.

White, Helene Raskin, Robert J. Pandina, and Randy L. LaGrange. 1987. "Longitudinal Predictors of Serious Substance Use and Delinquency." *Criminology* 25,3 (August), pp. 715–740.

Wikler, Abe. 1952. "Mechanisms of Action of Drugs that Modify Personality Function." *American Journal of Psychiatry* 108, pp. 590–599.

Wish, Eric D. and Bernard A. Gropper. 1990. "Drug Testing by the Criminal Justice System: Methods, Research, and Applications." Pp. 321–391 in Michael Tonry and James Q. Wilson (eds.) *Drugs and Crime.* Chicago: University of Chicago Press.

Woods, S.C. and J.G. Mansfield. 1983. "Ethanol and Disinhibition: Physiological and Behavioral Links." In R. Room and G. Collins (eds.), *Alcohol and Disinhibition: The Nature and Meaning of the Link.* Research Monograph #12, National Institute on Alcohol Abuse and Alcoholism. Washington, D.C.: Department of Health and Human Services, U.S. Public Health Service.

Woody, George E., Harold Persky, A. Thomas McLellan, Charles P. O'Brian and Isabelle Arndt. 1983. "Psychoendocrine Correlates of Hostility and Anxiety in Addicts." Pp. 227–244 in E. Gottheil, K.A. Druley, T.E. Skoloda, and H.M Waxman (eds.), *Alcohol, Drug Abuse and Aggression.* Springfield, IL: Charles C. Thomas.

Zinberg, Norman E. 1984. *Drug Set and Setting: The Basis for Controlled Intoxicant Use.* New Haven, CT: Yale University Press.

Chapter 11

Abadinsky, Howard. 1993. *Drug Abuse: An Introduction.* Chicago: Nelson Hall Publishers.

Anti-Narcotics Force. n.d. "Reduction in Supply of Opium—Pakistan's Success Story" Available online: *http://www.anf.gov.pk/supplydeduction.htm* (Accessed May 25, 2001).

Barnett, Randy. 1987. "Curing the Drug-Law Addiction: the Harmful Side Effects of Legal Prohibition." Pp. 73–102 in Ronald Hamowy (ed.), *Dealing with Drugs: Consequences of Government Control.* Lexington, MA: D.C. Heath.

Bonnie, Richard. 1980. *Marijuana Use and Criminal Sanctions.* Charlottesville, VA: The Michie Company.

Bureau of Justice Statistics. 1997. *Sourcebook of Criminal Justice Statistics.* Washington, DC: U.S. Government Printing Office.

Carter, Jimmy. 1977. Message to Congress (August 2). Cited in NORML, "Special News Bulletin" June 15, 1999. Available online: *http://www.norml.org/news/ archives/99-06-15.shtml* (Accessed May 26, 2000).

Cuskey, Walter R., Lisa H. Berger and Arthur H. Richardson. 1978. "The Effects of Marijuana Decriminalization on Drug Use Patterns: A Literature Review and Research Critique." *Contemporary Drug Problems* 5,4, pp. 491–532.

Dombrink, John and James W. Meeker. 1985. "Racketeering Prosecution: the Use and Abuse of RICO." *Rutgers Law Journal* 16, pp. 633–654.

———. 1986. "Beyond 'Buy and Bust'" Nontraditional Sanctions in Federal Drug Law Enforcement." *Contemporary Drug Problems* 13,4, pp. 711–740.

Drug Enforcement Administration. n.d. "Operations Pipeline and Convoy." Available online: *http://www.usdoj.gov/dea/programs/pipecon.htm* (Accessed May 29, 2000).

———. 2000. "Drug Law Enforcement Statistics." Available online: *http://www.usdoj.gov/dea/stats/ lawstats.htm* (Accessed May 1, 2000).

Evans, John L. 1996. "International Money Laundering: Enforcement Challenges and Opportunities." *Southwestern Journal of Law and Trade in the Americas* 3. Available online: *http://members.tripod.com/~orgcrime/genmlchall.htm* (Accessed May 31, 2000).

Gallup Organization. 2000. "Racial Profiling Is Seen as Widespread, Particularly Among Young Black Men." Available online: *http://www.gallup.com/poll/releases/pr991209.asp* (Accessed May 19, 2000).

Garcia, Maria Isabel. 1999. "DRUGS-LATAM: Globalization Hampers Crop Substitution Programmes." Inter-Press Service, October 18. Available online: *http://www.oneworld.org/ips2/oct99/18_26_125.html* (Accessed May 25, 2001).

Goldstein, Avram and Harold Kalant. 1990. "Drug Policy: Striking the Right Balance." *Science* 249 (September 28), pp. 1513–1521.

Goldstein, Paul J. 1985. "The Drugs/Violence Nexus: A Tripartite Conceptual Framework." *Journal of Drug Issues* 15, pp. 493–506.

Gusfield, Joseph. 1967. "Moral Passage: The Symbolic Process in Public Designations of Deviance." *Social Problems* 15, pp. 175–188.

Hall, S.W. 2000. *Statement to the Hearing Before the Subcommittee on Treasury, Postal Service, and General Government Committee on Appropriations U.S. House of Representatives.* April 4. Available online: *http://www.customs.ustreas.gov/top/search.htm* (Accessed April 24, 2000).

Harris, David A. 1994. "Factors for Reasonal Suspicion: When Black and Poor Means Stopped and Frisked." *Indiana Law Journal* 69, pp. 659–688.

———. 1998. "Car Wars: The Fourth Amendment's Death on the Highway." *The George Washington Law Review* 66, pp. 556–591.

———. 1999. "Driving While Black: Racial Profiling on Out Nation's Highways." An American Civil Liberties Union Special Report (June). Available online: *http://www.aclu.org/profiling/report/index.html* (Accessed May 29, 2000).

Inciardi, James A. 1981. "Marijuana Decriminalization Research." *Criminology* 19, pp. 145–159.

Inciardi, James A. and Duane C. McBride. 1989. "Legalization: A High Risk Alternative in the War on Drugs." *American Behavioral Scientist* 32, pp. 259–289.

———. 1990. "Debating the Legalization of Drugs." Pp. 283–299 in James A. Inciardi (ed.), *Handbook of Drug Control in the United States.* New York: Greenwood Press.

Inciardi, James A., J. Bryan Page, Duane C. McBride, Dale D. Chitwood, Clyde B. McCoy and H. Virginia McCoy. 1995. "The Risk of Exposure to HIV-Contaminated Needles and Syringes in Shooting Galleries." Pp. 277–283 in James A. Inciardi and Karen McElrath (eds.) *The American Drug Scene: An Anthology* (1st ed.). Los Angeles: Roxbury Publishing Co.

Inciardi, James A. and Christine A. Saum. 1996. "Legalization Madness." *The Public Interest,* 123, pp. 72–82.

Jacobs, James. 1990. "Imagining Drug Legalization." *The Public Interest.* 101, pp. 28–42.

Johnston, Lloyd D., Patrick M. O'Malley, and J.G. Bachman. (December 2000). "Ecstasy" Use Rises Sharply Among Teens in 2000; Use of Many Other Drugs Steady, but Significant Declines are Reported for Some. University of Michigan News and Information Services: Ann Arbor, MI. Available online: *http://www.monitoringthefuture.org* (Accessed May 24, 2001).

Kaplan, John. 1983. *The Hardest Drug: Heroin and Public Policy.* Chicago: University of Chicago Press.

Kleber, Herbert D. 1994. "Our Current Approach to Drug Abuse–Progress, Problems, Proposals." *The New England Journal of Medicine* 330 (February 3), pp. 361–365.

Kleiman, Mark A.R. 1985. "Drug Enforcement and Organized Crime." Pp. 67–87 in Herbert E. Alexander and Gerald E. Caiden, *The Politics and Economics of Organized Crime.* Lexington, MA: D.C. Heath.

Kleiman, Mark A.R. and Kerry D. Smith. 1990. "State and Local Drug Enforcement: In Search of a Strategy." Pp. 69–108 in Michael Tonry and James Q. Wilson (eds.), *Drugs and Crime.* Chicago: University of Chicago Press.

Lama, Abraham. 2000. "DRUGS-PERU: Rising Coca Prices Threaten Crop Substitution Plans." Inter-Press Service, May 21. Available online: *http://www.oneworld.org/ips2/may00/16_46_012.html* (Accessed May 25, 2001).

Lindesmith Center. 1997. "Research Brief: Needle and Syringe Availability." Available online: *http://www.lindesmith.org/cites_sources/brief15.html* (Accessed May 29, 2001).

Martello, Thomas. 1999. "New Jersey Report Admits Racial Profiling by State Cops." Court TV Online. Available online: *http://www.courttv.com/national/1999/0420/profiling_ap.html* (Accessed May 24, 2001).

Massing, Michael. 1999. "Beyond Legalization: New Ideas for Ending the War on Drugs—It's Time for Realism. *The Nation* (September 20), pp. 11–15.

McCaffrey, Barry. 1997. *National Drug Control Strategy, 1997.* February. Washington, D.C.: U.S. Government Printing Office.

Mill, John Stuart. 1956. *On Liberty.* (Currin v. Shields, ed.) Indianapolis: Bobbs-Merrill Co.

Moore, David. 1999. "Americans Oppose General Legalization of Marijuana." Gallup News Service. Available online: *http://www.gallup.com/poll/releases/pr990409b.asp* (Accessed May 22, 2000).

Murphy, Sheigla and Dan Waldorf. 1991. "Kickin' Down to the Street Doc: Shooting Galleries in the San Francisco Bay Area." *Contemporary Drug Problems* 18, pp. 9–29.

Nadelmann, Ethan. 1988. "The Case for Legalization." *The Public Interest*, 92, pp. 3–31.

_____. 1989. "Drug Prohibition in the United States: Costs, Consequences, and Alternatives." *Science* 245 (September 1), pp. 939–947.

_____. 1995. "Drugs, Prohibition of." *Collier's Encyclopedia*, Vol. 8, pp. 395–398.

_____. 1997. "Reefer Madness 1997: The New Bag of Scare Tactics." *Rolling Stone* (February 20), pp. 51–53, 77).

_____. 1998. "Commonsense Drug Policy." *Foreign Affairs* 77, pp. 111–126.

Nadelmann, Ethan, Jennifer McNeely and Ernest Drucker. 1997. "International Perspectives." Pp. 22–39 in Joyce H. Lowinson, Pedro Ruiz, Robert B. Millman and John G. Langrod (eds.), *Substance Abuse: A Comprehensive Textbook.* (3rd ed.). Baltimore, MD: Williams & Wilkins.

Nadelmann, Ethan and Jann S. Wenner. 1994. "Toward a Sane National Drug Policy." *Rolling Stone*, May 5, pp. 24–26.

National Commission on Marihuana and Drug Abuse. 1972. *Marihuana: A Signal of Misunderstanding.* Washington, D.C.: U.S. Government Printing Office.

National Organization for the Reform of Marijuana Laws. 2002. "The NORML State Guide to Marijuana Laws. Available online: *http://www.norml.org/index.cfm* (Accessed October 28, 2002).

Office of National Drug Control Policy. 1992. "Needle Exchange Programs: Are They Effective?" *ONDCP Bulletin, No. 7* (July).

President's Commission on Organized Crime. 1986. *America's Habit: Drug Abuse, Drug Trafficking, and Organized Crime.* Washington DC: U.S. Government Printing Office.

Schur, Edwin M. 1965. *Crimes Without Victims: Deviant Behavior and Public Policy.* Englewood Cliffs, NJ: Prentice-Hall.

Schwartz, Richard H. and Michael J. Sheridan. 1997. "Marijuana to Prevent Nausea and Vomiting in Cancer Patients: A Survey of Clinical Oncologists." *Southern Medical Journal* 90, pp. 167–172.

Singer, Merrill, Ray Irizarry and Jean Schensul. 1991. "Needle Access as an AIDS-Prevention Strategy for IV Drug Users: A Research Perspective." *Human Organization* 50, pp. 142–153.

Sterling, Eric. 1990. "Is the Bill of Rights A Casualty of the War on Drugs?" Remarks delivered to the Colorado Bar Association, 92nd Annual Convention, Aspen CO, September 14.

Thies, Clifford F. and Charles A. Register. 1993. "Decriminalization of Marijuana and the Demand for Alcohol, Marijuana and Cocaine." *The Social Science Journal* 30, pp. 385–399.

Trebach, Arnold. 1987. *The Great Drug War.* New York: MacMillan.

Tyler, Tom. 1990. *Why People Obey the Law.* New Haven, CT: Yale University Press.

U.S. Coast Guard. nd. "Drug Interdiction" Available online: *http://www.uscg.mil/hq/g-o/g-opl/mle/drugs.htm* (Accessed April 24, 2000).

U.S. Customs. 2000. "Millions Enter U.S. Through South Texas Ports of Entry in FY 2000" November 22. Available online: *http://www.customs.ustreas.gov/top/search.htm* (Accessed May 6, 2001).

Wenner, Jann S. and Ethan A. Nadelmann. 1997. "Clinton's War on Drugs: Cruel, Wrong, Unwinnable." *Rolling Stone* April 17, p. 54.

Westermeyer, Robert W. n.d. "Reducing Harm: A Very Good Idea." Available online: *http://www.habitsmart.com/harm.html* (Accessed May 24, 2000).

Wisotsky, Steven. 1986. *Breaking the Impasse in the War on Drugs*. New York: Greenwood Press.

Chapter 12

Andrews, D.A., Ivan Zinger, robert D. Hoge, James Bonta, Paul Gendreau and Francis T. Cullen. 1990. "Does Correctional Treatment work? A Clinically Relevant and Psychologically Informed Meta-Analysis." *Criminology* 28, pp. 369–404.

Anglin, M. Douglas, Michael Prendergast and David Farabee. 1998. "The Effectiveness of Coerced Treatment for Drug-Abusing Offenders." Paper Presented at the Office of National Drug Control Policy's Conference of Scholars and Policy Makers, Washington, D.C., March 23–25.

Anglin, M. Douglas and Yih-Ing Hser. 1990. "Treatment of Drug Abuse." Pp. 393–460 in Michael Tonry and James Q. Wilson (eds.), *Drugs and Crime*. Chicago: University of Chicago Press.

Associated Press. 2000. "Two Doctors May Lose Licenses Over Fast-Detox Method Medicine." (December 31) Available online: *http://www.doctordeluca.com/Documents/UROD_MDs_License.htm*

Baumohl, Jim. 1986. "On Asylums, Homes, and Moral Treatment: The Case of the San Francisco Home for the Care of the Inebriate, 1859–1870." *Contemporary Drug Problems*, 13, 3, pp. 395–445.

Beschner, George and Peggy Thompson. 1981. *Women and Drug Abuse Treatment: Needs and Services*. Rockville, MD: National Institute on Drug Abuse.

Brown, Barry. 1979. *Addicts and Aftercare: Community Integration of the Former Drug User*. Beverly Hills, CA: Sage Publications.

Cole, Steven G. and Lawrence R. James. 1975. "A Revised Treatment Typology Based on DARP." *American Journal of Drug and Alcohol Abuse* 2, pp. 37–49.

Cook, L. Foster and Beth A. Weinman. 1988. "Treatment Alternatives to Street Crime." Pp. 99–105 in Carl G. Leukefeld and Frank M. Tims (eds.), *Compulsory Treatment of Drug Abuse: Research and Clinical Practice*. National Institute on Drug Abuse Research Monograph Series #86. Washington, DC: U.S. Government Printing Office.

Cuccia, A.T., et. al. 1998. "Ultra-Rapid Opiate Detoxification Using Deep Sedation: Short and Long Term Results." *Journal of Drug and Alcohol Dependence* 52, 3, pp. 243–250.

Cuskey, Walter R., Lisa H. Berger and Judianne Densen-Gerber. 1977. "Issues in the Treatment of Female Addiction: A Review and Critique of the Literature." *Contemporary Drug Problems* 6, pp. 307–322.

Davidson, Jeffrey. 1981. "Location of Community-based Treatment Centers." *Social Service Review* (June), pp. 221–241.

De Leon, George. 1985. "The Therapeutic Community: Status and Evolution." *The International Journal of the Addictions* 20, pp. 823–844.

De Leon, George, Henry K. Wexler, and Nancy Jainchill. 1982. "The Therapeutic Community: Success and Improvement Rates 5 Years After Treatment." *The International Journal of the Addictions* 17, pp. 703–747.

Dembo, Richard, James A. Ciarlo and robert W. Taylor. 1983. "A Model for Assessing and Improving Drug Abuse Treatment Resource Use in Inner-City Areas." *The International Journal of the Addictions* 18, pp. 921–936.

Doweiko, Harold E. 1990. *Concepts of Chemical Dependency*. Pacific Grove, CA: Brooks/Cole.

Dunham, Roger G. and Armand L. Mauss. 1982. "Reluctant Referrals: the Effectiveness of Legal Coercion in Outpatient Treatment for Problem Drinkers." *Journal of Drug Issues* 12, pp. 5–20.

Faupel, Charles E. 1981. "Drug Treatment and Criminality: Methodological and Theoretical Considerations." Pp. 183–206 in James A. Inciardi (ed.) *The Drugs-Crime Connection*. Beverly Hills, CA: Sage Publications.

———. 1985. "A Theoretical Model for a Socially Oriented Drug Treatment Policy." *Journal of Drug Education* 15, pp. 189–203.

———. 1991. *Shooting Dope: Career Patterns of Hard-Core Heroin Addicts*. Gainesville, FL: University of Florida Press.

Faupel, Charles E. and Penelope J. Hanke. 1993. "A Comparative Analysis of Drug-Using Women with and without Treatment Histories in New York City." *The International Journal of the Addictions* 28, pp. 233–248.

French, M.T., G.A. Zarkin, J.W. Bray and T.D. Hartwell. 1999. "The Cost of Employee Assistance Programs: Comparison of National Estimates from 1993 and 1995." *Journal of Behavioral Health Sciences and Research* 26, pp. 95–103.

Friedman, Jennifer and Marixsa Alicea. 2001. *Surviving Heroin: Interviews with Women in Methadone Clinics.* Gainesville, FL: University of Florida Press.

Gil-rivas, Virginia, Robert Fiorentine, M. Douglas Anglin and Ellise Taylor. 1997. "Sexual and Physical Abuse: Do They Compromise Drug Treatment Outcomes?" *Journal of Substance Abuse Treatment* 14, pp. 351–358.

Glasscote, R., J.N. Sussex, J.H. Jaffe, J. Ball, and L. Brill. 1972. *The Treatment of Drug Abuse: Programs, Problems, Prospects.* Washington, DC: American Psychiatric Association.

Graff, Harold and John C. Ball. 1976. "The Methadone Clinic: Function and Philosophy." *International Journal of Social Psychiatry* 22, pp. 140–146.

Green, Lesley L., Mindy Thomson Fullilove and Robert E. Fullilove. 1995. "Stories of Spiritual Awakening: The Nature of Spirituality in Recovery." *Journal of Substance Abuse Treatment* 15, pp. 325–331.

Hanke, Penelope J. and Charles E. Faupel. 1993. "Women Opiate Users' Perceptions of Treatment Services in New York City." *Journal of Substance Abuse Treatment* 10, pp. 513–522.

Hartjen, Clayton A., S.M. Mitchell and N.F. Washburne. 1981. "Sentencing to Therapy: Some Legal, Ethical and Practical Issues. *Journal of Offender Counseling, Services and Rehabilitation* 6, pp. 21–39.

Hawkins, J. David. 1979. "Reintegrating Street Drug Abusers: Community Roles in Continuing Care." Pp. 25–79 in Barry S;. Brown (ed.), *Addicts and Aftercare.* Beverly Hills, CA: Sage.

Hobbs, Thomas R. 1978. "Managing Alcoholism as a Disease." *Physicians News Digest*, February. Available online: *http://www.physiciansnews.com/commentary/298wp.html* (Accessed August 28, 2002).

Horowitz, Alan. 2000. "Narcotics Anonymous." Pp. 438–442 in Clifton D. Bryant (ed.) *Encyclopedia of Criminology and Deviant Behavior*, Vol. 4. Philadelphia: Taylor and Francis.

Hser, Yih-Ing, M. Douglas Anglin and Chih-Ping Chou. 1988. "Evaluation of Drug Abuse Treatment: A repeated Measures Design Assessing Methadone Maintenance." *Evaluation Review* 12, pp. 547–570.

Hser, Yih-Ing, M. Douglas Anglin and Bennett Fletcher. 1998. "Comparative Treatment Effectiveness: Effects of Program Modality and Client Drug Dependence History on Drug Use Reduction." *Journal of Substance Abuse Treatment* 15, pp. 513–523.

Hubbard, Robert L., Gail Craddock, Patrick M. Flynn, Jill Anderson and Rose M. Etheridge. 1997. "Overview of 1-Year Follow-up Outcomes in the Drug Abuse Treatment Outcome Study (DATOS). *Psychology of Addictive Behaviors* 11, pp. 261–278.

Hubbard, Robert L., Mary Ellen Marsden, J. Valley Rachal, Henrick J. Harwood, Elizabeth R. Cavanaugh, and Harold M. Ginzburg. 1989. *Drug Abuse Treatment: A National Study of Effectiveness.* Chapel Hill, NC: The University of North Carolina Press.

Inciardi, James A. 1988. "Compulsory Treatment in New York: A Brief Narrative History of Misjudgment, Mismanagement, and Misrepresentation." *Journal of Drug Issues* 18, pp. 547–560.

———. 1977. *Methadone Diversion: Experiences and Issues.* Rockville, MD: National Institute on Drug Abuse.

Institute of Medicine. 1995. *Federal Regulation of Methadone Maintenance.* Washington, DC: National Academy Press.

Internet Mental Health. Nd. "Disulfiram." Available online: *http://www.mentalhealth.com/drug/p30-a02.html* (Accessed March 20, 2000).

Jellinek, Elvin M. 1960. *The Disease Concept of Alcoholism.* Highland Park, NJ: Hillhouse.

Julius, Demetrios. 1976. "NIDA's Naltrexone Research Program." Pp. 5–11 in Demetrios Julius and Pierre Renault, *Narcotics Antagonists: Naltrexone.* Rockville, MD: National Institute on Drug Abuse.

Kaplan, John. 1983. "Heroin Maintenance." *The Hardest Drug: Heroin and Public Policy.* Chicago: University of Chicago Press, pp. 153–187.

Karan, Lori D. 1989. "AIDS Prevention and Chemical Dependence Treatment Needs of Women and Their Children." *Journal of Psychoactive Drugs* 21, pp. 395–399.

Khantzian, E.J. and John E. Mack. 1994. "How AA Works and Why It's Important for Clinicians to Understand." *Journal of Substance Abuse Treatment* 11, pp. 77–92.

Kleber, Herbert D. and Frank Slobetz. 1979. "Outpatient Drug-Free Treatment." Pp. 31–38 in Robert DuPont, Avram Goldstein, and John O'Donnel (eds.), *Handbook on Drug Abuse*. Rockville, MD: National Institute on Drug Abuse.

Kleber, J. 1998. "Ultrarapid Opiate Detoxification (an editorial)." *Addiction* (Vol. 93, No. 11), pp. 1629–1633.

Laign, Jeffrey. 1987. "How Far Have We Really Come, Baby? Women's Addiction Treatment in 1987. *Focus* 10, 5, pp. 14–15, 29–31.

Laundergan, J. Clark. 1982. *Easy Does It: Alcoholism Treatment Outcomes, Hazelden and the Minnesota Model.* Center City, MN: Hazelden Foundation.

Leukenfeld, Carl G. and Frank M. Tims. 1990. "Compulsory Treatment for Drug Abuse." *The International Journal of the Addictions* 25, pp. 621–640.

Lewis, Ricki. 1999. "Products to Help Smokers Quit." Available online: *http://www.wellweb.com/SMOKING/SMPATCH.HTM* (Accessed March 17, 2000).

Lindesmith Center. 1997. "Research Brief: Methadone Maintenance Treatment." Available online: *http://www.lindesmith.org/cites_sources/brief14.html* (Accessed March 17, 2000).

Lipton, Douglas S. and Michael J. Maranda. 1983. "Detoxification from Heroin Dependency: An Overview of Method and Effectiveness." *Advances in Alcohol and Substance Abuse* 2, pp. 31–55.

Lowinson, Joyce H. and Robert B. Millman. 1979. "Clinical Aspects of Methadone Maintenance." Pp. 49–56 in Robert DuPont, Avram Goldstein, and John O'Donnel (eds.), *Handbook on Drug Abuse*. Rockville, MD: National Institute on Drug Abuse.

Maddux, James F. 1988. "Clinical Experience with Civil Commitment." Pp. 35–56 in Carl G. Leukefeld and Frank M. Tims (eds.), *Compulsory Treatment of Drug Abuse: Research and Clinical Practice.* National Institute on Drug Abuse Research Monograph Series #86. Washington, DC: U.S. Government Printing Office.

Marion, Ira J. 1995. *LAAM in the Treatment of Opiate Addiction.* Substance Abuse and Mental Health Services Administration Treatment Improvement Protocol (TIP) Series 22. Washington, DC: U.S. Department of Health and Human Services.

Markel, Howard. 2002. "For Addicts, Relief May Be an Office Visit Away," *New York Times* (October 27, p. 14 of "Week in Review" section).

Marshall, Shelly. 2001. "Rapid Detox No Magic Pill: Program Has Its Shortcomings and Dangers." Available online: *http://alcoholism.about.com/library/weekly/aa010115a.htm*

McCrady, B. and S. Delaney. 1995. "Self-Help Groups" Pp. 173–175 in R. Hester and W. Miller (eds.) *Handbook of Alcoholism Treatment Approaches.* Boston: Allyn and Bacon.

McElrath, Karen. 1995. "Alcoholics Anonymous." Pp. 266–270 in James A. Inciardi and Karen McElrath (eds.) *The American Drug Scene: An Anthology* (2nd ed.). Los Angeles: Roxbury Publishing Co.

McGlothlin, William H., M. Douglas Anglin, and Bruce D. Wilson. 1977. *An Evaluation of the California Civil Addict Program.* Rockford, MD: National Institute on Drug Abuse.

McLellan, A. Thomas, Lester Luborsky, Charles P. O'Brien, George E. Woody and Keith A. Druley. 1982. "Is Treatment for Substance Abuse Effective?" *Journal of the American Medical Association*, 247, pp. 1423–1428.

Miller, N. and N. Hoffman. 1995. "Addictions Treatment Outcomes," in *Alcoholism Treatment Quarterly*, 12, 2, pp. 41–55.

Miller, Norman S., Mark S. Gold and A. Carter Pottash. 1989. "A 12-Step Treatment Approach for Marijuana (Cannabis) Dependence." *Journal of Substance Abuse Treatment*, 6, pp. 241–250.

Nadelmann, Ethan. 1995. "Switzerland's Heroin Experiment." *National Review* (July 10), pp. 46–47.

National Institute on Drug Abuse. 1977. *Securing Employment for Ex-Drug Abusers: An Overview of Jobs.* Services Research Report DHEW #(ADM)78-467. Washington, DC: U.S. Government Printing Office.

_____. 2000. "Gender Differences in Drug Abuse Risks and Treatment. *NIDA Notes* 15, 4 (September).

Nordenberg, Tamar. 1997. "It's Quitten' Time: Smokers Need Not Rely on Willpower Alone." *FDA Consumer Magazine.*

ONDCP. 2001. "Demonstrating the Effectiveness of Drug Treatment." An online fact sheet from the White House Office of National Drug Control Policy.

Peterson, Russell W. 2000. "A Cure Worse Than Crime (an op-ed piece)." *Wilmington (DE) News Journal* (June 18).

Platt, Jerome J., G. Buhringer, C.D. Kaplan, Barry S. Brown and D.O. Taube. 1988. "The Prospects and Limitations of Compulsory Treatment for Drug Addiction. Special Issue: A Social Policy Analysis of Compulsory Treatment for Opiate Dependence. *Journal of Drug Issues* 18, pp. 505–525.

Reed, Beth Glover. 1987. "Developing Women-Sensitive Drug Dependence Treatment Services: Why So Difficult?" *Journal of Psychoactive Drugs* 19, pp. 151–164.

Resnick, Richard B., Elaine Schuyten-Resnick and Arnold M. Washton. 1979. "Treatment of Opioid Dependence with Narcotic Antagonists: A Review and Commentary. Pp. 97–104 in Robert DuPont, Avram Goldstein, and John O'Donnel (eds.), *Handbook on Drug Abuse.* Rockville, MD: National Institute on Drug Abuse.

Room, R. and T. Greenfield. 1993. "Alcoholics Anonymous, Other 12-Step Movements and Psychotherapy in the U.S. Population, 1990. *Addiction* 88, pp. 555–562.

Rosenbaum, Marsha and Sheigla Murphy. 1981. "Getting the Treatment: Recycling women Addicts." *Journal of Psychoactive Drugs* 13, pp. 1–13.

Rosenberg, Chaim M. and Joseph Liftik. 1976. "Use of Coercion in the Outpatient Treatment of Alcoholism." *Journal of Studies on Alcohol*, 17, pp. 58–65.

Rosenthal, Michael P. 1988. "The Constitutionality of Involuntary Civil Commitment of Opiate Addicts." *Journal of Drug Issues* 18, pp. 641–661.

SAMHSA. 2001. *Unpublished Results from the 2000 National Household Survey on Drug Abuse.* U.S. Department of Health and Human Services (August).

Schneider, Joseph. 1978. "Deviant Drinking as Disease: Alcoholism as a Social Accomplishment." *Social Problems* 25, pp. 361–372.

Schoemaker, Bernadette. 1995. "Treatment with Heroin." *Jellinek Quarterly* (July 2), pp. 2–3.

Sells, S. B. 1979. "Treatment Effectiveness." Pp. 105–118 in Robert DuPont, Avram Goldstein, and John O'Donnel (eds.), *Handbook on Drug Abuse.* Rockville, MD: National Institute on Drug Abuse.

Shaw, Elton. 1910. *The Curse of Drink (or Stories of Hell's Commerce).* Albion, MI: Prohibition Party National Committee.

Sheldon, T. 1997. "Dutch and Swiss Support Heroin on Prescription." *British Medical Journal* 315, (October 4), p. 835.

Simpson, D. Dwayne and H. Jed Friend. 1988. "Legal Status and Long-Term Outcomes for Addicts in the DARP Followup Project." Pp. 81–98 in Carl G. Leukefeld and Frank M. Tims (eds.), *Compulsory Treatment of Drug Abuse: Research and Clinical Practice.* National Institute on Drug Abuse Research Monograph Series #86. Washington, DC: U.S. Government Printing Office.

Simpson, D. Dwayne, Joe, G.W. and Bracy, S.A. 1982. "Six-Year Follow-up of Opioid Addicts After Admission to Treatment." *Archives of General Psychiatry 39*, pp. 1318–1323.

Simpson, D. Dwayne, L. James Savage, Michael R. Lloyd and S. B. Sells. 1978. *Evaluation of Drug Abuse Treatments Based on First Year Followup.* Rockville, MD: National Institute on Drug Abuse.

Simpson, D. Dwayne, and Sells, S. B. (eds.). 1990. *Opioid Addiction and Treatment: A 12-year Follow-up.* Malabar, FL: Krieger Publishing Co.

Stevens, S., V. Arbiter and P. Glider. 1989. "Women Residents: Expanding Their Role to Increase Treatment Effectiveness in Substance Abuse Programs. *The International Journal of the Addictions* 24, pp. 425–434.

Terry, Charles E. and Mildred Pellens. 1928. *The Opium Problem.* New York: The Committee on Drug Addictions in Collaboration with the Bureau on Social Hygiene, Inc.

Tonry, Michael and James Q. Wilson. 1990. *Drugs and Crime.* Chicago: University of Chicago Press.

U.S. Department of Health and Human Services. 1980. "Alcohol, Drug Abuse, and Mental Health Administration and Food and Drug Administration. Methadone for Treating Narcotic Addicts: Joint Revision of Conditions for Use." *Federal Register* 45 (September 19), pt. 3.

Waldorf, Dan. 1983. "Natural Recovery from Opiate Addiction: Some Social-Psychological Processes of Untreated Recovery." *Journal of Drug Issues*, 13 (Spring), pp. 237–280.

Waldorf, Dan and Patrick Biernacki. 1981. "The Natural Recovery from Opiate Addiction: Some Preliminary Findings." *Journal of Drug Issues*, 11 (Winter), pp. 61–74.

Winick, Charles. 1962. "Maturing Out of Narcotic Addiction." *Bulletin on Narcotics*, 14 (January–March), pp. 1–7.

Wolkstein, Eileen. 1979. "The Former Addict in the Workplace." Pp. 103–114 in Barry S. Brown (ed.) *Addicts and Aftercare: Community Integration of the Former Drug User.* Beverly Hills, CA: Sage Publications.

Yablonsky, Lewis. 1965. *Synanon: The Tunnel Back.* New York: Penguin.

Chapter 13

Ackerman, Deborah L. 1995. "Drug Testing." Pp. 473–489 in Robert H. Coombs and Douglas Ziedonis (eds.), *Handbook on Drug Abuse Prevention: A Comprehensive Strategy to Prevent the Abuse of Alcohol and Other Drugs.* Boston: Allyn and Bacon.

———. 1991. "A History of Drug Testing." Pp. 3–21 in Robert H. Coombs and Louis Jolyon West (eds.), *Drug Testing: Issues and Options*. New York: Oxford University Press.

American Civil Liberties Union. 2000. "Citing 'Dangerous Precedent,' Federal Judge Blocks MI's Plan to Drug Test Welfare Recipients" Available online: *http://www. aclu.org/issues/drugpolicy/cases/Marchwinski%20v%20Michigan/Marchwinski_v_ Michigan.html* (Accessed July 17, 2001).

———. 2001a. "Continuing National Trend, Appeals Court Rejects Oklahoma School Drug Testing Policy." Available online: *http://www.aclu.org/issues/drugpolicy/cases/Earls%20v%20Tecumseh/ Earls_v_Tecumseh.html* (Accessed July 17, 2001).

———. 2001b. "Texas Court Strikes Down First-Ever Mandatory School Drug Testing Policy" Available online: *http://www.aclu.org/issues/drugpolicy/cases/Tannahill_v_Lockney/Tannahill_v_Lockney.html* (Accessed July 17, 2001).

American Management Association. 1992. *AMA Survey on Workplace Drug Testing and Drug Abuse Policies*. New York: American Management Association.

Anglin, M. Douglas and C.A. Westland. 1989. "Drug Monitoring in the Workplace: Results from the California Commercial Laboratory Drug Testing Project." Pp. 81–96 in Steven W. Gust and J. Michael Walsh, *Drugs in the Workplace: Research and Evaluation Data*. NIDA Research Monograph #91. Rockville, MD: National Institute on Drug Abuse.

Arkin, Rise Morgenstern, Helen F. Roemhild, C. Anderson Joyhnson, Russell V. Luepker and David M. Murray. 1981. "The Minnesota Smoking Prevention Program: A Seventh-Grade Health Curriculum Supplement." *The Journal of School Health* 51, 9, pp. 611–616.

Bandura, Albert. 1977. *Social Learning Theory*. Englewood Cliffs, NJ: Prentice Hall.

Banta, William F. and Forest Tenant. 1989. *Complete Handbook for Combating Substance Abuse in the Workplace*. Lexington, MA: Lexington Books.

Bompey, Stuart H. 1986. "Drugs in the Workplace: From the Batter's Box to the Boardroom." *Journal of Occupational Medicine* 28, pp. 825–832.

Bordin, Ruth. 1981. Woman and Temperance: The Quest for Power and Liberty, 1873–1900. Philadelphia: Temple University Press.

Brown, Joel H., Marianne D'Emidio-Caston, Karen Kaufman, Teddy Goldsworthy-Hanner, and Maureen Alioto. 1995. *In Their Own Voices: Students and Educators Evaluate California School-Based Drug, Alcohol, and Tobacco Education (DATE) Programs*. Sacramento, CA: California State Department of Education.

Bukoski, William J. 1991. "A Definition of Drug Abuse Prevention Research." Pp. 3–19 in Lewis Donohew, Howard E. Sypher and William J. Bukoski (eds.), *Persuasive Communication and Drug Abuse Prevention*. Hillsdale, NJ: Lawrence Erlbaum Associates, Publishers.

Bureau of Justice Assistance. 1995. "Drug Abuse Resistance Education (DARE)." *Bureau of Justice Assistance Fact Sheet*. Washington, DC: U.S. Department of Justice.

Bureau of Labor Statistics. 1989. *Survey of Employer Antidrug Programs*. Washington, DC: U.S. Bureau of Labor.

Clayton, Richard R., Anne Cattarello, L. Edward Day and Katherine P. Walden. 1991. "Persuasive Communication and Drug Prevention: An Evaluation of the DARE Program." Pp. 295–313 in Lewis Donohew, Howard E. Sypher and William J. Bukoski (eds.), *Persuasive Communication and Drug Abuse Prevention*. Hillsdale, NJ: Lawrence Erlbaum Associates, Publishers.

Clayton, Richard R., Anne Cattarello and Bryan M. Johnstone. 1996. "The Effectiveness of Drug Abuse Resistance Education (Project DARE): 5-Year Follow-Up Results." *Preventive Medicine* 25, pp. 307–318.

Cohn, Jason. 2001. "Drug Education: The Triumph of Bad Science," *Rolling Stone*, May 24, pp. 41–42.

Coombs, Robert H. and Carol J. Coombs. 1991. "The Impact of Drug Testing on the Morale and Well-Being of Mandatory Participants." *International Journal of the Addictions* 26, pp. 981–992.

Coombs, Robert H. and Douglas M. Ziedonis. 1995. *Handbook on Drug Abuse Prevention: A Comprehensive Strategy to Prevent the Abuse of Alcohol and Other Drugs*. Boston: Allyn and Bacon.

DeAngelis, Gerald G. 1976. *Testing and Screening for Drugs of Abuse: Techniques, Issues and Clinical Implications*. New York: Marcel Dekker.

Donohew, Lewis, Howard E. Sypher and William J. Bukoski. 1991. *Persuasive Communication and Drug Abuse Prevention*. Hillsdale, NJ: Lawrence Erlbaum Associates.

Duncan, David F., Thomas Nicholson, Patrick Clifford, Wesley Hawkins and Rick Petosa. 1994. "Harm Reduction: An Emerging New Paradigm for Drug Education." *Journal of Drug Education* 24, pp. 281–290.

Eggert, Leona L. and Jerald R. Herting. 1991. "Preventing Teenage Drug Abuse." *Youth & Society* 22, pp. 482–524.

Eggert, Leona, Liela Nicholas and Linda Owen. 1995. *Reconnecting Youth: A Peer Group Approach to Building Life Skills*. Bloomington, IN: National Education Service.

Eggert, Leona L., Christine D. Seyl and Liela J. Nicholas. 1990. "Effects of a School-Based Prevention Program for Potential High School Dropouts and Drug Abusers." *The International Journal of the Addictions* 25, pp. 773–801.

Ellickson, Phyllis L. 1995. "Schools." Pp. 93–120 in Robert H. Coombs and Douglas M. Ziedonis (eds.), *Handbook on Drug Abuse Prevention: A Comprehensive Strategy to Prevent the Abuse of Alcohol and Other Drugs*. Boston: Allyn and Bacon.

Ellickson, Phyllis L., Robert M. Bell and Ellen R. Harrison. "Changing Adolescent Propensities to Use Drugs: Results from Project ALERT." *Health Education Quarterly* 20, pp. 227–242.

Ennett, Susan T., Nancy S. Tobler, Christopher L. Ringwalt and Robert L. Flewelling. 1994. "How Effective is Drug Abuse Resistance Education? A Meta-Analysis of Project DARE Outcome Evaluations." *American Journal of Public Health* 84, pp. 1394–1401.

Evans, Richard I., Richard M. Rozelle, Maurice Mittelmark, William B. Hansen, Alice L. Bane and Janet Havis. 1978. "Deterring the Onset of Smoking in Children: Knowledge of Immediate Psychological Effects and Coping with Peer Pressure, Media Pressure, and Parent Modeling." *Journal of Applied Social Psychology* 8, pp. 126–135.

Faley, Robert H., Lawrence S. Kleiman and Patricia S. Wall. 1988. "Drug Testing in the Public and Private-Sector Workplaces: Technical and Legal Issues." *Journal of Business and Psychology* 3, pp. 154–186.

Fay, Calvina L. 1996. "The Economic Value of Drug Prevention in Companies." Paper read in Zurich, Switzerland, June 22. Available online: *http://sarnia.com/groups/antidrug/srldnews/Economic.html* (Accessed July 10, 2001).

Fay, John. 1991. *Drug Testing*. Boston: Butterworth-Heinemann.

Flay, Brian R. 1987. "Mass Media and Smoking Cessation." *American Journal of Public Health* 77, pp. 153–160.

Freudenrich, Craig C. 2000. "How Breathalyzers Work." Available online: *http://www.howstuffworks.com/breathalyzer.htm* (Accessed July 2, 2001).

Gerstein, Dean R., and Lawrence W. Green. 1993. *Preventing Drug Abuse: What Do We Know?* Washington, DC: National Academy Press.

Gorman, D.M. 1998. "The Irrelevance of Evidence in the Development of School-Based Drug Prevention Policy, 1986–1996." *Evaluation Review* 22, pp. 118–146.

Haggerty, Kevin, Rick Kosterman, Richard F. Catalano and J. David Hawkins. 1999. "Preparing for the Drug Free Years." *Juvenile Justice Bulletin*, July. Washington, DC: Office of Juvenile Justice and Delinquency Prevention.

Hansen, William B., C. Anderson Johnson, Brian R. Flay, John W. Graham and Judith Sobel. 1988. "Affective and Social Influences Approaches to the Prevention of Multiple Substance Abuse Among Seventh Grade Students: Results from Project SMART." *Preventive Medicine* 17, pp. 135–154.

Hanson, Meredith. 1993. "Overview on Drug and Alcohol Testing in the Workplace." *Bulletin on Narcotics* 2, pp. 3–44.

Hartwell, Tyler D., Paul D. Steele, Michael T. French and Nathaniel F. Rodman. 1996. "Prevalence of Drug Testing in the Workplace." *Monthly Labor Review*, 119, 11, pp. 35–42.

Holden, Constance. 1990. "Hairy Problems for New Drug Testing Method." *Science* 249 (September 7), pp. 1099–2000.

Hurd, Peter D, C. Anderson Johnson, Terry Pechacek, L. Peter Bast, David R. Jacobs and Russell V. Luepker. 1980. "Prevention of Cigarette Smoking in Seventh Grade Children." *Journal of Behavioral Medicine*. 3, pp. 15–28.

Jacobs, James. 1989. *Drunk Driving: An American Dilemma*. Chicago: University of Chicago Press.

Janofsky, Michael. 2000. "Antidrug Program's End Stirs Up Salt Lake City," *New York Times,* September 15, p. B1.

Kim, Sehwan. 1981. "An Evaluation of Ombudsman Primary Prevention Program on Student Drug Abuse." *Journal of Drug Education* 11, pp. 27–36.

Kopstein, Andrea N. and Joseph C. Gfroerer. 1991. "Drug Use Patterns and Demographics of Employed Drug Users: Data from the 1988 National Household Survey on Drug Abuse." Pp. 11–24 in Steven W. Gust et al., *Drugs in the Workplace: Research and Evaluation Data*. NIDA Drug Abuse Research Monograph Series, No. 100. Rockville, MD: National Institute on Drug Abuse.

Kosterman, Rick, J. David Hawkins, Kevin P. Haggerty, Richard Spoth and Cleve Redmond. 2001. "Preparing for the Drug Free Years: Session-Specific Effects of a Universal Parent-Training Intervention with Rural Families." *Journal of Drug Education* 31, pp. 47–68.

Krauthamer, Gordon. 1998. "The Effectiveness of Preemployment Drug Testing." Paper prepared for the class *Drugs and American Society*, University of Maryland, College Park, Fall, 1998.

Lange, W. Robert, B. Rodrigo Cabanilla, Gerri Moler, Kiane L. Frankenfield and Paul J. Fudala. 1994. "Preemployment Drug Screening at The Johns Hopkins Hospital, 1989 and 1991." *American Journal of Drug and Alcohol Abuse* 20, pp. 35–46.

LeRoy, Michael H. "Discriminating Characteristics of Union Members' Attitudes Toward Drug Testing in the Workplace." *Journal of Labor Research*, 12, pp. 453–466.

Lundberg, George D. 1972. "Urine Drug Screening: Chemical McCarthyism." *New England Journal of Medicine.*" 287, 14, pp. 723–724.

Lynam, Donald R., Richard Millich, Rick Zimmerman, Scott P. Novak, T.K. Logan, Catherine Martin, Carl Leukefeld and Richard Clayton. 1999. "Project DARE: No Effects at 10-Year Follow-Up." *Journal of Consulting and Clinical Psychology* 67, pp. 590–593.

Maltby, Lewis L. 1999. *Drug Testing: A Bad Investment.* New York: American Civil Liberties Union.

McAlister, Alfred L. Cheryl Perry and Nathan Maccoby. 1979. "Adolescent Smoking: Onset and Prevention." *Pediatrics* 63, pp. 650–658.

McGuire, William. 1964. "Inducing Resistance to Persuasion." Pp. 191–229 in Leonard Berkowitz (ed.), *Advances in Experimental Social Psychology.* New York: Academic Press.

Mehay, Stephen L. and Rosalie Loccardo Pacula. 1999. *The Effectiveness of Workplace Drug Prevention Policies: Does 'Zero Tolerance' Work?* NBER Working Paper No. W7383. Boston, MA: National Bureau of Economic Research.

Mieczkowski, Tom and Kim Lersch. 1997. "Drug Testing in Criminal Justice: Evolving Issues, Emerging Technologies." *National Institute of Justice Journal* 234 (December), pp. 9–15.

Montagne, Michael, Carol B. Pugh and Joseph L. Fink III. 1988a. "Testing for Drug Use, Part 1: Analytical Methods." *American Journal of Hospital Pharmacy* 45, pp. 1297–1305.

———. 1988b. "Testing for Drug Use, Part 2: Legal, Social and Ethical Concerns." *American Journal of Hospital Pharmacy* 45, pp. 1509–1522.

Murray, David M., C. Anderson Johnson, Russell V. Luepker and Maurice B. Mittelmark. 1984. "The Prevention of Cigarette Smoking in Children: A Comparison of Four Strategies." *Journal of Applied Social Psychology* 14, pp. 274–289.

National Institute on Drug Abuse. 1989. *Model Plan for a Comprehensive Drug-Free Workplace Program.* Rockville, MD: National Institute on Drug Abuse.

Normand, Jacques, Stephen D. Salyards and John J. Mahoney. 1990. "An Evaluation of Preemployment Drug Testing." *Journal of Applied Psychology* 75, pp. 629–639.

Office of National Drug Control Policy. 1992. *National Drug Control Strategy: Budget Summaries.* Washington, DC: U.S. Government Printing Office.

Park, Jisuk, Rick Kosterman, J. David Hawkins, Kevin P. Haggerty, Terry E. Duncan, Susan C. Duncan and Richard Spoth. 2000. "Effects of the 'Preparing for the Drug Free Years' Curriculum on Growth in Alcohol Use and Risk for Alcohol Use in Early Adolescence." *Prevention Science* 1, pp. 125–138.

Pisani, Roger G. "Advertising Industry." Pp. 217–248 in Robert H. Coombs and Douglas M. Ziedonis (eds.), *Handbook on Drug Abuse Prevention: A Comprehensive Strategy to Prevent the Abuse of Alcohol and Other Drugs.* Boston: Allyn and Bacon.

Potter, Beverly A. and J. Sebastian Orfali. 1990. *Drug Testing at Work: A Guide for Employers and Employees.* Berkeley, CA: Ronin Publishing.

Ray, Oakley, and Charles Ksir. 1999. *Drugs, Society and Human Behavior.* Boston: WCB/McGraw-Hill.

Riley, Diane. 1993. *The Harm Reduction Model: Pragmatic Approaches to Drug Use from the Area Between Intolerance and Neglect.* Ottowa, Ontario: Canadian Center on Substance Abuse. Available online: *http://www.ccsa.ca/docs/harmred.htm* (Accessed August 13, 2001).

Rosenbaum, Marsha. 1999. *Safety First: A Reality-Based Approach to Teens, Drugs, and Drug Education.* San Francisco, CA: The Lindesmith Center.

———. 1996. *Kids, Drugs and Drug Education: A Harm Reduction Approach.* San Francisco, CA: National Council on Crime and Delinquency.

Shepard, Edward and Thomas Clifton. 1999. "Drug Testing and Labor Productivity: Estimates Applying a Production Function Model." Research Paper #18, LeMoyne College of Industrial Relations. Syracuse, NY: LeMoyne College.

Spoth, Richard and Cleve Redmond. 1996a. "A Theory-Based Parent Competency Model Incorporating Intervention Attendance Effects." *Family Relations* 45, pp. 139–147.

———. 1996b. "Barriers to Participation in Family Skills Preventive Interventions and Their Evaluations." *Family Relations* 45, pp. 247–254.

_____. 1995. "A Controlled Parenting Skills Outcome Study Examining Individual Difference and Attendance Effects." *Journal of Marriage and the Family* 57, pp. 449–464.

Spoth, Richard, Melissa Lopez Reyes, Cleve Redmond and Chungyeol Shin. "Assessing a Public Health Approach to Delay Onset and Progression of Adolescent Substance Use: Latent Transition and Log-Linear Analyses of Longitudinal Family Preventive Intervention Outcomes." *Journal of Consulting and Clinical Psychology* 67, pp. 619–630.

Swena, Dennis D. and Will Gaines Jr. 1999. "Effect of Random Drug Screening on Fatal Commercial Truck Accident Rates." *International Journal of Drug Testing* 1 Available online: *http://www.criminology.fsu.edu/journal/drugscreen.htm* (Accessed July 5, 2001).

Tobler, Nancy S. 1992. "Drug Prevention Programs Can Work: Research Findings." *Journal of Addictive Diseases* 11, pp. 1–28.

Tobler, Nancy S. 1986. "Meta-Analysis of 143 Adolescent Drug Prevention Programs: Quantitative Outcome Results of Program Participants Compared to a Aontrol or Comparison Group." *Journal of Drug Issues* 16, pp. 537–567.

Tobler, Nancy S. and Howard H.Stratton. 1997. "Effectiveness of School-Based Drug Prevention Programs: A Meta-Analysis of the Research." *The Journal of Primary Prevention* 18, pp. 71–128.

Wagner, Jon C. 1987. "Substance-Abuse Policies and Guidelines in Amateur and Professional Athletics." *American Journal of Hospital Pharmacy* 44, pp. 305–310.

Walsh, J. Michael and Jeanne G. Trumble. 1991. "The Politics of Drug Testing." Pp. 22–49 in Robert H. Coombs and Louis Jolyon West (eds.), *Drug Testing: Issues and Options*. New York: Oxford University Press.

Weil, Andrew and Winifred Rosen. 1983. *Chocolate to Morphine: Understanding Mind-Altering Drugs*. Boston: Houghton-Mifflin Co.

White, David and Marian Pitts. 1998. "Educating Young People About Drugs: A Systematic Review." *Addiction* 93, pp. 1475–1487.

Willette, Robert E. 1986. "Drug Testing Programs." Pp. 5–12 in Richard L. Hawks and C. Nora Chiang (eds.) *Urine Testing for Drugs of Abuse*. NIDA Research Monograph 73. Rockville, MD: National Institute on Drug Abuse.

Zemper, Eric D. 1991. "Drug Testing in Athletics." Pp. 113–139 in Robert H. Coombs and Louis Jolyon West (eds.), *Drug Testing: Issues and Options*. New York: Oxford University Press.

Zernike, Kate. 2001. "Antidrug Program Says it Will Adopt a New Strategy," *New York Times,* February 15, pp. A1.

Zwerling, Craig, James Ryan, and Endel John Orav. 1990. "The Efficacy of Preemployment Drug Screening for Marijuana and Cocaine in Predicting Employment Outcome." *Journal of the American Medical Association* 264, 20 (November 28), pp. 2639–2643.

_____. 1992. "Costs and Benefits of Preemployment Drug Screening." *Journal of the American Medical Association*. 267, 1 (January 1), pp. 91–93

Chapter 14

Abadinsky, Howard. 1993. *Drug Abuse: An Introduction* (2nd ed.). Chicago: Nelson-Hall.

Broadhead, Robert S., Yaël Van Hulst and Douglas D. Heckathorn. 1999. "The Impact of a Needle Exchange's Closure. *Public Health Reports* (September/October), pp. 446–447.

Burack, Jeffrey H. and David Bangsberg. 1998. "Epidemiology and HIV Transmission in Injection Drug Users." *HIV InSite Knowledge Base* Available online: *http://hivinsite.ucsf.edu/InSite.jsp?doc=kb-07-04-01&page=kb-07* (Accessed April 24, 2001).

Cuskey, Walter R., Lisa H. Berger and Arthur H. richardson. 1978. "The Effects of Marijuana Decriminalization on Drug Use Patterns: A Literature Review and Research Critique." *Contemporary Drug Problems* 5, 4 pp. 491–532.

Des Jarlais, Don C., Michael Marmour, Denise Paone, Stephen Titus, Q. Shi, Theresa Perlis, B. Hose and Samuel R. Friedman. 1996. "HIV Incidence Among Injecting Drug Users in New York City Syringe Exchange Programmes." *Lancet* 348 (October 12), pp. 987–991.

Faupel, Charles E. 1991. *Shooting Dope: Career Patterns of Hard-Core Heroin Addicts*. Gainesville, FL: University of Florida Press.

Friedman, Milton. 1972. "Prohibition and Drugs." *Newsweek* (May 1).

Goode, Erich. 1999. *Drugs in American Society* (5th ed.). New York: McGraw-Hill College.

Gostin, Lawrence O., Zita Lazzarini, T. Stephen Jones and Kathleen Flaherty. 1997. "Prevention of HIV/AIDS and Other Blood-Borne Diseases Among Injection Drug Users: A National Survey on the Regulation of Syringes and Needles." *Journal of the American Medical Association* 277, pp. 53–62.

Inciardi, James A. 1981. "Marijuana Decriminalization Research: A Perspective and Commentary." *Criminology* 19, pp. 145–159.

Institute for Social Research. 1981. "Marijuana Decriminalization: The Impact on Youth 1975–1980. *Occasional Paper #13.* Ann Arbor: University of Michigan.

Lurie, P., A. Reingold and D. Bowser. 1994. *The Public Health Impact of Needle Exchange and Bleach Distribution Programs in the United States and Abroad.* Washington, DC: National Academy Press.

Nadelmann, Ethan. 1998. "Commonsense Drug Policy." *Foreign Affairs* 77, pp. 111–126.

Nadelmann, Ethan, Jennifer McNeely and Ernest Drucker. 1997. "International Perspectives." Pp. 22–39 in Joyce H. Lowinson, Prdro Ruiz, Robert B. Millman and John G. Langrod (eds.), *Substance Abuse: A Comprehensive Textbook.* Baltimore: Williams and Wilkins.

National Treasury Employees Union v. Von Raab. 1989. 489 U.S. 656.

Ray, Oakley. 1978. *Drugs, Society and Human Behavior* (2nd ed.). St. Louis: C.V. Mosby.

Ray, Oakley and Charles Ksir. 1999. *Drugs, Society and Human Behavior* (8th ed.). Boston: WCB/McGraw-Hill.

Singer, Merrill, Ray Irizarry and Jean Schensul. 1991. "Needle Access as an AIDS-Prevention Strategy for IV Drug Users: A Research Perspective." *Human Organization* 50, pp. 142–153.

Skinner v. *Railway Labor Executives' Association.* 1989. 489 U.S. 602.

Sourcebook of Criminal Justice Statistics. 1999. *Sourcebook of Criminal Justice Statistics, 1998.* Washington, DC: Office of Justice Programs.

Thies, Clifford F. and Charles A. Register. 1993. "Decriminalization of Marijuana and the Demand for Alcohol, Marijuana and Cocaine." *The Social Science Journal* 30, pp. 385–399.

United States v. *Oakland Cannabis Buyers Cooperative.* 2001. United States Supreme Court.

Vernonia Sch. Dist. 47J v. *Acton.* 1995. 515 U.S. 646.

Watters, John K., Michelle J. Estilo, George L. Clark and Jennifer Lorvick. 1994. "Syringe and Needle Exchange as HIV/AIDS Prevention for Injection Drug Users." *Journal of the American Medical Association* 271 (January 12), pp. 115–120.

Westermeyer, Robert W. n.d., "Reducing Harm: A Very Good Idea." Available online: *http://www.habitsmart.com/harm.html* (Accessed April 2, 2001).

TEXT, LINE ART, AND PHOTO CREDITS

TEXT AND LINE ART CREDITS

Chapter 2

P. 56 From *The Times They Are A-Changin'.* Copyright © 1963 by Warner Bros. Inc. Copyright renewed 1991 by Special Rider Music. All rights reserved. International copyright secured. Reprinted by permission.

Chapter 3

Table 3.2 From *Drugs, Society and Human Behavior, 8th Edition* by Charles Ksir and O. Ray. Copyright © 1999 by the McGraw-Hill Companies. Reprinted by permission.

Chapter 4

Table 4.1 Adapted from Mary C. Ritz and Michael J. Kuhar, "Psychostimulant Drugs and a Dopamine Hypothesis Regarding Addiction: Update on Recent Research" in S. Wonnacott and G.G. Lunt (eds.) *Neurochemistry of Drug Dependence,* Portland Press, 1993. Used with permission.

P. 121 From *Shooting Dope: Career Patterns of Hard-Core Heroin Users* by Charles E. Faupel. Copyright © 1991 by Charles Faupel. Reprinted with permission of the University Press of Florida.

Chapter 5

P. 147 text, Figs. 5.1, 5.2 From *Shooting Dope: Career Patterns of Hard-Core Heroin Users* by Charles E. Faupel. Copyright © 1991 by Charles Faupel. Reprinted with permission of the University Press of Florida.

Chapter 8

Fig. 8.2 From http://www.norml.org. Reprinted with permission of NORML Foundation.

Fig. 8.3 From "Just Say Yes: The Use of Opioids for Managing Pain at the End of Life" by Steven Z. Pantilat in *The Western Journal of Medicine,* 171, 4, pp. 257–259. Reprinted by permission of BMJ Publishing Group Ltd.

Chapter 9

P. 293 From www.voy.com. Reprinted with permission.

Chapter 10

P. 328 From Richard P. Rettig, Manual J. Torres, Gerald R. Garrett, *Manny, a Criminal Addict's Story*, Houghton-Mifflin, 1977. Reprinted by permission of the author.

T.10.2 Adapted from Bruce D. Johnson, et al, *Taking Care of Business: The Economics of Crime by Heroin Users*, pp. 77 & 81, Tables 7-2 & 7-4. Copyright © 1985 by Bruce D. Johnson. Reprinted by permission of Lexington Books.

Chapter 11

T.11.1 From http://www.norml.org/index.cfm. Reprinted with permission of NORML Foundation.

T.11.2 Adapted from Ethan Nadelmann, Jennifer NcNeely, Ernest Drucker, "International Perspectives" 1997 Table 4.1 (pp. 22–39) in Joyce H. Lowinson et al, (eds.) *Substance Abuse: A Comprehensive Textbook, 3rd Edition*. Reprinted with permission from Lippincott, Williams & Wilkins.

Chapter 12

Figs. 12.1, 12.2, 12.3 From *Drug Treatment: A National Study of Effectiveness* by Robert Hubbard et al. Copyright © 1989 by University of North Carolina Press. Used by permission of the publisher.

P. 388 Reprinted with permission from www.anonymousone.com/stories.

PHOTO CREDITS

Page #	Credit	Page #	Credit
3	Benjamin Rondel/Corbis	239	Jeff Albertson/Corbis
25 left	The Kobal Collection	258	Brand X Pictures
25 right	Stockbyte	273	Francoise de Mulder/Corbis
31	The Granger Collection	290	PhotoDisc
40	The Granger Collection	303	Brand X Pictures
65	Artville	317	PhotoDisc
68	Bonnie Kamin/PhotoEdit	337	Bettman/Corbis
107	Stockbyte	341	AP/Wide World Photos
118	Image100/Punchstock	373	Jeff Greenberg/PhotoEdit
135	Najlah Feanny/Corbis Saba	379	Mary Kate Denny/PhotoEdit
190	David Wells/The Image Works	409	Mary Kate Denny/PhotoEdit
201	Kathleen Kliskey-Geraghty/Index Stock Imagery/Picturequest	423	Reuter NewMedia Inc./Corbis
		439	AP/Wide World Photos
232	AFP/Corbis	453	Michael Newman/PhotoEdit

NAME INDEX

SUBJECT INDEX